The Routledge Companion to Visual Organization

The visual constitutes an increasingly significant element of contemporary organization, as post-industrial societies move towards economies founded on creative and knowledge-intensive industries. The visual has thereby entered into almost every aspect of corporate strategy, operations and communication; reconfiguring basic notions of management practice and introducing new challenges in the study of organizations.

This volume provides a comprehensive insight into the ways in which organizations and their members visualize their identities and practices and how they are viewed by those who are external to organizations, including researchers.

With contributions from leading academics across the world, *The Routledge Companion to Visual Organization* is a valuable reference source for students and academics interested in disciplines such as film studies, entrepreneurship, marketing, sociology and organizational behaviour.

Emma Bell is Professor of Management and Organisation Studies at Keele University, UK.

Samantha Warren is Professor in Management at the University of Essex, UK.

Jonathan Schroeder is the William A. Kern Professor of Communications at Rochester Institute of Technology, USA.

Routledge Companions in Business, Management and Accounting

Routledge Companions in Business, Management and Accounting are similar to what some publishers call 'handbooks', i.e. prestige reference works providing an overview of a whole subject area or sub-discipline, and which survey the state of the discipline including emerging and cutting-edge areas. These books provide a comprehensive, up-to-date, definitive work of reference, which can be cited as an authoritative source on the subject.

One of the key aspects of the Routledge Companions in Business, Management and Accounting series is their international scope and relevance. Edited by an array of well-regarded scholars, these volumes also benefit from teams of contributors that reflect an international range of perspectives.

Individually, Routledge Companions in Business, Management and Accounting provide an impactful one-stop-shop resource for each theme covered, while, collectively, they represent a comprehensive learning and research resource for researchers and postgraduates and practitioners.

Published titles in this series include:

The Routledge Companion to Fair Value and Financial Reporting
Edited by Peter Walton

The Routledge Companion to Nonprofit Marketing
Edited by Adrian Sargeant and Walter Wymer Jr

The Routledge Companion to Accounting History
Edited by John Richard Edwards and Stephen P. Walker

The Routledge Companion to Creativity
Edited by Tudor Rickards, Mark A. Runco and Susan Moger

The Routledge Companion to Strategic Human Resource Management
Edited by John Storey, Patrick M. Wright and David Ulrich

The Routledge Companion to International Business Coaching
Edited by Michel Moral and Geoffrey Abbott

The Routledge Companion to Organizational Change
Edited by David M. Boje, Bernard Burnes and John Hassard

The Routledge Companion to Cost Management
Edited by Falconer Mitchell, Hanne Nørreklit and Morten Jakobsen

The Routledge Companion to Digital Consumption
Edited by Russell W. Belk and Rosa Llamas

The Routledge Companion to Identity and Consumption
Edited by Ayalla A. Ruvio and Russell W. Belk

The Routledge Companion to Public-Private Partnerships
Edited by Piet de Vries and Etienne B. Yehoue

The Routledge Companion to Accounting, Reporting and Regulation
Edited by Carien van Mourik and Peter Walton

The Routledge Companion to International Management Education
Edited by Denise Tsang, Hamid H. Kazeroony and Guy Ellis

The Routledge Companion to Accounting Communication
Edited by Lisa Jack, Jane Davison and Russell Craig

The Routledge Companion to Visual Organization
Edited by Emma Bell, Samantha Warren and Jonathan Schroeder

The Routledge Companion to Visual Organization

*Edited by Emma Bell,
Samantha Warren and
Jonathan Schroeder*

LONDON AND NEW YORK

First published 2014
by Routledge
2 Park Square, Milton Park, Abingdon, Oxon OX14 4RN

and by Routledge
711 Third Avenue, New York, NY 10017

Routledge is an imprint of the Taylor & Francis Group, an informa business

© 2014 Emma Bell, Samantha Warren and Jonathan Schroeder

The right of the editors to be identified as the authors of the editorial material, and of the authors for their individual chapters, has been asserted in accordance with sections 77 and 78 of the Copyright, Designs and Patents Act 1988.

All rights reserved. No part of this book may be reprinted or reproduced or utilized in any form or by any electronic, mechanical, or other means, now known or hereafter invented, including photocopying and recording, or in any information storage or retrieval system, without permission in writing from the publishers.

Trademark notice: Product or corporate names may be trademarks or registered trademarks, and are used only for identification and explanation without intent to infringe.

British Library Cataloguing in Publication Data
A catalogue record for this book is available from the British Library

Library of Congress Cataloging-in-Publication Data
The Routledge companion to visual organization / edited by Emma Bell, Samantha Warren and Jonathan Schroeder.
    pages cm.—(Routledge companions in business, management and accounting)
    Includes bibliographical references and index.
1. Organizational change—Research. 2. Social media. 3. Management—Technological innovations. I. Bell, Emma, 1968- II. Title: Companion to visual organization.
HD58.8.R6936 2013
658.4'06—dc23   2013003477

ISBN: 978-0-415-78367-5 (hbk)
ISBN: 978-0-203-72561-0 (ebk)

Typeset in Bembo
by Cenveo Publisher Services

Printed and bound in Great Britain by
TJ International Ltd, Padstow, Cornwall

Contents

List of figures	x
List of tables	xii
List of contributors	xiii
Acknowledgements	xx
Introduction: The visual organization Emma Bell, Samantha Warren and Jonathan Schroeder	1

PART I
Thinking visually about organization — 17

1. Between the visible and the invisible in organizations — 19
   Wendelin Küpers

2. The visual organization: Barthesian perspectives — 33
   Jane Davison

3. The method of juxtaposition: Unfolding the visual turn in organization studies — 46
   Bent M. Sørensen

4. The limits of visualization: Ocularcentrism and organization — 64
   Donncha Kavanagh

PART II
Strategies of visual organization — 77

5. Constructing the visual consumer — 79
   Lisa Peñaloza and Alex Thompson

Contents

6. Cultural production and consumption of images in the marketplace 96
Laurie A. Meamber

7. Portraiture and the construction of 'charismatic leadership' 116
Beatriz Acevedo

8. The signs and semiotics of advertising 130
Norah Campbell

9. Art, artist, and aesthetics for organizational visual strategy 146
Pierre Guillet de Monthoux

PART III
Visual methodologies and methods 163

10. Methodological ways of seeing and knowing 165
Dvora Yanow

11. Navigating the scattered and fragmented: Visual rhetoric, visual studies, and visual communication 188
Kelly Norris Martin

12. Using videoethnography to study entrepreneurship 202
Jean Clarke

13. Ethnographic videography and filmmaking for consumer research 214
Ekant Veer

14. Drawing as a method of organizational analysis 227
David R. Stiles

15. Visual sociology and work organization: An historical approach 243
Tim Strangleman

PART IV
Visual identities and practices 259

16. Arts-based interventions and organizational development: It's what you don't see 261
Ariane Berthoin Antal, Steven S. Taylor and Donna Ladkin

17. Towards an understanding of corporate web identity 273
    Carole Elliott and Sarah Robinson

18. Visual workplace identities: Objects, emotion and resistance 289
    Harriet Shortt, Jan Betts and Samantha Warren

19. Managing operations and teams visually 306
    Nicola Bateman and Sarah Lethbridge

20. Social media and organizations 322
    Pauline Leonard

21. Simulated realities (Or, why boxers and Artificial Intelligence scientists do mostly the same thing) 335
    Steve G. Hoffman

PART V
Visual representations of organization   351

22. The organization of vision within professions 353
    Alexander Styhre

23. Visual authenticity and organizational sustainability 365
    Emma Bell and McArthur

24. (Seeing) organizing in popular culture: Discipline and method 379
    Martin Parker

Index *391*

Figures

3.1	*The Conversion of Saint Paul* (inverted), Caravaggio	52
3.2	Mintzberg's 'basic model of the organization'	52
3.3	Aalbæk and the office clerk	54
3.4	Aalbæk and the office clerk	56
3.5	Four Nigerians	56
3.6	Jewish Ghetto, Warsaw 1943	58
3.7	Jewish Ghetto, Warsaw 1943	59
3.8	*Angelus Novus*, Paul Klee	59
4.1	Meta-theoretical trajectories	64
4.2	The categorical distinction between m-vision and e-vision	66
4.3	The double inversion of ocularcentrism	72
5.1	Playing cowboy	83
5.2	Grocery shopping	85
5.3	Testing blood sugar while smoking	88
5.4	Painful insulin injection	89
8.1	Self-organizing technology, Siemens *Building Blocks* (Publicis, New York 2005)	137
8.2	*Hey Genius* Microsoft Recruitment Campaign, Wexley School for Girls, Seattle 2010	139
8.3	Recruitment card for Apple Inc., circa 2010	140
10.1	The analytic triad during fieldwork (with 1st and 2nd hermeneutics)	172
10.2	The nesting of artefacts and interpretations: 1st, 2nd and 3rd hermeneutics, from the researcher's perspective	173
11.1	Comparison of three visual approaches	189
11.2	Definitions and criticisms	190
14.1	Individual free-drawn personality image: Katie, lecturer	234
14.2	Individual free-drawn personality image: Darren, lecturer	235
14.3	Individual free-drawn personality image: Mark, full professor	235
14.4	Group free-drawn personality image: MBA students	237
17.1	Royal Bank of Scotland, website homepage, 10 November 2012	284
18.1	Rampant personalization of space	292
18.2	Homely desks	293
18.3	Objects as talking points	294

18.4a, 18.4b, 18.4c	Unprofessional clutter	296
18.5a, 18.5b, 18.5c	Professional and proficient	297
18.6	Hidden briefcase	298
18.7	Football fixtures	299
18.8	Brian's monkey	299
19.1	Visual Management Principles, developed by Cardiff University, of 'Lean University' project	309
19.2	Implementation in Assa Abloy	310
19.3	Research overlaying implementation	310
19.4	Assa Abloy communications board, KPI side	313
19.5	Management board for University of St Andrews Web Services	315
19.6	Sefton Magistrates' Court's team information board	316
19.7	Visual bed management	317
19.8	Example of page 7 from IDEAS prescription chart	319
19.9	Use of red to highlight key features	319
21.1	Three dimensions of simulation	342

Tables

2.1	Oppositions in 'Rhetoric of the image' and *Camera Lucida*	43
7.1	Categories for the analysis of portraits	123
10.1	Three genres of visual materials, by creator/source and purpose	167
10.2	Logics of enquiry	176
17.1	Summary of different foci, approaches and methodology	282

Contributors

Beatriz Acevedo is a Colombian academic living and working in the United Kingdom. Her research interests integrate the areas of visual studies, aesthetic and organizational symbolism. In addition, she is an artist and illustrator and she is passionate about the practical aspects of aesthetics and the use of art-based methodologies in management development. Beatriz is the director of GoGreen Movement, an action learning project concerning education for sustainability, and she works as a Senior Lecturer in Sustainable Management at Anglia Ruskin University in Cambridge.

Nicola Bateman is a Senior Lecturer in Operations Management. Her main research interests are flexibility and lean implementation, particularly sustainability and visual management. She gained her PhD at De Montfort University in modelling flexibility and went on to Cardiff University's Lean Enterprise Research Centre. She has been asked to speak to a range of industrial and academic organizations including: CBI, Said Business School (Oxford University), Rexel Staples, LG, Landrover and the Institute of Operations Management. Her research into lean implementation has taken her to a wide range of sectors and organizations including: Mars, RAF, Assa Abloy and drinks carton fillers and manufacturers. She has written two books and many conference and journal papers. The current focus for her personal research is examining how visual management can contribute to sustainability of change, process improvement and team-based decision-making.

Emma Bell is Professor of Management and Organisation Studies at Keele University. Her research focuses on understanding organizational cultures and meaning-making at work. She also teaches and writes about methods of management research. She is the author of *Reading Management and Organization in Film* (2008), co-author of *Business Research Methods* (3rd edition, 2011) and *A Very Short, Fairly Interesting and Reasonably Cheap Book About Management Research* (2013). Emma is a founding member of *in*Visio – the International Network of Visual Studies in Organisations (www.in-visio.org) – and part of an ESRC Researcher Development Initiative to promote the development of visual analysis in management research.

Ariane Berthoin Antal leads the research stream on 'Artistic Interventions in Organizations' in the Research Unit 'Cultural Sources of Newness' at the Social Science Research Center Berlin, Germany (WZB). She is Distinguished Research Professor at Audencia Nantes School of Management, France, and Honorary Professor at the Technical University of Berlin. She is particularly grateful to the Institute for Advanced Studies Konstanz for offering the ideal conditions for working on this chapter in 2012.

Contributors

Jan Betts is an organizational psychologist currently undertaking her PhD at the University of Essex. Her research interests have included reflective practice, organizational learning and material culture at work. Her PhD research is focused on materiality and the impact of objects in the workplace, at both individual and corporate levels.

Norah Campbell is Assistant Professor of Marketing at Trinity College, Dublin. She is interested in the philosophy of technology, the philosophy of service, and imaginations of the future in consumer culture.

Jean S. Clarke is an Associate Professor at Leeds University Business School, the University of Leeds. Her research focuses on how entrepreneurs use visual cues in interactions with relevant stakeholders such as investors, customers and employees to develop legitimacy for their new venture. This work is divided into two main streams. One focus is on understanding how entrepreneurs use and manipulate visual symbols (dress, props, settings, etc.) and the second is on how entrepreneurs use body language and, in particular, hand gestures to communicate. She uses a variety of visual methodologies in her research including visual ethnographic work, micro-analysis of body language and gesture, and more recently video-based experimental studies.

Jane Davison is Professor of Accounting at Royal Holloway, University of London, UK. Her research interests include visual and narrative perspectives on accounting. She is widely published in major international journals, co-editor of several journal special issues, co-founder of the *in*Visio research network and associate director of the Bangor Centre for Impression Management in Accounting.

Carole Elliott is Senior Lecturer in Management at Durham University Business School. She has previously worked at Hull University Business School and Lancaster University Management School, where she was awarded her PhD in 2004. Her research interests lie in three main areas: critical approaches to management and leadership learning; critical human resource development; and qualitative research methods, particularly the development of critical hermeneutic and visual methods in management and organization research. She is currently working on papers examining visual representations of women's leadership in the media and popular culture. She is associate editor for the Routledge journal *Human Resource Development International*.

Pierre Guillet de Monthoux is Professor of Management, Politics and Philosophy at Copenhagen Business School. Pierre's proposition for both research and teaching goes: Art is a way to come closer to creativity in organizations and aesthetics is the philosophical approach best suited to articulate how it works! His main research focus areas include management philosophy, art and aesthetics. His books include *The Art Firm: Aesthetic Management and Metaphysical Marketing from Wagner to Wilson* (Stanford Business School Press).

Steve G. Hoffman received his PhD in Sociology from Northwestern University, where he learned the craft of rigorous yet eclectic interpretive sociology from some of the best in the business. He is a social theorist and ethnographer whose research lies at the intersection of organizational studies, social psychology, and science and technology studies. His primary research develops an organizational and interpretive approach to how simulation techniques and technologies, and scientific knowledge more broadly, are imagined, made legitimate and disseminated across complex organizational fields. Most recently, this has lead Hoffman to write about how academic capitalism is remaking twenty-first-century academic culture and practice. His scholarship spans a wide variety of empirical cases, ranging from ethnographic research on boxing gyms and Artificial Intelligence labs, interview- and survey-based research on gay-affirming churches and conservative working-class towns, and multi-method research on conflicting ideas about how to implement fairness in the law. In the near future, he plans to conduct ethnographic research on socio-technical disasters, and is currently teaching classes on the topic.

Donncha Kavanagh is Senior Lecturer in Management at University College Cork, Ireland. He has published widely in the fields of management, marketing, organization studies and engineering. His research interests include the history and philosophy of management thought, pre-modern and postmodern modes of organizing, and the sociology of knowledge and technology.

Wendelin Küpers is an Associate Professor at the School of Management, Massey University in Auckland, New Zealand. Previously, he has been affiliated to various universities in Europe. In his phenomenological and intertransdisciplinary research, he focuses on embodied, emotional and creative/aesthetic dimensions in organizational life-worlds and leadership as well as its integration. Based on advanced phenomenology, he is developing an integral 'pheno-practice' in organizing and leading.

Donna Ladkin is Professor of Leadership and Ethics at Cranfield School of Management in the UK. A philosopher and musician by background, her research focuses on the aesthetic and ethical dimensions of leading and organizing. Her interest in how the visual arts can enhance moral perception and moral imagination has sparked a unique approach to teaching business ethics on Cranfield's MBA programme. This method is highlighted in her upcoming book, *Mastering the Ethical Dimension of Organizations* (Edward Elgar, 2014).

Pauline Leonard is Professor of Sociology at University of Southampton. She studied sociology at the University of Reading and qualified as a teacher at the Institute of Education, University of London. She gained a Masters Degree in Education from the University of Southampton and then completed her PhD, also at the University of Southampton. She has taught at further and higher education level in both the UK and Hong Kong.

Sarah Lethbridge joined the Health and Services Team in the Lean Enterprise Research Centre in 2005. She has worked on numerous lean projects in hospitals, universities, and public and private services. Sarah specializes in helping to develop the knowledge of continuous improvement teams and has worked with the Ministry of Justice's Lean Academy, their Shared Service Centre in Newport, the Value for Money team in the Home Office, Legal & General, Principality Building Society and, most recently, Nestlé, to ensure that organizations approach lean in a holistic, sustainable way. Her passion is to explore the interconnection of lean concepts and tools, helping people to understand how all of the lean ideas support and inform each other.

Laurie A. Meamber is an Associate Professor of Marketing at the School of Management, George Mason University. She writes on the intersection of art, aesthetics, marketing and consumption in today's economy, including design and aesthetic value. Her work has appeared in *Consumption Markets & Culture, Journal of Business Research, Marketing Theory,*

Advances in Consumer Research, among other publications. She serves on the editorial advisory board of *Consumption Markets & Culture*, and is a Regional Editor for *Arts Marketing: An International Journal*. She holds a BA in sociology-organizational studies with a minor in dramatic art from the University of California, Davis; an MBA from the University of California, Riverside; and a PhD in Management from the University of California, Irvine.

McArthur worked in design and communications for 15 years and loves to create smart blends of aesthetics and effective ideas. At Free Range, she managed the organizational growth and business development from a small, 2-person design studio to a highly prestigious, 25-person strategic firm. Her communications background, business acumen and non-profit experience combine to make her a valuable asset to communications projects and a sought-after consultant and speaker. Among other venues, she has spoken at Harvard Medical School's New Media Forum, American University's 'Filmmakers for Conservation', AIGA's Design Unbound, University of Michigan and The BYU Marriott School of Management. Driven by her passion for real world change, McArthur now does independent consulting and storytelling from her base in India.

Kelly Norris Martin is an Assistant Professor in the Department of Communication at Rochester Institute of Technology. She earned her PhD in Communication, Rhetoric and Digital Media at North Carolina State University. Her research focuses on the intersections of visual communication, rhetorical criticism and design. Recent journal publications include: 'A Visual World Demands Design Sense: Advocating for Visual Communication Across the Curriculum' in *International Journal of Design Education* (2013) and 'You Make it Amazing: The Rhetoric of Art and Urban Regeneration in the Case of *The Public*' in *Journal of Visual Literacy* (2012).

Martin Parker is Professor of Organisation and Culture at the School of Management, Leicester University. His training is mostly in sociology, with some anthropology and cultural studies, and he has a particular interest in various meanings of the word 'culture'. He has worked on a variety of topics, including social and organizational theory, market managerialism and higher education, culture and popular culture, utopianism, conspiracy theory, the Apollo space programme, business ethics, critical management studies and alternative organizations. At the moment, he is working on various topics in culture and organization as well as *The Routledge Companion to Alternative Organizations* (with George Cheney, Valerie Fournier and Chris Land) (Routledge, 2013).

Lisa Peñaloza joined Kedge Business School in Bordeaux, France in 2012, as Professor-researcher. Over the past 20 years, she has held academic positions in the US at the University of Colorado, University of Illinois and University of Utah; and at EDHEC Business School in France. Her research and teaching interests emphasize the use of qualitative methods for better understanding of the complex interplay of cultural signification and economic valuation in families, communities and marketing strategy. Recent studies include the negotiation of identity among elderly consumers (with Barnhart); the importance of organizational identity in international marketing (with Cayla); trust in rural buyer–seller relationships in India (with Abdul); the normalization of credit among US consumers (with Barnhart); the bittersweet role of remittances in Mexican transnational families (with Cavazos Arroyo); and the nature of value co-creation in sustainable businesses (with Mish). Her work has been published in such journals as the *Journal of Marketing, Journal of Consumer Research, Consumption Markets & Culture*, and *Marketing Theory*. She is a former editor of the journal *Consumption Markets & Culture* and coedited the MBA text *Marketing Management: A Cultural Approach*. She has produced two films, *Generaciones: Cultural Memory, Identity, and the Market* and *Inside the Mainstream: Credit in the U.S. White Middle Class* (with Barnhart), and written a one-act play, *Dinner with Marx and Baudrillard*.

Sarah Robinson is Senior Lecturer in Management and Organisation Studies at Leicester University School of Management. She has previously worked at Lancaster Management School and the Open University Business School. She has a keen interest in the development of hermeneutic and visual methodologies as applied to critical approaches to the study of leadership and international management learning. Her work includes the semiotic analysis of Business School websites (Elliott and Robinson, 2012), and she is currently working on papers using visual data on the media representations and scapegoating of banking leaders and the rise and fall of corporate campuses.

Jonathan Schroeder is the William A. Kern Chair in Communications at Rochester Institute of Technology. Prior to this, he was Chair in Marketing at the University of Exeter, UK and has held visiting appointments at a wide range of institutions. He has published widely on branding, communication, identity and visual issues. He is the author of *Visual Consumption* (Routledge, 2002) and co-editor of *Brand Culture* (Routledge, 2006). He is Editor-in-Chief of *Consumption Markets & Culture*, and serves on the editorial boards of numerous journals, including *Advertising and Society Review*, *European Journal of Marketing*, *Innovative Marketing*, *Journal of Business Research* and *Marketing Theory*.

Harriet Shortt is a Senior Lecturer in Organisation Studies at Bristol Business School, University of the West of England. Her research focuses on the often overlooked and under-researched people in organizations, specifically the work of hairdressers and other service workers. She has an expertise in innovative visual methodologies including participant-led photography and collaborative photo-interviews.

Bent Meier Sørensen is Professor of Organizational Philosophy at Copenhagen Business School. He believes very much in the power of the visual, which is why we have to bend it, pull it apart, cut it up and, perhaps, juxtapose it, not to stay too faithful to its – in the final analysis – rather enigmatic message. Nietzsche's warning that, if you gaze into the abyss, the abyss gazes back is, however, also an invitation to keep experimenting with that gaze, and with that abyss.

David Stiles is Senior Lecturer in Management Strategy and International Business in the Management Department at University of Canterbury, Christchurch, New Zealand. His current research focuses on organizational identity, image and culture, strategy-as-practice, strategy implementation in emerging countries and higher education strategy. David has published in such journals as *British Journal of Management*, *Public Administration*, *Public Management Review*, *Financial Accountability and Management* and *Culture and Organization*. He previously lectured at Cardiff University, UK, and has worked as a senior manager and consultant in a variety of private and public sector organizations.

Tim Strangleman is Professor in Sociology at the University of Kent. His research interests are in the sociology of work and its historiography, work identity and meaning, deindustrialization and nostalgia. He is the author of two books, *Work and Society: Sociological Approaches, Themes and Methods,* with Tracey Warren (Routledge 2008), and *Work Identity at the End of the Line? Privatisation and Culture Change in the UK Rail Industry* (Palgrave, 2004). He has been developing visual aspects of his work for more than a decade, collaborating with a number of artists and photographers and working on projects funded by the ESRC and British Academy. His work combines contemporary and archive material and explores what the visual adds to our sociological imagination. He has recently been involved in making a documentary film, *Watermark*, which tells the story of the closure and workplace culture of a former paper mill in Dover, Kent. He is currently working on two books that draw extensively on visual material: *Corroding Capital: Work, Place, Culture and the Meaning of Deindustrialisation* and *Imagining Work in the Twentieth Century*, which is a study of the Guinness Brewery at Park Royal in West London.

Alexander Styhre (PhD, Lund University) is Chair of Organization Theory and Management, Department of Business Administration, School of Business, Economics and Law, University of Gothenburg. Alexander has published widely in the field of organization theory and his work has appeared in *Journal of Management Studies, Organization Studies, Human Relations, Organization*, and elsewhere. In addition, Styhre is author and co-editor of several research monographs and textbooks including the most recent *Organizations and the Bioeconomy* (Routledge, 2012) and *Assembling Health Care Organizations* (co-authored with Kajsa Lindberg and Lars Walter) (Palgrave Macmillan, 2012). Alexander is the Editor-in-Chief of *Scandinavian Journal of Management*.

Steven S. Taylor is an Associate Professor in the School of Business at the Worcester Polytechnic Institute (WPI) in Worcester, Massachusetts, USA. His research focuses on the aesthetics of organizational action and reflective practice. Recently, his academic work has focused on theorizing what business can learn from the arts and management as craft. He is the author of the book *Leadership Craft, Leadership Art*, and is the editor of the journal *Organizational Aesthetics*. Steve is also a playwright whose work has been performed in England, France, Poland, Canada, Denmark, New Zealand, Italy, Australia and the USA.

Alex Thompson is a Lecturer in Marketing at the University of Exeter Business School. Alex specializes in commercial market research methods and consumer representation. His background is in the field of anthropology and socio-cultural approaches to marketing. Alex's ethnographic approach to marketing seeks to address the mechanism through which consumer knowledge is produced, contested and generated through an understanding of videoethnographic research practices.

Ekant Veer is an Associate Professor of Marketing at the University of Canterbury, New Zealand. His research looks to understand consumer culture and consumption practices in various offline and online contexts. His research specifically focuses on how marketing can be used to improve consumer wellbeing and welfare. He is the current Editor of the *Journal of Research for Consumers* (www.jrconsumers.com) and has been published in various international journals, such as *Marketing Letters, Journal of Marketing Management, European Journal of Marketing, Consumption Markets & Culture* and *Advances in Consumer Research*.

Samantha Warren is Professor in Management at the University of Essex. She is a leading writer on visual methodologies in organization studies, has co-edited several journal special issues and has convened a major international management conference (Standing Conference on Organizational Symbolism) on the theme of 'Vision'. In 2007, she co-founded *in*Visio: the International Network for Visual Studies in Organisations, and she has been the recipient of four recent research grants relating to the sensory dimensions of organization and management.

Her published research spans subjects as diverse as organizational aesthetics, the management of pregnancy, the iPod, workforce drug-testing, flash-mobbing as a contemporary organizational form, the organization of Christmas and the professional identity of accountants. She is currently working on a project to explore the social role of smell in office contexts.

Dvora Yanow, Visiting Professor in Wageningen University's Faculty of Social Sciences, Communication, Philosophy, and Technology Department, is a policy/political and organizational ethnographer and interpretive methodologist whose research and teaching are shaped by an overall interest in questions of the generation and communication of knowing and meaning in organizational and policy settings. Research topics include state-created categories for race-ethnic identity, immigrant integration policies and citizen-making practices, research regulation (ethics board) policies, practice theory and the life cycle, science/technology museums and the idea of science, and built space/place analysis. Her most recent book, *Interpretive Research Design: Concepts and Processes* (Routledge, 2012), with Peregrine Schwartz-Shea, is the first volume in their co-edited Routledge Series on Interpretive Methods.

Acknowledgements

This project benefited from support from the Economic and Social Research Council, UK, in the form of a seminar series grant to develop the International Network for Visual Studies in Organisations, 2007–2009, and a Researcher Development Initiative grant for Advanced Visual Methodologies in Business and Management, 2010–2012. We thank the members of the grant teams: Chris McLean, Caroline Scarles, Russ Vince, Jane Davison, Bill Lee, Harriet Shortt, as well as the speakers, attendees and organizers of the 2008–2009 ESRC seminars, which served as a basis for many of the chapters in this volume, including: Susanne Tietze, Gill Musson, Susan Hayward, Julian Burton, Jan Betts, Harriet Shortt, Burkard Sievers, Susan Halford, Craig Prichard, Lee Parker, Jon Prosser, Sharon Schembri, Albena Yaneva, Andrew Hill, Susie Howarth, Rafael Alcadipani, Amelia Jones, Cathy Johnson, Nina Kivinen, Karen Dale, Eric Guthey, Helen Couchman and Claus Noppeney. Special thanks go to Sarah Pink, Alexander Thompson, Sarah Warnes, Sarah Robinson, Pauline Leonard, Norah Campbell, Dvora Yanow, Nicola Bateman, Janet Borgerson, Sarah Watts, Tim Strangleman, and Charlotte Smith for constructive feedback on early drafts of the chapters. We also thank Alexander Krause, David Varley, Peter Lloyd and Rosie Baron at Routledge for their interest, support and guidance. Finally, we thank Lasse Lychnell for kindly granting us permission to use his photograph for the front cover of the book.

Introduction

The visual organization

Emma Bell, Samantha Warren and Jonathan Schroeder

> Images are now as much a material force in and between societies as are economic and political forces.
>
> *(Victor Burgin 1996: 21)*

> [In organizations] there is a frantic production of images which are circulated; a frantic translation of incoming images into collages of 'ideal companies'; less frantic but steady attempts to translate those images into the local practices and vice-versa; and once again a production of self-images to be sent around.
>
> *(Barbara Czarniawska 2000: 216)*

> Images are more real than anyone could have supposed.
>
> *(Susan Sontag 1977: 180)*

Why 'visual organization'?

The visual is a pervasive feature of contemporary organization. Visually rich, digital, Internet and new social media technologies have revolutionized the ways in which organizations interact with their stakeholders. Visual brands drive value creation in an 'experience society' that increasingly prizes the 'look and feel' of products and services (La Salle and Britton 2003). Organizations hire employees to project the right visual aesthetic in service encounters (Pettinger 2004; Warhurst et al. 2012); managers commission visually striking workspaces to engender creativity and commitment from employees (Myerson and Ross 2006); accountants design annual reviews and financial reports to project the right image (Davison 2008); visual artists deploy corporate strategies in building their 'brand' (Schroeder 2006); and product designers and marketers create alluring visual brands to promote goods and services (Charters 2006). These trends are amplified in post-industrial societies moving towards economies founded on creative and knowledge-intensive industries.

Image management is not just big business in the private sector, but is also a leading concern for other kinds of organization, such as charities, universities and governments (e.g. Czarniawska 2000; Harper 2012). The visual enters into almost every aspect of organizational strategy, operations and communication, reconfiguring basic notions of management practice and introducing new challenges into the study of organizations. Enabled by connective technologies, the management of image has become a vital task that cuts across traditional geographical and cultural boundaries (Müller 2008). As well as presenting new vistas for visual organizational communication, these technologies have opened up a potentially more democratic space for image production and circulation, particularly through platforms such as YouTube, Twitter and Facebook, requiring organizations to deal with the 'scattered images' that result (Price *et al.* 2008). This *Companion* serves as an introduction to some of these developments.

Organizations and individuals inhabit (and generate) a visually saturated culture where visual communication, based on showing, or mimesis, has come to occupy a parallel status to verbal communication, based on telling, or diegesis. This, combined with the ubiquity of the image as a cultural construction as outlined above, implies that organizational researchers cannot avoid studying them (Bell and Davison 2013; Meyer et al. 2013). Yet, to date, a corpus of literature addressing the empirical and conceptual issues in researching visual organization has at best been disparate or missing altogether. Across the social sciences and humanities, however, the visual in recent years has become 'more acceptable, more viable and more central' (Pink 2012: 3) to the development of theoretical, empirical and methodological understandings. In this volume, we draw on interdisciplinary insights to establish a fundamental resource base for the visual organizational researcher.

In compiling *The Routledge Companion to Visual Organization*, our aim was to assemble the latest research and current thinking on the role of the visual in understanding organizations from a range of perspectives. Through this, we seek to provide comprehensive insight into the ways in which organizations and their members visualize their identities and practices and how these practices are understood by those external to the organization, including researchers. Visual organization studies includes researchers in the traditional management sub-disciplines of marketing and consumer behaviour, accounting, organization studies, operations management and tourism, as well as those working in areas of social policy, sociology of work, media and cultural studies. It is thus a highly interdisciplinary, or perhaps even post-disciplinary, field of scholarship and practice.

Visualizing the linguistic turn

The *Companion* also focuses on the visual as a necessary counterweight to redress the privileging of language in organizational research (Holliday 2001; Strangleman 2008). This 'way of seeing' argument (Bell and Davison 2013) invites researchers to take images seriously as legitimate objects of enquiry, rather than merely viewing them as an adjunct to linguistic meaning-making activities (Biehl-Missal 2012; Pink 2001; Rose 2007). It implies that visual communication is fundamentally different from verbal communication through the immediate, multi-sensory impact that comes from viewing an image that combines rationality with emotionality (Spencer 2011). This draws attention to the epistemological aspects of the visual, by focusing on the potential for creating new forms of knowledge and understanding.

The visual turn in organizational analysis can therefore be seen as a response to and a reaction against the linguistic turn (Rorty 1979), which positions language at the heart of social interaction and the construction of meaning. The linguistic turn represented a major shift in twentieth-century thought, through proposing that language shapes our understanding of reality, and that meaning can never be understood independently of language. These ideas have been immensely influential in organizational studies, particularly through the development of

Introduction

discourse, narrative and conversational methodologies, which invite a view of organizations as 'socially constructed verbal systems' that are 'actively constructed through discursive activity' (Rhodes and Brown 2005: 178).

Bell and Davison (2013) argue that the linguistic turn may now have gone too far in asserting the primacy of language in the constitution of socially constructed organizational realities. Consequently, visuality and vision remain under-explored and under-theorized in the organizational literature (Styhre 2010). A focus on the visual thus opens up areas that have been less explored by management researchers, such as embodiment (Emmison and Smith 2012), and reveals insights relating to established topics, such as corporate branding, that cannot be accessed by studying language alone (e.g. Davison 2009; Schroeder 2002; Warren 2008). And yet organizational researchers on the whole have been relatively slow to respond to this 'visual turn', causing some to suggest that it remains something of a 'blind spot' in our field (Cohen et al. 2006; Guthey and Jackson 2008; Strangleman 2004).

However, there have been signs of a growing interest in the study of visual organization in recent years. Since 2000, the EIASM (European Institute for Advanced Studies in Management) has supported three workshops on aesthetics, art and management, two workshops on the theme of *Imag[in]ing business*, three on architecture, and a workshop on fashion. In 2008, the UK ESRC (Economic and Social Research Council) supported a seminar series, organized by the *in*Visio research network (International Network for Visual Studies in Organisations, www.in-visio.org), which the editors of this *Companion* were active in founding.

More recently, we have been working with colleagues on a UK ESRC Researcher Development Initiative to develop a comprehensive online resource base for visual organizational researchers. Many of the authors in this *Companion* have also contributed methodological resources relating to their areas of interest, which *in*Visio members can access from the *Inspire* project website (http://moodle.in-visio.org) (see www.in-visio.org for details on how to become a member of *in*Visio). Publishers have also commissioned several books on the visual and organizations, including Jonathan Schroeder's (2002) *Visual Consumption*; Emma Bell's *Reading Management and Organization in Film* (2008); *Visual Culture in Organizations: Theory and Cases* (2010) by Alexander Styhre; and Puyou, Quattrone, McLean and Thrift's edited collection, *Imagining Organizations: Performative Imagery in Business and Beyond* (2012). Special issues on the visual have also appeared in various management journals including *Accounting, Organizations and Society* (1996), *Organization* (2004), *Accounting, Auditing & Accountability Journal* (2009), *Culture and Organization* (2012) and *Qualitative Research in Organizations and Management* (2012), several of which Samantha Warren has been involved in editing. We see this *Companion* as building on the work these publications have developed, but also consolidating disparate pockets of interest in the visual to create a state-of-the-art reference text for the field.

The *Companion* comprises 24 chapters written by established and developing scholars of visual organization from a wide variety of disciplinary perspectives. It is organized into five parts. The rest of this introductory chapter introduces the structure of the book, along with an overview of the intellectual landscape sketched out in each part. It closes with some thoughts on the future of visual organization as both organizational phenomena and a field of enquiry.

Part I: Thinking visually about organization

As the title of this part suggests, the visual occupies a primary place in what it means to think about organization. Psychoanalytic theory, for example, places the image at the centre of

3

thought itself, through dreams or fantasy (Ehrenzweig 1965), and visual methodologies such as freehand drawing seek to access this unconscious strata of mental life (Broussine and Simpson 2008; Vince and Warren 2012). Since the Enlightenment, the role of sight has also been privileged over other sense impressions in what comes to stand for valid knowledge (Corbett 2006), and natural science's preoccupation with what is empirically observable – and therefore measurable and amenable to prediction – permeates everyday culture as what we can *see* is understood as evidence or other proof of reality, even though we also know that photographs are partial, constructed and subject to manipulation (Goldstein 2007). CCTV cameras in public places, photographs on passports and driving licences, and controversies around privacy and 'tagging' in personal photographs displayed on social media sites are all testament to the importance our societies place on images and the role of the visual (in the developed world at least). The four chapters in this part all interrogate the status of the visual as knowledge in various ways, some addressing more theoretical agendas, and others focusing on the mechanics of *how* images function. This is important in extending the focus of visual organization studies beyond a potentially narrow preoccupation with analysing particular instances of images as divorced from wider organizational practices, for, as Burri reminds us, 'an adequate sociology of images should not exclusively focus on how best to interpret and use an image in social sciences – thus revealing its meanings – but as well examine how images themselves shape cultural meanings' (2012: 54).

Recent developments in visual communication studies have sought to explain the operation of images, ranging from approaches that parallel linguistic equivalents to more performative theories based on the 'aesthetic gestalt' of the image. Proponents of the linguistic perspective put forward theories of 'visual literacy' (Avgerinou and Pettersson 2011), which can be extended to the moving image through the idea of 'videocy' (Goldfarb 2002), while semioticians seek to embed a structuralist understanding of images into a social context, such as the extensive work emerging from media communication studies (e.g. Kress and van Leeuwen 2006). At the more performative end of the spectrum, organizational symbolists (Gagliardi 1990) and scholars of organizational aesthetics (Strati 1999) argue that the visual is but one mode of apprehending the sensory realm of organizational life and, moreover, that this realm is not available to us in the bite-size chunks of linguistic syntax, but as a whole whose elements interact with one another to generate affect (Hancock 2005; Langer 1957). Finally, contemporary thinking from the field of geography insists on the non-representational analysis of images and treats them not as mimetic correspondences with what they claim to depict, but as circulating artefacts with past, current and future trajectories (Thrift 2007). Many of these themes are picked up in the later chapters of this *Companion* as applied to a range of organizational images and issues. The intention of the four chapters in this part is to lay some broader epistemological foundations to support them.

The opening chapter, by Wendelin Küpers, firmly reminds us that vision is of the body. Taking a phenomenological stance, inspired by Merleau-Ponty (1962), he argues that what we see is a constructed artefact of our being-in-the-world, and not a situation whereby we stand outside of and/or apart from that which we gaze upon. Nonetheless, in organizational life, he suggests that this is forgotten; instead, we treat vision as an objectifying phenomenon, ignoring the material conditions – such as gender, seniority, power, occupational position and so on – that enable certain kinds of seeing while others are prevented (see also Styhre 2010). These 'scopic regimes' also rest on what we do *not* see (Acevedo and Warren 2012) and Küpers invokes Merleau-Ponty's idea of the 'chiasma' to explain how the blind spot in our vision is what allows us to see in the first place. After reviewing a range of practical organizational possibilities, he concludes the chapter by stressing the importance of *in*visibility as much as visibility in organizational life.

Chapter 2, by Jane Davison, operationalizes some of these ideas by drawing together strands of the work of Roland Barthes in relation to the visual, showing how his oeuvre has been a popular choice for visual organizational scholars to date. Addressing both Barthes' structuralist and post-structuralist writings, she puts forward a comprehensive framework for analysing images and applies these ideas to the study of corporate annual reports. Beginning with Barthes' semiotic system of linguistics, denotation and connotation (Barthes 1982), she brings to life the utility of the linguistic approach to analysing visuals through interpretation of the annual reports of Ernst & Young, showing how their strategic use of images carries important and persuasive organizational messages. Davison then turns to Barthes' more post-structuralist theory found in *Camera Lucida* (1980) to engage in exploration of those aspects of images that are less amenable to systematic classification. She concludes by noting how useful Barthes' ideas are to organizational disciplines, as they can be applied to a host of different visual forms, from everyday images to fine art, for example.

Staying with the idea that images can tell us more than we know, or are able to express, Bent Meier Sørensen explores what he calls 'the method of juxtaposition' in Chapter 3. Here we start to see the overlaps between epistemology, theory and method that so characterize 'the visual' as an organizational discipline – in this case, it is only by effecting a practical method that the conceptual underpinning of juxtaposition can be understood. As the label indicates, the approach here is to place one image alongside another and view them simultaneously. Interpretation does not arise from consideration of a single image, nor from each member of the pair in turn, but from an oscillation *between* the two pictures, which draws on the viewer's stock of cultural knowledge as well as the features of the images themselves – in what Belova (2006) calls 'the event of seeing'.

Donncha Kavanagh's discussion in Chapter 4 asks how the visual came to be so prominent in Western thought, as noted above. Dealing with an ocularcentric critique of 'the visual organization', he skilfully shows how ocular metaphors have infiltrated language to the extent that they have come to stand for knowledge itself (e.g. in *sight* or *view*point in English and the verb sa*voir* – to know – in French). This, he contends, shapes the way we are able to conceive of organization, noting that language constructs the object it purports to describe, and tends to objectify it. In common with Küpers' opening chapter, Kavanagh calls for greater cognisance of other sensory modalities in understanding organizational life (e.g. see Pink 2007; Mason and Davies 2009). However, as Warren (2012) has argued, holding such a position in mind might allow us to consider the extent to which vision as a faculty of perception evokes sensory experience beyond immediate apprehension with the eyes. Indeed, the division of sight from the 'other' senses may rest on a Western-centric idea of 'the senses' as separate organs generating discrete information about the world, rather than combined receptors of a flow of experience. In research practice, this has thoughtfully been critiqued by Wheeler (2012) who, writing as a blind ethnographer, questions this hierarchical division. All of which returns us to where this part of the *Companion* began, that sight (as other sensory modalities) is an artefact of the body-in-the-world. We continue this theme of divisibility and interconnectedness into Part II of the book.

Part II: Strategies of visual organization

When this *Companion*'s editors were helping to create the *Inspire* Researcher Development webpages (http://moodle.in-visio.org/), we were faced with many decisions about where the various materials should go – what should we call them to make them useful and recognizable? Several of the proposed sections – including 'Visual Theory', 'Visual Methods' and 'Visual

Analysis' – seemed quite similar, and thus we needed a rationale for dividing the content among them. In our reckoning, 'Visual Methods' generally refers to research techniques that employ photography, film, video or other methods to produce images – images that can serve as data for analysis. 'Visual Analysis' implies researching images that already exist – corporate images, advertising, corporate films, websites, and so on. This distinction, which we all understood theoretically and perhaps intuitively, became clearer to us when attempting to communicate it to beginning researchers. Of course, these categories are not perfect, and many projects may involve multiple 'visuals' – encompassing pre-existing imagery as well as visual 'data' obtained expressly for a particular research study. Nonetheless, we find thinking about visual analysis and visual methods as differing realms useful.

This part of the *Companion* is largely concerned with visual analysis. As influential visual theorist John Berger reminds us, 'seeing comes before words' (1972: 7). Hence, the visual offers a means of generating multi-sensory impact through communicating in a way that is more immediate and emotionally powerful than that enabled by words. The visual can enable understanding of social action in cultural contexts and embodied experience of actions as they unfold in space and over time. This has not gone unnoticed by contemporary organizations that use increasingly sophisticated visual approaches to interact with stakeholders, formulating their core business and prominent stakeholders as visually apprehended artefacts. This part of the *Companion* addresses these organizational processes through suggesting that we have overlooked other forms of organizational meaning-making and alternative possibilities for generating knowledge about organizations. This is in part because interpretive organizational research over the past decade has been primarily concerned with what Boden (1994) calls 'the business of talk' in organizations, and what the use of language achieves. While there is no doubt that everyday talk is an important medium through which people make sense of organizations and get things done, there is a danger in treating talk as 'central to what organizations *are*' (Boden 1994: 9, original emphasis) and ignoring the visual strategies that are central to organization. However, to do so relies on overcoming the deep mistrust of visual communication in the social science disciplines, which is traditionally seen as subservient to linguistic structures of meaning (Holliday 2001). One of the reasons for this is that visual rhetoric and corporate communication require new research approaches, concepts and frameworks (Campbell and Schroeder 2011; Phillips and McQuarrie 2008).

As art historians Sturken and Cartwright (2009) note, because we are all immersed in our own visual cultures and continually bombarded by a stream of images in our organizational lives, there is a tendency to assume that we are automatically visually literate. This has two effects: first, we tend not to notice how images are constructed, operate, circulate and are consumed, since they are backdrops and props we take for granted in everyday life; and, second, we can assume that we need no special training or critical expertise in order to incorporate visual methods into a research design. Yet visual images are culturally and historically contingent. In writing about photography, philosopher Vilém Flusser argues:

> images come between the world and human beings. They are supposed to be maps but they turn into screens: Instead of representing the world, they obscure it until human beings' lives finally become a function of the images they create. Human beings cease to decode the images and instead project them, still encoded, into the world 'out there', which meanwhile itself becomes like an image – a context of scenes, of state of things.
>
> *(2000: 10)*

This state of affairs is, in turn, exacerbated by the traditional role of images as illustrations for accompanying text and the subordinate/decorative role images have often played throughout history (Davis 2011; Emerling 2012; Mitchell 1994). These tendencies are particularly prevalent in organizational life where principles of scientific management and rational, scientific modes of knowledge have tended to hold the greatest power and influence (Gagliardi 1996).

The chapters in this part address a number of questions. What does the production and consumption of images mean for marketing, organization and society? How do organizations conduct visual research? What are the connections between artistic and organizational use of images? How does the handling of images in the allied fields of advertising, aesthetics, ethnographic research and corporate identity shed light on the relationships between visual processes and organization? Strategies of visual organization cut across disciplinary lines, thus we turn to researchers from marketing and consumer research as well as organization studies for answers.

In Chapter 5, Lisa Peñaloza and Alex Thompson draw upon their extensive experience in ethnographic consumer research to discuss how visual images inform consumer research as well as corporate ethnographic research. They present a notion of the 'visual consumer' to describe how consumers are represented, in academic studies as well as corporate research on consumer behaviour. They show how ethnographers deploy visual images in situating consumers as active agents in negotiation with organizations and the market by drawing on two studies, one looking at how consumers interact with the National Western Stock Show and Rodeo in the US, the other a commercial study investigating how diabetes patients manage their disease with blood-monitoring technology. They offer useful insights into how visual research frames consumers, how consumption is embodied visually and how organizations visually conceptualize their customers.

The next chapter, by Laurie Meamber, provides a thorough review of visual consumption, focused on how images are produced, circulated and consumed. She addresses key theoretical topics of *co-creation* – how consumers and organizations work together to produce meaning and value; the role of aesthetics in productive consumption, and how consumers consume the images that organizations produce. In this way, she provides a useful connection between marketing and organization, and points the way towards interdisciplinary work to uncover how the visual 'works'.

Beatriz Acevedo, in Chapter 7, delves deeper into the realm of aesthetics and imagery by showing how portraiture interacts with leadership. She offers an in-depth, historically minded example of how portraiture reveals aspects of leadership that show how art history provides a useful addition to the visual organization researcher's toolbox. She foregrounds *charisma* as a key attribute that artists visually highlighted, and provides an illuminating example of the Spanish painter Velázquez's portraits of famous leaders.

In Chapter 8, Norah Campbell calls advertising 'the most readily recognized, ubiquitous and contentious symptom of organization'. She diagnoses that symptom by providing a theoretically rich account of the signs and semiotics of advertising, working against the grain of much analysis that dwells in an 'advertising as persuasion' paradigm, rather than understanding that advertising also functions as visual representation (see also Chapter 2). She focuses on images of technology, and reveals how they offer visions of fantasy, couched in cultural narratives, myths and fables. She closes with some insightful thoughts on new forms of visual advertising, including social media.

The final chapter in this part, by Pierre Guillet de Monthoux, offers an historically grounded analysis of how organizations and artists have used aesthetics, and argues that organizations can be productively seen as art projects. He also shows how visual artists, writers and performing artists work in response to one another, revealing the interconnectedness of the visual with the other senses (see also Chapters 6, 7 and 16). He provides an intellectual genealogy of current concerns of the visual organization, replete with historical and contemporary examples drawn from the lively world of the art market.

Together, these chapters reveal the interdisciplinarity of the visual organization. They suggest that understanding organizations visually involves several tasks: (1) cultural and historical contextualization; (2) including consumers and other stakeholders; (3) connecting to other sensory and aesthetic forms; and (4) dealing with the market.

Part III: Visual methodologies and methods

As the field of visual organizational studies expands, there is a need to reflect on how different methods and methodologies are required in order to understand the wealth of visual data that organizations generate. This forms the focus for the third part of this *Companion*. The ease with which visual data can be digitally captured, stored and shared, whether in the form of static or dynamic images, opens up possibilities for organizational researchers to apply these methods of data generation, analysis and dissemination to a far greater extent, as addressed by all the chapters in this part in various ways. This includes analysis of already existing visual material and ways of doing research that generate visual material. It encompasses a wide variety of forms of visual data, including two-dimensional (e.g. websites, photographs, graphs and diagrams) and three-dimensional or lived media (such as dress and architecture).

Visual studies of organization alter the focus of methodological enquiry and, through this, have the potential to generate different conceptual and theoretical possibilities, so that 'hitherto unknown and non-apparent things become visible' (Knowles and Sweetman 2004: 7). The chapters in this part of the *Companion* highlight some of the theoretical and empirical possibilities enabled by visual organizational analysis, showing how systematic study using visual methodologies and methods has the capacity to reveal the inner mechanisms through which organizational life is ordered and understood. The chapter authors adopt different paradigms (Knowles and Sweetman 2004) in their approach to visual organizational studies. Some are predominantly realist in orientation, regarding images as evidence that provides a record of existing phenomena and events. Others adopt a more post-structuralist stance, analysing how visual communication can be used to construct and privilege a particular version of reality in a way that is supportive of particular ideological interests. A third group lies within the semiological paradigm, focusing on analysis of existing images which are regarded as texts that can be read to uncover the cultural and ideological messages that they communicate; this is the approach taken by Dvora Yanow in the first chapter in this part of the *Companion* (see also Chapter 8).

As these different possibilities highlight, visual methodologies involve more than simply collecting and analysing visual data. Instead, they rely on adopting a methodological framework that enables the visual to be taken seriously as a means of communication and a source of meaning. Although the chapter authors in this part all take a broadly interpretive approach in their visual organizational research (which is consistent with the application of visual methodologies across the social sciences, cf. Rose 2007), they acknowledge the possibilities for positivistic application of visual methods, for example in relation to scientific management (see Chapter 10) or via content analysis (see Chapter 15). The six chapters in this part thus illustrate the considerable methodological and paradigmatic diversity that characterizes the visual study of organizations, a point reinforced further by the *Companion* as a whole.

In Chapter 10, Dvora Yanow provides a wide-reaching analysis of visual studies and organization. She makes an important distinction between methodology and method: the former relating to epistemological and ontological presuppositions about the nature of reality and how we understand it, and the latter concerning the data generation and analysis possibilities that particular methodologies imply. She further outlines the triadic relations upon which visual communication relies. Finally, she identifies a series of procedural logics that underpin the use of visual methods in studying organizations and concludes by stressing the need to avoid naive realism.

Chapter 11, by Kelly Norris Martin, draws on communication studies to offer a conceptual framework for understanding the visual that has relevance across the social sciences. Her chapter illustrates the extent to which methodological opportunities and challenges in visual studies cut across disciplinary boundaries and demonstrates the strengths and limitations associated with three main theoretical approaches: visual rhetoric, visual studies and visual communication.

The practical and methodological implications associated with the use of video in organizational research are explained by Jean Clarke in Chapter 12, through focusing on her application of this method in studying entrepreneurship. Clarke discusses some of the messy aspects of conducting this type of research that often get written out of methodological accounts in journal articles. She also highlights the strengths of the method in focusing on the symbolic aspects of entrepreneurial impression management, while also recognizing the ethical challenges that video-based research raises.

Chapter 13 by Ekant Veer provides a complement and a contrast to Clarke's chapter, by focusing on ethnographic videoethnography in the field of consumer research, where such methods have been taken up enthusiastically. Veer argues that researchers need to be open to the creative and aesthetic opportunities for data collection, analysis and dissemination that videoethnography offers, but not to get carried away by this – the purpose of such methods being ultimately to produce an academic rather than an artistic product.

In Chapter 14, David Stiles explains the role of the drawing method as a data collection and analysis tool in organizational research. As an interpretive researcher, his aim is to encourage participants to produce pictorial representations that provide insight into how they understand organizational identity. This metaphorical approach to meaning-making relies on semi-structured interviewing in order to elicit research participants' own interpretations of their drawings.

An historical, sociological approach to visual organizational studies is offered by Tim Stangleman in Chapter 15. Strangleman argues that sociologists of work have been reluctant to acknowledge the visual and provides numerous fascinating historical examples to demonstrate the importance of corporate photography as a resource in understanding organizations. His emphasis is on the analysis of already existing visual material but also in understanding the socio-historical conditions under which particular corporate images were created and the ideological interests they served.

The visual turn in organizational research is relatively nascent. By bringing together the authors in this part, we have sought, in the spirit of interdisciplinarity, to coalesce some of the strands of work currently being done within different fields and create a dialogue between them. However, there is considerable potential for greater use of visual methodologies and methods in organizational research (see Bell and Davison 2013 and Meyer et al. 2013 for examples). The chapters in this part illustrate some of the innovative approaches and practices that have so far been adopted. We hope this provides inspiration to other organizational researchers in exploring visual methodologies and methods as possible means of knowledge creation.

Emma Bell, Samantha Warren and Jonathan Schroeder

Part IV: Visual identities and practices

In this part of the *Companion*, we shift attention away from methodology and towards the subject matter of visual investigations. These chapters are grouped together as exemplars of the ways in which visual organizations are produced through the practices of their members, such as arts-based organizational development (Berthoin Antal, Taylor and Ladkin, Chapter 16), visual management (Bateman and Lethbridge, Chapter 19) and Hoffman's excursion into the fascinating world of simulations in Chapter 21. We have also included the descriptor 'identities' in the heading for this part, since half the chapters here address this in some way, either corporate – as in Elliott and Robinson's exploration of company websites in Chapter 17 and organizational identities performed through visual social media discussed by Leonard in Chapter 20 – or the more individual work identities elucidated by Shortt, Betts and Warren in Chapter 18.

Image-based research lends itself well to the study of identity since much can be learned about individuals and organizations by studying the ways in which they choose to present themselves to the outside world (e.g. Goffman 1959). The image of accountants, for example, has been studied on an individual level using auto-photographic methods (Parker and Warren 2012) and on a profession level through industry advertisements (Baldvinsdottir *et al.* 2009). Likewise, hairdressers' workplace identities have been researched using photo-narratives (Shortt and Warren 2012) and visual identity-scapes (Shortt 2012). Acevedo (2011; see also Chapter 7, this volume), Guthey and Jackson (2008) and Chatterjee and Hambrick (2007) have all attended to the visual dimensions of CEO and/or leader portraits in the media. Enduring organizational dimensions such as gender (im)balance (Benschop and Meihuizen 2002) and the diversity of workforces (Swan 2010) have also been studied in relation to how organizations choose to portray themselves in visual media. Campbell *et al.* (2009) reveal how individual faces are employed in the service of ethical identities of corporations through their inclusion in annual reports and, somewhat alarmingly, studies are emerging from psychology disciplines that study bone structure and the physiognomy of faces, purporting to 'demonstrate that static physical attributes can indeed serve as reliable cues of immoral action, and provide additional support for the view that evolutionary forces shape ethical judgement and behaviour' (Haselhuhn and Wong 2011: 1). Taking a corporate-level view, Schroeder's work on branding (2012) has established the centrality of the visual to engendering appropriate representations of branded products and services as well as the identities of the organizations that produce them, as discussed in Part III of this *Companion*. This small snapshot of contemporary research on identities gives a flavour of some key themes to be found in wider literature relating to identity, some of which are further explored in the chapters in this part.

We begin with a case study of organizational theatre drawn from the field of arts-based organizational development. In Chapter 16, Ariane Berthoin Antal, Steven Taylor and Donna Ladkin remind us that arts-based organizational interventions do not employ just the visual arts in their practice and, on the contrary, it is what you do *not* see happening – that which is invisible and below the surface – that is of value in organizational development using these methods.

Next, Carole Elliott and Sarah Robinson (Chapter 17) assemble a framework to investigate company websites and develop what they call 'corporate web identity' (CWI). They map out a useful summary of existing research on corporate websites, contrasting the different methodological approaches hitherto taken in this emerging field. Consisting of five elements: mobility, accessibility, visuality, interactivity and customization, Elliot and Robinson's CWI framework is a development of corporate visual analysis based on semiotics (e.g. see Melewar and Karaosmanoglu 2006), but importantly takes account of both the dynamism of web-based media and its multi-modality. Their framework also allows analysis of user interaction with the site and, as such, represents an important development in bridging the producer vs. viewer divide that is common in visual organizational analysis.

Chapter 18, by Harriet Shortt, Jan Betts and Samantha Warren, takes a micro-level perspective on visual identity in an organizational context, this time in relation to the objects that workers display and/or hide in the course of their everyday lives. Using three photographic case studies, they show how possessions and workplace tools variously assist with the creation of individual workplace identities. First, through the display of personal effects on desks in an office environment; second, how attachment to certain functional objects in the open-plan workspace of the hair salon surfaces in the relationship between individual identity and that projected by the organization. Finally, they draw on data that illustrates how items hidden from view act as a buffer against the colonization of individual identity by the employer in a wide variety of workplaces. They conclude with interesting reflections about the future of individuals' visual organization practices.

Staying with visual practices, the next chapter by Nicola Bateman and Sarah Lethbridge reports on the use of 'visual management boards' to organize and manage operations and teams in a range of organizational settings. In this chapter, they give an overview of this approach as a development from 'lean' production techniques and reflect on what it is that the visual adds in this context. This chapter is an interesting departure from others in the *Companion*, in that it does not focus on pictorial or expressive media, but on more traditional forms of graphical presentation of information as elegantly elucidated by Tufte (1986). Bateman and Lethbridge remind us that managers have been using 'the visual' to organize for a lot longer than management researchers have been studying this!

Chapter 20, by Pauline Leonard, takes us from traditional visual practices to the cutting edge of corporate identity management through social media. In a chapter that complements Bell and McArthur's discussion of Free Range Studios in Chapter 23, Leonard's discussion takes us down a more technological path, through arguing that we are witnessing the birth of 'org/borgs' (Haraway 1991) and that 'social media is contributing to a blurring of, and even a challenge to, previously established boundaries in organizational practices, positions and identities'. Encompassing a review of literature on 'corporate visual identity' and an overview of social media technologies used by organizations at the time of writing, Leonard's comprehensive discussion serves as a valuable foundation for the development of what is perhaps the least theorized visual organizational practice of all those included in this volume.

The final chapter in this part of the *Companion* (Chapter 21) stays with technology to some degree through Steve Hoffman's mapping of the role of simulations in producing organizational action. Using examples as diverse as boxing sparring and Artificial Intelligence scientists, Hoffman builds a three-dimensional conceptual model on which to map different kinds of simulations according to their degree of virtuality, realism and pre-enactment. He concludes that simulations involve a greater degree of experiential engagement – despite being marked off from 'normal' organizational interaction as play or 'not serious' – that goes beyond a superficial focus on the visual.

Thus, the writers in this part consider the myriad resources and techniques used by organizational members, employees as well as managers, to construct identities, visualize their organizational experiences and communicate them to others, often in emergent and unplanned ways.

Part V: Visual representations of organization

The *Companion* concludes with three chapters that deal with the diverse and expanding ways in which organizations and their members represent themselves using visual media and analyse how these representations are understood culturally. As others have noted, there is significant potential in studying how organizations and their members are represented visually, whether this involves television, printed media, film, websites or social media (Hassard and Holliday 1998; Hassard and Buchanan 2009). Such images constitute already existing visual data that often circulates globally, as an aspect of popular culture that is consumed by mass audiences. Images of organization are also produced by and for internal audiences, such as employees, as a way of representing their experience and shared identity in relation to their work, whether or not this is consistent with the image that managers would like them to represent to external audiences (see Bell 2012a; Brannan *et al.* 2011 for examples).

Earlier chapters in this *Companion* have highlighted the ways in which organizations seek to influence and control these representations, for instance through managing brand identity. However, the polysemic nature of the visual means that images can be read in very different ways, depending on the reader's positionality, cultural knowledge and life experience (Spencer 2011). In many instances, images are thus highly resistant to control, since they form part of a nonlinear circuit of communication (Hall 1980), in which the producer of the image is only partially in control of the message. This draws attention to the role of audiences as active agents in the construction of meaning, and the need for organizational researchers to remain cautious about privileging their own reading of an image and to pay attention to the ways in which diverse audiences make sense of it (Bell 2012b).

A further dynamic that increases the complexity of interpreting visual representations of organizations relates to intertextuality, or the tendency for images to refer and relate to other image texts, genres and visual codes. This encourages a focus on the provenance of images, as continually imported from one social context to another 'in order to signify ideas and values which are associated with that other context by those who import the sign' (Kress and van Leeuwen 2001: 10). Individual images can thus be understood semiotically as constituting elements in an overall sign system, the meaning of which is derived experientially based on what is done to produce them and how they are read. The three chapters in this part explore this process of sign-making and its cultural consequences.

In Chapter 22, Alexander Styhre explores how professional groups use visual culture, which he defines as the totality of practices, traditions, beliefs and assumptions about visuality in organizations, to construct shared expertise. Using case study material relating to medical professionals, he shows how medical visualizing technologies, such as the microscope, form the basis for constructing 'professional vision' as a source of expertise. Drawing on diverse historical and theoretical sources, he argues that these visual skills are acquired through embodied practice as a form of collectively shared, experiential knowledge. Styhre thus highlights the contextual specificity of sign systems and the role of professionals in producing and providing authoritative readings of images.

Chapter 23, by Emma Bell and McArthur, focuses on the construction and contestation of organizational authenticity based on a case study of a US-based creative design company. It is argued that authenticity is a contested issue in digital Web 2.0 image world where visual representations are no longer understood as providing evidence that something exists or happened in the way that the image claims (Sontag 1977). Their analysis focuses on short films disseminated via YouTube that communicate critical messages about corporate social responsibility. Through the involvement of McArthur, who was an author of some of these texts, in the analysis of this circuit of visual communication, insight is gained into the role of the producer as well as the audience, as sites of meaning.

The final chapter, by Martin Parker, calls into question the capacity of the visual to adequately deal with representations of organization such as those found in popular culture.

Parker is resistant to the idea of methods as a way of structuring our understandings of the visual, arguing that a focus on the visual falsely imposes a sense of order on organizational culture and thus constitutes a way of *not* seeing organizations, so creating new blind spots (as also highlighted by the chapter by Küpers with which we opened this *Companion*).

Towards the future

In closing, we suggest some issues that are likely to shape the future of visual organization. First, is the growing digitalization of the image. The Internet has demanded that almost every aspect of organizations is visualized – not just customer-facing operations such as marketing, but also accounting, finance, investor relations, human resources and public relations. Many organizations exist as virtual entities, and most organizations use the Internet for an increasing number of functions, including training, benefit management, evaluation and purchasing. What does this imply for the visual (digital) organization? Gone are the days when an organizational website merely 'represented' the organization – now many organizations exist entirely via their website. Furthermore, older understandings of websites tend to imply some form of mimesis to the 'real' or physical organization. This distinction is collapsing.

Second, and closely related to the digital, is the rise and rise of social media. Our own use of social media often refers to the logic of organizations and marketing, in that we build our reputation, gather an audience and market ourselves via various platforms and emerging applications. Organizations now seem compelled to engage with social media, as discussed by Leonard in Chapter 20, which have their own emerging 'logic'.

Third, one side effect of digitalization is the growing use of cameras, in the form of webcams, mobile phone cameras, iPads and computer cameras to capture our experience, including our experience at work or on the job. Formerly, snapshot photography was generally focused on leisure activities – few 'amateur' photographs showed mundane aspects of organizational life. Now, however, the camera is everywhere (and the lines between 'work', 'home' and 'play' are blurring). What might this mean for the visual organization? Certainly, visual methods encompass so-called 'consumer-generated' and employee-generated photographs, and many researchers have used photo elicitation tools of having informants photograph their work (Warren 2012). However, the explosion of images – many relevant to concerns of organization researchers – heralds a new era of visual organization.

Fourth, surveillance images abound. Apart from workers and researchers recording images, our lives are constantly being visually recorded by traffic cameras, security cameras and web cameras – some of which we are aware of, many of which we are not. Security and surveillance images, for the most part, are recorded 'automatically', that is, without an active photographer or camera operator, making their agency and hence ontological status fragmentary. These images may provide fertile ground for visual organization researchers, particularly those interested in ethical issues of identity, privacy and personal control of one's image. In any case, surveillance images are certain to play an important roles in the visual organization of the future.

Finally, the ubiquity of visual images does not necessarily improve one's ability to see – to actively engage one's senses in reflective analysis in thinking about the visual in organization (cf. Schroeder and Borgerson 2005). Thus, issues of visual literacy, which hover over many of the *Companion*'s chapters, may become (even) more important, both for researchers and for everyone involved in organizations, as we come to depend ever more on visual images.

To conclude this introduction, we hope that *The Routledge Companion to Visual Organization* will provide comprehensive insight into the ways in which organizations and their members visualize their identities and practices and how they are viewed by those who are external to organizations, including researchers. We have endeavoured to provide a useful, cutting-edge *Companion* that will be useful to students and researchers in business and management disciplines, including organization studies, marketing and accounting, as well as in other fields of organizational or visual study, including health and social care, film, communication, sociology, media and cultural studies. Academics and students seeking convenient access to an expanding and innovative area should find this *Companion* a comprehensive, yet detailed introduction to the visual organization. The web-based *Inspire* resources associated with this book will also continue to evolve, providing further commentary as the field develops. Through this we aim to provide established researchers with insight into the current state of knowledge, current debates and relevant literature in this rapidly emerging field.

References

Acevedo, B. (2011) 'The Screaming Pope: imagery and leadership in two paintings of Pope Innocent X', *Leadership* 7(1): 27–50.
Acevedo, B. and Warren, S. (2012) 'Vision in organization studies', *Culture and Organization* 18(4): 277–284.
Avgerinou, M. and Pettersson, R. (2011) 'Towards a cohesive theory of visual literacy', *Journal of Visual Literacy* 30(2): 1–19.
Baldvinsdottir, G., Burns, J., Nørreklit, H. and Scapens, R. (2009) 'The image of accountants: from bean counters to extreme accountants', *Accounting, Auditing & Accountability Journal* 22(6): 858–882.
Barthes, R. (1980) *La Chambre Claire*, Paris: Le Seuil. (Barthes, R. (2000) *Camera Lucida*, trans. R. Howard, London: Vintage.)
——(1982) 'Rhétorique de l'image', in *L'obvie et l'obtus*. Paris: Le Seuil, 25–42. (Originally published in 1964.) (Barthes, R. (1977) 'Rhetoric of the image', in *Image, Music, Text*, trans. S. Heath, London: Fontana Press, 32–51.)
Bell, E. (2008) *Reading Management and Organization in Film*, Basingstoke: Palgrave Macmillan.
——(2012a) 'Ways of seeing death: a critical semiotic analysis of organizational memorialization', *Visual Studies* 27(1): 4–17.
——(2012b) 'Understanding audiences', in J. Billsberry, J. Charlesworth and P. Leonard (eds) *Moving Images: Effective Teaching with Film and Television in Management*, Charlotte, NC: Information Age Publishing.
Bell, E. and Davison, J. (2013) 'Visual management studies: empirical and theoretical approaches', *International Journal of Management Reviews*, forthcoming.
Belova, O. (2006) 'The event of seeing: a phenomenological perspective on visual sense-making', *Culture and Organization* 12(2): 93–107.
Benschop, Y. and Meihuizen, H. (2002) 'Keeping up gendered appearances: representations of gender in financial annual reports', *Accounting Organizations and Society* 27(7): 616–636.
Berger, J. (1972) *Ways of Seeing*, London: BBC and Penguin.
Biehl-Missal, B. (2012) 'The atmosphere of the image: an aesthetic concept for visual analysis', *Consumption Markets & Culture*, [online]. Available at http://www.tandfonline.com/doi/abs/10.1080/10253866.2012.668369.
Boden, D. (1994) *The Business of Talk: Organizations in Action*, Cambridge: Polity Press.
Brannan, M.J., Parsons, E. and Priola, V. (2011) *Branded Lives: The Production and Consumption of Meaning at Work*, Cheltenham: Edward Elgar.
Broussine, M. and Simpson, P. (2008) *Creative Methods in Organizational Research*, London: Sage.
Burgin, Victor (1996) *In/Different Spaces: Place and Memory in Visual Culture*, Berkeley: University of California Press.
Burri, R. (2012) 'Visual rationalities: toward a sociology of images', *Current Sociology* 30(1): 45–60.
Campbell, D., McPhail, K. and Slack, R. (2009) 'Face work in annual reports: a study of the management of encounter through annual reports, informed by Levinas and Bauman', *Accounting, Auditing & Accountability Journal* 22(6): 907–932.
Campbell, N. and Schroeder, J.E. (2011) 'Visual culture', in D. Southerton (ed.) *Encyclopedia of Consumer Culture*, Thousand Oaks, CA: Sage, 1506–1510.
Charters, S. (2006) 'Aesthetic products and aesthetic consumers: a review', *Consumption Markets & Culture* 9(3): 235–255.

Chatterjee, A. and Hambrick, D. (2007) '"It's all about me": narcissistic CEOs and their effects on company strategy and performance', *Administrative Science Quarterly* 52: 351–386.

Cohen, L., Hancock, P. and Tyler, M. (2006) 'Beyond the scope of the possible: art, photography and organisational abjection', *Culture and Organization* 12(2): 109–125.

Corbett, J.M. (2006) 'Scents of identity: organisation studies and the cultural conundrum of the nose', *Culture and Organization* 12(3): 221–232.

Czarniawska, B. (2000) 'The European capital of the 2000s: on image construction and modeling', *Corporate Reputation Review* 3(3): 202–217.

Davis, W. (2011) *A General Theory of Visual Culture*, Princeton, NJ: Princeton University Press.

Davison, J. (2008) 'Rhetoric, repetition, reporting and the "dot.com" era: words, pictures, intangibles', *Accounting, Auditing & Accountability Journal* 21(6): 791–826.

——(2009) 'Icon, iconography, iconology: visual branding, banking and the case of the bowler hat', *Accounting, Auditing & Accountability Journal* 22(6): 883–906.

Ehrenzweig, A. (1965) *The Hidden Order of Art: A Study in the Psychology of the Artistic Imagination*, London: Weidenfeld & Nicolson.

Emerling, J. (2012) *Photography: History and Theory*, New York: Routledge.

Emmison, M. and Smith, P.D. (2012) *Researching the Visual*, 2nd ed., London: Sage.

Flusser, V. (2000) *Toward a Philosophy of Photography*, trans. A. Mathews, London: Reaktion Books.

Gagliardi, P. (1990) *Symbols and Artefacts: Views of the Corporate Landscape*, Berlin: de Gruyter.

——(1996) 'Exploring the aesthetic side of organizational life', in S.R. Clegg, C. Hardy and W.R. Nord (eds) *Handbook of Organization Studies*, London: Sage Publications, 565–580.

Goffman, E. (1959) *The Presentation of Self in Everyday Life*, Harmondsworth: Penguin Books.

Goldfarb, B. (2002) *Visual Pedagogy: Media Cultures in and Beyond the Classroom*, Durham: Duke University Press.

Goldstein, B. (2007) 'All photos lie: images as data', in G. Stanczak (ed.) *Visual Research Methods: Image, Society and Representation*, London: Sage.

Guthey, E. and Jackson, B. (2008) 'Revisualizing images in leadership and organization studies', in D. Barry and H. Hansen (eds) *New and Emerging Approaches in Management and Organization*, London: Sage, 84–92.

Hall, S. (1980) 'Encoding/decoding', in S. Hall, D. Hobson, A. Lowe and P. Willis (eds) *Culture, Media, Language: Working Papers in Cultural Studies 1972–79*, London: Routledge, 128–139.

Hancock, P. (2005) 'Uncovering the semiotic in organizational aesthetics', *Organization* 12(1): 29–50.

Haraway, D. (1991) *Simians, Cyborgs and Women*, New York: Routledge.

Harper, D. (2012) *Visual Sociology*, New York: Routledge.

Haselhuhn, M. and Wong, E. (2011) 'Bad to the bone: facial structure predicts unethical behaviour', *Proceedings of the Royal Society (B)* doi:10.1098/rspb.2011.1193.

Hassard, J.S. and Buchanan, D.A. (2009) 'From modern times to Syriana: feature films as research data', in D.A. Buchanan and A. Bryman (eds) *Sage Handbook of Organizational Research Methods*, London: Sage.

Hassard, J. and Holliday, R. (1998) *Organization-Representation: Work and Organizations in Popular Culture*, London: Sage.

Holliday, R. (2001) 'We've been framed: visualising methodology', *Sociological Review* 48(4): 503–521.

Knowles, C. and Sweetman, P. (2004) *Picturing the Social Landscape: Visual Methods and the Sociological Imagination*, London: Routledge.

Kress, G. and van Leeuwen, T. (2001) *Multimodal Discourse: The Modes and Media of Contemporary Communication*, London: Arnold.

Kress, G. and van Leeuwen, T. (2006) *Reading Images: The Grammar of Visual Design*, London: Routledge.

Langer, S. (1957) *Philosophy in a New Key*, Milton Keynes: Open University Press.

La Salle, D. and Britton, T. (2003) *Priceless: How to Turn Ordinary Products into Extraordinary Experiences*, Cambridge, MA: Harvard Business School Press.

Mason, J. and Davies, K. (2009) 'Coming to our senses? A critical approach to sensory methodology', *Qualitative Research* 9(5): 507–603.

Melewar, T.C. and Karaosmanoglu, E. (2006) 'Seven dimensions of corporate identity: a categorisation from the practitioners' perspective', *European Journal of Marketing* 40(7/8): 846–869.

Merleau-Ponty, M. (1962) *Phenomenology of Perception*, London: Routledge.

Meyer, R.E., Höllerer, M.A., Jancsary, D. and van Leeuwen, T. (2013) 'The visual dimension in organizing, organization, and organization research', *Academy of Management Journals* 7(1): 487–533.

Mitchell, W.J.T. (1994) *Picture Theory*, Chicago: University of Chicago Press.

Müller, M. (2008) 'Visual competence: a new paradigm for studying visuals in the social sciences', *Visual Studies* 23(2): 101–112.

Myerson, J. and Ross, P. (2006) *Space to Work: New Office Design*, Aldershot: Gower.

Parker, L. and Warren, S. (2012) 'Personal life values and the accountant's stereotype', Interdisciplinary Perspectives on Accounting Conference, Cardiff, 11–13 July.

Pettinger, L. (2004) 'Brand culture and branded workers: service work and aesthetic labour in fashion retail', *Consumption Markets & Culture* 7(2): 165–184.

Phillips, B. and McQuarrie, E. (eds) (2008) *Go Figure: New Directions in Advertising Rhetoric*, Armonk, NY: M.E. Sharpe.

Pink. S. (2001) *Doing Visual Ethnography: Images, Media and Representation in Research*, London: Sage.

——(2007) *Doing Sensory Ethnography*, London: Sage

——(ed.) (2012) *Advances in Visual Methodology*, London: Sage.

Price, K., Gioia, D. and Corley, K. (2008) 'Reconciling scattered images: managing disparate organizational expressions and impressions', *Journal of Management Inquiry* 17(3): 173–185.

Puyou, F.-R., Quattrone, P., McLean, C. and Thrift, N. (eds) (2012) *Imagining Organizations: Performative Imagery in Business and Beyond*, London: Routledge.

Rhodes, C. and Brown, A. (2005) 'Narrative, organizations and research', *International Journal of Management Reviews* 7(3): 167–188.

Rorty, R. (1979) *Philosophy and the Mirror of Nature*, Princeton: Princeton University Press.

Rose, G. (2007) *Visual Methodologies: An Introduction to the Interpretation of Visual Materials*, London: Sage.

Schroeder, J.E. (2002) *Visual Consumption*, London: Routledge.

——(2006) 'Aesthetics awry: The Painter of Light™ and the commodification of artistic values', *Consumption Markets & Culture* 9(2): 87–99.

——(2012) 'Style and strategy: snapshot aesthetics in brand culture,' in F.-R. Puyou, P. Quattrone, C. McLean and N. Thrift (eds) *Imagining Organizations: Performative Imagery in Business and Beyond*, London: Routledge, 129–151.

Schroeder, J.E. and Borgerson, J.L. (2005) 'An ethics of representation for international marketing communication', *International Marketing Review* 22: 578–600.

Shortt, H. (2012) 'Identityscapes of a hair salon: work identities and the value of visual methods', *Sociological Research Online* 17: 2.

Shortt, H. and Warren, S. (2012) 'Fringe benefits: valuing the visual in narratives of hairdressers' Identities at Work', *Visual Studies* 27(1): 18–34.

Sontag, S. (1977) *On Photography*, New York: Farrar, Straus and Giroux.

Spencer, S. (2011) *Visual Research Methods in the Social Sciences*, London: Routledge.

Strangleman, T. (2004) 'Ways of (not) seeing work: the visual as a blind spot in WES?', *Work, Employment and Society* 18(1): 179–192.

——(2008) 'Representations of labour: visual sociology and work', *Sociological Compass* 2(4): 1491–1505.

Strati, A. (1999) *Organization and Aesthetics*, London: Sage.

Sturken, M. and Cartwright, L. (2009) *Practices of Looking: An Introduction to Visual Culture*, 2nd ed., New York: Oxford University Press.

Styhre, A. (2010) *Visual Culture in Organizations: Theory and Cases*, London: Routledge.

Swan, E. (2010) 'Commodity diversity: smiling faces as a strategy of containment', *Organization* 17(1): 77–100.

Thrift, N. (2007) *Non-representational Theory: Space, Politics, Affect*, London: Routledge.

Tufte, E.R. (1986) *The Visual Display of Quantitative Information*, Cheshire, CT, USA: Graphics Press.

Vince, R. and Warren, S. (2012) 'Qualitative, participatory visual methods', in C. Cassell and G. Symons (eds) *The Practice of Qualitative Organizational Research: Core Methods and Current Challenges*, London: Sage, 275–295.

Warhurst, C., van den Broek, D., Hall, R. and Nickson, D. (2012) 'Great expectations: gender, looks and lookism at work', *International Journal of Work, Organisation and Emotion* 5(1): 72–90.

Warren, S. (2008) 'Empirical challenges in organizational aesthetics research: towards a sensual methodology', *Organization Studies* 19(4): 559–580.

——(2012) 'Having an eye for it: aesthetics, ethnography and the senses', *Journal of Organizational Ethnography* 1(1): 107–118.

Wheeler, P. (2012) 'Sightless vision: reflections on a paradox', *Culture and Organization* 18(4): 285–304.

Part I
Thinking visually about organization

1
Between the visible and the invisible in organizations

Wendelin Küpers

Introduction

To explore visibility in organizations, this chapter takes a phenomenological approach, attending to the lived experience of visibility at work. Phenomenology aims to investigate the conditions of the appearance of phenomena and therefore what is taken as reality. In particular, it tries to reveal the difference between *what* appears and *how* something appears or becomes visible as something, as well as the interplay between these two modes. It also considers the invisible in this process. Following a phenomenological perspective, this chapter discusses specifically the status, distinct qualities and entwinement of visuality and the invisible in organizational life-worlds and how they function together as sources of perceiving, knowing, performing and understanding in and about organizations.

Vision, visuality, visual culture, and visual consumption are playing an increasingly important role in present-day societal and economic contexts as well as in organizational and managerial life-worlds (Campbell, Chapter 8, this volume; Fuery and Fuery 2003; Schroeder 2005). Apparently, we are living – and organizations are situated – in a visually over-saturated culture (Gombrich 1996), moving in the light and shadows of a visual or pictorial turn, towards an intensifying and ambiguous ocularcentric orientation (Jay 1993, 2002; Kavanagh, Chapter 4, this volume; Mitchell 1994, 2005b). Yet, despite the proliferation of powerful visual forms and relationships, the influence and production of various images or impacts of visual technologies in everyday working life, research on visuality and visual culture seems to be peripheral to the study of organizations. In part, this may be caused by organization studies' self-image, that is, what it regards as its identity, 'object' and methodologies – in other words, traditionally, 'the visual' is not seen as part of organizational analysis. However, as this chapter explains, visuality and the power to make visible are shot through all organizational action.

The phenomenon of vision and concepts of visualities are complicated and implicated experiences and notions, with a long history of contested philosophical and scientific thinking and analysis, with regard to their ontological and epistemological status. Due to specific orders of visibilities, members of, as well as entire, organizations are framed in a certain way of looking. To explore this further, the chapter first presents a brief discussion of epistemologies of the eye and the act of seeing as performative practice. The role of vision in processes of organizational objectification, as well as concrete practices of seeing in organizations, are then critically discussed, before the phenomenology of 'visio-corporeality' by Merleau-Ponty (1962, 1995) is put forward as a way to 're-member' and 're-view' organizations beyond objectified and instrumentalized forms. In particular, this shows how phenomenology helps understanding of the sensuous embodied socio-cultural 'life-worlds' of organization with its visible and invisible dimensions. Afterwards, some theoretical, methodological and practical implications for organization studies and practice will be put forward and the chapter concludes with an outline of some limitations and future perspectives.

Epistemologies of eyes and practices of seeing: how do we see and enact seeing?

Vision and visually related phenomena are conceptualized, analysed, understood and interpreted in various ways. Seeing, sight and vision are embroiled in different, ambivalent, sometimes contradictory approaches. Visuality can be characterized as 'how we see, how we are able, allowed or made to see, and how we see this seeing or the unseen therein' (Foster 1988: ix). Instead of taking seeing and visualizing or vision for granted, visual processes need to be explored in the way they appear, and then problematized, theorized, historicized and critiqued (Mitchell 2005a: 264).

For theorizing critically and developing a methodological conceptualization, it makes analytical sense to differentiate between 'epistemologies of the eye' and 'practices of seeing' (Daston and Galison 2007; Brighenti 2007: 323).

Epistemologies of modern science attribute a fundamental role to the sense of sight, in the forms of vision and evidence that are taken as intellectual apprehension. 'Epistemologies of the eye' refer to the theoretical body of elaborations that address the philosophical and scientific theories of what vision 'is'. These perspectives explore 'how vision can be used to formulate and generate "representational" knowledge as well as how perceptions of subjects and scientific selves and their scientific gaze are constituted' (de Bolla 1996: 76).

While the 'epistemologies of the eye' are concerned with theories of how knowledge claims are made on the basis of the inter-relationships between seeing, saying and previous knowing, 'practices of seeing' are studied in how vision and visuality happen, structure and inform everyday working life more concretely. Accordingly, 'practices of vision' refer to actual practicalities and day-to-day engagements with visual presentations and ways of seeing, serving specific purposes (Styhre 2010: 187). In contrast, 'practices of seeing' explore how visual practices are occurring, developed and used in various domains of presentation.

Epistemologies and practices are interrelated. On the one hand, theorizing is a form of practice. Interestingly, the Greek word for theory – *theoria* – shares a root with *theatron* or *theatre*, which literally means 'a place for seeing' (Sennett 2008: 124). Seeing in this sense is a theoretical affair that can be related to practice, as it is a kind of doing. On the other hand, practices of seeing do not occur in a social and cultural vacuum, but are always structured and organized in accordance with specific conditions, processes and epistemic regimes. How we acquire, interpret and transform what (and the way) we see is always contingent on the cultural and historical context of the seer and of seeing. Practices of presentational performative seeing are always that which is 're-presentative' of and formed by a particular regime of vision, which is predominant in a locally situated and embodied setting. There is no 'seeing *per se*' detached from other embodied practices and procedures. In turn, vision and visuality are of essential significance for exploring how practices are constituted and how they engender organizational practices, processes and effects.

The role of vision and practices of seeing in organizations

Driven by the need for security and a quest for certainty, gazing vision (for example, by management (systems) on employees' actions) is often instrumentalized so as to posit a distance and exert mastering control. Accounting systems, production statistics and the reduction of human endeavour to, say, performance management metrics are all examples of how organizations make some activities and actions visible (but not others) and, in doing so, render them as objects. The passion and drive of the employee's commitment to the organization is only made visible as a point on a Likert scale that can be ranked and contrasted with others' scores, for example. Following a 'frontational' ontology, this representational regime is characterized by an enframing and foreclosing of the viewer, which makes him/her 'stand-over-against' the world (Heidegger 1977 [1938]). This stance makes phenomena or things that organizations seek to visualize and our relationship to them sub-stances, standing under the masterful transfixing and possessing gaze in search of surveillance, security, control – thereby objectifying them. The operationalization of this objectifying vision therefore 'sees' only what can be measured, in other words, what can come to count as an object to be used. Intentionally or otherwise, this leads towards obscuration, occlusion or even suppression of other ways of seeing.

For example, Oswick (1996) develops a diagnostic approach for organization development including pattern recognition, spatial localization and visual imagery, illustrating vision as effect of an objectifying approach – including blind spots, visual accommodation or visual acuity. In diagnosing various forms of 'impaired vision' in organization, such as blindness, blurred or tunnel vision, as well as short- and long-sightedness, Oswick (1996: 148) argues we can consider the unseen, the unseeable and the overlooked in organizational life. Furthermore, these objects are posited as a 'naturalized' vision; they are taken as evidential proof of how things are, while overlooking the generative dimensions of visibility that allow objects to come into focus, forgetting the diacritical systems and meaning that are at play in object-formation. The logic of objectification tends to ignore, exclude or omit the social-historical horizon and material and affective or subjective dimensions, which, however, motivates and impacts the seeing. In other words, we forget that we are socialized into what is worth looking at and how we see it, which is *learned* and not given.

This powerful practice of vision can be seen in what has been called 'professional vision'. This orientation refers to a specific and contingent 'way of seeing' that is embedded in professional identities, ideologies, formal training and everyday work experience (Goodwin 1994, 1995; Styhre 2010: 43). Accordingly, knowing and knowledge is always already embedded in practices of seeing that are highly specialized and based on membership of communities and collectives. Importantly, for Goodwin (1995), vision is a professional skill that is neither individual nor innate, but always based on collective agreements and acquired through training and actual practice in the field of expertise. Visuality can also be observed as being executed in formal ceremonies and rituals of organizations with its visible language and visual labour or contexts. Practically, various depicting forms of graphs, ratios and other forms of mathematized vision or ways of visualizing time manifest an objectifying orientation (Styhre 2010: 18).

Echoed in the work of Spoelstra: 'some things can be seen only through organizations, other things can be organized only through seeing, and yet other things can only be hidden through organizations' (2009: 376). Spoelstra refers to this organizational 'hiddenness' as 'black blindness'. Organizations produce this 'darkness' of deprived sight for their members through the division of labour and the creation of distance – in other words, they prevent certain people from seeing certain things. In contrast to this dark form, a white blindness manifests as an excess of vision, as if taken away by light. Similar to Benjamin's concept of 'phantasmagoria' as a deceptive image

('*Blendwerk*'), designed to dazzle, whitening blindness refers to a 'brilliance that conceals in its shining but which also produces its own singular attraction' (Spoelstra 2009: 379), such as, for example, overly brilliant leaders or products or employees or shining corporate image-work in times of crisis (de Cock *et al*. 2011). Being ruled by a scopic regime, seeing has been systematically sharpened and disembodied, becoming an errant, clinically fixed but clouded gaze (Jütte 2005: 186). Accordingly, the gaze in organizations, with their orientation towards abstraction, masculinity, coldness and detachment, is used as a disciplinary mechanism and technique of disembodied panoptic eyes and social panoptical control and visio-governmentality (Foucault 1977; McKinlay and Starkey 1998).

Correspondingly, within organization studies, the objectivist and disembodied understandings of phenomena are connected to an ocularcentric orientation (e.g. Belova 2006; Kavanagh 2004), using vision instrumentally, for example, to produce a 'functionalist transparency' (Bloomfield and Vurdubakis 1997). Dale (2000) argues that the scientist's 'eye' dissects what it sees in order to perform an invasive investigation. It fragments and reorganizes the object of study, and this anatomizing urge pervades almost all areas of knowledge, both as a metaphor and as a form of representation. Thus, the critique of the 'culture of dissection' presents vision as an incising, objectifying and ordering activity aimed at seizing and appropriating the other.

Politics of visibility

In contemporary, supposedly more transparent society, organizations are required to become more visible, and thus accountable, through reporting, disclosure and, of course, unintentionally through Internet activity by those who their operations affect. This implies a specific politics of visibility (Tapscott and Ticoll 2003; Zyglidopoulos and Fleming 2011). Exploring such politics would consider the controlling and contested in-visibilities of power (Simpson and Lewis 2005) and seeing that organizations and their members are situated in a tension between 'transparency-as-secrecy' and 'secrecy-as-transparency' with its inherent mutual dependencies and contradictions (Birchall 2011). As Birchall argues, considering a possible symbiotic relationship between secrecies and transparencies means invoking a politics of opacity and openness, which is able to work with the inherent tensions involved. In other words, organizations display in order to conceal and vice versa. All is not what it first appears. For example, forms of organizational perception management practices, such as organizational aesthetics, architecture and design or marketing/branding, use a variety of manipulations of the visual in organizational spaces or settings to produce desirable effects in a market or the public (Styhre 2010: 13). Imageries are used as persuasive communication for apparently rendering organizations visually, but adopting a politics of visibility asks 'what is simultaneously obscured?' by these practices (Dale and Burrell 2003; Messaris 1997).

Accounting practices in organization, for example, are shaped and experienced as a series of images that undertake political work on behalf of organizations (Belkaoui 1987; Brown 2010; Davison 2011). Accounting reports are ostensibly artefacts providing visual traces (or drivers) of past, present and future activities (e.g. budgets) or other organizational action, processes and culture. They use words, diagrams, tables, charts and pictures to create images that render tangible and intangible values or specific organizational activities visible or invisible (Hines 1988). Yet re-presentational aspects of accounting are a symbolic, cultural and hegemonic force (Lehman and Tinker 1987). For example, corporate sustainability reports contain unsubstantiated visual rhetoric on 'clean, green images' and manifest a 'reporting-performance' gap (Adams 2004). For instance, the journey metaphor related to sustainability can be used as visual rhetoric that masks issues of what it is that businesses are actually or even supposedly moving 'towards', thus paradoxically reinforcing business-as-usual (Milne et al. 2006).

However, critical scholars in this field have begun to document different accounting(s) than those of, for and by this visual instrumentality, potentially providing new envisioning, and stimulating new imag(in)ings (Brown 2010). Although there has been some myopia with regard to the importance of the visual in accounting and accountability (Davison and Warren 2009), some social and environmental accounting reports incorporate externalities and non-monetary (re)presentations and delineate consensual meaning-making processes, whereas others proactively seek to represent marginalized views and develop alternative professional bodies and digital technologies to challenge mainstream accounting (Brown 2010).

In another political move, 'vision', and especially visualization of strategy (Eppler and Platts 2009) and strategic envisioning, is seen as one of the critical tasks transformational or visionary leaders claim to perform to demonstrate their competencies (Larwood et al. 1995). However, this is often merely a rhetorical vision without authentic involvement or recognition of followers that then can result in disillusionment and distrust, instead of inspiration and motivation (Coulson-Thomas 1992) or various forms of resistance (Westley 1990). When we take recognition as a form of social visibility embedded in interaction between leader and followers, the lack of recognition has disempowering effects: in formulating strategic visions, the followers become paradoxically *in*visible. We can see this as having very real effects. In post-Fordist, more competitive workplaces, the conditions for genuine, intersubjective recognition have been eroded as supposedly counter-productive (Dejours 2003). Instead of recognition, managerial regimes of 'sur-veillances' (literally: to view from above) can function as subjugation and means of control through disciplinary regimes. Inherent in such one-way managerial gaze is a kind of dehumanization of the observed – and possibly, although indirectly, of the observer, too. Performance appraisals are an example par excellence of so-called 'recognition' in neoliberal organizations, which actually function as surveillance, control and objectification as also outlined earlier in this chapter.

The mono-gaze of the modern subject or agencies in organization is, thus, a 'grasping' look that advances political agendas by calculating, looking at in order to objectify and control, intentionally or otherwise, towards obscuration, occlusion or even suppression of other ways of seeing. For critically exploring underlying conditions of vision and regimes of visual representation and how practices of seeing serve as an influencing factor within organizations, a phenomenological approach is therefore helpful. It not only allows alternating between the two registers of epistemologies and practices, but also integrates them (Styhre 2010: 187). Merleau-Ponty, in particular, provides a post-Cartesian epistemology and relational ontology of embodied vision and an extended understanding of seeing and the invisible as part of embodied practice and somatic infrastructures in organizations, as opposed to the partial, political and 'enframed' vision this chapter has put forward thus far.

Merleau-Ponty's phenomenology of perception and ontology: between visible and invisible

Phenomenology has developed a profound critique of the hegemony of an optical paradigm in everyday vision. In critical distancing from the Husserlian transcendental visualism with its rectilinear, centred gaze of '*Wesensschau*' (intuitive glance upon essences), Heidegger (1962) showed that our 'visionary-being-in-the-world' is part of our endowment as an attunement. Accordingly, he developed a critique of the re-presentational orientation of enframed vision. He tried to show that this enframing is a mode of revealing – when we understand the concealment and unconcealment of what is happening; when seeing those moments when *Being* reveals itself as event we will be able to catch its hiding.

Like Heidegger, Merleau-Ponty (1962) disclosed other ways of experiencing the field of perception from a post-representational perspective, particularly by attending to the living body. For Merleau-Ponty, embodiment and perception – including seeing – are pre-reflexive openings onto a world. As such, these are not merely a screen of ideas or stage of Cartesian theatre, what we see 'out there' with us gazing upon it like an audience. Rather, processes of perceiving are incarnated through bodies as living media, especially mediating a crossing where matter, nature and culture, self and world as well as forces and meaning meet and unfold. Importantly, such an approach helps to bridge these divisions without effacing the differences between these poles of perception, knowledge and living.

Thus, he argues for a vision as being embodied. That is, when we see, we feel the presence of the thing we are looking at viscerally and are part of a 'carnal formula': a matrix of embodiment. By means of our bodily perceptive insertion into reality, we are always already vitally responsive to the demands of our situation upon our body. With this orientation, he aims at rediscovering and uncovering the system of inseparable 'self-other-things' (Merleau-Ponty 1962: 57) that create visual experience all together. The sensible and thus visual world is not comprised of a distinct subject that perceives distinct objects, but, rather, seeing is formed in the midst of the world and, as it were, in (relation to) phenomena experienced. Perception is not something that provides the embodied subject with access *to* the world, but rather embodied perception is only possible because it is *of* the world, whereby 'he who sees cannot possess the visible unless he is possessed by it, unless he is of it' (Merleau-Ponty 1995: 134–135).

By returning to this primordial experience, Merleau-Ponty is trying to find a third position beyond an empiricist-objectivist realism or materialism, as well as discount a rationalistic-subjectistic idealism or intellectualism. Both of these strands are reductive, reducing live-worldly phenomena, perception and sensation either to the realm of matter or to that of ideas of absolute subjectivity. He accused materialistic empiricism of reducing vision to observations of sensualistic in- and output mechanisms, and rationalistic intellectualism of turning vision to a function of thought and judgement. Instead, he argued for decentring perception and for a perspectivism, which are undermining the vision-generated dualism of subject and object.

Correspondingly, bringing the 'becoming visible' of the seen into the glance is not to take substantive sensualities, nor atomic sense data or a reason-oriented transcendentalism as a starting point. Rather, it requires considering the *process* of sensual experience of the entwined and embodied world-situated experiencing within a horizon and Gestalt figure-back-ground.

For Merleau-Ponty, perceiving and seeing is not holding an object egological with a frontational glance in a re-presentational way. Rather, the perceiver is embedded and delivered over to a field of the sensible and vision, which is structured in terms of the difference between things and colours, as a momentary crystallization of coloured being or visibility (Merleau-Ponty 1995: 132).

According to Merleau-Ponty, it is through a pre-cognitive multi-sensorial contact that the world appears within the perceptual field. Embodied visual sensing is mediating a pre-reflexive, yet active communion (Merleau-Ponty 1962: 212) and thereby meanings. Moreover, sensual and especially visual perception re-creates or reconstitutes the world at every moment (ibid.: 207). Seeing is not an act of the subject, but an event, which interplays between the one who sees, the visual and co-seeing in the sphere of visuality and performance. When we perceive things, we are constantly sensitive not only to what we perceive, but also, and essentially, to how well our experience measures up to our perceptual needs and desires. As sensing is embedded and related to a horizon of meaning, visual sensing and its making of sense are bound by historical and cultural perspectives as well as social practices. Therefore, the seeing body and the embodiment of senses are always already culturally mediated (Merleau-Ponty 1995: 147) and to make visible cannot be conceived without (reflecting) a specific order of visibility and field of indeterminate vision, which is then endowed with meaning (Merleau-Ponty 1962: 5, 9). The glance is itself an incorporation of the one who sees and searches into a given visibility, to which s/he always already belongs.

For Merleau-Ponty, embodied perception, vision, consciousness and the world are all intricately intertwined. Focus on bodily experiences and embodiment not as 'objects' or 'representations', but as constitutive and 'open' media led Merleau-Ponty to an anti-foundationalism, anti-essentialism and non-dualism, and philosophy of ambiguities. These orientations characterize his non-reductionistic approach and post-metaphysical ontology of visibility. The patterns of meaningful being and action, as base or media for visuality, exist neither in the mind nor in the external world. They are neither subjective nor objective, but constitute rather a kind of world *in between*, an inter-relationality of individual, social and trans-subjective practices. It is this 'between' within an ongoing continuity of ourselves, others and the natural world in what Merleau-Ponty calls 'flesh' that needs to be considered to understand vision, as both are enfolded ontologically.

Vision and chiasmic flesh: the invisible in organization

For Merleau-Ponty, habitual ways of seeing and vision – entwined with other senses, especially touch – belong to a certain style or mode of fleshly being and primordial expression. Metaphorically, this elemental flesh refers to a textile or common connective tissue. As such, it mediates between exterior and interior horizons as well as functions as an 'anonymous visibility' (Merleau-Ponty 1995: 131, 142). Thus, this elemental being manifests a kind of invisible ontological processual 'foundation' out of which things, selves and others arise in reciprocal relations in search for an expression. This reversible dynamic inter-relationship and its in(ter)- between of flesh is processed and described by Merleau-Ponty with the post-dichotomous metaphor of chiasm. Derived from the Greek letter '*chi*' (א), chiasm implies a criss-crossing structure, as is found at the point in the brain where the optic nerves from the right visual field cross to the left side and vice versa. Since these perception-enabling nerves are not photosensitive, they 'create hidden blind spots in the periphery of our field of vision before the chiasm reversibly rejoins the two sides of the visual field in one unified visibility' (Cataldi 1993: 73). The chiasm in Merleau-Ponty's thinking is a point of diffraction and a mediating link between different sides, like a connecting lacuna of intersection, i.e. giving and taking that constitutes all perception and communication without a final synthesis (Merleau-Ponty 1995: 143).

Metaphorically, the affective chiasm is like a wave that encounters sand at the seashore before flowing back to the sea. Through a constantly reversible flow, they form an interlaced circular movement; each advances by turn, folding over and coiling back through divergence and overlap(ping) as an 'identity-encompassing-difference' (Dillon 1988: 159). Within this fabric of experience or 'flesh' pre-personal, personal and interpersonal dimensions are processed and serve as a milieu of visibility; 'the place of emergence of a vision' (Merleau-Ponty 1995: 272). In this way, flesh serves as a reflexive sensibility of things (Carman 2008: 123). It carries or mediates the perceptibility of the environment and of ourselves as perceivers simultaneously. The intertwining and reversible chiasm of the visibility of vision is much the same as the tangibility of touch. Even more, flesh sensibly reflects the exposure of anything to which the world itself can be exposed and related in experience, including the bodily sense or experience of motor intentionality and movement, as well as the inter-folding of things and words, language and meaning.

Merleau-Ponty's phenomenology and indirect, chiasmic 'inter-ontology' not only allows understanding of phenomena and its ambiguous visibility as multiform and multivalent. His philosophy also makes it possible to integrate both: a critical post-representational epistemology of the eye-world-contact and practices of pre-cognitive, moving-touching gestures. Accordingly, the space of vision both surrounds us and passes through us. Phenomena meet our embodied eyes in such ways of expressing or speaking as if they are looking upon us, as if objects stare back while we look at them (Elkins 1996).

As perceivers, therefore, we partake in the 'enfleshed visible' that makes us see and be seen, but, crucially, the medium that brings this reversible relation about remains hidden. For Merleau-Ponty, this invisible is not only part of being in the visible; it is also what makes visible or visibility possible in the first place. Specifically, there are two interrelated forms of invisibilities (Al-Saji 2009): on the one hand, there is the invisibility of the historical and material genesis of vision and, on the other hand, there are what Merleau-Ponty call 'the invisibles of the visible' (1964: 181), which concern the formal conditions of how objects appear to us, like colour, line, depth and movement, themselves conditioned through social structures and hierarchies of power. Thus, the invisible is not a transcendental or mystical realm, but rather the effaced medium, through which vision is realized, like the seeing-enabling blind spot in the eye. Therefore, the invisible is not simply something visible that happens to be contingently away from sight. Rather, the invisible is what is given, without being an 'object'. Both the visible and invisible are like a crossing-over 'fold' in Being, as Merleau-Ponty explains, 'the invisible is a hollow in the visible a fold' (1995: 235); therefore, the invisible is intrinsic to the visible.

How the invisible accompanies or makes something visible is present also in organizing and organization. For Cooper, in all acts of form-making in organizing, what is visible and communicable is a 'pre-sense' of an originary absence: 'it is the vague sensing of an invisible that lies beyond – and yet within – all the visible, positive objects and forms that make up the visuality of our everyday being' (2006: 63). Thus, 'vision is always constituted by that which it is not' (ibid.: 64). An illustrating example of this neutral omnipresence and latency is the very co-organizing white space of this page, on which this very text has been written and which you read at this moment. Here meaning and visibility of meaning is co-constituted by the present absence conveyed b e t w e e n letters and lines.

In the same vein, according to the theory of social systems (Luhmann 1986: 180), organizations are fundamentally grounded in a paradox: they continuously require both to visibilize and to invisibilize the alternativity of processes in order to allow for interconnectivity between them. For example, as Schoeneborn (2008, 2010) found in an empirical case study of a project organization in a globally operating business consulting firm, vast inherently constitutive contingencies were disguised or made opaque to non-participants (i.e. 'hiding the elephant'). As he showed, all that remains after a project has been completed is a collection of highly condensed PowerPoint documents, manifesting narratives that focused on consistency, e.g. 'best practices' or 'success stories', rather than contingency, e.g. doubts, mistakes or alternative paths.

Visualizing the invisible can be approached instrumentally or critically. Following an instrumental orientation visualizing of intangibles can be analysed. These refer to assets or resources, intellectual capital or cognitive property, but also unconscious structures and processes, which are identified, measured, reported and thus appropriated for their economic benefits (Epstein and Mirza 2005; Kristandl and Bontis 2007; Zambon and Marzo 2007). However, as Davison and Warren (2009), showed, a visual analysis of intangible values is not reflected in accounts and accounting. A more critical approach refers to the dynamics of visible and especially invisible social identities in organizations, such as religion, national origin, social group memberships, illness or sexual orientation, and how they influence and complicate workplace interactions, especially in relation to stigmatization (Clair *et al.* 2005). Furthermore, there exists an invisibilization of banalized suffering of employees in relation to their intensified work, for example, not being able to cope with or the fear of losing one's job as part of the precariousness of existence in an intrinsically pathogenic, neoliberal society (Deranty 2008: 458–459).

The visual field of and in organizations, then, is not only a means for knowing the world, but also the invisible and preconceived ideas, beliefs and ideologies are always already present in the act of bodily seeing and embodied regimes of visibility.

Some implications for organization studies

Theoretical and political

Research is using lenses to perceive, frame, make distinctions and to ask different kinds of questions, develop research designs and pursue empirical studies related to phenomena or meta-studies. Lenses are sharpening filters of seeing and theorizing that select, categorize and interpret experiences, empirical findings and theories. Importantly, as we have seen, lenses are not passive neutral tools, but play an active, shaping role. They need to be seen in a network of lens relationships as part of a meta-theoretical integral approach to knowledge (Edwards 2010). By providing the means for an emancipatory visibilization via the act of 'seeing through', theory functions as an interrogative tool for seeing, i.e. for insights. They can function as an intermediary; an opportunity for practitioners to see beyond the current horizon of their own practice and expand the existing practice in new directions and explore new ways of doing, saying and being (Eikeland and Nicolini 2011).

Critical research on vision in organization explores how specific visual experiences, meanings and corresponding practices are discriminated, marginalized, degraded or ignored, excluded, dominated or subordinated, exploring how visual strategies are used to achieve and maintain power and control (e.g. Warhurst *et al.* 2012). This implies critically considering the ordering and normalizing of disciplinary techniques or governing functional and instrumental orientations within the organizational system. Interrogating the visual and the invisible in relation to organizations needs to include a critical investigation of how organizational members see (or not) ideological biases or power relations that arise in the construction and dissemination of visual representations or communication, like websites or blogs in daily life (see, for example, Elliott and Robinson, Chapter 17, this volume).

Furthermore, the conceptualization of vision as part of the 'political life of sensation' (Panagia 2009) that phenomenology affords thus opens space for a potential reconfiguration of the sensible. A phenomenological look at vision helps in re-interrogating the sensory world (Porcello *et al.* 2010), which implies understanding senses as complex and perplexing phenomena anew. Recognizing them both in their own right and as guide, a phenomenological exploration and disclosure can contribute to moving towards a regained integral sensorial culture, considering fascinating new developments such as ambient intelligence (Verbruecken 2003). This kind of sense-constituted culture is particularly relevant, for example, for experiential workspaces as characterized by dynamic mutability, emergent norms and epistemic openness (Talero 2008).

Methodological

A sensually oriented methodology can contribute to visual possibilities and interpretations in organization studies (Warren 2002, 2008) and towards a more 'seeing' research (Prosser 2011). For collecting and analysing embodied, sensuous pre-reflective 'data', the integration of visual methodologies and methods (Rose 2007), particularly videography, into research methodologies helps to study and present the visual experiences and processes, but also 'unrepresentable' dimensions of the invisible (Merchant 2011). Visual methods can help to capture embodied fieldwork; they complement and extend written and spoken textual forms, thereby 'enabling the researcher to reflect more deeply on their embodied and emotional experience in the field in relation to other social actors' (Kunter and Bell 2006: 192). Thus, they facilitate the collection, interpretation and communication of insights and findings about organizational phenomena in more inclusive and accessible ways.

Other methodological possibilities opened up by a phenomenological stance towards the visual include an 'art of visual inquiry' (Knowles *et al.* 2007), employing images and art forms as part of the inquiry process and representation, including photography, painting, installation art, collage, film or video, and sculpture. Where 'method meets art' in this way (Leavy 2009), researchers can include experimenting with alternative forms of expression and audio-visual possibilities, like image elicitation, photos, sounds, videos, scenes, stories, and so forth, some of which are discussed in this *Companion* (e.g. Berthoin Antal *et al.*, Chapter 16; Shortt *et al.*, Chapter 18; Stiles, Chapter 14) and which were used in an empirical study that revealed phenomenologically the embodied narrative practice of strategies (Küpers *et al.* 2013).

Practical

Phenomenological seeing can be cultivated through an 'education of attention' (Ingold 2001: 139) with and to the body. Specifically, a critical phenomenology of visuality aims to cultivate an ability to see and explore embodied visual experiences 'purposefully' by deconstructing elements of images and reconstructing them in their social, environmental and cultural contexts (Campbell and Schroeder 2011). One important practical implication, therefore, refers to the ability to create, read and respond to visual images as active viewers, questioners and critical producers of meaning (Falihi and Wason-Ellam 2009: 410). This entails a co-presence of verbal and visual literacies as interlacing modalities, which complement one another in the meaning-making process. This learning to see implies developing attentive, connective and loving eyes (Pattison 2007). These organs are not only responsive and responsible, but also critical in being able to see what cannot be seen directly, while going beyond recognition towards nourishing otherness (Kelly 2001: 219, 221), seeing the unseen, and to see differently. For example, experiences of arresting aesthetic practices such as those discussed by Sørensen in his method of juxtaposition (Chapter 3, this volume), and those described by Matilal and Höpfl (2009) in their anti-narrative account of the Bhopal tragedy, contribute to a learning to 'see with' the body (Al-Saji 2009: 391) – which is, in fact, the original meaning of intuition (*intueri*) – and which may overturn ossified attitudes and categories. Such aesthetic practices, especially as somaesthetics (Shusterman 2008) may bring to new expressions previously unnoticed features of the world (Dillard-Wright 2011: 210) or facilitate the reconfiguring of the territory of the visible, the thinkable and the possible (Rancière 2004: 41).

Conclusions

> True philosophy consists in relearning to look at the world.
>
> *(Merleau-Ponty 1962: xx)*

This chapter has called for the body to be reinstated as an active medium of meaning in the experiencing and (re-)structuring of the visible, which, in turn, cannot be separated from the invisible. Based on a critique of epistemologies of the eye and showing the significance of seeing as practice, the phenomenological perspectives presented here offered possibilities for re-learning to look at and interact in the life-world of organizations differently. Importantly, vision needs to be seen not as compartmentalized or isolated, but can be reconceived in relation to and in the context of other embodied senses and their interplay as a sensorium. Phenomenologically, perception is a whole-body phenomenon and part of a dynamic, hybrid embodiment and supplementing inter-affects (Küpers 2013), sensing, gesturing, and seeing as well as saying, and acting.

Vision then is more than just the visual, as it is inseparable from the aural, the tactile, the kinaesthetic, the temporal, and thus co-constituted by the entire bodily existence, synaesthetic perceptions and shared social experiences. Such interconnected understanding of senses can then become the processual base for an extended and more integral sense-making in embodied organizations (Küpers 2013a). Foreseeably, the need to embrace this 'new sensoriality' and a further exploration of the sensory potential and forms of sensory cooperation in organizational and societal cultures will become even more important as the desire for more intensive experiences and deeper meanings of employees in organizational life-worlds grow. Increasingly, it will become more significant to understand senses as rich, complex and perplexing phenomena, both in their own right and because of where they may guide us, moving towards a more sensorial culture (Verbruecken 2003) that will be strongly focused on all senses and their integration.

However, considering the complexities of current organizations and their systemic infrastructures, it remains important to realize that not all of what is involved in them can be understood and interpreted adequately by the senses and bodily or embodied visual processes alone. The corpus of the 'corporation' is more and different to what can be captured and shaped by sensual dimensions and visual experiences. Therefore, falling into a trap of a devaluing anti-ocularism is to be avoided as much as the fallacy of hypervaluing visualism. A critical approach for exploring the intricacies of vision does not follow monocular scopic regimes, nor does it discursively collapse embodied vision into denaturalized visuality. Instead, it sees embodied vision and its meaning as part of an interdependent, caring interaction and 'inter-visuality' (Mirzoeff 2000: 7) and as a creative interplay with present and possible conditionings of vision. To realize this kind of integration, there is a need to shift our attention from the individual to the enacted encounter and understanding of an affective 'participatory sense-making' (De Jaegher and Di Paolo 2007) and participatory spectatorship as a kind of 'democracy of the eye' (de Bolla 2003).

Because our bodily and visual involvement with things is indeterminate, we encounter meaningful things in an interconnected and patterned, though ever open-ended world. Accordingly, what is made visible here is *pro-visional* in the double sense of providing or supplying the means for transmission and of being transient. Moving at the edge of vision between the visible and invisible, without losing sight of the potentiality to see new sights and creative insights, the re-visioning of vision can be part of rehabituated sensual culture and practice in organization. Such a re-vision may become a medium for envisioning different organization studies and practices, which integrate sensual ways of relating towards a more sustainable, responsive and responsible organizing (Küpers 2012). If social and organizational change happens through 'constantly negotiated imaginary space' (Michelis 2002), a re-visioned imagination can play an important role in developing new visibilities (Soussloff 1996) or visual possibilities within practices as well as cultivating embodied and reflective embodied visions and visual cultures in organizations and beyond.

References

Adams, C. (2004) 'The ethical, social and environmental reporting–performance gap', *Accounting, Auditing & Accountability Journal* 17: 731–757.

Al-Saji, A. (2009) 'A phenomenology of critical-ethical vision: Merleau-Ponty, Bergson, and the question of seeing differently', *Chiasmi International* 11: 375–398.
Belkaoui, A. (1987) *Inquiry and Accounting*, Connecticut: Greenwood Press.
Belova, O. (2006) 'The event of seeing: a phenomenological perspective on visual sense-making', *Culture and Organization* 12: 93–107.
Birchall, C. (2011) 'Introduction to "secrecy and transparency": the politics of opacity and openness', *Theory, Culture & Society* 28: 7–25.
Bloomfield, B. and Vurdubakis, T. (1997) 'Visions of organisation and organisations of vision: the representational practices of information system', *Accounting, Organizations and Society* 22: 639–668.
Brighenti, A. (2007) 'Visibility: a category for the social sciences', *Current Sociology* 55: 323–342.
Brown, J. (2010) 'Accounting and visual cultural studies: potentialities, challenges and prospects', *Accounting, Auditing & Accountability Journal* 23: 482–505.
Campbell, N. and Schroeder, J.E. (2011) 'Visual culture', in D. Southerton (ed.) *Encyclopedia of Consumer Culture*, Thousand Oaks, CA: Sage, 1506–1510.
Carman, T. (2008) *Merleau-Ponty*, London and New York: Routledge.
Cataldi, S. (1993) *Emotion, Depth, and Flesh: A Study of Sensitive Space Reflections on Merleau-Ponty's Philosophy of Embodiment*, Albany, NY: SUNY Press.
Clair, J.A., Beatty, J.E. and MacLean, T.L. (2005) 'Out of sight but not out of mind: managing invisible social identities in the workplace', *Academy of Management* 30: 78–95.
Cooper, R. (2006) 'Making present: autopoiesis as human production', *Organization* 13: 59–81.
Coulson-Thomas, C. (1992) 'Strategic vision or strategic con?: Rhetoric or reality?', *Long Range Planning* 25: 81–89.
Dale, K. (2000) *Anatomising Embodiment and Organisation Theory*, Basingstoke: Palgrave.
Dale, K. and Burrell, G. (2003) 'An-aesthetics and architecture', in A. Carr and P. Hancock (eds) *Art and Aesthetics at Work*, London: Palgrave, 155–173.
Daston, L. and Galison, P. (2007) *Objectivity*, New York: Zone Books.
Davison, J. (2011) 'Barthesian perspectives on accounting communication and visual images of professional accountancy', *Accounting, Auditing & Accountability Journal* 24: 250–283.
Davison, J. and Warren, S. (2009) 'Imag[in]ing accounting and accountability', *Accounting, Auditing & Accountability Journal* 22: 845–857.
de Bolla, P. (1996) 'The visibility of visuality', in T. Brennan and M. Jay (eds) *Vision in Context: Historical and Contemporary Perspectives on Sight*, New York: Routledge, 63–79.
——(2003) *The Education of the Eye: Painting, Landscape and Architecture in Eighteenth-Century Britain*, Stanford, CA: Stanford University Press.
de Cock, C., Baker, M. and Volkmann, C.R. (2011) 'Financial phantasmagoria: corporate image-work in times of crisis', *Organization* 18: 153–172.
De Jaegher, H. and Di Paolo, E. (2007) 'Participatory sense-making: an enactive approach to social cognition', *Phenomenology and the Cognitive Sciences* 6: 485–507.
Dejours, C. (2003) *L'évaluation du travail à l'épreuve du reel*, Paris: INRA.
Deranty, J. (2008) 'Work and the precarisation of existence', *European Journal of Social Theory* 11: 443–463.
Dillard-Wright, D.B. (2011) 'Figurations of the ecstatic: the labor of attention in aesthetic experience', *Janus Head* 12: 203–221.
Dillon, M. (1988) *Merleau-Ponty's Ontology*, Bloomington: Indiana University Press.
Edwards, M.G. (2010) *Organizational Transformation for Sustainability: An Integral Metatheory*, New York: Routledge.
Eikeland, O. and Nicolini, D. (2011) 'Turning practically: broadening the horizon', *Journal of Organizational Change Management* 24: 164–174.
Elkins, J. (1996) *The Object Stares Back: On the Nature of Seeing*, New York: Harvest Books.
Eppler, M.J. and Platts, K. (2009) 'Visual strategizing', *Long Range Planning* 42: 42–74.
Epstein, B. and Mirza, A. (2005) *IAS 2005: Interpretation and Application of International Accounting and Financial Reporting Standards*, Hoboken, NJ: Wiley.
Falihi, A. and Wason-Ellam, L. (2009) 'Critical visuality: on the development of critical visual literacy for learners' empowerment', *The International Journal of Learning* 16: 409–418.
Foster, H. (1988) *Vision and Visuality*, Seattle, WA: Bay Press.
Foucault, M. (1977) *Discipline and Punish: The Birth of the Prison*, London: Penguin.
Fuery, P. and Fuery, K. (2003) *Visual Cultures and Critical Theory*, London: Hodder Arnold Publications.
Gombrich, E.H. (1996) *The Essential Gombrich: Selected Writings on Art and Culture*, London: Phaidon.

Goodwin, C. (1994) 'Professional vision', *American Anthropologist* 96: 606–33.
——(1995) 'Seeing in depth', *Social Studies of Science* 25: 237–74.
Heidegger, M. (1962) *Being and Time*, New York: Harper & Row.
——(1977 [1938]) 'The age of the world picture', in *The Question Concerning Technology and Other Essays*, New York: Harper.
Hines, R. (1988) 'Financial accounting: in communicating reality, we construct reality', *Accounting, Organizations and Society* 13: 251–261.
Ingold, T. (2001) 'From the transmission of representations to the education of attention', in H. Whitehouse (ed.) *The Debated Mind: Evolutionary Psychology versus Ethnography*, Oxford: Berg, 113–153.
Jay, M. (1993) *Downcast Eyes: The Denigration of Vision in Twentieth-Century French Thought*, Berkeley: University of California Press.
——(2002) 'That visual turn', *Journal of Visual Culture* 1: 87–92.
Jütte, R. (2005) *A History of the Senses: From Antiquity to Cyberspace*, Cambridge, UK: Polity Press.
Kavanagh, D. (2004) 'Ocularcentrism and its others: a framework for metatheoretical analysis', *Organization Studies* 25: 445–464.
Kelly, O. (2001) *Witnessing: Beyond Recognition*, Minneapolis: University of Minnesota Press.
Knowles, J.G., Luciani, T., Cole, A.L. and Neilsen, L. (eds) (2007) *The Art of Visual Inquiry*, Halifax, Nova Scotia/Toronto, Ontario, Canada: Backalong Books/Centre for Arts-Informed Research.
Kristandl, G. and Bontis, N. (2007) 'Defining intangible assets and intellectual capital', *Management Decision* 45: 1510–1524.
Kunter, A. and Bell, E. (2006) 'The promise and potential of visual organizational research', *M@n@gement* 9: 177–197.
Küpers, W. (2012) 'Integral response-abilities for organising and managing sustainability', in G. Eweje and M. Perry (eds) *Business and Sustainability, Concepts, Strategies and Changes, Critical Studies on Corporate Responsibility, Governance and Sustainability, Volume 3*, London: Emerald, 25–58.
Küpers, W. (2013a) 'Phenomenology of embodied senses and "sense-making" and the making of sense in organisational culture', *International Journal of Work, Organization and Emotion*, Special issue on: 'Sensually exploring culture and effect at work', *Emotion, Embodiment, Research* 6 (forthcoming).
Küpers, W. (2013) 'Inter-passion – embodied affect in organisational life-worlds', *Critical Horizons – A Journal of Philosophy and Social Theory* (forthcoming).
Küpers, W., Mantere, S. and Statler, M. (2013) 'Strategy as storytelling: a phenomenological exploration of embodied narrative practice', *Journal for Management Inquiry* 22(1): 83–100.
Larwood, L., Falbe, C.M., Kriger, M.P. and Miesling, P. (1995) 'Structure and meaning of organization vision', *Academy of Management Journal* 85: 740–769.
Leavy, P. (2009) *Method Meets Art: Arts-Based Research Practice*, New York: Guilford Press.
Lehman, C. and Tinker, T. (1987) 'The "real" cultural significance of accounts', *Accounting, Organizations and Society* 12: 503–522.
Luhmann, N. (1986) 'The autopoiesis of social systems', in F. Geyer and J. van der Zouwen (eds) *Sociocybernetic Paradoxes: Observation, Control and Evolution of Self-Steering Systems*, Berkeley, CA: Sage, 172–192.
Matilal, S. and Höpfl, H. (2009) 'Accounting for the Bhopal Disaster: footnotes and photographs', *Accounting, Auditing & Accountability Journal* 22(6): 953–972.
McKinlay, A. and Starkey, K. (1998) *Foucault, Management and Organization Theory: From Panopticon to Technologies of Self*, London: Sage.
Merchant, S. (2011) 'The body and the senses: visual methods, videography and the submarine sensorium', *Body & Society* 17: 53–72.
Merleau-Ponty, M. (1962) *Phenomenology of Perception*, London: Routledge.
——(1964) *Eye and Mind, The Primacy of Perception*, trans. James M. Edie, Evanston: Northwestern University Press.
——(1995) *The Visible and the Invisible*, Evanston: Northwestern University Press.
Messaris, P. (1997) *Visual Persuasion: The Role of Images in Advertising*, London: Sage.
Michelis, A. (2002) 'Art histories and visual culture studies', *The Year's Work in Critical and Cultural Theory* 9: 175–195.
Milne, M.J., Kearins, K. and Walton, S. (2006) 'Creating adventures in wonderland: the journey metaphor and environmental sustainability', *Organization* 13: 801–839.
Mirzoeff, N. (2000) 'Introduction: the multiple viewpoint – diasporic visual cultures', in N. Mirzoeff (ed.) *Diaspora and Visual Culture*, London: Routledge.

Mitchell, W.J.T. (1994) *Picture Theory*, Chicago: University of Chicago Press.
——(2005a) 'There are no visual media', *Journal of Visual Culture* 4: 257–266.
——(2005b) *What Do Pictures Want? The Lives and Loves of Images*, Chicago: Chicago University Press.
Oswick, C. (1996) 'Insights into diagnosis: an exploration using visual metaphors', in C. Oswick and D. Grant (eds) *Organisation Development: Metaphorical Explorations*, London: Pitman, 137–153.
Panagia, D. (2009) *The Political Life of Sensation*, Durham and London: Duke University Press.
Pattison, S. (2007) *Seeing Things, Deepening Relations with Visual Artefacts*, Canterbury: SCM Press.
Porcello, T., Meintjes, L., Ochoa, A.M. and Samuels, D. (2010) 'The reorganization of the sensory world', *Annual Review of Anthropology* 39: 51–66.
Prosser, J. (2011) 'Visual methodology toward a more seeing research', in N.K. Denzin and Y.S. Lincoln (eds) *The Sage Handbook of Qualitative Research*, Thousand Oaks, London and New Delhi: Sage.
Rancière, J. (2004) *The Politics of Aesthetics: The Distribution of the Sensible*, New York: Continuum.
Rose, G. (2007) *Visual Methodologies: An Introduction to the Interpretation of Visual Materials*, 2nd ed., London: Sage.
Schoeneborn, D. (2008) *Alternatives Considered But Not Disclosed: The Ambiguous Role of PowerPoint in Cross-Project Learning*, Wiesbaden: Verlag für Sozialwissenschaften.
——(2010) 'PowerPoint and the invisibility of contingency in project organizing', 17 December 2010, IOU Working Paper No. 124. Available at http://papers.ssrn.com/sol3/papers.cfm?abstract_id=1833943.
Schroeder, J. (2005) *Visual Consumption*, London and New York: Routledge.
Sennett, R. (2008) *The Craftsman*, New Haven: Yale University Press.
Shusterman, R. (2008) *Body Conciousness: A Philosophy of Mindfulness and Somaesthatics*, New York: Cambridge University Press.
Simpson, R. and Lewis, P. (2005) 'An investigation of silence and a scrutiny of transparency: re-examining gender in organization literature through the concepts of voice and visibility', *Human Relations* 58: 1253–1275.
Soussloff, C.M. (1996) 'The turn to visual culture: on visual culture and techniques of the observer', *Visual Anthropology Review* 12: 77–83.
Spoelstra, S. (2009) 'Organizational brilliance: on blinding visions in organizations', *Journal of Organizational Change Management* 22: 373–385.
Styhre, A. (2010) *Visual Culture in Organizations: Theory and Cases*, London: Routledge.
Talero, M. (2008) 'The experiential workspace and the limits of empirical investigation', *International Journal of Philosophical Studies* 16: 453–472.
Tapscott, D. and Ticoll, D. (2003) *The Naked Corporation: How the Age of Transparency Will Revolutionize Business*, New York: The Free Press.
Verbruecken, M. (2003) 'Towards a new sensoriality', in E. Aarts and S. Marzano (eds) *The New Everyday: Views on Ambient Intelligence*, Rotterdam, The Netherlands: 010 Publishers, 54–59.
Warhurst, C., van den Broek, D., Hall, R. and Nickson, D. (2012) 'Great expectations: gender, looks and lookism at work', *International Journal of Work, Organisation and Emotion* 5: 72–90.
Warren, S. (2002) 'Show me how it feels to work here: using photography to research organizational aesthetics', *ephemera: theory & politics in organization* 2: 224–245.
——(2008) 'Empirical challenges in organizational aesthetics research: towards a sensual methodology', *Organization Studies* 19: 559–580.
Westley, F.R. (1990) 'Middle managers and strategy: micro-dynamics of inclusion', *Strategic Management Journal* 11: 337–351.
Zambon, S. and Marzo, G. (2007) *Visualizing Intangibles: Measuring and Reporting in the Knowledge Economy*, Burlington, VT: Ashgate.
Zyglidopoulos, S. and Fleming, P. (2011) 'Corporate accountability and the politics of visibility in "late modernity"', *Organization* 18: 691–706.

2
The visual organization
Barthesian perspectives

Jane Davison

Roland Barthes is one of the great figures of late twentieth-century French philosophy and critical theory, a writer of gargantuan appetite for enquiry, encompassing linguistics, semiology, structuralism and post-structuralism, and its manifestations across a broad range of media, from verbal text to visual image and music, and from classical literature to architecture, film, fashion and advertising. His work is largely concerned with the philosophy of communication, and not only ranges across a broad spectrum of communicative media, but also moves between opposite poles of scientific rationalism and creative pleasure.

In broad terms, Barthes' work is driven by two main but contradictory impulses: science and pleasure. The first phase of his work is largely devoted to demystification and to a search for a science of communication, inspired by the linguistic enterprise of Saussure (1995 [1916]), and resulting in a formal semiology and the systems and patterns of *structuralism*. The later phase is paradoxically characterized by a revival of hedonism that 'seems to indulge in some of the mystifications he had effectively exposed' (Culler 1983: 99) and which privileges pleasure and creativity over scientific rationalism, in the movement known as *post-structuralism*.

One of Barthes' strengths lies in the provision of universal models and ways of thinking that may be fruitfully exploited in many domains, especially since they often take the form of loose frameworks and pointers rather than prescriptive guidelines. Barthes' principal analyses of the visual image are to be found in four short essays translated in *Image, Music, Text* (1977) and in his work *Camera Lucida* (*La chambre claire*) (1980). This chapter discusses two of these models: 'Rhetoric of the image' (1982 [1964]) from his structuralist phase (where he suggests a framework based in *linguistics*, *denotation* and *connotation*) and *Camera Lucida* (1980) from his post-structuralist work (where he formulates a framework of the *Studium* – the realm of rational codes – and the *Punctum* – more personal and subjective elements). In each case, discussion of the theoretical model is followed by visual semiotic readings of annual report front covers, guided by elements of Barthesian thought. 'Rhetoric of the image' is applied to three annual report front covers of professional accountancy firm Ernst & Young: dual messages are highlighted of a profession portrayed as simultaneously an art and a science, creative and measured, both business-aware and traditionally professional (Carnegie and Napier 2010). Accountancy is not often regarded as a 'people business', yet the intangible values of people are indicated to be fundamental to accountancy. *Camera Lucida* is applied to the annual report front cover of a charity, and assists in revealing Oxfam's crossroads of activity between the corporate and the charitable and between the developed and developing worlds, together with the manner in which the front cover photograph arouses our compassion.

Barthes' 'Rhétorique de l'image' ['Rhetoric of the image']: linguistics, denotation, connotation

One of Barthes' early short essays, 'Rhetoric of the image' (1982 [1964]), gives navigational tools for the analysis of visual images. 'Rhetoric of the image' concerns not fine art, but advertising images, of a similar *genre* to the promotional images that frame annual reports. In offering guidance for the analysis of visual images, Barthes suggests a tripartite structure: *linguistics, denoted iconic image, connoted iconic image* (1982 [1964]: 32–37).

Linguistics (ibid.: 37–41) is, for Barthes, a prime element of visual images in modern times. He reasons that, since the appearance of the book, few pictures in contemporary civilization are bereft of words, and the linking of image and text is almost *de rigueur*. In mass communication, the linguistic message is omnipresent, as title, caption, speech bubble and so on. The linguistic message has two functions with regard to the (twofold) iconic message: *anchorage* and *relay*. *Anchorage* is an effort to 'fix the floating chain of signifieds': as images are always polysemous, and the reader is able to choose some meanings and ignore others, text provides stability; it answers the question 'what is it?', elucidates, illuminates, directs, reduces uncertainty, but also reduces, controls and represses. *Relay* – more generally a feature of picture series such as cartoons, rather than isolated pictures – advances the action, and adds narrative and sequence and meanings that are not necessarily to be found in the image itself.

Barthes then divides the iconic part of the visual image into two signifying modes: *denotation* and *connotation*, which are inextricably interlinked. *Denotation* (ibid.: 42–46) is the analogical representation of external realities, their 'natural being-there', where the photograph comes the closest to providing a literal imitation without transformation. The denoted image is descriptive and dis-intellectualized. However, this notion of pure denotation remains largely an idealistic aspiration, as even the denoted image is coded, by conventions (for example, perspective) and choice (what is included and excluded), and can present a false innocence, such that 'The more technology develops the diffusion of information (and notably of images), the more it provides the means of masking the constructed meaning under the appearance of the given meaning' (ibid.: 46).

Connotation (ibid.: 46–51) is the realm of symbolic associations and codes, which may, for example, be *practical, national, cultural* or *aesthetic*, terms that Barthes does not define. The interpretation of these codes will vary according to the reader, but there will be a body of recognizable signs and stereotypes. Barthes suggests that rhetorical figures may be apprehended in the icon as formal relations of elements, of which the most common could be said to be *metonymy* and *repetition*.

Barthes illustrates his model by reference to a Panzani pasta advertisement. The iconic message *denotes* a string bag, vegetables, packets of pasta and a tin of sauce. These objects are signifiers, *and* at the same time furnish the signifieds of *denotation*. The visual message is thus to some degree uncoded (and therefore cross-cultural) in a formal sense; it requires little from the viewer other than basic knowledge bound up with perception. Barthes further suggests that the element of *denotation* in the image 'disintellectualizes the message' in furnishing a 'natural being-there of objects', apparently suffused with innocence. However, the iconic message at the same time transmits *connoted messages*, which Barthes interprets as follows: the half-open bag connotes an idyll of fresh domestic shopping and preparation; the tomato, pepper and tri-coloured hues of the poster evoke 'Italianicity' in tourist stereotypes; the composition of the image recalls the artistic convention of 'still-life'; finally, the labels together with the caption connote the medium of advertising. The connoted message depends more than the denoted message on levels of practical, national, cultural and aesthetic knowledge.

Ernst & Young *Annual Review* front covers[1]

The following analysis takes three front covers of an international professional accountancy firm and provides a detailed study of their intermingled signals of the firm's activities guided by 'Rhetoric of the image' (Barthes 1982 [1964]).

Ernst & Young's 2005 *Annual Review* front cover is a complex construction that lies between snapshot, studio photograph, documentary record, promotional image and work of art. Apart from the titular information, its *linguistics* are twofold. A caption 'WHAT PEOPLE CAN DO', where 'PEOPLE' is highlighted in a different colour, underscores the role played by the firm's human resources, an invisible intangible in the firm's accounts. Additionally, and more interestingly, the cover deliberately retains the linguistic traces of a mass-produced Kodak film negative, with its brand name, film type and numbering; while being the carefully constructed photograph of photographs, and further example of *mise en abyme* (Dällenbach 1977), these traces convey an impression of untouched amateur snapshot authenticity (Schroeder 2008).

As photographs, there is a strong *denotative* element to the icons; they provide a variety of visual portraits (faces, hands, upper torsos, full length), sometimes only partially seen, sometimes singly, sometimes in pairs or threes, of mixed ethnicity and carefully balanced gender, but exclusively of young people, in City garb or conventional casual dress. From their poses, the photographs also *denote* movement and enjoyment. Despite their verbal anonymity, the presumption is that they represent the firm's staff.

The *connoted* message is that the Ernst & Young workplace is dynamic, young and presents equal opportunities. It is a cliché that the accounting profession has suffered from a stereotypical image of dullness, parodied by John Cleese; research has investigated the ways in which accounting firms and professional institutes have more recently endeavoured in their recruitment literature to promote in its place an image of the 'trendy and fun-loving accountant' (Jeacle 2008: 1296). The *Annual Review* offers the opportunity of constructing just such a visual identity (Davison 2010). Although the subjects are anonymous, they are numbered, but in a sequence that is left incomplete, and infers the existence of many more; they are members of a large team. There are intimations of the photo-booth, and, like *Identity* (Rideal 1985), the small images represent the kinship of everyday life, while simultaneously demonstrating the individuality of members of the group (Rideal 2005: 10). At the same time, the presentation has resonances of Evans' earlier parody of the banality of the passport photo *genre*, entitled *Penny Picture* (1936). And yet the messages remain dual: the partying poses are tempered by the conventional dress (the significance of dress in the workplace is well recognized; see, for example, Rafaeli and Pratt 1993); the spontaneity is countered by the catalogued rows and the constructed nature of the image.

The front cover is moreover a metapicture, providing self-referential comment on the photographic medium; such metacommentary, or what Barthes would term *metatexte*, is a general feature of twentieth-century art and literature. The presentation of the photographic portraits adds to the *connotations*. They are in black and white, for a long time considered to be the medium of art photography (Badger 2007), and thus indicative of higher artistic status and quality; at the same time, in the digital age, this is an outmoded photographic form, yet one still used for high-quality results. Additional *connotations*, therefore, are of tradition combined with quality.

In the photomontage that forms Ernst & Young's 2006 *Annual Review* front cover, the photographs, again in black and white, again *denote* a gendered mix of young people, through visual portraits of the face and upper torso. The emphasis on people is verbally articulated on the inner front page, again making prominent use of repetition:

> People who demonstrate integrity, respect and teaming.
> People with energy, enthusiasm and the courage to lead.
> People who build relationships based on doing the right thing.

Here, however, a word is centre-stage, and has become a visual artefact, an object in its own right. Language is made visible, letters become images, but at the same time photographs become letters, and thus the boundary between text and image is disturbed (Barthes 1982 [1964]; Mitchell, 1994). Behind the 11 letters of OPPORTUNITY have been transposed the portraits of seven individuals, sometimes straddling several letters, sometimes including blank areas, resulting in a sense of fragmentation, pluralism and multiple points of view. The fragmentation also infuses movement and contributes to a sense of narrative that overcomes the motionless nature of the photograph. Yet, paradoxically, these 'photo-letters' also have an air of frozen blocks, a frieze that has been turned to stone.

Almost in the manner of Magritte's *Carte Blanche*, the letters and portraits of the Ernst & Young front cover play visual hide and seek with the spectator. Barthes, whose *Le plaisir du texte* (1973) reminds readers and spectators of the sheer hedonistic pleasure of text, insisted on the pleasure provided by intermittence: 'It is intermittence, as psychoanalysis has noted, that is erotic … the staging of appearance-disappearance' (1973: 19). The people and words *denoted* in this front cover have been fused to *connote* the abstract and intangible quality of *opportunity*, which needs to be recognized by client and professional adviser alike, thus stressing the business professional role of accountancy (Carnegie and Napier 2010). The photomontage has emphasized opportunity, and simultaneously provided a visual metaphor of something that by its very nature is only half-seen.

Ernst & Young's 2007 *Annual Review* front cover puts Barthes' visual figure of *metonymy* to the fore in *denoting* two unassuming objects that are *connotative* of the firm's identity: a dark-coloured jacket hanging on a coat-hook that is utilitarian in character. This bare scenario is everyday, and spare, indeed spartan or even clinical. The *connotations*, however, are again rich. Human presence is once more indicated, although now indirectly through absence, and through a male City dress code (Rafaeli and Pratt 1993); as in the photographic work of Walker Evans, garments epitomize their owners (Badger 2007). Moreover, the jacket and hook have the flavour of what the surrealists termed a 'found object', an everyday thing that signifies beyond its immediate appearance, as in, for example the repetitive stuffed suits and ghostly, indeed ghastly, shop mannequins of Atget's *Magasin, avenue des Gobelins* (1925).

The normality, security and stability of a reassuring and repetitive daily routine is intimated; indeed, the coat-hook is a familiar symbol of order and belonging from early childhood schooldays. Repetition is associated with renewal, ritual and regeneration (Davison 2008; Eliade 1965). Interplay with the caption 'Another day at the office …' *anchors* and reinforces the notion of daily repetition from past to present, strengthened still further by the ellipsis, which extends the routine into the future. The photograph of a static moment is thus given a temporal dimension through the *relay* function of a continuing narrative. The firm's motto, stressing the intangible attribute 'Quality in Everything We Do', is exemplified in this photographic depiction of routine professionalism, which seems to revert to a traditional grey but trustworthy image of accountancy.

These three *Annual Review* front covers are a testament to the expressive powers of the visual image, and especially photography. Consistent patterns have emerged of antithetical messages regarding accountancy, which is portrayed as simultaneously an art and a science, creative and measured, dynamic yet reliable, spontaneous while constrained, alert to surprise and opportunity as well as being grounded in well-worn professional care and routine; it is shown as both business-aware and traditionally professional (Carnegie and Napier 2010). Accountancy is not often regarded as a 'people business', yet people, and their intellectual capital and associated qualities, are fundamental to accountancy; the front covers of their *Annual Reviews* have provided prime opportunities to communicate such abstract intangibles

Barthes' *La chambre claire* [*Camera Lucida*]: '*Studium*' and '*Punctum*'

Camera Lucida is Barthes' most extended analysis of the photograph. The text is a many-angled meditation; in part, it is also intensely autobiographical, in its anguished searching for a true image of his recently deceased mother. Warren (2005) refers to *Camera Lucida* in the context of visual elicitation. The following summarizes its key notions regarding the photograph, referring to *Camera Lucida*'s own section numbers in brackets.[2]

Barthes notes the paucity of guidance regarding the interpretation of the photograph, which 'eludes classification' (Section 2, p. 14). There are books on photographic techniques, which are focused too narrowly, and books in historical and sociological traditions, which are written at too much of a distance (Section 2). In seeking a set of general principles, Barthes is torn between the discourses of sociology, semiology and psychoanalysis, but dissatisfied with them all and their essential reductionism (Section 3).

In finding himself, therefore, '"scientifically" bereft' (Section 3, p. 20), he aims to sketch what he refers to as an 'eidetic science of the Photograph' (Section 8, p. 40), but without losing the power of emotion; he aims to follow a formal path of logic, but without losing the pathos and sentimentality inherent in the photograph (Section 8). He resolves to make himself the 'mediator for all Photography', in order 'to try to formulate the fundamental feature, the universal without which there would be no photography' (Section 3, pp. 21–22).

He structures the practice of photography into three parts: the *Operator* is the photographer, the *Spectator* is the viewer and the *Spectrum* is the person or thing photographed (Section 4). Barthes is reticent on photography where the *Operator* and *Spectrum* are intentionally conflated (see, for example, the work of Cindy Sherman discussed in Harvey 1990: 7–8). He uses the word *Spectrum* designedly, in that it contains the idea of 'spectacle' and, more disconcertingly, the notion of the 'spectre', or return of the dead, the absent presence in all photographs (Section 4); here, he follows Sontag's sense of the elegy of photographs, which she describes as all being *memento mori* (Sontag 1971: 15). Barthes goes on to point out that the fact of posing further contributes to the lifeless nature of the *Spectrum*; the self becomes other, joins a social game, is inauthentic. The photographer fears this death, and does everything to make his photograph lifelike, perhaps by avoiding the formal pose, by posing outdoors rather than indoors, or by including children (Section 5).

The current study is, like Barthes, unconcerned with the technical world of the *Operator*, but takes the part of the *Spectator* to analyse the *Spectrum*. Barthes distinguishes two elements within the *Spectrum*: the *Studium* and the *Punctum*.

Studium

The *Studium* refers to a recognizable body of information. Here, emotion is filtered by the rational intermediary of codes, which might be political, ethical or cultural. It may be more or less stylized, depending on the photographer and is invested with the *Spectator*'s active consciousness (Section 10). The *Studium* follows conventions that are intentional on the part of the photographer and recognized by the *Spectator*, a contract arrived at between creators and consumers (Section 11). It might, for example, provide an ethnological knowledge, such as details of dress or a social and historical record. The *Studium* derives from training, invites rational liking and polite interest.

In these ways, photography resembles painting. Yet, whereas in painting the referent may be memorized or imagined, in photography direct links are retained with the referent, so that, even when subsequently manipulated, photography possesses a super abundance of realism (Section 12). Photography comes closer to the art of theatre, in its setting of a stage, posing of subjects, and in being the realm of the mask (Sections 13 and 15). Further, in attempting to defeat the inauthenticity of the pose, the photographer may contrive a variety of surprises: rarity value (for example, a man with two heads); capturing a moment (for example, a woman jumping out of a window); or contortions of technique (for example, superimpositions) (Section 14).

Punctum

The *Studium* and the *Punctum* exist as co-presences. The *Punctum* is a less rational, more personal and subjective element, which breaks or punctuates the conventional and coded harmony of the *Studium*. Rather than being actively sought, it rises from the scene and 'pierces' the *Spectator*. It is a 'wound ... sting, little mark, little hole, small cut' (Section 10, p. 49). It may be poignant, delightful, painful or thought-provoking (Section 10). The *Punctum* evades analysis (Section 18), and is probably unintentional or only partly intentional; it is disturbing (Section 20). It is a moment of intense immobility, which is what distinguishes the photograph from the film (Section 21). It is not coded; indeed, it cannot be put into words and is often revealed after the event when thinking back to a photograph and withdrawing it from the 'critical claptrap' that surrounds it (Section 22, p. 89). It may point to a subtle beyond, which takes the *Spectator* outside the frame (Section 23).

Yet there is more to the 'eidos' of photography, which Barthes set out to define, and again it is related to the fact that 'Reference is the founding order of Photography' (Section 32, p. 120). Near the beginning of *Camera Lucida*, Barthes emphasizes the part played by sentiment in the photograph: 'I was interested in photography only for sentimental reasons' (Section 8, p. 42), and he returns to the theme near the end. Presence in photographs is never metaphoric; someone has seen the referent in its flesh and blood or concrete reality; that presence is resurrected through the alchemy of photographic chemistry or digital recreation (Sections 33 and 34) (see also Sontag 1971). The *Punctum* thus additionally consists of an apprehension of the defeat of time (Section 39). The resurrected photographic subject has the power of looking the *Spectator* straight in the eye; yet this is an illusion, for the subject is not seeing the *Spectator*, and is looking at no one. This 'Look' touches, arouses emotion, has a mysterious moral quality, which endows the photograph and its subject with life values, or with a soul, an aura of goodness (Section 45). The 'Look' may possess an affection, innocence or a sense of profound 'goodwill'.

Barthes' dual analysis of the photograph is thus invested with two sets of characteristics: one rational, coded and cultural (*Studium*), the other emotional, uncoded and personal (*Punctum*). It therefore provides a fitting framework for the examination of photographs provided as part of the accountability statement of a charity, where, in addition to formalized and codified responsibilities, more intangible and subjective qualities of 'trust, emotion, social contracts and mutuality' (Gray et al. 2006) also necessarily enter into play.

Oxfam *Annual Review* front cover[3]

Designing a front cover to the *Annual Review* that reflects Oxfam's complex cocktail of the charitable and the corporate, and captures Oxfam's crossroads of activity between the developed and developing worlds, presents a rare challenge. Oxfam has created an arresting image for its front cover. The following detailed study, guided by Barthes' *Camera Lucida*, examines the ways in which such interwoven messages of accountability can be interpreted as being signalled in the photograph.

The image, a colour photograph, is described inside the document as 'New lessons from old bottle-tops', and features a close-up of children from Kibera in Kenya learning to read and write with teaching aids recycled from old bottle-tops. The image appears to have been carefully composed by the *Operator* from the fact that the camera is above the table; this allows the camera additionally to capture the arms of a third child whose face is not seen, and give the *Spectator* more of a sense of being present in the scene. In the hard copy, a circular part of the table has been cut out and replaced with a compact disc bearing similar but not identical images to those of the removed section. The *Spectator* is thus presented with a *Spectrum* consisting of people and things. Following Barthes, the analysis is concerned with the way in which the *Spectrum* may be received by the *Spectator*. The *Spectrum* may be analysed from two contrasting points of view: that of the *Studium* and that of the *Punctum*.

Studium

The *Studium* is Barthes' realm of recognizable codes, which might be political, cultural or ethical, among others. The codes are implicit in the human and inanimate elements of the Oxfam front cover photograph, and the interplay between them. Both the children and the objects portrayed convey ethical and cultural codes, which are considered in turn below.

People

The subjects are children. This immediately implies an ethical or charitable code, which is recognized across the globe and embedded in UN thinking and strategy. The UN 1948 Convention recognizes that the child, by reason of his physical and mental immaturity, needs special safeguards and care (Addison 2002). The *Spectator* sees the faces of what appear to be a boy and a girl, in accordance with Oxfam's stated advocacy of equality between the genders and improved access to education for girls. The children are dignified, neither happy nor sad, in harmony with objectives of support through self-help, focus on rights and a sustainable livelihood. Moreover, they are depicted as sharing their play or learning, in conformity with principles of giving and cooperation.

There is, further, a cultural code attached to the children. From their physical appearance, they represent the children of Africa, and thus the recipients of much Oxfam funding. Their dress, on the other hand, is neither traditionally African nor obviously Western, but a mélange: the bright primary colours of the garb of the left-hand child could come from either culture; the large floral or leaf pattern of the right-hand child is perhaps more African in inspiration.

Things

There are two contrasting sets of objects, and whose codes are intricate, cross-cultural and far-reaching. The boy is playing with a small set of artefacts, which are not readily distinguishable. They appear varied and uneven in nature, but whether they are perhaps made of bone, metal or even dough cannot be discerned. Their purpose is also unclear; they might be a game, they might represent some religious symbol, or a system of writing or counting (see, for example, Jean 1987, 1989). However, despite being mysterious to Western eyes, they serve to represent some form of local culture, albeit a somewhat hackneyed image ('It is no longer quite so easy to claim that there is nothing to ethnic art but knocking a couple of bones together' (Eagleton 2003: 13)). In contrast, the bottle-tops, overwhelming in their standard multiplicity, proclaim their identity. Trifling on the surface, they are heavily and ambiguously laden with coded interpretations. Whether their source is local or Western is irrelevant; they are a concrete manifestation of Western industrial mass production. The bottle-tops are not anonymous, but bear the decipherable brand name and logo of 'Pilsner'; thus, they represent the consumer culture of the Western corporate and retail sector.

To this is added a moral code. The image is one not only of plenty, but also of luxury, or even degeneracy. Yet this Western-style waste and excess is being recycled, and not to produce more of the same, but to be put to quite a different, educational purpose. A literacy project that uses bottle-tops rather than pen or paper, or indeed computers, is indicative of Oxfam's cost-effectiveness and innovation. Moreover, the soulless repetitive uniformity of the machine has been tempered by the human effort that has inscribed the uneven handwritten letters, thereby coming closer to the local culture. Messages of corporate social responsibility, 'Green Oxfam', mingle with charitable messages of educational aid; the developed world is intertwined with its developing counterpart.

As society in general, and corporations and NGOs, come under increasing moral and political pressure to minimize the wasteful use of resources (Jegers and Lapsley 2001), so is recycling a recurring theme in contemporary art, and particularly the art of developing countries. A recent major exhibition (Hayward Gallery 2005) entitled *Africa Remix* displayed a number of contemporary works of art based on the notion of salvage, including an immense patchwork 'cloth of gold' by the Ghanaian-born sculptor El Anatsui. Composed of thousands of aluminium and wire bottle-tops, the large ceremonial cloak is a prime example of a striking use of recycling, in transforming discarded materials.

The Oxfam bottle-tops' letters are symbols *par excellence* of literacy, of systems of writing, and all the connotations of culture, history and civilization, including accounting and accountability. The letters are those of the western Roman alphabet, but whether the children are learning to write an African language in Roman characters or a European language is left unsaid. It is interesting that primacy is given to letters rather than numbers, and hence to the qualitative rather than the quantitative. However, again, the status of the bottle-tops is ambiguous: they could well be seen as counters, and thus instruments of numeracy as well as literacy. From a philosophical stance, the alphabet is symbolic, for example, of the human desire to order, and of the manner in which thinking is necessarily and intrinsically linked with classification. As Barthes has observed, the alphabet is not neutral and represents a choice against other possible systems of classification; it is the classification of appropriation, particularly of knowledge and encyclopaedias (Barthes 1964).

The coded messages of the *Studium* of the photograph have thus engaged the *Spectator*'s rational consciousness and informed him or her of key elements of Oxfam's accountability. Oxfam is symbolically shown to be engaged in both the corporate and NGO sectors, the developed and developing worlds. The people and things of the *Studium* exemplify best practice (Edwards and Hulme 1995) and illustrate Oxfam's stated goals.

Punctum

Punctum at first sight

The *Punctum* is Barthes' more disturbing realm, which punctuates the more readily recognizable and accepted codes of the *Studium*, by introducing sometimes incongruous elements. A first interpretation might focus on the unusual manner in which, in the case of the Oxfam report, the codes are cracked literally by the cutting open of the front cover and insertion of a compact disc. Moreover, whether deliberately or not, the replacement picture on the compact disc does not co-relate precisely with the missing circle in subject matter or in colour. The sense of fragmentation is compounded by the disembodied arms, now additionally deprived of their hands. Such fragmentation, disjunction and plurality is typical of Western late modernity. Codes are also cracked metaphorically, as the two-dimensional convention of the photograph becomes three, and a real thing leaves the image to be present in the hands of the *Spectator*.

Barthes has observed the rapprochement between photography and the dramatic arts, for example, in its use of staged sets and lighting (*Camera Lucida*, Section 13). The Oxfam cover could be interpreted as having a theatrical, game-playing or magical dimension. Theatre is a live art, and in extracting the disc the *Spectator* becomes actively involved in the childish delights and game-play of pop-up books, hide and seek, jigsaws and finding the missing piece (Barthes 1973; Picard 1986). The *Spectator*'s sense of intrigue and mystery is aroused, together with the desire to explore this magic circle, its aperture itself symbolic of the photographer's lens or even of secret doors to other worlds.

Through the compact video disc, the world of the front cover is expanded and takes the viewer outside the frame (Section 23). By handling and watching the video, the senses of touch and hearing are added to that of sight already involved in receiving the photograph. The disc is a concrete representative of the advanced information technology of Western society, and its distribution a sign of the general availability of computer hardware among those receiving the *Annual Review*. To the two contrasting systems of communication of the photograph (the unidentified local artefacts and the bottle-tops) is added the high-technology communication of modern Western society.

In exploring further, the aperture or peephole at the centre of the disc becomes, on the disc's removal, an enlarged circular window through which is seen a partial round section of the front cover photograph. The *Spectator*'s sense of order is satisfied, in finding that this is the missing piece that correctly fits the absent section of the front cover. On turning the page, the eye is led directly to two more circles, each presenting a different perspective of the globe. Both of the perspectives that have been selected focus on the developing parts of the world. The Oxfam message is thus expanded from Africa to all corners of the developing world. Once again, therefore, the Oxfam charitable programme has elements in common with the corporate sector.

Yet, on reflection, does this apparent *Punctum* at first sight conform to Barthes' understanding of this intuitive realm? As Barthes writes, often the *Punctum* is not revealed at first sight, but only when thinking back, eyes literally or metaphorically closed (Section 23). In retrospect, this carefully composed scene belongs rather to the *Studium*, in its theatricality, trick elements and coded messages. Barthes devotes one section under *Studium* in *Camera Lucida* to the photograph's affinity with theatre (Section 13) and another to contrived surprises, or contortions of technique, such as superimpressions, deceptive blurring, deceptive perspectives and trick framing (Section 14).

Punctum on reflection

To reiterate from Barthes, the *Studium* and the *Punctum* exist as co-presences. The *Punctum* is a less rational, more personal and subjective element, which, rather than being actively sought, rises from the scene and 'pierces' the *Spectator*. It is a poignant, delightful, painful or thought-provoking moment of authenticity (Sections 10, 11 and 15). The *Punctum* evades analysis (Section 18), and is a moment of intense immobility (Section 21). It is not coded; indeed, it cannot be put into words.

It might be objected, therefore, that the *Punctum* does not lend itself to academic and rational discussion of organizational documents. Yet the fact of its occupying a more personal and affective terrain does not mean that the *Punctum* does not exist in such documents. Further, Barthes' statement that it 'evades analysis' should not be interpreted as meaning that it is insusceptible to analysis, but rather that it is more difficult to nail down in rational discourse; indeed, Barthes himself subjects the notion of *Punctum* to considerable careful analysis in *Camera Lucida*. Finally, such a personal dimension is fitting to the NGO, where 'trust, emotion, conscience, social contracts and mutuality all enter into the relationship' (Gray *et al.* 2006: 335).

As Barthes says, the *Punctum* is often revealed when thinking back to a photograph and reliving it in a purely intuitive manner (Section 22). When thinking back to the Oxfam cover, the lasting image is that of the two children. Children are often said to represent philosophical and religious codes of innocence, of a fundamental belief in the goodness of humankind (see, for example, Rousseau 1968 [1782]; Jankélévitch 1986). From a photographic point of view, their innocence makes children good subjects, and helps to prevent what Barthes sees as the deathly nature of the pose and its potentially stale inauthenticity. One child looks up at the camera. Even though we know the child does not see us, as Barthes says, we suffer from the illusion that he is looking directly at us. Simultaneously, the private has become public, and the public is consumed privately (Section 40). This 'Look' (Section 46) pierces us with its appeal to raw sentiment. Here the charitable rather than the corporate is in ascendancy.

The Oxfam front cover photograph is a *tour de force* as a statement of the multiple nature of the non-governmental organization's operations and advocacy. It fulfils all the functions of the photograph formulated by Barthes as being 'to inform, to represent, to surprise, to cause, to signify, to arouse desire' (Section 11, p. 51). It informs us of Oxfam's activities, both represents and signifies its interwoven worlds, surprises us with high-technology hide and seek, causes us to think about Oxfam and the plight of those in the developing world, and provokes charitable instinct. As well as satisfying rational codes and expectations, it possesses more elusive qualities of surprise, magic and moral sensibility.

Summary

'Rhetoric of the image' (Barthes 1982 [1964]) has been useful in steering an analysis of both *linguistics* and the *iconic* in Ernst & Young's front covers, and demonstrating their often inextricable intermingling and interdependence, as the words provide *anchoring* and *relay* to the more free-floating meaning of the visual. The notions of *denotation* and *connotation* are useful, together

Table 2.1 Oppositions in 'Rhetoric of the Image' and *Camera Lucida*

Visual model	Term	Sense
'Rhetoric of the Image'	Denotation	Description
	Connotation	Symbolism
Camera Lucida	*Studium*	Rational codes
	Punctum	Intuition

with the seeking of codes, such as the *practical, national, cultural* and *aesthetic* suggested by Barthes. They have been used in other analyses of organizational images, for example, in US annual reports (Preston *et al.* 1996), in magazine advertisements displaying accountants (Baldvinsdottir *et al.* 2009) or in the bowler-hat branding of a British bank (Davison 2009, 2012). Barthes' *Camera Lucida* has provided a fitting framework for the Oxfam image for the following reasons: the *Studium* has been useful in revealing the coded messages of Oxfam's crossroads of activity between the corporate and the charitable and between the developed and developing worlds; the *Punctum* has provided insight into the manner in which the photograph arouses our compassion.

The sets of oppositions in the two models (see Table 2.1) represent a shift in Barthes' thinking. 'Denotation' and 'connotation' are useful in highlighting the distinction between representation (although even the apparent objectivity of representation needs to be treated with great care) and symbolism. '*Studium*' is similar to 'connotation' in highlighting secondary messages. '*Punctum*' is more difficult, but arguably also more interesting: its very personal and intuitive nature is beneficial for endeavouring to capture elusive moral qualities of trust, compassion or reputation, particularly in photographic communications related to issues of social conscience. While both Barthes' models well suit figurative images, they are reticent on abstract art, and on areas of blurred definition, such as where photography and painting come together in collage, or in work where the *Operator* and *Spectrum* are intentionally conflated.

However, as Eagleton (2003) observes, no set of theoretical concepts can be all-embracing, and notwithstanding these limitations, the models have the potential for wide application. Barthes' frameworks provide useful models for the analysis of organizational images since they encompass all manner of visual images from those of everyday media to fine art, provide elements of universal models, that are both structured and flexible, and give primacy to the interpretative action of the viewer over that of the designer.

Acknowledgement

This chapter is based on articles previously published in *Accounting, Auditing & Accountability Journal*: 'Photographs and accountability: cracking the codes of an NGO' (Davison 2007) and 'Barthesian perspectives on accounting communication and visual images of professional accountancy' (Davison 2011).

Notes

1 Images available to view in Davison 2011.
2 For the sake of keeping notes to a minimum, author's paraphrases of the text in *La chambre claire* refer simply to section numbers. Quotations are translated by the author.
3 Images available to view in Davison 2007.

References

Addison (2002) *Smoke and Mirrors? Corporate CSR Reporting, Claims and Reality*, London: Addison.
Badger, G. (2007) *The Genius of Photography. How Photography has Changed our Lives*, London: Quadrille.
Baldvinsdottir, G., Burns, J., Nørreklit, H. and Scapens, R.W. (2009) 'The image of accountants: from bean counters to extreme accountants', *Accounting, Auditing & Accountability Journal* 22(6): 858–882.
Barthes, R. (1964) 'Littérature et discontinu', in *Essais critiques*, Paris: Le Seuil, 175–187.
——(1973) *Le plaisir du texte*, Paris: Le Seuil. (Barthes, R. (1976) *The Pleasure of the Text*, trans. R. Miller, London: Jonathan Cape.)
——(1977) *Image, Music, Text*, trans. S. Heath, London: Fontana Press.
——(1980) *La chambre claire*, Paris: Le Seuil. (Barthes, R. (2000) *Camera Lucida*, trans. R. Howard, London: Vintage.)
——(1982 [1964]) 'Rhétorique de l'image', in *L'obvie et l'obtus*, Paris: Le Seuil, 25–42. (Barthes, R. (1977) 'Rhetoric of the image', in *Image, Music, Text*, trans. S. Heath, London: Fontana Press, 32–51.)
Carnegie, G.D. and Napier, C.J. (2010) 'Traditional accountants and business professionals: portraying the accounting profession after Enron', *Accounting, Organizations and Society* 35(3): 275–392.
Culler, J.D. (1983) *Barthes*, London: Fontana.
Dällenbach, L.L. (1977) *Le récit spéculaire: essai sur la mise en abyme*, Paris: Le Seuil.
Davison, J. (2007) 'Photographs and accountability: cracking the codes of an NGO', *Accounting, Auditing & Accountability Journal* 20(1): 133–158.
——(2008) 'Rhetoric, repetition, reporting and the "dot.com" era: words, pictures, intangibles', *Accounting, Auditing & Accountability Journal* 21(6): 791–826.
——(2009) 'Icon, iconography, iconology: visual branding, banking and the case of the bowler hat', *Accounting, Auditing & Accountability Journal* 22(6): 883–906.
——(2010) '[In]visible [in]tangibles: visual portraits of the business élite', *Accounting, Organizations and Society* 35(2): 165–183.
——(2011) 'Barthesian perspectives on accounting communication and visual images of professional accountancy', *Accounting, Auditing & Accountability Journal* 24(2): 250–83.
Eagleton, T. (2003) *After Theory*, London: Penguin.
Edwards, M. and Hulme, D. (1995) 'NGO performance and accountability: introduction and overview', in M. Edwards and D. Hulme (eds) *Non-Governmental Organizations – Performance and Accountability: Beyond the Magic Bullet*, London: Earthscan Publications Limited, 3–16.
Eliade, M. (1965) *Le sacré et le profane*, Paris: Gallimard.
Gray, R., Bebbington, J. and Collison, D. (2006) 'NGOs, civil society and accountability: making the people accountable to capital', *Accounting, Auditing & Accountability Journal* 19(3): 319–348.
Harvey, D. (1990) *The Condition of Postmodernity: An Enquiry into the Origins of Cultural Change*, Oxford: Blackwell.
Hayward Gallery (2005) *Africa Remix. Contemporary Art of a Continent*, London: Hayward Gallery Publishing.
Jankélévitch, V. (1986) *L'innocence et la méchanceté*, Paris: Flammarion.
Jean, G. (1987) *L'écriture, mémoire des hommes*, Paris: Gallimard.
——(1989) *Langage de signes, l'écriture et son double*, Paris: Gallimard.
Jeacle, I. (2008) 'Beyond the boring grey: the construction of the colourful accountant', *Critical Perspectives on Accounting* 19(8): 1296–1320.
Jegers, M. and Lapsley, I. (2001) 'Making sense of non-profit organizations', *Financial Accountability and Management* 17(1): 1–3.
Mitchell, W.J.T. (1994) *Picture Theory*, Chicago and London: The University of Chicago Press.
Picard, M. (1986) *La lecture comme jeu*, Paris: Minuit.
Preston, A.M., Wright, C. and Young, J.J. (1996) 'Imag[in]ing annual reports', *Accounting, Organizations and Society* 21(1): 113–137.
Rafaeli, A. and Pratt, M. (1993) 'Tailored meanings: on the meaning and impact of organizational dress', *Academy of Management Review* 18(1): 32–55.
Rideal, L. (1985) *Identity*, London: National Portrait Gallery.
——(2005) *Insights: Self-portraits*, London: National Portrait Gallery.
Rousseau, J.-J. (1968 [1782]) *Les Confessions*, Paris: Garnier-Flammarion.

Saussure, F. de (1995 [1916]) *Cours de linguistique générale*, Paris: Payot.
Schroeder, J. (2008) 'Strategic analysis of images in brand culture', in B.J. Phillips and E. McQuarrie (eds) *Go Figure: New Directions in Advertising Rhetoric*, Armonk, NY: M.E. Sharpe, 277–296.
Sontag, S. (1971) *On Photography*, London: Penguin.
Warren, S. (2005) 'Photography and voice in critical qualitative management research', *Accounting, Auditing & Accountability Journal* 18(6): 861–882.

3

The method of juxtaposition

Unfolding the visual turn in organization studies

Bent M. Sørensen

> In the most sophisticated critical works, content and form are intimately linked
> *(Marcus and Fischer 1986: 137)*

For now we see through a glass, darkly

To state that we live in an image-saturated world borders on the trivial, and is obvious. The word obvious is defined in *Oxford English Dictionary* as 'clearly visible', but also as 'banal' and 'predictable'. So, we may ask, how can we pass the banal and the predictable, indeed the obvious, of the visual and render it intriguing again? A renewed engagement with the visual cannot, of course, take it at face value. What you see is very seldom what you get. However, this is not a function of late modernity being saturated, for some to the point of nausea, with images. In the first century AD, St Paul had already noted the visual's non-trivial character: 'For now we see through a glass, darkly' (I Cor. 13:12). To Paul, the visual is puzzling, and not only because ancient glass was less clear than today's transparent technology. In his warning, Paul uses a particular Greek word for 'darkly', namely αινιγματι, enigmatic: the visual is, in this perspective, at least as enigmatic as any other empirical matter or discourse, for all that the visual is connected to clarity and truth in what Jay (1986) calls modernity's 'empire of the gaze'.

It is a fact, whether one likes 'the optics of it' or not, that the visual reigns superior in contemporary life and in the life of organizations. Outside the field of organization studies, the visual has attained a dominant position as what expresses and, concomitantly, informs and controls our joint 'social imaginaries' (C. Taylor 2004). This may be conceived as the engine of Debord's (1994) society of the spectacle or Baudrillard's (1994) equally uncanny age of the simulacrum. It is, moreover, true to such a degree that one would assume a 'visual turn' in organization studies to have superseded the 'linguistic turn'. Yet, while discourse analysis, which is focused on language and linguistic representation, had a deservedly easy entry into organization studies (Alvesson and Kärreman 2000), this has been the case only to a lesser extent for the analysis of the visual (Strangleman 2004). There are, however, reasons for optimism. The publication of this *Companion* testifies in any case to the fact that the visual in its own right is gaining ground within organization studies as a (set of) field(s) and method(s); visual analysis is what may both complement and transgress discursive and more traditional, social scientific analysis (Fuery and Fuery 2003).

Whether one chooses to be optimistic or not in this regard, it is a curious fact that organization studies still remains about 20 years behind cultural studies scholarship, where the visual is a much more central category. Moreover, organization studies possibly still struggles with a Romantic yearning for depth and profundity as opposed to surface and superficiality. Organization scholars prefer to deal with the *meaning* of the words uttered over the executive desk, rather than with the designed *visuality* of the shiny desk itself and the room's accompanying CEO portraits (for exceptions, see Betts 2006; Guthey and Jackson 2005). Organization studies remains more inclined to deal with the *inside* of the body from where thoughts and language on this account would 'stem from', rather than with the imagery through which, today, this body is expressed and disciplined, our time's 'social imageries' (C. Taylor 2004). The inside and the depth are still considered the sites where truth ultimately is to be found (psychoanalysis is a qualified example of this, as expressed in Gabriel's *Organizations in Depth*, 1999). Nietzsche, however, would have it differently, as expressed in his praise for 'the Greeks': 'They knew how to *live*: what is needed for that is to stop bravely at the surface, the fold, the skin; to worship appearance, to believe in shapes, tones, words – in the whole Olympus of appearance!' (2001: 8).

The surface and the apparent – the visual – was Nietzsche's way to profundity. As Deleuze says: 'Nietzsche was able to discover depth only after conquering the surfaces' (1990: 147). Visual analysis of organizations, in my view, is especially well suited to 'stop bravely at the surface' in order to 'conquer' it, to sense and unfold what goes on nearby and find its profundity in a meticulous superficiality.

This is in line with Paul's insight that, while the visual is important, it is still an enigma through which one must travel to reach Deleuze's profundity. Paul considers – much in line with Debord and Baudrillard – the enigmatic quality of our vision to be an *ethical* issue. The 'now' of the dark vision he speaks of is a time before the light of God, as it were, becomes 'all in all' (I Cor. 15:28). The now, then, is a time in which the visual is deceptive and seductive, doubled and barred. When Jesus was led astray by the devil, it happened in the desert, the place for hallucinations and *fata morganas*; eventually, Jesus was offered a total view from a mountain top of the world that could fall under his reign, if he would succumb to the seduction. However, and staying with this theological inroad to the visual, one observes that the true deity cannot be approached in full light, as spelled out in Matthew 6:6: 'But when you pray, go into your room, close the door and pray to your Father, who is unseen. Then your Father, who sees what is done in secret, will reward you.'

The truth, as it turns out, is not necessarily directly approachable in the visual range. The visual is bent on pretending that what you see is what you get. But you see 'through a glass, darkly', and you are not going to get what you expect (from Latin *expectare*, to look out for). To Paul, who will be part of one of the 'visual unfoldings' in this chapter, this issue is ethical to the point of damnation and disgrace: only a conversion, as we will see in the analysis of Caravaggio's *Conversion of St Paul*, can make one 'see the light' and receive Truth (or, in a perhaps more modest *Companion*-style, experience an interesting, organizational analysis). Light will, in any case, as Kavanagh (Chapter 4, this volume) argues, be connected to insight, while, still, the visual itself is unreliable and covered in (an ethical and spiritual) darkness. Descartes, Caravaggio's contemporary, will come to share Plato's, the Semites' as well as Paul's distrust of the visual, but the Cartesian alternative – the sovereign power of reason – was, ironically, in itself 'a model based on the metaphorics of vision (the mind's eye) in which the properties of the visible were transferred into the mental domain' (Kavanagh, Chapter 4, this volume).

Yet, Paul did not consider the ethical issue of visuality – that you don't get what you see – solved by moving it into the domain of a superior reason: it remains enigmatic and, theologically and ethically, *fallen*. While perhaps not calling for a traditional conversion, this chapter presents a method of *experimental juxtaposition*, which intends to challenge the obviousness of the visual by rendering visible, ideally, forces that exist in secrecy, veiled in the all too obvious. This is, at any rate, how Deleuze and Guattari read Paul Klee's idea of the role of art: 'The visual material must capture nonvisible forces. Render visible, Klee said; not render or reproduce the visible' (1987: 342).

This is very much in line with Berthoin Antal *et al.*'s observation regarding artistic interventions in organizations, which 'work with the powerful intangible forces in people and organizations' (Chapter 16, this volume). However, as such, organizational researchers are not artists; neither should we pretend to be: our ethical task is more closely connected to the political than to the artistic, yet may from time to time bridge the two. We may become craftsmen and deploy *the force* of art – its ability to render visible and its ability to create 'new sensations' (Deleuze and Guattari 1994). Such effects stem from an engagement with 'knowledge that is not entirely verbal, nor entirely sayable' (Strati quoted in Warren 2008: 561). This enables us – and this is the idea with the method of juxtaposition – to invoke other ways to understand a given visual, organizational artefact and blow up its significance. Such visual or aesthetic method is a strategy that pertains directly to the ethical and hence political side of organizational analysis, directly intervening in the virtual and invisible, yet 'powerful intangible forces' of organizing.

In this chapter, I want to walk the reader through three juxtapositions,[1] which intend to intervene in the configuration of these forces, each intervening, as it were, on various 'levels' of organization. The first pertains to the level of the organization itself, as it juxtaposes the famous Renaissance painting *Conversion of St. Paul* (1601) by Caravaggio with an also quite well-known organizational chart by Henry Mintzberg, namely his 1983 chart of 'The Six Basic Parts of the Organization'. The second juxtaposition pertains to the level of 'management', as it juxtaposes an image of a naked CEO of Zentropa, Lars von Trier's production company, with a photo of four Nigerians from a festival in 1944. The third juxtaposition, then, puts the iconic photo of a little Jewish boy coming out of the Jewish Ghetto in Warsaw with his hands in the air taken in 1943 side by side with Paul Klee's painting *Angelus Novus* from 1920. In some respect, this juxtaposition pertains to the individual level (the boy), yet its ambition is to intervene in the 'collective instruction' of memory.

The following ambition counts for all the juxtapositions: while they may set off at a certain 'level', as normally understood in analyses of organizations (say, individual, group or organizational level), they illustrate how visual organizational analysis is able to move by simple (and, at times, by more complicated) means between different levels of analysis. Following this introduction, the method of juxtaposition is discussed methodologically, after which the three examples of juxtapositions are presented and discussed. A brief afterword closes the chapter.

The method of juxtaposition

The method of juxtaposition is quite simple, as it will place visual artefacts side by side. One may juxtapose any visual material and any organizational artefacts, a strategy that could involve photos, paintings, charts, material items, models, slogans, logos, architectural designs, the corporative rules and the company games, brands and commercials, etc. The point and aim is to let the collision of the two items make the reader/viewer stand back and think anew. The methodological challenge is to construct rich juxtapositions that produce new sensory experiences in those that are subjected to them, freeing them from the way these subjects have been disciplined regarding how they may perceive and interpret the world (Warren 2008; Gagliardi 1996).

Juxtaposition analyses visual material in organization through the double lenses of aesthetics: two different experiences and two different habits of viewing collide and conjoin into a new experience. This new experience is a somewhat alienated one: the familiar becomes strange and, at times, uncanny, and breaks up the ways in which we, as Sontag (2003) sees it, have been 'instructed' to see and memorize what we see. The anthropologists Marcus and Fischer (1986) address such 'instructional' tendencies in Western culture through constructing a new type of enquiry, which works through 'defamiliarization'. In their view, this can be accomplished in two ways: defamiliarization by 'cross-cultural juxtaposition' (technical and organizational) and defamiliarization by 'epistemological critique' (juxtaposing forms of knowledge formation) (for a discussion, see Banerjee and Linstead 2004).

For the purpose of this chapter, it is especially Marcus and Fischer's method of 'cross-cultural juxtaposition' that is interesting; it forms the theoretical background for the method of juxtaposition here proposed. In order to illustrate their point, they discuss the well-known study by Margaret Mead (2001) of young people coming of age in Samoa, where she juxtaposes her study of Samoan youth with that of US youth. Yet as convincing as her study is – it practically came to define anthropology in the US – it is only a 'weak' variant of juxtaposition, since Mead only actually explored and researched the Samoan side of the juxtaposition, and relied on common knowledge when it came to US youth. In the 'strong' version of cross-cultural juxtaposition, which is the version I am championing here, both sides of the juxtaposition must be researched, analysed and explored in order to reap the full fruits of the exercise.

Marcus and Fischer's cross-cultural juxtaposition aims to defamiliarize the familiar and habitual by a 'disruption of common sense, doing the unexpected, placing familiar objects in unfamiliar, or even shocking, contexts' in order 'to make the reader conscious of difference' (1986: 137). This procedure produces new differences and remains a 'more explicit empirical' and 'more dramatic, upfront kind of cultural criticism' (ibid.: 138). Within organization studies, Alvesson offers an astute reading of Marcus and Fischer's method, explaining that 'the trick ... is to locate one's framework (cultural understanding) *away* from the culture being studied, so that significant material to "resolve" emerges' – and this is, Alvesson continues, 'of course to a large extent a matter of creativity' (1995: 53).

Such creation of new differences and consciousness, in my view, is exemplarily attained in Ian King's (2003) juxtaposition of a painting by Mondrian with an organizational chart taken from Mary Jo Hatch. King says that 'In placing these two figures together we should not be entirely surprised by their bond' (2003: 197), which is an insight the carefully crafted juxtaposition always should aim at. In King's case, the two images obviously belong to two different archives or imaginaries; they are both, each in their way, indebted to a view of science that is closely linked to Scientific Management and parallel, early modernist ways of thinking. Following what Marcus and Fischer refer to as the 'strong' version of their programme, in which both sides of the juxtaposition are explored equally, King establishes a set of genuine connections between what first appear disparate.

> The suggestion that these two figures possess similar characteristics has become more understandable as our discussion has continued – both have emerged and have in their different ways responded to the writings of F.W. Taylor and others advocating a scientific approach to organization and management.
>
> *(King 2003: 203)*

In the most productive juxtaposition, the 'strong version' as Marcus and Fischer call it, both sides of the juxtaposition are researched and explored. When the two parts or two sides of the fold are both unfolded (they may be inside/outside of the same fold, or the next fold in a manifold that would consist of more images from, possibly, the same archives), new similarities are seen and new differences are produced. It is in this positive sense that King 'does not rely on mere defamiliarization for an effect, but rather tries to engage the reader in a prolonged, dialectic discourse about the open-ended nature of similarities and differences' (Marcus and Fischer 1986: 161). This dialectical discourse must traverse both sides of the juxtaposition and create a third site where the 'new sensations' that Deleuze and Guattari (1994) talk about become possible.

In the juxtaposition between Caravaggio's second version of *The Conversion of Saint Paul* (from 1601) and Mintzberg's (1983) chart of 'The Six Basic Parts of the Organization', Sørensen (2010) points out how Mintzberg's model and Caravaggio's painting both partake in and depart from a long tradition of naturalizing contingent divisions between labour and management, expressed through darkness and light. Also a number of more or less explicit juxtapositions have emerged in organization studies. Departing from Kristeva's discussion of the body and law, Matilal and Höpfl (2009) juxtapose images of the Bhopal disaster with the 'dry' accounts of the disaster. Perhaps being less programmed in the collision it engenders in the empirical material, it still strives to 'find the relationship' between the two expressions of disaster and 'set [them] against each other' (Matilal and Höpfl 2009: 953).

In a more radical vein, Burrell's *Pandemonium* also deploys the form of juxtaposition in the book's very layout, where the upper and lower part of the pages must be read in different directions, so that the book will become 'a divided highway in which the meridian or central reservation separates reading which is moving in one direction from reading which is moving in the other' (Burrell 1997: 30).

In addition, organization scholars may get inspiration from avant-garde artists, who, in the twentieth century, developed the 'art of juxtaposition', which has produced 'disconcerting, fragmented works' (Shattuck quoted in Broughton 1981: 48). But we are still faced with the pressing methodological question of what material to juxtapose. The first rule is that the image or artefact you want to change the perception of – be it a Renaissance masterpiece, an image of a CEO in the creative sector, or a victim of a crime against humanity – must be selected because of its quality of being remarkable, interesting, or even iconic.

The second rule is experimentation: find a counter-image or artefact and place it beside the first item. Now, the field of this experimentation is not just limitless. Great art is not chaotic or haphazard; neither is a strong and compelling, empirical analysis. On the contrary; the form and the content of an analysis are equally important as Marcus and Fischer observe: 'In the most sophisticated critical works, content and form are intimately linked' (1986: 137). One cannot, in other words, just juxtapose a chosen item with anything and assume this to be productive. Ultimately, of course, one only knows after the fact whether one's juxtaposition is productive or not, but one necessary and, as it were, productive constraint is that both images (texts, symbols, artefacts, etc.) must belong to what Deleuze (1988) in his reading of Foucault refers to as the same 'archive': it must be feasible to construct an archive where both images/artefacts can be said to belong.

In the final case of this chapter, the juxtaposition between a photo of a genocide and a piece of art, both images may be said to stem from the archive termed 'children close to death', or 'subjects faced with the horror of war'. Yet, while the images must belong to the same archive, and 'repeat' the basic figure comprising and traversing the archive, they must at the same time be 'different' in a significant way. The one must, as Marcus and Fischer argue, be able to defamiliarize the other in a reciprocal and ultimately circular process. This also counts for the first juxtaposition, where a painting by Caravaggio is juxtaposed with Mintzberg's basic model of the organization (Figures 3.1 and 3.2). Such a juxtaposition opens up, in Roland Barthes' (1977) words, a third space or an 'obtuse meaning', which, as he stresses, is 'sensually produced'.

Another methodological or, perhaps, technical question is how one goes about analysing and developing a juxtaposition. Here the rule is: everything is already there, although it may be enigmatic, veiled, not yet unfolded. So work detail by detail: what is different between the two items, and what is repetitive. The written analysis may – as with the boy and the angel – consciously try to effect the production of a third space or figure 'between' the two images, which both unites them and makes them stand out on their own: both transforms them and anchors them in their original zone of solidarity.

Marcus and Fischer are quite explicitly aware of the dangers of the method and point out that it may produce 'off-balance, even unwieldy texts, by conventional standards' and they observe that the enterprise is often 'received as merely fanciful, cute, or eccentric, rather than really consequential, persuasive, or biting' (1986: 138). Yet, the productive and persuasive juxtaposition recreates the world as an open-ended event, and in some way remarkable or interesting becoming (Deleuze and Guattari 1987).

Finally, one particular promising consequence within organization studies is, as I see it, the method's ability to change the organization of memory, or, to be more specific, to change the organizational memory. Organizational Memory Studies (Rowlinson *et al.* 2010; Booth *et al.* 2007) identifies the role organizations and organizational artefacts play in subjecting memory and history to specific dominating systems of memory and in this way participates in its ongoing 'instruction' (Sontag 2003). This is especially critical when it comes to photos, which, as we once were told, convey reality. But photos do not convey reality, rather, they instruct our memory: 'Photographs objectify: they turn an event or a person into something that can be possessed. And photographs are a species of alchemy, for all they are prized as a transparent account of reality' (Sontag 2003: 81).

It is this alchemical process that a productive juxtaposition should intercept. This way another space where another understanding of a photo and hence the entire organization of memory may open up. Sontag here wants to *free the image*, but not from Halbwachs' (1992) 'collective memory', a concept which Sontag rejects. Rather, she wants to free the image from the 'collective instruction', which has tied down the possibility of memory to predisposed structures. Juxtaposition is a way of countering this collective instruction by intercepting the rational argument by aesthetic means, not least of our memories of guilt and horror-ridden atrocities.

Three juxtapositions

Caravaggio juxtaposed with Mintzberg: the Catholic Church creating the appropriate worker

This chapter's first juxtaposition (Figures 3.1 and 3.2) aims at exposing the way an aesthetic artefact, a painting, participates in the organization and production of the 'appropriate individual' (Alvesson and Willmott 2002), here the appropriate 'believer' in the Catholic Church; the painting was created in 1601 and has since 1609 been exposed in the Church Santa Maria del Popolo in Rome. Yet, the specific modern and exceptionally profound insights that Caravaggio

Bent M. Sørensen

is working with in this painting reach further than Church politics: the appropriate believer will transmute into the image of the appropriate modern worker, shaped in line with the composition of the art piece. The painting works directly on the sentiments of the church-goers, and this way naturalizes their idea of what a natural and necessary organization of the social fields looks like. These political issues may be less obvious when the painting is viewed in isolation, and it is the point of the juxtaposition to highlight such perspectives. Of course, this reading in no way precludes any other reading of Caravaggio's masterpiece, and to seek in it a particular organization of labour does remain a rare reading of this iconic Renaissance masterpiece.

For the purpose of juxtaposing, I have turned *St Paul's Conversion* upside down compared to the normal exposition of the painting. Caravaggio's painting depicts Paul's conversion as he had set off to Damascus but was thrown to the ground by Christ's voice: 'Why are you persecuting me?' This version of the conversion is the painter's second, as the first was rejected by the Catholic Church, which had commissioned it: this more realistic version, I think, was deemed more adequate in the ensuing Counter-Reformation. What the juxtaposition exposes is a strong isomorphism between the accepted version and the Church understood as a corporation in Mintzberg's 'basic model of the organization' sense. The Strategic Apex is – and we are here helped by the mentioned 'conversion' of the canvas itself – the head of Paul; his arms as they ambiguously connect to the horse's legs are the supporting Technostructure and Staff; and the enormous animal's torso is the Operating Core. Despite the fact that a forceful hoof is threatening Paul's genitals, he is not concerned: Paul stays calm in the belief that power in the modern world is not exercised primarily through brute force, but through knowledge and discipline (Foucault 1977). This light is represented by the bright areas of Paul's head, arms and the one leg of the peasant and the front of the animal.

Figure 3.1 The Conversion of Saint Paul (inverted), Caravaggio
Source: Rome, Church of Santa Maria del Popolo. © 2013. Photo Scala, Florence/Fondo Edifici di Culto – Min. dell'Interno.

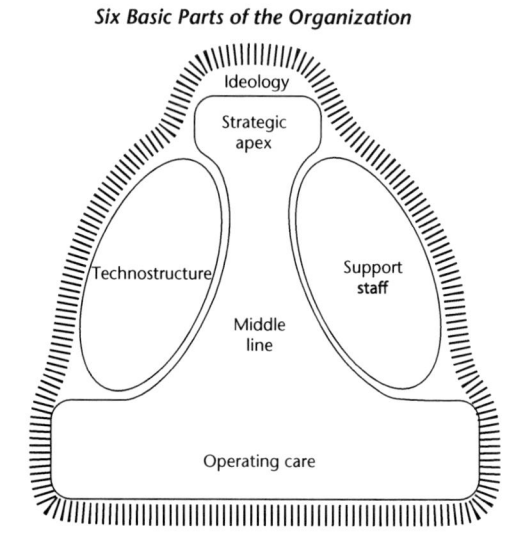

Figure 3.2 Mintzberg's 'basic model of the organization'

Paul, on his side, is not primarily engaged with the physical production, which is relegated to the horse and the peasant, i.e. the workers and the middle managers, who both are in severe need of management. To consider the Operating Core to be a monstrous crowd incapable of self-control is far from unknown in the history of ideas. Marx observed that the economic science 'knows the worker only as a working animal – as a beast reduced to the strictest bodily needs' (1972: VII). We also observe that Caravaggio had a more cynical but also more adequate view on (middle) management than Mintzberg. The manager who *is* visible in the painting is the groom. Whereas in the rejected version he was an active and centrally placed *soldier*, he is now a marginal part of the man–animal assemblage of the Operating Core, depicting how middle management is caught between an almighty board of directors and a crowd of workers/professionals, both groups having little regard for the middle manager who is neither a specialist nor a person with great influence and visibility in the organization, despite the grave responsibility. The groom's hand leads the horse. The word *manus*, Latin for hand, is the well-known etymological root of *manager*, from the Italian *maneggiare*, a term directly connected to handling things, especially horses (Wensley 1996). But, while the groom's hand may be said to '*maneggiare*' the horse, it is constantly controlled and administered by Paul's hand, and finds itself subjected to a Catholic knowledge economy where it is only a spare part in the overall division of labour. Paul's authority becomes visible in the light surrounding him as a charisma, one of Weber's (1947) three forms of authority, what strikingly reappears in Mintzberg's drawing as the 'Ideology' glowing from the corporation. Naturally, today, Florida's (2002) 'creative class' no longer handles *horses*; the creative class handles *thoughts*. This then happens, if we are to take Caravaggio's analysis seriously, in splendid isolation: Paul's conversion has become a primarily *psychological* and *cognitive* event that takes place within Paul's head, behind his closed eyes. The overarching insight is modernity's general displacement of the event (of conversion, of miracles, of meaning, of management, of thinking, *etc*.) from being an externality imposing itself on man to be what happens (only) inside man's brain: 'the site of control is … displaced to a significant extent from external to inner attributes of the subject who is urged to self-manage' (Costea *et al.* 2008: 673).

This splendid isolation, however, alienates the middle manager, the Operating Core's subjected workers as well as the Strategic Apex's creative directors. The middle manager and the workers as they find themselves inside the actually rigid divisions of modern organizations as physical labour; the directors as they find themselves disconnected from affects and passions. The 'passions' have been turned into 'interests' (as argued by Hirschman 1977), and thus also prepared the modern knowledge worker for modern capitalism, which can work only if the fiery passions of the collective crowd of humanity is broken down and privatized into appropriate, individual self-interest and rational calculi, that is, restricted self-management under the aegis of a supreme market (which has substituted the supreme deity, cf. M. Taylor 2004).

It is not entirely satisfactory to categorize this juxtaposition as pertaining to the organizational level: the genius of Caravaggio and the deftness of Mintzberg reside partly in their ability to imbue their work with multiple layers of meaning and in their aptitude to simultaneously deal with issues that transgress such categorizations. Caravaggio's painting discusses not only the nature of the Catholic Church's bureaucracy and, by implication, the nature of the modern corporation, but also how this nature predisposes the appropriateness of the modern employee and the psycho-cognitivist cosmology to which this employee is subjected. Mintzberg's model not only encapsulates (the dominant idea of) the internal logic of the corporation, but also draws up a symbol of what it means to labour and to manage in modernity. Juxtaposed, they show the continuity in the cultural icons that shape our everyday activity and thoughts and produce our 'social imaginaries' (C. Taylor 2004).

Bent M. Sørensen

The postmodern manager juxtaposed with four Nigerians

The second juxtaposition I want to present pertains, at the outset, directly to the level of management, in fact *a* manager: the Danish COE Peter Aalbæk, who is a producer and managing director in renowned film director Lars von Trier's (*Dancer in the Dark* from 2000, *Antichrist* from 2009) film company Zentropa. Peter Aalbæk is something like a celebrity/manager in the Danish media, and would often stage himself and the company in excessive and eccentric ways, which often would be connected to nudity and smoking cigars and the like. However, his ability to create an imaginary of creativity cannot be denied.

While both von Trier and Aalbæk are trained film directors, Aalbæk has taken on the more administrative side of their joint enterprise, a company located in some old but very characterful military barracks in a suburb of Copenhagen. These barracks work very well as the background for the movie from which the juxtaposition in question is taken: the documentary *One Day with Peter*, a 16-minute movie directed by Pablo Tréhin-Marçot was produced in 2004. The movie follows Peter Aalbæk for what seems to be one day of work at Zentropa. After a morning song session with the whole company, Peter walks around in the corridors and offices and greets everyone: a kiss for the female employees, and a handshake for the boys. Says Aalbæk in the voiceover, 'There is no system there ... but I do not kiss the men. I think that's disgusting.' There are signs of mutual disgust as some of the women seem taken considerably aback by the kissing and hugging. When Aalbæk reaches his destination, the steam bath and the outdoor pool swim, he is alone. Figure 3.3 is taken from a particular

Figure 3.3 Aalbæk and the office clerk
Source: Screenshot from *One Day with Peter*.

The method of juxtaposition

scene in the movie where Aalbæk enters a (male) employee's office and undresses in order to be ready for the steam bath and swimming. The screenshot is actually a juxtaposition in its own right.

To the left, one has the naked, free and liberated CEO, shaking his penis in front of the camera. To the right, one sees a bureaucratic worker, solemnly attending to his business, talking on the phone. He did not react on the actual undressing scene, but, after Aalbæk left, he went and picked up his boss's clothes, and put them on a hanger in the closet. A more comprehensive account of this bureaucratic knowledge worker and his share of creative work is told elsewhere (Sørensen 2012). Here, we will stay with Aalbæk: if we cut the screenshot in half, we have isolated our manager, and are free to juxtapose him with something other than his employee. One guiding analytical question could be: what other images of 'creative nakedness' can we find, and in this way construct the 'social imaginary' that is the background for Aalbæk's type of creative management?

In this juxtaposition, the image of Aalbæk is brought together with a photograph from 1944 depicting four (not identified) Nigerians at a traditional Dunbar festival (Levine 2008). Again, another note on the choice of juxtaposition. The choice of Aalbæk as naked is not, in a national context, anything peculiar, as Aalbæk as mentioned has turned it into a brand to undress: it is a mainstream choice. But it did not, I must admit, fare well with the publisher of a previous publication based on the same images. They wanted me to censor Peter Aalbæk's penis with a black box, whereas the Nigerians, who are hardly more 'dressed', were 'suitable' as they appeared. This very reaction – which the publisher reversed after I insisted in describing their reaction in the very same chapter – gave me the sense that I had found the right counter image: Aalbæk, a white, Anglo-Saxon, Protestant male CEO is real and must be censored, whereas the Nigerians are only representatives of our fantasy about them, unreal to the core of their existence, hence it is no problem to visualize them (much the same way one may 'visualize' just anything in one's own mind.)

For this occasion, then, the Nigerians have dressed up to meet the imperial governor, but their dressing up parades the most ridiculous outfit *they* could imagine that the governor (or, at least, 'the imperial gaze') could think of: white painting, odd headgear and penis sheaths. The crowd around them laughed heartedly in appreciation of their mockery: they match the category 'savage indigenous people' with great precision. In many, if not all, regards, this category had already worn out. In 1960, there was no longer a British governor in Nigeria.

With the same if only somewhat unconscious precision, Aalbæk mirrors what could be our fantasy of the postmodern, creative boss. And this fantasy is quite parallel to the supposed fantasy of the imperial gaze: with his nakedness and free desire, Aalbæk signals a proximity to the original creativity, creation before the Fall, when Adam and Eve were naked and had no shame. Such creative naivety (a word stemming from French for 'native') Westerners connect to women, children and, of course, natives. Consider the Nigerian in the forefront. Just as Aalbæk, he has caught the attention of the camera, and, although he does not hold his penis with his hand, but rather has it managed by his penis sheath, he does, with clear signs of victory and dominance, hold an upright stick. Both men know that a flaccid penis is an embarrassment when it is to appear in front of the gaze, be it imperial, corporate, medical or whatever. They both know that a flaccid penis is in need of a helping hand or a penis sheath: it is in need of *management*. The word management stems, as already developed above, from the Latin *manus*, hand, through Italian *maneggiare*, a term directly connected to handling things and objects (Wensley 1996). The penis needs management in order to appear as a phallus. The unmanaged penis is a disgrace, or, today, when 'graciousness' has been outdated as a relevant aesthetic quality, a farce.

Bent M. Sørensen

Figure 3.4 Aalbæk and the office clerk
Source: Screenshot from *One Day with Peter*.

Figure 3.5 Four Nigerians
Source: John Gwilym Davies, 1944. The Bodleian Library, University of Oxford. Ms.Afr. s. 310(1) no. 20.

Marx (1972) mocked Hegel by claiming that history appears twice: first as tragedy, then as farce. Both the first appearance of modern management in the early industrialization as well as the global imperial zeal were truly tragic as they proudly and erect mistreated the subjected and marginal classes, workers and indigenous people, respectively. In the juxtaposition, we see their second, farcical and impotent appearance: the soft, all-embracing manager who (at least wants to appear as if he) manages by immediate impulses and lust is just as ridiculous as the fantasy of the imperial gaze. The imperial zeal, on its side, is in its second (if not last) appearance met with active sarcasm and contempt.

That the post-bureaucratic manager is farcical does not mean that he or she does not create fantasies that inform the subjectivity of the employees in the creative sector. Zizek expresses this ambivalence well; an ambivalence played out to its fullest extent through Peter Aalbæk's choreographed mix between parading as a French *Roi Soleil* and as your next-door buddy with a tapped beer. Zizek's (2009: 202) analysis of such a managerial character runs as follows:

> A 'postmodern' boss insists that he is not a master but just a coordinator of our joint creative efforts, the first among equals; there should be no formalities among us, we should address him by his nickname, he shares a dirty joke with us ... but during all this, he remains our master.

The postmodern boss appeals to his or her employees in order to make them adopt a certain ironic stance towards themselves as well as towards their colleagues and their work. This is what Fleming and Spicer (2003) refer to as a 'cynical distance' adopted towards management: you live out management's fantasy, just as the Nigerians are living out the fantasy of the empire. The juxtaposition with the Nigerians in this regard is instructive, as they perform what Zizek (2008) refers to as 'parodic overidentification' (see also Contu 2008). In the post-bureaucratic corporation, the employee must somehow 'mirror' the orgone *jouissance* of the boss (even when he appears *not* to be the boss). In order to fill this open space of fantasy, the employee becomes a permanent opportunist, who constantly must self-evaluate the opportunities (Maravelias 2009).

Both Aalbæk and the Nigerians parade nakedness in a way that seems to be significant of their character. It has been suggested to me by students at my courses that Albæk's nakedness is connected to his creativity, and at least such sentiment is supported in the literature on creativity and entrepreneurship. For instance, Po Bronson's bestseller *The Nudist on the Late Shift, and other Tales of Silicon Valley* (1999) describes the California programmer community where 'eccentricity is de rigueur' and where the entrepreneur 'David Coons and his wife held skinny-dipping parties, to which Mr. Coons invited his friends from work. So nobody made much of it that he took his clothes off at the office after ten p.m.' While nakedness as such becomes connected to creativity, it also lives on in the Victorian bourgeoisie's idea of freedom, ultimately the freedom gained through escaping from rationality and civilization, deep into, one may imagine, the dark heart of Nigeria, of Kenya, of the earliest human evolution said to have begun in the mythological Rift Valley. Postcolonial theory describes the ambiguous relation between the knowledge of the gaze and its phantasmagorical Other, the Orient, which is 'at once both completely knowable through the "scientific" gaze of the colonizer, but at the same time it is an object of desire, a danger and a threat that is mysterious and unknowable' (Bhabha 1994: 75).

The clothed body has historically been connected to the two qualities of rationality and civilization, to such an extent that Mark (5:15) lets people that are 'Clothed and in their right mind' be destined to salvation and sanity. As Levine observes regarding the colonial view on the 'natives': they were considered, on account of their lack of shame at being naked, to be 'people whose souls were in danger' (2008: 191).

Zentropa's corporate values expressed in the triumvirate 'Christianity, Communism and Capitalism' (see www.zentropa.dk) have obvious predecessors in the missionaries' triumvirate 'Christianity, Civilization and Clothing' (Levine 2008). Levine also observes that the images of colonialized natives that circulated throughout the British Empire and beyond were by default oversexualized:

> The non-Western body, with its absence of shame and its apparent normalizing or incomprehension of nudity, re-mapped that violation [of taboo], creating a safe space for observing naked bodies belonging to nameless, over-sexualized people to whom shame could not, allegedly, attach.
>
> *(2008: 210)*

However, in addition, this second return of nudity has changed valour. Peter Aalbæk does not come forward as oversexualized, but rather as *under*sexualized: the tragedy of violent potency and rape has now returned as the farce of impotence and noisy gestures, a 'parodic overidentification' (Zizek 2008) with free desire, which becomes utterly untrustworthy and appeals to our pity rather than, as would be the case earlier, to our piety.

The juxtaposition of the screenshot with Peter Aalbæk and the four festive Nigerians at the Dunbar festival again points to the fact that the analytical 'level' of organizational analysis only refers to an analytical construct. The juxtaposition sets to work a complicated flow of foldings and unfoldings, which, far from pertaining only to management, come to take up issues of significance to our entire civilization and its history.

The dark side of organization: a little boy juxtaposed with an angel

The final juxtaposition I want to present departs from a photo which, like the screenshot of Peter Albæk, in itself is a significant juxtaposition between the deportees and their deporting adversaries (see Figure 3.6).

Bent M. Sørensen

Figure 3.6 Jewish Ghetto, Warsaw 1943
Source: Photo © The Israel Museum, Jerusalem by Elie Posner.

The storm trooper to the right in the picture from World War II's Jewish Ghetto in Warsaw in 1943 is Josef Blösche of the *Sicherheitsdienst* (SD) of the SS. In 1969, Blösche was interrogated about his role in the event: 'The picture shows how I, as a member of the Gestapo office in the Warsaw Ghetto, together with a group of SS members, am driving a large number of Jewish citizens out of a house' (Blösche quoted in Raskin 2004: 95). Blösche becomes juxtaposed in the frame with what is arguably the most famous child from World War II, a little frightened boy stretching his arms in the air, possibly with parts of his family surrounding him. We don't know this. Blösche is the only person identified beyond doubt in the photo, and, although the identity of some of the refugees is somewhat certain, the identity and destiny of the boy is unknown (Raskin 2004; Porat 2010). Following the logic of this picture, there appears really no way out for him, he is already a victim of circumstances. But the logic of photographs is highly ideological; Paul is more right today than ever: we see enigmas through dark glasses. Sontag maintains a counter-intuitive reading of this very photo: 'Photographs of the suffering and martyrdom of a people are more than reminders of death, of failure, of victimization. They invoke the miracle of survival' (2003: 72). In Figures 3.7 and 3.8, I juxtapose the little boy with another little creature, an angel painted by Paul Klee more than 20 years earlier.

Although Klee painted *Angelus Novus* two decades before the outbreak of World War II, he did paint it in the debris of World War I. Moreover, as he painted at home with his family surrounding him, a child in anguish was well known to him. *Angelus Novus* was for a period of time owned by the philosopher and cultural critic Walter Benjamin, who wrote some of his most powerful and vivid texts on this painting. Benjamin's 'Ninth Thesis', in his *Theses on the Philosophy of History*, opens as follows: '*Angelus Novus* shows an angel looking as though he is

The method of juxtaposition

Figure 3.7 Jewish Ghetto, Warsaw 1943
Source: Photo © The Israel Museum, Jerusalem
by Elie Posner.

Figure 3.8 *Angelus Novus*, Paul Klee

about to move away from something that he is fixedly contemplating. His eyes are staring, his mouth is open, his wings are spread' (1999: 245ff).

As the angel is caught in a storm (as Benjamin specifies), it can't get back to 'us', but sees us caught in 'one single catastrophe which keeps piling wreckage upon wreckage and hurls it in front of [the angel's] feet' (ibid.). The little boy is also caught in wreckage, although he also is 'about to move away': the catastrophe that the angel sees is *his* catastrophe, or, in the eyes of the angel, *our*, that is, *humanity's joint catastrophe*. But we, humans as such, keep looking away from our catastrophe and the little boy caught in it, because we, humans as such, are looking for progress instead, no matter whether we are Marxists or liberalists (Gray 2003). While through this juxtaposition we may become witnesses of the boy's fate, he remains, by way of the same juxtaposition, *our* witness to the catastrophe itself. Benjamin speculates that the angel would want to stay in order to awaken the dead and redeem the crushed world, but this is not going to happen. The angel cannot stay – and so ends Benjamin's (1999: 249) 'Ninth Thesis' – because:

> a storm is blowing from Paradise; it has got caught in his wings with such violence that the angel can no longer close them. This storm irresistibly propels him into the future to which his back is turned, while the pile of debris before him grows skyward. This storm is what we call *progress*.

Progress makes impossible both the boy's escape from the catastrophe as well as the angel's return to it, and progress 'irresistibly propels' both of them into a nameless future. We observe, however, that the boy carries a rucksack, as is pointed out by artist and Holocaust survivor Samuel Bak, who has used parts of the photo extensively in his own paintings: 'A rucksack

59

is something that you take along only if you believe that the next day you will still be alive. In this photo it symbolizes the persistence of hope' (Bak quoted in Raskin 2004: 149). While I maintain that this juxtaposition harbours hope, there is always the risk that hope is being turned into wishful thinking or ideology, as experienced by Dan Porat, author of another book about the photo *The Boy* (2010). Porat personally saw the photo of the Warsaw boy when visiting the Yad Vashem Holocaust Museum in Jerusalem. The official guide was showing it to a group consisting of a Slovenian minister and his civil servants:

> 'Do you know that this picture tells a good story of the Holocaust?' The surprised men's faces turned toward her. She continued unequivocally: 'This boy survived. After the Holocaust, he studied medicine, became a doctor, and settled in New York. A year ago, he immigrated to Israel.' The men nodded in approval, and the delegation disappeared down the dark museum hall.
>
> *(Porat 2010: 3)*

This is a clear and quite practical example of what Sontag (2003) refers to as collective instruction, and, in regards to the Nazi holocaust, it is such instruction that resides at the heart of what Finkelstein (2000) refers to as 'the Holocaust industry'. The photo of the little boy has itself become a central player in this industry as an 'emblem of suffering' (Sontag 2003: 119), at least for Western generations born prior to, say, 1970, for whom it is still a part of their 'social imaginaries' (C. Taylor 2004). The organization studies scholar Yannis Gabriel experimented recently with showing the photo to an international group of fifteen doctoral students: only one recognized the picture, and only two connected it to specific Jewish suffering. In one way, the juxtaposition contributes to such 'defamiliarization' of the photo: while it, of course, remains important that historically it was a Jewish boy led out of a Jewish ghetto, the juxtaposition with Klee's angel points to an ahistorical surplus, a suffering that is universal and which begs us to contemplate it in unfamiliar contexts of which the most prominent is our present.

Afterword

In this chapter, I have introduced a concrete method for visual organizational analysis, which I find is applicable to a very broad array of different types of material. The simplicity of the method does not make it an easy one. Both the selection of the items to juxtapose, the concepts with which to analyse the juxtaposition, and the ensuing questions: What do the two items do to each other? Which kind of new space or new production of meaning do they allow for? How does this pertain to organization or organizational memory? Does it pertain to repressed or not so easy accessible material? Did the juxtaposition fail? In a productive or unproductive way?

It may happen that a juxtaposition allows for a reintegration of experiences that in Kristeva's expression have been 'abjected' from the common-sense vocabulary (Kristeva 1982; Cohen *et al.* 2006; Stokes and Gabriel 2010) and hence become ethical and political. Not all juxtapositions would produce ethical or political 'spaces', but one necessary assessment of the value of a given juxtaposition is its ability to turn organizational problems, through such aesthetic analysis, into ethical or political questions. That we live in an image-saturated world only makes us so much more susceptible to control, substantiating Cooper's (1989) insight that what characterizes the 'labour of division' in the disciplinary society is a matter of performing control 'over the social and material world through enhanced clarity, transparency and visual certainty at a distance'. Visual analysis should be concerned with this disciplining, and allow, possibly through juxtaposition, the breaking up of this gridlock. Unfortunately, much management theory has been tied to an 'appreciative, aesthetically elevated conception of aesthetics and art' (Schroeder 2006: 87), where it instead should follow Contu's (2008: 367) injunction to 'investigate the hidden transcripts, the offstage discourse' of (aesthetic) organizational practice.

Juxtaposition may liberate memory both through its inbuilt iconoclasm and through its creation of new visual imaginaries. In Parr's (2006) vision, this is where an ethical potential lies for such experimentation with what we may term our present past. As students of the visual, we are again reminded of Benjamin's warning: 'every image of the past that is not recognized by the present as one of its *own concerns* threatens to disappear irretrievably' (1999: 247, emphasis added).

Notes

1 All three juxtapositions are discussed much more comprehensively in articles that also deal with these issues elsewhere (Sørensen 2010, 2012, under review). The current reproductions of the juxtapositions basically follow the same logic as the original; they are, perhaps, nothing more than slightly different unfoldings and refoldings of the same surface as their 'origin'.

References

Alvesson, M. (1995) *Cultural Perspectives on Organizations*, Cambridge, MA.: Cambridge University Press.
Alvesson, M. and Kärreman, D. (2000) 'Taking the linguistic turn in organizational research', *Journal of Applied Behavioral Science* 36(2): 136–158.
Alvesson, M. and Willmott, H. (2002) 'Identity regulation as organizational control: producing the appropriate individual', *Journal of Management Studies* 39(5): 619–644.
Banerjee, S.B. and Linstead, S. (2004) 'Masking subversion: neocolonial embeddedness in anthropological accounts of indigenous management', *Human Relations* 57(2): 221–247.
Barthes, R. (1977) *Image, Music, Text*, New York: Hill and Wang.
Baudrillard, J. (1994) *Simulacra and Simulation*, Ann Arbor: The University of Michigan Press.
Benjamin, W. (1999) *Illuminations*, London: Pimlico.
Betts, J. (2006) 'Framing power: the case of the boardroom', *Consumption Markets & Culture* 9(2): 157–167.
Bhabha, H.K. (1994) *The Location of Culture*, New York: Routledge.
Booth, C., Clark, P., Delahaye, A., Procter, S. and Rowlinson, M. (2007) 'Accounting for the dark side of corporate history: organizational culture perspectives and the Bertelsmann case', *Critical Perspectives on Accounting* 18(6): 625.
Bronson, P. (1999) *The Nudist on the Late Shift: and other Tales of Silicon Valley*, London: Secker & Warburg.
Broughton, P.R. (1981) 'The Cubist novel: towards defining the genre', in Doreen Fowler and Ann J. Abadie (eds) *'A Cosmos of My Own': Faulkner and Yoknapatawpha, 1980*, Jackson: University Press of Mississippi.
Burrell, G. (1997) *Pandemonium. Towards a Retro-organization Theory*, London: Sage.
Cohen, L., Hancock, P. and Tyler, M. (2006) '"Beyond the scope of the possible": art, photography and organisational abjection', *Culture and Organization* 12(2): 109–125.
Contu, A. (2008) 'Decaf resistance: on misbehavior, cynicism, and desire in liberal workplaces', *Management Communication Quarterly* 21(3): 364–379.
Cooper, R. (1989) 'The visibility of social systems', in M.C. Jackson, P. Keys and S.A. Cropper (eds) *Operational Research and the Social Sciences*, New York: Plenum, 51–59.
Costea, B., Crump, N. and Amiridis, K. (2008) 'Managerialism, the therapeutic habitus and the self in contemporary organizing', *Human Relations* 61(5): 661–685.
Debord, G. (1994) *The Society of the Spectacle*, New York: Zone Books.
Deleuze, G. (1988) *Foucault*, Minneapolis: University of Minnesota Press.
——(1990) *The Logic of Sense*, New York: Columbia University Press.
Deleuze, G. and Guattari, F. (1987) *A Thousand Plateaus*, Minneapolis: University of Minnesota Press.
Deleuze, G. and Guattari, F. (1994) *What is Philosophy?* New York: Columbia University Press.
Finkelstein, N.G. (2000) *The Holocaust Industry: Reflections on the Exploitation of Jewish Suffering*, London: Verso.

Fleming, P. and Spicer, A. (2003) 'Working at a cynical distance: implications for power, subjectivity and resistance', *Organization* 10(1): 157–179.
Florida, R. (2002) *The Rise of the Creative Class and How it's Transforming Work, Leisure, Community and Everyday Life*, New York: Basic Books.
Foucault, M. (1977) *Discipline and Punish: The Birth of the Prison*, New York: Pantheon Books.
Fuery, P. and Fuery, K. (2003) *Visual Cultures and Critical Theory*, London: Arnold.
Gabriel, Y. (1999) *Organizations in Depth*, Thousand Oaks, CA: Sage.
Gagliardi, P. (1996) 'Exploring the aesthetic side of organizational life', in S.R. Clegg, C. Hardy and W.R. Nord (eds) *Handbook of Organization Studies*, Thousand Oaks, CA, US: Sage, 565–580.
Gray, J. (2003) *Al Qaeda and what it Means to be Modern*, New York: New Press.
Guthey, Eric and Jackson, Brad (2005) 'CEO portraits and the authenticity paradox', *Journal of Management Studies* 42(5): 1057–1082.
Halbwachs, M. (1992) *On Collective Memory*, Chicago: University of Chicago Press.
Hirschman, A.O. (1977) *The Passions and the Interests: Political Arguments for Capitalism before its Triumph*, Princeton, NJ: Princeton University Press.
Jay, M. (1986) 'In the empire of the gaze: Foucault and the denigration of vision in twentieth-century French thought', in D.C. Hoy (ed.) *Foucault: A Critical Reader*, Oxford: Blackwell, 175–204.
King, I.W. (2003) 'Reassessing organizational structure as a painting of space', *Culture and Organization* 9(3): 195–207.
Kristeva, J. (1982) *Powers of Horror: An Essay on Abjection*, New York: Columbia University Press.
Levine, P. (2008) 'States of undress: nakedness and the colonial imagination', *Victorian Studies* 50(2): 189–219.
Maravelias, C. (2009) 'Freedom, opportunism and entrepreneurialism in post-bureaucratic organizations', in D. Hjorth and C. Steyaert (eds) *The Politics and Aesthetics of Entrepreneurship*, Cheltenham: Edward Elgar, 13–30.
Marcus, G.E. and Fischer, M.M.J. (1986) *Anthropology as Cultural Critique: An Experimental Moment in the Human Sciences*, Chicago: University of Chicago Press.
Marx, K. (1972) *The Eighteenth Brumaire of Louis Bonaparte*, New York: International Publishers.
Matilal, S. and Höpfl, H. (2009) 'Accounting for the Bhopal Disaster: footnotes and photographs', *Accounting, Auditing & Accountability Journal* 22(6): 953–972.
Mead, M. (2001) *Coming of Age in Samoa: A Psychological Study of Primitive Youth for Western Civilisation*, Perennial Classics edn, New York: Perennial Classics.
Mintzberg, H. (1983) *Structure in Fives: Designing Effective Organizations*, Englewood Cliffs, NJ: Prentice-Hall.
Nietzsche, F.W. (2001) *The Gay Science*, Cambridge, UK: Cambridge University Press.
Parr, A. (2006) 'Deterritorialising the Holocaust', in I. Buchanan and A. Parr (eds) *Deleuze and the Contemporary World*, Edinburgh: Edinburgh University Press, 125–145.
Porat, D. (2010) *The Boy: A Holocaust Story*, 1st ed., New York: Hill and Wang.
Raskin, R. (2004) *A Child at Gunpoint: A Case Study in the Life of a Photo*, Aarhus: Aarhus University Press.
Rowlinson, M., Booth, C., Clark, P., Delahaye, A. and Procter, S. (2010) 'Social remembering and organizational memory', *Organization Studies* 31(1): 69.
Schroeder, J.E. (2006) 'Aesthetics awry: The Painter of Light™ and the commodification of artistic values', *Consumption Markets & Culture* 9(2): 87–100.
Sontag, S. (2003) *Regarding the Pain of Others*, 1st ed., New York: Penguin.
Sørensen, B.M. (2010) 'St Paul's Conversion: the aesthetic organization of labour', *Organization Studies* 31(3): 307–326.
——(2012) 'Management as farce: entrepreneurial subjectivity and the creative industries', in D. Hjorth (ed.) *Organizational Entrepreneurship*, London: Edward Elgar.
——(under review) 'Rendering suffering visible: an organizational aesthetics for the dark side' for *Organization Studies*, Special Issue on The Dark Side of Organization.
Stokes, P. and Gabriel, Y. (2010) 'Engaging with genocide: the challenge for organization and management studies', *Organization* 17(4): 461.
Strangleman, T. (2004) 'Ways of (not) seeing work: the visual as a blind spot in WES?', *Work, Employment and Society* 18(1): 179.
Taylor, C. (2004) *Modern Social Imaginaries*, Durham: Duke University Press.
Taylor, M.C. (2004) *Confidence Games: Money and Markets in a World without Redemption*, Chicago: University of Chicago Press.
Tréhin-Marçot, P. (2004) *One Day with Peter*, Copenhagen: Zentropa Productions.

Warren, S. (2008) 'Empirical challenges in organizational aesthetics research: towards a sensual methodology', *Organization Studies* 29(4): 559–580.
Weber, M. (1947) *The Theory of Social and Economic Organization*, New York: The Free Press.
Wensley, R. (1996) 'Isabella Beeton: management as "everything in its place"', *Business Strategy Review* 7(1): 37–46.
Zizek, S. (2008) *In Defense of Lost Causes*, London: Verso.

4
The limits of visualization
Ocularcentrism and organization

Donncha Kavanagh

Introduction

We live in a spectatorial society, where we are bombarded by visual images, and where conversations are littered with visual metaphors. This chapter seeks to ground this empirical reality through considering the position in discourse of visual or ocular metaphors. Succinctly, it seeks to understand ocularcentrism – a paradigm or epistemology based on visual or ocular metaphors – and its limits. The chapter begins by outlining the characteristics and development of the paradigm, and the different ways in which it has been critiqued by philosophers, social theorists and political scientists. These critiques are classified into three trajectories which, informed by the original paradigm, constitute a 'meta-theoretical' framework – schematically depicted in Figure 4.1.

The bulk of the chapter considers the three different trajectories that the critiques of ocularcentrism have taken. The first consists of writers who have critiqued the vision metaphor by taking it to its extreme, but who also, somewhat paradoxically, retain the metaphor's central position in their own texts. This trajectory is referred to as *ocularcentrism extended*. The second trajectory seeks to excoriate the root metaphor, and *ocularcentrism displaced* traces the metaphoric redescriptions and displacements that have been effected through this approach. The third

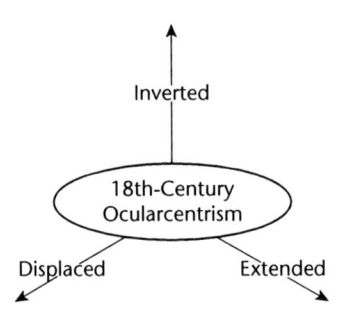

Figure 4.1 Meta-theoretical trajectories

trajectory, *ocularcentrism inverted*, effectively inverts some of the categorical distinctions on which ocularcentrism is founded, in particular the understanding that theory is pure, in contrast to the impurity of the 'real' world. Together, these three trajectories provide a frame for organizing how we might think about visualization, while it also frames limits on what visual organization might, or might not, mean.

The ascendancy of the eye

With considerable justification, we can characterize Western culture as an ocularcentric paradigm, based as it is on a vision-generated, vision-centred interpretation of knowledge, truth and reality. At the outset, it is worth summarizing the key contributions to the ocularcentric paradigm made by Plato, Descartes and the philosophers of the Enlightenment (for more extensive discussions on the philosophical roots of ocularcentrism, see Jay 1993a; Levin 1993b; Jonas 1966).

Plato made the important distinction between the sense of sight, which he grouped with the creation of human intelligence and soul, and that of the other senses, which he placed with man's material being. Not only was sight 'by far the most costly and complex piece of workmanship which the artificer of the senses ever contrived' (Plato 1974:VII/S507), but also sight, unlike the other senses, had a theological dimension as it was directly connected, via light, to the sun deity: 'the sun is not sight, but the author of sight who is recognised by sight' (ibid.:VII/S508). Plato also made the critical division between the visible world and the intelligible world (ibid.:VII/S509–10), although his description of the latter is always based on ocular metaphors: for him, the 'soul is like the eye' (ibid.:VII/S508) and things in the intelligible domain 'can only be seen with the eye of the mind' (ibid.:VII/S510). His well-known myth of the cave was especially important in the development of the ocularcentric paradigm because it demonstrated how the immediately experienced sight of one's eyes (the visible world) is impure, in contrast to the pure Truth that is only attainable through the speculative ability of the mind's eye (the intelligible world). Plato's interpretation of the allegory is that 'the prison-house is the world of sight, the light of the fire is the sun, and ... the journey upwards [is] the ascent of the soul into the intellectual world', which, importantly, he always describes using light, sight, shadows and vision, for example:

> the world of knowledge ... [which] when seen is also inferred to be the universal author of all things beautiful and right, parent of light and of the lord of light in this visible world, and the immediate source of truth in the intellectual; and that this is the power upon which he who would act rationally either in public or private life must have his eye fixed.
> *(ibid.: VII/S517)*

Because ocular metaphors are primordial in both the visible and intelligible worlds, we will restate Plato's demarcation as a distinction between the 'eyes on one's head' (which we will refer to as *e-vision*) and the 'eye in one's mind' (*m-vision*). Ever since, the ocularcentric paradigm has been driven by a constant play between these different 'eyes'. This distinction, as depicted in Figure 4.2, came to be foundational in modern thought.

So impressed was Democritus by Plato's reasoning that he supposedly blinded himself in order to better 'see' with his intellect and thus discern truths denied to his normal vision. Likewise, Plato's suspicion of e-vision was the reason for his hostility to all mimetic arts, which he saw as a form of deception. Many centuries later, Descartes was equally distrustful of what he saw and, like Plato, he rejected the visible world (e-vision) as a potential or actual illusion. Ironically, his alternative – the sovereign power of reason – was essentially a model based on the metaphorics

	Modern Thought
m-vision (theory)	Pure
e-vision (practice)	Impure

Figure 4.2 The categorical distinction between m-vision and e-vision

of vision (the mind's eye) in which the properties of the visible were transferred into the mental domain. The ocular paradigm was further enhanced by the discovery of perspectivism in the sixteenth century and Newton's work on optics in the seventeenth century. As Berger put it:

> [p]erspective makes the single eye the center of the visible world. Everything converges on to the eye as to the vanishing point of infinity. The visible world is arranged for the spectator as the universe was once thought to be arranged for God.
>
> *(1972: 16)*

In time, the modern individual (the 'I') came to be centred on, if not abbreviated to, the eye ('I' = eye).

This infatuation with the visual reached a new zenith during the Enlightenment – a term that is itself based on an ocular metaphor – when the rationalist understanding that the mind's eye (Reason) could potentially 'see' the Truth came to dominate intellectual thought. For rationalists, 'a certain class of reasons … carry their own credibility with them: they will be visible because they glow by their own light' (Barnes and Bloor 1982: 29). What is interesting for our purposes is that many of the Enlightenment's central precepts, such as objectivism, reflection, critical rationality and subjectivism, are fundamentally based on the primacy accorded to the visual. In particular, the dominant ocularcentric paradigm promulgated during the Enlightenment worked to elevate static Being over dynamic Becoming and fixed essences over ephemeral appearances. This ontological consequence is because, as Jonas (1966) has explained, sight is essentially the sense of simultaneity, of seeing a wide field at one moment, while hearing is significantly more temporal because it operates through intertwining past, present and future into a meaningful whole. And sight, unlike hearing, leaves the visible undiminished by its action, creating a unique sense of otherness. Moreover, the phenomenon of distancing, which is the most basic function of sight, helps create the belief that objects are distant from and neutrally apprehended by sovereign subjects, which, in turn, provides the basis for the subject–object dualism that is so typical of Greek and Western metaphysics.

The dominance of visual metaphors continues to this day in contemporary academic discourse: in conceptualizing, we seek insight and illumination; we speculate, inspect, focus and reflect; and, when we speak of points of view, synopsis and evidence, we may forget or be unaware of these concepts' sight-based etymology. The 'spectatorial' nature of modern epistemology is also evident when we consider that the word theory has the same root as the Greek word for 'theatre', *theoria*, meaning to look at attentively, or to behold. Likewise, writing is largely a visual exercise, in contrast to speaking, which is centred on the sense of hearing. Thus, in modern philosophy, the eye is the hinge point between the subjective and the objective, the window to the world and the mirror of the soul. In this spectatorial epistemology, the ocular subject has become the ultimate source of all being, with 'the world' being seen, reflected in, represented by, objectified and instrumentalized by the sovereign subjective self. As Derrida put it:

the metaphor of darkness and light (of self-revelation and self-concealment) [is the] founding metaphor of Western philosophy as metaphysics… [I]n this respect the entire history of our philosophy is a photology, the name given to a history of, or treatise on, light.

(1978: 27)

Ocularcentrism extended

If rationalism reached its high-water mark in the eighteenth century, it was subsequently critiqued by both Romantics and conservatives in the nineteenth century, and by most everyone else in the twentieth century. However, with respect to the root ocular metaphor of rationalism, it is useful to distinguish between those critiques that seek to displace the metaphor and those that retain it. In this section, we consider the latter, namely the Romantics (including Nationalists and Socialists) who concoct and follow utopian visions, and the postmodern counter-visionaries who, while they critique ocularcentrism, still remain within its thrall.

In their attempt to move away from Enlightenment rationality, the Romantics of the nineteenth century stressed the imaginative, the irrational and fantastic aspects of the human creative mind. Yet, insofar as Romanticism retains the primordial position of the human mind, it is best seen as an extension and deepening of the Enlightenment rather than an alternative philosophy. Thus, the Romantics presented mental pictures of what the world *might be* like – instead of the rationalist picture of what the world *was* like. To emphasize the difference, Abrams (1953) used the metaphors of mirror and lamp to distinguish between the two movements. For Abrams, the rationalist mind is a 'reflector of external objects', while the Romantic mind is:

> a radiant projector which makes a contribution to the objects it perceives. The [mirror metaphor] was characteristic of much of the thinking from Plato to the eighteenth century; the [lamp metaphor] typifies the prevailing romantic conception of the poetic mind.
>
> *(1953: viii)*

While Abrams asserts that the two metaphors are 'antithetic' to one another, for us, they are both fundamentally ocular, or sight based. Moreover, the Romantics followed in the tradition of the rationalists by invariably presenting optimistic, progressive – and one might say innocent – visions of the future. Prototypical of these creative and imaginative visions was the nineteenth-century catalogue of utopian texts that provided a life-force and inspiration for many subsequent political and social movements.

The Romantic movement of the early nineteenth century provided an important philosophical basis for both socialism and nationalism, the two primary movements of radical political change in the late nineteenth century and throughout the twentieth century (Jones 1974). In particular, Romantic literature, with its celebration of the vernacular and folk traditions, certainly inspired nationalistic feeling throughout Europe in the nineteenth century. Moreover, in terms of ocular metaphors, both nationalism and socialism were still founded on a 'fixed point of view', or what Trimble (1998) refers to as 'the Platonic pursuit of abstract perfection'.

Marshall McLuhan identified a further connection between ocularcentrism and nationalism when he noted the important role played by print technology during the nineteenth century: 'by print a people *sees* itself for the first time. The vernacular in appearing in high visual definition affords a glimpse of social unity co-extensive with vernacular boundaries' (McLuhan 1962: 217, original emphasis). Elsewhere, he reiterated the link when he asserted that '[n]ationalism depends upon or derives from the "fixed point of view" that arrives with print, perspective, and visual quantification' (ibid.: 220).

While the Romantics of the early nineteenth century critiqued Enlightenment rationality, Nietzsche was perhaps the first writer to attack *ocularcentrism* when he argued against the philosopher's presupposition of an eye outside time and history, 'an eye that no living being can imagine, an eye required to have no direction, to abrogate its active and interpretative powers' (1969 [1887]: 255). As early as the eighteenth century, the import of an individual historian's perspective on history was well understood, but Nietzsche took this further by asserting that *every* discourse could only be understood as a perspective – 'all seeing is essentially perspective and so is all knowing' (ibid.) – and he developed this insight to present a radical critique of both philosophy and science. Nietzsche's rhetorical device was to subvert the visual by turning it in on itself through extending and multiplying its logic. As Jay put it: 'Plato's singular sun of truth illuminating a reality of forms was replaced by a thousand and one suns shining on a multitude of different realities' (1993a: 190). What is important for our purposes is that the visual metaphor is still central in Nietzschean multi-perspectivalism.

Foucault was just as averse to the 'spectator' theory of knowledge, but his line of argument was quite different. Foucault's insight was that, while the subject was constituted as a detached, contemplative, disinterested, autonomous entity in a spectatorial epistemology, his historical studies showed how the subject was better understood as being incarcerated and indeed constituted by various technologies of visualization. For him, vision becomes supervision: 'the gaze that sees is the gaze that dominates' (Foucault 1973: 39). In other words, the power to see, to make visible, is the power to control, which is why Foucault sees knowledge and power as fundamentally indwelling. In the *Birth of the Clinic* (subtitled *An Archaeology of Medical Perception*), he argued that the medical gaze took hold once pathological anatomy and the autopsy – which was essentially a project of spatializing disease – came to be accorded central status in medical practice after 1800. In *Discipline and Punish*, he mapped out the nineteenth-century shift from sovereign to disciplinary power: the shift from 'governmentality organized around the gaze of the sovereign to governmentality organized by surveillance, panopticism, the normalizing gaze dispersed throughout the social system, maintaining civil order' (Levin 1993a: 20–21). In a disciplinary regime, 'power is exercised by virtue of things being known and people being seen … by surveillance rather than ceremonies' (Foucault and Gordon 1980: 154), and, in this regime, individuals are no longer autonomous entities, but are better understood as being constituted by technologies of visualization, such as the examination, which, in turn, includes self-observation, self-examination and self-monitoring. Notwithstanding Foucault's antipathy to vision, his archaeological and genealogical methods are fundamentally ocular – insofar as they make visible the correlations between vision and truth, and vision and power, respectively – and he makes generous use of spatial metaphors throughout his writings.

Other writers have also followed a similar path, critiquing modern epistemology but still retaining the ocular metaphor as central to their 'new' paradigm. Typical of this approach would be the so-called 'reflexive turn' taken by many sociologists of science during the 1980s on the back of the postmodern critique of modern epistemology (see, for example, Woolgar 1988). One difficulty with this project is that the concept of reflection is itself based on an ocular metaphor, which is precisely why Winner dismissed the reflexive turn as 'that endlessly enchanting hall of mirrors' (1993: 373). Within this group, we might also locate the more self-indulgent and self-centred of the postmoderns.

Ocularcentrism displaced

Writers in this category are equally hostile to Enlightenment rationality, but what makes them more radical than those in the previous category is that not only do they reject the ocular metaphor but they also attempt to replace it with different metaphors and vocabulary. We begin by summarizing the more significant endeavours to place other senses – especially hearing but also the sense of touch – at the centre of philosophical discourse. The chapter then proceeds to explain why it is appropriate, if paradoxical, to place conservatives and postmodern radicals within this category on the basis that they both seek to jettison the visual metaphor from political discourse.

The linguistic turn: from sight to sound

Over the last century or so, a succession of philosophers have revolted against the legacy of Cartesianism and the Enlightenment, and have denounced the 'spectatorial and intellectualist epistemology based on a subjective self reflecting on an objective world exterior to it' (Jay 1993b: 143). One of the most significant shifts occurred in the early part of the twentieth century with the development of structuralism. In particular, the contribution of the linguist Ferdinand de Saussure proved hugely influential as it marked a profound shift towards language and narrative. Since language is fundamentally about speaking – and hearing – structuralism constitutes a 'metaphorical redescription' from a paradigm based on vision and sight to one based on speaking and hearing (even if language and communication is not exclusively based on speech).

Others soon applied Saussure's ideas beyond the domain of language. Indeed, what links the various forms of structuralism is the common use of Saussure's ideas to study a variety of symbolic relations – understood as an underlying system of differences – whether these be structured by language, class or whatever. So, for instance, Hans-Georg Gadamer argued for a shift from seeing to a conversation-based hermeneutics, while Jürgen Habermas' work can similarly be interpreted as a project to move from a rationality grounded in a detached-spectator paradigm to one based on communication, speech and democratic participation. Centrally, the subject in Habermas' philosophy is neither the dominating observer nor an observed subject, but a speaking, listening subject participating in democratic practices. The same theme is to be found in the so-called 'voice discourse', which asserts the primacy of speech (experience) over writing (theory) and which counters knowledge claims based on a spectatorial epistemology with narratives of the silenced and excluded (see, for example, Spivak 1988 [1985]). Likewise, the American pragmatist Richard Rorty (1979) has rigorously refuted the picture of the mind as a mirror of theoretical reflection. Instead of ocular theories of truth that make truth a matter of correspondence, he proposed a conception of truth and mind based on discourse. And, if we see, as Rorty does, 'the history of language, and thus of the arts, the sciences, and the moral sense, as the history of metaphor' 1989: xvi), then we can understand the profound shift in philosophical discourse away from theory and towards narrative as a move in metaphorics from sight to hearing.

One of the significant limitations of structuralism, and it is a limitation that the post-structuralists have sought to transcend, is its tendency to focus on the *synchronic* aspects of linguistic difference at the expense of the more processual, *diachronic* elements. This critique led to an increasing and ongoing engagement, throughout the century, with processual understandings. This shift, in our sense-based framework, can be seen as a shift towards the senses of hearing and touch, since these senses necessarily involve change over time.

The process philosophers

One of the first modern philosophers to dispute the noble position accorded to sight was Henri Bergson, writing around the same time as Saussure. Bergson asserted that both idealists and materialists, the massive polar anchors of philosophical debate, were both too cognitive, and were incapable of appreciating that the body was not just an object of contemplation but was actually the primary site of lived action. Hannah Arendt set the measure of Bergson's influence when she asserted that, '[s]ince Bergson, the use of the sight metaphor in philosophy has kept dwindling, not unsurprisingly, as emphasis and interest has shifted entirely from contemplating to speech, from *nous* [mind] to *logos* [word]' (1978: 122). In particular, Bergson railed against the spatialization of time and the profound mistake of reducing the *qualitative* difference between past, present and future to a simple *quantitative* distinction. The particular problem with reducing temporality to a number-line was that it privileged sight, since 'every clear idea of number implies a visual image in space' (Bergson and Pogson 1971 [1889]: 79). This was hugely important to Bergson because, for him, experienced time depended more on the non-visual senses, such as hearing and touch, which intertwine past, present and future into a meaningful whole.

Contemporaneous with Bergson, the American pragmatists (Peirce, Dewey, James) also celebrated action, change, negotiation and the 'plastic' nature of reality over fixed principles, abstractions and essentialist beliefs. A.N. Whitehead was another 'process philosopher' who drew the various strands of this emergent philosophy together in his vast book *Process and Reality* (1929). Around the same time, Martin Heidegger published *Being and Time* and he continued to make sustained attacks on the ocularcentrism of Greek and Western philosophy throughout his career. His language and vocabulary were different but his central point was that ocularcentrism had reduced being to being-represented or being-imaged. In other words, the very being of the world had come to be equated with our images and representations, which, for him, was an inauthentic existence:

> Metaphysics thinks about beings as beings. Whenever the question is asked what beings are, beings as such are in sight. Metaphysical representation owes this sight to the light of Being. The light itself, i.e., that which such thinking experiences as light, does not come within the range of metaphysical thinking ... Metaphysics, insofar as it always represents only beings as beings, does not recall Being itself.
>
> *(1975: 207–208)*

Heidegger was extremely critical of the visually orientated Greek notion of *theoria*, and he lamented the reduction of *theoria* to observation in modern empiricism. He contested the privileging of a spectatorial vision that made subject and object distant and estranged from one another, and, like Bergson, he repudiated ontologies that made spatial existence prior to temporality. He also contrasted the early Greek attitude of *wonder* – which lets things be – with the modern sense of *curiosity* – which is symptomatic of a predatory possessiveness and a calculating, self-interested will to power. Instead, Heidegger preferred to give ontological primacy to 'speaking', 'listening to' and 'silence': 'listening to ... is Dasein's existential way of Being-open as Being-with for Others. Indeed hearing constitutes the primary and authentic way in which Dasein is open for its ownmost potentiality for Being' (1962 [1927]: 206); 'language stands in essential relation to the uniqueness of being ... Being is the most said and at the same time a keeping silent' (ibid. 1993 [1981]: 54).

Heidegger employed novel linguistic and hermeneutical techniques, coining new words at will to aid his attempt at comprehending being in new ways. Other philosophers have continued this tradition, which we can now see as a metaphoric revolt against the dominant ocular metaphor in Western philosophy. In organization theory, this turn to process is also evident in, for instance, the influence of constructivism, actor-network theory and the more philosophical writings of Chia (1995) and Cooper and Law (1995) to name but three of the more prominent writers. More broadly, this interest in process (means) rather than ends (visions, utopias) is a feature of contemporary political discourse, whether it be articulated by conservatives or what we might refer to as postmodern radicals.

The displacement of vision in political discourse

Vision, and especially any form of radical vision, has been shunted to the margins of political discourse. Many in society, it seems, are at one with David Trimble (1998), who, on receiving the Nobel Peace, stated that '[i]nstinctively, I identify with the person who said that when he heard a politician talk of his vision, he recommended him to consult an optician'. In his Nobel speech, David Trimble drew extensively on Edmund Burke's conservative thesis that the pursuit of 'abstract perfection' had to be rejected, for the simple reason that humans are imperfect. In terms of the ocularcentric paradigm, we can understand Burkean conservatives as *radical* insofar as they reject the vision metaphor that underpins both rationalism and Romanticism (and, in turn, socialism and nationalism). Burke's (and Trimble's) philosophy was to remain true to tradition and the status quo, imperfect and all as it might be. Of course, some might say that the ruling 'caste', because of their standpoint, will be blind to the problems that others can see all too clearly: namely differential relations of power and equality.

In many respects, Burkean conservatism has been the dominant political movement in the second half of the twentieth century. The success of conservatism and the reluctance to extol alternative visions of the future is understandable, since many have linked the totalitarianism and fascism, which have punctuated the twentieth century, with the Romantic pursuit of utopian visions. The compelling conservative argument is that Romanticism leads not to utopia but instead creates Hitlers and the dystopias of Nazi Germany, ethnically cleansed of those that don't fit the perfect vision.

Such antipathy to visionary thinking is maybe to be expected from conservatives who axiomatically reject any alternatives to the status quo, but today even socialists seem unable to articulate a clear vision of what society should be like, having largely lost faith in the utopian beliefs that propelled their common projects for over a century. As Giddens put it, 'the hopes of radicals for a society in which, as Marx said, human beings could be "truly free" seem to have turned out to be empty reveries' (1994: 1). This eclipse of past visions now leaves the Left unsure and tentative, and few today, even those that still claim to be radicals, believe in revolutionary change towards a socialist ideal of what society should be like. Donna Haraway, one of the more radical thinkers of our age, summed up the situation when she admitted that: 'I think that the most difficult problem that I face, if I own up to it, is I have almost lost the imagination of what a world that isn't capitalist could look like. And that scares me' (Harvey and Haraway 1995: 519). Moreover, what it means to be radical is further obscured by the fact that conservatism has become radical, under Thatcher's neoliberal reforms, while socialism has become conservative, insofar as socialism's practical activity is now largely centred on maintaining the welfare state (Giddens 1994, 1998).

Notwithstanding the threat of implosion, some have sought to continue the tradition of radical socialist thinking, while being careful to avoid the problems with utopian, vision-centred teleologies or grand narratives. We refer to these writers as 'postmodern radicals' because of the uneasy conjunction that they straddle. The 'post-Marxist' scholars Laclau and Mouffe are representative of this position.

Following in the tradition of Lyotard and Foucault, the postmodern radicals reject meta-narratives or big teleological stories, and hence have little truck with either Romantic utopias or political ideologies as a basis for understanding social change. For example, Laclau and Mouffe

(1985) have critiqued the eschatological dimension in Marxist thought as a 'dangerous illusion' and likewise they reject the myth of social progress towards some great vision. They stress the importance of the chance event and the contingent, or, as Smith has put it, 'instead of an endpoint, we have an infinite series of contestations, and the role of the theorist is to incite these' (1998: 23). Thus, radical democratic theory, which might traditionally have been associated with utopian thinking and social engineering, now 'rejects teleologies, "scientific" predictions and eschatological prophecies' (ibid.: 24). Where Laclau and Mouffe differ from Lyotard is that they advocate a linking of different language games into a 'hegemony'.

Ocularcentrism inverted

In this section, we introduce a framework that provides a useful understanding of how one strand of postmodernism has effected a profound change in the relative understanding of the Platonic–Cartesian distinction between the world as seen by the eyes on one's head (e-vision) and the world of the mind's eye (m-vision). In the modern period, which we can approximate as spanning from 1600 to 1900, m-vision (which loosely equates to the theoretical world) was understood as pure in contrast to the impurity of the visual world, e-vision (see Figure 4.2).

As Figure 4.3 shows, postmodernity is characterized by an interesting double inversion (shown as 1 and 2 in the figure). In this section, we will briefly discuss each of these.

The first inversion shows how the modern understanding of theoretical purity – which we can trace to Platonic idealism – has effectively been replaced to the point where clarity of thought is no longer afforded primacy in theoretical discourse. Symptomatic of this shift is the introduction of a large catalogue of terms that emphasize impurity and the repudiation of any theory based on fixed essences or pure Truth. Thus, Derrida has employed a vocabulary of terms like 'difference', 'supplementarity', 'trace', 'deconstruction' and 'decentring' to emphasize the instability, ambiguity or impurity of language. Likewise, Rorty (1989) uses the concept of 'irony' to stress the contingency of all beliefs and concepts, while Foucault and others have shown how the project of modernity, far from creating a society that was transparent to its members, has actually created a carceral, irrational society. The cumulative effect of these and other writings is that we now have, in terms of theory, what Habermas (1989) refers to as a 'new obscurity'.

The second inversion is the translation of e-vision, the world of practice, from the impurity of the modern era to the purity of the postmodern (shown as translation 2 in Figure 4.3). As discussed earlier, the moderns were hostile to the illusory nature of the visible world (i.e. they understood it as imperfect), and consequently their utopias were very much fictions, located in the imaginary (m-vision). In contrast, what might be called a postmodern argument is that the history project (as a singular project) has ended, and that we now live in a postmodern meta-utopia (a meta-utopia being an environment wherein different utopian visions are permitted). According to some marketing scholars (see, for instance, the collection edited by Brown *et al.* 1998), marketing has been central to this project of creating contemporary utopias, since its very essence is the development, dissemination and manipulation of image:

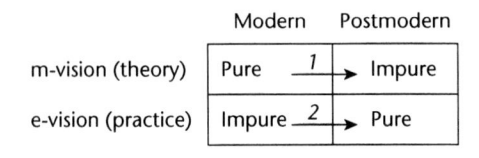

	Modern	Postmodern
m-vision (theory)	Pure	→1→ Impure
e-vision (practice)	Impure	→2→ Pure

Figure 4.3 The double inversion of ocularcentrism

With its boundless ability to invent 'imaginary worlds of perfect appearances, perfect personal relationships, perfect families, perfect personalities, perfect careers, perfect holidays, perfect pizzas, perfect personalities and perfect imperfections' (Brown 1995: 137), marketing, more than any other contemporary cultural institution, is arguably the keeper of the late-twentieth-century utopian flame.

(Brown and Maclaran 1996: 266)

Martins makes much the same point when she says that, 'in the absence of stronger illusions, the public needs to invest its dreams somewhere. Replacing other vendors of illusions that progress has dislodged from their traditional positions, advertising appears at the right time to fill the vacuum' (1995: 51).

Thus, we can understand postmodernism as Romanticism without vision (Livingston 1997; Power and Stern 1998). Similarly, Belk asserts that '[o]ur primary source of hope has shifted from religion, to art and science, and finally to consumption' (1996: 93) and that 'we must face the fact that for many of us, perhaps all of us in one way or another, some of our strongest and most readily available hopes for transcendent and transformational experiences lie in consumer goods and services' (ibid.: 102). According to Baudrillard, America is the ultimate consumer world, which he, appropriately, sees as a 'paradise', albeit a 'mournful, monotonous and superficial' paradise (1989: 98). In this non-teleological world, we have no future vision but live instead in the perpetual present: like the traffic on America's freeways we are 'coming from nowhere, going nowhere' (ibid.: 125). Elsewhere, Baudrillard argues that, as we draw upon and use all of our resources, we only end up destroying 'metaphors, dreams, illusions and utopias by their absolute realization' (1994: 102). For Baudrillard, the complete clarity of the postmodern world, where everything is filmed, broadcast, videotaped, etc., is *obscene*, because it leaves the totality of the world exhibited and visible. Instead, he prefers the *scene* that involves both absence and illusion: '[f]or something to be meaningful, there has to be a scene, there has to be an illusion, a minimum of illusion, of imaginary moment, of defiance of the real, which carries you off, seduces or revolts you' (Baudrillard and Fleming 1990: 65).

Reflections

Notwithstanding the extensive criticisms of Enlightenment rationality and ocularcentrism, summarized above, the evidence is that the ocularcentric paradigm continues. New information and communication technologies permit spectacularizations that have not been possible before (Debord 1983 [1967]; Baudrillard 1983; Vattimo 1992). Globalization and just-in-time production, which are both predicated on the existence of intensive surveillance and supervisory technologies, constitute a new form of electronic panoptica. Vision continues to be privileged across domains, from strategic management to fervent nationalism, indicating that teleological metanarratives based on a 'fixed point of view' still provide a pervasive and potent organizing logic across the world. And Western thought has colonized new locales and discourses, creating an *audit society* that seeks to make everything visible (Power 1999). It is clear that, no more than nuclear technology can be 'unlearned', one cannot simply drop-kick Western philosophy into oblivion because one is uneasy about its ocularcentrism. Likewise, this text is peppered with the language of a spectatorial epistemology – aspect, insight, points of view, perspective, clear, see, focus, etc. – although, if we were to dispense with this language totally, we would probably be either silent or unintelligible. The lesson, maybe, is that it is just as inappropriate to dismiss the vision metaphor – which would be impossible anyway – as to be transfixed by it.

Ocular metaphors are privileged in organizational discourse, not just in terms of epistemology and methodology, but also in terms of constructs that filter through to management thinking (for example, the notion of organizational vision). This way of thinking about the world is not so much deficient, as necessarily partial. The implication is that there is significant potential for the other senses to contribute, in terms of pedagogy, research methods and modes of results dissemination, to organization studies. This echoes similar calls in the nascent literature of organizational aesthetics – where Antonio Strati has suggested that 'smell sheds light [sic] on an aspect that the organizational literature habitually ignores' (2000: 17) – and in the literature on emotion and organizations – where emotion is presented as a more sensual mode of enquiry that is at odds with the cognitivist paradigm in organization studies (Fineman 2000). Likewise, the recent turn to 'sensory marketing' and 'sensory branding' (Lindstrom 2005; Hultén et al. 2009; Krishna 2010) may indicate a growing challenge to the hegemony of the ocular paradigm. According to Lindstrom, '99 percent of all brand communication today is focused on our two senses: what we hear and see. In sharp contrast, 75 percent of our emotions are generated by what we in fact smell' (2005: 85). Even if one might be sceptical of this claim, it is typical of the rhetoric that companies use when highlighting the limits of visualization and the need to use scent, sound and texture when building brand identity. Beyond the world of branding, touch, smell and sound seem to have regained some lost status within the hierarchy of senses that constitute the human condition. Most obviously, perhaps, the personal computer has evolved from an almost exclusively visual interface into a multi-sensory environment. In particular, the design of Apple's iPod was premised on the simple idea that touch matters and that 'computing' could – and perhaps should – be a viscerally tactile experience. Similarly, many of the most recent advances in the computer gaming industry, such as the Xbox and Wii, are centred on somatic rather than visual technologies. More broadly, our own lived experiences remind us how limiting it is to reduce the human condition to the sense of sight, and that our more intimate human relations typically revolve around senses other than the sense of sight.

This is an important cautionary note in a book on visual organization, written by academics for academics, who tend to valorize the creation of texts and visual representations of the world. Yiannis Gabriel (2005) has famously invoked the alluring metaphor of the 'glass cage' to capture much of what it means to live in late modernity, where we are surrounded, if not constituted, by visual images and spectacle. Yet, it is important to remember that, while alluring, this and other ocular metaphors can never shed light on that which is lost to sight. Which is a lot. The glass cage that is the ocular world *is* a prison that contains us, but there is also a world beyond the cage, beyond the visual, beyond the text.

At the very least, the ideas and framework introduced in this chapter should stimulate a deeper understanding of debates and positions in organization theory, and the limitations and exclusions created by the ocular metaphors on which our own contribution to discourse is based. Of course, one should not expect radical change, at least in the short term, since our current practices and preferred meta-metaphors are the sedimented effect of ancient institutionalizing practices. Nevertheless, the conjunction of similar arguments across disparate discourses suggests that metaphors based on sight and light will have a diminished role in the future of our discipline. We shall see.

References

Abrams, M.H. (1953) *The Mirror and the Lamp: Romantic Theory and the Critical Tradition*, New York: Oxford University Press.
Arendt, H. (1978) *The Life of the Mind/Thinking*, New York: Harcourt Brace Jovanovich.

Barnes, B. and Bloor, D. (1982) 'Relativism, rationalism and the sociology of knowledge', in M. Hollis and S. Lukes (eds) *Rationality and Relativism*, Oxford: Basil Blackwell, 21–47.
Baudrillard, J. (1983) *Simulations*, New York: Semiotext(e).
——(1989) *America*, London: Verso.
——(1994) *The Illusion of the End*, Cambridge: Blackwell.
Baudrillard, J. and Fleming, J. (1990) *Fatal Strategies*, New York: Semiotext(e).
Belk, R.W. (1996) 'On aura, illusion, escape, and hope in apocalyptic consumption: the apotheosis of Las Vegas', in S. Brown, J. Bell and D. Carson (eds) *Marketing Apocalypse: Eschatology, Escapology and the Illusion of the End*, London: Routledge, 87–107.
Berger, J. (1972) *Ways of Seeing*, London: BBC and Penguin.
Bergson, H. and Pogson, F.L. (1971 [1889]) *Time and Free Will: An Essay on the Immediate Data of Consciousness*, London: Allen & Unwin.
Brown, S. and Maclaran, P. (1996) 'The future is past', in S. Brown, J. Bell and D. Carson (eds) *Marketing Apocalypse: Eschatology, Escapology and the Illusion of the End*, London: Routledge, 260–277.
Brown, S., Doherty, A.-M. and Clarke, B. (1998) 'Stoning the romance: on marketing's mind-forged manacles', in S. Brown, A.-M. Doherty and B. Clarke (eds) *Romancing the Market*, London: Routledge, 1–20.
Chia, R. (1995) 'From modern to postmodern organizational analysis', *Organization Studies* 16(4): 579–604.
Cooper, R. and Law, J. (1995) 'Organisation: distal and proximal views', *Research in the Sociology of Organisations* 13: 237–274.
Debord, G. (1983 [1967]) *Society of the Spectacle*, Detroit: Black & Red.
Derrida, J. (1978) *Writing and Difference*, London: Routledge and Kegan Paul.
Fineman, S. (ed.) (2000) *Emotion in Organizations*, London: Sage.
Foucault, M. (1973) *The Birth of the Clinic: An Archaeology of Medical Perception*, New York: Random House Vintage Books.
Foucault, M. and Gordon, C. (1980) *Power/Knowledge Selected Interviews and Other Writings 1972–1977*, Brighton: Harvester.
Gabriel, Y. (2005) 'Glass cages and glass palaces: images of organization in image-conscious times', *Organization* 12(1): 9–27.
Giddens, A. (1994) *Beyond Left and Right: The Future of Radical Politics*, Cambridge: Polity Press.
——(1998) *The Third Way*, Cambridge: Polity.
Habermas, J. (1989) 'The new obscurity: the crisis of the welfare state and the exhaustion of utopian energies', in S.W. Nicholsen (ed.) *The New Conservatism: Cultural Criticism and the Historian's Debate*, Cambridge MA: MIT Press, 48–70.
Harvey, D. and Haraway, D. (1995) 'Nature, politics, and possibilities: a debate and discussion with David Harvey and Donna Haraway', *Environment and Planning D, Society & Space* 13(5): 507–527.
Heidegger, M. (1962 [1927]) *Being and Time*, Oxford: Basil Blackwell.
——(1975) 'The way back into the ground of metaphysics', in W.A. Kaufmann (ed.) *Existentialism from Dostoevsky to Sartre Revised and Expanded*, New York: New American Library, 206–221.
——(1993 [1981]) *Basic Concepts*, Bloomington: Indiana University Press.
Hultén, B., Broweus, N. and van Dijk, M. (2009) *Sensory Marketing*, Basingstoke: Palgrave Macmillan.
Jay, M. (1993a) *Downcast Eyes: The Denigration of Vision in Twentieth-Century French Thought*, Berkeley: University of California Press.
——(1993b) 'Sartre, Merleau-Ponty, and the search for a new ontology of sight', in D.M. Levin (ed.) *Modernity and the Hegemony of Vision*, Berkeley: University of California Press, 143–185.
Jonas, H. (1966) 'The nobility of sight: a study in the phenomenology of the senses', in H. Jonas (ed.) *The Phenomenon of Life: Towards a Philosophical Biology*, New York: Harper & Row, 135–156.
Jones, H.M. (1974) *Revolution and Romanticism*, Cambridge, MA: Belknap Press.
Krishna, A. (2010) *Sensory Marketing: Research on the Sensuality of Products*, London: Routledge.
Laclau, E. and Mouffe, C. (1985) *Hegemony and Socialist Strategy: Towards a Radical Democratic Politics*, London: Verso.
Levin, D.M. (1993a) 'Introduction', in D.M. Levin (ed.) *Modernity and the Hegemony of Vision*, Berkeley: University of California Press, 1–29.
——(1993b) *Modernity and the Hegemony of Vision*, Berkeley: University of California Press.
Lindstrom, M. (2005) 'Broad sensory branding', *The Journal of Product and Brand Management* 14(2/3): 84–87.

Livingston, I. (1997) *Arrow of Chaos: Romanticism and Postmodernity*, Minneapolis: University of Minnesota Press.
Martins, M.C. d. S. (1995) *Humor and Eroticism in Advertising*, San Diego: San Diego State University Press.
McLuhan, M. (1962) *The Gutenberg Galaxy: The Making of Typographic Man*, Toronto: University of Toronto Press.
Nietzsche, F. (1969 [1887]) *On the Genealogy of Morals*, New York: Vintage Books.
Plato (1974) *The Republic*, London: Pan Books.
Power, M. (1999) *The Audit Society: Rituals of Verification*, Oxford: Oxford University Press.
Power, P. and Stern, B.B. (1998) 'Advertising illumination: romantic roots of postmodern promises', in S. Brown, A.-M. Doherty and B. Clarke (eds) *Romancing the Market*, London: Routledge, 202–215.
Rorty, R. (1979) *Philosophy and the Mirror of Nature*, Princeton: Princeton University Press.
——(1989) *Contingency, Irony and Solidarity*, Cambridge: Cambridge University Press.
Smith, A.M. (1998) *Laclau and Mouffe: The Radical Democratic Imaginary*, London: Routledge.
Spivak, G.C. (1988 [1985]) 'Can the subaltern speak?', in C. Nelson and L. Grossberg (eds) *Marxism and the Interpretation of Culture*, Urbana: University of Illinois Press, 271–313.
Strati, A. (2000) 'The aesthetic approach in organization studies', in S. Linstead and H. Höpfl (eds) *The Aesthetics of Organizations*, London: Sage, 13–34.
Trimble, D. (1998) 'Nobel speech on receiving the Nobel Peace Prize'. Available at http://www.nobel.se/peace/laureates/1998/trimble-lecture.html.
Vattimo, G. (1992) *The Transparent Society*, Baltimore: Johns Hopkins University Press.
Whitehead, A.N. (1929) *Process and Reality: An Essay in Cosmology*, Cambridge: Cambridge University Press.
Winner, L. (1993) 'Upon opening the black box and finding it empty: social constructivism and the philosophy of technology', *Science, Technology and Human Values* 18(3): 362–378.
Woolgar, S. (ed.) (1988) *Knowledge and Reflexivity: New Frontiers*, London: Sage.

Part II
Strategies of visual organization

5
Constructing the visual consumer

Lisa Peñaloza and Alex Thompson

> Seeing and representing are 'material,' insofar as they constitute means of intervening in the world. We do not simply 'see' what is there before us. Rather, the specific ways in which we see (and represent) the world determine how we act upon that world and, in so doing, create what that world is.
>
> *(Poole 1997: 7)*

Introduction

The quote above is taken from Deborah Poole's insightful visual economy of the Andean image world. In her introduction, Poole explains how she had come to be the resident community photographer in the village in southern Peru where she conducted an ethnographic study of the development of family portraits as the means of accounting for modern understandings of race. Photographs turned out to be the one thing that was 'useful' to the people she studied, as they repeatedly asked her to take pictures of their families in ways different from her everyday portrayals of them.

An important consideration for Poole regarding images and image-objects is how people inscribe meaning from a multitude of perspectives. Unlike 'the gaze,' which, according to Poole, represents a singular representation embedded in power and control, she argues that a visual economy yields a holistic understanding of the mechanisms that convey a 'complexity and multiplicity of images.' Poole's aim is to try to understand the intersections between how photographers depict others and how others choose to represent themselves. For Poole, the visual economy represents a visual meaning system where the images act as self-referential devices in the context of other representations that hold different meanings for different actors. Thus, she instructs visual ethnographers to work to understand how these images operate both inter- and intra-culturally, as they have important socio-political meaning considerations for the visual ethnographer and the people with whom they study.

In the text, Poole marvels at the formal poses her willing subjects chose for their photographs, decked in their finest clothes, their bodies stiff and their faces serious. She notes that all informants preferred these staid images to the *natural* shots she routinely took of them engaged in their everyday activities. Poole compared the formal poses informants preferred, the portraits of ancestors they proudly displayed in their homes, and the images of colorful advertisements and calendars that graced the adobe walls of their homes, and even her own photos of herself and her family, in trying to better understand how people develop ideas of how they want to be represented.

More importantly for our purposes, Poole came to question how she was thinking about and incorporating the people she was studying in her work almost by accident. Poole had showed her informants photography books, such as Sebastiao Salgado's (1986) *Other Americas*. While aesthetically appealing and technically flawless, Salgado's depictions of sad, destitute people had disturbed Poole, and she expected informants to share her reaction. She was surprised when Olga, a key informant, found beauty in the photographs, expressing particular appreciation for the way Salgado conveyed the texture of the tattered clothes of an elderly couple. 'Poverty is beautiful,' Olga mused, indicating a photo of cracked, weathered feet among her favorites.

Poole credits the surprise she felt in hearing Olga's reaction to the photographs in stimulating her to interrogate her own ideas and aesthetics of poverty, economic development and race/ethnicity. In her research, she subsequently examined more explicitly what she shared with informants in ways of seeing each other and knowing their respective worlds, and where they differed. The images, then, were a key tool for Poole in learning about how she produced knowledge about other people and ways of being different from her own.

Overview: constructing the visual consumer

Multicultural learning is fundamental to market development globally, in the exchanges, interactions and understandings among people of different cultures. In ways somewhat similar to Deborah Poole's research, scores of ethnographers canvass the globe using visual methods to study consumers. Some work for a single firm full time; others work for a short duration for various corporate clients – manufacturers, advertising agencies, research firms and strategy groups – while still others work in universities and business schools as faculty and students.

The overall objective of this chapter is to help readers better understand the use of visuals in learning about consumers and consumption. Achieving such understanding is necessarily predicated on appreciating the visual faculties of consumers and exploring how such faculties constitute consumption in particular ways. For example, in Poole's account, we can see how respondents take agency over how she represents and inscribes them. Thus, key considerations in constructing the visual consumer are to appreciate more explicitly how consumers see themselves and how they want to be represented and to incorporate explicitly their perspectives and interests. In bringing these considerations to the fore, we discuss the challenges and prospects of using visuals to incorporate more strongly consumer agency into marketing representations and, in turn, into marketing strategy. We further argue for the importance of interrogating market agents and organizational cultural understandings of consumers.

The term *visual consumer* refers to a particular set of approaches used to represent consumers and consumption that brings to the fore visual imagery, material artifacts, virtual and physical environments, and their understandings in ways that explicitly entail a negotiation among multiple agents. This perspective considers representation as an inherently 'political act' (Schroeder 1998) with economic significance (Schroeder 2011) and gives special consideration to the visual faculties of researchers as well as those with whom they work – consumers, as well as sponsors and strategists. This chapter is as much about how researchers inscribe the consumer in visual constructions as it is about how consumers inscribe themselves in their interactions with market agents in ways that create meaningful value in the marketplace.

We address the use of visual research approaches and materials regarding consumers and consumption for two main audiences: corporate and academic. Our distinction between academic and corporate visual constructions is not meant to polarize the two, but to suggest how the different uses of visual methods by academics and practitioners offer distinct opportunities in constructing the visual consumer. Our aim is to better understand the role that the visual plays in consumer meaning-making at both a consumer and organizational level.

Much visual ethnographic work in business schools has taken place in the interdisciplinary domain of Consumer Culture Theory (Arnould and Thompson 2005), and published in the form of various journal articles and book chapters, many of which we cite below. We also highlight the special video issues of *Consumption Markets & Culture* edited by Russell Belk and Robert Kozinets (2005, 2007). At present, this work is increasingly common in corporations as well (e.g. Zwick and Cayla 2011); Sunderland and Denny 2007). Both academics and corporate practitioners can benefit from this discussion of the use of visual data in learning more about different peoples across the globe, in making knowledge claims, and in developing strategic courses of action. Visual materials are invaluable sources of knowledge on consumers, and so it is vital to be able to read critically and evaluate their use by others. Further, it is useful to understand key differences between the use of visuals in corporate and academic settings, in terms of time pressures, foci on contributing to knowledge and/or developing strategic marketing or management recommendations, and deployment in bringing colleagues/clients 'to the field' to better explain phenomena, to support knowledge claims, and to justify a particular course of action as appropriate and viable.

We initiate our discussion by drawing from visual studies in ethnography and in culturally oriented consumer research. Here our focus is on how ethnographers leverage visual images and image objects to situate consumers as active producers in marketplace discourses. We use images from the first author's work to explore how consumers proactively use visual imagery to navigate, negotiate, and create meaning in marketplace exchanges. In this discussion, we give sensitivity to our role as ethnographic researchers and how we leverage multiple modes of representation in our own constructions of the visual consumer.

We then turn our attention to images from the second author's visual studies in corporate settings to offer some suggestions in advancing a more visual understanding of consumers and consumption. The use of visual ethnography in corporate circles is a key site for constructing the visual consumer as it sheds light on how organizations go about producing consumer knowledge through visual representation. We discuss the ways in which commercial ethnographers seek to embody consumer insights with their clients, and to become a source point for the joint production of cultural meaning, and we highlight the mechanisms through which these agents incorporate consumers' agency and perspectives in how they are to be represented and understood in marketing strategy.

As illustrated in the opening vignette, reflecting explicitly about the content and contexts of visuals and their use by informants and others are necessary steps to provide a more holistic understanding to the visual constructions of consumers. Specifically, we encourage researchers to make iterative comparisons between their own culture(s) and those of the persons with whom we work – research participants, clients, sponsors, even readers – to better distinguish between their interests. Reflecting upon the multiple perspectives and interests at work in reproducing visual constructions are, as Poole astutely observes, vibrant means of intervening in the world.

Lisa Peñaloza and Alex Thompson

What is the visual consumer?

> [T]he power of symbols in modern society derives not only from the technological virtuosity of the creators of messages but from the human need to search for meaning.
>
> (Jhally 1990: 189)

A way of being a consumer and 'doing' consumption. We use the term visual consumer to emphasize the visual skills and abilities of consumers. Every moment, consumers utilize their visual faculties: at home in getting up, dressing, and preparing and eating meals; in commuting to work, school or play, whether bustling with fellow commuters on subways or buses or jockeying with other drivers past colorful billboards; in shopping, in provisioning foodstuffs, seeking an appropriate gift, home furnishing, or something to wear; back at home reveling in the pleasures of intimate family life, toiling in daily chores, or simply relaxing with friends or family or with a film or book; in leisure, in catching up with friends and loved ones online or at a local pub, exercising, or experiencing other places. While often taken for granted, the steady barrage of visual stimuli from which consumers make 'sense' of themselves and their social and market environments is nothing short of amazing!

To use the word visual is to emphasize certain sensory and aesthetic processes and activities as ends in themselves and as the means of knowing. Sight is a crucial bodily capability for consumers in navigating transitory, complex apps and websites, and physically demanding material social and market environments. It is a vital cognitive input in meaning-making as well, with profound emotional and mnemonic dimensions. Here our emphasis begins with consumers' faculties of perception, categorization, and interpretation and those of researchers to study these important consumption elements. For example, in one research project, the first author examined the activities of western ranchers and the consumers who come to see them at the National Western Stock Show and Rodeo. Importantly, the pictures 'speak' in the languages of their takers and subjects, and, because of their vast differences, it is vital that researchers access the interpretations of those depicted (Heisley and Levy 1991) and make transparent their own views. Figure 5.1 depicts a man tossing a lariat, while his son looks on. In interviews, the researcher learned of the connections of 'city slickers' to ranch and farm life, which was typically two generations back in many families, and that, while ranchers come there to play, many worked two jobs to be able to afford the lifestyle they described as free (Peñaloza 2000). Such play is quite serious for consumers as well, as they come for amusement that includes learning about and teaching their kids where their food comes from and showing respect for those who 'put their food on the table' (Peñaloza 2001).

That such meaning-making is an active, productive exercise is intimated in the quote by Jhally opening this section. It is consciously and unconsciously selective, as mental processes organize visual stimuli, and, in doing so, reproduce ways of thinking and believing. Jhally (1990) further emphasizes consumers' compulsion to know and participate in visual codes, because, in lacking these skills, they risk novel forms of illiteracy that consist of social misrecognition and alienation.

Among the most important visual lessons is that images and objects do not contain meanings; people attribute meanings to them. And yet, because such meaning-making is so pervasive, as profound as it is subtle, and learned over time by consumers and marketers, their productive work in associating and bonding meanings to images and objects is often taken for granted and is thus difficult for researchers to access.

In their extensive work on visual aspects of advertising, Scott and Vargas (2007) detail the complex, rhetorical processes through which consumers interpret images. An ad conveying the softness of toilet paper by featuring a fluffy white kitten is anything but simple, these scholars

Figure 5.1 Playing cowboy

explain. Instead, visual literacy enacts a complex and rapid process akin to writing, in which consumers review multiple associations for signs, including those associations taught to them by marketers over time, and then narrow down and transfer meanings among the signs to produce complex ideas appropriate to their lives. The implications of this work are profound in illuminating the visual skills of consumers and marketers in navigating ever dense, increasingly market-mediated online and physical social environments.

A way of viewing consumers and consumption. To emphasize consumers' visual faculties stems from particular approaches to research as well, those grounded in an episteme that emphasizes visuals as a means of knowing oneself and others, and enacting and making sense of the world. This viewpoint conceives of consumers as conscious, meaning-making entities who use visuals in performing and enacting themselves and their relations to others and to their surroundings.

Usage of visuals by consumers captures only part of the way the consumer is constructed, however. As important is the set of ideas and activities regarding what a consumer is and does, that academic and corporate researchers routinely 'pack' into and draw from visual images, artifacts, and environments. Thus, an evolving consideration in constructing the visual consumer is to explicitly attend to the way consumers choose to construct themselves, as this may contrast with the views of researchers and marketers. Such work goes beyond the use of pictures and video to represent the worldview of a consumer. The goal is to place the agency associated with representation in consumers' hands to utilize collages or video diaries as tools to tell their story. Begun as an anthropological 'experiment' in the late 1980s (Marcus 1986), this ethnographic convention has diffused into contemporary corporate usage, such that consumers are invited to use the visual more directly as a mechanism to represent their consumption practices and articulate their belief systems.

More recent techniques in consumer research, such as photovoice, seek to empower consumers further to control how their image and likeness are produced (Wray-Bliss 2003).

A good example of pioneering work in constructing the visual consumer can be found in Blanchette's study of full-figured women. Blanchette invites women to use photovoice as a visual tool in placing themselves into the roles of model and image producer. Similar to Poole's account in the opening vignette of this chapter, respondents are provided with a platform with which to represent themselves. After completion of a photo-shoot, respondents comment on their representations, which elicits further discussion with the researcher, at times challenging the discourses and practice that researchers and other social and market agents routinely and often unconsciously 'pack' into visual images, artifacts, and environments of full-figured women (Blanchette 2012). This form of constructing the visual consumer represents an important sociopolitical shift in how ethnographers represent the worldview of their respondents by providing respondents with powerful tools to control their own forms of representation and speak on their behalf.

Where and how the visual consumer is constructed

Moisander and Valtonen succinctly summarize the importance of visual representations in constituting consumer culture, 'The cultural meanings and narratives that these images evoke provide consumers not only with norms, standards, ideals and role models, but also cultural knowledge, a visual vocabulary and interpretive resources that help them to make sense of their lives' (2006: 84). Evoke is the key word here – as consumers, academics, and practitioners use visual images as material resources that serve as provocative, tangible markers summoning intricate webs of social roles and market obligations within which consumers are implicated.

Using the word construction in tandem with visual directs attention to how consumers develop constitutive capabilities and characteristic ways of being, as aided and/or thwarted by market agents, objects, environments, and media. The next section deals particularly with the productive activities by corporate and academic researchers. The place of work matters, as it impacts the kind of visual research methods used, as well as the timeframes, goals, format, and uses of visual data.

Academic constructions of visual ethnography. Academic visual studies tend to be carried out over a longer period of time, focus on social/market processes or phenomena, and culminate in a literary work contributing to knowledge in a particular scholarly discipline and/or satisfying requirements for an academic degree. Like other forms of research, visual studies produce knowledge by building upon what is already known. Where the studies depart somewhat lies in the way visual researchers forge new insight(s). Let's break this point down in further detail with an example. It sounds simple, but is actually quite complex.

The first goal in building upon what is known is to draw explicit attention to existing knowledge claims and how they are established and recognized to be true. Here the objective is twofold: (1) to identify the types of data; and (2) to make explicit the rhetorical strategy employing these data as evidence in support of the claims.

The second goal is to build a logical 'bridge' from extant to new knowledge. The objectives are also twofold: (1) to direct attention to phenomena 'overlooked' by existing research; and (2) to employ visuals as types of data that support the new insight(s).

This sounds very logical and is all very linear. What we've just described are the steps to follow in *writing up* visual data, however. The way the visual insights are generated is often directly the opposite! That is, the researcher sees things that are somehow different, things that catch his/her attention without necessarily knowing why, as with Poole's photos, and works backwards through the above steps to explain them.

Now let's take an example. Take a look at Figure 5.2. What do you see?

Figure 5.2 Grocery shopping

As noted by John and Malcolm Collier in their classic *Visual Anthropology*, photography is a recording and accounting tool, a 'mirror with a memory' (1986: 7). It is also an analytic aid that helps ethnographers document and categorize their observations, review their findings, and develop theoretical explanations by comparing their data to those in other field sites (ibid.: 164). These authors underscored the *realism* of photographs, directing attention to the dynamics in which viewers (such as you) attribute to people action, intention, and emotion as they engage with the images.

Take a closer look. Do you see anything unusual? Who is shopping? What section of the store is this? Can you see what is in the cart? We see two gallons of milk, two flats of eggs, eight or nine packages of corn tortillas, three bags of flour tortillas, one to two large bags of chicharrones (fried pork skins), two bags of bolillos (white bread rolls, the term is also slang for white person), a bag of pan dulce (sweet bread), a box of Reynolds Wrap aluminum foil, and a bottle of cooking oil on the lower rack of the cart.

To uncover consumers' productive uses of products/services and the productive effects of these cultural artifacts on consumers, it is important to take descriptive research findings, such as these about people, cart, and store, and interrogate their *conditions of possibility*. How do you explain all this? A large family, perhaps more than one family? Seeing this cart and trying to formulate adequate explanations pushed the first author to ask people *in the store*, and from their answers to revisit the previous studies for their understandings of immigrant consumption. In bringing out key differences between the literature and what was observed *in situ*, she reformulated the interview questions for Mexican immigrant consumers beyond household size, composition, and food consumption to include market details along with who cooked what meals for whom and how often they ate at home, as well as who did the shopping, what did they buy, where, and for whom in the US and in Mexico. Observation of two refrigerators side by side in one apartment generated further questions about the use of space in the home.

There one family 'occupied' each of the two bedrooms, while a single man rented the couch (formerly the back seat of a car) and stored his few possessions in the living-room closet.

Both photographs and fieldnotes are crucial in the construction of the visual consumer, with each bringing distinct advantages and constraints. Peñaloza and Cayla (2007) noted that researchers use fieldnotes to detail observation of physical settings, activities, and occurrences, translating visual phenomena to verbal texts as they proceed. The camera can be more obtrusive than observation and can compromise the researcher's relations with informants, and must be used carefully and with prior explanation and consent. Its advantage is greater detail. Even so, as researchers translate visual observation to visual images in taking pictures, it is helpful to record such translations and to further transcribe the images into words for textual analysis.

Refer again to Figure 5.2. In writing the 'contents' of the first picture, the first author became more attuned to other shoppers in the store, documenting their characteristics and what was in their carts. She carried out further observation in parking lots in the US and in grocery stores in Mexico.

Attempting to visualize previous research findings was another useful theoretical exercise. Previous work emphasized consumers' cognitive learning processes, hedonic responses to store design and layout, and nuclear families, in contrast to more observable aspects of consumption, bustling markets and neighborhoods, and extended families. Making this contrast more explicit was crucial for her in developing a behavioral account of immigrant consumers' adaption that featured prominently the characteristics of the stores, neighborhoods, and marketplaces. Notably, reinterpreting what is already known and the basis for how it is known is critical in forging the visual consumer.

Paul Rabinow (1986) detailed the way ethnographic representations operate as social 'facts,' with an authority and currency that depends upon shared conventions of representation and interpretation shared by members of distinct academic communities. This authority is at once tentative and powerful. Visual data are powerful in providing their producers with evidence that they 'were there,' in the field, which, in turn, becomes the support for knowledge claims. And yet, visual data are tentative because they are subject to multiple interpretations. This is why it is so crucial to 'write' the visual data, that is, to explain what they depict to those featured in the visuals and how the researcher uses the depictions to support his/her knowledge claims.

The photo of the shopping cart in Figure 5.2 was part of the first author's doctoral dissertation defense. She had put together a slide presentation, coordinated with music to simulate the four-block commercial area that served as the field site for the research. The music ranged from Mexican corridos (El Chicano Mexicano) to popular songs making reference to immigration (the soundtrack from the film *West Side Story*; and the recording 'Walking the Line' by rock artists Face to Face). Her intentions were to shift the audience from their lives and from the previous literature by recreating the spirit and ambiance of that field site in order to make credible her account of consumer acculturation (Peñaloza 1994). Looking back now, she readily admits such a feat was elusive, not in the sense of something false, but rather as an exercise in productive imagination, as the visuals and the research discussions traversed boundaries in ways not unlike the phenomena – boundaries between nations, between informants and the researcher, and with other academics, with all the complications that translation entails.

As Pink (2007) notes, 'scientific realism' was challenged during the late 1980s and through the 1990s by the 'postmodern' turn that held that all research was, in its very nature, produced, and, as such, was unavoidably partial and interested. 'Fiction' was the term advanced by James Clifford (1986) in noting the imaginative work fundamental in building theory, in the sense of telling a story that hasn't been imagined before.

The ability of photographs to convey something real remains, as Susan Sontag (1977) noted, their greatest accomplishment and their most serious epistemological challenge. In response to criticism in anthropology of using photographs to build knowledge, Collier and Collier (1986) went to great lengths to establish procedures to ensure that, when used as a research tool, visual methods (photography, as well as film and video) are systematic in data collection, with well-documented and explicit provision of analytical procedures. In consumption and market studies, through the 1990s, interpretive scholars, like those in anthropology, labored to incorporate visuals into the top research journals as more than stimuli (Scott 1994) and illustration (Peñaloza 1998) and to push the boundaries of understanding how visuals work when employed by consumers and by advertisers (Schroeder and Salzer-Mörling 2006; Scott and Vargas 2007). More recent work continues to strive to incorporate consumers in visualizing data and bringing audiences into the wide and varied worlds of consumers, marketers, and markets (Blanchette 2012; Thompson 2011).

To date, ethnographers in the academic fields of anthropology and business speak less of the ability of visuals to capture an objective reality and more about how researchers create with them to learn about those they study, and to foster consumer wellbeing in more viable, sustainable markets. Even so, both fields continue to grapple with the legacy in which knowledge claims are to be substantiated, and thus systematic data collection and well-documented analysis remain important in using visuals.

Corporate constructions of ethnography. The visual consumer is of increasing interest in various corporate departments – design/innovation, advertising, and marketing strategy – to name a few. In general, corporate visual studies tend to be of shorter duration and to focus more narrowly on specific goals, such as developing a new product, exploring user interactions with existing products, copy testing an advertisement, or personifying existing consumer segmentation models. Visual methods in corporate ethnography are similar to their academic counterparts in including various combinations of photographs, video, collage, together with on-site interviews, diaries, and pantry/refrigerator audits. Where they differ from academic ethnographies is the use of visual materials to develop knowledge claims towards the end goal of strategic insights.

Corporate ethnographers often leverage the visual to bring to the fore how organizational members characterize their consumers as an implicit part of developing marketing strategy (Cayla and Peñaloza 2012). The visual can be used to challenge existing assumptions about organizational personas (Sunderland and Denny 2011), and proprietary notions of 'my customers' (Flynn 2009). As Tim Strangleman highlights in his chapter on visual sociology (Chapter 15, this volume), the visual represents an important 'intervention' in corporate understanding that challenges organizational thinking and facilitates new ways of thinking that transcend the written report and challenge dominant, strongly held organizational views.

Corporate ethnographers use visuals to bring their clients and coworkers into consumers' lives and provide them with direct 'evidence' of consumers' relations to products and services, which typically goes beyond functional uses. A good example is the second author's study of the use of videography by a market research firm working for a manufacture of diabetic testing meters. Blood-monitoring systems are important tools that help diabetic patients monitor their blood sugar levels and give them valuable feedback of how well they are managing the disease. In our study, visual ethnography was used as a tool to expose research and development members to 'real diabetic patients' in environments where the metering technologies they design (i.e. blood-testing meters, injection pens, and testing strips) were used in 'real life conditions.' As part of this study, the commissioning client accompanied the ethnographer on 12 in-home visits in northern Scotland.

During the in-home visits, R&D members met a variety of diabetic patients from different socio-economic and educational backgrounds. In some cases, they witnessed patients drop cigarette ash on their meters (see Figure 5.3) and dispose of the expensive devices when the battery ran out. Throughout the study, patients demonstrated an inability to deal with some of the complex features built into their testing meters. It quickly became apparent to R&D members that the conditions for the use of diabetic testing meters in the field were drastically different from those in the labs. A core recommendation from the visual ethnographic team was to develop a low-priced, disposable meter that diabetics could throw away, which contrasted markedly with company efforts to design more technologically innovative meters with additional functionality. This recommendation provided this diabetic manufacturer an opportunity to introduce a distinctive testing meter not currently available within the UK market.

This example features the use of visual methodologies that involve bodily activity, which complements the previous discussion of the use of cultural artifacts such as pictures, video, and objects in ethnographic consumer research. Here visual ethnography in the form of observation serves as a transformative device that situates clients into the homes of diabetic patients. By creating a platform in which socio-cultural practices, ritual activities and accouterments, categories of use and competition, and the host of symbolic associations and meanings can be witnessed first-hand, such work fosters dialogue among researchers and strategists that effectively 'unpacks' the *productive force* of the product.

All products and services, when examined carefully, may be seen to 'consume' people, in the sense that consumption 'structures' people's lives in particular ways (Firat and Dholakia 2003). Such structuring, while formative in consumers' lives and vital ingredients in strategic marketing, is often difficult to access and articulate. Successful corporate ethnographers work with partners to articulate consumers' assumptions, worldviews, and their relations with each other and with products and services to develop appropriate strategy (Cayla and Peñaloza 2012).

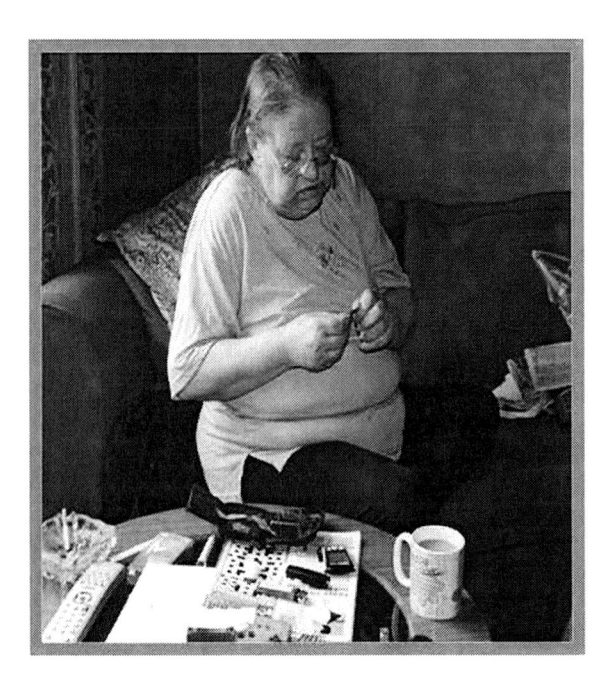

Figure 5.3 Testing blood sugar while smoking

Constructing the visual consumer

This cultural approach to marketing positions products and services into a symbolic field of meaning negotiation where consumers, clients, agencies, and corporate ethnographers 'inject' brands with meaning that is visually constructed and negotiated (Schroeder and Salzer-Mörling 2006).

The productive force of market artifacts is especially notable in another example, a study conducted by the second author in order to better understand the diabetic experience (Thompson 2011). In this study, thirty-six diabetic patients in three major US cities were filmed going about their daily routines over the course of one full day. The videos depicted patients at work and at play, and highlighted the pain of the insulin injections (see Figure 5.4), the effort to constantly self-monitor diet and activity levels, the way patients carry out daily activities, and even their physical surroundings.

Yet even video wasn't enough for ethnographers, who, in their desire to represent the disease experience, insisted that clients enact the disease. It was only when the clients engaged with the physical product – used the actual diabetes kits to sample and record their blood sugar levels over a two-week period – that they 'got' the productive force of their product. Finally, they understood diabetes not just as an abstract concept, and no longer as a consumer 'experience,' but also as a disease that imposes itself upon the body, their body. Clients were able to better understand through their own experience what their product felt like and did. They now understood the repeated pricks, the bruised and discolored skin, the need to explain why they had these marks, to watch what they ate, and to keep an eye on the clock. This embodied, situated consumption knowledge is what corporate ethnographers strive to render intelligible in using visuals in collaboration with marketers in co-producing marketing strategies that will resonate with consumers.

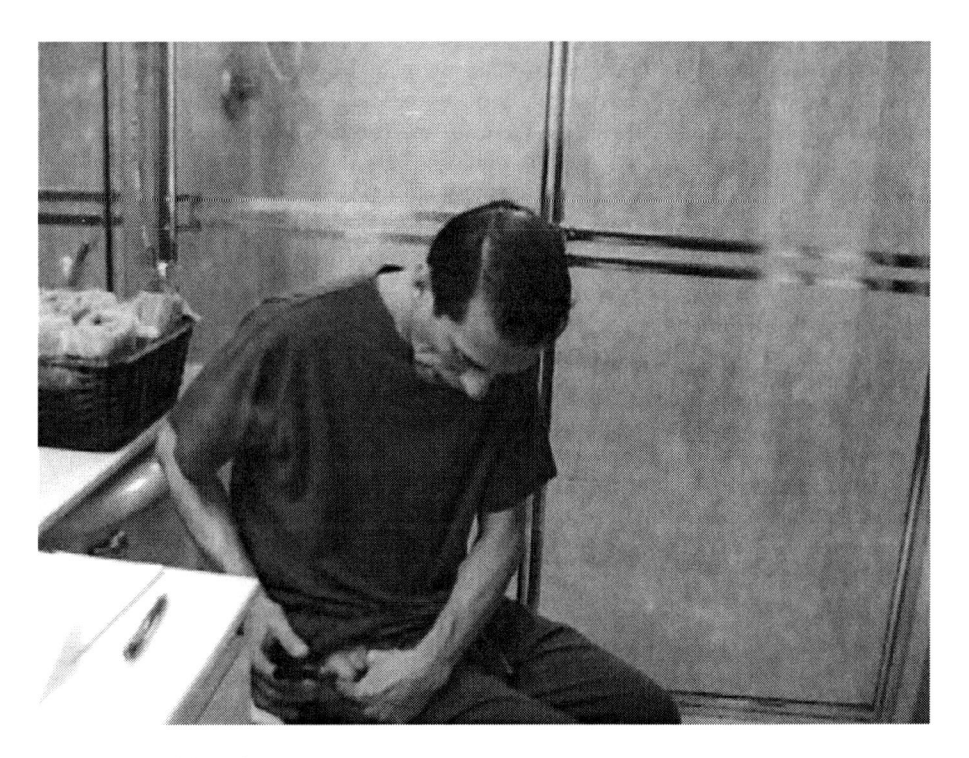

Figure 5.4 Painful insulin injection

Market meaning-making thus draws from and is interwoven into institutionalized social codes for appropriate dress, roles, codes of comportment, even driving. A final example of corporate ethnography is James Glasnapp and Ellen Isaacs' (2011) work with PARC. Their presentation was thoroughly visual, beginning with historical photos of the first Parc-o-meter 1935 from Carl McGee, Oklahoma City, and ending with depictions of color-coded meters that changed color, depending on particular usage patterns and times of day. Laughter erupted from the audience in viewing a sequence of images showing a horse 'parked' at one of the meters, followed by its owner playing cards and pointing to a paid parking meter in response to an inquiring police officer.

The clients in this example are several US cities; their task was to improve the use of parking areas, increase consumer convenience, and raise revenue for the cities. Their method consisted of observation, video, and photographs, which they cleverly dubbed REACT (Rapid Ethnographic Assessment and Communication Technique) in seeking to derive insights in a short period of time and communicate them via video podcast. Among their strategic recommendations were various parallel, head-in, and multi-level parking designs and private rental options to remedy various problems including accessibility for emergency vehicles, consumer irritation and site avoidance, and lost revenue for merchants. In the course of their work, the ethnographers made explicit multiple users' (clients, consumers, delivery truck drivers, police and fire departments) ways of thinking about parking, and detailed how design and technology could reconfigure the space to achieve their objectives.

In conclusion, constructing the visual consumer in corporate ethnography strives for a fundamental shift in thinking within an organization regarding how they conceptualize consumers. Organizations adept in visual literacy are willing to use visual data in decision-making and give it equal weight with other forms of consumer data, such as quantitative segmentation profiles and sales reports. Constructing the visual consumer in corporate settings strives to include, even empower, consumers by featuring prominently their voice and being during the research process and by providing them with the means to choose and alter their modes of representation and to take an active, primary role in how the story is told. The role of the corporate ethnographer is to bring that story to life (Martin *et al.* 2005) and disseminate that information in credible and persuasive ways across an organization to facilitate the co-creation of actionable strategy that at the same time remains true to the respondents featured within the study (Cayla and Peñaloza 2012; Thompson 2011).

Corporate ethnographers use visuals for data collection, analysis, strategic development, and, not least importantly, in conveying, justifying, and implementing the strategic recommendations. Visuals are vibrant, sensory, and engaging ways of overcoming the standard objections of people to research in stating the obvious, not reading reports, and fostering breakdowns in dissemination among geographically dispersed clients.

Important in data collection is recording people in relation to a specific product/service or phenomenon of interest. Returning to the PARC example, we list among the ethnographers' visual data: bird's eye images of dizzying urban sprawl, the same cars driving around and around, consumers perplexed in using parking payment systems, ticket-density patterns, and even parking 'time shares' rented by the hour. Important in analysis is categorizing users and uses, such as service delivery, emergency vehicles, consumers, pedestrians, and design aesthetics as the basis upon which to develop a system synchronizing the users/uses with holding capacity and turnover for the parking spaces. Ultimately, getting it 'right' means designing a workable strategy – be it an advertisement, product development, or service system design (this is not an exhaustive list) – in collaboration with clients by bringing together their views and those of the users of the product/service system.

Discussion: towards a more visual understanding of consumers and consumption

In an insightful essay concluding his book *Picturing Culture*, Jay Ruby writes of the importance of ethnographic film in confounding the expectations of ethnographers (2000: 239). In ways somewhat like those just discussed in producing another way of seeing, ethnographic film shows people in their environments doing things and relating to other people and objects, and does not just feature ethnographic writing about what people are saying and doing.

Our discussion offers some suggestions in encouraging readers to use visuals to construct other ways of seeing consumers and consumption. Here we refer specifically to the transgressive potential of visual academic and corporate ethnography in confounding the expectations of market researchers and marketing practitioners. We see visual methods not solely as a mechanism of representation, but also as the means for intervening in the world, as Poole noted in the opening quote. Constructing the visual consumer empowers consumers and researchers to represent consumption in modalities that go beyond characterizing consumption activities as dependent variables and reducing them to the domain of market exchanges. Instead, when consumers are given agency in co-producing those representations, such visuals are better able to serve as a promising means to challenge existing understandings and strategic practices.

We again refer to Poole's opening quote to emphasize multiple modalities in seeing constructing the visual consumer. According to Poole, 'the metaphor of an image world through which representations flow from place to place, person to person, culture to culture, and class to class also helps us to think more critically about the politics of representation' (1997: 7). It is our argument that critically understanding visual imagery is not just an ethical way of understanding the role of the visual; it is a fundamental prerequisite in generating new consumer insights, academic and corporate.

We build upon the ideas of Joy *et al.* (2006) and Arnould *et al.* (2006) in formulating a more explicitly visual and collaborative reflexivity capable of intervening on the world. We underscore the importance of taking into consideration how the ways of seeing and knowing of informants, researchers, and their academic/corporate colleagues come together and are affected by their interests in the varied settings in which they live and work.

Joy *et al.* (2006) elaborate at length the importance of reflexivity on the part of consumer researchers. Drawing from a rich and extensive bibliography of writings across several disciplines including anthropology, sociology, education, and feminist and science and technology studies, these authors address such issues as authorial power, voice, and writing style, with an eye to whose perspectives are included in textual accounts, how they are included, and how the results, be they knowledge creations and/or strategic interventions, impact the lives of those studied. This work provides a valuable list of considerations for textually oriented research, which we extend to visual research techniques and materials. We encourage researchers to reflect upon the conditions of production for the visuals to better include consumer interests and views and to ensure that those depicted understand and may benefit from their use.

In other work, Arnould *et al.* (2006) address systematically the relationships between context and theory. The authors encourage researchers to think more carefully in selecting contexts to develop theoretical insights and to avoid getting caught up in the context to the point of losing sight of the theoretical contribution. Such loss of perspective, dubbed 'going native' in anthropology, is due to the ways contexts – lived habitats and the people and activities in them – engage our emotions and senses. These authors call for more explicit foregrounding and/or backgrounding of neglected peoples, phenomena, relationships, variables, and processes to stimulate discovery, invite description, and excite innovative thought. The suggestions of these authors extend those of C. Wright Mills (1959) in his classic *The Sociological Imagination* in explicitly encouraging researchers to shift their scale and scope, and alter perspectives, contexts, and peoples in ways that draw out and help formulate robust and compelling explanations for puzzles and paradoxes in consumption and market phenomena.

We suggest that a *double contextualization of images* is helpful in rendering more explicit visual ways of seeing and knowing consumers and consumption. The first step of this visual reflexivity entails situating the images within informants' lives per their testimony and reflection to highlight their ways of seeing and priorities, as suggested by Heisley and Levy (1991) in academic settings, and elaborated by Sunderland and Denny (2007) in corporate ones. As Foley (2002) noted, informant testimony can be a useful 'corrective' to the exoticization and distanced othering of the experiences of those studied that happens in ethnographic accounts cast solely in the voices of researchers.

The second step is a re-contextualization of images, artifacts, and environments by researchers in relation to their own lives and socio-market system(s). We strongly encourage academic and corporate visual ethnographers to take note of the geographic, economic, and socio-cultural distances between ourselves and those we study in order to be more aware of the act of power we perform in incorporating the images and meanings of others into our visual and textual accounts. For Poole, the photographs were insightful when she elaborated her own expectations regarding how people should be represented in her photographs. In featuring images of others as they wanted to be seen, she was able to recognize and reconsider her own assumptions regarding aesthetic tastes, poverty, and high levels of development, not as isolated phenomena, but rather as related aspects of a singular, multi-level socio-economic system within which her own social and academic positions are implicated. Here Foley's (2002) caution regarding researcher reflexivity is relevant. As long as such reflexivity does not redirect attention to the researcher(s) and away from those under study, it can offer a thoughtful qualification of authorial power and even a conscientious undermining of the objectivity and infallibility of the scientific method.

In providing instruction for visual anthropologists, MacDougall (1997) calls for researchers to 'rethink' through visual media, to suspend the dominant non-visual orientation in words and sentences, and to develop instead categories of socio-cultural life that are drawn from sequences of visual images and people's relations with material artifacts. Our task is somewhat similar, to use visuals to develop categories and processes from our visual data that reformulate understandings of motives, decisions, and intentions in order to more fully account for the conditions of possibility for the productive force of products and services on consumers and consumption.

We have a long way to go towards the above goal. In 1984, Russell Belk anticipated marketers' ideal consumer. His 'manifesto' featured a computer chip embedded in a consumer's brain that gave marketers direct access to the consumer's thoughts and consumption preferences (Belk 1984). The representation of consumers then was basically an information processor that was highly rational and utilitarian, somewhat emotional, autonomous nonetheless. A lot has changed since then, and yet many consumer researchers and market agents continue to portray consumers in ways that essentially bypass sight and consciousness. At best, consumers are conceived of as textual responders in most experimental 'treatments' and non-visual ethnographic accounts; they are limited to lists of purchases in scanner panel data, and depicted as brain scans in neuromarketing studies. And yet, as consumers disclose their most intimate thoughts and activities in social media and in our studies, we have tremendous opportunities to show such consumption phenomena and to provide the perspective(s) from which to view the images and use them to challenge and extend extant knowledge with novel insights.

Ruby (2000: 241) suggests that showing the conditions of production can snap us out of a realistic posturing and help us to envision alternative, imaginative possibilities. Directing attention to the logic by which we arrange, script, and pattern visuals may help us accomplish a more explicit comparison with the way the life-worlds of consumers are depicted and understood in the literature versus in households and corporations. Such explicit comparisons are useful in decentering implicit assumptions regarding consumers, the marketplace, and marketers that circumscribe and support much of the canon in consumer research. For visuals specifically, this comparison is intended to serve as one means of confounding assumptions and expectations and to foster *extrospection*, as an external, collaborative endeavor with those we study to complement internal, introspective reflexivity.

Conclusion

At the 2011 Consumer Culture Theory conference, plenary speaker Ken Anderson, an anthropologist at Intel Corporation, encouraged consumer researchers to inspire and craft the worlds we want to live in. The future promises engaging, 'game-changing' academic and corporate visual ethnographies in combining photography, film, music, and text, and culminating in research and/or strategic insights. It is likely that few academic or corporate ethnographers are as reflexive as consumers themselves are on Facebook; certainly few are as quick or of this magnitude in making visible the contours and dynamics of consumer subjectivity as consumers want to be represented. And yet, as stores, malls, museums, and other consumer venues and social media become ever more experiential and interactional, the more marketers depend upon consumers to put their imaginations to work to glean 'benefits' and produce meanings. In turn, the more consumers 'work' in research and in the marketplace, the more opportunities there are for academic and corporate visual ethnographers to work as 'market midwives' and critics imagining, interpreting, and enacting the super-visual, super-interpretive endeavor that contemporary consumers and consumption is becoming.

References

Arnould, E. and Thompson, C. (2005) 'Consumer Culture Theory: twenty years of research', *Journal of Consumer Research* 31(4): 868–882.
Arnould, E., Price, L. and Moisio, R. (2006) 'Making contexts matter: selecting research contexts for theoretical insights', in Russell Belk (ed.) *Handbook of Qualitative Research in Marketing*, Cheltenham, UK: Edward Elgar, 106–125.
Belk, R.W. (1984) 'A manifesto for consumer behavior of consumer behavior', in Paul F. Anderson and Michael J. Ryan (eds) *Scientific Method on Marketing*, Chicago, IL: American Marketing Association, 163–167.
Belk, R.W. and Kozinets, R.V. (2005) 'Introduction to the Resonant Representations Issue of *Consumption Markets & Culture*', *Consumption Markets & Culture* 8(3): 195–203.
Belk, R.W. and Kozinets, R.V. (2007) 'Resonant Representations 2', *Consumption Markets & Culture* 10(2): 75–76.
Blanchette, A. (2012) '(Re)presenting full-figuredness: poetics and politics of representation', presentation, University of Exeter Doctoral Symposium, Exeter, UK, 12 June.
Cayla, J. and Peñaloza, L. (2012) 'Mapping the play of organizational identity in strategic market adaptation', *Journal of Marketing* 76(6): 38–54.
Clifford, J. (1986) 'Introduction: partial truths,' in J. Clifford and G. Marcus (eds) *Writing Culture: The Politics and Poetics of Ethnography*, Berkeley: University of California Press, 1–27.
Collier Jr., J. and Collier, M. (1986) *Visual Anthropology: Photography as a Research Method*, Albuquerque, NM: University of New Mexico Press.
Firat, A.F. and Dholakia, N. (2003) *Consuming People: From Political Economy to Theaters of Consumption*, London: Routledge.

Flynn, D. (2009) 'My customers are different! Identity, difference and the political economy of design', in M. Cefkin (ed.) *Ethnography and the Corporate Encounter: Reflections on Research in and of Corporations*, New York: Berghahn, 41–57.

Foley, D. (2002) 'Critical ethnography: the reflexive turn', *Qualitative Studies in Education* 15(5): 469–490.

Glasnapp, J. and Isaacs, E. (2011) 'No more circling around the block: evolving a rapid ethnography and podcasting method to guide innovation in parking systems', presented at the 2011 Ethnographic Praxis in Industry Conference (EPIC), Boulder, Colorado, 18–21 September.

Heisley, D. and Levy, S.J. (1991) 'Autodriving: a photoelicitation technique', *Journal of Consumer Research* 18 (December): 257–272.

Jhally, S. (1990) *The Codes of Advertising: Fetishism and the Political Economy of Meaning in the Consumer Society*, London: Routledge.

Joy, A., Sherry, J.F., Troilo, G. and Deschenes, J. (2006) 'Writing it up, writing it down: being reflexive in accounts of consumer behavior', in R. Belk (ed.) *Handbook of Qualitative Research in Marketing*, Cheltenham, UK: Edward Elgar, 345–360.

MacDougall, D. (1997) 'The visual in anthropology', in M. Banks and H. Morphy (eds) *Rethinking Anthropology*, New Haven, CT: Yale University Press, 276–295.

Marcus, G. (1986) 'Afterword: ethnographic writing and anthropological careers', in J. Clifford and G. Marcus (eds) *Writing Culture: the Politics and Poetics of Ethnography*, Berkeley: University of California Press, 262–265.

Martin, D., Schouten, J. and McAlexander, J. (2005) 'Reporting ethnographic research: bringing segments to life through movie making and metaphor', in R. Belk (ed.) *Handbook of Qualitative Research in Marketing*, Cheltenham, UK: Edward Elgar, 361–370.

Mills, C.W. (1959) *The Sociological Imagination*, New York: Oxford University Press.

Moisander, J. and Valtonen, A. (2006) *Qualitative Marketing Research: A Cultural Approach*, London: Sage.

Peñaloza, L. (1994) 'Atravesando fronteras/border crossings: a critical ethnographic exploration of the consumer acculturation of Mexican immigrants', *Journal of Consumer Research* 21(1): 32–54.

——(1998) 'Just doing it: a visual ethnographic study of spectacular consumption behavior at Nike Town', *Consumption Markets & Culture* 2(4): 337–400.

——(2000) 'The commodification of the American West: marketers' production of cultural meanings at the trade show,' *Journal of Marketing* 64 (October): 82–109.

——(2001) 'Consuming the American West: animating cultural meaning and memory at a stock show and rodeo', *Journal of Consumer Research* 28 (December): 369–398.

Peñaloza, L. and Cayla, J. (2007) 'Writing pictures; taking fieldnotes,' in R. Belk (ed.) *Handbook of Qualitative Research in Marketing*, Cheltenham, UK: Edward Elgar, 279–290.

Pink, S. (2007) *Doing Visual Ethnography*, London: Sage.

Poole, D. (1997) *Vision, Race, and Modernity: A Visual Economy of the Andean Image World*, Princeton, NJ: Princeton University Press.

Rabinow, P. (1986) 'Representations are social facts: modernity and postmodernity in anthropology', in J. Clifford and G. Marcus (eds) *Writing Culture: The Politics and Poetics of Ethnography*, Berkeley, CA: University of California Press, 234–261.

Ruby, J. (2000) *Picturing Culture: Explorations of Film and Anthropology*, Chicago: University of Chicago Press.

Salgado, S. (1986) *Other Americas*, New York: Pantheon.

Schroeder, J.E. (1998) 'Consuming representation: a visual approach to consumer research', in B.B. Stern (ed.) *Representing Consumers: Voices, Views and Visions*, London: Routledge, 193–230.

——(2011) 'Value creation and the visual consumer', in K. Ekström and K. Glans (eds) *Beyond the Consumption Bubble*, New York: Routledge, 137–148.

Schroeder, J.E. and Salzer-Mörling, M. (eds) (2006) *Brand Culture*, New York: Routledge.

Scott, L.M. (1994) 'Images in advertising: the need for a theory of visual rhetoric', *Journal of Consumer Research* 21 (September): 252–274.

Scott, L.M. and Vargas, P. (2007) 'Writing with pictures: toward a unifying theory of consumer response to visuals', *Journal of Consumer Research* 34 (October): 341–56.

Sontag, S. (1977) *On Photography*, New York: The Noonday Press.

Sunderland, P. and Denny, R. (2007) *Doing Anthropology in Consumer Research*, Walnut Creek, CA: Left Coast Press.

Sunderland, P. and Denny, R. (2011) 'Consumer segmentation in practice: an ethnographic account of slippage', in J. Cayla and D. Zwick (eds) *Inside Marketing: Practices, Ideologies, Devices*, Oxford: Oxford University Press, 137–161.

Thompson, A. (2011) 'Videography as an embodied form of knowledge production', presentation, 2011 Consumer Culture Theory Conference, Chicago, IL, 7–10 July.

Wray-Bliss, E. (2003) 'Research subjects/research subjections: the politics and ethics of critical research', *Organization* 10(2): 307–25.

Zwick, D. and Cayla, J. (eds) (2011) *Inside Marketing*, London: Oxford.

6
Cultural production and consumption of images in the marketplace

Laurie A. Meamber

Introduction and overview

In the aesthetic or image economy of today, marketing strategies focus on creating and communicating appealing images of organizational offerings. Consumers respond to these images, and productively consume them in order to mold themselves and their everyday consumption experience. Take, for example, Jim, a 49-year-old executive, married with children, who comments on his visual experience inside a retail store that he likens to an art gallery.

> [There was a lot] of the stuff, so you were attracted by the whole kind of 'gestalt' of the whole thing. ... But what the guy really made the money on was the small items, the under $5 items of which he had a lot of, kind of cutesy things that might have been dime store items but in the context suddenly became something else. So [it] was very much kind of a show in there and he was very successful ... Like if you go to an art gallery, you may not buy a picture. If you went to this place, you may not buy that [high-priced artistic piece] but you would buy something else.
>
> *(Meamber 1997b)*

The purpose of this chapter is to review current scholarship pertaining to the cultural production and visual consumption of images within the market. The specific organizational offerings that are highlighted in the chapter include: advertisements, products (design and material artifacts), brands, and everyday consumption experiences, such as shopping and tourism. The major topics and key questions that will be addressed include: (1) 'productive consumption' – what is the association between cultural production and consumption in the marketplace?; (2) 'aesthetic consumption' – what is role of aesthetics in productive consumption?; and (3) 'marketplace image consumption' – how is the visual content offered by organizations within the market consumed productively by consumers? The chapter concludes with a discussion of future research directions on image production and consumption for the visual organization.

It is essential that research on visual organization takes into account the processes by which images are produced and consumed – i.e. the interdependent and aesthetically driven processes of cultural production and productive consumption. There are numerous participants, roles, and meanings generated by the cultural actors involved in the creation and interpretation of visual images. Understanding the actors involved in this complex process as well as the issues that arise, such as multiple (and perhaps competing) interpretations of these images by the organizations that use them to create value, the marketers that present them to the marketplace, and the consumers who seek out and transform them to fulfill their own identity projects, is critical for visual scholars.

In the first part of the chapter, I explore the relationship between cultural production and visual consumption. There are many different approaches to cultural production as related to visuality, including critical and strategic approaches. Critical views highlight issues such as power and control of image content. From a strategic perspective, organizations attempt to use images in order to create value, representing themselves and their offerings to various stakeholders and to the market. These images are intended to communicate specific meanings to these audiences. Yet, meanings are never fixed; and the recipients of these images, to some extent, may determine the meanings of these images. While consumers (and visual scholars) may actively and perhaps critically resist the prearranged meanings, organizations nevertheless employ visual content in an attempt to shape their relationship with consumers in the marketplace. Therefore, I ask the following questions in the context of an organization's internal and external strategy. What is cultural production in the realm of the market? How does consumption become productive? How can a consumer be considered both a producer and consumer?

Productive consumption: the cultural production and consumption relationship

Cultural production is the process of creating, transforming, and diffusing cultural products. While some scholars study 'cultural production' and 'cultural products' in the domain of the arts, the broader usage of these terms in this chapter encompasses the production of all products and experiences, such as advertising images, consumer products, brands, and consumption experiences that are created by organizations for the marketplace. The traditional view of cultural production within the market is based on the work of anthropologist Grant McCracken (1986, 1988, 1989, 1993) and Solomon (1988). According to McCracken (1986), producers take pre-existing symbols from culture to create cultural products that are then passed on to cultural intermediaries. Producers in the cultural production process include designers, artists, architects, and others involved in creation of the cultural product, including other image makers, such as website developers, brand advisors, and others. Cultural intermediaries include those involved in the meaning transfer of the cultural products from producers to consumers, such as marketers and communication specialists (see also Bourdieu 1984). These cultural intermediaries generate meanings for these cultural products and communicate them to consumers who, in turn, consume these meanings.

Likewise, in consumer researcher Michael Solomon's (1988) modeling of the cultural production system, the creative subsystem that generates cultural products works in conjunction with the managerial subsystem to select and produce them, and also in tandem with a communication subsystem, which provides suggested meanings. These meanings are expressed to consumers via cultural intermediaries that he names 'cultural gatekeepers.' According to both McCracken and Solomon, consumers take cultural products and receive their intended meaning(s) in the act of consumption. Culture is reified when these consumed meanings are linked back to the culture or symbolic pool that was the genesis of the cultural products.

Therefore, within the cultural production process itself, organizations act as cultural agents in the creation and dissemination of cultural products, such as visual images, in the form of many marketplace offerings including advertising campaigns, physical products, brands, and shopping and tourism experiences. Organizations seek to develop and manage these cultural products via marketing practices to further organizational objectives. For example, organizations generate attention-getting advertising and develop appealing visual brands to promote the material goods, services, and experiences for sale in the marketplace. Organizations may also use cultural products to advance and communicate organizational identities to internal and external stakeholders (Davenport *et al.* 2009; Schroeder 2011). For example, Schroeder discusses how the Toyota Motor Corporation's Japanese website (as cultural product) visually represents the company to the world – 'its brand, products, dealer showrooms and customer service' (2004: 231). Management studies illustrate the importance of organizational aesthetics (e.g. Warren 2008), and visualization practices through which organizations operate. For example, the chapters in this volume written by Jane Davison and Norah Campbell (Chapters 2 and 8) focus on organizational identity as expressed through websites, annual reports, and corporate communication.

While acknowledging its importance in identifying the participants in the process, including the roles of organizations and their marketing activities, some scholars argue that McCracken and Solomon's work is one-way in orientation; that is, it proposes a top-down process of meaning creation and transfer beginning with an extant 'symbol pool' or 'culturally constituted world' at the beginning of the process, and consumers and consumption at its end. Instead of treating the ad, product, brand, or experience as an active agent in constituting culture, the cultural product is merely constituted with a pre-codified meaning. This viewpoint also ignores the role of consumer agency in determining meaning, as well as the idea that meaning is never fully present until constructed by the consumer (e.g. Borgerson and Schroeder 1997; Scott 1994a, 1994b).

In our research, my co-author and I set forth an alternative perspective of cultural production (Meamber 1997b; Venkatesh and Meamber 2006). In conceptualizing the relationships between art, aesthetics, cultural production, and marketing, we proposed a conceptual model of the cultural production process that was grounded in the institution of marketing. Marketing, because it is concerned with the development of cultural products and their diffusion in the marketplace, as an institution, relies upon the cultural production process (Meamber and Venkatesh 1999). This re-conceptualization of the cultural production process includes cultural producers, cultural intermediaries, and consumers, but, in this model, the relationships between these cultural actors are conceptualized to operate in a dynamic fashion. Therefore, consumers and consumption are no longer at the end of the process, but are actors equal to the other cultural actors and elements of the process. In this model, production and consumption are inextricably linked, and cultural products, organizations, and consumers play constructive roles in the process.

This newer model of cultural production takes into consideration scholarship that suggests that consumers' approach to consumption is productive at several levels – including the individual, organizational, and societal. First, at the individual level, consumption is related to identity formation when consumers select, secure, use, and possess cultural products in part or whole, for their symbolism, and as images for identity formation. Research on the relationship between symbolism, material objects, and meaning finds that consumers purchase and consume products (brands) because of what they mean, in addition to or rather than for their function (Arnould and Thompson 2005; Douglas and Isherwood 1979; Hirschman and Holbrook 1982; Kozinets 2002; Levy 1959, 1981; Mick 1986; Tharp and Scott 1990; Venkatesh 1992). Consumer researchers maintain that consumption also contributes to identity formation (Arnould and Thompson 2005; Carù and Cova 2007; Ekström and Brembeck 2004; Firat and Venkatesh 1995; Thompson and Haytko 1997; Thompson *et al.* 1990). In contemporary consumer culture, individual identities are shaped by consumers' engagement with cultural objects, including images (brands) corresponding to material possessions (Arnould and Thompson 2005; Belk 1988; Firat and Venkatesh 1995; Gergen 1991; Wallendorf and Arnould 1988). Consumers rework and transform symbolism, signs, and images encoded in marketplace products (such as material goods, brands, retail settings, and other experiences) to further their identity goals as they construct and negotiate their existence.

As Shankar and colleagues (2009) note, identity is no longer thought of as unitary, fixed, or stable, but as a project that is constantly assembled, reassembled, produced, and re-reproduced in the act of consumption. Identity is a social construct, realized through interactions in consumer culture. Consumer culture provides the materials for identity projects, including the symbolism of advertising campaigns that promote a particular lifestyle, products, brands, and consumer experiences.

Therefore, the updated perspective of cultural production challenges the notion that the consumer is a passive recipient of products, experiences, services, and ideas in everyday life (de Certeau 1984; du Gay 1997). In this view, the consumer is an active agent in the cultural production process. Consumers produce culture when they use cultural products and other market-generated content to construct a self-definition. Consumers can create meanings for themselves that incorporate or subvert the cultures of production, in terms of the original intended meanings. This is not to argue that consumer identity is a matter of complete free choice, as consumers may be constrained by age, race, class, and other demographic characteristics (except perhaps in cyberspace) (Schau and Gilly 2003; Turkle 1995), although consumer freedom may be limited by marketers (see Venkatesh et al. 1997). The social and historical realities impacting identity projects cannot be completely disregarded either (Thompson and Hirschman 1995), including, for example, the issue of cultural capital constraints on consumption practices (Bourdieu 1984; Holt 1998). Rather, in contemporary life, consumers, to some extent, are able to choose symbolic content to construct identity that can also link them to others, including consumer 'tribes' or communities organized around symbolic content or shared meanings, such as brand images (Cova et al. 2007; Maffesoli 1996 [1988]; Muñiz and O'Guinn 2000; Muñiz and Schau 2005; Schau and Gilly 2003). In this sense, then, consumers are co-producers of meaning, whether it is personal, identity-related meaning and/or group-level meaning, including communities and organizations.

When consumers absorb the intended meaning of the cultural object into their lives, as defined by the 'producers' and cultural intermediaries, they are not only enacting their own sense of identity but also reaffirming the identity of the organization (or of 'corporate brands' as defined by Balmer 2006) from which it came. For example, Björkman (2002), writing on *aura*, says that, in the consumption of the cultural product, such as designer brand clothing, consumers are also appropriating the designer as brand into their lives. Extending this idea, consumers in the act of consuming (wearing) the clothing are incorporating the brand or designer symbolism into their own identities, the meanings of which are subject to (re-)interpretation. In wearing the clothing, consumers communicate its brand symbolism to others, and simultaneously develop, encode, and reinforce the organizational (designer, brand) identity in the marketplace. Consumption, therefore, acts at the organizational level as well as the individual level, and can help establish and maintain the organization and its visuality and organizational image.

However, if consumers choose to construct an alternate meaning for the cultural object, this can also change or even undermine the intended organizational or marketplace identity (Brown 2006; Featherstone 1991; Fiske 1989; Hall 1993; Holt and Thompson 2004; Kozinets 2002; Süerdem 1994). As Süerdem writes, the focus of contemporary culture is reading, watching, seeing, and consuming signs, but consumers can subvert the meanings that are imposed by others and institutions. Consumers may resist predetermined meanings of an organization and its market offerings, undermining and transforming them into new meanings (Kozinets and Handleman 2004; Thompson 2004; Thompson and Arsel 2004). For example, as Thompson and Arsel 2004) mention, consumers who resisted the Starbucks brand developed and promoted the image of 'Frankenbucks' to signify their fear surrounding the organization's use of dairy products containing genetically modified hormones prior to 2008.

At the societal or cultural level, consumption also plays an active role in the constitution of society or culture (Simmel 1971 [1903], 1978 [1900]). Cultural theorists maintain that cultural products are central to the constitution of culture and, therefore, a key premise of cultural production is that culture itself is (re-)constructed by producers, intermediaries, and consumers participating in the process. Culture is the sum of shared meanings, rituals, norms, and traditions (Geertz 1973), and culture can come into being through cultural production. Through the dynamic process of meaning creation, transmission, consumption (including appropriation and/or interpretation) via cultural products, meaning flows at all levels – from individual 'producers' and/or organizations to consumers to the culture at large. Kaplan (2008) illustrates how images of traumatic events (e.g. war in Iraq, Hurricane Katrina, and artwork by two artists) produce what she terms a 'culture of trauma' in which private and public feelings become intermixed. In this example, the cultural product, consisting of images of trauma created and disseminated by cultural 'producers' and intermediaries, is consumed by members of society (consumers) leading to the creation of personal and public, social and political meanings, which constitute culture.

In summary, the construction of meaning is an active process of cultural production. In the cultural production process within the market, production and consumption are linked, in that production does not end, but, even in consumption, production is taking place. The cultural production process allows consumers to make sense of their cultural world, themselves, and their place in it. Consumers are not conceptualized as being passive receivers of meanings, but are part of the ongoing process of symbolic construction and meaning generation as they productively consume the cultural products offered by organizations in their everyday lives. Meaning is created and negotiated in the consumption experience, as much as it is in the production experience. Therefore, all consumption can be conceptualized as productive, giving rise to the concept of 'productive consumption.' The term productive consumption, in this context, differs from its use in economics to refer to the employment of human labor in the production process. The meaning of productive consumption in the present context refers to the generative nature of consumption for consumers.

Turning specifically to the cultural production process involving image production and consumption, and to the creation of visual culture, and of the visual consumer, what occurs when consumers are engaged in the productive consumption of images, brands, and experiences generated by the organization is an aesthetic process of visualizing their everyday world. Therefore, it is important to step back to position the visual consumer as an aesthetic subject. The following questions will be addressed in the next section of the chapter. What is aesthetics? How are aesthetics and cultural production linked in the consumption of organizational offerings in the marketplace? Why is aesthetics important to our understanding of visual culture and of the visual consumer?

Aesthetic consumption: the current period of productive consumption

Aesthetics is a term that originated in the eighteenth century. Its Greek etymological origin translates to sensory experience. Aesthetic scholars explain that, in its original use, aesthetics refers to any kind of sensory experience, regardless of whether or not it is beautiful. Aesthetics, as a philosophy or set of philosophies, as explained by organization theorists, then came to mean a concern for art and beauty (Strati 1996; White 1996). Both notions of aesthetics are accepted by scholars. In contemporary usage, aesthetics (or esthetics) has a multiplicity of meanings (Koren 2010; Townsend 1997). One definition concerns sensory experience or response as related to the arts, media, or entertainment including its visual forms (Holbrook and Huber 1979; Holbrook and Zirlin 1985; Schroeder and Borgerson 2002). A second meaning of aesthetics, which extends the first, refers to sensory experiences of everyday objects (Forty 1995 [1986]; Heilbrun 2002). A third use of the term concerns the concepts that often define aesthetics, including visual forms, such as form, expression, harmony, order, symbolism, imagery, and others (Carroll 2001). All three of these definitions are integral to understanding the productive consumption of images.

The idea that aesthetics concerns the sensory engagement with the arts or of everyday objects brings us back to the cultural production process. The production and consumption of cultural objects is premised on use of the senses. Producers, cultural intermediaries, and consumers cannot engage with symbols, signs, or images and create, disseminate, interpret, and construct meaning from them without utilizing one or more of the senses, such as vision. While aesthetics is often explored in the context of the arts, other work has examined sensory experiences involving the arts and of everyday consumption experiences, combining the first and second definitions of aesthetics (Dewey 1934; Dickie 1971).

According to Dewey (1934), aesthetic consumption pertains to all experiences, whether traditionally classified as aesthetic or non-aesthetic, because they have a similar structure. In Dewey's discussion, ordinary experience has an aesthetic component when objects and events arrange themselves in a pattern that is perceived through emotion. Other writers have delineated extraordinary experience as distinct from ordinary experience (Carù and Cova 2003). Nevertheless, in our research, my co-author and I find that aesthetic consumption of either the arts or of everyday experience or of both can contribute to identity formation and the construction of meaning (Venkatesh and Meamber 2008). Aesthetics and cultural production are interrelated, in that aesthetics as understood as sensory experience is how cultural actors produce and consume cultural products offered in the market. As discussed in the previous section, cultural products are by definition made up of signs, symbols, and images, making their productive consumption an interpretive process involving the senses.

As noted earlier, the term aesthetics also relates to the constructs that delineate aesthetics or, more accurately, aesthetic content. These terms – form, expression, harmony, order, symbolism, imagery, and so on – originate within the visual art world, and, therefore, one of the common uses of the word aesthetics is the visual content of an artwork or design – i.e. appearance or style (Koren 2010). Consumer scholars have, therefore, used this idea of aesthetics to describe consumers, and what they consume in visual terms, such as clothing, advertisements, and places, among other topics (Schroeder 2002; Thompson and Haytko 1997; Maclaran and Brown 2005). In fact, this notion of the aesthetic as visual content becomes central to understanding life in the present image economy. Aesthetics is important as consumer culture has become more of a visual culture (Schroeder 2002).

> Many battles of the brands take place within the visual domain. Design, in particular, depends upon visual understanding and aesthetic expertise. The Web mandates visualizing almost every aspect of corporate strategy, operations and communication; web design has brought visual issues into the mainstream of strategic thinking, and spurred research and thinking about perception and preference of visual displays.
>
> (Schroeder 2006c: 5)

In summary, even an ordinary or everyday experience or object offered by the market can be aesthetic due to its reliance upon a sensory interpretation. Following this logic, aesthetics are part of the everyday experience of consumers, and, therefore, consumers can be called 'aesthetic subjects' (Meamber 1997b; Venkatesh and Meamber 2006, 2008) when they productively consume cultural products as part of how they conduct their lives. The sensory experience of everyday objects, including the consumption of images, includes the symbolic aspects of consumption – i.e. the exchange of symbols, images, signs, and meanings. The aesthetic nature of life (Cova and Svanfeldt 1993; Debord 1983 [1967]) makes it necessary to consider aesthetics and the aesthetic subject, the visual consumer, within the context of everyday activities, that is, of everyday consumption experiences. In the next section of this chapter, I will more formally introduce the concept of the visual consumer and how this visual consumer engages with image consumption in the market. Key questions that I will address are: What is visual consumption? What are some important marketplace domains for the productive consumption of images – including advertising campaigns, products, brands, and experiences?

Marketplace image consumption: the productive consumption of visual content

Visual consumers productively consume images or other visual material and experiences offered by organizations. The etymology of the word 'image' from the Greek indicates that it is a verbal creation of a visual representation of what one sees (in the mind's eye). In conventional usage, Stern and colleagues (2001) find multiple uses of the term in the dictionary and in marketing thought. In the end, these authors conclude that image can be equated with the idea of gestalt, a whole. This whole is more than the sum of its parts. Therefore, the consumption of images is predicated on interpreting in the entire visual message, including its historical, cultural, ideological connotations, which may or may not be obvious.

The concept of visual consumption was established by Schroeder (2002) to discuss the production and consumption of images in consumer culture. As defined by Schroeder: 'Visual consumption, then is a perceptual process of making sense and integration, and a consumer process of gazing, looking and categorizing visual experience' (2011: 138). Visual consumption encompasses such activities as touring, watching, and viewing. Through visual consumption, consumers construct, maintain, and communicate their identities by looking, seeing, observing, and interpreting visual material. In contemporary consumer culture, vision is perhaps the most important of the five senses, although historically vision has always been both elevated and debased as compared to written knowledge in thought and scholarship (Campbell and Schroeder 2011; Jay 1993; Kant 1964 [1791]; Kellner 1990; Scott 1994a; Stern 1989, 1991). In contemporary consumer culture, vision assumes importance because marketers rely upon the visual. This is not to deny the long history and predominance of visual consumption experiences in earlier times, but to acknowledge the ubiquitous nature of images, signs, and symbols in consumers' daily lives, and the visual turn in research on visual consumption issues in the late twentieth and early twenty-first century.

In everyday life, consumers are ensconced in visual content that they consume productively in order to mold flexible identities and give meaning to their lives (Ahuvia 2005; Ahuvia and Izberk-Bilgin 2011; Venkatesh *et al.* 2006). Organizations are reliant upon the productive consumption of its signs, symbols, and images in terms of its marketplace offerings. Signs, symbols, and images supersede materiality and use value in terms of their visuality. This is not to argue that cultural products and experience have no functional utility, but that ideas such as function and utility are treated as signs (Askegaard and Firat 1996) and symbols (Levy 1959,

2003) that signal particular meanings that can be appropriated and reinterpreted. This refers to the semiotics or the sign value of a cultural product (Barthes 2000 [1957]; Mick 1986, 1997; Nöth 1988). According to Baudrillard (1988 [1968], 1993 [1976]), consumption in the current period involves the exchange of signs. Image consumption allows consumers to signify aspects of the self to themselves and to others in a complex code of symbolic meaning. Consumers continuously (re-)construct their identities, in part, through the consumption of symbols, images, and signs.

Conferring meaning upon symbols, images, and signs, as articulated in the previous sections of the chapter, is a negotiated, aesthetic (sensory)-oriented, constructivist process of productive consumption. In the case of providing meanings to organizational offerings in the marketplace, the cultural actors are: marketers (producers, cultural intermediaries), consumers, and the cultural product itself. The interaction between these entities gives rise to meaning, but where does this meaning reside? With the marketers that attempt to create and communicate intended meanings? With the consumers who appropriate the signs, symbols, and images to construct their own meanings? With the cultural product itself that can construct culture through the production and consumption process? The answer is all of the above, potentially. Although still open to debate, current thought suggests that cultural products are inscribed with particular meanings and associations that are (initially) formed and circulated by marketers with the conscious attempt to generate desire (Ewen 1988; Lash and Urry 1994). Consumers can consume these suggested meanings, which often come in the form of competing representations and identity positions (Shankar *et al.* 2009) associated with different cultural products in the marketplace. As noted already, consumers can also manipulate and hybridize marketer-created meanings (Muñiz and Schau 2005) and cleverly, and perhaps cynically, resist these meanings (Mikkonen *et al.* 2011). This polysemic nature of meaning (Putoni *et al.* 2010) is the essence of productive consumption, and has been studied extensively in the research on advertising.

The productive consumption of advertising

Image interpretation in advertising and organizational communication, while it may be circumscribed through representational practices that attempt to anchor images with particular meanings, remains unfixed and incomplete. As discussed previously, meaning construction is constrained by a number of forces – including the culture, history, background, and social forces that impact the choices made by consumers. Consumer interpretations of advertising campaigns may also be reduced because of expectations, intentions, and preferences or because of a lack of awareness, attention, or knowledge concerning the background of the image (Schroeder 2004). Yet, signs, symbols, and images are never neutral, but exist within the milieu of extant signs, symbols, images, and meanings – i.e. a system of representation.

Representation constitutes a language, and visual representation is the visual language of visual content. Schroeder (2002) defines 'consuming representation' as consumer engagement with signs, symbols, and meaning in the visual marketplace. The visual marketplace can include any cultural product offered in the market, but, traditionally in marketing and consumer research, it is defined as advertisements, products, brands, and marketer-designed consumer experiences (including services). Much of the work on representation relates to the study of advertising campaigns. A number of conceptual, theoretical, and methodological traditions can be employed to the study of representation in advertisements, including but not limited to: psychology, art history, ethics, visual studies, visual criticism, and critical race theory (Borgerson and Schroeder 2002, 2005; Borgerson *et al.* 2009; Schroeder 1998, 2002, 2006b, 2008, 2010; Schroeder and Borgerson 1998, 2005; Schroeder and Zwick 2004).

Many studies draw upon semiotics, as discussed in Norah Campbell's chapter 'The signs and semiotics of advertising' (Chapter 8, this volume). Some work is interdisciplinary, combining several or all of the above, under the rubric of 'critical visual analysis' (Schroeder 2006b), such as the analysis of an advertising campaign for a brand of rum that used the imagery of vampires to communicate meaning (Schroeder 2002). After describing the ad, Schroeder (2002) addresses the possible associations of power, danger, and mystery of the image with the product. He then employs discursive analysis to link vampires with blood, infection, death, and blood diseases like AIDS to show that advertising produces meaning beyond the product, brand, or experience that is being advertised.

Images convey an ideological stance – what consumers notice, attend to, interpret, and value. Advertising campaigns often rely upon photographic images, and therefore research by Schroeder and others on advertising images also notes the linkages between representation, photography, consumption, and identity. As Schroeder (2002) contends, photography is an essential visual information technology in advertising, in particular, and in everyday life, in general. Photographs are often considered objective, visual records, and, with the advent of digital photography, consumers can easily and instantly create and share these photographic experiences that represent their identities with other visual consumers (and organizations). Photography is a powerful agent in shaping consumers' view of the world, yet its power is often invisible to those who use it (Schroeder 2012). For example, Schroeder's (2012) work illuminates how snapshot imagery that portrays consumers in what appears to be real, spontaneously captured, everyday life experiences are, in reality, posed and carefully controlled by the organizations that use the imagery as a strategic tool in the marketplace.

Photographs are, however, constructions that are defined by cultural actors – photographers, advertisers, and consumers and by the culture in which they circulate and re-circulate. This present era, what Baudrillard (1993 [1976]) describes as the 'code-governed' phase of post-industrial capitalism or the third order of simulacra, is a period of reproduction in that signs are created and recycled over and over to signify disparate meanings. Images, signs, and symbols can have histories and can be put to use repeatedly to signify particular meanings for consumers who interpret them, such as in relation to cultural products (e.g., products, brands, and experiences). The act of reproducing images has been made easier with the advent of more and more sophisticated technology. Critical theorist Walter Benjamin (1969) recognizes the implications of the process of reproduction in contemporary culture in his writings; namely, how new technologies, including cinema and photography, transform the traditional notions of originality and the cultural production process itself. These technologies are mediums of representation and reproduction. Berger also notes, 'Consequently, a reproduction, as well as making its own references to the image of its original, becomes itself the reference point for other images' (1972: 29). Today, contemporary organizations appropriate cultural referent systems from the past to develop advertising campaigns, products, brands, or experiences.

In the realm of art, consumption is predicated upon viewing images (Schroeder 2000, 2005, 2006a). Taking Renaissance art as an exemplar, Schroeder and Borgerson (2002) discuss how it, as a technology, enabled viewers to imagine themselves as subjects in artworks, having implications for the personal collection of art and for arts patronage. Renaissance artists appropriated earlier symbols and forms of Christian religious art. Visual theorist John Berger (1972) also traces visual representation from fifteenth-century painting to twentieth-century advertising. Much recent work has focused upon developing a 'visual genealogy' of contemporary images, showing how images can have meaning based on their construction and linkage to earlier images, technologies, and meanings (Borgerson and Schroeder 2003; Schroeder 2004; Schroeder and Borgerson 2002). For example, digital architecture, such as the Internet, relies upon classical principles of physical architecture (Schroeder 2003), and photography is influenced by the representational conventions of painting (Schroeder and Borgerson 2002). In his analysis of a famous CK One fragrance advertising campaign, Schroeder (2002, 2006b) illustrates how the campaign images combine principles of group portraiture in Dutch painting and of fashion photography to signify a genderless brand and allow for 'consuming difference' (such as different multicultural identities and gender relations in advertising and branding campaigns).

Images, whether they are in the form of advertisements, products, brands, or experiences, serve as the 'face of capitalism' in the current period (Schroeder 2004). Through advertising, products and brands are linked to the performance of identity and of living (lifestyles), and therefore constructing a brand is a key to product success in the market (Schroeder 2002). In today's world, consumers act as tourists, seeking out experiences, especially visual experiences, sights, and sensations in terms of their interactions with products, brands, advertising, services, and other types of consumption experiences (Schroeder 1998).

The productive consumption of products and brands

Turning to the role of products and brands in the processes of cultural production and image consumption, vision came to be linked with marketing in the selling of products, especially in the late nineteenth century with the advent of new consumer experiences and visual displays of merchandise. The first department store opened in Paris in 1852, based on outdoor arcades. Engendering desire through vision was central to the Great Exhibition of 1851. Inside the Crystal Palace, 100,000 goods were exhibited to showcase that all human life and cultural endeavor could be represented in manufactured goods (Meamber 1997a; Richards 1990).

Vision continues to assume a primary role in the material products in the marketplace (Meamber 1995, 2001). It is well established that companies, such as Apple, have achieved success over recent decades, in part through their design-based approach to marketing. 'Design is often misunderstood by marketers or managers, who marginalize it as a cosmetic intervention or face lifting to a product ... With the aesthetization of everyday life, design becomes central to the innovation process' (Carmagnola 1991, quoted in Cova and Svanfeldt 1993: 307). Koenenn (1997) writes that, in the contemporary world, consumers are sensitive to visual communications and thus design aesthetics is becoming a part of everyday objects. Konicus (2000) notes that home appliances are being designed with aesthetic appeal as a goal. In the current period, product design is concerned with the celebration of the image – 'It is this image which, represented through the planned interplay of a multitude of signs, then reflects on the surface and becomes the "essence" that the consumer seeks in adopting a product' (Firat and Venkatesh 1993: 232). In our research, my co-author and I found consumers can articulate the role of design in their purchase and consumption of products (Venkatesh and Meamber 2008). The aesthetics of these products becomes a key factor in some consumers' assessment of value.

Concerning the productive consumption of specific products, Borgerson and Schroeder (2006), for example, examine books as material and design artifacts. They find that used books challenge extant notions of consumer desire through the value consumers place upon the pleasures of consuming the (visual) content that appears outside of organizational (publisher, author) control. Using the Peter Pauper Press as the example, these authors decode these books as representing cultural storytelling during the Cold War era – allowing consumers to explore new cuisines and cultures, and to simultaneously gain cultural capital. While the study discusses many material aspects of book consumption, including collecting, gift giving, and selling, the authors also focus upon the visual consumption of the covers, inside content, and notes made by other consumers. In particular, they show how owner inscriptions add meaning and aesthetic value to the book.

Physical products, such as the books of Peter Pauper Press are not only material objects that signify meaning, but also, in many instances, are subsumed under 'brands.' The word 'brand' comes from an Old Norse word meaning 'to burn.' Livestock owners mark (burn) their animals to identify them. In marketing, a brand refers to a name, symbol, or design, or combination of these, that distinguishes an organizational offering from others in the marketplace (Keller 2003). A brand, therefore, takes the discussion of product design one step further, in that a brand designates differentiation from other products, and this difference is often based on the brand alone. Yet, brands are more than just ways to identify products or the organizations that own them. Brands, because they are communicative, are also cultural, ideological, and political objects (Askegaard 2006; Schroeder and Salzer-Mörling 2006). Brands, especially powerful brands (strong or iconic), become ideological referents that shape culture, such as the way consumers 'see' life (Heilbrun 2006; Holt 2004; Schroeder 2009). Images are critical in brand building, and often products or brands are created to reflect particular images (Firat *et al.* 1994; Reynolds and Gutman 1984).

At the individual level, consumers can use the content of brands (images, symbols, signs) to construct, perform, and communicate identities (Borgerson and Schroeder 2002; Elliott 2004; Elliott and Wattanasuwan 1998; Wikström 1996). At the organizational level, brands serve as mediators between organizations and consumers, that is, vehicles by which organizations interact with consumers. Brand imagery colonizes and appropriates existing reference systems within culture, turning signs into myths designed to sell lifestyles (Schroeder 2005). At the cultural level, as Holt (2004) expresses, certain brands become iconic (strong or powerful) in consumer society because they serve as channels for expressing collective desire and for resolving tensions or collective anxiety. For example, research conducted over the last decade on the Hummer brand suggests that it expresses the desire of Americans to feel powerful and yet secure within a wide range of cultural, legal, economic, ecological, political, and social meanings (Luedicke and Giesler 2007; Lukas 2007; Meamber and Sussan 2009; Miller 2007).

Brands, as visual referents, can be, and have been, studied from various perspectives, including managerial, psychological, and interpretive perspectives, and with various tools developed to understand culture, politics, history, aesthetics, and ideology. Most recently, scholars have examined issues and processes that impact the productive consumption of the brand, such as culture, history, and ethics (Schroeder 2009). Schroeder and Salzer-Mörling (2006) have advanced the idea of 'brand culture' to focus upon the role of historical and cultural codes that influence branding, its production, its productive consumption, meaning, and value. The study of brand culture, in conjunction with research on brand identity and brand image, provides a more complete portrait of the branding process as related to cultural production and productive consumption.

> The brand culture concept occupies the theoretical space between strategic concepts of brand identity and consumer interpretations of brand image, shedding light on the gap often seen between managerial intention and market response, in other words, between strategic goals and consumer perceptions.
>
> *(Schroeder 2009: 124)*

The productive consumption of everyday consumer experiences

In addition to the negotiation of brand meanings, everyday productive consumption experiences, such as shopping, tourism, and so on, are replete with visual organization issues.

Holbrook and Hirschman (1982) established that the consumption experience allows consumers to experience fantasy, feelings, and fun. Consumer experiences, much like advertising and branding, are often designed by organizations to engender particular meanings that can be taken and used or re-interpreted for identity projects. In the realm of shopping, research has focused on the nature of the shopping experience as being premised upon the idea of 'gaze' or the visual consumption of people and space, and its temporary pleasure (Brottman 1997), on how the space allows for resistance of predetermined meanings (Maclaran and Brown 2005), among other topics. For example, Schroeder (2011) discusses the evolution of self-service retailing and how this retail revolution alters the shopping experience to one that is more visually oriented. Consumers are required to look and recognize brands and products in order to shop and make purchases.

Other groundbreaking work on spatial aesthetics (e.g. Peñaloza 1998; Sherry 1998) examines consumers' movement through space and interactions with the architecture, photographs, products, and other intertextual shopping displays, providing multi-sensorial but, above all, visual experiences. Shopping environments and other servicescapes often take mythologies and rework them to serve commercial aims and channel consumer experiences along certain lines. For example, Peñaloza's (1998) paper on Chicago's Nike Town illustrates how the design of the retail space and the displays produced materials for interpretation, which consumers drew from and productively consumed. Mythologies surrounding competition, peak performance, style, and recreational activity all were on display and readily consumed in the shopping experience.

Work on tourism has also addressed the visual aspects of consumption, such as my and my co-author's visual ethnographic research on representations of culture and history at Disney, and how these representational practices have been applied at historical sites (Houston and Meamber 2011; Meamber 2011). The tourist experience itself has also been studied in relation to the visual practice of taking photographs (Schroeder 2002) as signaling expertise, insider knowledge, and elite tastes. Also fitting into the study of consumer experiences are papers by Borgerson and Schroeder (1997, 2002) on the marketing representations of Hawaii. These texts contribute to broadening the perspective of marketing to include the packaging of a place, in this case, an entire state. In this work, Borgerson and Schroeder (1997, 2002) discuss Hawaii itself, as a retroscape consisting of signs, sounds, and lifestyle that is visually, acoustically, and sensually consumed. In addition, Borgerson and Schroeder link their discussion to the constitution of culture via consumption. The authors apply critiques from art history and advertising to illustrate the colonizing discourse contained in these visual artifacts. These pieces together deconstruct the marketed image of Hawaii and its power to influence how consumers 'see' the place, and to make it attractive as a vacation destination.

Work on visual consumers and visual consumption has expanded in recent years. Yet, much more attention deserves to be paid to the analysis of visual images in marketing, and newer technologies for aesthetic, visual consumption, such as social media. In the final section of this chapter, I ask; what are the avenues for future research on visual consumers?

Image production and consumption: future research directions

Research on visual consumers and visual consumption is far from complete. The discipline of consumer research has examined images as stimuli engendering a consumer response, photography as a data-gathering tool, and, more recently, images themselves and their role in contemporary consumer culture and marketing. The use of images in marketing and consumer research has expanded over the last few decades beyond the subjects touched upon in this chapter. For example, in the realm of art, in addition to exploring how art functions within the marketing system (Guillet de Monthoux 2000), scholars have used artists and artworks to look at branding and variety of other marketplace and consumption topics (e.g. Belk 1986; Ger and Belk 1995; Schroeder (1992, 2000, 2005, 2006a; Schroeder and Borgerson 2002; Witkowski 1996, 2004, 2010).

Similar to its use in understanding management (e.g. Bell 2008), researchers have often used film as material to unpack consumer behavior (e.g. Hirschman 1992, 1993; Hirschman and Stern 1994; Holbrook and Grayson 1986; Kates 2000; Meamber and Sussan 2011), as well as to disseminate knowledge, such as the September 2005 and June 2007 DVD issues of *Consumption Markets & Culture*, and conference film festivals (Belk and Kozinets 2005, 2007). Research methodologies adopted by marketing and consumer scholars have also advanced to include images as data (e.g. Heisley and Levy 1991; Dion *et al.* 2011), images as visual metaphors (e.g. Zaltman 2003), the use of video diaries (e.g. Brown *et al.* 2011), and the use of visual ethnography (e.g. Houston 2007; Houston and Meamber 2011; Meamber 2011; Peñaloza 1998). In-depth discussions of photography and ethnography are also making their way into scholarship, such as Peñaloza and Thompson's chapter in this volume (Chapter 5).

Scholars of visual culture point out that there are many other domains outside of those traditionally addressed by organizational or consumption studies that rely upon the production and consumption of visual images that have yet to be studied. For example, Campbell and Schroeder (2011) identify law, science, technology, and mathematics as areas that deserve further attention. Images in these domains are also sites of productive visual consumption and of negotiated meanings. Already marketing and consumer scholars are redefining traditional ideas such as competition premised on the visual economy. Competition in contemporary consumer culture is predicated on images in the form of advertising, brand images, websites, and social media, all of which merit additional study.

In particular, the concept of value in the marketplace deserves further exploration as related to consumer empowerment versus enslavement (Firat and Dholakia 2006; Izberk-Bilgin 2010). For example, writing on value creation and the visual consumer, Schroeder (2011) highlights that, while scholars maintain that consumers are free to create or co-create the identities and meanings for themselves while engaging with the organizations, brands, and communities to which they belong (Fitchett 2004; Manolis *et al.* 2001; Vargo and Lusch 2004), some work suggests that consumers are 'aesthetic laborers' (or 'working consumers') who work for, and are exploited by, organizations that use consumer-generated images in advertising, on websites, and now through social media, without providing any compensation to these consumers (Cova and Dalli 2009; Prahalad and Ramaswamy 2000; Zwick *et al.* 2008). As long as images continue to drive the economy, marketing, and organizations, there are ample subjects for researchers to study.

Summary and conclusion

In summary, organizations employ signs, images, and symbols strategically – to communicate with its public through the images and cultural products offered in the market – including advertising campaigns, products, brands, and consumer experiences. In presenting current scholarship on cultural production and visual consumption of images in the marketplace, this chapter illustrated that meaning is generated through the interactive and interdependent processes of cultural production and what may be termed 'productive consumption,' in which the consumer is simultaneously both a producer and consumer of marketplace images. Productive consumption is an aesthetically oriented, dynamic process that occurs when the consumer engages with (i.e. senses) organizational images, signs, and symbols and uses these to shape his or her identity and sense of the world. The meaning that the consumer creates depends on the image, sign, or symbol itself, its cultural history, referents, associations, and intended purpose, the organizational goals, as well as the consumer's background, interests, and social constraints. This means that the consumption is a productive act, and to consume is not merely 'to use up' as its etymology and traditional definitions suggest.

In the current era, sources of value for organizations and consumers include the visual, sensory content of cultural products offered within the market. The cultural production and productive consumption of this visual aesthetic material by consumers may be considered of value to both the consumer and the organization. In today's world, the visual dominates our experience of life and how consumers interact with the organization through its offerings. The study of images, and the interactions and power relations between consumers, cultural products, and organizations to produce value is paramount to our understanding of the aesthetic age now, and for the time to come.

References

Ahuvia, A. (2005) 'Beyond the extended self: loved objects and consumers' identity narrative', *Journal of Consumer Research* 31: 171–184.

Ahuvia, A. and Izberk-Bilgin, E. (2011) 'Limits of the McDonaldization thesis: eBayization and ascendant trends in post-industrial consumer culture', *Consumption Markets & Culture* 14: 361–384.

Arnould, E.J. and Thompson, C.J. (2005) 'Consumer Culture Theory (CCT): twenty years of research', *Journal of Consumer Research* 31: 868–882.

Askegaard, S. (2006) 'Brands as a global ideoscape', in J.E. Schroeder and M. Salzer-Mörling (eds) *Brand Culture*, London and New York: Routledge.

Askegaard, S. and Firat, A.F. (1996) 'Material culture and symbolic consumption', working paper, Odense University.

Balmer, J.M. (2006) 'Corporate brand cultures and communities', in J.E. Schroeder and M. Salzer-Mörling (eds) *Brand Culture*, London and New York: Routledge.

Barthes, R. (2000 [1957]) *Mythologies*, trans. J. Cape, London: Random House.

Baudrillard, J. (1988 [1968]) 'The system of objects', in J. Thackera (ed.) *Design After Modernism*, New York: Thames and Hudson.

——(1993 [1976]) *Symbolic Exchange and Death*, Thousand Oaks, CA: Sage Publications.

Belk, R.W. (1986) 'Symbolic consumption of art', in D.V. Shaw, W.S. Hendon and C.R. Waits (eds) *Artists and Cultural Consumers*, Akron, OH: Association for Cultural Economics.

——(1988) 'Possessions and the extended self', *Journal of Consumer Research* 15: 139–168.

Belk, R.W. and Kozinets, R.V. (2005) 'Introduction to the Resonant Representations issue of *Consumption Markets & Culture*', *Consumption Markets & Culture* 8: 195–203.

Belk, R.W. and Kozinets, R.V. (2007) 'Resonant Representations 2', *Consumption Markets & Culture*, 10: 75–76.

Bell, E. (2008) *Reading Management and Organization in Film*, Basingstoke: Palgrave Macmillan.

Benjamin, W. (1969) 'The work of art in the age of mechanical reproduction', in *Illuminations*, trans. H. Zohn, New York: Schocker Books.

Berger, J. (1972) *Ways of Seeing*, London: British Broadcasting Corporation and Penguin Books.

Björkman, I. (2002) 'Aura: aesthetic business creativity', *Consumption Markets & Culture* 5: 69–78.

Borgerson, J.L. and Schroeder, J.E. (1997) 'The ethics of representation: packaging paradise: consuming the 50th state', *Cooley Law Review* 14: 473–489.

Borgerson, J.L. and Schroeder, J.E. (2002) 'Ethical issues of global marketing: avoiding bad faith in visual representation', *European Journal of Marketing* 36: 570–594.

Borgerson, J.L. and Schroeder, J.E. (2003) 'The lure of paradise: marketing the retro-escape of Hawaii', in S. Brown and J.F. Sherry (eds) *Time, Space and Place: The Rise of Retroscapes*, Armonk, NY: M.E. Sharpe.

Borgerson, J.L. and Schroeder, J.E. (2005) 'Identity in marketing communications: an ethics of visual representation', in A.J. Kimmel (ed.) *Marketing Communication: New Approaches, Technologies, and Styles*, Oxford: Oxford University Press.

Borgerson, J.L. and Schroeder, J.E. (2006) 'The pleasures of the used text: revealing traces of consumption', in S. Brown (ed.) *Consuming Books: The Marketing and Consumption of Literature*, London: Routledge.

Borgerson, J.L., Schroeder, J.E., Escuderdo Magusson, M. and Magnusson, F. (2009) 'Corporate communication, ethics, and operational identity: a case of Benetton', *Business Ethics – A European Review* 18: 209–223.

Bourdieu, P. (1984) *Distinction: A Social Critique of the Judgment of Taste*, Cambridge: Harvard University Press.

Brottman, M. (1997) 'The last stop of desire – Covent Garden and the spatial text of consumerism', *Consumption Markets & Culture* 1: 45–79.

Brown, C., Costley, C., Friend, L. and Varey, R. (2011) 'Capturing their dream: video diaries and minority consumers', *Consumption Markets & Culture* 13: 419–436.

Brown, S. (ed.) (2006) *Consuming Books: The Marketing and Consumption of Literature*, New York: Routledge.

Campbell, N. and Schroeder, J.E. (2011) 'Visual culture', in D. Southerton (ed.) *Encyclopedia of Consumer Culture*, Thousand Oaks, CA: Sage, 1506–1510.

Carroll, N. (2001) *Beyond Aesthetics: Philosophical Essays*, Cambridge: Cambridge University Press.

Carù, A. and Cova, B. (2003) 'Revisiting consumption experience: a more humble but complete view of the concept', *Marketing Theory* 3: 267–286.

Carù, A. and Cova, B. (eds) (2007) *Consuming Experience*, London: Routledge.

Cova, B. and Dalli, D. (2009) 'Working consumers: the next step in marketing theory', *Marketing Theory* 9: 315–319.

Cova, B. and Svanfeldt, C. (1993) 'Societal innovations and the postmodern aesthetization of everyday life', *International Journal of Research in Marketing* 10: 297–310.

Cova, B., Kozinets, R.V. and Shankar, A. (eds) (2007) *Consumer Tribes*, Oxford: Elsevier.

Davenport, S., Leitch, S., Motion, J. and Renton, M. (2009) 'Mobilizing scientific discourse to rebrand organizational identity', paper presented at the 25th EGOS (European Group for Organizational Studies) Colloquium, Barcelona, July 2009.

Debord, G. (1983 [1967]) *Society of the Spectacle*, Detroit: Black and Red.

de Certeau, M. (1984) *The Practice of Everyday Life*, Berkeley and Los Angeles: University of California Press.

Dewey, T. (1934) *Art as Experience*, New York: Minton, Balch and Company.

Dickie, G. (1971) *Art and the Aesthetic*, Ithaca, NY: Cornell University Press.

Dion, D., Sitz, L. and Rémy, E. (2011) 'Embodied ethnicity: the ethnic affiliation grounded in the body', *Consumption Markets & Culture* 14: 311–331.

Douglas, M. and Isherwood, B. (1979) *The World of Goods*, NY: W.W. Norton & Co.

du Gay, P. (1997) *Production of Culture/Cultures of Production*, London: Sage.

Ekström, K. and Brembeck, H. (eds) (2004) *Elusive Consumption*, Oxford: Berg.

Elliott, R. (2004) 'Making up people: consumption as a symbolic vocabulary for the consumption of identity', in K.M. Ekström and H. Brembeck (eds) *Elusive Consumption*, New York: Berg.

Elliott, R. and Wattanasuwan, K. (1998) 'Brands as symbolic resources for the construction of identity', *International Journal of Advertising* 17: 131–144.

Ewen, S. (1988) *All Consuming Images: The Politics of Style in Contemporary Culture*, New York: Basic Books.

Featherstone, M. (1991) *Consumer Culture and Postmodernism*, Newbury Park: Sage Publications.

Firat, A.F. and Dholakia, N. (2006) 'Theoretical and philosophical implications of postmodern debates: some challenges to modern marketing', *Marketing Theory* 6: 123–162.

Firat, A.F. and Venkatesh, A. (1993) 'Postmodernity: the age of marketing', *International Journal of Research in Marketing* 10: 227–250.

Firat, A.F. and Venkatesh, A. (1995) 'Liberatory postmodernism and the reenchantment of consumption', *Journal of Consumer Research* 22: 239–267.

Firat, A.F., Sherry Jr., J.F. and Venkatesh, A. (1994) 'Postmodernism, marketing and the consumer', *International Journal of Research in Marketing* 11: 311–316.

Fiske, J. (1989) *Understanding Popular Culture*, New York: Routledge.

Fitchett, J.A. (2004) 'The fantasies, orders and roles of sadistic consumption: game shows and the service encounter', *Consumption Markets & Culture* 7: 285–306.

Forty, A. (1995 [1986]) *Objects of Desire: Design and Society, 1750–1980*, London: Thames and Hudson.

Geertz, C. (1973) *The Interpretation of Cultures*, New York: Basic Books.

Ger, G. and Belk, R.W. (1995) 'Art, art collecting, and consumer culture: a cross-cultural and historical analysis', in A. Joy, K. Basu and Z. Hangsheng (eds) *Marketing & Development*, Beijing: International Society for Marketing & Development.

Gergen, K.J. (1991) *The Saturated Self*, NY: Basic Books.

Guillet de Monthoux, P. (2000) 'The art management of aesthetic organizing', in S. Linstead and H. Höpfl (eds) *The Aesthetics of Organization*, London: Sage.

Hall, S. (1993) 'Encoding, decoding', in S. During (ed.) *The Cultural Studies Reader*, New York: Routledge.

Heilbrun, B. (2002) 'Alessi: Italian design and the re-enchantment of everyday objects', in M. Solomon, G. Bamossy and S. Askegaard, *Consumer Behavior: A European Perspective*, Harlow, UK: Prentice Hall.

——(2006) 'Brave new brands: cultural branding between utopia and a-topia', in J.E. Schroeder and M. Salzer-Mörling (eds) *Brand Culture*, London and New York: Routledge.

Heisley, D. and Levy, S.J. (1991) 'Autodriving: a photoelicitation technique', *Journal of Consumer Research* 18: 257–272.

Hirschman, E.C. (1992) 'Mundane addiction: the cinematic depiction of cocaine consumption', in J.F. Sherry Jr. and B. Sternthal (eds) *Advances in Consumer Research*, 19, Provo, UT: Association for Consumer Research.

——(1993) 'Consumer behavior meets the nouvelle femme: feminist consumption in the movies', in L. McAlister and M.L. Rothschild (eds) *Advances in Consumer Research*, 20, Provo, UT: Association for Consumer Research.

Hirschman, E.C. and Holbrook, M.B. (1982) 'Hedonic consumption: emerging concepts, methods and propositions', *Journal of Marketing* 47: 92–101.

Hirschman, E.C. and Stern, B.B. (1994) 'Women as commodities: prostitution as depicted in *Pretty Baby* and *Pretty Woman*', in C.T. Allen and D.R. John (eds) *Advances in Consumer Research*, 21, Provo, UT: Association for Consumer Research.

Holbrook, M.B. and Grayson, M.W. (1986) 'The semiology of cinematic consumption: symbolic consumer behavior in *Out of Africa*', *Journal of Consumer Research* 13: 374–381.

Holbrook, M.B. and Hirschman, E.C. (1982) 'The experiential aspects of consumption: consumer fantasies, feelings, and fun', *Journal of Consumer Research* 9: 132–140.

Holbrook, M.B. and Huber, J. (1979) 'Separating perceptual dimensions from affective overtones: an application to consumer aesthetics', *Journal of Consumer Research* 5: 272–283.

Holbrook, M.B. and Zirlin, R.B. (1985) 'Artistic creation, artworks, and aesthetic appreciation: some philosophical contributions to nonprofit marketing', in R.W. Belk (ed.) *Advances in Nonprofit Marketing*, 1, Greenwich, CT: JAI Press.

Holt, D.B. (1998) 'Does cultural capital structure American consumption?', *Journal of Consumer Research* 25: 1–25.

——(2004) *How Brands Become Icons*, Boston, MA: Harvard Business School Press.

Holt, D.B. and Thompson, C.J. (2004) 'Man-of-action heroes: the pursuit of heroic masculinity in everyday consumption', *Journal of Consumer Research* 31: 425–440.

Houston, H.R. (2007) 'Medicine, magic, and maternity: an ethnographic study of ritual consumption in contemporary, urban Japan', unpublished dissertation, UMI Publications, Inc., Ann Arbor, Michigan.

Houston, H.R. and Meamber, L.A. (2011) 'Consuming the "world": reflexivity, aesthetics and authenticity at Disney World's EPCOT Center', *Consumption Markets & Culture* 14: 177–191.

Izberk-Bilgin, E. (2010) 'An interdisciplinary review of resistance to consumption, some marketing interpretations, and future research suggestions', *Consumption Markets & Culture* 13: 299–323.

Jay, M. (1993) *Downcast Eyes: The Denigration of Vision in Twentieth-Century French Thought*, Berkeley: University of California Press.

Kant, I. (1964 [1791]) 'Critique of judgment', reprinted in A. Hofstadter, and R. Kuhns (eds) *Philosophies of Art & Beauty: Selected Readings in Aesthetics from Plato to Heidegger*, Chicago: University of Chicago Press.

Kaplan, E.A. (2008) 'Global trauma and public feelings: viewing images of catastrophe', *Consumption Markets & Culture* 11: 3–24.

Kates, S. (2000) 'Gay men on film: a typologic of the scopophilic consumption pleasures of cultural text', *Consumption Markets & Culture* 4: 281–313.

Keller, K.L. (2003) *Strategic Brand Management: Building, Measuring, and Managing Brand Equity*, Upper Saddle River, NJ: Prentice Hall.

Kellner, D. (1990) 'Critical theory and ideology critique', in R. Roblin (ed.) *The Aesthetics of the Critical Theorists: Studies on Benjamin, Adorno, Marcuse, and Habermas*, Lewiston, NY: The Edwin Mellen Press.

Koenenn, C. (1997) 'Extra ordinary', *Los Angeles Times*, 2 September: E2.

Konicus, J. (2000) 'Tangerine dreams in home design', *The Washington Post Online*, 2 February (accessed March 2000).
Koren, L. (2010) *Which 'Aesthetics' Do you Mean? Ten Definitions*, Point Reyes, CA: Imperfect Publishing.
Kozinets, R.V. (2002) 'Can consumers escape the market? Emancipatory illuminations from Burning Man', *Journal of Consumer Research* 29: 20–38.
Kozinets, R.V. and Handleman, J.M. (2004) 'Adversaries of consumption: consumer movements, activism, and ideology', *Journal of Consumer Research* 31: 691–704.
Lash, S. and Urry, J. (1994) *Economies of Signs and Space*, London: Sage.
Levy, S.J. (1959) 'Symbols for sale', *Harvard Business Review*, July: 117–124.
——(1981) 'Interpreting consumer mythology: a structural approach to consumer behavior', *Journal of Marketing* 45: 49–61.
——(2003) 'Roots of marketing and consumer research at the University of Chicago', *Consumption Markets & Culture* 6: 99–110.
Luedicke, M.K. and Giesler, M. (2007) 'Brand communities and their social antagonists: insights from the Hummer case', in B. Cova, R.V. Kozinets and A. Shankar (eds) *Consumer Tribes*, New York, NY: Butterworth-Heinemann.
Lukas, S.A. (2007) 'The Hummer as cultural and political myth: a multi-sited ethnographic analysis', in E. Cardenas and E. Gorman (eds) *The Hummer: Myths and Consumer Culture*, Lanham, MD: Lexington Books.
Maclaran, P. and Brown, S. (2005) 'The center cannot hold: consuming the utopian marketplace', *Journal of Consumer Research* 32: 311–323.
Maffesoli, M. (1996 [1988]) *The Time of Tribes: The Decline of Individualism in Mass Society*, trans. Don Smith, Thousand Oaks: Sage Publications.
Manolis, C., Meamber, L.A., Winsor, R.D. and Brooks, C.M. (2001) 'Partial employees and consumers: a postmodern, meta-theoretical perspective for services marketing', *Marketing Theory* 1: 225–243.
McCracken, G. (1986) 'Culture and consumption: a theoretical account of the structure and movement of the cultural meaning of goods', *Journal of Consumer Research* 13: 71–84.
——(1988) *Culture and Consumption*, Bloomington: Indiana University Press.
——(1989) '"Homeyness": a cultural account of one constellation of consumer goods and meanings', in E.C. Hirschman (ed.) *Interpretive Consumer Research*, Provo, UT: Association for Consumer Research.
——(1993) 'The value of the brand: an anthropological perspective', *Brand Equity & Advertising: Advertising's Role in Building Strong Brands*, Hillsdale, NJ: Lawrence Erlbaum Associates.
Meamber, L.A. (1995) 'Mosaics of consumption experiences: entertainment in postmodernity', *Proceedings*, 1995 Winter AMA Marketing Educators' Conference, La Jolla, California.
——(1997a) 'Commentary "The last stop of desire – Covent Garden and the spatial text of consumerism"', *Consumption Markets & Culture* 1: 81–90.
——(1997b) 'The constitution of the arts as cultural production: the role of the consumer, artist, and cultural intermediary as producer/consumer of meaning', unpublished dissertation, UMI Publications, Inc., Ann Arbor, Michigan.
——(2001) 'Visual issues and the market: product design aesthetics', *Proceedings*, Globalization and Equity: 26th Annual Macromarketing Conference, Williamsburg, Virginia.
——(2011) 'Disney and the presentation of Colonial America', *Consumption Markets & Culture* 14: 125–144.
Meamber, L.A. and Sussan, F. (2009) 'Hummer: The H3 Model and the end of a brand icon', *Proceedings*, 34th Annual Macromarketing Conference, University of Agdar, Kristiansand, Norway.
Meamber, L.A. and Sussan, F. (2011) 'Student centered learning about consumer behavior using feature films', *Proceedings*, 2011 AMA Summer Educators' Conference, San Francisco, California.
Meamber, L.A. and Venkatesh, A. (1999) 'The flesh is made symbol: an interpretive account of contemporary bodily performance art', in E.J. Arnould and L.M. Scott (eds) *Advances in Consumer Research*, 26, Provo, UT: Association for Consumer Research.
Mick, D.G. (1986) 'Consumer research and semiotics: exploring the morphology of signs, symbols and significance', *Journal of Consumer Research* 13: 196–213.
——(1997) 'Semiotics in marketing and consumer research: balderdash, verity, pleas', in S. Brown and D. Turley (eds) *Postcards from the Edge of Consumer Research*, London: Routledge.
Mikkonen, I., Moisander, J. and Firat, A.F. (2011) 'Cynical identity project as consumer resistance – the Scrooge as a social critic?' *Consumption Markets & Culture* 11: 99–116.
Miller, D. (2007) 'Forward', in E. Cardenas and E. Gorman (eds) *The Hummer: Myths and Consumer Culture*, Lanham, MD: Lexington Books.

Muñiz, A. and O'Guinn, T.C. (2000) 'Brand communities', *Journal of Consumer Research* 27: 412–432.
Muñiz, A. and Schau, H. (2005) 'Religiosity in the abandoned Apple Newton brand community', *Journal of Consumer Research* 31: 737–747.
Nöth, W. (1988) 'The language of commodities: groundwork for a semiotics of consumer goods', *International Journal of Research in Marketing* 4: 173–186.
Peñaloza, L. (1998) 'Just doing it: a visual ethnographic study of spectacular consumption behavior at Nike Town', *Consumption Markets & Culture* 2: 337–400.
Prahalad, C.K. and Ramaswamy, V. (2000) 'Co-opting customer competence', *Harvard Business Review* 78: 79–87.
Putoni, S., Schroeder, J.E. and Ritson, M. (2010), 'Meaning matters: polysemy in advertising', *Journal of Advertising* 39: 51–64.
Reynolds, T.J. and Gutman, J. (1984) 'Advertising is image management', *Journal of Advertising Research* 24: 27–37.
Richards, T. (1990) *The Commodity Culture of Victorian England: Advertising and Spectacle 1851–1914*, Stanford: Stanford University Press.
Schau, H.J. and Gilly, M.G. (2003) 'We are what we post? Self-presentation in personal web space', *Journal of Consumer Research* 30: 385–404.
Schroeder, J.E. (1992) 'Materialism and modern art', in F. Rudmin and M. Richins (eds) *Meaning, Measure, and Morality of Materialism*, Provo, UT: Association for Consumer Research.
——(1998) 'Consuming representation: a visual approach to consumer research', in B.B. Stern (ed.) *Representing Consumers: Voices, Views and Visions*, New York: Routledge, 193–230.
——(2000) 'Édouard Manet, Calvin Klein and the strategic use of scandal', in S. Brown and A. Patterson (eds.) *Imagining Marketing: Art, Aesthetics, and the Avant-Garde*, London: Routledge, 36–51.
——(2002) *Visual Consumption*, London and New York: Routledge.
——(2003) 'Building brands: architectural expression in the electronic age', in L. Scott and R. Batra (eds) *Persuasive Imagery: A Consumer Response Perspective*, Mahwah, NJ: Lawrence Erlbaum, 349–382.
——(2004) 'Visual consumption in the image economy', in K. Ekström and H. Brembeck (eds) *Elusive Consumption*, Oxford: Berg.
——(2005) 'The artist and the brand', *European Journal of Marketing* 39: 1291–1305.
——(2006a) 'Aesthetics awry: The Painter of Light™ and the commodification of artistic values', *Consumption Markets & Culture* 9: 87–99.
——(2006b) 'Critical visual analysis', in R. Belk (ed.) *Handbook of Qualitative Research Methods in Marketing*, Aldershot, UK: Edward Elgar, 303–321.
——(2006c) 'Introduction to the Special Issue on Aesthetics, Images and Vision', *Marketing Theory* 6: 5–10.
——(2008) 'Visual analysis of images in brand culture', in E. McQuarrie and B.J. Phillips (eds) *Go Figure: New Directions in Advertising Rhetoric*, Armonk, NY: M.E. Sharpe, 277–296.
——(2009) 'The cultural codes of branding', *Marketing Theory* 9: 123–126.
——(2010) 'The artist in brand culture', in D. O'Reilly and F. Kerrigan (eds) *Marketing the Arts: A Fresh Approach*, London: Routledge, 18–30.
——(2011) 'Value creation and the visual consumer', in K. Ekström and K. Glans (eds) *Beyond the Consumption Bubble*, London: Routledge, 137–148.
——(2012) 'Style and strategy: snapshot aesthetics in brand culture', in C. McLean, P. Quattrone, F.R. Puyou and N. Thrift (eds) *Imagining Organisations*, London: Routledge, 129–151.
Schroeder, J.E. and Borgerson, J.L. (1998) 'Marketing images of gender: a visual analysis', *Consumption Markets & Culture* 2: 161–202.
Schroeder, J.E. and Borgerson, J.L. (2002) 'Innovations and information technology: insights into consumer culture from Italian Renaissance art', *Consumption Markets & Culture* 5: 153–169.
Schroeder, J.E. and Borgerson, J.L. (2005) 'An ethics of representation for international marketing communication', *International Marketing Review* 22: 578–600.
Schroeder, J.E. and Salzer-Mörling, M. (2006) 'Introduction: the cultural codes of branding', in J.E. Schroeder and M. Salzer-Mörling (eds) *Brand Culture*, London: Routledge, 1–12.
Schroeder, J.E. and Zwick, D. (2004) 'Mirrors of masculinity: representation and identity in advertising images', *Consumption Markets & Culture* 7: 21–52.
Scott, L.M. (1994a) 'Images in advertising: the need for a theory of visual rhetoric', *Journal of Consumer Research* 21: 252–273.
Scott, L.M. (1994b) 'The bridge from text to mind: adapting reader-response theory to consumer research', *Journal of Consumer Research* 21: 461–480.

Shankar, A., Elliott, R. and Fitchett, J. (2009) 'Consumption, identity and narratives of socialization', *Marketing Theory* 9: 75–94.

Sherry Jr., J.F. (1998) 'The soul of the company store: Nike Town Chicago and the emplaced brandscape', in J.F. Sherry Jr. (ed.) *Servicescapes*, Chicago, IL: NTC Business Books.

Simmel, G. (1971 [1903]) 'The metropolis and mental life', reprinted in D. Levine (1971) *On Individuality and Social Form*, Chicago: University of Chicago Press.

——(1978 [1900]) *The Philosophy of Money*, trans. T. Bottomore and D. Frisby, London: Routledge.

Solomon, M.R. (1988) 'Building up and breaking down: the impact of cultural sorting on symbolic consumption', in J. Sheth and E.C. Hirschman (eds) *Research in Consumer Behavior*, Greenwich, CT: JAI Press.

Stern, B.B. (1989) 'Literary criticism and consumer research: overview and illustrative analysis', *Journal of Consumer Research* 16: 322–334.

——(1991) 'Advertising to the "Other" culture: women's use of language and language's use of women', in B.G. Englis and D. Frederick Baker (eds) *Advertising and Consumer Psychology: Cross-Cultural Advertising*, Hillside, NJ: Lawrence-Erlbaum Publishers.

Stern, B., Zinkhan, G.M. and Jaju, A. (2001) 'Marketing images: construct definition, measurement issues, and theory development', *Marketing Theory* 1: 201–224.

Strati, A. (1996) 'Organizations viewed through the lens of aesthetics', *Organization* 3: 209–218.

Süerdem, A. (1994) 'Social de(re)construction of mass culture: making (non)sense of consumer behavior', *International Journal of Research in Marketing* 11: 423–444.

Tharp, M. and Scott, L.M. (1990) 'The role of marketing processes in creating cultural meaning', *Journal of Macromarketing* 10: 47–60.

Thompson, C.J. (2004) 'Marketplace mythology and discourses of power', *Journal of Consumer Research* 31: 162–175.

Thompson, C. and Arsel, Z. (2004) 'The Starbucks brandscape and consumers' (anticorporate) experiences of glocalization', *Journal of Consumer Research* 31: 631–642.

Thompson, C.J. and Haytko, D.L. (1997) 'Speaking of fashion: consumers' uses of fashion discourses and the appropriation of countervailing cultural meanings', *Journal of Consumer Research* 24: 15–42.

Thompson, C.J. and Hirschman, E.C. (1995) 'Understanding the socialized body: a poststructuralist analysis of consumers' self-conceptions, body images, and self-care products', *Journal of Consumer Research* 22: 139–153.

Thompson, C.J., Locander, W.B. and Polio, H.R. (1990) 'The lived meaning of free choice: an existential-phenomenological description of everyday consumer experiences of contemporary married women', *Journal of Consumer Research* 17: 346–361.

Townsend, D. (1997) *An Introduction to Aesthetics*, Oxford: Blackwell.

Turkle, S. (1995) *Life on the Screen: Identity in the Age of the Internet*, New York: Simon and Schuster.

Vargo, S.L. and Lusch, R.F. (2004) 'Evolving to a new dominant logic for marketing', *Journal of Marketing* 68: 1–17.

Venkatesh, A. (1992) 'Postmodernism, consumer culture and the society of the spectacle', in J.F. Sherry and B. Sternthal (eds) *Advances in Consumer Research*, 19, Provo, UT: Association for Consumer Research.

Venkatesh, A. and Meamber, L.A. (2006) 'Arts and aesthetics: marketing and cultural production', *Marketing Theory* 6: 11–39.

Venkatesh, A. and Meamber, L.A. (2008) 'The aesthetics of consumption and the consumer as an aesthetic subject', *Consumption Markets & Culture* 11: 45–70.

Venkatesh, A., Firat, F. and Meamber, L. (1997) 'Cyberspace the next marketing frontier (?): questions and issues', in Stephen Brown (ed.) *Consumer Research: Postcards from the Edge*, New York: Routledge.

Venkatesh, A., Peñaloza, L. and Firat, A.F. (2006) 'The market as a sign and the logic of the market', in R. Lusch and S. Vargo (eds) *The Service-Dominant Logic of Marketing*, New York: M.E. Sharpe.

Wallendorf, M. and Arnould, E.J. (1988) '"My favorite things": a cross-cultural inquiry into object attachment, possessiveness, and social linkage', *Journal of Consumer Research* 14: 531–547.

Warren, S. (2008) 'Empirical challenges in organizational aesthetics research: towards a sensual methodology', *Organization Studies* 19: 559–580.

White, D.A. (1996) 'It's working beautifully! Philosophical reflections on aesthetics and organization theory', *Organization* 3: 195–208.

Wikström, S. (1996) 'The consumer as co-producer', *European Journal of Marketing* 30: 6–19.

Witkowski, T.H. (1996) 'Farmers brand selling as a subject in American genre painting, 1835–1868', *Journal of Macromarketing* 17: 84–101.

——(2004) 'Re-gendering consumer agency in mid-nineteenth-century America: a visual understanding', *Consumption Markets & Culture* 7: 261–283.
——(2010) 'A brief history of frugality discourses in the United States', *Consumption Markets & Culture* 13: 235–238.
Zaltman, G. (2003) *How Customers Think*, Boston: Harvard Business School Press.
Zwick, D., Bonsu, S.K. and Darmody, A. (2008) 'Putting consumers to work: "co-creation" and new marketing govern-mentality', *Journal of Consumer Culture* 8: 163–196.

7
Portraiture and the construction of 'charismatic leadership'

Beatriz Acevedo

The leader rests on his luxurious chair, his piercing eyes looking at the viewer. He is a mature, strong man; his experience and wisdom impress the viewer who is captured by his inquisitive gaze. In this portrait, he looks severe, and his competitors know it: he is not a man to play with. His clothes are carefully chosen, exquisite garments of Italian craft. Holding an item of the latest technology, one can see his command on the latest technology and his high level of education. Indeed, the elements of this portrait show a strong man, a charismatic leader able to lead us all to that hopeful future.

This description can be applied to a contemporary picture of a multinational CEO posing in his office; and it may be indeed the case of this portrait of Pope Innocent X, painted by Spanish painter Diego Velázquez in 1650. At the time, Innocent X was the equivalent of the CEO of, perhaps, one of the first global corporations in the competitive market of faith and religion. In spite of the historical distance, similar elements in the depiction of leadership can be found in the contemporary portraits of business leaders: a particular pose of the body, showing strength and confidence; the latest brand of computers placed in office settings of alluring interior design in a composition carefully organized to have a desired effect. In both cases, the intention of the image is clear: to reveal the power and charisma of the individual portrayed.

As argued by Guthey and Jackson, images of contemporary leaders like CEOs are 'produced and disseminated by commercial organizations, and many seek to convey a visual impression of commercial organizations themselves' (2005: 1057). Even though the media is very different to the oil and canvas of the portrait of the Pope, the main elements in the depiction of power seem to remain throughout the centuries. Examining portraits as a particular kind of 'text' can provide some interesting insights regarding the understanding of 'leadership' and its representation through images.

During the history of Western art, the link between portraits and status or power has been widely documented. Commissioned portraits have been traditionally the privilege of certain groups and individuals occupying positions of authority (West 2004). The possibility of understanding portraits as a tool for what Weber has called the 'routinization of charisma' offers an interesting avenue to link portraits and the field of leadership studies. The term 'charisma' applies to 'a certain quality of an individual personality by virtue of which he is set apart from ordinary men and treated as endowed with supernatural, superhuman, or at least specific powers or qualities' (Weber 1968: 48). This chapter aims at presenting some elements of the analysis of portraiture as a form of art that can illuminate the understanding of leadership in contemporary organizational studies. It follows the growing field of organizational aesthetics (Strati 1999; Linstead and Höpfl 2000); vision in organizational studies (Warren 2002; Acevedo and Warren 2012) and some ideas of aesthetic leadership (Taylor and Hansen 2005).

The questions inspiring this chapter include:

- How can portraiture reveal aspects of leadership in Western cultures?
- Which notions of leadership are highlighted through portraits in contemporary culture?
- What are the contributions of art history in the analysis of images of leadership?

In order to address these questions, this chapter presents a brief summary of how portraiture can be an instrument for what has been called the 'routinization of charisma' and how Western leaders throughout history have used portraits and images as a way of extending, disseminating and asserting their power. The second part sets out an analytical framework to understand images drawing upon Guthey and Jackson's (2005, 2008) work on CEO portraits, and including some aspects from art history that can expand the way in which images of leaders can be understood. The third part of the chapter concerns the main aspects of a critical approach to the images in relation to a visual genealogy, which allows the viewer to reveal the mechanisms of power and image underlying the presentation of images in certain contexts and historical periods. Some examples comparing the portrait of Pope Innocent X by Diego Velázquez and some contemporary photographs of business leaders will be presented in order to illustrate this approach. Finally, the chapter will offer some conclusions and further suggestions on the intersections between art history frameworks to understand the construction of particular forms of leadership.

Portraits of power

A portrait is a work of art that represents the features or likeness of a unique individual. As a work of art, a portrait is also influenced by certain aesthetic conventions and the social expectations of a particular time and place (West 2004: 22). When analysing a portrait, it is important to take into account not only the imagination of the artist, the technique involved and the modality, but also the perceived social role of the sitter and the qualities emphasized in the portrait according to convention, status, hierarchy and political intent. In Western cultures, images of rulers have become a powerful tool for political domination. This tradition was inaugurated by Alexander the Great, as a way of being present in every corner of his vast empire:

> Alexander's face was the most influential in history. His artists constructed a multifaceted image of the ruler, his dealing with friend and foe, his place in history, and his relationship with the divine that was unprecedented in its richness and diversity. They inaugurated not only the multiple commemoration of the myriad 'worthies' of the Hellenistic world and Rome, but the genres of charismatic ruler portraiture and royal narrative in the West.
>
> *(Stewart 1993: 55)*

Alexander's portraits represent a concrete testimony to his power, since they serve both to establish the identity of the sovereign and to consolidate that authority by making his appearance omnipresent. It can be said also that this use of portraits represents a new means of depicting and transmitting ideas about 'charisma' and 'power' (Stewart 1993). Portraiture had a particular social meaning, normally conveying a number of symbols, meanings and moral messages in the depiction of sitters and their institutional position. As a power tool, portraiture had been the exclusive privilege of those who held a prominent position in society, the court or the Church, normally depicting the figure's social status or institutional worth (Bürger 2007). When analysing portraits, it is important to consider both the 'body' of the sitter, but also his 'status' as part of an institutional regime. As Mariana Jenkins has stated in her groundbreaking work on portraiture: '[its] primary purpose is not the portrayal of an individual as such, but the evocation through his (sic) image of those abstract principles for which he (sic) stands' (1947: 1).

Portraits act as signifiers of the status of the individuals and institutions represented. They convey certain symbols of power and status, expressed through gestures, dress, props, the background, etc., thus they serve a clear political and social function. The use of certain symbols also corresponds to particular historical periods, where the meanings can be easily understood. For instance, in order to understand the portrait of Innocent X, we need to consider the wider socio-political context dominated by the instructions of the Catholic Church who held a tight grip on the way in which images should be constructed. The [Trento] Council's *Decree on the Invocation, Veneration, and Relics of Saints, and on Sacred Images* was held as the main strategy against the competition posed by Protestants, thus, visual images were tools for 'instructing the mind and elevating the spirit' and the act of artistic creation was interpreted almost as a form of religious worship (Véliz 2002: 11–12). Such deification is transferred to the figure of the rulers – both monarchs associated with the Catholic Church or high officers in Rome – as part of a complex political game. For example, King Philip IV, the most powerful monarch of the time, and a close associate of Pope Innocent X, used portraiture as a way of exerting his authority in the recently colonized New World. Such was the power of his image that the elites of the viceroyalty of Peru took oaths of loyalty and adoration for the king in a highly charged ceremony where a portrait of the king, framed in gold and 'seated' on a throne beneath a canopy, presided over the ritual (Feros 2002). Nowadays, British embassies and some offices of the Commonwealth exhibit the portrait of Queen Elizabeth II as a powerful symbol of their allegiance to the monarch.

The use of portraits for political purposes is widely exemplified by the use of visual imagery produced by the Habsburg dynasty in Europe (Wheatcroft 1996). Emperor Maximilian continued the Hellenistic tradition of Alexander the Great, by commissioning artists such as Albrecht Dürer for his 'marketing' campaign (Silver 2008). Applying early techniques of mass production through woodcuts, the 'image' of the leader was available for popular consumption. In these portraits, Maximilian's distinctive features were normally fused with the attributes of saintly or revered figures, thus linking him as an individual with an ideal type (Silver 2008: 23). For Maximilian and the lineage of the Habsburgs, imperial publicity through paintings, woodcuts and poems became a '*raison d'être*': they provided the general public presentation of the emperor and the routinization of his charisma, while simultaneously being aimed at gaining popular support for their policies. Charles V, King of Spain, had in Titian one of his most important allies in his political agenda. Titian distanced his portraits from Dürer's depiction of the Emperor as a Christian knight; instead, he portrayed Charles V as a Majestic, Universal Emperor and Crusader, but also as a Prince of Peace (Wheatcroft 1996: 104).

Apart from the political purposes of portraiture illustrated above, its prevalence in Western culture can be explained by the fact that this type of art tends to flourish in regimes that grant privilege to the notion of the individual over that of the collective (West 2004: 17). The Renaissance in Western Europe was a period of increased self-consciousness, in which concepts of individual identity began to be represented and verbalized (Greenblatt 1984). The focus on the individual gained prominence during the seventeenth and eighteenth centuries; consequently, portraiture flourished during that period both as an artistic practice and as a cultural commodity.

The importance of portraiture in depicting authority and status continued well into the eighteenth century and the first part of the nineteenth century. During this period, the visual conventions and language may have varied. For instance, the eighteenth-century English artist Sir Joshua Reynolds used to depict his sitters in the poses of ancient sculpture following the old masters, adding grandeur and 'charisma' to the people represented (Allard and Rosenblum 2007). By using certain gestures and timeless costumes, these paintings addressed 'mythical' characteristics associated with heroes and charismatic leaders throughout history.

With changes in social and economic contexts, merchants, traders and bankers began to commission portraits as a celebration of their growing status and power, and portraits became an important instrument in the formation of the bourgeois identity (West 2004). In fact, each historical period favours certain ways of characterizing and depicting leadership and status. From the theatrical poses of Van Dyck, for example, the eighteenth-century rulers in Britain favoured the commission of portraits in domestic settings and displaying the family's attributes, while providing a moral example (Schama 1988).

This variety in the possibilities of portraiture may have influenced artists in their choices of representing their own realities. By the nineteenth century, artists were approaching portraits as a means of their own expression, rather than of the representation of an exclusive group of people. Impressionism used portraits for their experiments into light, as well as other explorations regarding form and volume. Cézanne painted his wife as a way of deconstructing the figure towards a more essential form; Matisse approached portraits in his experiments of explosive colour; and Picasso used the human figure to establish his cubist language (Allard and Rosenblum 2007). Although portraiture was somehow neglected in favour of abstract expressions during the first half of the twentieth century, images were widely used to depict authority and charisma. For instance, the Fascist and Nazi regimes used aesthetics extensively in their rise to power (Spotts 2003). Falasca-Zamponi (1997) emphasizes the symbolic aspects of the Fascist regime concerning the 'sacralization' of politics, and the use of visual images to reinforce its message. In this regard, Walter Benjamin argued that, in the age of mechanical reproduction, 'the total function of art is reversed. Instead of being based on ritual, it begins to be based on another practice [-] politics' (1973: 224).

As well as the political aspects of portraits, it is important to consider the intention of the portrait and how the composition will be read by certain audiences. For instance, the portrait of Innocent X emphasized the luxurious clothes appropriate to his status, whereas a portrait of a modern CEO may stress certain colours or settings, depending on the intention: thus, a modern office with a view to a modern capital of the world may emphasize the institution's global power; while a frontal pose may highlight the 'authenticity' of the leader's profile. As argued by Guthey and Jackson 'top executive portraits now appear so commonplace that they have become hidden in plain sight, with the result that scholars of management, organization and leadership have not explored the issues they raise in any depth' (2005: 1058). They suggest looking at visions of leadership, not as metaphors, but as actual images, such as portraits, as a source for enquiry about leadership in contemporary organizations.

Portraits and the routinization of charisma

Weber, in his seminal study of sources of authority, identified 'charisma' as a way of exercising power, alongside tradition and legal rational frameworks. The importance of this notion in defining leadership is matched also with the wide range of views held about how charisma should be defined and from where it originates (Ladkin 2006: 166). For Yukl, traits and behaviours explain how a charismatic leader influences the attitudes and behaviour of followers by, among others:

> articulating an appealing vision, using strong, expressive forms of communication when articulating the vision, taking personal risks and making self-sacrifices to attain the vision, communicating high expectations, managing follower impressions of the leader, building identification with the group of organization, and empowering followers.
>
> *(2002: 244)*

In modern leadership studies, the concept of charisma continues to be a subject for analysis, although Weber's view has been revised and adapted to contemporary organizational and social settings (Bryman 1992; Conger and Kanungo 1988). As summarized by Ladkin (2006), charisma remains a key notion in leadership studies. Further, the literature on charismatic leadership identifies self-image and self-presentation as two key dispositional elements in the construction of leadership (Sosik *et al.* 2002). *Self-image* is the articulation of traits and characteristics perceived in association to the self. These traits can be expressed in relation to others by *self-presentation* as a set of ways and means to monitor and control expressive behaviour – self-monitoring – and employ behavioural strategies to regulate one's identity – also known as impression management (Schlenker 1985). The use of certain clothes, words, institutional symbols and other means can contribute to the construction of the leader's identity. Portraits, thus, are the ideal place to show these elements aimed at impressing a particular audience: followers, competitors, customers or stakeholders. These strategies help create a charismatic relationship between the leader and follower (e.g. attributions of charisma) by influencing dispositional, perceptual and motivational aspects of the follower/audience (Sosik *et al.* 2002: 221).

The stress on the individual aspects of leadership, as popularized by portraiture in Western art, evidences the accepted notion of leadership as an individual trait (Taylor 1989; Greenblatt 1984; Grint 2007). Although the notion of charisma has been 'watered down' to cohere with contemporary renderings (Beyer 1999) and it is possible to argue that charismatic leadership is normally associated with the notion of the 'great man', Ladkin (2006) contests this individual approach to leadership by noting that the emphasis on a psychological paradigm for researching charisma (as opposed to a sociological one) has resulted in an overemphasis on individual traits of 'the leader' without sufficiently accounting for the impact of context on this phenomenon. She suggests instead considering charismatic leadership as a 'relational encounter', in which contextual factors are acknowledged.

A contrasting view on traditional views on leadership is advanced by Michel Foucault in his consideration of power, not as the privilege of a single individual or group, but as a form of energy omnipresent in society: '[it] is the moving substrate of force relations, which by virtue of their inequality constantly engender states of power' (1978: 93). Foucault's main question is to explore how power is exercised through complex *dispositifs*. Following this view, it would be possible to consider portraiture a 'dispositif of power' for the visual representation of charisma and status. Indeed, Weber acknowledged that charisma is only possible when it is 'perceived' as such by followers. Following Foucault's views, it is possible to understand portraits, such as those of Alexander, as a new 'technology of power serving as testimony of an overwhelming power' (Stewart 1993: 60).

This brief review of art scholarship and portraiture evidences the strong relationship between portraiture and the 'routinization of charisma', and how this association has varied across historical periods. For instance, it is interesting to note that leadership is normally depicted in the form of individuals' adopting certain poses or visual configurations. This also may be understood within the conceptualization of leadership as charisma, focused on the characteristics of 'the great man'. In leadership studies, the great man theory holds that legitimacy resides in the greatness of the man, in his being great (Harter 2008: 70). A similar understanding of leadership seems to have been adopted by classic portraiture concerning the depiction of individuals with certain status or charisma.

In the context of leadership studies, specifically, attention has shifted from the personal characteristics of leaders (trait theory) towards more relational aspects of leadership and its development (Marturano and Gosling 2008). Bryman (2004) identifies two standing aspects in the evolution of leadership research: first, the methodological diversity in leadership studies and, second, a greater optimism regarding the potentialities of leadership as a practice. He mentions the increasing use of qualitative methods and the bridging of leadership studies with other disciplines, such as organizational symbolism and cultural studies (Turner 1990). From the work by Moore and Beck (1984) in their research into metaphorical imagery among bank managers towards the rising interest in the use of storytelling (Cuno 2005) and dramaturgy in leadership development (Gardner and Avolio 1998), as well as the increasing number of articles stressing the potentialities of an aesthetic approach in both developing leadership and exploring its meaning (Bligh and Schyns 2007), the theoretical and methodological landscape seems ripe for exploring newer and more daring connections between leadership and other areas such as art and painting.

In recent years, scholars and researchers have suggested enhancing the understanding of leadership by including an aesthetic approach (Hansen *et al.* 2007) considering the sensorial aspects of the exercise of leadership. In particular, Ropo and Parviainen (2001) suggest that leadership work is largely a matter of embodied performance aimed at rendering visible traits of credibility and trustworthiness. Some others have suggested concentrating on the formation of a 'vision' as a key trait for ideological and charismatic leadership (Mumford *et al.* 2007; Avolio and Gardner 1999). Topics such as 'the articulation of a clear vision', the leader as 'visionary', the 'clairvoyant' talents of a leader, etc. seem to confirm the 'visual turn' in organizational studies (Styhre 2010). On the other hand, Guthey and Jackson (2008) challenge the metaphorical aspects of vision as the 'picture in our heads', inviting us to 'look at the pictures in front of our eyes as well'. The following section considers some elements from art history in the interpretation of portraits.

Analysing portraits: a framework

Taking into account the generous tradition of portraiture in Western art, it is possible to say that art history frameworks may contribute to the study of social and organizational phenomena such as leadership. Guthey and Jackson, drew upon Baxandall's (1986, 1988) pioneering work of art history and interpretation. Baxandall said that

> if we wish to explain pictures, in the sense of expounding them in terms of their historical causes, what we actually explain seems likely to be not the unmediated picture but the picture as considered under a partially interpretative description.
>
> *(1986: 11)*

It is nevertheless possible to suggest a framework for interpreting portraits following the framework proposed by Guthey and Jackson (2008) in their analysis of CEOs' portraits. For them, portraits are 'complex forms of visual communication, interaction, and conflict over the representation of individual leaders and business leadership writ large'. In their view, images of leaders are representational conventions aiming to produce meaning. Indeed, 'photograph is already in itself a holistic reading of reality … it isolates fragments of surrounding reality and reproduces them with their particular visual language' (Strati 1997: 315). Guthey and Jackson (2008) argue that visual images function as complex sites of social struggle over meaning and that CEO portraits should be understood as complex forms of visual communication, interaction and conflict over the representation of individual leaders and business leadership at large. Further, they say that a focus on visual images also makes clear that all approaches to image involve interpretation, and that no interpretation enjoys a monopoly of meaning. Quoting Rosenblum (1978), they add that not only the content of visual images, but also their aesthetic and stylistic aspect can be understood productively as forms of social process and interaction.

In order to reveal the connections of how images of leadership are produced, as well as how their meaning is socially constructed within a particular context of power configuration, it is important to enquire about the 'visual genealogy' of such images (Schroeder 2002). In other words, a visual genealogy aims at revealing how certain images of leadership are constructed as a form of exercising power following certain aesthetic conventions in particular historical periods. Guthey and Jackson investigate these conventions through the analytical categories of frame, gaze and period eye, expounding a most specific way of addressing this visual genealogy. As they suggest:

> The concept of frame foregrounds the multiple ways in which images can be viewed. The concept of gaze highlights the interaction of multiple viewing subjects within any given image. The notion of period eye places limits on the potential meanings these active subjects can produce by specifying the context-bound habits, skills, and predispositions that influence image production and consumption.
>
> *(2008: 85)*

In their analysis, the category of *frame* refers to an 'objective' representation. In this case, it concerns the depiction of Innocent X: the pictorial techniques, the use of colours, textures and patterns, and the configuration of certain elements on the canvas surface. Further, this category should consider the technical aspects present in the productive process of the painting (Benjamin 1973).

Second, the *gaze* refers to a socially constructed event mediated by the intersection of gazes between the viewer and the painting. This *gaze* is produced by the exchange of meanings, located in a language that 'speaks' to the different parts. For Guthey and Jackson, *gazes* subjectify: the concept emphasizes the active looking that must occur in and around an image to produce meaning. Such an exchange of meanings – the unveiling of significances, resonances and emotions – is determined by certain 'ways of seeing' (Berger 1972).

Finally, the construction of meaning is related to what Baxandall (1988) has called the 'period eye', referring to some of the mental equipment through which a person orders his/her visual experience. The equipment is 'variable and culturally relative, in the sense of being determined by the society which has influenced his experience'. Consequently, the painter responds to his/her public's visual capacity. Baxandall develops the theme: '[w]hatever [the artist's] own specialized professional skills, he is himself a member of the society he works for and shares its visual experience and habit' (1988: 40). The artist does not act in isolation; his/her actions respond to influences and forces, questions and demands, themselves in turn determined by a wider configuration of power relationships. Baxandall also suggests that the artist actually responds to a particular market or *truc*, in which certain institutions, authorities or instances validate or acknowledge the artist's work. For some painters, it may be their patrons; for others, the art market or the art critic.

In addition to Guthey and Jackson's approach to the 'period eye', it is important to consider how the visual experience is actually regulated by power mechanisms. Rose (2007: xv) reminds us that there is no such thing as an 'innocent picture'; thus, the interpretation of visual images must address questions of cultural meaning and power. In other words, the category of 'period eye' must also include the deciphering of a 'visual genealogy', aimed at revealing the cultural significance, social contexts and power relationships in which portraits are embedded.

In summarizing, Guthey and Jackson's categories for the analysis of portraits may be represented as in Table 7.1.

Using this framework, Acevedo (2011) advances a comparison between two paintings of Pope Innocent X as depicted by Diego Velázquez in 1650 and Francis Bacon in 1950. Using this example as a basis, the next section will illustrate how this framework can be used to understand the construction of charismatic leadership in different historical periods.

Analysing Velázquez's portrait of Pope Innocent X

Frame: In 1649, Velázquez began painting the portrait of Innocent X, soon after the former had arrived in Rome as part of the diplomatic mission sent by King Philip IV of Spain. Although Innocent X was in his sixty-seventh year when he sat for Velázquez, he really does not show such an advanced age in the painting. In the portrait, Innocent X is not a benevolent leader; rather, he looks more like a watchful man, very efficient in the conduct of his office (Brown 1986: 199). His prominent head crowned by the red cap (*camauro*) denotes intelligence and authority; his hands appear relaxed under the *manteletta* and are covered in exquisitely shimmering lace. On one of his hands, the commanding ring of authority gleams in sole splendour; in the other hand, the Pope holds a folded piece of paper, a document, a token of the endemic bureaucracy of which the Pope is the absolute Head. The document is a prayer made by the painter in petition regarding this portrait: '*Alla Santa di Nro. Sigre Inocencio Xo. per Diego de Silva Velázquez*

Table 7.1 Categories for the analysis of portraits

Category of analysis	Definition	Elements
Frame	Objective description, includes the composition and the technical devices used by the artist	The Figure (as in Deleuze's analysis) and the body Technical aspects
Gaze	Subjective construction of meaning, created by the intersection of an 'intention' (personal or dictated by the market) and the perception of the audience (visual language and cultural equipment to decipher meanings)	Intention Perception
Period Eye	Wider consideration in the artistic production, including power relationships linked to particular historical conditions, and the artistic and pictorial languages available for the audience and the artists	Visual genealogy Power relationships Market/*truc*

de la Camera de S. Mta. Catt.co.' The Pope has just read it and gazes inquisitively at the writer of the missive.

The pose of the sitter follows the convention in portraiture, given definitive form in Raphael's *Portrait of Julius II* and used thereafter by many artists. Here, Velázquez chose strong, symbolic colours to emphasize the importance of his sitter: red and white, with some touches of gold on the papal throne, thus compose the tonality of the picture. He expanded this simple combination into infinite tones and textures, from the shiny crimson of the *manteletta* to the grave maroon of the cap, thence the impressionist brushstrokes of the creamy *rochetta* (Brown 1986). This notwithstanding, the figure is not adorned by these devices; on the contrary, the Pope appears more human in virtue of the emphasis given by the artist on his human body. Another important element concerns the technical devices available to the painter. The techniques used in Velázquez's portrait derive from his apprenticeship and artisan practice, including drawing skills, rapid sketches and, as previously mentioned, the classical conventions in the art of portraiture established by Raphael.

It is important to note that, in categorizing the 'frame', one must include most of the elements of the composition, the technique and the descriptive aspects of the image. In contemporary portraits favouring photography, Rose (2007: 13) recommends including three modalities that can contribute to a critical understanding of images: technological, compositional and social. For instance, the use of technology dictates the way in which images can be manipulated. A good example is Cecil Beaton's portraits of the young Queen Elizabeth, who took some kilos off her plump figure, while emphasizing the colour of her eyes and luscious lips appropriate of a fairy princess.

Constructing visual meaning: The intention of the portrait was to flatter the Pope's attributes, since Velázquez indeed was part of a diplomatic mission. The Pope's portrait shared a common language of symbols and imagery with the portraits of King Philip IV also executed by Velázquez. These portraits present an image of the leadership that is carefully crafted, serving specific purposes.

As a painter in a Catholic-centred world, Velázquez was aware of the conventions and symbols attached to each of the icons or saints, by highlighting their virtues or their martyrdom, including certain symbols (flowers, animals, books, utensils or props) that were easily understood by a mostly illiterate audience. As argued by Baxandall: 'the public mind was not a blank tablet on which the painters' representations of a story or a person could impress themselves; it was an active institution of interior visualization with which every painter had to get along' (1988: 43).

In particular, the seventeenth century marks a period of transition from a 'God-centred' world towards a more 'humanistic' centrality, propelled by the Renaissance ideology in Europe – an early milestone towards modernity. In the Velázquez representation of the Pope, the virtues of the good pontiff are highlighted in the painting: the bodily humanity of the person is central and exerts its powerful influence through the exchange of glances contextualized within a series of conventions and pre-understandings. It is possible that Velázquez was influenced by the precepts formulated by Erasmus de Rotterdam concerning 'the good prince', thus the leader is (or should be) a human being invested with very special characteristics (Feros 2002). Curiously, the painter's skill was such that he actually captured the real character of the sitter: it is said that, when the Pope saw the finished portrait, he said that it was *troppo vero*, too truthful! (Manchip-White 1969).

For contemporary portraits, it is important to consider the relationship between sitters and artists. Guthey and Jackson (2005) question the 'authenticity' of CEO images, as portraits are commissioned and executed by publicity agencies or renowned photographers. They focus on the work of Per Morten Abrahamsen, a celebrated photographer and his work with CEOs and business leaders. For Guthey and Jackson: 'CEO portraits taken by recognised photographer/artists seek to associate both the executive and the corporation with this ideal artistic self and with his or her own cache of individual personality, authentic human presence and creative agency' (2005: 1068–1069).

Although not all CEO portraits are taken by such renowned artists, it is important to consider the process of negotiation and commission, between the sitter and the artist. It will be important to consider who takes part in the negotiations, what are the elements of the composition that are highlighted: the pose, the props, the intention; as well as the media and audience targeted by the portrait. Like traditional portraiture, the images convey a particular message to be deciphered or read by contemporary audiences. For instance, images of USA President Barack Obama as a pop-icon following conventions of advertising or Andy Warhol silk-screens are easily understood by certain audiences, and the intention is to create a certain impression in the public.

The period eye: Baxandall defines 'period eye' as the system of exchanges and understandings that facilitate the conveyance of a message. During the fifteenth and sixteenth centuries, the art of portraiture focused on the representation of rulers. Powerful leaders adopted certain poses and devices, intended to convey their authority and status (West 2004). The political requests linked to the art of portraiture and the personal demands of Philip IV and Innocent X can be seen as part of the bargain made by Velázquez. Further, as argued by Brown, Velázquez himself pursued a deeply personal ambition: to become a gentleman, a knight of one of the exclusive brotherhoods endorsed by the Catholic Church. In this endeavour, the journey to Rome and the support of the influential pontiff formed an invaluable opportunity for the painter.

In terms of a visual genealogy, it is important to acknowledge the configuration of power and knowledge, or in this case power and representation, and how the visual repertoire available for artists was conditioned by overarching powers linked to religion or tradition. As we mentioned before, Innocent X as Head of the Catholic Church was aware of the power of images. In the counter-strategy against the growing competition from the Protestants in the North of Europe, the Catholic Church had favoured images, visuality and icons. Consequently, Velázquez's painting was ruled by the institutional conventions, the traditions of religious portraiture and the intentions of portraiture in depicting status, authority and hierarchy. Although our contemporary perception considers artists as innovators or tradition breakers, at the time of Velázquez, painters were not more than artisans at the service of their masters. In considering this painting, the period eye is determined by three main factors: first, the regulated conventions of portraiture at this particular historical moment regulated by Catholic perceptions on art and painting. Second, there is an emerging paradigm in the understanding of leadership: from a leader invested by divine design, the new leader is a human being, thus his attributes are focused on his human body rather than on symbols of divinity. And, third, the *truc* or exchange is dictated not in terms of money but favours and alliances, since the portrait is part of the diplomatic mission in which the artist is a key player.

Similar elements need to be considered when analysing modern portraits: what are the conventions in portraiture of contemporary leaders? For instance, communication experts and marketers decide whether or not to produce pictures of politicians as caring 'family men' or as 'working-class fellows' depending on the intention, the audience and the market. In addition, visual languages vary depending on the media: social networks, newspapers or television appearances. In all of these decisions, we must not forget that there is a clear intentionality and power relationships selecting and discerning what exactly is available for the 'eye' to see and the mind to understand about leadership.

Synthesis and conclusions

This chapter shows how the manipulation of images as a way of constructing charismatic leadership is nothing new, yet their power in conveying status and power are still pervasive. Art history allows us to understand the context and power configurations through which certain representations of power and status are possible. In spite of the changes in visual language, available techniques and mediums of expressions, the depiction of leadership as an individual of charismatic features persists. This view is engraved and reproduced in current images of leaders, top managers and CEOs as instrumental heroes of the capitalistic system.

As mentioned before, portraits – throughout history – seem to emphasize the idea of charismatic leadership as an individual trait, invested in certain individuals – great men or women who can lead corporations, governments or communities to certain aims. However, this view neglects the fact that leaders are working within organizations and teams, and that their actions are part of a wider political and cultural environment. As argued by Grint (2007: 232) this individualistic approach dismisses the possibility of learning to lead as a 'social process' rather than an individual event. Portraits deploy a variety of conventions and exchanges that contribute to the routinization of charisma as an individual trait.

It is thus important to have appropriate tools to reveal the sometimes hidden meanings of portraits in their conveyance of leadership. In the example, the portrait of Innocent X by Velázquez deploys ecclesiastic and symbolic conventions through the use of the figure, the pose and the pictorial composition. Innocent X, as the Head of the Catholic Church, is depicted as an efficient and rational leader, which in contemporary terms resembles the characteristics of a successful CEO. However, his authority and leadership are limited by the boundaries of the organizational space they represent. The organization or the context is suggested yet the focus remains on the individual. As noted above, the situation of the sitter is dictated by wider conventions regarding the 'virtues' of the leader, shifting from a traditional (religious) leadership towards a charismatic type of leadership as underlined by the emphasis on the human body.

Second, this chapter alerts us to the intentionality and symbolic elements of portraits relevant to the understanding of contemporary leadership. As argued by Fisher and Fowler, the re-imagination of business leaders as 'heroes' clearly uses the symbols and significance of 'graphic or visual images and their roles in contemporary culture as a starting point for normative reflection on leadership in general, and business leadership in particular' (1995: 30). We must not forget that any image (as worthy of a thousand words) is charged with meanings and intentions. Misquoting (playfully) Baxandall's (1986) explanation about the influence of the Catholic Church in the regulation of images and paintings actually may reveal the business world's intentionality of using images in the reconfiguration of the identities of their leaders:

> Know that there were three reasons for the institution of images [in the mass media/advertising]. First, for the instruction of simple people ... Second, so that the mystery of [capital/capitalism] and the examples of the [CEOs] may be the more active in our memory through being presented daily to our eyes. Third, to excite feelings of devotion [consumption], these being aroused more effectively by things seen than by things heard.
>
> *(cf. p. 41)*

Third, this chapter offers a practical framework based on Baxandall's (1986) approach to art history and updated by Guthey and Jackson (2008). This framework is not exhaustive but it offers a comprehensive approach to the analysis of images, in particular, those in portraits. Moreover, in the context of contemporary discussions on visuality and leadership, this chapter invites the exploration of aesthetic expressions as a means of enquiry into organizational and social issues, such as the case of leadership. It stresses the potentialities of considering certain forms of artistic expressions, such as portraiture, as heuristic devices towards reaching an understanding of some of the processes through which leadership is socially constructed and the mechanisms that promote one or other idea of leadership in different historical periods.

The exploration of aesthetic products as a means of enquiring provides an interesting avenue for scholars of organization and leadership. In a world overpopulated with images of economic depression, financial crises and political scandals, we should question to what extent the focus on the figure of the leaders disregards crucial elements in the equation, such as the context, the organizational setting, the socio-political environment and the power relationships. In this chapter, the power of art is emphasized in the artists' quest to stimulate these types of questions on how we *see* leadership both as visual images and also as themes for further study and understanding.

Acknowledgement

This chapter is based on an article previously published in *Leadership*: 'The Screaming Pope: imagery and leadership in two paintings of Pope Innocent X'(Acevedo 2011).

References

Acevedo, B. (2011) 'The Screaming Pope: imagery and leadership in two paintings of Pope Innocent X', *Leadership* 7: 27–50.
Acevedo, B. and Warren S. (2012) 'Vision in organizational studies', *Culture and Organization* 18(4): 277–284.
Allard, S. and Rosenblum, R. (2007) *Citizens and Kings: Portraits in the Age of Revolution 1760–1830*, London: Royal Academy of Art.
Avolio, B.J. and Gardner, W. (1999) 'Perceptions of leader charisma and effectiveness: the effects of vision, content, delivery and organizational performance', *The Leadership Quarterly* 10: 345–373.
Baxandall, M. (1986) *Patterns of Intention: On the Historical Explanation of Pictures*, New Haven and London: Yale University Press.
——(1988) *Painting and Experience in Fifteenth-Century Italy*, Oxford: Oxford University Press.
Benjamin, W. (1973) 'The work of art in the age of mechanical reproduction', in *Illuminations*, edited and with Introduction by H. Arendt, trans. H. Zohn, New York: Schocken Books.
Berger, J. (1972) *Ways of Seeing*, London: A Pelican Original.
Beyer, J.M. (1999) 'Taming and promoting charisma to change organisations', *The Leadership Quarterly* 10(2): 307–331.
Bligh, M.C. and Schyns, B. (2007) 'Leading question: the romance lives on: contemporary issues surrounding the romance of leadership,' *Leadership* 3: 343–360.
Brown, J. (1986) *Velázquez: Painter and Courtier*, New Haven and London: Yale University Press.
Bryman, A. (1992) *Charisma and Leadership in Organizations*, London: Sage.
——(2004) 'Qualitative research on leadership: a critical but appreciative review', *The Leadership Quarterly* 15: 729–769.
Bürger, P. (2007) 'The portrait as a problem for modernist art', in *Francis Bacon: The Violence of Real*, edited by Armin Zweite in collaboration with Maria Müller, London: Thames and Hudson, 29–36.
Conger, J.A. and Kanungo, R.N. (1988) 'Behavioral dimensions of charismatic leadership', in J.A. Conger and R.N. Kanungo (eds) *Charismatic Leadership: The Elusive Factor in Organizational Effectiveness*, San Francisco, CA: Jossey-Bass.
Cuno, J. (2005) 'Telling stories: rhetoric and leadership, a case study,' *Leadership* 1(2): 205–213.
Falasca-Zamponi, S. (1997) *The Aesthetics of Power in Mussolini's Italy*, London: University of California Press, Ltd.
Feros, A. (2002) 'Sacred and terrifying gazes: languages and images of power in early modern Spain', in S. Stratton-Pruitt (ed.) *The Cambridge Companion to Velázquez*, Cambridge: Cambridge University Press, 68–86.

Fisher, D. and Fowler, S. (1995) 'Re-imagining moral leadership in business: image, identity and difference', *Business Ethics Quarterly* 5(1): 29–42.
Foucault, M. (1978) *The History of Sexuality*, Vol. 1, London: Penguin.
Gardner, W.L. and Avolio, B.J. (1998) 'The charismatic relationship: a dramaturgical perspective', *Academy of Management Review* 23: 32–58.
Greenblatt, S. (1984) *Renaissance Self-fashioning: From More to Shakespeare*, Chicago: University of Chicago Press.
Grint, K. (2007) 'Learning to lead: can Aristotle help us find the road to wisdom?' *Leadership* 3: 231–246.
Guthey, E. and Jackson, B. (2005) 'CEO portraits and the authenticity paradox', *Journal of Management Studies* 42(5): 1056–1082.
Guthey, E. and Jackson, B. (2008) 'Revisualizing images in leadership and organization studies', in D. Barry and Hansen, H. (eds) *The Sage Handbook of New Approaches in Management and Organization*, London: Sage, 84–92.
Hansen, H., Ropo, A. and Saure, E. (2007) 'Aesthetic leadership', *The Leadership Quarterly* 18: 544–560.
Harter, N. (2008) 'Great Man Theory', in Antonio Marturano and Jonathan Gosling (eds) *Key Concepts in Leadership Studies*, London: Routledge, 67–71.
Jenkins, M. (1947) *The State Portrait, Its Origins and Evolution*, New York: College Art Association in Conjunction with the Art Bulletin, No. 3: New York.
Ladkin, D. (2006) 'The enchantment of the charismatic leader: charisma reconsidered as aesthetic encounter', *Leadership* 2: 165–179.
Linstead, S. and Höpfl, H. (eds) (2000) *The Aesthetics of Organization*, Sage: London.
Manchip-White, J. (1969) *Diego Velázquez: Painter and Courtier*, Hamish Hamilton Ltd.: London.
Marturano, A. and Gosling, J. (eds) (2008) *Key Concepts in Leadership Studies*, London: Routledge.
Moore, L.F. and Beck, B.E.F. (1984) 'Leadership among bank managers: a structural comparison of behavioral responses and metaphorical imagery', in J.G. Hunt, D.M. Hosking, C.A. Schriesheim and R. Stewart (eds) *Leaders and Managers: International Perspectives on Managerial Behavior and Leadership*, New York: Pergamon.
Mumford, M., Espejo, J., Hunter, S., Bedell-Avers, K., Eubanks, D. and Connelly, S. (2007) 'The sources of leader violence: a comparison of ideological and non-ideological leaders', *The Leadership Quarterly* 18: 217–235.
Ropo, A. and Parviainen, J. (2001) 'Leadership and bodily knowledge in expert organizations: epistemological rethinking', *Scandinavian Journal of Management* 17: 1–18.
Rose, G. (2007) *Visual Methodologies: An Introduction to the Interpretation of Visual Methods*, London: Sage.
Rosenblum, B. (1978) 'Style as social process', *American Sociological Review*, June, 43: 422–438.
Schama, S. (1988) 'The domestication of Majesty: Royal Family Portraiture 1500–1850', in R.I. Rotberg and T.K. Rabb (eds) *Art and History: Images and Their Meaning*, Cambridge: Cambridge University Press, 155–184.
Schlenker, B.R. (1985) 'Identity and self-identification', in B.R. Schlenker (ed.) *The Self and Social Life*, New York: McGraw-Hill, 15–99.
Schroeder, J.E. (2002) *Visual Consumption*, New York: Routledge.
Silver, Larry (2008) *Marketing Maximilian: The Visual Ideology of a Holy Roman Emperor*, Princeton, NJ: Princeton University Press.
Sosik, J., Avolio, B. and Jung, D. (2002) 'Beneath the mask: examining the relationship of self-presentation attributes and impression management to charismatic leadership', *The Leadership Quarterly* 13(3): 217–242.
Spotts, F. (2003) *Hitler and the Power of Aesthetics*, New York: Overlook Press.
Stewart, A. (1993) *Faces of Power: Alexander's Image and Hellenistic Politics*, Berkeley: University of California Press.
Strati, A. (1997) 'Organizations as hypertext: a metaphor from visual cultures', *Studies in Cultures, Organizations and Societies* 3: 307–324.
——(1999) *Organization and Aesthetics*, London: Sage.
Styhre, A. (2010) *Visual Culture in Organizations: Theory and Cases*, Abingdon: Routledge.
Taylor, C. (1989) *Sources of the Self: The Making of Modern Identity*, Cambridge, MA: Cambridge.
Taylor, S.S. and Hansen, H. (2005) 'Finding form: looking at the field of organizational aesthetics', *Journal of Management Studies* 42: 1211–1231.
Turner, B.A. (ed.) (1990) *Organizational Symbolism*, Berlin: de Gruyter.

Véliz, Z. (2002) 'Becoming an artist in seventeenth-century Spain', in S. Stratton-Pruitt (ed.) *The Cambridge Companion to Velázquez*, Cambridge: Cambridge University Press, 11–29.

Warren, S. (2002) '"Show me how it feels to work here": using photography to research organizational aesthetics', *Theory and Politics in Organizations* 2: 224–245.

Weber, M. (1968) *On Charisma and Institution Building*, edited by S.N. Eisenstadt, Chicago: University of Chicago Press.

West, S. (2004) *Portraiture*, Oxford: Oxford University Press.

Wheatcroft, A. (1996) *The Habsburgs: Embodying Empire*, New York: Viking.

Yukl, G. (2002) *Leadership in Organizations*, Harlow: Prentice Hall (original from the University of Michigan).

8
The signs and semiotics of advertising

Norah Campbell

> I think we have higher aspirations for our clients, and are more passionate about what our clients can be, should be, should try to be than they are. We're trying to tell them … 'Hey, you can be more than just a pet food company. You can aspire to loving dogs rather than just feeding dogs'.
>
> *Agency Director at Chiat/Day*

> Advertising is the rattling of a stick inside a swill bucket.
>
> *George Orwell*

Introduction

Advertising, in its print and media forms, in its direct and ambient modes, in its contemporary and age-old instantiations, is the most readily recognized, ubiquitous and contentious symptom of organization. Advertising acts as the 'aesthetic ambassador' of the organization (Campbell 2012). It is the way through which anyone outside the organization mythologizes an imaginary inside. Think the words 'apple', 'axe' or 'Amazon' – chances are that the images these words conjure are not a common fruit, a household tool or a river, but silver smoothness, girls on a beach, or a black and orange dotcom sign. Advertising *envisions and organizes meaning* for the viewer, the organization and society at large. In this chapter, I leverage that double-sense of organization – both as a corporate entity and as a common practice. I try to make the point that advertising organizes meaning in the world in the most powerful and generic of ways, as well as being a symptom of the organization, that is, something that indicates the existence of the organization.

Providing a simple definition of advertising risks reducing its complexity, but it is important to say that a famous definition does exist, describing advertising as 'a paid, mediated form of communication from an identifiable source, designed to persuade the receiver to take some action, now or in the future' (Richards and Curran 2002; O'Barr 2008). This has traditionally helped us to understand some aspects of advertising that make it different from other messages, though it could be argued that some messages have lost their 'paid' element; many media, including YouTube and Twitter, allow advertisements to be uploaded for free on the Internet. The second substantial dimension to this famous definition is that an advertisement must use a medium to transmit a message; such media can be as diverse as the bombastic and direct appeal of made-for-cinema advertisements and corporate communications, to the amorphous and indirect messages of public relations that are embedded deep in the heart of non-advertising genres.

What has *not* been said about advertising? Despite changes in paradigms, there are two things about advertising that seem to remain constant: first, we are fascinated by it. A Google search of the term 'advertising' returns over a billion hits; there are over half a million advertisements uploaded on YouTube; my library holds 38 academic journals directly dealing with advertising; most marketing students want to work in advertising agencies. You can be quite certain that every university department in business, media studies, cultural studies, sociology, communication, journalism and graphic design has a module dedicated to advertising. This is even more remarkable when one considers how advertising used to be scorned as a practice and profession. Marchand (1986) recounts how it gained respectability in American culture in three ways – it became instrumental in enlisting soldiers during World War I, lending it a moral force which served more noble purposes besides commerce; it was elevated through its incorporation into education (Harvard University's first course in advertising was in 1924); and it became adept at referencing styles and commissioning work from the realm of high culture.

Today, advertising is a subject of intense fascination for the general public. We have reached an era where advertising does not just produce culture, but culture produces advertising. This is evidenced in the creation of entertainment products based on the advertising profession itself, such as hit television series like *Mad Men*, which depicts life on Madison Avenue in the glory days of the 1950s, or the multi-award-winning 2009 documentary of advertising *Art & Copy*. Indeed, one of the central questions of advertising in contemporary times has been the extent to which it enframes everything within its discourse and logic. Advertising has been shown to be implicated in even the loftiest and most removed spheres of high art and used in even the most ancient of times, as wine advertising uncovered on the walls of ancient Rome shows (O'Barr 2008; see Schroeder 2006). Other research has explored the extent of non-obvious genres of advertising, including scientific advertising (Haraway 2000) and medical advertising (Cartwright 1995). If advertising is everything, what is it *not*? This is a crucial question about advertising and it is part of a larger, global and crucial debate about the commodification of life and previously inalienable aspects thereof, to which we will return later.

Second, advertising works. It was estimated that nearly half a trillion dollars were spent globally on advertising in major media in 2012, up nearly 5 per cent on 2011 (AdAge 2011). Of course, we are all familiar with the statistic that the average person living in the Western world is exposed to 3,000 advertisements a day. However, this actually tells us quite little, because it is debatable as to whether we process or can even attend to such huge amounts of data. Rather, it seems more appropriate to consider the deeper psychological impact of advertising. Every day, on many occasions, it transports me from this world to an imaginary one for a moment; I observe people exercising, eating, interacting with other people, working and sleeping. I see their bedrooms, cars, bathrooms and streets. I have been inside more houses through advertising than I ever have in real life. Advertising affects me in a non-obvious way; it offers, through a constant stream of visual cameos, implicit standards of cleanliness, sociality, family life, health and happiness, and a great many other values. Advertising does not work by making people feel like dupes or clones, nor does it depict fantastical scenarios completely out of reach. To do so would alienate its audience. Modern advertising works in the strangest way – by appearing not to care if it works. Thus, when someone utters the immortal phrase 'advertising doesn't affect me' – advertising has achieved its ultimate goal. Advertising *empowers* us to feel distant to it.

This chapter considers advertising as a primarily visual sign system, that is, an institution that organizes meaning as powerful as other systems at work to organize meaning – medicine, law or education. I am trying to leverage the double-sense of organization; it is both a corporate entity and a common, indispensable practice of human beings. I want to make the point that advertising organizes meaning in the most powerful and generic of senses, as well as being a symptom of the organization, that is, something that indicates the existence of the organization. We will first consider how this visual sign system has evolved by surveying a hundred-year history. We will then take the most obvious statement that can be made about signs in advertising – that they communicate – and examine the philosophical underpinnings of such a statement. The importance of semiotics – the formal study of sign systems – will be discussed using an emblematic but quite neglected example from Roland Barthes and highlighting how similar conventions continue today. We will overview the range of research conducted on the most represented object in advertising – the human body. One of the reasons why advertising is intensely interesting to the public is because it is such a highly visible, accessible site of ideological contest; therefore, we shall briefly discuss how advertising can be thought to be ideological. By way of concluding, we will point to three ways advertising might evolve in the future.

The history of advertising signs

Histories of advertising are useful because they trace this sign system in its context – economic, political and socio-cultural. This enables us to observe shifts in how advertising signs change over time. The vast majority of such studies are centred on the emergence of advertising in the United States (Leiss *et al.* 2005; Lears 1994; Schudson 1985; Marchand 1986).[1] Marchand's historical study places the 1920s and 1930s as modern advertising's coming of age. Advertising was always there of course, but it is around this time that its signs underwent a qualitative shift in sophistication. This ushered in a new era in advertising when personalized testimonials began to be more common than the simple hard-selling ads of the time; social dramas around objects trumped mere announcement, and a participatory tone of voice was adopted, which became more widespread than the direct imperative command to purchase that characterized many previous advertisements. Through the system of advertising, consumer goods became more than mere economic entities; they embodied values that had normally been attributed to humans and the natural world. This must be seen in context in order to appreciate the enormity of the change. As Freud and many others have shown, the pace and scale of rationalization, depersonalization and urbanization brought about by modern industrial capitalism had exerted a toll on the human psyche. Ironically, rather than being the hallmarks of identity, the products produced came instead to offer mini-solutions to the dilemmas of modernity. This was possible only through the system of advertising, which recalibrated the meaning of the good by focusing not on the mere material product, but rather by imagining the product as a *benefit sought* by the consumer. Or, in Marchand's words, advertising brought 'illumination instead of lighting fixtures, prestige instead of automobiles, sex appeal instead of mere soap' (1986: 10). The sign system of advertising had become more mobile, more creative with potentially boundless ways to create compelling signs.

If advertising's golden era was the 1920s and 1930s, its nadir came in the 1950s and 1960s when its public image turned sour. Advertising, it was widely suspected, had moved from its public role of sign identification, to the private and psychological space of one's mind and interior life. Perhaps the most famous example of this proposition was Vance Packard's 1957 book *The Hidden Persuaders* (1983), which became one of the biggest-selling books in the field. Packard's book depicted the rise of 'depth men' – people in advertising agencies that reportedly used psychoanalytical techniques to uncover the subconscious needs, desires, insecurities and fears of consumers. Their job was to create advertisements that would present products as the unconscious fulfilments, solutions, comforts and fantasies to them. In the book, Packard plays the role of a detective, looking for clues about signs that a consumer does not consciously process, only decoding them on a deeper, unconscious and emotional level. Packard's implicit theory of signs is an interesting one – far from consciously visible, logically rational marks, signs existed at the emotional level of human consciousness. Some examples that Packard uses in the book – from Betty Crocker cake mix to Esso's 'Tiger in your Tank' campaign – have become staple short-hands in popular culture for the alleged power of small groups of people to organize meaning on a massive and uncontrolled level.

Let us take a lesser-known example from *Hidden Persuaders* to demonstrate the dynamic of Packard's analysis of signs. In the book, Packard argues that advertising agencies had become suspicious of the rational answers they were receiving from respondents buying home freezers. Post-World War II sales in home freezers had dramatically increased, despite the fact that the initial investment and the cost of energy to run them had made them uneconomical. Interested in this apparent contradiction, Packard describes how the Weiss and Geller advertising agency conducted psychiatric studies of home-freezer owners. The agency concluded that the freezer was not a device for cooling foodstuffs. Rather, it was a nostalgic site of security in a threatening environment. People who were insecure, they argued, needed more food around than they could eat. Freezer advertisements had to leverage the anxiety about food shortages resulting from post-World War II rationing. They had to link freezers to a nostalgic childhood, which, according to motivational research, was when the giving of food was linked to love.

Histories of advertising reveal the crudeness of visual sign systems in the early part of the twentieth century, replete with simple psychology and bald appeals to status and social acceptance (Williams 2000 [1980]), only to be followed by this type of more sophisticated motivational research and appeals. What this reminds us of, of course, is that people were not more naive or inexperienced than they are today, but rather advertising is a form of literacy that, like any grammar, had to be learned. As Lears attests, advertisements in the early twentieth century 'constituted a new and bewildering code, a set of verbal and visual signs for which the referents were unclear … As frequency of exposure mushroomed, the underlying advertising codes become familiar, taken for granted and unproblematic' (1983: 21, in Goldman 1992: 68). The sign system of advertising is not static; an historical perspective reminds us that, as sure as we look back at the obviousness of early modern advertising sign systems, generations to come will regard contemporary sign systems as rudimentary and easy to decode. Ultra-sophisticated images will appear antiquated and perhaps even humorous. Images that seem to us mundane today will be pored over for their sophisticated sign systems. The way in which advertising today visualizes software, the environment or nanotechnology as seemingly undeconstructible and transparent, will be staple examples in classroom curricula. We will return to this idea later.

Advertising as communication

The most obvious and immediate way to conceptualize advertising is as a system that creates signs with the purpose of communicating meaning. It has been argued that focusing on, and developing theories around, the advertising image itself could only ever tell one part of the dynamics of signs and their meaning. In comparison to the fields of sociology and cultural studies, the discipline of marketing has been the most supportive of the investigation of image consumption. A raft of qualitative and quantitative research has been conducted proposing various strategies for factoring in the consumer's response to the sign.

Early models of advertising – the so-called 'ancestral' models – followed hugely important developments at the time in information theory, which reflected, and continue to reflect, how we understand the philosophy of what information and communication are. In 1949, Bell Laboratories technician Claude Shannon sought to provide a theory of communication using the term 'information' as a technical measurement. Up until then, 'information' was a rather poetic and spiritual term, more at home in philosophy than engineering. In Shannon's (1971 [1949]) work, information became universalized as a component of any system that communicated. This simple but powerful notion was adapted to the field of advertising by researchers who argued that advertising works by a sequence of stages, or a so-called 'hierarchy of effects' – cognitive to affective to behavioural, or a variation thereof – which a person goes through following exposure to the advertisement (Strong 1925; Lavidge and Steiner 1961). Such a powerful theory resulted in numerous acronyms over the last century as new refinements were developed; the advertising landscape is filled with AIDA models, DAGMAR models, AIETA models and STARCH models, as well as more recent models and scales such as ADTRUST, AdSam and PrEMo. Such work was concerned with the effectiveness of advertising developing scales to informationalize and measure aspects of advertising such as the rate of advertising wear-out, the effectiveness of advertising during the product's life cycle, effect on price sensitivity, attitude formation and the impact of advertising on emotional states.

It is important, and fascinating, to understand the informational theory of communication as a reflection of larger scientific and philosophical aims at the time. The goal of mathematical theories of information and communication was to apply scientific measurability to an ineffable phenomenon, to universalize and standardize a dynamic with the aim of providing codified models that predict response, and to enframe communication within a logic of relative effectiveness or ineffectiveness. Such theories dominate managerialist discourses and practices of advertising, and, despite their theoretical weaknesses, are extremely influential precisely because of their underlying goals.

Further, theories of communication that dominated advertising textbooks in the last 60 years are gradually being supplemented with measurement techniques stemming from neuropsychology (see Plassmann *et al.* 2007). A number of issues are of interest here: first, the extent to which neuroscientific techniques locate areas in the brain that are purportedly associated with different emotions. For example, Daimler-Chrysler measured people's reactions to different cars using magnetic resonance imaging (MRI), a technique that measures brain function. It was found that the reward areas of the brain were significantly active when viewing sports cars compared with sedans (Erk *et al.* 2002, in Plassmann *et al.* 2007). Second, the question arises as to whether there are far too many extraneous factors in the environment to monitor causal links between advertising and behaviour, particularly when it comes to more long-term behaviour and affect, such as brand memories or brand equity, where the pathways to this are so numerous and complex that only the crudest approximations are possible within laboratory settings. Third, neuroscientific measurement seems not so much concerned with originality of results but with finding a neurological basis for what is already intuitively well known. Finally, the drive for empirical results in neurological advertising is driven by the goal of gaining economic advantage for organizations. Thus, there has been relatively little critique in the use of neurological measurement in advertising (Kenning 2007).

Qualitative research in advertising has better recognized that the act of reading advertisements is likely to call for research designs that acknowledged the holistic nature of the human, the fluid boundary between advertising and everyday life, and the multitude of often contradictory interpretations people could simultaneously hold about signs – research that, in other words, focused on 'real readers reading' (Mick and Buhl 1992; see, for example, O'Donohoe 1997; Otnes and Scott 1995; Scott 1994; Hirschman and Thompson 1997). However, this is not to say that qualitative advertising research does not have a managerialist axiology (Zaltman 2003).

The a priori assumption of advertising as informative communication is argued by many to be a reductive procedure that neglects how advertising has other uses, as part of the 'spectacular vernacular' of social fabric (Scott 1993). In researching advertising, one could argue that there are three sites of investigation; one is the site of consumption or 'reception', the field of meaning from a consumer's perspective, and primarily the one that managerialist research deems most important. The second is the site of production, taking a route to understanding by investigating the processes involved in making ads – something that is favoured in media studies and ethnographic approaches to advertising. The third is what could be called the site of the 'image itself' (van Leeuwen and Jewitt 2006). As van Leeuwen and Jewitt argue, '[a] mode of analysis which restricts itself to the evidence of the text may not ... by itself demonstrate how viewers understand and value what they see or hear or what producers, deliberately or otherwise, intend to communicate' (2006: 7). On the other hand, they argue that analyses of the image itself, independent of intention and reception, are the most powerful way to show what images include and exclude, drawing influence primarily from the disciplines of history, philosophy, sociology and linguistics. In each site, the advertisement plays a different role.

Although primarily concerned with the managerialist implications of advertising, business disciplines have slowly seen the merit of investigating the advertisement itself. One of the most influential writers that moved beyond the thrall of measurement is Grant McCracken. In 1986, he published a model of how meaning moved from the world of advertising to the world of the consumer, offering an insight into the complex and subtle ways in which advertising is integrated into the life-world of people. McCracken's model, despite its theoretical weaknesses (see Otnes and Scott 1995; Mick *et al.* 2004; Venkatesh and Meamber 2006), is influential because it sees advertising as a powerful translator of the cultural world and a central arbiter of meaning in consumer worlds. As critiques and elaborations of the model have since elucidated, advertising is also a two-way process, where consumers affect the process of advertising as much as they are affected by it. For example, advertising is not mere communication; people incorporate advertising so that it functions as a social glue within groups (Ritson and Elliott 1999).

The semiotics of advertising

In the 1950s and 1960s, advertising theory began to be influenced by the semiotic turn, in other words, the study in other disciplines of the formal properties of signs and their meaning, and emanating from the work of semioticians such as Barthes, Saussure, Peirce and Jacobsen. Semiotics can be regarded as one of the most comprehensive studies of sign systems. The work under its various manifestations provided a conceptual vocabulary to talk about the formal properties of signs and codes and their relevance within social groups.

Semiotics proposed that advertisements were, in fact, bundles of signs that formed finely constructed conventions. In semiotics, the image is a text, and, like any language, possesses its own grammar; understanding the grammar will give us access to the language. And this grammar is articulated through the image's composition, lighting, framing, focus, gestures, spacing of forms, and so on. Mick *et al.* (2004) break down this grammar into three levels of sign analysis:

the micro-, mid- and meta-level. The micro-level conceives advertising signs as tiny units, such as the vectors, colours and forms within the visual plane (Kress and van Leeuwen 2006). Mid-level analysis decomposes signs into human-level characteristics of gender, hairstyle, posture, facial expression, buildings, as well as rhetorical devices in the image such as metaphor and troping (McQuarrie and Phillips 2005; McQuarrie and Mick 1996; Scott 1994), A meta-level range of semiotics reflects on the narrative structure of the advertisement, one that is often mythic in nature (Holt 2004; Stern 1995). One of the most important characteristics of semiotics was its ability to see embodied in the properties and dynamics of the image the macro properties and dynamics of the social world; a characteristic that made semiotics a political and ethical intervention into the interrogation of images. As Davison (Chapter 2, this volume) notes, semiotics presents a system for looking at images that is both structured and flexible, and shows how it can be used as a tool to deconstruct the ordinariness of organizational images, from annual accounting reports to food labels. It is this structured flexibility that semiotic approaches offer that allows the researcher the scope to find patterns in very diverse data.

The French semiotician Roland Barthes was, of course, particularly good at showing how the new medium of the photographic advertisement was not a transparent reflection of the world, but a codified structure. His two-page description of the advertisement of Italian pasta brand Panzani is surely the most referenced analysis in the whole field of semiotics. It is worth turning briefly to a less-known, but still powerful example of semiotic analysis by Barthes – that of the Citroën, DS,[2] a car model where the product is its own advertisement. We will then show how Barthes' semiotic analyses are still valid in contemporary advertising.

Barthes makes a number of strikingly insightful remarks in his short reading of the new car model by Citroën, DS. First, the car appears to us in a state of almost impossible newness; it 'appears at first sight as a superlative *object*' (Barthes 1977 [1972]: 88). What is fascinating is that Barthes argues, like others after him, that objects which appear at first sight as completely finished present to us 'at once a perfection and an absence of origin, a closure and a brilliance, a transformation of life into matter ... and in a word a *silence* which belongs to the realm of fairytales'. Barthes examines not just the impact of an image on the eyes, but also what a visual image *sounds* like. Further, as is the case so often in Barthes' work, it is not just the substance of the image that is examined, but also *how* it is composed. Here, he points out that the DS erases any signs of its construction through the presentation of extreme smoothness. To Barthes, smoothness is not a property of a material, but a social value:

> [S]moothness is always an attribute of perfection because its opposite reveals a technical and typically human operation of assembling: Christ's robe was seamless, just as the airships of science-fiction are made of unbroken metal ... there are in the DS a new phenomenology of assembling, as if one progressed from a world where elements are welded to a world where they are juxtaposed and hold together by sole virtue of their wondrous shape, which of course is meant to prepare one for the idea of a more benign Nature.
>
> *(1977 [1972]: 88)*

In a single analytic gesture, Barthes uncouples the car from its mundane and obvious denotation, or first-order signification and describes how its image follows longer lines of visual convention, from religious painting, science-fiction film and the politics of nature. This second level or order of analysis – this *connotation* – exposes that linkage not to be a natural one, but rather one that has been slowly constructed over the past 2,000 years of Western culture.

The signs and semiotics of advertising

The traditional privileging of single, synchronic advertisements of units for analysis is a weakness of semiotics that can be compensated by the building up of visual genealogies, which trace the use of visual conventions across long time periods. For example, Donna Haraway's work, which analyses contemporary images of technology and science, argues that most so-called high-tech and ideologically neutral images of science 'quote, point to, and otherwise evoke a small, conventional, potent stock of Renaissance visual analogues, which provide a legitimate lineage and origin story for technical revolutions at the end of the Second Christian Millennium' (Haraway 2000: 237). In an attempt to highlight how a visual convention continues through time, let us provide a contemporary visual analogy to Barthes' Citroen reading – an advertisement for Siemens entitled *Building Blocks* (2005). This advertisement draws attention to what Barthes so insightfully termed the 'phenomenology of assembling'. In other words, Barthes asks the right question of the image – what sign constructions do Westerners use to tell the story of how technology comes to be present in the world.

In Siemens' advertisement, a band of technology – in the forms of panelling, vents, wheels and bolts – moves silently through the sky, floating to earth to form office blocks, hospitals, street lights, airports, shuttles and stadia. The striking absence of labour heralds a universe of self-organizing, invisible agency. Technology is an invisible force that is lighter than air, rearranging itself into whatever seems to be needed (Figure 8.1). By removing the visibility of human labour from the equation, we no longer see a world where technology is fashioned, melted, hammered, soldered and generally forced into the natural order; instead, Siemens' technological products are so natural they fit the world like a glove. The agency that organizes is non-pollutant, non-disruptive and non-energetic. The Siemens products float into place, as naturally as a pure white snowflake falling to the earth. These calm, precise movements seem to be guided by an invisible hand, lending the scenes an almost divine sense of inevitable fate. The white aesthetic, the soundtrack and the voiceover serve to anchor this message as the music passes from slightly cacophonous (as technology seeks its home) to harmonious and melodic as it finds its rightful place. The voiceover follows:

> Our innovations make the world brighter, safer, more efficient and better connected. Siemens. We're turning the dreams of business and communities into reality.

Figure 8.1 Self-organizing technology, Siemens *Building Blocks* (Publicis, New York 2005)

137

Like the Citroën reading, technology in this advertisement possesses the quality of weightlessness; it emanates from the sky above rather than the ground below. *Infra*structure, literally meaning structure from below, has been replaced by an orientation of an imagined *supra*-structure. Since at least Barthes' time, images of technology have followed a similar geometric orientation. In *Building Blocks*, technology is apotheosized by extending its self-organizing capabilities, lending it a divinity which is universal, inevitable, natural and just. Let us now turn from an under-investigated site of advertising – technology – to perhaps the most visually studied object in the universe – the human body.

The sign of the human

Much of the interest in advertising is generated from the representation of the human body – especially the female body and the racially marked body. Indeed, the human body is by far the most depicted object in advertising – evidence of our fascination with images of ourselves. Neurological research has shown that we humans have more synapses for interpreting the human face and body than we have for any other object in the universe. The body in advertising has revolved around a number of debates; the depiction of the female body in advertising (Kilbourne 2000; Scott 2005); the mainstreaming of research on the representation of male bodies (Patterson and Elliott 2002); sex in advertising (Reichert and Lambaise 2003); and advertisements that depict futuristic human bodies (Buchanan-Oliver *et al.* 2010; Campbell 2010), the racially marked body (Merskin 2001) and the disabled body (Shakespeare 1994). All this work centres on the important, and unresolved, question of whether advertising reflects the world, or shapes it. Such work focuses on how signs such as the human body's poise, gesture, positioning, gender role, and interaction with other bodies and objects reproduce, create, normalize or subvert the often unequal power structures that exist between male and female bodies, old and young bodies, white and black bodies, able and disabled bodies, rich and poor bodies.

Research in this tradition tells us that, despite potential ambiguity in images, we as visual consumers are always presented with a 'preferred reading' (Hall 1980: 134) or a 'potentialized meaning' (Mick *et al.* 2004: 4). All images, it is suggested, are controlled by discursive limits, and these limits tacitly frame the range of possibilities within an image. Indeed, it is claimed that this is the subtlest ideological weapon of advertising; images give us the impression that we can freely create and form new identities. But, in fact, the narrow range of identities has already been determined in advance (Arvidsson 2006; Williamson 1978). This is the paradox of identity construction; the consuming subject chooses among a limited repertoire of 'iterated' or pre-existing identities provided by marketing and advertising (Schroeder and Borgerson 2003), all of which – despite nods to the contrary – serve to consolidate traditional identity roles (Schroeder and Zwick 2004). Advertisers sequester meaning by 'mortising' or 'steering' viewers in preferred directions (Goldman 1992), or through the process of co-optation – where advertising pretends to acknowledge a competing discourse or ideology, but only pays lip service to it, ignoring its real, radical challenge (Williamson 1978). It is at the site of the human body where much research focuses on the concept of the ideology of advertising.

Ideology and the advertising sign – is advertising magic?

Advertising is a system that instils products and services with cultural and social values that are not intrinsic to them. One of the reasons why advertising is intensely interesting to the public is because it is such a highly visible display of ruling-class interests. Advertising is the site where capitalism and aesthetics merge – indeed, it has been described as the 'face of capitalism'

(Schroeder 2002: 141). Many academics of advertising and public intellectuals alike have argued that advertising is the pre-eminent way in which the interests of the powerful minority maintain the docility, alienation or servitude of the majority (Elliott and Ritson 1997; Pollay 1986, Herman and Chomsky 1988; Williams 2000 [1980]; Berger 1972). Raymond Williams famously declared advertising to be a magic system, possessing the power that magic objects had in primitive societies. Appealing to the supernatural ability of advertising is an interesting strategy; magic can conjure an object from its immediate material rootedness and animate it with a much more potent energy. For example, an advertisement for a mobile phone is not an *announcement* about a technological device; it is a *suggestion* about a certain design aesthetic, a certain role in professional life, a certain sexual appeal and a certain social network. Advertising, some argue, is magic not just because of its transformative power on objects, but because it is also able to *erase* human experience of the monotony of consumption with its transient satisfactions, and reinvigorate it anew with fresh promise-claims. Thus, advertising, as Williams (1980) argues, 'operates to preserve the consumption ideal from the criticism inexorably made of it by experience'.

Such critique, diverse as it is, centres on the idea that advertising's signs are not simple reflections of the state of the world, but carefully constructed, highly selective and distortive ways of seeing. Such critiques are theoretical, exploring how advertising produces false consciousness, commodity fetishism, docility, passivity, manipulation of unconscious desire and environmental degradation (Adorno and Horkheimer 1979 [1947]; Marcuse 1991 [1964]; Klein 1999; Curtis 2002; Jhally 2005). It is also technical, in that some research analyses the processes by which signs actually achieve their aims, through mortise and framing work, cropping, reification, interpellation, co-optation, the gaze, face-ism and individuation (Althusser 1970; Williamson 1978; Goldman 1992; Jhally 2005; Schroeder and Borgerson 2005).

For the sake of making concrete these quite technical terms, let us take one of these processes and show its dynamics in advertising. Interpellation is a concept developed in the writings of the political philosopher Louis Althusser on ideology in the early 1970s. Althusser argued that subjects are created through material practices; going to church and kneeling down to pray precedes my subjecthood as a spiritual person. Interpellation is the process by which we are called or 'hailed' into subjecthood through practices – and these practices may be imposed onto us from outside interests. In his work on interpellation, Althusser uses the oft-cited example of the police officer hailing someone on the street: 'Hey, you there!' The person makes a 180-degree turn, stops, looks at the policeman, and becomes a subject of interest to the law.

Recruitment advertising is the interpellative genre *par excellence*. The more authoritative and convincing the source of interpellation, the more likely we are to disregard the framing work that is done to legitimize and de-legitimize positions within the interpellation. Through the practice of response, we enter into the predefined parameters of relation with the organization. The advertisements in Figures 8.2 and 8.3 show recent recruitment drives by both Apple Inc. and Microsoft. Both have very similar stylistic qualities that are worth noting.

Figure 8.2 Hey Genius Microsoft Recruitment Campaign, Wexley School for Girls, Seattle 2010

Figure 8.3 Recruitment card for Apple Inc., circa 2010

In these cases, the act of interpellation has three dimensions – the first is the act of defining the subject – one who is special, unique, an individual among the masses. The second is the use of the collective pronoun, 'we', which serves to close the subject and the organization within a circuit of common purpose. The third and most important is what is missing – a concrete visualization of working life in the organization, an absence which allows the reader to project his/her own fantasy onto the space. Instead of images of people in the workplace, these advertisements powerfully evoke this intended future in the most understated manner – through the typography of the interpellative text – comic book, childlike and disarming in one case, lowercase, understated and sexually suggestive in the other. Interpellation is ideological in both cases because it infantilizes the organization in order to empower the subject, which represents an imaginary relationship to the real conditions of our existence. The act of interpellation functions to empower the potential applicant, but it also subjects him/her to the circuit of identity produced within the address; he/she must willingly take his/her predefined place within it in order for it to have meaning.

The future of the field

The disappearance of advertising, the reappearance of advertising

Trends in advertising suggest a disappearance of the advertisement in its traditional form of billboard, print and television, and its intensification and hybridization in oblique ways and through new media, such as adver-gaming, twitter-piccing or virtual-worlding. As we saw at the beginning of this chapter, advertising as a rhetorical force moved from information-heavy selling to dramatic persuasion. We could say that we are now in a third era of advertising, characterized not by communication through information or persuasion, but through entertainment.

Product placement – the unobtrusive embedding of branded goods and services primarily in films and video games – does not begin to describe the scope and sophistication of this era of advertising. The practice of staging products in films is surpassed by an embedding of brands so deeply into the fabric of the film's narrative that they serve not as *props*, but as *object-actors* that propel the plot. HBO's *Sex and the City* is emblematic of such a practice. To give another example: some major brands leverage the creativity of consumers to create artistic output in the form of short stories, films and poems, the only stipulation being that they mention the product category within them. Advertisements thus have another rhetorical purpose: they do not inform or persuade as much as they entertain. The original function of advertising was 'to warn' – stemming as it does from the French verb *avertir* in the early fifteenth century. In the future, advertising will lose its original function as warning or announcement and become entertainment.

Advertisements are alive

All work in advertising revolves around the ways in which the image seems to produce something that is more than the sum of its parts. Images are ontologically cryptic, in other words, we conceive images to be both agentic *and* passive, residing in *and* affecting many spheres simultaneously. The image is variously used to mean 'visuality, apparatus, institutions, discourse, bodies, and figurality' (Mitchell 1994: 16). It exists 'within a distinctive socio-legal environment – unlike textual or verbal statements, such as product claims or political promises, pictures cannot be held to be true or false … elud[ing] empirical verification' (Schroeder 2006: 7). Such multiple ontologies move images beyond simple categories of analysis, because it is difficult to say *what* an image is to begin with, or *where* it resides, what constitutes the border between the image and not-image, whether they are active agents or passive conduits. Images are extra-organizational entities; they are designed by the organization but become quixotic and uncontrollable.

Images are often referred to as 'complex' without paying due attention to what this concept requires in terms of methodological and epistemological approaches. In thinking of images as complex, theorists often begin by arguing that there exists something about the image that is beyond analytic investigation. Mitchell says that the question of meaning has been exhaustively explored by hermeneutics as well as semiotics, 'with the result that every image theorist seems to find some residue or "surplus value" that goes beyond communication, signification, and persuasion' (2005: 9). There exists an ineffable extra in images, impossible to put into words (van Eck and Winters 2005), which remains 'in excess' of the processes of mediation and connotation (Jay 1994: 275).

In defending images from simplistic comparisons with text, Schroeder attests that, ironically, 'the vast body of writing *about* art confirms nothing more than that words fail miserably to "account for" the communicative and expressive power of images' (2002: 19). In a similar vein, Rose points out that there exists in art historical methods an acknowledgement of the overall 'feel' of an image, its 'expressive content' as she calls it, which is elusive and slippery because 'breaking an image into its component parts – spatial organisation, colour, content, light – does not necessarily capture the look of the image' (2007: 48–49). Barthes talks about the vitalistic qualities of images that cannot be pinned down, and terms this surplus value 'the third meaning' – that magic within the image that cannot be explained away, as Davison explains in Chapter 2 in this volume. Images are complex precisely because they exceed the sum of their parts. Through their very complexity, they are constantly mutating in meaning and significance. Second, they cross aesthetic borders and are not confinable to a particular domain; they are at once aesthetic, political and social, artefactual and imaginary. Third, they act on all domains recursively, which means it is impossible to describe in linear fashion how the aesthetic life of images affects the political life of images. Instead, we could see this as a recursive, infinite gesture; the aesthetic affects the political affects the aesthetic affects the political.

In this context, we could argue that it is better to think of advertising images as *alive*. This argument follows recent philosophical debates about the ascription of life to previously lifeless entities. For example, the visual theorist W.J.T. Mitchell wonders if it is not better to regard the image as a *species*; a species that reproduces, desires and holds us in thrall; one that seeks attention, one that has power:

> Images are, then, like *species*, and pictures are like organisms whose kinds are given by the species ... Perhaps, then, there is a way in which we can speak of the value of images as evolutionary or at least co-evolutionary entities, quasi life-forms (like viruses) that depend on a host organism (ourselves), and cannot reproduce themselves without human participation ... 'Does [this image] go anywhere?' 'Does it flourish, reproduce itself, thrive and circulate?'
>
> *(2005: 84–87)*

Thus, it might be fruitful to consider advertising images as alive. The first reason why is because it inverts the relationship between humans and their images, enabling us to reconceive them more realistically as something not fully under human control, but rather able to spread through the host organism (humans themselves) using any suitable carrier. It accounts for why some die and some become pandemic; they reproduce themselves in order to survive with varying degrees of success.

Second, thinking this way helps us give a different account of the evolution of new media forms. New media come into existence because of the ever-growing impetus of advertising to reproduce itself in new forms, to the extent that advertising *creates new media to propagate itself*. Consider phenomena as diverse as search engines and social networking sites – two globally pervasive and path-changing forms of media that would not exist without advertising revenue. A generation ago, the media theorist Marshall McLuhan made his famous pronouncement that the medium was the message; that we should look at the structural nature of the media, rather than what it contains, to observe how it changes social behaviour and values. But, inverting this, we could contend that in the twenty-first century the message is the medium. In other words, advertising is a species that creates media in order to allow it to replicate. Such a conceptualization repositions advertising from a thing that we humans create and put in media as an incidental extra to an originary agent of meaning.

Visualizing the invisible – the task of advertising in the twenty-first century

Finally, in many respects, the task of advertising in the twenty-first century will be to render the invisible into compelling visualities. Advertising will play a large role in visualizing the qualities that organizations privilege today, qualities such as 'complexity'. The term complexity is used in organizational discourse to articulate the unpredictable, multi-layered, decentred, emergent and globalized world of the twenty-first century, and organizations are keen to highlight products themselves as complex while at the same time responding to complexity by making life simpler. Complexity is thus a metonym for the technological, adaptable and multi-layered, and the organizations that can best visualize the complexity of their products will be the most successful. Therefore, a task for advertising research will be to investigate how complexity and other privileged but invisible qualities such as 'network' or 'information' are translated into the public imagination through the advertising image.

In a similar vein, corporate advertising will play a vital part in creating legitimacy for new, as yet unvisualized technosciences such as nanotechnology. This is a crucial, though unexplored avenue of investigation. An interesting contribution in this direction is Goldman *et al.*'s six-year media project Landscapes of Capital (1998–2003). Landscapes of Capital explores how advertising, particularly corporate advertising, visually depicts the phenomenon of globalization. The authors' goal is to investigate how such representations affect the cultural imaginary and shape our political sensibilities with respect to life in high-tech globalism. Despite the massive and global private and state investment into sciences like nanotechnology, little work has investigated the *imaging* of such sciences. Given the fact that technosciences such as nuclear fusion and genetic crop modification have a bad *image* in the public imagination, it would be useful to explore the evolution of corporate images of nanotechnology and citizens' perceptions of it. This is equally true for other amorphous phenomena such as counter-terrorism or climate change, which in the future will require high-stakes visualization work on the part of various stakeholders.

Conclusion

This chapter considers advertising as a primarily visual sign system, that is, an institution that organizes meaning as powerful as other systems at work to organize meaning – medicine, law or education. It presents a potted history of the past hundred years of advertising in order to show that it is a form of literacy that is learned, and a lexicon and grammar that can be fruitfully investigated using semiotic approaches, and this chapter takes examples as diverse as automobiles and recruitment advertising. Advertising is shown to have three sites – the site of production, the site of consumption and the site of the image itself. This chapter argues that the site of the image itself offers the most insight into what advertising is. It makes the argument that advertising is the realm where capitalism and aesthetics merge; this makes research in advertising one of the most important research priorities in any discipline today.

Notes

1 Historical databases such as Duke University's *Ad Access* (http://library.duke.edu/digitalcollections/adaccess) and the British History of Advertising Trust (http://www.hatads.org.uk) are noteworthy archives of advertising over the last centuries in both countries, and provide ample evidence that advertising is a visual instantiation of social life.
2 'DS' when pronounced in French sounds like 'goddess'.

References

AdAge (2011) 'The Ad Age Annual 2012'. Advertising Age. Available at http://adage.com/article/datacenter-top-line-data/ad-age-annual-2012/231396/ (accessed 1 December 2011).
Adorno, T.W. and Horkheimer, M. (1979 [1947]) *Dialectic of Enlightenment*, London: Verso.
Althusser, L. (1970) 'Ideology and ideological state apparatuses'. Available at http://www.marxists.org/reference/archive/althusser/1970/ideology.htm#n16 (accessed 28 January 2012).
Arvidsson, A. (2006) *Brands: Meaning and Value in Media Culture*, New York and London: Routledge.
Barthes, R. (1977 [1972]) 'The third meaning', in *Image-Music-Text*, edited and translated by Stephen Heath, New York: Hill and Wang.
Berger, J. (1972) *Ways of Seeing*, London: British Broadcasting Corporation and Harmondsworth: Penguin.
Buchanan-Oliver, M., Cruz, A. and Schroeder, J.E. (2010) 'Shaping the body and technology: discursive implications for the marketing communications of technological products', *European Journal of Marketing* 44(5): 635–652.
Campbell, N. (2010) 'Future sex: cyborg bodies and the politics of meaning', *Advertising and Society Review* 11(1). Available at http://muse.jhu.edu/login?auth=0&type=summary&url=/journals/advertising_and_society_review/v011/11.1.campbell.html.
——(2012) 'Regarding Derrida: the tasks of visual deconstruction', *Qualitative Research in Organizations and Management* 7(1): 105–124.
Cartwright, L. (1995) *Screening the Body: Tracing Medicine's Visual Culture*, Minneapolis: University of Minnesota Press.
Curtis, A. (2002) *The Century of the Self*, London: BBC Four Productions.
Elliott, R. and Ritson, M. (1997) 'Post-structuralism and the dialectics of advertising: discourse, ideology, resistance', in S. Brown and D. Turley (eds) *Consumer Research: Postcards from the Edge*, London: Routledge, 190–219.

Goldman, R. (1992) *Reading Ads Socially*, London: Routledge.
Goldman, R., Papson, S. and Kersey, N. (1998–2003) 'Landscapes of Capital: representing time, space and globalisation in corporate advertising'. Available at http://it.stlawu.edu/~global/ (accessed 12 January 2006).
Hall, S. (1980) 'Encoding/decoding', in S. Hall, D. Hobson, A. Lowe and P. Willis (eds) *Culture, Media, Language: Working Papers in Cultural Studies 1972–79*, London: Routledge, 128–139.
Haraway, D.J. (2000) 'The virtual speculum in the new world order', in G. Kirkup, L. James, K. Woodward and F. Hovenden (eds) *The Gendered Cyborg: A Reader*, London: Routledge/Open University, 221–246.
Herman, E.S. and Chomsky, N. (1988) *Manufacturing Consent: The Political Economy of the Mass Media*, New York: Pantheon.
Hirschman, E.C. and Thompson, C.J. (1997) 'Why media matter: towards a richer understanding of consumers' relationships with advertising and the mass media', *Journal of Advertising* 26(1): 28–43.
Holt, D.B. (2004) *How Brands Become Icons: The Principles of Cultural Branding*, Boston: Harvard Business School Press.
Jay, M. (1994) *Downcast Eyes: The Denigration of Vision in Twentieth-Century French Thought*, Berkeley: University of California Press.
Jhally, S. (2005) 'Advertising at the edge of the apocalypse'. Available at http://www.sutjhally.com/articles/advertisingattheed/.
Kenning, P. (2007) 'What advertisers can and cannot do with neuroscience', *International Journal of Advertising* 26(3): 472–474.
Kilbourne, J. (2000) *Killing Us Softly 3: Advertising Images of Women*, Northampton, MA: Media Education Foundation.
Klein, N. (1999) *No Logo: Taking Aim at the Brand Bullies*, Toronto: Random House.
Kress, G. and van Leeuwen, T. (2006) *Reading Images: The Grammar of Visual Design*, London: Routledge.
Lavidge, R.J. and Steiner, G.A. (1961) 'A model for the predictive effects of advertising effectiveness', *Journal of Marketing* 25 (October): 59–62.
Lears, T.J.J. (1983) *The Culture of Consumption: Critical Essays in American History 1880–1980*, New York: Pantheon.
——(1994) *Fables of Abundance: A Cultural History of Advertising in America*, New York: Basic Books.
Leiss, W., Kline, S., Jhally, S. and Botterill, J. (2005) *Social Communication and Advertising: Consumption in the Mediated Marketplace*, Abingdon: Routledge.
Marchand, R. (1986) *Advertising the American Dream: Making Way for Modernity 1920–1940*, Berkeley: University of California Press.
Marcuse, H. (1991 [1964]) *One Dimensional Man: Studies in the Ideology of Advanced Society*, London: Routledge.
McCracken, G. (1986) 'Culture and consumption: a theoretical account of the structure and movement of the cultural meaning of consumer goods', *Journal of Consumer Research* 13(1): 71–84.
McQuarrie, E.F. and Mick, D.G. (1996) 'Rhetorical figures in advertising language', *Journal of Consumer Research* 22(3): 424–438.
McQuarrie, E.F. and Phillips, B.J. (2005) 'Indirect persuasion in advertising: how consumers process metaphors presented in pictures and words', *Journal of Advertising* 34(2): 7–20.
Merskin, D. (2001) 'Winnebagos, Cherokees, Apaches, and Dakotas: the persistence of stereotyping of American Indians in American advertising brands', *The Howard Journal of Communications* 12: 159–169.
Mick, D.G. and Buhl, C. (1992) 'A meaning-based model of advertising experiences', *Journal of Consumer Research* 19 (December): 317–338.
Mick, D.G., Burroughs, J.F., Hetzel, P. and Brannen, M.Y. (2004) 'Pursuing the meaning of meaning in the commercial world: an international review of marketing and consumer research founded on semiotics', *Semiotica* 152(4): 1–74.
Mitchell, W.J.T. (1994) *Picture Theory: Essays on Verbal and Visual Representation*, Chicago: University of Chicago Press.
——(2005) *What Do Pictures Want? The Lives and Loves of Images*, Chicago: University of Chicago Press.
O'Barr, W.M. (2008) 'What is advertising?' *Advertising and Society Review* 6(3). Available at: http://muse.jhu.edu/journals/advertising_and_society_review/v006/6.3unit01.html (accessed: 1 September 2011).
O'Donohoe, S. (1997) 'Raiding the postmodern pantry: advertising intertextuality and the young adult experience', *European Journal of Marketing* 31(3/4): 234–253.

Otnes, C. and Scott, L.M. (1995) 'Something old, something new: exploring the interaction between ritual and advertising', *Journal of Advertising* 25(1): 33–50.

Packard, V. (1983 [1957]) *The Hidden Persuaders*, New York: IG Publishing.

Patterson, M. and Elliott, R. (2002) 'Negotiating masculinities: advertising and the inversion of the male gaze', *Consumption Markets & Culture* 5(3): 231–246.

Plassmann, H., Ambler, T., Braeutigam, S. and Kenning, P. (2007) 'What can advisers learn from neuroscience?' *International Journal of Advertising* 26(2): 151–175.

Pollay, R.W. (1986) 'The distorted mirror: reflections on the unintended consequences of advertising', *Journal of Marketing* 50(2): 18–36.

Reichert, T. and Lambaise, J. (eds) (2003) *Sex in Advertising: Perspectives on the Erotic Appeal*, London: Routledge.

Richards, J.I. and Curran, C.M. (2002) 'Oracles on "advertising": searching for a definition', *Journal of Advertising* 31(2): 63–77.

Ritson, M. and Elliott, R. (1999) 'The social uses of advertising: an ethnographic study of adolescent advertising audiences', *Journal of Consumer Research* 26(3): 260–277.

Rose, G. (2007) *Visual Methodologies*, London: Sage.

Schroeder, J.E. (2002) *Visual Consumption*, London: Routledge.

——(2006) 'Aesthetics awry: The Painter of Light™ and the commodification of artistic values', *Consumption Markets & Culture* 9(2): 5–10.

Schroeder, J.E. and Borgerson, J.L. (2003) 'Identity and iteration: marketing images and the constitution of consuming subjects', paper presented at Critical Management Conference, Stream 23: Critical Marketing: Visibility, Inclusivity, Captivity, Lancaster Management School, July.

Schroeder, J.E. and Borgerson, J.L. (2005) 'An ethics of representation for international marketing communication', *International Marketing Review* 22(5): 578–600.

Schroeder, J.E. and Zwick, D. (2004) 'Mirrors of masculinity: representation and identity in marketing communication,' *Consumption Markets & Culture* 7: 21–52.

Schudson, M. (1985) *Advertising, the Uneasy Persuasion: Its Dubious Impact on American Society*, New York: Basic Books.

Scott, L.M. (1993) 'Spectacular vernacular: literacy and commercial culture in the postmodern age', *International Journal of Research in Marketing* 10(3): 251–275.

——(1994) 'Images in advertising: the need for a theory of visual rhetoric', *Journal of Consumer Research* 21 (September): 252–273.

——(2005) *Fresh Lipstick: Redressing Fashion and Feminism*, New York: Palgrave Macmillan.

Shakespeare, Tom (1994) 'Cultural representations of disabled people: dustbins for disavowal?' *Disability and Society* 9(3): 283–299.

Shannon, C.E. (1971) *The Mathematical Theory of Communication*, Champaign, IL: University of Illinois Press.

Stern, B.B. (1995) 'Consumer myths: Frye's Taxonomy and the structuralist analysis of consumption text', *Journal of Consumer Research* 22(2): 165–185.

Strong, E.K. (1925) *The Psychology of Selling*, New York: McGraw-Hill.

van Eck, C. and Winters, E. (2005) 'Introduction', in C. van Eck and E. Winters (eds) *Dealing with the Visual: Art History, Aesthetics and Visual Culture*, Aldershot, UK: Ashgate, 1–13.

van Leeuwen, T. and Jewitt, C. (eds) (2006) *The Handbook of Visual Analysis*, London: Sage Publications.

Venkatesh, A. and Meamber, L.A. (2006) 'Arts and aesthetics: marketing and cultural production', *Marketing Theory* 6(1): 11–39.

Williams, R. (2000 [1980]) 'Advertising: the magic system', *Advertising and Society Review* 1(1). Available at http://muse.jhu.edu.elib.tcd.ie/journals/advertising_and_society_review/v001/1.1williams.html (accessed 13 September 2011).

Williamson, J.E. (1978) *Decoding Advertisements: Ideology and Meaning in Advertising*, London: Marion Boyars.

Zaltman, G. (2003) *How Consumers Think*, Boston, MA: Harvard Business School Press.

9

Art, artist, and aesthetics for organizational visual strategy

Pierre Guillet de Monthoux

Introduction

What are the underlying implications in seeing organizations as art? Are artists participants in such visual organizing, and, if so, how do they engage in the process? In organization studies, questions pertaining to art and artists gained relevance when the aesthetic angle began to gain respectability as a valid benchmark for sizing up the visual in organizing (Ramirez 1991; Strati 1999; Linstead and Höpfl 2000; Guillet de Monthoux 2004). Although studies of organizational 'symbols' and 'culture' touched upon the subject first, it was when organization scholars began to take 'aesthetics' seriously that art and artists became central to their work (e.g. Strati 2009). In the 1980s, it took future organizational strategy professor Rafael Ramirez considerable effort to make his thesis supervisor Eric Trist – at the time 'guru' of the dominating social systems approach – accept his pioneering doctoral work on organizational beauty in organization studies (Ramirez 1991). Eventually, however, the 'aesthetic turn' in organization studies made fields traditionally associated with the humanities and liberal arts relevant to organization scholars as well. But how can philosophy, art history, and details from contemporary art scenes inform our investigation and understanding of the visual strategies for organizing?

In an attempt to provide a systematic answer to these questions, this chapter follows a then-and-now chronology. The first part, *classical aesthetics strategies*, is an overview of typical cases where art and organization strategy have been connected in the Western Hemisphere over the past two centuries; the second part deals with *contemporary aesthetics strategies*.

Classical strategy focuses on two classical uses of visual strategies: the official aesthetic organizing of the political *state* and the commercial *market*. What can we learn from art organizing in the formation of nation states and what sort of artist is likely to be a good organizer? After that, we account for how marketing aesthetics inspired the emergence of commercial markets and this, in turn, heralded the role of artists who designed products into coherent brands and helped to frame the market as an art show exposing the work of artist marketers.

The second part, on *contemporary strategy*, explores art and artists who accomplish new visual organizing by differentiating themselves from the classics of the past. Artists after the 1980s increasingly have engaged in visual strategies that strikingly transcend the classic official use of art by artists in the last two centuries. While mainstream media, marketing, and advertising today perpetuate this classic official art in a global postmodern spirit, recent examples help demonstrate how contemporary artists do it in new ways. They are sick and tired of the postmodern condition and now propose their help as researchers to rediscover reality as art. Therefore, a new kind of reality art is emerging, and, in addition to the standard curriculum, artists gain competency as reality coaches during their tenure in art school. When art and artists get involved and apply the new kind of aesthetics contemporaries label 'relational,' new visual strategies for organizing emerge.

Throughout the chapter, we will apply aesthetics to describe the value that only art and artists can add to visual strategies. In one example, we will see how the role of artists as organizers of the state was interdependent on the emergence of a German aesthetic philosophy that made public sense of their work. In Anglo Saxon-rooted marketing aesthetics, we will see how artists and art became valued as visually organizing commercial activity. As we consider the implications of seeing organizations as art, we will place different aesthetic spectacles on the nose of the reader; this will hopefully enable him/her to reflect on and consider what qualities and what competencies turn something into art or someone into an artist. When it comes to art and artists, the visual is never a matter of direct perception only. Where a philosophical, aesthetic point of view is lacking, what we see will remain aesthetically invisible! Perception and philosophy must go hand in hand for an aesthetics strategy to have a chance to work ... as artwork!

Classical aesthetics strategies

Organization as a work of art: the case of the nation state

Currently, the primary venues for the movies of German filmmaker Leni Riefenstahl (1902–2003) are community art cinema clubs. For many years after World War II, however, her 1934 film *Triumph of the Will* and her 1937 picture *Olympia* were not available for circulation and viewing, as they had been banned for celebrating Nazi ideology.[1] To be sure, Riefenstahl was one of Hitler's favorite artists, but, when she was charged with being a Nazi propagandist, she denied the accusation with what seemed to her a perfectly plausible explanation: Hitler had explicitly *selected* her, a free artist, not a party hack, to film the Nuremberg Party Congress in 1933 and the Berlin Olympic Games of 1936. While her statement implied that being an artist freed her of any guilt for the content of her films, the very fact that she was an artist provided her with the leverage to empower the Nazi cause. And, while she was no advertising consultant *per se*, her mesmerizing scenes on the silver screen projected far beyond what Hitler and his propaganda minister Joseph Goebbels could ever imagine. The aesthetic value she added to the visual was devastating.

Riefenstahl was certainly not alone; she had numerous colleagues whose works have filled art film archives with movies that aesthetically mobilized political organizations. In addition to the Nazis, other totalitarian regimes like the Fascists and the Communists have used cinematic art to galvanize twentieth-century moviegoers into political enthusiasts. Walter Benjamin (1892–1940), a philosophical critic of this totalitarianism, wondered if art would lose its magical attraction in times of mass-media art. To the contrary, of course, art grew into an even more powerful strategic-visual instrument. While it might be claimed that the magical attraction of single art pieces waned, the growth of the organizational power of mediated art is without challenge. Unfortunately, Benjamin was terribly wrong!

When watching the pseudo-documentaries of Russian director Sergei Eisenstein (1898–1948) – I recommend his masterpiece *The Battleship Potemkin* and *Ten Days that Shook the World* – contemporary students of filmography are, in fact, viewing the Stalinist visual art strategy that helped organize Soviet society. In addition, when viewers get carried away by the films of Stanley Kubrick (1928–1999), they also need to remember the respect Kubrick had for the uncle of his German-born wife. Furthermore, at the same time the Nazis were executing their Holocaust genocide, Veit Harlan (1899–1964) wrote and directed his infamous movie *Jud Süss* (1940),[2] which promoted pro-German anti-Semitism. Politicians traditionally have made a very efficient as well as a very terrifying use of art as an organizational power. At the outset, it is important to understand that tradition and its supporting aesthetics.

'Deutschland, Deutschland über alles,' sing the victorious Germans – yesterday on the battlefield and today mostly at World Cup soccer matches. In 1952, German President Theodor Heuss (1884–1963) agreed to reinstate the old hymn as the national anthem of the new GFR, although by that time it had been mixed with the infamous Horst-Wessel song and used as Hitler's national-socialist anthem. Heuss wanted a brand-new anthem, but Konrad Adenhauer (1876–1967) insisted upon the old one. Adenhauer did, however, substitute a revised third verse that began with more democratic words 'Einigkeit und Recht und Freiheit' (Unity and Justice and Freedom) in place of the earlier nationalistic 'Deutschland, Deutschland.' The fact that the third democratic verse and not the earlier pompously patriotic one became legally protected in 1990 as a symbol of the GFR indicates that the real organizational power survived in the music and not in words. In 1967, the German publishing house Bote & Bock made public the latest official military band arrangement of the old song. This case provides an excellent example of how closely an audio-visual strategy for organizing is connected to how artists work inside organizations long before the modern nation state employed strategizing.

On the 12 February birthday of Roman-German Emperor Franz II in 1797, the 'Deutschland' version of the song was first performed at the old Burgtheater in Vienna. Shortly afterward, its proud composer Joseph Haydn (1732–1809) blended it into his string quartet Op.76, no. 3, which was printed in 1799 and subsequently became famous as the Kaiserquartett (see Guillet de Monthoux 2009). By then, the work was already known as Haydn's hymn. Its text was conceived as a prayer for the Kaiser and almost immediately became a powerful and widely diffused musical symbol in service of the Austrian monarchy. Haydn had an impressive track record for successfully hailing and celebrating both divine and worldly powers in his creations, and, while his works gave glory to specific elites, they also loosened up and animated otherwise stiff feudal organization. One reason why some politicians hesitate to retain artists is that aesthetics strategies are more risky than other safer though less powerful propaganda techniques.

This makes art special in comparison with other strategic instruments of power, domination, and propaganda. Art does not just harness ruling power, however, and its legitimizing effect must always be considered in tandem with its propensity for organizational change. This might be one lesson drawn from the case of an Austrian Kaiserlied now in service of German democracy. Haydn can serve as a prototype for artist-organizers who easily provide special audio-visual powers to their organization. What kind of artist is likely to be a strategic asset though? Let us try to build a profile of this individual by considering Haydn as a paradigmatic artist-organizer and discern how different he was from the virtuoso Mozart and the genius Beethoven, both less suited to the task.

Looking for the 'artist-organizer'

Haydn's contemporary colleagues such as Wolfgang Amadeus Mozart and Ludwig van Beethoven knew the composer simply as 'Papa Haydn.' They saw him as an artist respected for his gentle character and orderly style of life; he was certainly not perceived as a misunderstood rebel. With the exception of an eight-year period in Vienna between 1749 and 1757, Haydn spent his immensely productive life as an artist-organizer. He landed a tenured contract in the service of the court of Prince Esterhazy and quickly rose from the position of Vice Kapellmeister to Kapellmeister, a position that put him in charge of the Esterhazy orchestra and its 20–25 musicians and gave Haydn all the responsibilities of a full-fledged art manager. As was the protocol in such princely households, Haydn became an artist kept firmly in check by precise rules and regulations carefully written down in a very detailed document. His life was regulated by the hierarchy of the estate of Esterhazy and his castle Esterhaza, which had been recently erected in the spirit of Versailles, the most glorious court of Europe. In addition to the halls and salons, a large theatre and a smaller stage for puppet performances were parts of the court property. In the summer season, Haydn was responsible for programming, rehearsing, and staging a performance at each venue every night. Prince Nikolaus graciously offered free tickets to all performances to his party, subjects, and occasional guests. In reality then, Haydn at Esterhaza was actually the director of a huge audio-visual performance manufacture with an impressive output: the seasons of 1782 and 1783, for example, offered 90 and 105 performances. Out of the 125 shows produced in 1786, only 9 operas were recycled, while 8 were brand-new creations for that season only. Haydn presumably wrote at least one of these operas. During his tenure, Haydn composed 14 operas for Esterhaza, but this was only a part of the commitment specified by his contract. In addition to these tasks, Haydn was also responsible for music for the church and chapels of the castle, and this resulted in many masses and oratorios. Hiring and firing performing artists was also on his 'to-do' list. Above all, however, his first priority was helping to develop Esterhazy's audio-visual strategy, which was so important for maintaining public image and political relations.

In 1773, for example, Empress Maria Theresa attended an opera performed by marionettes and was so impressed she invited the show to Schönbrunn, her Vienna residence. And in 1763, when the Prince was on a mission to elect a new Kaiser in Frankfurt am Main, his fireworks and illumination of the city were reportedly an exquisite event. All the electors put on impressive shows, but the young Johann Wolfgang Goethe noted that Nikolaus' offering was the most beautiful and magical of all. As an artist-organizer Haydn received routine payment far exceeding the scattered earnings he had obtained freelancing in Vienna. His organizational importance is underlined by his listing in the 'house officers' of the Prince, where Haydn's position of Kapellmeister was ranked third. As a bonus, he seemed to have enjoyed great freedom to do projects for performances and publication outside of his main duties.

His primary responsibility, however, was inside the organization where music in all its forms accompanied all worldly and religious projects of the Prince. As inconceivable as it would be to marry, christen, or bury without music, secular events such as masked balls, hunting parties, and sundry anniversaries also demanded music specifically composed for the event. Haydn's impressive productions catered to all these audio-visual demands, especially those of the Prince himself, the CEO-proprietor of Haydn's courtly corporation and the one who proudly played new music written by his beloved artist-organizer Haydn.

A comparison of Haydn with technical virtuoso Wolfgang Amadeus Mozart (1756–1791) reveals that not all good artists are fit to organize. Mozart was born and drilled to become the main attraction of Leopold Mozart's Musical Touring Circus. Young Mozart wrote his first composition at the age of five. When he was six, he went on his first tour and was received by Maria Theresa as the *wunderkind* of the day. Since Wolfgang's childish charm was a magnet for audiences, his family lost no time in capitalizing on it. In 1763, he set out on a tour that was to last for more than three years, and by the time he was nine he had performed for royalties in England and France. Two years later, he composed his song plays, which today would be called musicals, and these were soon to be followed by both opera *seria*-serious and *buffa*-humorous.

Mozart spent most of his youth on tour, and, when he did return home to his native Salzburg, he almost immediately had to begin another project. Due to the low pay for steady positions as Konzertmeister or Hoforganist, he could not afford to stay in Salzburg for long.

Whether Mozart found himself in Munich, Mannheim, Vienna, or Berlin, he tried hard to obtain a dependable inside position similar to the one old Papa Haydn had. In his youth, he had traveled to get rich and, as he grew older, poverty pushed him out onto the roads. Not even in Vienna did he find peace. One can trace almost 20 addresses among which he constantly had to move his poor little family and his old tattered pianoforte. His nomadic life as an outsider was more of necessity than by intention, and his early death in 1791 was probably due in part to the physical hardship he had had to endure beginning at the time of his youthful tours as a *wunderkind*. Even though Mozart died a famous composer, his honor and fame came from his reputation as an exceptionally gifted and technically brilliant craftsman, not from his success as an artist-organizer. The fact that no organization found it worthwhile to keep him on its tenured payroll supports this conclusion.

Let us now turn to another artist icon, Ludwig van Beethoven (1770–1827), in order to get an even better understanding of the artist-organizer. On Beethoven's second visit to Vienna in 1792, Haydn accepted him as a pupil, and their teacher–student relationship seems to have been the principal thing they had in common. Haydn, for example, gladly spent 28 years in the loyal service of his Prince, but, when Prince Karl Lichnovsky, also a good friend and admirer of the late Mozart, paid Beethoven 600 gulden to enter his service in 1800, this Prince was up against an entirely different temperament. Beethoven responded to his position by whining, 'Now I have to be home at half past three to shave and put on something better; can't stand it!' (Geck 2001: 28). At that time Beethoven was much hailed as a piano virtuoso and composer, but, in the words of Johann Wolfgang Goethe (1749–1832), he was also known for his heroic 'Napoleonic' stubbornly uncompromising personality. When Beethoven approached the managers at Breitkopf & Härtel to get a lifelong exclusive contract similar to the one 'Goethe has … with Cotta' and 'Händel had with his London publisher' (Geck 2001: 47), he received the harsh reply that, as far as the impresario knew, Beethoven was neither a Goethe nor a Händel.

This rejection made Beethoven even more determined to obtain support as an independent artist, and, after ten years of persistent effort, he finally did it. His success came when his three most influential Viennese patrons – Archduke Rudolph and the two Princes Lobkowitz and Kinsky – by written contract granted him an annual lifelong rent of 4,000 gulden. In addition to this, Beethoven continually earned money on the side, not only selling his compositions but also capitalizing on his popularity by peddling dedications for his compositions to Viennese nobility. Beethoven was not an artist lending his audio-visual organizational skills to an organization, however; he was an entrepreneur hedging market risk through a fixed income from rich donors. He also incorporated the idea of the 'genius' with a divine mystical gift that accounts for his qualitative jump from brilliant technique to sublime art. Even though the stubborn struggle for independence makes it difficult for a genius to serve an organization, the rise of a new kind of German philosophy during this period fostered a new look at artists and art from an organizational point of view.

Aesthetics of the state: seeing the value of art and artists to organizing

Around the time of Haydn, Mozart, and Beethoven, a branch of German philosophy began to reflect on the roles of art in society. A figure central in this development of German aesthetics was poet and philosopher Johann Wolfgang Goethe. Goethe actually lived through and took an active part in the formational period of German aesthetic philosophy, and, in addition, he knew personally the trio of Haydn, Mozart, and Beethoven. Goethe believed that the acknowledgment of the power of art was closely connected to philosophical reflection. To Goethe, Haydn's creation of his string quartet was stimulating as a philosophical discussion 'because you hear four reasonable men converse, [and] get both the impression of grasping their discussion and becoming familiar with the special character of each participating instrument' (Knispel 2003: 90).

In Frankfurt am Main, Goethe had once noticed 'the little man in wig and dagger' (Hennenberg 1992: 14), alias *wunderkind* Mozart, on his first tour. Goethe had no problem with the art of Haydn and Mozart, but he became seriously concerned when clarity and playful beauty were overshadowed by introverted rebellion in the work of Beethoven. Goethe once remarked that Beethoven's *Fifth* was 'grandiose, though completely insane' (Salomon 2003: 285). The composer actually met Goethe several times and wrote several pieces inspired by Goethe's writing. Goethe was an elegant and witty celebrity, but he had difficulty comprehending the uncompromising artist. Beethoven had once revolted Goethe by childishly urging him, an innate aristocratic gentleman, to ignore the Czar in an idiotic attempt to make the ruler of Russia salute Beethoven before Beethoven greeted the monarch. Regardless of this, Goethe accepted most of Beethoven's whimsy and even played the game of spelling his name '*von* Beethoven' even though his 'van' clearly signaled that he was, in fact, a 'bourgeois gentilhomme.'

Beethoven admired Goethe immensely and also held Goethe's protégé poet Georg Friedrich Schiller in high regard. Schiller's poetry survives today primarily in the lyrics of Beethoven's *Ninth*. In 1795, Schiller recorded some of his reflections in his *On the Aesthetic Education of Man* (Schiller 1982), as he investigated how Immanuel Kant's third critique could be used as a theory for how art and artists could help organizing an 'aesthetic state' (Chytry 1989). Had Schiller published his 'aesthetics' it would have undoubtedly provided Goethe with the philosophical frame needed to completely acknowledge the organizational and constructive function of even a too wild genius like Ludwig van Beethoven. In Schiller's rendering of Kant, it makes aesthetic sense that Beethoven cut himself loose from much of the musical tradition of his time by inventing a third form of music somewhere between noble opera and religious oratorio. The fact that Beethoven emphasized the independent character of his music and branded it 'absolute' art is equally understandable in light of Schiller's aesthetic theory.

Schiller's organizing aesthetics defined art as the modern expression of our innate drive for play. *Play*, in turn, is a third kind of absolute force that balances two other innate drives for *form* and *matter*. Without this balance, individuals run the constant risk of getting hooked on either form, defined as our love of logical thinking, or matter, our lust for physical pleasure. When form or matter rules, human organization turns dogmatic or materialistic. Only play is able to keep a check on these forces. According to Schiller, artists are the guides to play and the guardians of playfulness, and he maintains therefore that artists are the true organizers of a good society. By upholding playfulness as a third constructive power controlling the two destructive powers of form and matter, art can save us. When this belief becomes influential, which was the case during the nineteenth century in the German-speaking world, art and artists turn good candidates toward leading societal positions.

In 1830, when Felix Mendelssohn-Bartholdy (1809–1847) visited old Goethe in Weimar, this aesthetic philosophy had flourished for more than 30 years. From the time Mendelssohn first spent some time in Weimar at the age of 12, Goethe had admired his way of doing art, first asking him to 'make some noise' (Rolland 2011 [1864]: 7) at the pianoforte. Goethe then sallied forth into a philosophical conversation about the role of art and disclosed that 'you the young have all made such progress in art; so now you have to explain it all to me; for I am no longer informed ... we really have to talk reasonably' (ibid.: 6–7).

Goethe's specific interest, however, was hearing about the philosophy of Hegel, and Felix Mendelssohn was a reasonable person to explain Hegel's ideas, for the great Prussian state philosopher was a frequent guest in the house of Mendelssohn's father, a famous Berlin banker. Hegel enjoyed both concerts and philosophical conversations; to him, art might be politically significant because philosophical aesthetics could explain art's role in helping to unify scattered German states under Prussian rule. Hegel saw to an even greater extent than Kant did that art was an important pillar for a perfect modern state. Here was a new philosophical system that gave leading roles to art and artists, and even Prussian elites read aesthetics as a theory for organizing the new state. Hegel provided artists with an amazing expansion of Schiller's theory and made them key organizers of the evolving bourgeois state.

The Mendelssohn family métier was deeply conditioned by organizational aesthetics. Felix Mendelssohn was nothing but the offspring of humble craftsmen, but his music making had a philosophical grounding that led to his getting a central position in the state. He ran the famous Leipzig Gewandthaus concert house and managed its orchestra. In addition, he was an important state bureaucrat who administered the first public conservatory for state-supported music education. It was no coincidence that Felix was the grandson of Kant's friend the Jewish philosopher Moses Mendelssohn. German idealism and its aesthetic philosophy paved the way for how new art institutions operated. This new aesthetic state granted powerful inside positions to those that rank and faith had made outsiders before. The Hegelian positioning of art at the core of a new idealistic state made it possible to dispose of church as well as court without jumping into a market system void of any institutional protection for art and artists.

Today, two centuries later, the differences in cultural policies between English- and German-speaking Europe can probably be accounted for by the same Hegelianism that made it possible for art and artists to be counted as state insiders, protected and in charge of a new kind of cultural institution. Son of a wealthy banker and a recent convert to Christianity, grandson of a philosopher who secretly learned the German language to escape from an outsider position in a ghetto sealed off by orthodox Jewish rabbis, Mendelssohn had orchestrated his career as artist-organizer perfectly in tune with dominant organizing aesthetics. Hegel welcomed artists that made art in the spirit of Schiller. Arthur Schopenhauer hailed even further the artists' claim to the throne of the new philosopher king. It was no coincidence that Hitler was devoted to Richard Wagner who retained his own private philosopher-coach or that Friedrich Nietzsche, as long as he was publicly acknowledged as the new Dionysus, turned opera into an audio-visual scenario for an aesthetic state. This became the Nazi scenario to the extent that Hitler considered Wagner his 'religion' and in the 1930s considered marrying Winifred Wagner, widow of Richard's son. Felix Mendelssohn-Bartholdy strolled up the same broad road of organizing aesthetics as all the Riefenstahls and Eisensteins had. In the middle of the nineteenth century, he spelled out the constitutional duty of an artist-organizer to develop audio-visual strategies since

> we have to acknowledge that there exists no art of the same high standards as our German art ... no other people is able to understand art as we although I cannot explain why that is so ... In music a work of art of that stature (as Schiller's Wilhelm Tell [*my example*]) is still lacking, and music still needs one day to bring forth a work of that similar perfection.
>
> (Rolland 2011 [1864]: 248–249)

The artful market: designing products as pieces of art

Marketing aesthetics

The rise of German bourgeois art and its organizing aesthetics is a prelude to contemporary 'cultural policy.' From the German aesthetic philosophy of Immanuel Kant forward, it was directly conceived as a theory for organizing a public sphere. Artists educated in art academies and conservatoires were primarily trained to make official public art in the service of an aesthetic state. Meanwhile, other parts of Europe like Britain and France saw the birth of a different aesthetics with a focus on visual strategies. While state aesthetics concentrated on the public sphere, a new marketing aesthetics contended that art and artists have an important role to play in private markets.

During successful tours in England, both Haydn and Mendelssohn experienced early 'marketing aesthetics.' They found musical life in England fundamentally different from their publicly embedded careers on the continent. In Haydn's case, in addition to shaping audio-visual strategy for the House of Esterhazy, he had freelanced in 'academies' of the Vienna Palais and the court theatres. In England, and to some extent in France, a third type of venue had opened up in public chambers between church and court, and this was a market for performances open to a paying audience. On the British Isles, Haydn's music was presented in venues such as the Hanover Square Rooms, and music lovers of the thriving bourgeoisie began to unite in consumer associations. Professional concerts were supplied in this new commercial market where artists supplied pieces of art as products in a marketplace. Single products were designed so that they naturally fit the artist's signature.

At the same time, art and artists became central to the making of markets for manufactured products. Adam Smith, the moral philosopher of modern markets, provided an account of art-based visual strategies of the market in his *Theory of Moral Sentiments*. The book, published in 1759, sets in place the philosophical footing for his treatise on *The Wealth of Nations* published in 1776. He provides an aesthetic explanation for the demand for the luxury products we are attracted to:

> We are ... charmed with the beauty of that accommodation which reigns in the palaces and economy of the great; and admire how every thing is adapted to promote their ease, to prevent their wants, to gratify their wishes, and to amuse and entertain their most frivolous desires.
>
> (Smith 1979: 183)

Smith declared 'the eye to be larger than the belly,' pointing out that what drives the 'wealth of nations' is the visual. Our physical needs or the practical usefulness of what we demand is secondary. He laid the foundations for a marketing aesthetics that pinpointed the 'something' that made the manufacturers and workshops do business by 'charm' and 'beauty.' Moreover, Smith believed that what spurred demand for private goods was connected to what determined preferences in the public sphere. For what determines both private and public choices, in political states as well as in commercial marketplaces, is our visually triggered attraction to beautiful organization or in Smith's words:

> the same principle, the same love of system, the same regard to the beauty of order, of art and contrivance, [that] frequently serves to recommend those institutions which tend to promote public welfare ... They make up part of the great system of government,

> and the wheels of political machines seem to move with more harmony and ease by means of them.
>
> *(ibid.: 185)*

German state aesthetics differ from the Scottish aesthetics of marketing, however. The contention that the desire for beauty and charm motivates the modern consumer as well as the modern citizen makes an aesthetics of the 'pleasure principle.' Smith's reason for including art and artists as visual marketers is, therefore, somewhat distant from Kant's or Schiller's aesthetic theories. Smith offers a different, and also potentially conflicting, rationale for making art and artists shape visual strategies. Kant (1991) was adamant that aesthetics aimed at making judgment about higher truths, and Schiller dubbed the artist an organizer responsible for stopping formalism and materialism in the ideal state. Kant felt that Smith's Scottish friend and inspiration David Hume diminished the role of higher ideals in human action when he focused on sense perception and factual experience in his empiricist philosophy. Hume's empiricism made us skeptical of the existence of any higher values. In addition, Smith saw all of society as a theatrical stage, a vanity fair, where actors showed off to each other and where no underlying values or honest intentions could ever be read into it with full certainty. In the world of Adam Smith, little room exists for enabling overwhelming enthusiasm to sweep away doubts and mobilize observers into spontaneous actors in the way organizing aesthetics interprets how visual happenings like a Wagner opera or an Eisenstein movie can affect masses.

Marketing aesthetics became a social science on the same plane as Newton's discovery of gravitation. Visually attractive actions and beautiful goods had the power to cluster people into groups and communities. This interest in social effects caused by using beauty and charm made modern 'marketing,' a term already used by Smith to provide psychological rationales for why art and artists are important. On the other hand, the more philosophically bent investigations stemming from state aesthetics led to more sociologically tainted rationales approaching societies and organizations as a whole as artworks *per se*. In matters of art and of artists, perception is always accompanied by philosophy; the German school, however, generally put the emphasis on philosophy while the Scots relied mostly on perception. Marketing aesthetics at the most hypothetical level assumes that the design of individual products connects and organizes them into brands in the mind of the consumer-spectator. In English marketplaces, buyers saw what they knew, while Prussian citizens rather knew what they saw.

Market as an art show for designed pieces

What was offered in the markets of early industrialization people often saw as art. It often even looked like a performing artist. Karl Marx, for example, pictured factory goods on the shop counter as performance-pantomime between a coat and a piece of cloth arguing their relative value as if on the stage of a commercial theatre. It was taken for granted that the commercial success of early industrial wares depended on colorful stage makeup, as in the case of the vividly printed fabrics that seduced buyers in the textile markets of the first monster mills. When the moral/market philosopher Smith explained how poor traders got their hands on primitive gold treasures from rich tribes, he took it for granted that glittering glass pearls, baubles, and trinkets would do the aesthetic trick. No wonder that nineteenth-century world exhibitions made no difference in exposing industrial hardware, blueprint software for better social organizations, as well as spectacular pieces of art by famous artists.

Smith's early lesson in visual marketing aesthetics was later interpreted by Karl Marx as how the appearance of wealth can be exchanged for what really is! Marx leaned heavily toward the German focus on philosophy behind perception, and the Marxian interpretation indeed hinges on the Platonic idea of artists as visual tricksters who cunningly fool by projecting visual shadows on the walls of our caves. This Platonic idea of art fits naturalistic artists who depict the masterpieces of craftsmen. Flemish still-life art, which shows plates and cutlery on an exquisite tablecloth, was often actually an early version of commercial posters and ads visually representing value in real goods. In Plato, this is clear; he saw artists as providing illusions by mirroring only the values others produced, therefore deeming the visual worthless. In that Platonic perspective, artists were at the bottom of the value-making pyramid; they just mirrored objects produced by honest craftsmen according to the ideal blueprints of philosopher-designers. Smith's aesthetics in fact put artists making attractive visual impressions at the top of the commercial-value pyramid.

The advent of industrial mechanization, first in the mass manufacturing of products and then by industrial depiction of this visual reality in the form of photography and motion pictures, posed the problem of reinforcing the Platonic callout of artists as visual parasites on material production and formal philosophizing. Where Platonic philosophy prevailed – and it did gain considerably in importance through industrialization due mainly to its modernization in Marxian philosophy – the recognition of value in art depended on aesthetics that would explain it as something more than just visual mirrors of the real or ideal. The Marxian tried to escape the problem by postulating that modern states should be split up into a commercial and a cultural sector. But even that imaginary iron curtain has cracked due to the fact that industrial factory and services workers look more and more like art and artists. German aesthetics had tried to turn Plato's argument on its head by claiming that artists represented a third way that made the world tick smoothly, while philosophers of form and materialists would ruin it if left alone. This argument worked well where the elite often aspired to govern an 'aesthetic state' (Chytry 1989) as a 'total work of art' (Groys 1992), but early industrialization took place elsewhere.

Artist marketers

England, the very cradle of industrialization, recognized other strategies like the 'Arts and Crafts' movement promoting the artist-artisan as paramount to the production process. Similarly, Austria's 'Werk-Bund' organization invited factory owners to look at old masterpieces that might be copied using new machinery, thereby reconnecting mass manufacturing to ancient craftsmanship. Much in the spirit of Smith's marketing aesthetics, early industrial design made art museums and art schools interact with industry. Nineteenth-century European art academies opened special programs for drawing patterns for textiles, like the 'flower class' in French silk-city Lyon. Much later, the same motivating force caused visual artists such as Andy Warhol and Michelangelo Pistoletto, each with a background in marketing and advertising, to team up as pop artists operating in a market where the overlap between commerce and culture was an empirical fact. Museums and art collections interacted with design and production in a spirit fostering young artists such as John Galliano, who scouted for new Dior collections mining the Victoria and Albert Museum. Small companies grew visually large brands by inviting artists to play in their factories and then, as artists, to sign limited edition products as Marcel Duchamp once jokingly had signed 'ready-mades.' This old tradition of melding manufacturing and art has recent successors in arty furniture companies such as the German Vitra, Swedish Källemo, Italian Alessi or Finnish Artek. Signature designers became visual experts for companies functioning as artists associated with galleries. In the French-speaking world, these new artists-marketers have the professional name of their 'createurs,' vaguely alluding to the old-time art genius. This is how the Italian Alessi presents its product designers who are usually Italian architects who earned degrees from art academies and then opted to make small articles instead of big houses.

The marketing artist then does not 'do art' dictated by the market. He/she does not simply decorate or embellish by painting on boxes and advertisements instead of on canvas. While the organizing artist is good at maneuvering in a state and its bureaucracy, the marketing artist instead navigates in markets. This implies – and this is an important qualification – that marketing artists do not produce art *for* the market but *in* the market. Marketing artistry stands in sharp contrast to earlier artists living a double life as both breadwinners and artists. Salvador Dali (1904–1989) worked as a department store window dresser, Henri de Toulouse Lautrec (1864–1901) sold dance hall posters, and René Magritte (1898–1967) earned his living by way of his Studio Dongo advertising firm. They lived double lives making the commercial pay for the cultural.

For marketing artists such as American Andy Warhol (1928–1987) and German Joseph Beuys (1921–1981), there was no longer such a split. Warhol successfully fought his way out of his first profession as an advertising artist to begin making his art in close interplay with markets (e.g. Schroeder 2005). Instead of cloistering himself in a secluded studio, he founded a factory of his own as well as a glamorous commercial-looking magazine, declaring to the world that he wanted to become a real 'business artist' doing true 'business art.' His screen prints feature Campbell soup cans and Coke bottles that paradoxically offer individual portraits of mass wares. Beuys, the German friend of Warhol, focused his creative effort on 'enlarging' the concept of art, making it work far outside the world of fine arts. He launched his ideas through extremely efficient public event marketing accompanied by catchy ad slogans such as 'Art is Capital' and 'Everyone is an artist' and by defining doing art as 'Social Sculpture.'

Michelangelo Pistoletto (1933–), another prominent marketing artist, today focuses on managing his foundation and promoting experiments in 'socially responsible art' in cooperation with regions, corporations, and single firms. He locates visual experiments in art spaces and biennales, partly financing them through gallery sales of his own artwork; for example, his Illy projects are shown in the Venice Biennale. The commercial and the cultural are now fundamentally blurred. In the second part of the chapter, it will become clear that even the last three artists belong to the classical era.

Contemporary aesthetics strategies

Art and the real

A new contemporary aesthetics strategy still half-baked and still much in the making is evolving in a world where Western art is permeating globally. YouTube stores art classics of Riefenstahl, Haydn, and even Wagner opera. Shoppers know art they constantly see on the markets. Impressionist painting, the exquisite detail of early Salvador Dali drawings, and the color of Andy Warhol prints belong to contemporary folklore. Our visual experience is forged by the calligraphy of Apple, the baroque of Dolce & Gabbana, or the Schinkel neo-classicism of a banking palace. We have no problem integrating art history in our reading of everyday reality. When thus an organization studies lecturer displays art icons by Matisse, Picasso, and Dali to her students asking them, 'Where would you like to work; in Matisse, Picasso or Dali-organization?', they seem to have no problem interpreting what kind of atmospheres such masterpieces may convey. Media provide us today with aesthetics spectacles from very early on.

Most large cities invest in art fairs and hold biennales, so that the man on the street has an easy pathway to visual experience. The number of art students is increasing exponentially as new forms of art take advantage of new visual technologies. This, in turn, implies that visual art is being explained, interpreted, analyzed, and reflected upon by an equally growing global army of theorists, curators, and critics. It has been said that a picture is worth a thousand words. Today, these words reappear in the art-connected publications and one may ask: which ones are not? We live in Societies of Spectacle (Debord 1995) entrenched in the postmodern conditions (Lyotard 1979) that make it unproblematic for even a child to discern the difference between a Fauvist or Cubist or Surrealist organization! Marcel Duchamp had in the neighborhood of 3.5 million Google hits as of early March 2012. Businesses are art firms, managers are artists, and museum and art galleries but bleak copies of markets and organizations (Guillet de Monthoux 2004). Managers pride themselves on doing 'business art' a la Candy-Andy and cool corporate communication artfully turns loss to profit and old hats to new caps by creative tricks many artists have derided in their work over the past two decades (e.g. Mir 2003). In short, there are plenty of reasons why those who want neither Guy Debord nor Jean Baudrillard (1994) to have the final say today should avoid classic aesthetics strategies. How then do contemporary aesthetics strategies attempt to invent new roles for art and artists in visual organizational strategies?

Inventing is actually an inappropriate term to use in context with contemporary aesthetics strategies; the movement is rather about discovering or finding. The classics, philosophers and artists united, were constantly looking for how to make the general or universal visible in the everyday. Contemporaries seem to imply that, when art and artists focus on making the universal visible, they unfortunately end up exposing idealistic clichés, which are increasingly removed from the truth Kant claimed aesthetic judgment could help detect. That said, contemporaries do not claim they can pull a correct idea out of some Marxist top hat nor do they want art or artists to present visuals with an alternative symbolism or from different imageries. One of their novel battles against the classics claims that art and artists will help organize a better world only when they make us see what is really out there. By seeing, they mean *observing* rather than just viewing. They see classics lost in a museum of images, visions, and ideals. To the contrary, contemporaries envision art museums that feature scientific observation of the world. The science they propose is one based on human beings and their concrete conditions.

The mega art show dOCUMENTA takes place every fifth year in Kassel, Germany. At dOCUMENTA 13, which ran from 9 June until the end of September 2012, the German-based artist Omer Fast presented a piece of video art critically exploring the narrative process demonstrated during the take reunion between a German soldier returning from Afghanistan and his middle-aged parents. The video records how, after being informed that their son had been killed in combat the couple takes an assortment of young men home with them as surrogate sons. What initially presents itself as a comment on a macro political event turns into a complex drama disclosing effluvia of human behavior, as single close-up micro events send the viewer far into the muck and mayhem of the subject. An overwhelming impression of dOCUMENTA 13, a show that traditionally offers a good sample of contemporary artwork in general, is that art and artists quite often resolve to zero in on the individual close up and personal. It seems to take very little effort to assume the opposite position of blowing up something from its singularity to a universal meta-level, as if the contribution of art and artist would be to critically check the real substance of the general by putting it to a singularity test. Does this exist or is it a myth, an ideal or an empty vision? Earlier such tests were performed by giving the artist the privilege to put herself, as a subject, on the scene of art. Contemporary aesthetics strategy, however, consciously avoids the subjective and opts for what is now labeled the 'singular.'

The focus is no longer on individual feelings or emotions but on the possibility to marinate something in a general form, a special unique content. This is what artists attempt, this is what art should offer, and this is how contemporary aesthetics strategy attempts to eliminate the postmodern mist polluting overexploitation of classic strategies.

Implicit in this new strategy is the desire to maintain but refine special art spaces. This new kind of art necessitates a special visual experiment, and the laboratory or observatory supporting such an investigation has to be organized carefully. Remember how art spaces and performance venues were designed as white cubes or black boxes to focus the attention – of eye and mind – on pieces of art. Such observatories could be single buildings or whole cities like the dOCUMENTA in Kassel, the Biennale of Venice, or the European cultural capitals. The visual strategy of putting us in the picture in a very physical sense seems highly efficient, for a large number of people go to art spaces. This tells us that the visuality of contemporary aesthetics strategies is a physical consideration. The art space works on us, or, in the words of artist Olafur Eliasson (1967–), museums are really 'reality machines.' Art is a return to intensively complete sense experiences beyond the audio-visual limitation and the isolated ideal daydream. In that vein, artists become reality coaches to facilitate this new strategy of embodied vision. How does one become an artist able to put this sort of visual strategy into action?

Artists as reality coaches

When we look at art schools nurturing a contemporary aesthetics strategy, we no longer see comfortable nests for hippy dreamers fueled by outmoded 'alternative' utopias of freedom or tolerance. Art schools today encourage students to get inside the real world and face its constraints and conflicts. Young artists need to get used to a mix of monastery and mob scene and develop the practical skills necessary to function in the challenging fusion in art worlds. Before they leave art school, students should role-play how they will react to collectors who want to put them under long-term contracts and decide for themselves to what extent it is worthwhile to follow all the whims of curators and gallerists. An artist today must always be able to negotiate position in practical situations where freedom is always relative and contingent.

The contemporary art student knows there are no theoretical shortcuts to developing visual strategies. They usually have to familiarize themselves with the real-world practices of managing and curating, and what older artists confidently delegated to other art-world specialists like gallerists and art dealers, the contemporary art student now must master and integrate into his skill set. Today's young artists participate in and gain direct inside experience with the complex organizational exercises involved in the development of visual strategies and assessment of their impact on audiences and critics. Artists like Danish Olafur Eliasson and Chinese Ai Weiwei are deeply involved in constructing and delivering their complex installations, always keeping in mind the effect of these strategies on direct spectators and indirect media.

Gone are the days when fledgling art students shared a crowded common studio; in the past, it was only after years of study or upon graduation that students were told they had reached the top and were then able to move – usually alone – to a single isolated studio. The house shared by Eliasson and Weiwei in Berlin exhibits the reverse; here there are two masters in a well-organized space that allows many different specialists to cooperate productively in the quest not for new dreams but for rediscovering the reality lost to classical dreamers.

The workspace of the reality coach artist is a place for generating social knowledge that cannot be transferred by assigning 'passwords' to isolated artists. A reality coach acts as if the social capital that integrates art with society will be destroyed if it is managed as individual property. It is both produced and shared in a cooperative experience.

Relational aesthetics

The young contemporary artist actually has more in common with Haydn than with Picasso or Mozart. Eccentricity verging on egocentricity resonates with the old artist myth but has no place in a contemporary art school fostering reality coaches fit to help develop visual strategies. What turns the contemporary artist into a potentially good reality coach is a preoccupation with experience and its meaning. Respect for this kind of practical knowledge can only emerge if it is liberated from the model of knowledge as information to single individuals. It rests on acknowledging the embodiment of vision and the importance of sensual knowledge (Bourriaud 2002). The implication, of course, is that learning in social interaction is the right way to grasp aesthetics.

The reality coach artist constructs shows, makes installations, and arranges performances and stage encounters where vision is continuously interwoven with interpretation, and the visual is continuously mixed with the intellectual. What Beuys prophetically alluded to as 'social sculpture' found its philosophical articulation nearly half a century later in Nicolas Bourriaud's 'relational aesthetics.' Bourriaud is not a philosopher; he is a Parisian critic-curator who found it important to articulate the ideas of the artists he has exhibited. The same goes for the aesthetic investigation of Boris Groys who has elaborated a theory to show that novelty in contemporary art is a matter of transferring objects from the index of general archives to those of art institutions (Groys 2007). It is in close cooperation with installation artist Iliya Kabakov that Groys has developed his arts practice-based aesthetics (Groys 1996).

These are but two of the many cases illustrating the new way of doing aesthetics. Some would say this new way got off the ground when philosopher Arthur Danto began reflecting on the work of Warhol he had encountered in some New York gallery half a century earlier (Danto 1999). While Kant and Smith wrote for philosophers, the readers of this new kind of aesthetics are mainly artists in search of intellectual reflections on their own practice. This aesthetics also gets published and read in art magazines, and museum bookstores now disperse this type of aesthetics globally. In contrast to state and marketing aesthetics of the classical strategy, evidently it is also global simply because it follows visual art on tour as its intellectual catalogue companion.

Relational aesthetics is perfectly in tune with Mayor Bloomberg's commissioning Olafur Eliasson to create an eye-catching New York Waterfalls installation in 2008.[3] It could easily defend the choice of Ai Weiwei as the designer of the Beijing Olympic Stadium in 2007. Relational aesthetics delivers explanations why art is able to open our eyes to reality. Bourriaud further claimed that art has the relational power to make people meet and interact. Instead of engaging the service of an advertising firm to make a social impact, people should involve the artist in their visual strategies. Groys described the almost erotic sensitivity of installation artists and pointed out how they might touch us with their art in much more sensitive ways than any event-manager would be able to. Note how Danto minted an aesthetic term for how something like Duchamp's ready-made bottle rack suddenly perceived as a piece of art undergoes a 'transfiguration of the commonplace' (Danto 1981). Blinded by our grand visions and dreams, we tend to disregard our observation of visual art in the form of the real.

Summary: art, artist, and aesthetics for organizational visual strategies

Some art and artists practicing visual organization strategy operate consciously, while others spin off it to their main concern. We have seen how what was called the classic approach has been taken over by a number of communication professionals using, or maybe abusing, art as the main raw material of postmodern productions. We have also discovered the contemporary aesthetics strategist, who helps organize but does it differently than those who stage aesthetic promotions of nation states or big corporations or transform products into designer wares in markets. The contemporaries are a bit tired of the classics' focus on the general and universal ideals. They are not convinced that their own subjectivity can make them escape the dream world of a society of spectacles.

Instead, the contemporaries go for the singular and try to frame art as snapshots of reality that can perhaps capture cracks in the media wall of myths. They see no difference between art and society and hate having double careers as media gurus and art stars. They are like Swedish filmmaker Roy Andersson[4] who gladly collects golden eggs, the prizes awarded for making commercial movies promoting insurance firms, political parties, and business firms, in the same basket as golden palms, the prizes awarded at the Cannes film festival.

While classics tend to think they can offer us dreams and visions, the contemporaries are after reality. This strangely echoes the art epoch in which realists such as French painter Courbet and writer Zola teamed up with positivist scientists to expose nature true and unmasked. Maybe the contemporaries are our new positivists, and maybe our so-called classics masquerade as romantics.

Finally, the chapter has attempted to explain that art and artists depend on aesthetics. In order to have practical effectiveness, the visual strategies we employ must be viewed through the glasses of aesthetics. If we forget aesthetics, we miss the whole point of connecting art and artists to such strategizing. Put bluntly, Stalin would never have paid Eisenstein, Alessi would never have hired either Mendini or Sottsass, and Bloomberg would never have given a thought to having Olafur Eliasson add to the image of New York. Aesthetics translates and clearly articulates this creed into words and, in addition, supports art-loving spectators with intellectually convincing philosophical arguments. While there may be artists without art, there is not art without aesthetics. This goes for visual strategizing too.

Notes

1 A sample can be viewed on YouTube at http://www.youtube.com/watch?v=7TI6yIo-tcc.
2 Available on YouTube at http://www.youtube.com/watch?v=ZIvaBOxHDj0&skipcontrinter=1.
3 Olafur Eliasson's Waterfalls, New York, available on YouTube at http://www.youtube.com/watch?v=t7H-m5K06eM).
4 http://www.royandersson.com/

References

Baudrillard, J. (1994) *Simulacra and Simulation*, Ann Arbor: University of Michigan Press.
Bourriaud, N. (2002) *Relational Aesthetics*, Paris: Presses du Réel.
Chytry, J. (1989) *The Aesthetic State*, Berkeley: University of California Press.
Danto, A. (1981) *The Transfiguration of the Commonplace*, Cambridge; Harvard University Press.
——(1999) *Philosophizing Art*, Berkeley: University of California Press.
Debord, G. (1995) *The Society of the Spectacle*, New York; Zone Books.
Geck, M. (2001) *Ludwig van Beethoven*, Reinbek bei Hamburg: Rowohlt Taschenbuch Verlag.
Groys, B. (1992) *The Total Art of Stalinism: Avant-Garde, Aesthetic Dictatorship, and Beyond*, trans. C. Rougle, Princeton: Princeton University Press.
——(1996) *Die Kunst der Installation*, München: Carl Hanser Verlag.
——(2007) *Über das Neue: Versuch einer Kulturoekonomie*, München: Hanser Verlag.
Guillet de Monthoux, P. (2004) *The Art Firm: Aesthetic Management and Metaphysical Marketing*, Palo Alto, CA: Stanford University Press.
——(2009) 'Papa Haydn and the Amadeus Myth', *Aesthesis* 3(1).

Hennenberg, F. (1992). *Mozart*, Reinbek bei Hamburg: Rowohlt Taschenbuch Verlag.
Kant, I. (1991) *The Critique of Judgement*, Oxford; Clarendon Press.
Knispel, C.M. (2003) *Joseph Haydn*, Reinbek bei Hamburg: Rowholt Taschbusch Verlag.
Linstead, S. and Höpfl, H. (eds) (2000) *The Aesthetics of Organization*, London: Sage.
Lyotard, J.-F. (1979) *La Condition Postmoderne*, Paris: Les Editions de Minuit.
Mir, A. (ed.) (2003) *Corporate Mentality – An Archive Documenting the Emergence of Recent Practices within a Cultural Sphere Occupied by both Business and Art*, New York: Lukas & Sternberg.
Ramirez, R. (1991) *The Beauty of Social Organization*, München: Accedo.
Rolland A.A. (ed.) (2011 [1864]) *Lettres Inédites de Mendelssohn*, Paris: Collection Hetzel.
Salomon, M. (2003) *Beethoven*, Paris: Librairie Artheme Fayard.
Schroeder, J.E. (2005) 'The artist and the brand', *European Journal of Marketing* 39: 1291–1305.
Schiller, F. (1982) *On the Aesthetic Education of Man*, Oxford: Oxford University Press.
Smith, A. (1979) *The Theory of Moral Sentiments*, Oxford: Clarendon.
Strati, A. (1999) *Aesthetics and Organization*, London: Sage.
——(2009) 'Do you do beautiful things? Aesthetics and art in qualitative methods of organization studies', in D.A. Buchanan and A. Bryman (eds) *The Sage Handbook of Organizational Research Methods*, London: Sage, 230–245.

Part III
Visual methodologies and methods

10
Methodological ways of seeing and knowing

Dvora Yanow

Seeing comes before words. ... It is seeing which establishes our place in the surrounding world; we explain that world with words, but words can never undo the fact that we are surrounded by it. The relation between what we see and what we know is never settled. ... [T]he knowledge, the explanation, never quite fits the sight.

(John Berger 1972: 7)

The crunch of the crostini, the slitheriness of the penne alla vodka – a question preoccupying philosophers is where these personal experiences ... [of] qualia, the raw, subjective sense we have of colors, sounds, tastes, touches and smells ... fit within a purely physical theory of the mind.

(Syracuse University, NY, philosopher Robert Van Gulick, in a talk at the Association for the Scientific Study of Consciousness, Las Vegas conference, mentioned by reporter Johnson 2007)

And because I brought a critical approach to thinking about photography, I was interested in what these photographs were – not as windows through which you would look at a life and a world, but as cultural artifacts in their own right.

(Barbara Kirshenblatt-Gimblett, quoted in Gruber 2011)

That organizational activities include the visual, as do methods for studying organizations and organizing, is, or should be, evident. From the moment a researcher physically enters the setting of a field research project, the eye is, or can be, confronted with a multitude of stimuli. Manufacturing, governing, educating and other forms of organized life take place in built spaces that are seen, experienced and responded to, from corporate headquarters to individuals' offices to the shop floor. Working artists and university art major graduates advise executives on the purchase of paintings and sculptures intended to evoke just the right mood for visiting clients or customers, board members or community members. Employees adorn their desks, cubicles or lockers with cartoons, postcards, pinups, photographs, and more, giving visual voice to selected aspects of their identities. Organizations do the same with logos and brands. Designers generate images for annual reports, college catalogues and political campaigns to convey the organization's identity, as it wishes to be perceived publicly. Marketing has its own long tradition of symbolic representations of human social meanings, especially in the design of advertising (see, e.g., Cone 1960; Goffman 1979). And so on. Many organizational members are aware of the role of the visual in representing organizational values. As Dino Olivetti wrote half a century ago, reflecting on his company's role as a symbol of this notion, 'Respect for our customers is reflected in the design of our products, of our advertising, and of our showrooms' (1960: 42). The key methodological and methods questions in this arena are: what to look at in this vast array of sine waves that can stimulate the retina's cones; how to 'see', systematically, when we do look; and what informs and hangs on these ways of seeing and knowing.

For all the prominence of 'observation' in methods talk, visual elements have long taken a back seat in studies of organizations and in their dissemination, both of which have tended to privilege words, whether written or spoken.[1] Consider the kinds of evidentiary sources most commonly drawn on in organizational studies analyses: written documents of various sorts, from annual reports to memoranda, correspondence to webpages; formal interviews with managers and CEOs; water-cooler chats with staff, bar or kerb-side talk with workers. In this logocentrism, organizational researchers have tended to ignore, or forget, or simply turn a blind eye to the visual elements of the physical settings in which work takes place, with their varying spatial designs, contrasting building materials and landscaping, and wide-ranging types of furnishing and other decor, internal and external.[2] In turning to 'take language seriously' (White 1992), we have tended to forget that people do things not only with words (Austin 1962), but also with objects: the gold watch presented on retirement after 50 years' service to one company or the trophy awarded for a job well done (e.g. Kunda 1992, ch. 4), the food selected for an annual party or the dress expected in particular work settings (e.g. Dougherty and Kunda 1990; Rafaeli *et al.* 1997; Rosen 2000), and so on. All of these visual elements may be studied visually, although even researchers who turn to visual studies may initially ignore what visual media make available for analysis, favouring, instead, transcriptions of spoken language (e.g. Bertoin Antal 2012).

What might it mean to study organizations' visual worlds, visually, and to do so systematically, considering both data generation (including potential data types and sources) and data analysis? The topic – often under the heading of 'visual anthropology', 'visual sociology' or, more broadly, 'visual methods' – has typically focused on researcher-generated materials recording individuals, acts, interactions and events observed in field research, using still photography, filmmaking or video-recording. Photography and film in the hands of the researcher are old tools in anthropology, dating to Margaret Mead and Gregory Bateson's early twentieth-century work and, subsequently, Tim Asch's, and a presence in sociology. Documentary in form, they constitute a point at which social science and journalism come perhaps closest (e.g. the 1930s US 'Dust Bowl' photographs of Dorothea Lange and Walker Evans). In organizational studies, these were pioneered a century ago by Frank and Dr Lillian Gilbreth, working with Frederick Winslow Taylor on time and motion studies.[3]

In this chapter, I take a broader approach. 'Visual studies' might also explore the meaning(s) of Khrushchev's shoe (banged on his speaker's desk during a United Nations debate, 1960), the shape of the Vietnamese peace talks table (oval vs. square, 1969), or military cemeteries (Ferguson and Turnbull 1999). They need not be done only with technological prostheses, such as cameras. In that sense, *analysing visual data* (tables, charts, various objects or [inter]actions observed) is not necessarily coterminous with *doing visual analysis*, to the extent that that entails mediated study. Visual 'recordings', from pencil and paper to video, help us 'capture' 'bodies in space', but modes of research can also include ethnographic and other forms of observation that are not usually thought of as 'visual studies'. Indeed, we use the language of all the senses

Methodological ways of seeing and knowing

to signal observation and understanding: 'Yes, I see'; 'I hear you'; 'It smells fishy'; 'It left a bad taste in my mouth'; 'I feel your pain' all signal a grasping of the other's meaning, although sight-related expressions predominate.[4]

Methodologically, it is useful to distinguish between two kinds of method. One set is used in locating visual materials that were created independently of the research project: the kinds of visual material 'found' in the field, like sherds in an archaeological dig – organizational artefacts that are 'collectable' and/or accessible visually, created by organizational members for organizational purposes, which may become evidentiary sources for a researcher. The other is used in creating visual data for research purposes, which can be further divided into two categories: materials created by organizational members at the researcher's request – maps, drawings, photographs, videos, and so on – and those created by the researcher for analysing those and other data (see Table 10.1).

Table 10.1 Three genres of visual materials, by creator/source and purpose

	'Found' [pre-existing the research project]	Generated [newly created for the research project]	
		Member-generated	Researcher-generated
Creator(s)	'the organization' or its 'agents' [individuals, teams, departments] acting for the organization or a unit within it	individual members, at the behest of the researcher	researcher
Purpose	created for organizational purposes [i.e. independent of the research project]; [assumed to have been] created to express organizational or sub-unit values, beliefs, feelings [meanings]; collected by the researcher as data for analysis or as evidence in support of the analytic argument	research [data generation, analysis]: intended to show the member's own views of the organization or part of it; collected by the researcher as data for analysis or as evidence in support of the analytic argument	research [analysis]: to record observed objects, acts, interactions, etc. for use as a visual aid in thinking through persons' locations, movement patterns, and other aspects of organizational life observed; writing [research dissemination]: to present data in textwork phase – to communicate to readers, in condensed fashion, vast amounts of observed data
Examples	annual or divisional reports [including photographs, layout]; brands, logos; building and/or interior design; ceremonies [graduation, retirement]; dress [including uniforms]; graphic displays [organizational charts, workflow charts, report tables, posters]; trophies [the gold watch; statues (the Oscar)]	photographs, videos/ films, drawings or other depictions of organizational life; photo elicitation [used to generate narrative evidence related to research question]	maps of movement through organizational space [who went where, interacted with whom, how frequently]; photographs, videos/films; sketches of interactions at meetings [e.g. Bales' interaction process analysis]

167

Before I turn to specific ways of seeing and knowing visually in organizational settings, a few initial questions – concerning the presuppositions underlying choices and uses of methods and the related issues they raise – need to be addressed, and, before that, some terminological clarification.

To begin with, this chapter rests on a distinction between methodology and method. The former enacts a researcher's ontological and epistemological presuppositions concerning the subject of study and processes of knowing it, along with knowledge claims issues arising from these. Methods themselves put those methodological presuppositions into play in everyday data generation activities and, later, in explicit, directed data analysis (by contrast with the less directed analysis that takes place in the course of field research or even in the process of formulating a research question). A second useful distinction differentiates between methods for generating data and methods for analysing them. In the context of visual methods, this distinction, although somewhat artificial in general, is particularly useful because of the need to attend to differences among organization-generated materials created for organizational purposes, materials generated by organizational members at the researcher's request for research analytic purposes, and researcher-generated materials created for research purposes.

Third, distinguishing, heuristically, among three phases of a field research project highlights the presence and role of visual methods in each: fieldwork, in which the researcher is busy with generating data, typically in interaction with situational members (although this could also include the interactions with texts characteristic of archival research); deskwork, in which the researcher is engaged explicitly in analysing those data, working from notes, recordings, transcripts, sketches, copies of original documents, etc.; and textwork, in which the researcher is actively transforming the analysis into a research text and disseminating it (Yanow 2000).[5] Treating research writing and/or reading themselves as methods (Richardson 1994; Yanow 2009) and, hence, presumably, also as enactments of methodological presuppositions (see also Schwartz-Shea and Yanow 2009) highlights the role of visual methods in 'textwork' as well as in 'fieldwork' and 'deskwork'. Further methodological ground-laying is called for before we take up visual methods for generating and analysing materials more directly.

Methodological priors

> Parfois les noms écrits dans un tableau désignent des choses précises, et les images des choses vagues; ou bien le contraire.
>
> *(René Magritte 1929)[6]*

Does the researcher consider visual materials to be transparent referents corresponding directly to, or mirroring, what they depict, or are they assumed to be interpretations – re-presentations – of that? Do the photographs of staff and students in a US college catalogue or on its webpage, for instance, depict the institution's population as it actually is – as an unannounced visitor might experience it? Or has each photograph been staged, the collected images carefully selected, and the layout strategically managed not only for aesthetic reasons, but in order to depict, publicly, the desired image of age, class, race-ethnic, sex or other demographic composition that a university sensitive to public opinion concerning diversity and affirmative action laws wishes to convey? How have changes over time in the series of photographs of prisoners of war held at US Naval Station Guantánamo Bay altered the image of the US military (Van Veeren 2011)? Parallel questions could (and should) be asked with respect to materials produced by or for the researcher: does he/she consider organizational members' videotapes or his/her own drawings and photographs to be mirrors of what transpired in meetings, in the corridors, wherever, or are they interpretations of organizational realities?

These are ontological questions concerning the 'reality status' of the materials produced with respect to what they depict, akin to what Magritte (in the epigraph) is pointing to concerning word and image. The first in each question pair above locates the researcher in a realist ontological realm; the second, in a constructivist one. Similar questions could be asked about organizational members' understandings of and/or attitudes towards the visual materials themselves: does the glass in the recently designed Scottish Parliament building in Edinburgh convey, in singular and possibly universal referential fashion, that governance is now transparent (glass = clear), as decision-makers wished it to (purportedly by contrast with non-transparent London-based decision-making)? Or might other interpretive communities interpret the use of glass there in other ways, thereby shaping, differently, their parsing of the building and the events and acts it houses? The one position rests on an understanding of direct correspondence between signifier (object) and signified (its meaning), to use semiotic terms; the other, on a presupposition of potential multiplicities of meaning-making shared within interpretive communities but not necessarily across different meaning-making groups, with conflict possibly arising from such differences.

Studying visual materials and their representations also entails epistemological questions concerning the 'know-ability' of visual elements by researchers and their analytic methods. If the objects or their portrayals are considered to be transparent (re)presentations of their underlying meanings, analysis can be made through observation alone. This is an objectivist epistemological realm: the researcher parses the object's, image's, event's or act's meaning by observing from a position *external* to it (the definition of objectivity), without necessarily involving the meaning-making of those who created or use(d) it. By contrast, if elements studied visually are understood as other than a direct capturing of what they depict, the researcher needs to discern their meanings through engaging with their creators and/or users – the research 'subjects' or participants for whom they have primary meaning(s). Context-specific meaning, rather than universal meaning, is central to this position: the researcher is seeking to understand organizational materials from the perspective of their customary (situated) users, the domain of 'subjective' meaning;[7] and the researcher is in an interpretivist epistemological domain (a position at odds, for instance, with psychiatrist Carl Jung's and mythologist Joseph Campbell's ideas about the universal meanings of archetypal symbols).

Consider, for instance, looking at an organization's building – its architectural design, construction materials, landscaping, furnishings, and the like (e.g. Berg and Kreiner 1990; van Marrewijk 2010; Wasserman and Frenkel 2011; Yanow 1993). Does the researcher hold that their significance for the organization can be established by analysing them objectively, drawing on established, general (and arguably universal) norms accepted throughout the design world, perhaps as an architecture critic might, without consulting the building's occupants or taking into account their values, beliefs and feelings? Or does the researcher hold that these elements' significance *for understanding aspects of organizational life* can only be established in the context of members' and/or stakeholders' experiences and meaning-making of the building and its furnishings, in their full, and perhaps conflicting, variety?

Alternatively, consider an editorial cartoon in an internal newsletter or a daily newspaper depicting an organizational decision that impacts on the local population. Cartoonists commonly exaggerate the features that, symbolically, denote that which they represent (Danjoux 2013) – whether of the Prime Minister or other actors (e.g. elongating Charles de Gaulle's nose) or of particular spaces or other objects, as in replacing the Statue of Liberty's torch of freedom with a carrot (Ilan Danjoux, personal communication, spring 2011). Does the researcher seek to ascertain 'the real story' masquerading in cartoon form? Or does analysis explore the multiplicities of possible meanings that the cartoon's symbolic elements – that carrot, for instance – might convey to various groups of readers, expressing their positions, giving voice or leading to conflict? This is one sense of Kirshenblatt-Gimblett's approach to photographs (see third epigraph above) 'not as windows through which you would look at a life and a world' representationally, providing a transparent view on to a singular organizational reality, 'but as cultural artifacts in their own right' (Gruber 2011), saying something about the values, beliefs and/or feelings of the photographer, perhaps, or of the organization.

Similarly, from such an interpretive methodological approach, researchers need to interrogate graphic representations of statistical data. As Drucker puts it, the 'simplicity and legibility' of graphic forms 'hides [*sic*] every aspect of the original interpretative framework on which the statistical data were constructed' (2011: 8). The vocabulary of bar graphs and other forms of visualizing quantitative information is not methodologically innocent: as she shows, charts' discrete bars, scale divisions, circles and rectangles, labels, arrows, vectors, paths, and their texture, proximity, grouping, orientation, and so on imply certainties about category definitions and quantities (nationalities, sex, time span, etc.), reifying them through the '*representational* force of the visualization as a "picture" of "data"' (ibid.: 12, original emphasis).[8] Even a map presumes a point of view, unarticulated, from which it was drawn (e.g. on mapping the US census category 'Asian-American', see Yanow 2003: 63–64).

Ontological and epistemological presuppositions intertwine; in 'ontoepistemological' fashion (Fuenmayor 1991), they position a researcher in either a realist-objectivist mode of enquiry or an interpretivist-intersubjectivist one (commonly referred to, these days, as 'positivist' and 'interpretive', respectively). These methodologies frame everything from the conception of a research question to its research design, from execution to analysis and writing (for an extended discussion, see Schwartz-Shea and Yanow 2012). This chapter proceeds mostly in keeping with the presuppositions that inform interpretive research, demarcating positivist approaches when appropriate and the differences between them. As meaning and meaning-making are central to interpretive methodology and methods, I turn next to the question of the locus of meaning, taking up hermeneutic approaches first and then phenomenological ones.

Locating meaning(s) I: creator, user, 'text analogue'

Where do the meanings of a visual representation of some aspect of organizational life reside? This is the sort of question that has long engaged literary critics or theorists concerning what texts mean, and how their theorizing can help us think systematically about analysing visual materials produced in or by organizations and their members for organizational purposes. It is a hermeneutic question, 'hermeneutics' referring originally to rules for interpreting biblical texts, these rules uniting members within an interpretive community and demarcating them from other interpretive communities, often in highly contentious ways. The concept was later extended beyond biblical passages to the interpretation of all manner of texts, and then beyond written words to all human artefacts, including film, architecture, art and other physical objects. Taylor (1971) and Ricoeur (1971) note that, in analysing human actions, we render them as texts – 'text artifacts', in Taylor's phrase – and apply to them the same hermeneutic processes that we bring to interpreting literal texts. This provides the philosophical ground-laying for methodological issues concerning the analytical applicability of literary theories to visual sense-making of physical objects and their representations.

Hermeneuticists argue that, in creating things, we embed in them the values, beliefs and/or feelings that comprise what is meaningful to us. The relationship thereby established is a symbolic one, the more concrete artefact (object, language or act) representing – symbolizing – its more abstract, 'underlying' meanings (values, beliefs, feelings). Every time we use or refer to an artefact, we sustain its established meaning(s) (although here is also where possibilities for change enter; Yanow 2000: 14–18). Hermeneutics sets out to decipher what these situated meanings might be.

To take a common example, the dove is often seen as a symbol of peace. For members of different epistemic-interpretive communities, it may symbolize other meanings or have solely instrumental meaning – as tonight's dinner. Or it may represent no particular meaning at all: the dove is just a dirty white bird. This example highlights several properties of artefacts and their symbolic representations: the meanings embedded in, carried by, and conveyed through artefacts are situation-specific; and, because the same artefact may have a 'situated' place in a range of settings, it can embody and convey multiple meanings.

In contemporary methods applications, 'hermeneutics' commonly refers more to the symbolic relationship between artefact and meaning and the idea of interpreting meanings embedded in and conveyed through those artefacts than to fixed sets of interpretive rules within interpretive-epistemic communities (whether of organizational members or researchers). Because of meaning's abstract character, interpretive research commonly begins with observing the artefacts themselves and their uses (including hands-on or other bodily 'observation'), inferring meaning, provisionally, and corroborating or rejecting those initial interpretations through further observations and/or conversations across persons, times, settings and/or written texts (depending on the research question). This is one of the central methodological differences demarcating 'interpretive' researchers from 'positivist' ones, who would commonly define their concepts and operationalize them a priori, before going to the field to test them (see Schwartz-Shea and Yanow 2012).

Ascertaining the meanings of texts has been of central concern to literary studies, and their approaches can be useful for analysing visual 'texts'. Initially, literary critics understood a text's meaning to reside in its author's life experiences (e.g. discerning whether his/her religious commitments influenced T.S. Eliot's crafting of *Four Quartets* or whether Shakespeare's possible homosexuality explains *Hamlet*), parallel to 'auteur theory' in film studies. Contesting that approach, in the mid-twentieth century, was the argument that textual meaning resides in the text itself – 'The author is dead!' (Barthes 1967) – conveyed through such devices as rhythm and rhyme, alliteration and metaphor (e.g. Ciardi 1959; consider light and shadow, angle, shot duration, and other filmic devices). Towards the end of that century, other theoretical approaches joined in opposing the relevance of authorial intent,[9] among them 'reader-response theory'. A more phenomenological orientation, this argues that meaning resides in the lived experiences that readers bring to their readings, thereby shaping textual meaning(s) (with some reader-response theorists arguing for interactions among all three sources; see, e.g., Iser 1989). In this view, meaning is indeterminate, potentially shifting not only from one reader/viewer to the next, but even from one reading/viewing to the next by the same reader.

The tripartite taxonomy of *creator* (author, painter, designer, etc.), *reader* (viewer, user, stakeholder, onlooker), and *text* or text-analogue (photograph, film) is useful in critically engaging visual artefacts' meanings. The researcher who explores intended meaning or his/her own meaning alone enacts a realist-objectivist methodological position. Meaning, in this instance, is assumed to be singular; and it is assumed that 'received' meaning (by those who engage with the artefact in question) is, or should be, identical to authored meaning. Discrepancies – e.g. a 'failed' brand image that is not being understood as its creators intended it to be – are attributed to poor design or some other 'noise' in the communications 'channel' between creator (the organization) and reader (e.g. customers).[10] On the other hand, the researcher who considers that the 'reception' of the artefact's meaning is not, or not necessarily, determined by and coterminous with its creator's intent – that, in other words, readers, viewers, users, passers-by and onlookers, near and far,[11] may have their own interpretations of the artefact – enacts an interpretivist-subjectivist position, assuming potential multiplicities of meaning. In addition, the symbolic repertoire of compositional elements – line, shape, form, colour, texture, size, weight, height, mass, and so on – can be studied to understand what meaning(s) they represent, for which interpretive communities. Each genre of visual material – built spaces, paintings, photographs, etc. – has its own meaning-communicating vocabulary.[12]

In asking about the meanings of organizational materials studied visually where 'authored' meaning does not predetermine 'constructed' meaning, analysis has to engage questions of 'whose meaning?' as well as 'where is meaning coming from?' Kenneth Burke's pentad (1945) contributes analytic systematicity here. Also a literary theorist, Burke identified five key elements in dramaturgical meaning, his key focus (but see Burke 1989 for extended sociological discussion), which lends itself directly to analysing films of organizational action: settings, actors, acts, agency and purpose (corresponding roughly to the journalist's where, who, what, how, and why or when). Adding objects (with or via what?) to the pentad expands the visual repertoire that can be analysed; growing the actors category to include both researchers and users/readers expands the hermeneutic realm. Analysis, then, needs to attend not only to who their creators are and the conditions of their use(s), but also to the purposes for which artefacts have been created: what their intended meanings were; who the intended 'users' ('readers', viewers) were/are, near and far; whether there are unintended users; what the interpreted uses and meanings are, perhaps unintended or unanticipated by their creators, and whether these generate tensions, and so on. Consider, for instance, the range of meanings expressed after the publication of the Abu Ghraib photographs or the Danish newspaper cartoon depicting the prophet Muhammad (on the latter, see Cohen 2009). Such questions might also engage creators' purposes and relative power vis-à-vis the full range of intended and unintended users, near and far, and the matter of strategic intentionality in artefact creation. And analysis might also explore interpretations not (readily) voiced, whether silent by choice or silenced through threat.

Still one more layer can be added to this interactive triad of creator, artefact, and user. So far, it has been treated at the level of the artefact in the field (see Figure 10.1). Here is the double hermeneutic (from the researcher's perspective) of creators' and/or users' interpretations of organizational artefacts and researchers' interpretations of those interpretations. When the research text is itself the artefact, the triad *entier* becomes the artefact in another triad – that of the researcher, the research manuscript, and the reader of that text (see Figure 10.2). This introduces a third hermeneutic (Yanow 2009): as the creator becomes the researcher-author of the text, the user becomes its reader or reviewer, interpreting the researcher's interpretations rendered in that text of users' interpretations of artefacts created by someone else. For that matter, to the extent that researchers can identify an artefact's creator and his/her intended meaning, we are in the realm of four hermeneutics: creator's, user's, researcher's and reader's.

Particular methodological questions arise concerning establishing the authorship of an artefact and its intended meaning. When working with organizational images (as with some written

| creator | artefact | user [1st hermeneutic] |
| [1st hermeneutic] | | researcher [2nd hermeneutic] |

Figure 10.1 The analytic triad during fieldwork (with 1st and 2nd hermeneutics)
Note: The 2nd hermeneutic – the researcher's interpretation of others' interpretations of field material (the 1st hermeneutic) – begins in the field, developing during desk- and textwork.

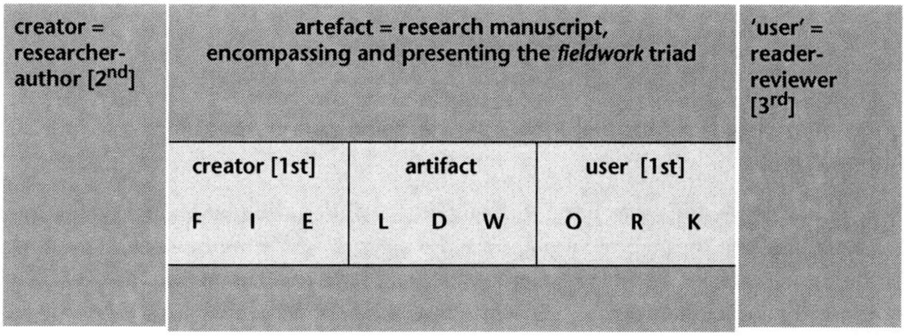

Methodological ways of seeing and knowing

creator = researcher-author [2nd]	artefact = research manuscript, encompassing and presenting the *fieldwork* triad			'user' = reader-reviewer [3rd]
	creator [1st]	artefact	user [1st]	
	F I E	L D W	O R K	

Figure 10.2 The nesting of artefacts and interpretations: 1st, 2nd and 3rd hermeneutics, from the researcher's perspective

Note: That readers' and other users' constructed 'texts' of others' authored texts are not, and cannot be, prescribed, delimited and controlled by those texts' creators is amply in evidence when we consider journal reviewers' readings of submitted research manuscripts, part of the dissemination phase of textwork.

artefacts), it may not be possible to identify their creators or *their* intended meanings for it: unlike modern fiction and poetry, such 'products' are often not signed. Indeed, authorship may be attributable to a team or some other group. In such a case, can meaning be attributed to the organization as a whole (or some unit within it)? Can a researcher claim, for instance, that an image used in an organizational publication represents the values of that organization, especially when the initial creator and/or adopter of that image cannot be located to attest to its (then) intended meaning? From an interpretive methodological perspective, Kirshenblatt-Gimblett's view concerning reading images for their broader, cultural meanings (see third epigraph above) once again comes into play. It is not necessary to identify the specific wizard-behind-the-curtain producing cartoons, photographs, films, and the like in order to assert intended meanings and attribute these to the collective or some part of it. Meaning is understood to be constructed collectively – intersubjectively – such that intended meanings are held by groups (epistemic-interpretive communities) and reflect their collective values, beliefs and/or feelings. Artefacts are not studied in isolation from other artefacts and other evidentiary genres; asserting intended, collective meaning is made possible by supporting evidence from other sources and, as with all analysis, a logic of argumentation that stands up against contradictory evidence. Conflicting interpretations held by other groups are also asserted, analytically, and supported through similar argumentation.

In my study of the Israel Corporation of Community Centers (1996), for example, I became confident that a statement about the meaning of their buildings' design elements written by one member of the founding board, a copy of which I found in correspondence files, reflected the meaning intended by the entire organization on the basis of his board membership, the board's role in developing the organization, and corroborating evidence from other sources (including observation, participation, interviews and other documents). Other evidentiary sources established other interpretive communities' conflicting interpretations of the same elements; my research manuscript brought these into conversation with each other. Historical analyses of visual materials where authorship is not always clear proceed similarly. In other words, members' interpretations are not necessarily uniform, nor are they necessarily identical with the researcher's. Meanings, whether authored or constructed, are inferred on the basis of mapping the organization for various, including contending, evidentiary sources and for the intertextual evidence these might yield or generate (Schwartz-Shea and Yanow 2012: 84–89), brought into conversation with each other for comparison, corroboration and refutation.

Locating meaning(s) II: not just looking – touching, phenomenology and body proxies

Studying visual materials puts us not only in the realm of hermeneutic interpretation. Because most, if not all, of the organizational objects and images we study are intended for *use*, we are also in the realm of phenomenological interpretation – analysis that engages the lived experiences of organizational members in and with those artefacts. We are looking, then, not only at aesthetic experiences, but also at pragmatic ones: visual analysis might include the feel of material objects as we heft and handle them, move them about and walk through them.

Note the use of 'we'. When it comes to the material world, 'we' researchers use our own bodily and other experiences (emotive, aesthetic) as proxies for the 'we' of human responses presumably shared with the inhabitants of, and visitors and onlookers to, the organizations we study (where we as researchers are somewhere between those statuses, balancing strangerness with familiarity in our search for understanding; Agar 1996 [1980]; Yanow 1996: 19–21; Schwartz-Shea and Yanow 2012: 29). This poses a conceptual-methodological problem for research projects conducted in keeping with realist-objectivist ontological-epistemological presuppositions, in which the researcher seeks to determine an artefact's meaning, objectively, in an a priori fashion (rather than 'bottom up' from the perspective of those who live and interact with it in everyday ways, including, at times, the participating researcher). This problem is especially evident in studying one particular constellation of visual materials: the built spaces that are the settings for organizational activities.

Here, phenomenological experience is key: researchers' experiences of spatial artefacts, along with those of situated members, become central to interpretive processes, as researchers and their bodies are the primary 'instrument' in sense-making[13] – at least in drawing initial, provisional inferences. Moving through organizational space, the researcher not only sees it but also 'feels' its meanings with, on and through his/her body, including aesthetic, emotional and other dimensions – attending, in other words, to 'pathos' and 'ethos' as well as 'logos' (Gagliardi 1990a; see also Strati 2003). The same process holds for office decor, dress, the ambience of a room or a meeting, and other visually observed materials in the organizational repertoire. Even though provisional sense-making would commonly be checked with situational members, drawing on 'body knowing' puts us irrevocably outside the realm of objective knowing.

In sum, the distinction between looking only for intended meaning in authored visual 'texts' – or even 'the real story' behind them – and looking for potentially multiple possible meanings they might have for a wide range of organizational actors has implications for how a researcher uses methods. Moreover, what can be studied visually are not only objects and images, but also events, acts and interactions that use and engage physical materials. Language, too, has visual dimensions: literally, in the sense of the graphic design of posters, flyers, graphs, and suchlike that are posted on office bulletin boards or included in print materials, something that Tufte (2001 [1983], 1990, 1997) has focused on at length; figuratively, in the form of non-verbal language – kinesics (hand and facial gestures), proxemics, personal 'decor' (dress, jewellery, eyeglass frames, hairstyle, etc.), and personal characteristics (physiognomy; skin quality, e.g. marked, smooth; hair, eye and skin colouring; height; weight; sex, etc.). Such a wealth of organizational material can be studied visually that it is difficult to provide a compendium of types. Equally complex is the question of where in the organization to look, but here we can be somewhat more systematic.

Turning to methods: systematic ways of looking

> Considering the tool-dependent nature of human reasoning and the ability of 'knowing,' the representational view of human action ... should be complemented with the acknowledgement that the use and making of these tools are inherent parts of human action itself.
>
> *(Van Herzele and van Woerkum 2008: 446)*

> An image is a social fact that may be applied as evidence to the task of historical or social analysis.
>
> *(Morgan 2009: 9)*

Listing visual elements for researchers to attend to in organizational settings is enticing, but impossible, as the range of artefacts (objects, mostly, but also events, etc. – anything that can be observed and studied visually) is innumerable, and perhaps inadvisable, given the temptation to use it as a checklist rather than as a set of potentialities whose realization is a function of the research context. Nonetheless, because this is an understudied area in organizational studies, such a suggestion of where and how a researcher, especially one who has never undertaken such a project, might look to find things that might constitute visual materials and, therefore, potential data for visual analysis might be useful.

From the perspective of designing a research project, different procedural logics suggest systematic ways of looking for visual artefacts that exist independently of the research project ('found objects') or that might be generated for research purposes. I organize these according to four procedural logics. The first three of these engage visual materials that a researcher might find in the research setting and/or generate him/herself to make a record of these 'found objects'. The fourth adds materials that researchers might ask situational members to generate. Table 10.2 includes examples for each. All four schemas are fairly basic, having been composed imagining a reader who has rarely, or never, contemplated visual methods, although I hope they might be of use to other researchers, as well. These might also be incorporated into a project that is not primarily a visual study.

'Geographic' logic. Entering a new research setting and moving through it, researchers can attend to an organization's 'geographic' features, beginning with mapping the organization's external physical plant and its relations, visual and proximal, to neighbouring buildings (for extended discussion, see Yanow 2013b). Inside the building, mapping can note spatial allocations of offices and roles, paths most and least travelled, interactions, and so on. Spatial allocations link organizational roles with power and status dimensions; mappings depict these graphically: the segregation of types of work and roles, for example, by location within a building and on a floor; departments or roles rendered 'invisible' by locational contrast with occupants of more prominently sited spaces. Similarities to or contrasts with neighbouring spaces may illuminate community–societal relations, power and status. And mapping may show up particular features of inter-organizational and network relations, whether between headquarters and dispersed sites or within an industry.

The geographic metaphor, then, references not only attention to 'topographical' and other spatial dimensions, but also to 'mapping' as a method. These can be literal maps, sketched out; photographed or videotaped paths of movement (e.g. Iedema et al. 2010); computerized movement maps (Bjerrum and Fangel 2012); narrative 'sketches' (e.g. 'ethnographic mapping', see Oliver-Velez et al. 2002; although an image can encompass and convey many more details, more quickly, than a word text; and unlike a videotape, at least with contemporary publishing techniques, a sketched image can also become part of the research report); or some other form.

Table 10.2 Logics of enquiry

Logic	Where to look	Examples
1. Geographic		
a. external	approach from the point of arrival	bus or tram stop, street or sidewalk leading to the main and other entrances, parking lot
	immediate surroundings	visual and proximal relationship of building design to design of neighbouring buildings [other enterprises, governmental agencies, residences; sight lines, similar or contrasting building and landscaping materials, design fit, setbacks]
	landscaping	number, height, colour, density, quality of plantings, or their absence; relationship to walkways, driveways
	parking lot	relationship of designated spaces to entrances [main, side, back]; the archetypal parking lot spaces reserved for organizational elites in close proximity to entrances versus more egalitarian spatial treatments
b. internal	hallways	floor-plans, usage maps [patterns of movement, who interacts with whom; e.g. Iedema et al. 2010]
	departments, offices, and roles in relation to each other across and within floors	elevations, layout of offices [the segregation of different work activities by labour type (e.g. Pachirat 2011: chapter 3); e.g. 'dirty' work relegated to the basement; organizational leaders on the first or top floors, depending on national cultural contexts (Yanow 1993: 311); workers' cafeteria sitings relative to executives' dining rooms]
2. Organizational design		
a. individual	non-verbal communication elements	dress and uniforms, personal 'decor' [jewellery, eyeglass frames, hair style], proxemics, etc.
b. interpersonal	interactions	schematic 'mappings', noting who collaborates with whom, who is bypassed [ignored, 'shunned']
c. group [department or other division]	meetings, interactions	schematic 'mappings', noting who initiates contact, who responds, who is sidelined, etc. [e.g. Bales' 1950 interaction process analysis coding method]
	planning offices, engineering and product design, other design practice-focused units	actor-network theorizing, other analyses exploring the role of boundary objects in mediating interactions [as epigraph to Section II suggests; see also e.g. Ewenstein and Whyte 2009]
d. intergroup	inter-departmental interactions	work flowcharts [adding time and timing to interaction processes]
e. organization	organizational charts	formal authority and responsibility relationships [which might contrast with other mapped observational data]

f. inter-organizational	systems flow charts	mapping interdependencies, information flows, and other such relationships
g. societal	wide range of 'low data' [Weldes 2013]	fiction, poetry, commercial films [including documentaries], political and other cartoons, paintings, etc. that depict, and comment on, organizational life [e.g. Panayiotou and Kafiris 2010]
3. Data genres		
a. objects	the full range of non-human artefacts that populate organizational life and which are used in practices	reports, including their photographs and graphic representations of facts, also treated as visual objects in their own right; analysed using STS [science and technology studies] or ANT [actor-network theory and its 'actants'] approaches [e.g. Barad 2003; Latour 1987; Orlikowski and Scott 2008; Suchman 2005]
b. acts	acts and interactions that have visual components [e.g. at meetings, ceremonies, in ordinary everyday work]	NASA-produced videos of the moon trips depicting astronauts' movements as they searched for a misplaced tool and interacted with engineers in Houston, analysed at the Institute for Research on Learning [Palo Alto, CA] by researchers studying organizational learning and other processes
c. language	signage; words used with visual images; non-verbal organizational language	photography, film/video, and/or drawing to study kinesics [facial and hand gestures], proxemics, posture and personal decor; non-verbal categories can be usefully extended, metaphorically, to include the rhetorical vocabularies of built space [Yanow 2013b], branding and logos [Hatch and Rubin 2006; Mortellito 1960; Ohlins 1989; Schroeder 2008], and other organizational phenomena
4. Research phase		
a. fieldwork	organization-generated materials	photographs and other materials for internal or promotional use, graphic displays of information, etc.
	researcher-generated materials	maps, diagrams, sketches or other graphic renderings, photographs, videos, etc.; walk-alongs that yield sketched or computer-drawn maps of movements, paths, etc. [e.g. Bjerrum and Fangel 2012; Ciolfi 2009; Jones et al. 2008; Kusenbach 2003; Pink 2008; Stavrides 2001]; shadowing
	member-generated materials, at researcher's invitation	photographs, videos/films, pen/pencil/crayon drawings, and other 'projective techniques' that capture members' views of activities, space use, and other aspects of organizational life, including related power, status or other issues [see, e.g., Pink 2007; Shotter and Katz 2006; Warren 2008]; 'photo-elicitation' techniques [Hinthorne 2012]
b. deskwork	using visual means to prompt and further analysis	sketching meetings, floor arrangements of work and tasks [Pachirat 2011], tabular data displays; studying photographs, films
c. textwork	data displays	drawings, sketches, photographs, maps, reproductions of original materials

Organizational design logic. Organizational 'building blocks', from individuals to groups to the organization as a whole, along with intermediary levels – interpersonal relations, inter-group relations, inter-organizational relations, and the broader socio-political context – can be used to structure observation and analysis. Whether the organizational design is a classic bureaucratic hierarchy or a flatter, more flexible 'amoeba', this approach can suggest various systematic foci. Any of these might enable power, powerlessness (Kanter 1993 [1977]), and status analyses, especially when compared with the geographic mappings described above.

Data genres logic. Visual materials are often multi-modal, and focusing on different genres of data suggests a range of data types to look for, as well as different analytic approaches:

- *objects*: the full range of non-human artefacts that populate organizational life. Adapting Latour (e.g. 1987) on following 'facts', organizational researchers might follow objects as an organizing device for a systematic study (e.g. mapping the objects used in a particular practice being studied; see Nicolini 2009 on the similar rhizomatic method);
- *acts*: visual methods of analysis also engage what people do, how they do these things, with whom, and with what, as in the expansion of Burke's pentad, described above;
- *language*: visual materials often use words alongside images, and the layout of a word-based document often has a visual (pictorial, designed) character. Non-verbal analytic categories – kinesics, proxemics, posture and personal decor – can also be useful in analysing recorded images or extended, metaphorically, to other organizational phenomena.

These three genres might be crossed with either of the previous logics. What kinds of objects, for instance, might be observed in particular geographic locations in an organization? What sorts of observable acts and interactions are found at what levels of the organization?

Research phase logic. At different phases of a research project, researchers might identify or generate different kinds of analytic visuals to analyse or present data:

- *Fieldwork*: Researchers commonly seek out *organization-generated materials* that (re)present the organization and its concerns visually, using one or more of the previous logics or some other system. *Researcher-generated* materials, such as sketches, photographs and/or films, and other visual recordings, are created during observational time or when making fieldnotes. De Rond (2012, min. 4:21 ff.), for example, reports taking one photograph of the field surgical team every 15 seconds or so, totalling over 1,000 photographs in the hospital alone, which he then used in interacting with team members to explore what was happening in a given moment of interaction and practice. Other methods include kinds of walk-alongs that social (human) geographers use to understand situational members' views of the spaces they inhabit, literally or figuratively (adding 'footwork' to the research phase taxonomy; Hall 2009). Researchers might accompany organizational members, learning their pathways and translating these into sketched maps or rendering them with computer graphics. This is a broader, 'upscale' technological version of the shadowing introduced by Wolcott (2003 [1973]), which is focused on a single individual and which can also be usefully 'translated' into visual renderings of paths traversed, persons encountered and acts engaged.

    Third, researchers might solicit *member-generated materials*, using 'projective techniques' in which members create their own representations of organizational life. These include giving members cameras, in what Wasson (2000) calls the 'roving camera' technique used for 'desk tours' and shadowing. Less 'naturalistic' and more interventionist, 'photo elicitation' techniques in which members are asked to respond to visual stimuli introduced by the researcher (a photograph, for instance), thereby generating data that the researcher can use in analysis (Harper 2002), might be appropriate in some research arenas or for some research questions.

- *Deskwork*: Researchers might also find various sorts of visual modes useful in analysing their data. Drawing maps, sketching interactions, or working up tables or other modes of graphic display can themselves trigger analytic insight (e.g. Pachirat 2011); some ethnographers use photographs to enable subsequent analysis.
- *Textwork*: Researchers may usefully present data in visual form in their research texts, reproducing organization- or member-generated materials (assuming permissions have been obtained or that images are in the public domain) or their own analytic graphics (such as the two hand-drawn maps used by Manderson and Turner (2006) to document movement in a designated space). Especially for ethnographic and other word-based, interpretive modes of analysis, which rest heavily on detailed descriptions of field experiences that take up lots of page space, a picture or other graphic rendering truly can be 'worth' a thousand words: much can be conveyed in the condensed format of visual renderings. Their use in traditional book and journal dissemination is limited only by current publishing technologies, and these are changing to keep up with multimedia techniques. Three things should be kept in mind in using such data displays. Design is crucial, requiring attention to more (and less) successful modes of rendering data (see Tufte 2001 [1983], 1990, 1997), as well as to the ontological presuppositions implied by the design vocabulary of graphic displays (Drucker 2011), discussed above. Second, such displays do not stand on their own – they need captioning, and the text needs to explain the work they are doing for the author's argument at that place in the manuscript. And third, their use entails ethical and legal issues, which space limitations preclude me from engaging. Suffice it to say, I am fully aware of the irony that a chapter on visual study has not a single image itself – in this case, due to permissions costs, as well as spatial limitations; but see also Van Veeren (2011) for another aspect of the ethical concerns.

Table 10.2 presents the four logics just discussed, with examples. I have not sought to encompass the full range of different visual modes and their analysis, each of which has its own semiotic and rhetorical vocabularies (on photography, e.g., see Becker 1998; Dougherty and Kunda 1990; on film, Iedema 2001; on painting, Morgan 2009; on built spaces, Yanow 2013b; on tables and charts, Drucker 2011; Roam 2011; and other chapters and references in this volume), as well as writings specific to each methods genre, e.g. semiotics. I have also engaged only those visual materials produced by organizational members or researchers, excluding the broader range of socio-cultural materials that might be studied for what they say, through visual means, about widespread assumptions concerning work and organizations.

Although the treatment of research methods presented here might suggest that visual material must constitute the sole focus of a study, both methods and materials lend themselves to projects whose focus lies elsewhere. I would hope that such researchers might consider that the meanings central to their analyses may also be being conveyed through visual means. Analyses of visual materials can be interwoven with other sorts of data and theoretical questions (see, e.g., Goodsell 1988, 1993; Mitchell 1991, 2002; Pachirat 2011), and a researcher pursuing an interview- or document-based project – the 'high data' of most organizational analyses – might also ask him/herself if visual elements – the 'low data' (Weldes 2013) – could also be worth exploring. For researchers accustomed to word-based studies who are not certain how to begin to contemplate the visual, a step taken by Forester (1999) might be helpful. Observing planners, whom he usually interviews, in action, he decided to stop listening for a moment and focus, instead, on what they were doing (which was pointing to one spot on a map and then another). It is an exercise that might prove useful as a pathway into the topic.[14]

Methodology redux: performing power, persuading of status

To link the methods discussion of the previous section back to methodological issues, I want to call attention to what might seem an unnecessarily articulated commonplace: that researchers cannot always bring back from the study setting the pre-existing artefacts – 'found objects' – whose visual properties and organizational implications, meaning(s) and/or significance they wish to assess. Workplace artwork, office decorations, built spaces, uniforms, and the like usually remain (or should) *in situ*, with the exception of mass-produced items intended for distribution, such as annual reports, posters, and other such 'organizational souvenirs' intended to travel beyond the organization's domain. What researchers commonly do bring back from the field are self-generated reproductions of primary source materials, created for research purposes: photographs, video-recordings, sketches, diagrams and/or detailed, descriptive 'word paintings' – more commonly called fieldnotes – of what they have seen and, perhaps, handled or used or touched. (They might also bring member-generated materials produced at the researcher's request for research purposes, discussed previously. Smells – e.g. in researching the perfume industry – and tastes – in studies of cuisine – require other sorts of 'recordings'; see, e.g., Endrissat and Noppeney 2013; Riach and Warren 2011; Gomez *et al.* 2003.)

Methodological consideration, then, also has to engage the notion that, whereas, in the field, researchers are observing, perhaps using, and interacting with originals, during deskwork and textwork phases, they are likely to be working with reproductions in various forms. Although both originals and reproductions can entail selectivity and composition in the framing of a shot or the making of a sketch, the researcher's use of self-generated images of events, interactions, etc. may mask the ontological issues discussed above concerning the character of the reproduction, in the researcher's eyes, as mirror or as interpretation of what it depicts. Methodological attention must, therefore, be paid, in advancing knowledge claims, to the assumed reality status of what those materials contain or (re)present.

This links to the hermeneutics of ownership and questions of power. Berger (1972) explores the ways in which issues of status and power played out, historically, in the commissioning and ownership of paintings, as well as in what was depicted in them.[15] From portraits backed by landscapes to paintings of galleries (e.g. Gainsborough's *Mr. and Mrs. Andrews*; Panini's *Picture Gallery of Cardinal Valenti Gonzaga*; Berger 1972: 106, 86), canvases displayed their owner's possessions and, thereby, (relative) status and power. Adding another dimension to the creator– 'text'–user triad, in intersecting with status, ownership and display, brings identity issues into the analytic domain. Cooper (1976) found this relationship in homes, which reminds us that the creator-designer and owner-inhabitant are not always identical. Berg and Kreiner (1990) explored these concerns in corporate headquarters, seeing not only their design and building materials but also the identity of the architect or firm selected to design them as symbolic of status and other power dimensions, linking to organizational identity and image. The reputation of the architect selected, in other words, has a halo effect, redounding on the occupant. Whether it works similarly for a successor occupant is an empirical question worthy of study.

Similar expressions of status and power are enacted through the acquisition and display of original artwork and its provenance (consider masterpieces and antiques), posters of renowned works of art (Yanow 1996: 167, 172–173), and office furnishings (their design and materials, quality of execution, size and quantity, and the space they command; Becker and Steele 1995; Ciborra and Lanzara 1990; Doxtater 1990; Hatch 1990; Steele 1981). Organizational manuals stipulating the precise dimensions and amounts of furnishing types by member rank render these relationships explicit. Dress also enacts such values (Pratt and Rafaeli 1997; Rafaeli *et al.* 1997), as do programmes and services made available to prospective clients and customers (such as the ballet courses offered to the children of rurally located development towns in Israel so that, as one of the organization's founders put it, 'the youngsters of the poor have an equal opportunity to be exposed to today's cultural activities as are the youngsters of the Tel Aviv residents'; Yanow 1996: 181).

Depictions and other visual materials, then, have both performative and persuasive dimensions, of which viewers tend to be more and less aware, depending on the genre. In the conflict between words and the visual data of deeds – between 'do what I say' and 'do what I do' – the power of the latter to compel belief in its greater truthfulness should not be ignored. We tend to consider pictures compelling in this way, but graphic displays can be equally persuasive, and even more subtly so, as we tend to miss the reality suppositions embedded in them (Drucker 2011). Because of visuals' immediacy and our interpretive capacity to bypass their translation into words, which would tie language to reason, these power dimensions may be overlooked.

Concluding 'observations'

Despite its dominant logocentrism, manifested in interviewing, document analysis, and the written presentation and dissemination of research, organizational analysis includes a long tradition of observational, participatory and ethnographic research that has not only looked at what people do and listened to what they say about what they do, but has also closely observed what they do things *with*, and *where* – objects, the physical artefacts of the material world, and their settings. Hermeneutics, phenomenology and other meaning-focused approaches – the interpretive dimensions of sense-making – treat artefacts as symbolic representations of what is meaningful to their creators and 'users', attending to similar and contested meanings. Visual analyses of things visual are not only a matter of aesthetic appreciation; the visual plays a key role in communicating other sorts of meaning. The idea that 'sight' (as with other observational modes) is always mediated by the figurative lens of prior knowledge and phenomenological experience lays the groundwork for methodology for analytic sense-making of things studied visually, including relationships of status, power, powerlessness, and the like, which are expressed and conveyed in visual, and visible, form.

Constructivist-interpretivist research, in which the researcher is present, in both research and narrative, to one degree or another, might be analogized to the drip canvases of Jackson Pollock, which retain traces of the artist's motions in time and space (Hatch and Yanow 2008). This analogy itself suggests that the movement arts might provide a source of insight for the visual study of visual materials. Ballet and text-based drama work with fixed 'scores' – written music plus Labanotation; the play script – by contrast with a more free-form dance and improvisational theatre (as well as Renaissance music and some forms of jazz), which have little or no written plan of action or record. Organizations' visual materials – photographs, films, paintings, cartoons, built spaces, and so on – present the researcher with a fixed 'score', but our challenge is to work out the 'notations' specific to each genre such that we can understand the types of meaning these various elements can embody and convey, in the context of the polysemic character of their organizational manifestations.

To conclude, then, on an ontological-epistemological note: can we study visual materials without reifying or essentializing their meanings? We have rejected the notion that words transparently designate what they represent. Let us not lose sight (*sic*) of the fact that images are no more transparent than words! In thinking about multiple meanings from a constructivist ontological position, the point is clear: meaning does not reside in the object itself, but is created – constructed, if you will – intersubjectively, through use and reuse. Organizational meanings are not independent of this process. An object may exist independent of its analysis – the sherd lying buried under 2,000 years of rubble – but its human, social – indeed, organizational – significance is called into being as evidentiary material for a study only once the research question is shaped and put into play in the research. Moreover, although interviews and documents also 'reproduce' and frame individuals' views of organizational matters, there is something in the verisimilitude of photographs, videos, and even drawings and sketches and in the relative immediacy with which we grasp their meanings that can lead a researcher to forget that these, too, are framing devices: interpretations from a particular point of view, which highlight and occlude at the same time. Even when intending to render a 'faithful' account of their observations (Yanow and Schwartz-Shea 2013: 438), researchers can develop blind spots concerning the interpreted character of visual 'found objects'. Keeping Burke's pentad in mind can help foreground the artefactual – created and interpreted – character of visual materials.

Finally, I hope that the renewed attention to visual studies of visual materials will not commit the counter-sin to what it corrects. Things visual do not have lives independent of other senses, other acts, other language. Whereas breaking out of our logocentrism is a welcome move, we should be admitting all of our sense observations into the realm of scientific enquiry. Meaning-making and its communication are multi-modal; and we would not be advancing our research processes in isolating and privileging the visual while ignoring its concomitant modalities. I hope we can add visual materials and methods to our analytic repertoire without losing the others.

Acknowledgements

A version of this chapter was presented at the 'Materialities, Visualities, Securities' workshop, School of Global Studies, University of Sussex (7 June 2012). My thanks to Elspeth Van Veeren and other participants there for the discussion and to Emma Bell, Jane Davison, Merlijn van Hulst, Ed Schatz and Sarah Warnes for comments on an earlier draft.

Notes

1. For some exceptions, see, e.g., Gagliardi (1990b); Kunter and Bell (2006); Rafaeli and Pratt (2006); Warren (2008). This point has also recently hit the popular management literature (see Roam 2011). The ignoring of visual materials is paralleled in the ignoring of spatial evidence, which might be considered a subfield of the broader category of visual materials; see Bell and Davison (2013) for a discussion of the point in general; and Yanow (2010) for its manifestation in spatial studies.
2. For exceptions, see, e.g., Iedema *et al.* (2010); Kenis *et al.* (2010); Wasserman and Frenkel (2011); Weir (2010); Yanow (1998) on spatial design; Berg and Kreiner (1990); van Marrewijk (2010); Yanow (1993) on building materials; Hatch (1990) and Panayiotou and Kafiris (2010) on furnishings and decor.
3. On Dr Gilbreth's contributions, see Krenn (2011). It is also worth looking at the films of documentarian Frederick Wiseman, many of which are, in effect, organizational and/or workplace or work practice studies (e.g. *Titicut Follies, High School, Hospital, The Store, Boxing Gym*; see Grant 1992).
4. For an interesting discussion of this 'ocularcentrism', see Kavanagh (2004).
5. As I say, for heuristic purposes. In research practice, the three are not as distinct as this typology might suggest; indeed, analysis often begins even before the researcher has entered the field, and it continues during fieldwork engagements and on through textwork. Van Maanen (2011) has recently added 'headwork' to fieldwork and textwork, which positions deskwork in a broader locational setting and, perhaps, scope. Wilkinson (2013) contributes 'legwork', in reference to the preparatory phase(s) during which desired field research is set up. And then there is 'footwork' (Hall 2009).

6 'Sometimes words written in a painting designate specific things, and images vague things; or, just as well, the opposite' (author's translation). Much of Magritte's work toys with the tension between image, language and representation, including the well-known 'This is not a pipe' (or *Ceci n'est pas une pipe*) canvases, 'This is not an apple' (*Ceci n'est pas une pomme*), and 'This is a piece of cheese'. See also Foucault's discussion (1983) of Magritte's work.
7 That is, 'subjective' is an epistemologically descriptive term, referencing meaning to a specific subject, not the pejorative one often invoked to criticize field and other qualitative or interpretive research for lacking in 'rigour'. Drucker (2011: 24) draws the distinction between observer-independent (objective) and observer-codependent (subjective) phenomena. For an intriguing argument that holds the primacy of sight (or visual metaphors) responsible for Enlightenment (seventeenth- to eighteenth-century) ideas about the possibility of objectivity, see Kavanagh (2004: 446–449). For more on the epistemological meanings of 'objective' and 'subjective', see Yanow (2013a).
8 And she shows graphic displays incorporating ambiguity and instability – 'expressive metrics and graphics' that 'reinsert the subjective standpoint of their creation' (Drucker 2011: 14, 20).
9 These included post-structuralist and Lacanian views. As Kirstie McClure (personal correspondence, 21–22 February 2012) notes, the debate over intentionality versus context also marks theories of intellectual history or the history of ideas.
10 This formulation parallels an older, realist-objectivist view of communication, with senders, signals, channels and receivers, and mis-communication attributable to 'noise' in the system (for an interpretive critique, see Putnam and Pacanowsky 1983).
11 Which is where researcher-as-human-proxy for organizational members and others comes in.
12 E.g. Roam (2012) identifies six building blocks of data representation, analogous to parts of speech: charts (adjectives of number); flow charts; timelines (tense: past, present, future); portraits (nouns: who, what); Venn diagrams; and maps (prepositions: position of objects in space).
13 Kavanagh, quoting Arendt, attributes to Bergson the understanding that the body is 'the primary site of lived action' (2004: 454). Van Maanen (1996) makes a similar point with respect to ethnography in general.
14 I am indebted to Merlijn van Hulst (personal communication, 26 July 2012) for this example and point.
15 See also Christian (1997) on links between managing and paintings.

References

Agar, M.H. (1996 [1980]) *The Professional Stranger: An Informal Introduction to Ethnography*, 2nd ed., New York: Academic Press.
Austin, J.L. (1962) *How To Do Things with Words*, Cambridge, MA: Harvard University Press.
Bales, R.F. (1950) *Interaction Process Analysis*, New York: Addison-Wesley.
Barad, K. (2003) 'Posthumanist performativity: Toward an understanding of how matter comes to matter', *Signs: Journal of Women in Culture and Society* 28(3): 801–31.
Barthes, R. (1967) 'The death of the author', trans. R. Howard, *Aspen* 5–6. Available at www.ubu.com/aspen/aspen5and6/threeEssays.html#barthes (accessed 19 July 2012).
Becker, F. and Steele, F. (1995) *Workplace by Design*, San Francisco: Jossey Bass.
Becker, H.S. (1998) 'Categories and comparisons: how we find meaning in photographs', *Visual Anthropology Review* 14(2): 3–10.
Bell, E. and Davison, J. (2013) 'Visual management studies: empirical and theoretical approaches', *International Journal of Management Reviews* 15(2): 167–184.
Berg, P.-O. and Kreiner, K. (1990) 'Corporate architecture: turning physical settings into symbolic resources', in P. Gagliardi (ed.) *Symbols and Artifacts: Views of the Corporate Landscape*, New York: Aldine de Gruyter, 41–67.
Berger, J. (1972) *Ways of Seeing*, London: British Broadcasting Corporation and Penguin.
Bertoin Antal, A. (2012) 'Visual methods and arts-based interventions: social entrepreneurship in Israel', in *Visio/inspire*. Available at http://moodle.in-visio.org/mod/resource/view.php?id=417 (accessed 1 June 2012).
Bjerrum, E. and Fangel, A.B. (2012) 'Reinventing ethnographic practise: the use of ethnographic methods in organisational development', presented at the International Conference on Organisational Learning, Knowledge, and Capabilities, Valencia (25–27 April).
Burke, K. (1945) *A Grammar of Motives*, New York: Prentice-Hall.

—— (1989) *On Symbols and Society*, edited and with an Introduction by Joseph R. Gusfield, Chicago: University of Chicago Press.

Christian, D. (1997) *Art de Diriger et Art de Peindre*, Paris: Editions DIFER.

Ciardi, J. (1959) *How Does a Poem Mean?*, New York: Houghton Mifflin.

Ciborra, C.U. and Lanzara, G.F. (1990) 'Designing dynamic artifacts', in P. Gagliardi (ed.) *Symbols and Artifacts*, NY: Aldine de Gruyter, 147–165.

Ciolfi, L. (2009) 'Mapping lived place', presented at the Spatial and Network Analysis in Qualitative Research Euroqual Conference, European University Cyprus, Nicosia (25–27 November).

Cohen, P. (2009) 'Danish cartoon controversy', *New York Times Topics* (updated 12 August). Available at http://topics.nytimes.com/top/reference/timestopics/subjects/d/danish_cartoon_controversy/index.html?emc=eta2 (accessed 1 August 2012).

Cone, F.M. (1960) 'Symbology in advertising', in E. Whitney (ed.) *'Symbology': The Use of Symbols in Visual Communications*, Hastings House, NY: Communication Arts Books, 69–86.

Cooper, C. (1976) 'The house as symbol of the self', in J. Lang, C. Burnette, W. Moleski, and D. Vachon (eds) *Designing for Human Behavior*, Stroudsberg, PA: Dowden Hutchinson and Ross, 130–146.

Danjoux, I. (2013) 'Don't judge a cartoon by its image: interpretive approaches to the study of political cartoons', in D. Yanow and P. Schwartz-Shea (eds) *Interpretation and Method: Empirical Research Methods and the Interpretive Turn*, 2nd ed., Armonk, NY: M.E. Sharpe, 353–367.

de Rond, M. (2012) 'Welcome to Bastion: warzone ethnography with the combat surgeons', video from photographs, published by Cambridge University (27 June). Available at www.youtube.com/watch?v=F0Ytealqv2g (accessed 31 July 2012).

Dougherty, D. and Kunda, G. (1990) 'Photograph analysis: a method to capture organizational belief systems', in P. Gagliardi (ed.) *Symbols and Artifacts: Views of the Corporate Landscape*, New York: Aldine de Gruyter, 185–206.

Doxtater, D. (1990) 'Meaning of the workplace', in P. Gagliardi (ed.) *Symbols and Artifacts: Views of the Corporate Landscape*, NY: Aldine de Gruyter, 107–127.

Drucker, J. (2011) 'Humanities approaches to graphical display', *DHQ: Digital Humanities Quarterly* 5(1). Available at http://www.digitalhumanities.org/dhq/vol/5/1/000091/000091.html (accessed 4 June 2012).

Endrissat, N. and Noppeney, C. (2013), 'Materializing the immaterial: relational movements in a perfume's becoming', in P.R. Carlile, D. Nicolini, A. Langley and H. Tsoukas (eds) *How Matter Matters: Objects, Artifacts, and Materiality in Organization Studies*, Oxford: Oxford University Press, 58–91.

Ewenstein, B. and Whyte, J. (2009) 'Knowledge practices in design: The role of visual representations as "epistemic objects"', *Organization Studies* 30(1): 7–30.

Ferguson, K.E. and Turnbull, P. (1999) *Oh, Say, Can You See? The Semiotics of the Military in Hawai'i*, Minneapolis: University of Minnesota Press.

Forester, J. (1999) 'Reflections on the future understanding of planning practice', *International Planning Studies* 4(2): 175–193.

Foucault, M. (1983) *This Is Not a Pipe*, with illustrations and letters by R. Magritte, trans. and ed. J. Harkness, Berkeley: University of California Press.

Fuenmayor, R. (1991) 'Truth and openness: an epistemology for interpretive systemology', *Systems Practice* 4(5): 473–490.

Gagliardi, P. (1990a) 'Artifacts as pathways and remains of organizational life', in P. Gagliardi (ed.) *Symbols and Artifacts: Views of the Corporate Landscape*, New York: Aldine de Gruyter, 1–38.

—— (ed.) (1990b) *Symbols and Artifacts: Views of the Corporate Landscape*, New York: Aldine de Gruyter.

Goffman, E. (1979) *Gender Advertisements*, Cambridge, MA: Harvard University Press.

Gomez, M.-L., Bouty, I. and Drucker-Godard, C. (2003) 'Developing knowing in practice: behind the scenes of haute cuisine', in D. Nicolini, S. Gherardi and D. Yanow (eds) *Knowing in Organizations: A Practice-Based Approach*, Armonk, NY: M.E. Sharpe, 100–125.

Goodsell, C.T. (1988) *The Social Meaning of Civic Space*, Lawrence: University Press of Kansas.

—— (ed.) (1993), 'Architecture as a setting for governance', Theme issue, *Journal of Architectural and Planning Research* 10(4) (Winter).

Grant, B.K. (1992) *Voyages of Discovery*, Urbana, IL: University of Illinois Press.

Gruber, R.E. (2011) 'The woman behind the Polish Jewry Museum', *The Jewish Daily Forward* (12 August). Available at http://forward.com/articles/140908/the-woman-behind-the-polish-jewry-museum/ (accessed 16 August 2011).

Hall, T. (2009) 'Footwork: moving and knowing in local space(s)', *Qualitative Research* 9(5): 571–585.

Harper, D. (2002) 'Talking about pictures: a case for photo elicitation', *Visual Studies* 17(1): 13–26.

Hatch, M.J. (1990) 'The symbolics of office design', in P. Gagliardi (ed.) *Symbols and Artifacts: Views of the Corporate Landscape*, New York: Aldine de Gruyter, 129–146.

Hatch, M.J. and Rubin, J. (2006) 'The hermeneutics of branding', *Journal of Brand Management* 14(1/2): 40–59.

Hatch, M.J. and Yanow, D. (2008) 'Methodology by metaphor: ways of seeing in painting and research', *Organization Studies* 29: 23–44.

Hinthorne, L. L. (2012) 'A picture is worth a thousand words: Using the visual interpretation narrative exercise to elicit non-elite perceptions of democracy', *Field Methods* 24(3): 348–64.

Iedema, R. (2001) 'Analysing film and television: a social semiotic account of *Hospital: An Unhealthy Business*', in T. van Leeuwen and C. Jewitt (eds) *The Handbook of Visual Analysis*, London: Sage, 183–204.

Iedema, R., Long, D. and Carroll, K. (2010) 'Corridor communication, spatial design and patient safety: enacting and managing complexities', in A. van Marrewijk and D. Yanow (eds) *Organizational Spaces: Rematerializing the Workaday World*, Cheltenham, UK: Edward Elgar, 41–57.

Iser, W. (1989) *Prospecting: From Reader Response to Literary Anthropology*, Baltimore, MD: Johns Hopkins University Press.

Johnson, G. (2007) 'Sleights of mind', *The New York Times* (21 August). Available at http://www.nytimes.com/2007/08/21/science/21magic.html (accessed 10 February 2012).

Jones, P.I., Bunce, G., Evans, J., Gibbs, H. and Hein, J.R. (2008) 'Exploring space and place with walking interviews', *Journal of Research Practice* 4(2), Article D2. Available at http://jrp.icaap.org/index.php/jrp/article/view/150/161 (accessed 22 February 2010).

Kanter, R.M. (1993 [1977]) *Men and Women of the Corporation*, NY: Basic Books.

Kavanagh, D. (2004) 'Ocularcentrism and its others: a framework for metatheoretical analysis', *Organization Studies* 25(3): 445–464.

Kenis, P., Kruyen, P.M. and Baaijens, J. (2010) 'Bendable bars in a Dutch prison: a creative place in a non-creative space', in A. van Marrewijk and D. Yanow (eds) *Organizational Spaces: Rematerializing the Workaday World*, Cheltenham, UK: Edward Elgar, 58–73.

Krenn, M. (2011) 'From scientific management to homemaking: Lillian M. Gilbreth's contributions to the development of management thought', *Management & Organizational History* 6(2): 145–161.

Kunda, G. (1992) *Engineering Culture*, Philadelphia: Temple University Press.

Kunter, A. and Bell, E. (2006) 'The promise and potential of visual organizational research', *M@n@gement* 9(3): 169–189.

Kusenbach, M. (2003) 'Street phenomenology: The go-along as ethnographic research tool', *Ethnography* 4(3): 455–85.

Latour, B. (1987) *Science in Action: How to Follow Scientists and Engineers through Society*, Cambridge, MA: Harvard University Press.

Magritte, R. (1929) *Les Mots et les Images*. Pages from the artist's notebook on exhibit in 'Magritte: Das Lustprinzip', Albertina Museum, Vienna, 9 November 2011–26 February 2012.

Manderson, D. and Turner, S. (2006) 'Coffee house: *Habitus* and performance among law students', *Law & Social Inquiry* 31(3): 649–676.

Mitchell, T. (1991) *Colonising Egypt*, Berkeley: University of California Press.

——(2002) *Rule of Experts*, Berkeley: University of California Press.

Morgan, D. (2009) 'Painting as visual evidence: production, circulation, reception', in R. Howells and R.W. Matson (eds) *Using Visual Evidence*, Maidenhead, UK: Open University Press, 8–23.

Mortellito, D. (1960) 'Symbology and the corporate image', in E. Whitney (ed), *'Symbology': the use of symbols in visual communications*, Hastings House, NY: Communication Arts Books, 103–14.

Nicolini, D. (2009) 'Zooming in and zooming out: a package of method and theory to study work practices', in S.B. Ybema, D. Yanow, H. Wels and F. Kamsteeg (eds) *Organizational Ethnography: Studying the Complexities of Everyday Life*, London: Sage, 120–138.

Ohlins, W. (1989) *Corporate Identity*, London: Thames and Hudson.

Oliver-Velez, D., Finlinson, H.A., Deren, S., Robles, R., Shedlin, M., Andia, J. and Colon, H. (2002) 'Mapping the air-bridge locations: the application of ethnographic mapping techniques to a study of HIV risk behavior determinant in East Harlem, New York, and Bayamon, Puerto Rico', *Human Organization* 61(3): 262–276.

Olivetti, D. (1960) 'Symbology in international industry', in E. Whitney (ed.) *'Symbology': The Use of Symbols in Visual Communications*, Hastings House, NY: Communication Arts Books, 41–48.

Orlikowski, W.J. and Scott, S.V. (2008) 'Sociomateriality: Challenging the separation of technology, work and organization', *Academy of Management Annals* 2: 433–74.

Pachirat, T. (2011) *Every Twelve Seconds: Industrialized Slaughter and the Politics of Sight*, New Haven, CT: Yale University Press.
Panayiotou, A. and Kafiris, K. (2010) 'Firms in film: representation of organisational space, gender, and power', in A. van Marrewijk and D. Yanow (eds) *Organizational Spaces: Rematerializing the Workaday World*, Cheltenham, UK: Edward Elgar, 174–199.
Pink, S. (2007) *Doing Visual Ethnography*, 2nd ed., London: Sage.
——(2008) 'An urban tour: the sensory sociality of ethnographic place-making', *Ethnography* 9(2): 175–196.
Pratt, M.G. and Rafaeli, A. (1997) 'Vested interests: dress as an integrating symbol', *Academy of Management Journal* 40: 860–896.
Putnam, L.L. and Pacanowsky, M.E. (eds) (1983) *Communication and Organization: An Interpretive Approach*, Beverly Hills, CA: Sage.
Rafaeli, A. and Pratt, M.G. (eds) (2006) *Artifacts and Organizations*, Mahwah, NJ: Lawrence Erlbaum Associates.
Rafaeli, A., Dutton, J., Harquail, C.V. and Lewis, S. (1997) 'Navigating by attire: the use of dress by female administrative employees', *Academy of Management Journal* 40: 9–45.
Riach, K. and Warren, S. (2011) 'Cultural osmologies: smell in the workplace', presented at the Critical Management Studies Conference, Naples (11–13 July).
Richardson, L. (1994) 'Writing: a method of inquiry', in N.K. Denzin and Y.S. Lincoln (eds) *Handbook of Qualitative Research*, Thousand Oaks, CA: Sage, 516–529.
Ricoeur, P. (1971) 'The model of the text: meaningful action considered as text', *Social Research* 38: 529–62.
Roam, D. (2011) *Blah Blah Blah: What to Do When Words Don't Work*, New York: Portfolio/Penguin.
——(2012) 'When words don't work', *TechNation*, (US) National Public Radio, original broadcast 15 May 2012. (Accessed 22 May 2012 at http://itc.conversationsnetwork.org/shows/detail5295.html, no longer available.) Cf. 'Dan Roam: What to Do When Words Don't Work', The Commonwealth Club of California: San Francisco (broadcast 31 January 2012). Available at www.commonwealthclub.org/events/archive/podcast/dan-roam-what-do-when-words-dont-work-13112 (accessed 8 April 2013).
Rosen, M. (2000) 'You asked for it: Christmas at the bosses' expense', in M. Rosen, *Turning Words, Spinning Worlds: Chapters in Organizational Ethnography*, Amsterdam: Harwood, 93–116.
Schroeder, J.E. (2008) 'Visual analysis of images in brand culture', in B.J. Phillips and E. McQuarrie (eds) *Go Figure: New Directions in Advertising Rhetoric*, Armonk, NY: M.E. Sharpe, 277–296. Available at http://papers.ssrn.com/sol3/papers.cfm?abstract_id=941431 (accessed 30 January 2012).
Schwartz-Shea, P. and Yanow, D. (2009) 'Reading and writing as method: in search of trustworthy texts', in S. Ybema, D. Yanow, H. Wels and F. Kamsteeg (eds) *Organizational Ethnography: Studying the Complexities of Everyday Life*, London: Sage, 56–82.
Schwartz-Shea, P. and Yanow, D. (2012) *Interpretive Research Design: Concepts and Processes*, New York: Routledge.
Shotter, J. and Katz, A. (2006) 'Making a practice visible from within the practice: a dialogically-structured "social poetics of inquiry" in health care settings', presented at the 2nd Organization Studies Summer Workshop on Re-turn to Practice, Mykonos (15–16 June).
Stavrides, S. (2001) 'Navigating the metropolitan space: Walking as a form of negotiation with otherness', *Journal of Psychogeography and Urban Research* 1/1. http://courses.arch.ntua.gr/stavrides.html (accessed 3 December 2009).
Steele, F.I. (1981) *The Sense of Place*, Boston: CBI Publishing Co.
Strati, A. (2003) 'Knowing in practice: aesthetic understanding and tacit knowledge', in D. Nicolini, S. Gherardi and D. Yanow (eds) *Knowing in Organizations: A Practice-Based Approach*, Armonk, NY: M.E. Sharpe, 53–75.
Suchman, L. (2005) 'Affiliative objects', *Organization* 12: 3379–99.
Taylor, C. (1971) 'Interpretation and the sciences of man', *Review of Metaphysics* 25: 3–51.
Tufte, E.R. (1990) *Envisioning Information*, Cheshire, CT: Graphics Press.
——(1997) *Visual Explanations: Images and Quantities, Evidence and Narrative*, Cheshire, CT: Graphics Press.
——(2001 [1983]) *The Visual Display of Quantitative Information*, 2nd ed., Cheshire, CT: Graphics Press.
Van Herzele, A. and van Woerkum, C.M.J. (2008) 'Local knowledge in visually mediated practice', *Journal of Planning Education and Research* 27: 444–455.
Van Maanen, J. (1996) 'Commentary: on the matter of voice', *Journal of Management Inquiry* 5: 375–381.
——(2011) 'Ethnography as work: some rules of engagement', *Journal of Management Studies* 48(1): 218–234.

van Marrewijk, A. (2010) 'The beauty and the beast: the embodied experience of two corporate buildings', in A. van Marrewijk and D. Yanow (eds) *Organizational Spaces: Rematerializing the Workaday World*, Cheltenham, UK: Edward Elgar, 96–114.

Van Veeren, E. (2011) 'Captured by the camera's eye: Guantánamo and the shifting frame of the Global War on Terror', *Review of International Studies* 37: 1721–1749.

Warren, S. (2008) 'Empirical challenges in organizational aesthetics research: toward a sensual methodology', *Organization Studies* 20(4): 559–580.

Wasserman, V. and Frenkel, M. (2011) 'Organizational aesthetics: caught between identity regulation and culture jamming', *Organization Science* 22(2): 503–521.

Wasson, C. (2000) 'Ethnography in the field of design', *Human Organization* 59(4): 377–388.

Weir, D. (2010) 'Space as context and content: the diwan as a frame and a structure for decision-making', in A. van Marrewijk and D. Yanow (eds) *Organizational Spaces: Rematerializing the Workaday World*, Cheltenham, UK: Edward Elgar, 115–136.

Weldes, J. (2013) 'High politics and low data: globalization discourses and popular culture', in D. Yanow and P. Schwartz-Shea (eds) *Interpretation and Method: Empirical Research Methods and the Interpretive Turn*, 2nd ed., Armonk, NY: M.E. Sharpe, 228–238.

White, J.D. (1992) 'Taking language seriously: toward a narrative theory of knowledge for administrative research', *American Review of Public Administration* 22: 75–88.

Wilkinson, C. (2013) 'Ethnographic methods', in Laura J. Shepherd (ed.) *Critical Approaches to Security: An Introduction to Theories and Methods*, London: Routledge, 129–145.

Wolcott, H.F. (2003 [1973]) *The Man in the Principal's Office: An Ethnography*, updated ed., Walnut Creek, CA: AltaMira Press.

Yanow, D. (1993) 'Reading policy meanings in organization-scapes', *Journal of Architectural and Planning Research* 10: 308–327.

——(1996) *How Does a Policy Mean? Interpreting Organizational and Policy Actions*, Washington, DC: Georgetown University Press.

——(1998) 'Space stories; or, studying museum buildings as organizational spaces, while reflecting on interpretive methods and their narration', *Journal of Management Inquiry* 7: 215–239.

——(2000) *Conducting Interpretive Policy Analysis*, Newbury Park, CA: Sage.

——(2003) *Constructing 'Race' and 'Ethnicity' in America: Category-making in Policy and Administrative Practices*, Armonk, NY: M.E. Sharpe.

——(2009) 'Dear author, dear reader: the third hermeneutic in writing and reviewing ethnography', in E. Schatz (ed.) *Political Ethnography: What Immersion Brings to the Study of Power*, Chicago: University of Chicago Press, 275–302.

——(2010) 'Giving voice to space: academic practices and the material world', in A. van Marrewijk and D. Yanow (eds), *Organizational Spaces: Rematerializing the Workaday World*, Cheltenham, UK: Edward Elgar, 139–158.

——(2013a) 'Neither rigorous nor objective? Interrogating criteria for knowledge claims in interpretive science', in D. Yanow and P. Schwartz-Shea (eds) *Interpretation and Method: Empirical Research Methods and the Interpretive Turn*, 2nd ed., Armonk, NY: M.E. Sharpe, 97–119.

——(2013b) 'A semiotics of built space', in D. Yanow and P. Schwartz-Shea (eds) *Interpretation and Method: Empirical Research Methods and the Interpretive Turn*, 2nd ed., Armonk, NY: M.E. Sharpe, 368–386.

Yanow, D. and Schwartz-Shea, P. (2013) 'Doing social science in a humanistic manner', in D. Yanow and P. Schwartz-Shea (eds) *Interpretation and Method: Empirical Research Methods and the Interpretive Turn*, 2nd ed., Armonk, NY: M.E. Sharpe, 433–447.

11

Navigating the scattered and fragmented

Visual rhetoric, visual studies, and visual communication

Kelly Norris Martin

Because of the attention devoted to the visual from a wide variety of disciplines, many of which use different approaches and techniques, visual research is often considered a place of turbulence and incoherence. As Smith *et al.* write, the field of visual communication 'is scattered and fragmented' (2005: xi). The term 'indiscipline,' proposed by Mitchell (1995) to describe inter-, cross-, and transdisciplinary work that is at the 'inner and outer boundaries of disciplines,' is therefore an accurate description of the visual research field. Although well-established disciplines such as art history, design history, and visual anthropology have established theoretical canons and methods, they too have entered conversations about the growth of visual research.

The purpose of this chapter is to provide a general understanding of three main analytical approaches to visual research. Though it focuses primarily on literature from visual communication and rhetoric, the types of approaches identified may have relevance to other fields that study the visual. A recent meta-study of visual research in communication studies found three prevalent approaches to the visual:

> Studies that take a primarily rhetorical approach consider images and designs key occasions of persuasion[;] ... studies that take primarily a semantic approach consider the visual as text in much the way that linguists look at language[;] ... [and] studies that take primarily a pragmatic approach consider the visual a practice.
>
> *(Barnhurst et al. 2004: 629–630)*

Research that takes a primarily 'rhetorical approach' could evidently be classified as visual rhetoric studies; research that takes a primarily 'semantic approach' ('toward an internal logic of the visual' and including *anything* visual) could be classified as simply visual studies; and research that takes a pragmatic approach could be classified as empirical visual communication.

In this chapter, I discuss these three primary approaches to visual research. Each of them offers a distinct theoretical perspective and asks particular kinds of questions that, in turn, should determine the methodological choices of the researcher. Some would argue that the distinctions between them amount to academic bickering and turf wars, and, in some sense, these critics

Navigating the scattered and fragmented

are correct. Much of the scholarship these approaches produce draws on common theorists and theories, and uses similar techniques, but there are slight differences – especially in regard to their history and treatment of the visual – that are important to acknowledge. For an illustration of these similarities and differences, see Figure 11.1.

In addition to outlining these three approaches and their corresponding methodological techniques, the chapter also reviews similarities and differences between them. Definitions of each of the three approaches and criticisms made of them are provided in Figure 11.2.

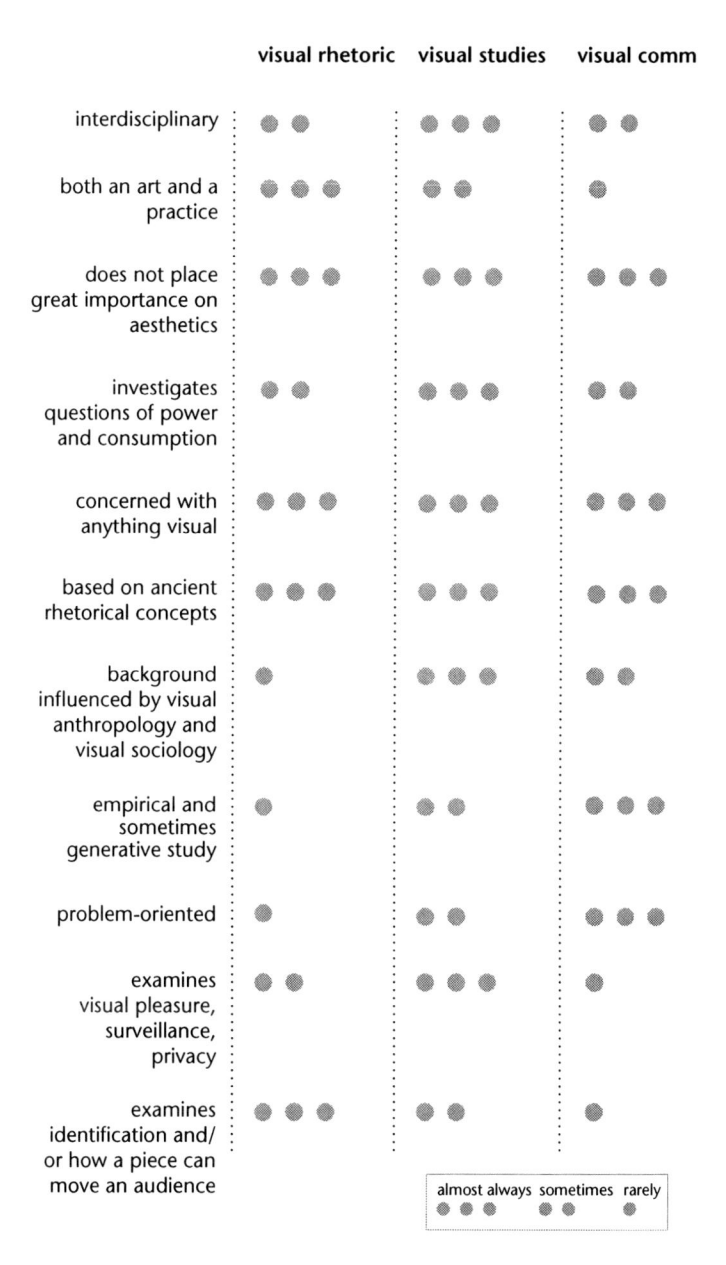

	visual rhetoric	visual studies	visual comm
interdisciplinary	●●	●●●	●●
both an art and a practice	●●●	●●	●
does not place great importance on aesthetics	●●●	●●●	●●●
investigates questions of power and consumption	●●	●●●	●●
concerned with anything visual	●●●	●●●	●●●
based on ancient rhetorical concepts	●●●	●●●	●●●
background influenced by visual anthropology and visual sociology	●	●●●	●●
empirical and sometimes generative study	●	●●	●●●
problem-oriented	●	●●	●●●
examines visual pleasure, surveillance, privacy	●●	●●●	●
examines identification and/ or how a piece can move an audience	●●●	●●	●

almost always   sometimes   rarely
●●●   ●●   ●

Figure 11.1 Comparison of three visual approaches

189

	visual rhetoric	visual studies	visual comm
definition	explores the connection between reflection and interpretation, historically situated ideas, and practices of design. It considers images as rational expressions of cultural meaning and examines the relationship between images and text	examines society's access to images and their entanglements in systems of meaning and power – "regards the visual image as the focal point in the processes through which meaning is made in a cultural context" (Dikovitskaya)	"an expanding subfield of communication science that uses social scientific methods to explain the production, distribution and reception processes, but also the meanings of mass-mediated visuals in contemporary social, cultural, economic, and political contexts" (Müller)
historic and potential criticisms	• may not be trained to deal with images or other forms of nondiscursive rhetoric • aesthetic concerns may be more important than some critics acknowledge • analyses may reveal only "stigmatized identity, crippled agency, distraction, diversion, nostalgia, self exhibition, exclusion, and the manipulation of collective memory" (Benson) • should try and support strategies and analyses by using findings from other areas of research such as cognitive studies • scholars do not test their analyses of rhetorical strategies against other findings using different strategies	• some analyses need deeper theoretical and methodological innovation • should be denser with existing visual theories and strategies • scattered subjects and untheorized choices of methods make it fairly simple to generate texts and unrewarding to compare one study to another • should be more attentive to neighboring and distant disciplines and less predictable in its politics • people may experience a type of looking that is different from voyeurism, fetishism and narcissism	• simply presents findings applicable to a specific group at a given time and even the more generalizable findings remain narrow in scope • there is the potential for critique but do not often arrive at philosophical, inventive, or artistic insight • rhetorical issues of framing and context would likely be valuable considerations • researcher may associate frequency of content with significance of content and also may use content categories without relating them to a theoretical perspective

Figure 11.2 Definitions and criticisms

I continue the chapter by investigating the key concepts and theories associated with the three approaches, including their methods and disciplinary origins and linkages.

Visual rhetoric

Key concepts and theoretical assumptions

When referring to visual rhetoric, scholars use one of two common definitions. The meaning of one refers to the visual impact of the object itself. An example of how someone would write about visual rhetoric in this manner would be: 'the visual rhetoric of the political poster (or the advertisement, or whatever indicated visual artifact) helped constitute the incendiary nature of the organization.' The second refers to an approach rhetorical scholars have adopted to analyze the visual. An example of how it might appear in this manner would be: 'Gallagher (2004) used expertise in visual rhetoric to analyze the Civil War memorial.' Ott and Dickinson advance a short list of principles about which scholars of visual rhetoric agree:

> Visual rhetoric is a meaningful set of visible signs and therefore a mode of communication ... 2) Visual rhetoric is rooted in looking, seeing, and visualizing and is fundamentally an optical process ... (although process is registered viscerally by the body as well as symbolically by the mind) ... 3) Forms of visual rhetoric are human constructions.
>
> *(2009: 392)*

Furthermore, visual rhetoric (as an approach for analyzing the visual) – which may also involve elements of semiotics, visual semantics, visual argument, and visual logic – explores the connection between reflection and interpretation, historically situated ideas, and practices of design. It considers images as rational expressions of cultural meaning and examines the relationship between images and text. It also assumes human beings are not passive recipients of messages but are active participants in shaping meaning. This is partly why visual rhetoric researchers do not assume function is synonymous with purpose. Therefore, they seek to discover how an image operates for its viewers instead of what was intended by the creator. Sometimes researchers of visual rhetoric self-identify as 'critics' because they believe the humanity of the critic is 'necessarily inherent' in the work (Sloan *et al.* 1971: 223), meaning that, because humans are not mechanical or electronic machines, there will always be a contextual influence in a study. The term 'critic' presents the researcher as an expert in the field but one who openly shares a critical viewpoint that naturally includes certain theoretical and social histories and perspectives.

Visual rhetoric involves persuasion, invention, and interpretation. Visual artifacts or images move an audience to action, awareness, or to certain values, but, through interpretive writing, the visual rhetoric critic may also persuade or enlighten his/her audience in regard to understanding the impact of the visual artifacts. It is suggested that rhetorical critics (as well as visual studies critics) have the power to advance stability or change based on their ability to provide a historical backdrop and social context.

Rhetorical critics also analyze visuals of the everyday. Once the field of rhetoric expanded to include other purviews, such as art and science (in addition to literature and speech), it also began to look at visuals encountered through mundane daily activities. In his analysis of the visual environment of Starbucks, Dickinson (2002) analyzed a Starbucks coffee shop by looking at the use of 'natural' colors, shapes, and materials. His goal was to determine how the visual and spatial elements of a coffee shop's interior make it a compelling place to visit. He found that the visual elements of the coffee's production and the interior design of the coffee house promote a sense of stabilized, localized authenticity. His argument was that Starbucks purposely draws on natural colors and materials in order to address society's growing dissatisfaction with mass production and feeling of up-rootedness to any particular geographical location. Because of Starbucks' consistency in their design elements throughout most of their stores, Dickinson's in-depth rhetorical analysis shows how material rhetoric can both constrain and enable interactions with our daily spaces.

Methodology

When rhetoric scholars met at the Speech Communication Association's Wingspread Conference in 1970[1] to reexamine how rhetorical criticism should be identified and to determine top priorities for the field, methodology was described as encompassing two poles: the 'critic-artist' and the 'critic-scientist' (Sloan *et al.* 1971). Visual rhetoric also incorporates these two poles methodologically. The rhetorical critic does not simply observe and report but takes his/her analysis a step further to illuminate contemporary rhetorical interactions. Although the concept of agency has lost momentum in the postmodern era,[2] it is traditionally an important notion for rhetorical critics because rhetorical criticism is both an art and a practice. Not only do critics espouse their agency within the interpretation and invention of their own writing,[3] but also they often make an effort to offer insights into how the visual artifact(s) may shed light on themes and possibilities that enhance agency in others.

Visual rhetoric critics will ask: how does this artifact move an audience to action? How does it teach? How does it exhibit certain values?[4] They also have the opportunity to evaluate an image, to assess whether it 'accomplishes the functions suggested by the image itself' (Foss 2004). Here, the critic would ask questions such as: What does it do? Is the image congruent with a particular ethical system? Does the image offer emancipatory options or improve the 'quality of the rhetorical environment?' (Foss 2005: 147). Instead of placing importance on the aesthetics of the visual, rhetorical critics examine how a piece can move an audience or how an audience may identify with a piece. They do not simply address their appreciation of the beautiful but inquire about the function of a visual artifact.

Olson *et al.* (2008) provide a useful review of some of the most common conceptual resources available to critics through the rhetorical tradition. These concepts, described as 'resources for analyzing and understanding symbolic acts of persuasion in context' (2008: 8), include visual argument, enthymeme, topoi, common rhetoric devices such as depiction and metaphor and Burke's notions of the tragic and comic frames, psychology of form, identification and representative anecdote. So, an organization, for example, might ask what kind of argument their website makes visually. Or what kind of messages does the visual environment of the workspace send to employees and clients? More recent concepts include ideograph, image event, rhetorical circulation, and iconic photograph. Olson *et al.* (2008) point out that critics of visual rhetoric also draw on transdisciplinary thinkers – who are also closely associated with visual culture/visual studies (see following section).

A familiar question posed to rhetorical researchers from scholars using other approaches is: why use rhetorical criticism to get at meanings of messages rather than just asking people what they think (by using a survey or interview)? One reason is that meaning is complex. A researcher might ask someone what he/she understood from a message multiple times and get a different answer every time. In addition, a researcher cannot rely on the intention of the message's creator because this is not the same message as may be interpreted by an audience. Another possible reason – though some scholars disagree with this argument – is that people may not be able to fully articulate meanings or articulate the meaning in enough detail or complexity.

Just as artists have the ability to capture our deepest sense of emotion, wellbeing, or fear into a piece of artwork, a rhetorical critic may offer an analysis that takes an audience to a deeper sense of meaning. The rhetorical critic also tries to articulate a message in ways that others may not have considered before, thereby illuminating alternative meanings.

Limitations

One of the most frequent criticisms of visual rhetoric is that critics do not know how to produce the visual artifacts they study. Most critics of visual rhetoric do not teach students how to produce visual texts such as photography, filmmaking, design, etc. Hence, critics do not produce visual texts but only know how to act as 'a consumer, an agent by proxy at best' (Benson 2008). What more can rhetorical critics offer than an art historian or designer who has had extensive training with the visual? One way rhetorical scholars address this question is to say that evaluating an image according to rhetorical standards is different from aesthetic standards. Where designers or art historians are concerned with the aesthetic merits of a visual piece, rhetorical critics are concerned with the influence of image and the 'way images are constructed to affect such influence' (Foss 1994: 214).

Another criticism of visual rhetoric researchers comes from scholars of a social scientific visual communication approach. These scholars suggest that visual rhetoric scholars do not test their analyses of rhetorical strategies. For the past couple of decades, the rhetoric scholar Leah Ceccarelli has been urging critics to use what she calls 'reception studies' to test analyses against actual audience responses. Similarly, from a visual communication approach background, Kenney and Scott call for critics to learn how people identify with an image 'at the time' (2003: 49) by conducting ethnographies of symbolic action like Geertz or Baxandall. Otherwise, they write, rhetorical critics are accused of articulating conscious and unconscious intentions and interpretations of an audience based only on personal inferences and insights. Obviously, as with much qualitative research, rhetoric is constrained in regard to generalizability at the level of each individual study but the opportunity rhetoric affords is based on the generalizability of the theoretical ideas it promotes.

Scholars from visual studies and visual communication approaches also believe that visual rhetoric critics should try to support their analyses by using findings from other areas of research such as cognitive studies or neuroscience. The implication here is that the field of rhetoric sometimes becomes too specialized and loses its generalizable significance. The claim, as explained by McKeon (1987), is that, by supporting rhetorical analyses with evidence from other areas of research, visual rhetoric critics could possibly make firmer conclusions and 'discover intelligible patterns' (Buchanan 2001). Although supporting findings from other research disciplines may very well be helpful, if rhetorical critics arrive at interesting and helpful findings through rigorous interrogation of a visual artifact without any kind of supporting data from an outside discipline, this does not indicate that the rhetorical analysis cannot offer something relevant of its own merit. Researchers using a non-rhetoric approach will sometimes cite findings from a rhetorical analysis because they offer insights not addressed using other approaches (and vice versa). For instance, Kjærgaard (2010) in her content analysis study of nanotechnology in a Danish newspaper cites Faber's (2006) article on the rhetoric of nanoscience, even though this study does not support all conclusions with evidence from other areas of research.

Furthermore, and perhaps the strongest argument for a rhetorical approach, is that the concepts and criteria used in oral and written rhetoric are based on approaches grounded in 'making,' that is, in observing and theorizing effective practice and instructing students to produce rhetorical artifacts. These ancient rhetorical concepts and criteria have been tested for effectiveness since at least the fifth century BCE and are still primary concepts taught to students in writing and public speaking courses today. Even the visual was addressed in the ancient rhetorical concept of *enargiea* (vividness and energy), where speakers were encouraged to create a vivid image of their topic or to bring it before the eyes of their audience.

Visual studies

Key concepts and theoretical assumptions

Interdisciplinary visual scholarship, often referred to as 'visual studies' or 'visual culture,' examines society's access to images and their entanglements in systems of meaning and power. According to the California College of the Arts Visual Studies bachelor degree program, visual studies scholars ask such questions as: 'How do images work to support political regimes, religious systems, or institutions? How do they assist in the consumption of goods? To what extent do they condition our understanding of people, races and ethnicities, gender and sexual orientation, abilities and disabilities?'[5]

Depending on the context, the terms 'visual studies' and 'visual culture' are either carefully distinguished or indifferently conflated. For instance, Dikovitskaya defines visual studies as:

> Visual culture, also known as visual studies, is a new field for the study of the cultural construction of the visual in arts, media, and everyday life. It is a research area and a curricular initiative that regards the visual image as the focal point in the processes through which meaning is made in a cultural context.
>
> *(2006: 1)*

Elkins (2003), on the other hand, suggests that the terms cultural studies, visual culture, and visual studies have vague but significant differences. Although arguments are made that the history of visual studies dates back hundreds of years, most assign the term visual culture to art historian Michael Baxandall, who is considered one of the founders of visual studies. Visual studies emerged as a field of study 20 years after the publication of Baxandall's 1972 book *Painting and Experience in Fifteenth-Century Italy*. His take on visual research was characterized by a fundamentally postmodernist point of view, a perspective taken up by many visual studies researchers. Baxandall argued that art historians should look at art through the experiences of viewers in the period. He urged artists to stop trying to control viewers' reactions and stop treating the exhibition as a static entity (Baxandall 1991: 40). Instead of writing about art from a viewpoint of connoisseurship, Baxandall studied artwork drawing from a variety of sources including the writing of ancient orators and mathematical manuals.

Today, cultural studies is defined as 'the search to understand the relationships of cultural production, consumption, belief and meaning, to social processes and institutions' (Lister and Wells 2001: 61). Along with Raymond Williams and Richard Hoggart, Stuart Hall is considered one of the founding figures of British cultural studies. One of Hall's (1997) main concerns is with the concept of representation. He makes the argument that, because culture is about shared meanings, and meanings can only be shared through our common access to language, language, as a representational system, constructs meanings. Studies of visual culture hold many of the same principles as cultural studies except that studies of visual culture argue for the centrality of vision (as opposed to a focus on language in the written and spoken sense) in everyday experience. Furthermore, visual cultural studies is not considered a sub-division of cultural studies but a new method of analysis for the visual field. Visual culture is younger than cultural studies by several decades. With the late twentieth-century explosion of imaging and visualizing technologies (digitization, satellite imaging, new forms of medical imaging, virtual reality, etc.), it is suggested that 'everyday life has become "visual culture"' (Lister and Wells 2001: 61). Visual culture also refers to the values and identities that are visually constructed and communicated by a particular culture and 'to the enormous variety of visible two- and three-dimensional things that human beings produce and consume as part of their cultural and social lives' (Barnard 2001: 2). For instance, photographs, advertisements, and television programming are the first things that come to mind for many people when they think of visual data but this can also include objects and buildings, not just images.

Methods

Because visual studies researchers investigate questions of power and consumption, much of their research examines the concept of visual pleasure. Visual pleasure has been discussed in connection with power issues because scholars (especially film scholars) have argued that conventions of popular media are structured according to someone's viewing pleasure (most often male), where the camera (or tool that creates the image) disempowers those before its gaze (who are the subject of the image). Researchers of visual pleasure discuss concepts such as scopophilia and the gaze to elucidate various types of visual pleasure such as voyeurism, fetishism, and narcissism. Subjects of visual pleasure, the person or persons being viewed, essentially hand over control to the spectator whose work is 'one of prolonged observation, performed at the margins of a particular activity or event' (Azoulay 2005: 44). This control, or more specifically the gaze, is historically connected to the power of the male in society with the 'acknowledgement that much imagery is produced by men for men' (Schroeder 2002: 10).

Investigating the relationships of cultural production, consumption, belief, and meaning to social processes and institutions as they are exhibited visually also reveals issues of surveillance, privacy, and use of space (Emmison and Smith 2000: ix). In general, visual studies, as compared to cultural studies, owes less to Marxist theory and devotes more attention to Barthes, Baudrillard, Foucault, Lacan, and Benjamin. Therefore, visual studies is distanced from analyses that might lead to social action and more closely connected to culturally oriented sociological analyses and in particular what is seen.

The age of reproduction is also especially important for visual studies theorists because, as the image travels to the spectator, the meaning of images is permanently changed. Continuous reproduction results in images that are 'ephemeral, ubiquitous, insubstantial, available, valueless, and free' (Berger 1972: 32). Most visual studies researchers mark this era, where the image changes status, at the invention of photography. However, today, visual studies scholars must consider another era where spectators, and not just the experts, commonly produce images using digital software and online dissemination.

It is difficult to describe specifically the types of methods used by visual studies researchers. According to the journal *Visual Studies*, visual studies promotes 'acceptance and understanding of a wide range of methods, approaches, and paradigms that constitute image-based research.' It also states that visual studies is committed to promoting 'an interest in developing visual research methodology in all its various forms' and encourages 'research that employs a mixture of visual methods and analytical approaches within one study.'[6] However, it is safe to say that there is a critical interpretive component to any visual studies research, no matter what mixture of methods and analytical approaches is used in the study.

Limitations

One of the most thorough and comprehensive discussions of the current state of visual studies is Elkins' 2003 book, *Visual Studies: A Skeptical Introduction*. Elkins claims that visual studies is 'too easy' and that '[the] scattered subjects and untheorized choices of methods make it fairly simple to generate texts and unrewarding to compare one study to another' (2003: 63). He proposes that visual studies needs to create texts of more lasting interest by balancing the innovative subject matter with strong theoretical and methodological innovation.

The three components of Elkins' arguments – that visual studies should be (1) 'Denser with theories and strategies,' (2) 'Warier of existing visual theories and more attentive to neighboring and distant disciplines,' and (3) 'less predictable in its politics' (ibid.: 65)[7] – are closely related and probably the harshest of his criticisms. However, many visual studies scholars argue that the field *does*, in fact, draw from dense theories and strategies. For example, one major resource for the canon of visual studies theory is Mirzoeff's *The Visual Culture Reader* (1998, 2002, 2012), a collection of essays that include works by Althusser, Balsamo, Barthes, Baudrillard, Debord, Descartes, Dubois, Lacan, Manovich, and many other writers. This thick collection of essays from well-respected authors (although Mirzoeff says it is impossible to represent the 'polymorphous field that visual culture is becoming' (2002: 21)) seems to indicate that visual studies does have its own set of theorists to draw from.

Communication scholars have also begun to question some of the assumptions made by visual studies scholars regarding power relationships. Finnegan (2006), a rhetorical critic from the discipline of communication, writes that there are three potential ways to frame 'communication as vision' – surveillance, spectacle and analogy. In her essay she argues that framing vision as surveillance is problematic because the dialectic of power relationships (e.g. 'the gaze' and someone being 'watched') impedes researchers' abilities to imagine relationships in different ways and 'blinds us to other interpretations' (2006: 62). Her problem with the notion of the spectacle (Debord's term for a 'social relationship between people that is mediated by images' (Debord 2000: 12)) is that audiences are passive viewers that absorb but do not engage. The spectacle turns attention away from materiality. Both visual studies concepts, surveillance and the spectacle, fall into the trap of iconophobia where vision is a dangerous one-way street. Instead, Finnegan argues that visual researchers should frame communication as vision through analogy, 'a perceptual process tied directly to how humans come to know and learn. It recognizes difference and attempts creatively to negotiate it by juxtaposing it with points of connection and similarity' (ibid.: 63).

An alternative to this could be a notion of visual wellbeing as described by Gallagher *et al.*: a 'state of feeling healthy, happy and content, of sensing vitality and prosperity, recognized precisely in one's experience of objects through the visual sense' (2011: 30). People may experience a type of looking that is different from the kinds of pleasures related to voyeurism, fetishism, and narcissism. They may experience visual pleasure that 'sustains them, that involves intersubjectivity and conscious experience' (ibid.: 30).

This commitment to a group of postmodern theorists inevitably results in visual studies analyses appearing predictable. Elkins notes, in his controversial *Skeptical Introduction* (2003), that an uncritical devotion to certain theoretical concepts makes the writing of the visual studies scholars predictable and uninteresting. However, the problem may not be that visual studies needs to move beyond its postmodern perspective but that it stops at a predictable conclusion without asking as Elkins puts it 'what distance from capitalist practices is optimal' (ibid.: 71). In other words, visual studies analyses are predictable because, like their contributions to theory, their insights do not go far enough. Visual studies does have great potential, but that is largely due to its openness to interdisciplinarity. As Finnegan points out, one of the strongest aspects of visual cultural studies is its focus on culture 'recognizes the ways that visuality frames our experience of the world' (2004: 244). Finnegan follows her assertion with a quote from W.J.T. Mitchell about visual culture: 'vision is a mode of cultural expression and human communication as fundamental and widespread as language' (Mitchell 1994: 540).

Visual communication

Key concepts and theoretical assumptions

Reviewing the literature, it becomes apparent that visual studies strongly influences and overlaps with visual communication research. However, visual studies research is not identical to visual communication. Visual studies and visual rhetoric perspectives are sometimes criticized for not using an entirely positivist or quantitative perspective as conceived by visual communication scholars. Critics argue that the material chosen for visual studies analyses appears to be selected to suit the analysis instead of illustrating a representative sample (Banks 2008). Visual communication scholars, on the other hand, conduct studies informed by a positivist perspective. The phrase 'visual communication' generally refers to the empirical and sometimes generative study of photography, television, film, advertising, drawing, illustration, etc. The purpose of these studies is to enable understanding of the creation, presentation, preservation, and support of media works as well as the effects and reception of audiences. Based on her understanding of visual communication as a problem-oriented approach, Müller offers this definition:

> Visual communication can be described as an expanding subfield of communication science that uses social scientific methods to explain the production, distribution and reception processes, but also the meanings of mass-mediated visuals in contemporary social, cultural, economic, and political contexts. Following an empirical, social scientific tradition that is based on a multidisciplinary background, visual communication research is problem-oriented, critical in its method, and pedagogical intentions, and aimed at understanding and explaining current visual phenomena and their implications for the immediate future.
>
> *(2007: 24)*

Methods

Because of this social scientific influence, research methods in visual communication are more empirical in design than in visual rhetoric or visual studies.[8] They use both qualitative and quantitative methods to 'explore the actual structuring, functioning and effects of visual phenomena in complex social, economic, political and cultural contexts' (Müller 2007: 19). The variety of contributing disciplines also results in the use of a variety of empirical methods – interviews, experiments, surveys, content analysis, diaries, visual ethnography, focus groups, visual-spatial intelligence tests, case studies, etc.

Limitations

With all of these research method options, scholars may ask what the specific methodological contribution of visual communication actually is. One of the most common methods used by visual communication researchers is content analysis. Most often viewed as a sophisticated method within communication science, content analysis is problematic in relation to images because of the difficulty of standardization. Visuals are not as easy to read because we do not have a dictionary or a grammar to apply to them as we do with written languages. Visual communication scholars sometimes use variations of traditional content analysis and employ interpretive and reception-based content analysis. According to Ahuvia, reception-based content analysis allows researchers 'to quantify how different audiences will understand text' (2001: 139) and, in interpretive content analysis, 'researchers go beyond quantifying the most straightforward denotative elements in a text' (ibid.: 139). With these two methods, the belief exists that readers' understanding of the artifact should be used as the basis for coding. The potential disadvantages to using content analysis with images (or using content analysis for any medium) are that the researcher may associate frequency of content with significance of content and also may use content categories without relating them to a theoretical perspective (Kenney 2009).

However, social semiotics theorists Gunther Kress and Theo van Leeuwen and cognitive psychologist Donald Norman argue that content analysis is not more difficult using images instead of text because society does, in fact, utilize a grammar of visuals. Even with the overwhelming shifts in technology and globalization, the idea is to search out a framework in which scholars and practitioners may create, organize and analyze visuals according to an established grammar. Although postmodernists react negatively to the idea of a universal way of describing visual forms and their universal significance, there may be some fundamental strategies for reading images, as is also suggested by the concept of visual literacy, where audiences are able to 'read' or successfully understand the intended meaning of an image. Form may be influenced by such quantifiable sciences as ergonomics or economics, but in the final analysis design choices are made to satisfy conscious and subconscious desires (Heller 2004).

Another criticism of visual communication, noted by scholars committed to a visual rhetoric approach, is the amount of attention the social sciences and visual communication scholars devote to issues of rhetoric. As Simon points out,

> Broadly speaking, virtually all scholarly discourse is rhetorical in the sense that issues need to be named and framed, facts interpreted and conclusions justified; furthermore, in adapting arguments to ends, audience, and circumstances, the writer (or speaker) must adopt a persona, choose a style, and make judicious use of what Kenneth Burke has called the 'resources of ambiguity' in language.
>
> *(1990: 9)*

This statement applies to visual communication scholarship because, just as a writer or speaker must 'adopt a persona' and 'choose a style,'[9] so does the creator of a visual image. Artists, photojournalists, designers, etc. are often identified by their style and this is created by certain choices the visual author has enacted. Therefore, when conducting a visual communication study, rhetorical issues of framing and context are likely to be important considerations.

In addition to these observations, scholars of visual rhetoric and visual studies approaches sometimes criticize visual communication studies for not arriving at philosophical, inventive, or artistic insight. They argue that the studies appear limited in that they simply present findings applicable to a specific group at a given time and even more generalizable findings remain narrow in scope (Hill 2004; Scott 1994). However, almost all visual communication scholars approach their research post-positivistically recognizing that discretionary judgment is unavoidable in their research and that 'proving causality with certainty in explaining social phenomena is problematic, that knowledge is inherently embedded in historically specific paradigms and is therefore relative rather than absolute' (Patton 2002: 92). Therefore, many believe that multiple methods, both quantitative and qualitative, are needed to generate and test theory.

Especially when using qualitative research methods, many, if not all, visual communication researchers embrace the interpretive skills needed to analyze the behaviors and beliefs of participants and situations. As Yanow mentions in Chapter 10 in this volume, the researcher needs to discern the meanings of visuals by engaging with their creators and/or users. Most visual communication researchers argue that, although their studies are specific to a certain context, if there is a sufficiently 'thick' description (Geertz 1973) in a study, two potentially similar contexts can be adequately assessed and transferability may be achieved. Transferability is a term proposed by education scholars Guba and Lincoln (1981) to account for the innate limit to naturalist generalizations. Their motivation for proposing the term stems from their belief that it is virtually impossible to imagine any human behavior that is not heavily influenced by context. They explain the concept: 'the degree of transferability is a direct function of the similarity between the two contexts ... If context A and context B are "sufficiently" congruent, then working hypotheses from the sending originating context may be applicable in the receiving context' (Lincoln and Guba 1985: 124).

Concluding thoughts

Visual research has grown considerably and continues to disperse throughout many fields and disciplines. Critics insist that, with the increase in visual phenomena, more studies are conducted without sufficient rigor and without contributing to theory (Elkins 2003; Finnegan 2004; Müller 2007). Other scholars such as Mitchell argue that studying images, especially artistic images, makes them objects of science and that is not how the work was meant to be treated (Grønstad and Vågnes 2006); by treating the works as objects of science, the researcher may completely miss the deeper meaning or appropriate wonder or pleasure. Michael Ann Holly alludes to Heidegger in his evaluation of research methods in an interview: 'the manipulations and maneuvers of any research paradigm can contribute to the process of stripping the work of its awe, the awe that makes art still matter' (Smith 2008: 180). However, by recognizing that methods should not be the focal point of analysis and by understanding instead a variety of approaches, researchers may develop a better understanding of visual artifacts and avoid losing sight of what makes the visual notable in the first place.

Notes

1 Report of the Committee on the Advancement and Refinement of Rhetorical Criticism. In *The Prospect of Rhetoric: Report of the National Development Project*. Ed. Lloyd F. Bitzer and Edwin Black. Englewood Cliffs, NJ: Prentice-Hall, 1971, pp. 220–227.
2 Famous postmodern thinkers, such as Michel Foucault, do not consider the individual subject as a creative autonomous being but instead consider humans to be 'hedged in on all sides by social determinations' (Layder 1994: 95).
3 Though an argument could be made that agency is espoused through all writing in many different approaches to research, the concept of agency for the rhetorical researcher or critic is arguably more important because its history can be traced back to the humanist perspective of the sophists in the fifth century BCE. The sophists boasted a sincere confidence in the creative power of the word in the hands of an individual (Crick 2011). As mentioned in the discussion of the critic-artist and critic-scientist, a critical-interpretive work is considered an artistic as well as a pragmatic activity whose results cannot be quantified or measured but is judged with respect to how it enriches and broadens the experience of the audience. As with public speakers who learn their art through speaking, most rhetorical critics believe their research is conducted and improved upon through their writing. They also firmly believe that, as an expert of persuasion, the rhetorical critic has something special to offer an audience through their individual insights.

4   Many theories provide the basis for addressing these rhetorical questions. For instance, activity theory would be a very useful theory to investigate how an object may rhetorically move someone to action.
5   See http://www.universities.com/edu/Bachelor_degree_in_Visual_Studies_at_California_College_of_the_Arts.html.
6   See http://visualsociology.org/journal.html.
7   Though he does not go into the specifics of the politics, judging from other writings and interviews, it is likely he is referring to societal politics that designated academia as the generator of critical thinking. Standard political ideologies that are typically referenced include Adorno's Marxist critique and the Kantian Kritik. Elkins argues that many interesting ideas happen outside of academia and that they should also be considered in visual studies.
8   Though social science is often considered more empirical, rhetorical scholar Edwin Black once said that rhetorical criticism is fundamentally empirical because it is always grounded in the particular case.
9   Style in this sense refers to the characteristics of the writing itself and has also been defined as those figures that ornament discourse and represent the person writing.

References

Ahuvia, A. (2001) 'Traditional, interpretive, and reception based content analyses: improving the ability of content analysis to address issues of pragmatic and theoretical concern', *Social Indicators Research* 54(2): 139–172.
Azoulay, A. (2005) 'The ethic of the spectator: the citizenry of photography', *Afterimage* 33: 38–44.
Banks, M. (2008) *Using Visual Data in Qualitative Research*, Thousand Oaks, CA: Sage.
Barnard, M. (2001) *Approaches to Understanding Visual Culture*, New York, NY: Palgrave.
Barnhurst, K.G., Vari, M. and Rodriguez, I. (2004) 'Mapping visual studies in communication', Special issue: The State of the Art in Communication Theory and Research, *Journal of Communication* 54(4): 616–644.
Baxandall, M. (1972) *Painting and Experience in Fifteenth-Century Italy: A Primer in the Social History of Pictorial Style*, Oxford, UK: Oxford University Press.
——(1991) 'Exhibiting intention: some preconditions of the visual display of cultural purposeful objects', in I. Karp and S.D. Lavine (eds) *Exhibiting Cultures: The Poetics and Politics of Museum Display*, Washington, DC: Smithsonian Institution Press, 33–41.
Benson, T. (2008) 'Afterword: look, rhetoric!', in L.C. Olson, C.A. Finnegan and D.S. Hope (eds) *Visual Rhetoric: A Reader in Communication and American Culture*, Newbury Park, CA: Sage.
Berger, J. (1972) *Ways of Seeing*, London: British Broadcasting Corporation and Penguin.
Buchanan, R. (2001) 'Design research and the new learning', *Design Issues* 17(4): 3–23.
Crick, N. (2011) *Rhetorical Public Speaking*, New York, NY: Pearson Education, Inc.
Debord, G. (2000) [1967] *Society of the Spectacle*, Detroit: Red & Black.
Dickinson, G. (2002) 'Joe's rhetoric: finding authenticity at Starbucks', *Rhetoric Society Quarterly* 32(4): 5–27.
Dikovitskaya, M. (2006) *Visual Culture: The Study of the Visual after the Cultural Turn*, Cambridge, MA: MIT Press.
Elkins, J. (2003) *Visual Studies: A Skeptical Introduction*, New York, NY: Routledge.
Emmison, M. and Smith, P. (2000) *Researching the Visual*, Thousand Oaks, CA: Sage.
Faber, B. (2006) 'Popularizing nanoscience: the public rhetoric of nanotechnology, 1986–1999', *Technical Communication Quarterly* 15(2): 141–169.
Finnegan, C.A. (2004) 'Review essay: visual studies and visual rhetoric', *Quarterly Journal of Speech* 90: 234–256.
——(2006) 'Vision', in G.J. Shepherd, J. St. John and Ted Striphas (eds) *Communication As…: Perspectives on Theory*, Thousand Oaks, CA: Sage, 60–66.
Foss, S. (1994) 'A rhetorical schema for the evaluation of visual imagery', *Communication Studies* 45: 213–224.
——(2004) 'Framing the study of visual rhetoric', in C.A. Hill and M.H. Helmers (eds) *Defining Visual Rhetorics*, New York, NY: Routledge, 303–312.
——(2005) 'Theory of visual rhetoric', in K. Smith, S. Moriarty, B. Gretchen and K. Kenney (eds) *Handbook of Visual Communication: Theory, Methods, and Media*, Mahwah, NJ: Lawrence Erlbaum, 141–152.

Gallagher, V.J. (2004) 'Memory as social action: cultural projection and generic form in civil rights memorials' in S.R. Goldzwig and P.A. Sullivan (eds) *Communities, Creations, and Contradictions: New Approaches to Rhetoric for the Twenty-first Century*, Thousand Oaks, CA: Sage, 149–171.

Gallagher, V.J., Martin, K.N. and Ma, M. (2011) 'Visual wellbeing: intersections of rhetorical theory and visual design', *Design Issues* 27(2): 25–39.

Geertz, C. (1973) *The Interpretation of Cultures*, New York, NY: Basic Books, Inc.

Grønstad, A. and Vågnes, Ø. (2006) 'An interview with W. J. T. Mitchell ', CVS Center for Visual Studies. Retrieved from http://www.visual-studies.com/interviews/mitchell.html.

Guba, E.G. and Lincoln, Y.S. (1981) *Effective Evaluation: Improving the Usefulness of Evaluation Results Through Responsive and Naturalistic Approaches*, San Francisco: Jossey-Bass.

Hall, S. (1997) 'The work of representation', in S. Hall (ed.) *Representation: Cultural Representations and Signifying Practices*, Thousand Oaks, CA: Sage.

Heller, S. (2004) *Design Literacy: Understanding Graphic Design*, New York, NY: Allworth Communications, Inc.

Hill, C.A. (2004) 'The psychology of rhetorical images', in C.A. Hill and M.H. Helmers (eds) *Defining Visual Rhetorics*, Mahwah, NJ: Lawrence Erlbaum, 25–40.

Kenney, K. (2009) *Visual Communication Research Designs*, New York, NY: Routledge.

Kenney, K. and Scott, L.M. (2003) 'A review of the visual rhetoric literature', in L. Scott and R. Batra (eds) *Persuasive Imagery: A Consumer Response Perspective*, Mahwah, NJ: Lawrence Erlbaum Publishers, 17–56.

Kjærgaard, R.S. (2010) 'Making a small country count: nanotechnology in Danish newspapers from 1996 to 2006', *Public Understanding of Science* 19(1): 80–97.

Layder, D. (1994) *Understanding Social Theory*, London: Sage Publications.

Lincoln, Y. and Guba, E.G. (1985) *Naturalistic Inquiry*, Thousand Oaks, CA: Sage.

Lister, M. and Wells, L. (2001) 'Seeing beyond belief: cultural studies as an approach to analyzing the visual', in T. van Leeuwen and C. Jewitt (eds) *Handbook of Visual Analysis*, Thousand Oaks, California: Sage, 61–91.

McKeon, R. (1987) *Rhetoric: Essays in Invention and Discovery*, edited with Introduction by Mark Backman, Woodbridge, CT: Ox Bow Press.

Mirzoeff, N. (1998, 2002, 2012) *The Visual Culture Reader*, New York, NY: Routledge.

Mitchell, W.J.T. (1994) *Picture Theory: Essays on Verbal and Visual Representation*, Chicago, IL: University of Chicago Press.

——(1995) 'Interdisciplinary and visual culture', *Art Bulletin* 70(4): 540–544.

Müller, M. (2007) 'What is visual communication?' *Studies in Communication Sciences* 7(2): 7–34.

Olson, L.C., Finnegan, C.A. and Hope, D.S. (eds) (2008) *Visual Rhetoric: A Reader in Communication and American Culture*, Thousand Oaks, CA: Sage.

Ott, B.L. and Dickinson, G. (2009) 'Visual rhetoric and/as critical pedagogy', in A.A. Lunsford, K.H. Wilson and R.A. Eberly (eds) *The Sage Handbook of Rhetorical Studies*, Los Angeles, CA: Sage, 391–405.

Patton, M.Q. (2002) *Qualitative Research and Evaluation Methods*, 3rd ed., Thousand Oaks, CA: Sage.

Schroeder, J. (2002) *Visual Consumption*, London and New York: Routledge.

Scott, L.M. (1994) 'Images in advertising: the need for a theory of visual rhetoric', *Journal of Consumer Research* 21(2): 252–273.

Simon, H. (1990) *The Rhetorical Turn: Invention and Persuasion in the Conduct of Inquiry*, Illinois: University of Chicago Press.

Sloan, T., Gregg, R., Nilsen, T., Rein, I., Simons, H., Stelzner, H. and Zacharias, D. (1971) 'Report of the committee on the advancement and refinement of rhetorical criticism', in L. Bitzer and E. Black (eds) *The Prospect of Rhetoric: Report of the National Developmental Project* [sponsored by Speech Communication Association], Creskill, NJ: Prentice-Hall, 220–227.

Smith, K., Moriarty, S., Gretchen, B. and Kenney, K. (2005) *Handbook of Visual Communication: Theory, Methods and Media*, New York, NY: Routledge.

Smith, M. (2008) *Visual Culture Studies*, Thousand Oaks, CA: Sage.

12
Using videoethnography to study entrepreneurship

Jean Clarke

Introduction

Organizational research has historically privileged text-based forms of communication over visual forms with most qualitative research in organizations focused on textual data-gathering techniques and representations, such as transcribed interviews and verbal observations of visual events published in text-based journals (Clarke 2011). This has led to a paradoxical situation where the majority of qualitative organizational research is based on text-based descriptions of situations, interactions and events, which originally took place in 'visual' and 'embodied' contexts (Hassard *et al.* 2000). While little attention has been given to visual methodologies in organizational research, in contrast, visual sociologists and anthropologists have a longstanding tradition stretching back over a hundred years of using photography, film and video as part of data collection and representation (Becker 1998; Harper 1989; McDougall 1997; Mead 1995; Prins 2002). More recently, there has been a reinvigorated 'visual turn' across the social sciences with the growing recognition that the visual is 'a pervasive feature not only of social life but of many aspects of social enquiry as well' (Emmison and Smith 2000: 2). As Secrist *et al.* (2002) highlight, despite all the thick description and linguistic detail researchers provide, words alone are often simply not enough to communicate the complex interactions that they encounter.

This has led to a burgeoning of interest in what visual methods may add to current text-based approaches, and the last two decades have witnessed a rapid growth in visual research in this domain (Prosser and Loxley 2007). This new wealth of academic scholarship includes journals such as *Visual Studies* and *Visual Communication*, and highly profiled international conferences, which offer insights into investigating the role that visual aspects of communication play in our cultural and societal lives. Despite this, many researchers of organizations remain suspicious over the utility of visual images, arguing that visual methods are subjective, partial and ultimately too difficult to interpret conclusively for any 'valid' research project. It seems, just as qualitative methodologies used for decades by our social science counterparts were once discounted by organizational researchers as being largely subjective and lacking 'validity' and transparency (Bryman 1994), visual methodologies currently appear to be enduring the same treatment. However, a small but growing community has started to make some inroads into incorporating visual research in organizational studies. This is evidenced by the increasing, if sporadic, examples of the use of visual approaches such as photographic representation into research designs (e.g. Buchanan 2001; Guthey and Jackson 2005; Warren 2002, 2009). Guthey and Jackson (2005), for example, examine the use of CEO portraits in the visual construction of corporate identity and image. These studies have begun to show that, by ignoring understandings in the visual domain, we continue to neglect a whole dimension of rich information about organizational processes.

One noticeable absence in these visual approaches to organization studies is any evidence of audio-visual material being encompassed into research designs. Video first emerged as a methodology alongside a developing tradition in ethnographic filmmaking that began in the mid-twentieth century (Ruby 1996). Aside from this specialist field, until recently, using video as a methodology remained quite rare, as the technical expertise and equipment it required made it prohibitively expensive for the majority of researchers (Harrison 2002). New technical innovations have now made it much easier for researchers to incorporate moving images into research designs (Heath and Hindmarsh 2002). The new digital video cameras are small, affordable and easy to use, and create good quality audio and visual data, which can be transferred on to a computer and edited easily and quickly. Video-based designs are now widely incorporated into a variety of social science disciplines interested in the ongoing production of social life and the interactions between people, artefacts and their environment (Shrum *et al.* 2005). More than ever before, participants are also willing to be videotaped, so accustomed are they to constant surveillance through CCTV and the ubiquity of amateur videos captured on mobile phones and handheld devices. Given these changing cultural and technological conditions and the potential video has to enhance the quality and insights of organizational research, it seems logical that we should become more methodologically capable in using this technology.

The goal of this chapter is to show how video may be incorporated into organizational research through an example of a video-based ethnography of three entrepreneurs. While a detailed discussion of this study can be viewed elsewhere (see Clarke 2011), here I wish to discuss some of the more 'messy' aspects of conducting this type of research that we don't have the space and perhaps the inclination to put into our journal articles – research is very rarely as sterile, ordered and clinical as it appears in journal form. Following a brief overview of the research upon which this chapter is based that outlines why it is important to examine the visual in interactions between entrepreneurs and their stakeholders, the chapter then considers the pragmatic, methodological and ethical dilemmas or problems that surround the collection of video-based data. This overview of an application and evaluation of a video-based ethnographic approach will benefit organizational researchers interested in understanding the constraints and opportunities associated with this kind of methodology.

Visual symbols in entrepreneurial interactions

Accessing adequate financial, material and human resources is regarded as central to the process of entrepreneurship, given that the vast majority of entrepreneurs are likely at some point to be faced with the challenge of obtaining external investment to initiate or expand their entrepreneurial venture (Starr and MacMillan 1990; Zott and Huy 2007). Yet entrepreneurs are likely to face much greater problems in engaging potential resource providers in their entrepreneurial ideas than those in more established organizations. This problem relates to the 'liability of newness' (Stinchcombe 1965) where resource providers are likely to be reluctant to become part of any novel or unorthodox undertaking for which there is no conclusive evidence that their efforts will eventually be rewarded (Brush *et al.* 2001). This liability is compounded by the information asymmetry (Zott and Huy 2007) between an entrepreneur and external resource providers in relation to the potential of a novel venture (Shane 2003). In an attempt to explain how entrepreneurs overcome the liabilities they face, many entrepreneurship scholars have turned to the literature on organizational legitimacy (Lounsbury and Glynn 2001; Zimmerman and Zeitz 2002). The development of legitimacy is seen as a social process whereby the entrepreneurial idea is judged and valued in relation to the cultural context resulting in a 'generalized perception or assumption that the actions of an entity are desirable, proper or appropriate within some socially constructed system of norms, beliefs and definitions' (Suchman 1995: 574). Entrepreneurs who are seen as legitimate benefit from this cultural support through having a higher probability of securing vital resources, while those who lack legitimacy are more vulnerable to their entrepreneurial ideas being viewed as 'negligent, irrational or unnecessary' (Meyer and Rowan 1991: 50).

Various symbols that legitimize entrepreneurial ventures have been identified, such as prior education and the calibre of the entrepreneur and founding team (Packalen 2007); the alignment of new ventures with traditional understandings of organizational forms (Tornikoski and Newbert 2007); use of rational business planning techniques (Delmar and Shane 2004); and certificates and endorsements (Rao 1994). While the cultural and symbolic dimensions of organizational forms and quality signals can make the new venture familiar and credible to key groups (Lounsbury and Glynn 2001), simply displaying certain organizational arrangements and appropriate signs of quality offers little insight into how entrepreneurs institute unorthodox or novel business forms or the actions entrepreneurs take to overcome a lack of certain quality symbols (Martens et al. 2007). Entrepreneurs must also be able to use these symbols effectively to persuade stakeholders of their venture's legitimacy during presentations and other interactions (e.g. Baron and Brush 1999). Some research has focused on how entrepreneurs use linguistic devices such as narrative, framing, and metaphor (Clarke and Holt 2010; Cornelissen and Clarke 2010; Martens et al. 2007) to symbolically represent their ventures as 'compatible with more widely established sets of activities' (Aldrich and Fiol 1994: 652). For example, Cornelissen and Clarke (2010) show how, in creating novel ventures, entrepreneurs use analogy and metaphor to make their new venture familiar to others by framing the venture in terms that are understandable and thus legitimate. However, as yet, no research has been conducted on how visual symbols are used in entrepreneurs' interactions with stakeholders.

From an impression management perspective, communication activities extend well beyond the use of traditional discourse, to include a wide range of meaning-laden actions and symbolic displays. Goffman (1959) uses the term performance to refer to the activities of an individual, which serves to influence a set of observers and suggests that individuals have the capacity to manage others' impressions through two different kinds of activity: (1) the expression that they give, which may be seen to be rooted in the language they use; and (2) the expression they give off, which relates to non-linguistic or visual aspects of this process (Goffman 1959). Gardner and Avolio similarly emphasize the integral role that visual symbols play in managing impressions, which they propose directs attention to the development and manipulation of 'physical appearances, settings, props and other types of artefactual displays' (1998: 43). This research suggests that human experience is never simply a linguistic experience, and that we use multiple modes of discourse to organize and communicate (Iedema 2007; Philips et al. 2004). In relation to this in the entrepreneurship domain, a number of theorists have highlighted the importance of what is being referred to as 'social competence', which emphasizes the importance of social skills that relate to entrepreneurial success (e.g. Baron and Brush 1999; Baron and Markman 2003; Chen et al. 2009; Cornelissen et al. 2012; Mason and Harrison 2000). The idea of social competence goes beyond ideas of persuasion through linguistic domains; as Vecchio outlines, social competence encompass[es] the ability to correctly gauge the current moods or emotions of others, proficiency in inducing positive reactions in others by enhancing one's own appearance and image, effectiveness in persuasion, and the ability to adjust to a range of social situations with a range of individuals.

(2003: 318)

The suggestion here is that entrepreneurship is an act of impression management, where the 'mood' of the audience must be gauged before any activities take place, and a number of tools applied, including but not limited to language, in order to accomplish the given task of engaging others in the venture.

In an attempt to access these non-linguistic dimensions of entrepreneurs' impression management, I conducted a study that investigated how entrepreneurs used visual symbols persuasively in their efforts to secure resources for their novel ventures (Clarke 2011). This was achieved through conducting a video-based ethnographic study (Pink 2001) of three male entrepreneurs in the North of England who were in the early stages of venture commercialization and seeking to attract funding. While the entrepreneurs involved in this study came from highly diverse industries and contexts, they all employed similar processes to create meaning visually. In particular, the data showed that a wide range of visual activities and physical or material contexts were used by the entrepreneurs in this study to convey symbolic meanings to others in their context, including their clothing, physical surroundings, such as their built environments, and artefacts, such as high-status vehicles and interior decor. The manipulation of these visual symbols helped entrepreneurs access much-needed resources through addressing low levels of legitimacy that typically exist when novel ventures are launched (e.g. Aldrich and Fiol 1994). By studying in detail across an extended period of time how entrepreneurs use the visual to persuade stakeholders to invest in their venture, this study shows that language is likely to be only one of the communication tools used by entrepreneurs. This expands previous understandings by accounting for how entrepreneurs create meanings outside the linguistic domain and illustrates the importance of bodily, material and physical modes of communication in the entrepreneurship process. It also suggests that future theoretical insights in the entrepreneurship domain should aim to account for how entrepreneurs engage others in their venture through visual modes of meaning-making. Now I turn to the collection and analysis of the video data and how the problems and issues I encountered along the way were overcome.

Introducing the camera

One of the main questions I am asked when I talk about this research is: 'How on earth did you get three busy entrepreneurs to agree that you could follow them around with a video camera!?' Initially, an email was sent to over a hundred entrepreneurs listed on a university database, explaining that I was interested in how entrepreneurs successfully accessed resources for new ventures. It also outlined the length of time that would be spent within the organization and stipulated that the entrepreneur needed to be in the process of commercializing a new technology/venture for which they were currently trying to attract funding. The use of the video camera was not mentioned at this stage, as I suspected that this would immediately discourage a large number of the entrepreneurs on the database from taking part. Videotaping the entrepreneurs was only discussed once I had selected the cases and met the participants in person. Surprisingly, perhaps, all three entrepreneurs accepted the use of the video, possibly because there was already some commitment on their part and they had become familiar with me through email and telephone conversations and trusted me and my motives to some degree.

Despite their agreement, I didn't introduce the camera immediately once I began fieldwork. The success of ethnography depends on the researcher developing and maintaining a positive personal relationship with participants and it was thought that to immediately introduce an intrusive device like a video camera could potentially damage the level of access to participants (Shrum *et al.* 2005). Over these first few days, I had many casual conversations with the entrepreneurs, employees and customers about my research and my interest in resource acquisition. I also explained that, in order to really understand these processes, I needed to video-record them during interactions; however, I didn't mention I was particularly interested in the visual aspects of this process as I wanted to limit my impact on the behaviour of participants as much as possible. One of the entrepreneurs compared my research to the BBC pseudo-documentary-style comedy series *The Office*, jokingly saying that he hoped he wouldn't be portrayed as a David Brent-style character – the irritating and offensive white-collar office middle manager and principal character of the series. While it was said humorously, these kinds of comparisons enabled participants to engage with the use of the video camera and, to some extent, to even enjoy the process of being observed and filmed.

Capturing natural interactions

It was also essential during those first few days in the organizations to begin to identify expectable patterns of action and analyse the situation even before the action took place (Mondala 2006). Following Collier and Collier's advice that 'good video and film records for research are ultimately the product of observation that is organised and consistent' (1986: 149), I explored a range of issues prior to capturing the videotaped data, including the optimum distance for researchers to videotape participants and the type of camera angle and view that is least distracting to participants (e.g. Collier and Collier 1986; Prosser 1998). These choices about perspectives and spots from which to record action often depend as much on technical and situational constraints (such as the length of the videotapes used, the possibility of placing the cameras in difficult angles and locations, etc.) as they do on research goals. As researchers, we must work within the constraints of the environment and adapt our data collection approaches as effectively as we can.

The camera used was the Sony Digital Camera Recorder HC94, which collected images onto mini DV tapes of up to 90 minutes. The technology has moved on somewhat from when I recorded the data and DV tapes are less often used now. Most people use hard drive or flash memory camcorders, which store videos as data files to a built-in hard drive or microchip, which can be directly transferred in file format on to a PC. The camera I used also had an LCD screen that could be flipped out so that I could view the scene as it unfolded and also what I was recording. As Pink (2001) argues, this creates distance between the researcher's eye and the camera, allowing the researcher to maintain better eye contact with participants as the camera is not hiding their face. At the same time, they can continue to view the scene unfolding through the LCD screen and assess whether the material that is being captured is usable and viewable. I found this aspect of the LCD screen particularly useful, as it allowed me to interview and question participants in a normal manner without having an instrument obscuring my face. The camera easily sat in the palm of my hand and participants often remarked that they had forgotten the camera was there. In meetings or at other times when I was involved in the research activity and therefore could not hold the video camera, it was positioned on a tripod in order to capture the interaction. Also, pragmatically, the video camera cannot be held for long periods of time as it is very tiring on the arms, so a tripod is definitely an essential tool of any would-be videoethnographer!

Although the camera was ideal in the situations described above where participants were sitting in meetings, or talking to me on a one-to-one basis, organizations are also noisy, busy places – people do not wait their turn to speak and are highly mobile and able to move out of view of the camera very easily. A larger microphone was introduced, which was attached to the camera in meetings, which helped to overcome the problem of multiple speakers as it allowed me to zoom into a particular speaker's dialogue. Yet it is difficult to capture the many events going on at the same time and the researcher needs to make constant judgements about the focus of attention and what should be recorded (Jordan and Henderson 1995). This is particularly problematic when the camera is situated on the tripod and therefore cannot adapt to these changes in conditions very easily – as Macbeth (1999) puts it, the camera cannot glance, it can only stare. Over the course of any ethnographic study, interaction is likely to take place sporadically and unannounced at any given moment in a number of different locations. Short of setting up some type of *Big Brother* environment, where cameras point in every direction, making no space unobservable, it is impossible to ensure that the researcher will always be close to where the interaction (or action!) occurs. This means that some degree of analysis is therefore taking place even as the material is being recorded, as the researcher must makes online judgements about where to locate their focus of attention, which are never made explicit in the reporting of the research. The problem for researchers is that such decisions are made instantaneously and important interactions cannot be recaptured if they are missed (Plowman 1996).

In relation to this, the main criticism levelled at this type of research is the influence that the researcher and their video camera have on the unfolding interactions. It is argued that participants will not 'act naturally' when the camera is around and, hence, the material that is collected is not representative of participants' 'normal' behaviour. In this project, I attempted as much as possible to reduce the 'reactivity' of participants (Harrison 2002; Prosser 1998). Given that I was placed in each organization for an extended period, over time the participants became accustomed to the use of the video camera and reacted less to its presence. Of course, this criticism cannot completely be dismissed and debates about whether research really represents 'reality' and 'truth' are evident across all types of ethnographic research. While we must strive to be as objective as possible, we must work on the assumption that we can only see 'with' the camera and not 'through it' (Büscher 2005). The choices we, as researchers, make about what and who should be recorded and our impact on the participants cannot be truly accounted for. For these reasons, we can never illustrate the whole situation but must make do with an account that is partial and constructed (Atkinson 1990; Watson 2000).

Ethical issues in video-based research

Incorporating a visual dimension into research projects also undoubtedly extends the ethical dilemmas inherent in the research process (Pink 2001). In particular, in visual research, it is not possible to protect participants' identities to the same extent as in a solely textual study, as people's faces and places of work are potentially identifiable. Although consent was obtained from the entrepreneurs and all other 'actors' who were to be videotaped, it became clear as the study unfolded that the use of a video camera was unacceptable to participants in certain organizational situations. For example, in one situation of conflict where tensions were running particularly high, I was asked to turn off the video camera but allowed to witness the event myself. On other occasions where sensitive material was being discussed, I was invited to join the discussion but asked not to videotape these interactions. Organizational participants are, therefore, often uncomfortable with the use of video in situations that we as researchers find interesting and informative, perhaps recognizing how insightful the tangible, concrete nature of a moving image can be. This emphasizes the importance of incorporating textual fieldnotes into visual research projects, as this ensures the researcher can, to some extent, record interactions and make observations in places where the video camera is forbidden (Clarke 2007).

Drawing on her experience of applying a video-based research approach in anthropological settings, Pink (2001) argues that it is difficult for researchers to have predetermined ideas and expectations of what they will be able to achieve through the use of visual methodologies in any research context. She proposes that it is often better to negotiate ethical issues as they appear in the field rather than having a fixed strategy (Pink 2001). Drawing on Simons and Usher's (2000) ideas on 'situated ethics', Flewitt (2006) argues that, rather than asking for 'informed consent' in video-based research, it is better to work with the idea of 'provisional consent'. Such an ethical stance evolves out of researcher/participant relationships where ethical dilemmas are resolved as they emerge in the field, in their local and specific contexts (Flewitt 2006). So, rather than adopting predetermined and fixed sets of values prior to the video-based research, we should respond reflexively to situations as we encounter them in the field. This is the approach that I adopted with my participants and we continually negotiated ideas of consent throughout the study. All participants were aware that they could stop the videotaping at any stage they felt uncomfortable or did not want the interaction to be recorded. Even now, if I want to use this material for conferences or other presentations, I will contact the individuals involved and ensure they are still happy for me to continue using the material captured in their organizations.

Analysing video data

Analysis of video can take multiple paths and will relate to the particular focus of your study and your research question (see van Leeuwen and Jewitt 2001 for a very useful overview of the various types of visual analysis). For example, if you focus in on the micro-dynamics of interactions, an in-depth analysis of the particular facial movements, body language and turn-taking may be required (e.g. Goodwin 2003; McNeill 2000). I have conducted an analysis of this kind, detailed elsewhere, which examined how entrepreneurs use hand gestures to communicate during interactions with stakeholders (see Cornelissen *et al.* 2012). For the purposes of the study outlined here, the focus was on entrepreneurs' use of visual symbols, so the micro-detail of their interactions and body movements was not as important. Rather, attention was focused on how they employed visual symbols during interactions with stakeholders and in interviews with the researcher. In addition, this was supplemented by instances when they *verbally* referred to their use of visual symbols and their importance. The sheer quantity of data that is collected using a visual ethnographic approach can feel overwhelming for a researcher new to this methodology and it is necessary to use your research questions to focus and guide what you're looking for. The researcher should, however, also try to remain open to unexpected or surprising results emerging from the videos. Many hours of mundane and uninteresting data may need to be observed before stumbling onto data that is useful and insightful. In this case, given the extensive amount of videotaped interactions generated over a total period of three months, it was necessary to reduce the data to material that was relevant to the research question. In order to facilitate and focus the analysis, I initially examined all of the video data and excluded any interactions where visual symbols were not relevant or important.

Approximately 60 hours of 'raw' videotaped interviews and interactions were transferred on to Windows Movie Maker, a free video-editing software system included in recent versions of

Microsoft Windows. The initial part of the analysis required me to repeatedly watch the videos, read the transcripts (annotated with notes from the videos) and fieldnotes, and examine collected documentation in order to become familiar with the data. A comprehensive write-up of each case was undertaken as a means of organizing my initial thoughts about each of the cases (Eisenhardt 1989). This allowed me to become familiar with each case as a standalone entity and allowed the unique patterns of each case to emerge before I moved towards generalizing across the cases (Zott and Huy 2007). This second part of the analysis involved a cross-case search for patterns. Each of the cases was compared in pairs, and the similarities and differences between each pair were listed. For example, the cases were compared in terms of previous experience, industry knowledge, occasions when visual symbols were used, and how frequently visual symbols were employed. This tactic forces the researcher to look for the subtle similarities and differences between the cases to go beyond mere impressions (Glaser and Strauss 1967; Miles and Huberman 1984). The next step of this process was to compare systematically the emerging dimensions with the evidence from each case in order to assess how well it fits with case data. Overall, six processes emerged: (1) concealment of setting; (2) exposure to setting; (3) wearing of business dress; (4) adapting dress to audience; (5) controlling personal expressiveness; and (6) managing stakeholders' emotions. Gradually, these six sub-categories were grouped into three, according to the function they fulfilled. For example, entrepreneurs' 'exposure' and 'concealment' of visual symbols were grouped together, as both processes function to control the visual scene that stakeholders are presented with, and are grouped under 'presenting an appropriate scene to stakeholders'. In total, three functions of visual symbols emerged: (1) presenting an appropriate scene to stakeholders; (2) creating professional identity and emphasizing control; and (3) regulating emotions.

Translating the data: transcription, analysis and publication

While it is necessary in order to code the data, in transforming video data into easily accessible, paper-based material for analysis, some of the richness of the original recording is lost. It is not fully possible to articulate through language a sense of the individual entrepreneurs and their idiosyncratic use of their visual surroundings without actually viewing the videotaped interactions. As Veer argues in Chapter 13 in this volume, 'to express what New Delhi's streets looked and sounded like, I could write thousands of words and not do the site justice'. The visceral nature of visual imagery often results in an inability to (verbally) articulate all that we find interesting about visual data and these preverbal, visceral hunches 'remain at the level of vague suspicion and intuitive response' (Iedema 2001: 201). In addition, while transcription is often treated as a practical, objective matter of simply scripting what participants said, the process of transcribing is also an act of representation (Oliver *et al.* 2005). This is particularly the case with video research, as the visual images need to be translated to another medium (i.e. text) to facilitate interrogation, and information is inevitably lost in the process. Our ability to transcribe talk is built upon a process of analysing relevant structure in the stream of speech and marking these distinctions with widely accepted written symbols that extend back thousands of years (i.e. text) (Goodwin 2001). In the case of transcribing visual phenomena, we are not so sophisticated, and, to make sense of visual data, we often translate our thought about the visual to text in order to record our evaluation of and insights into the visual material we are examining.

It is not only the practices and methods by which video-recordings are transcribed and analysed but also how they are edited and presented to an external audience in the form of a multimedia presentation or an ethnographic film. Representations are constructed through a process of selecting and excluding data and privileging different modes of communication, thereby presenting different perspectives on 'reality' (Plowman and Stephen 2008). This transformation of the data not only occurs during the process of analysis but also during the process of representing the outcomes of this analysis for dissemination to others. At conferences or seminars, it has been possible to show fellow academics the videos on which the findings of this study are built, yet in the article now published in *the Journal of Management Studies* (Clarke 2011) the videos were not produced. Given the newness of this type of study, there were no prior protocols for how these types of data could be represented. One suggestion was to have a link to the video embedded in the online version of the paper but the entrepreneurs involved in my study were against any suggestion of these videos being placed freely on the web. It may have been possible to print photographic stills of the recording but these do not illustrate effectively the complex video interactions. One solution to these problems would be to find ways of maintaining the original video format and avoid the loss of meaning by translating the images into text. A potential way of overcoming this is to begin using web-based 'papers', which integrate video sequences with written text and still images into one document (Olivero *et al.* 2004). This opportunity to view the raw material upon which observations are based allows a researcher's analysis to be scrutinized, adding another dimension of reflexivity to the research, as the author is not standing between the informants and the audience (Strecker 1997). With the advent of online journals, it may become increasingly common to integrate video-based research into published form, but at the moment this remains quite rare particularly in the domain of management studies.

Conclusion

This chapter has highlighted the deficiencies in a text-only approach to research and illustrated the potential utility of visual methodologies in the organizational domain through the example of a videoethnographic study in the field of entrepreneurship. By studying in detail, through the means of a videoethnographic approach, how entrepreneurs use their visual surroundings during interactions with stakeholders, this chapter and the study on which it is based show that language is only one of the symbols used by entrepreneurs. Using video allowed me to subject the data to repeated examination through the use of slow motion, still frames and zooming features, and created an enormous amount of micro-detail that could not have been caught through text as the situation emerged. These findings would therefore not have emerged if a video-based approach had not been incorporated into this research. Video produces data that can uniquely add to many research designs (Radcliffe 2003). Video can allow researchers to 'capture' interaction and behaviour in everyday settings, as well as allowing the researcher to once again experience the actual events as they occurred, which could not be provided by fieldnotes or audio tapes alone. The data produced can be micro-analysed allowing researchers to track the emergence of gesture, the use of artefacts, how participants interact with their environment, making it an ideal method for a range of research objectives and theoretical approaches. Images do not even need to be the focus of attention or topic to warrant researchers using video-based data. As Pink (2001) highlights, the relation of images to other sensory, material and linguistic details of the study will result in images potentially being of interest to most qualitative researchers.

While this methodology promises to bring new insights into our research investigations, the benefits of video-based data must also be tempered with a discussion of limitations of video-based methodologies. No hegemonic claims are being made about the superiority of video-based approaches over other types of research – video and other visual data should not replace text-based approaches, but rather they should be used as a complementary and additional source of data. Videoethnography is simply another tool in the organizational researcher's toolkit to be used alongside and to supplement other research methodologies. In particular, it is important to recognize that this form of research requires a skilled researcher who can record material, while at the same time probing participants for understandings, and reflect on the material as it is being captured. Other issues include access problems, methodological issues and issues of representation when translating the data. The aim of this chapter was to address several concerns for scholars considering this technique. Without more thought and discussion about these issues, it is not possible to come up with hard and fast answers about what is and is not appropriate with video-based research. In particular, there remains a raft of ethical and moral questions about video-based research, which need to be addressed before this technique becomes integrated into the way we conduct research. Despite these problems, what is clear is that it is highly probable that there are elements that a solely textual approach to the study of organizations may ignore, and applying such a methodology is likely to create fascinating insights into how organizational interactions are steeped in visual meaning.

References

Aldrich, H. and Fiol, C. (1994) 'Fools rush in? The institutional context of industry creation', *Academy of Management Review* 19(4): 546–671.
Atkinson, P. (1990) *The Ethnographic Imagination*, London: Routledge.
Baron, R.A. and Brush, C.G. (1999) 'The role of social skill in entrepreneurs' success: evidence from videotapes of entrepreneurs' presentations', 20th Babson-Kaufman Foundation Entrepreneurship Research Conference, Babson College, Wellesley.
Baron, R.A. and Markman, G.D. (2003) 'Beyond social capital: how social skills can enhance entrepreneurs' success', *Academy of Management Review* 14(1): 106–116.
Becker, H.S. (1998) 'Visual sociology, documentary photography, and photojournalism: it's (almost) all a matter of context', in J. Prosser (ed.) *Image-based Research: A Sourcebook for Qualitative Researchers*, London: Farmer Press.
Brush, C.G., Greene, P.G. and Hart, M.M. (2001) 'From initial idea to unique advantage: the entrepreneurial challenge of constructing a resource base', *Academy of Management Executive* 15: 64–78.
Bryman, A. (1994) *Research Design: Qualitative & Quantitative Approaches*, London: Sage.
Buchanan, D.A. (2001) 'The role of photography in organisation research: a re-engineering case illustration', *Journal of Management Inquiry* 10: 151–164.
Büscher, M. (2005) 'Social life under the microscope?', *Sociological Research Online* 10(1). Available at http://www.socresonline.org.uk/10/1/buscher.html.
Chen, X.P., Yao, X. and Kotha, S. (2009) 'Entrepreneur passion and preparedness in business plan presentations: a persuasion analysis of venture capitalists' funding decisions', *Academy of Management Journal* 52: 199–214.
Clarke, J. (2007) 'Video in management research', in R. Thorpe and Robin Holt (eds) *Dictionary of Qualitative Management Research*, London: Sage.
——(2011) 'Revitalizing entrepreneurship: how visual symbols are used in entrepreneurial performances', *Journal of Management Studies* 48(6): 1365–1391.
Clarke, J. and Holt, R. (2010) 'The mature entrepreneur: a narrative approach to entrepreneurial goals', *Journal of Management Inquiry* 19(1): 69–83.
Collier, J. and Collier, M. (1986) *Visual Anthropology: Photography as a Research Method*, Albuquerque: University of New Mexico Press.
Cornelissen, J. and Clarke, J. (2010) 'Imagining and rationalizing opportunities: inductive reasoning, and the creation and justification of new ventures', *Academy of Management Review* 35(4): 539–557.
Cornelissen, J., Clarke, J. and Cienki, A. (2012) 'Sensegiving in entrepreneurial contexts: the use of metaphors in speech and gesture to gain and sustain support for novel ventures', *International Small Business Journal* 30(3): 213–241.
Delmar, F. and Shane, S. (2004) 'Legitimating first: organizing activities and the survival of new ventures', *Journal of Business Venturing* 19: 385–410.
Eisenhardt, K.M. (1989) 'Building theories from case study research', *Academy of Management Review* 14: 532–550.

Emmison, M. and Smith, P. (2000) *Researching the Visual: Images, Objects, Contexts and Interactions in Social and Cultural Inquiry*, London: Sage.

Flewitt, R. (2006) 'Using video to investigate preschool classroom interaction: education research assumptions and methodological practices', *Visual Communication* 5(25): 25–50.

Gardner, W.L. and Avolio, B.J. (1998) 'The charismatic relationship: a dramaturgical perspective', *Academy of Management Review* 22: 32–58.

Glaser, B. and Strauss, A. (1967) *The Discovery of Grounded Theory: Strategies for Qualitative Research*, New York: Aldine de Gruyter.

Goffman, E. (1959) *The Presentation of Self in Everyday Life*, Garden City, NY: Doubleday.

Goodwin, C. (2001) 'Practices of seeing visual analysis: an ethnomethodological approach', in T. van Leeuwen, and C. Jewitt, *Handbook of Visual Analysis*, London: Sage.

——(2003) 'Pointing as situated practice', in S. Kita (ed.) *Pointing: Where Language, Culture and Cognition Meet*, Mahwah NJ: Lawrence Erlbaum.

Guthey, E. and Jackson, B. (2005) 'CEO portraits and the authenticity paradox', *Journal of Management Studies* 42(5): 1057–1082.

Harper, D. (1989) 'Visual sociology: expanding the sociological vision', in G. Blank, J. McCartney and E. Brent (eds) *New Technologies in Sociology: Practical Applications in Research and Work*, New Brunswick: Transaction.

Harrison, B. (2002) 'Seeing health and illness worlds – using visual methodologies in a sociology of health and illness: a methodological review', *Sociology of Health and Illness* 24(6): 856–872.

Hassard, J., Holliday, R. and Willmott, H. (2000) *Body and Organization*, London: Sage.

Heath, C. and Hindmarsh, J. (2002). 'Analysing interaction: video, ethnography and situated conduct', in T. May (ed.) *Qualitative Research in Action*, London: Sage.

Iedema, R. (2001) 'Analysing film and television: a social semiotic account of *Hospital: An Unhealthy Business*', in T. van Leeuwen, and C. Jewitt (eds) *Handbook of Visual Analysis*, London: Sage.

——(2007) 'On the multi-modality, materiality and contingency of organization discourse', *Organization Studies* 28(6): 931–946.

Jordan, B. and Henderson, A. (1995) 'Interaction analysis: foundations and practice', *The Journal of the Learning Sciences* 4(1): 39–103.

Lounsbury, M. and Glynn, M.A. (2001) 'Cultural entrepreneurship: stories, legitimacy and the acquisition of resources', *Strategic Management Journal* 22: 545–564.

Macbeth, D. (1999) 'Glances, trances, and their relevance for a visual sociology', in P.L. Jalbert (ed.) *Media Studies: Ethnomethodological Approaches*, Lanham: University Press of America & Int. Inst. for Ethnomethodology and Conversation Analysis, 135–170.

Martens, M.L., Jennings, J.E and Jennings, P.D. (2007) 'Do the stories they tell get them the money they need? The role of entrepreneurial narratives in resource acquisition', *Academy of Management Journal* 50: 1107–1132.

Mason, C.M. and Harrison, R.T. (2000) 'Investing in technology ventures: what do business angels look for at the initial screening stage?', 20th Babson-Kaufman Foundation Entrepreneurship Research Conference, Babson College, Wellesley.

McDougall, D. (1997) 'The visual in anthropology', in M. Banks and H. Morphy (eds) *Rethinking Visual Anthropology*, London: New Haven Press.

McNeill, D. (2000) *Language and Gesture*, Cambridge: Cambridge University Press.

Mead, M. (1995) 'Visual anthropology in a discipline of words', in P. Hockings (ed.) *Principles of Visual Anthropology*, 2nd ed., New York: Mouton de Gruyter.

Meyer, J.W. and Rowan, B. (1991) 'Institutionalized organizations: formal structure as myth and ceremony', in W.W. Powell and P.J. DiMaggio (eds) *The New Institutionalism in Organizational Analysis*, Chicago, IL: University of Chicago Press, 41–62.

Miles, M. and Huberman, M.A. (1984) *Qualitative Data Analysis: A Source Book of New Methods*, Beverly Hills, CA: Sage.

Mondala, L. (2006) 'Video recording as the reflexive preservation and configuration of phenomenal features for analysis', in H. Knoblauch, J. Raab, H. Soeffner and B. Schnettler (eds) *Video Analysis*, Bern: Lang.

Oliver, D.G., Serovich, J.M. and Mason, T.L. (2005) 'Constraints and opportunities with interview transcription: towards reflection in qualitative research', *Social Forces* 84(2): 1273–1289.

Olivero, F., John, P. and Sutherland, R. (2004) 'Seeing is believing: using video papers to transform teachers' professional knowledge and practice', *Cambridge Journal of Education* 34(2): 179–191.

Packalen, K. (2007) 'Complementing capital: the role of status, demographic features, and social capital in founding teams' abilities to obtain resources', *Entrepreneurship Theory and Practice* 31: 873–891.

Philips, N., Lawrence, T.B. and Hardy, C. (2004) 'Discourse and institutions', *Academy of Management Review* 29(4): 635–652.

Pink, S. (2001) *Doing Visual Ethnography: Images, Media and Representation in Research*, London: Sage.

Plowman, L. (1996) 'Narrative, linearity and interactivity: making sense of interactive multimedia', *British Journal of Educational Technology* 27(2): 92–105.

Plowman, L. and Stephen, C. (2008) 'The big picture? Video and the representation of interaction', *British Educational Research Journal* 34(4): 541–565.

Prins, S. (2002) 'Guidelines for the evaluation of ethnographic visual media: historical background', *American Anthropologist* 104(1): 303–305.

Prosser, J. (1998) *Image-based Research: A Sourcebook for Qualitative Researchers*, London: Falmer Press.

Prosser, J. and Loxley, A. (2007) 'Enhancing the contribution of visual methods to inclusive education', *Journal of Research in Special Educational Needs* 7(1): 55–68.

Radcliff, D. (2003) 'Video methods in qualitative research', in P. Camic, J. Rhodes and L. Yardley (eds) *Qualitative Research in Psychology: Expanding Perspectives in Methodology and Design*, Washington, DC: APA.

Rao, H. (1994) 'The social construction of reputation: certification contests, legitimation and the survival of organizations in the American automobile industry: 1895–1912', *Strategic Management Journal* 15: 29–44.

Ruby, J. (1996) 'Visual anthropology', in D. Levinson and M. Ember (eds) *Encyclopedia of Cultural Anthropology*, New York: Henry Holt and Company.

Secrist, C., de Koeyer, I., Bell, H. and Fogel, A. (2002) 'Combining digital video technology and narrative methods for understanding infant development', *Forum: Qualitative Social Research* [online journal], 3(2). Available at http://www.qualitative-research.net/fqs-texte/2-02/2-02secristetal-e.htm.

Shane, S. (2003) *A General Theory of Entrepreneurship: The Individual-Opportunity Nexus*, Cheltenham: Elgar.

Shrum, W., Duque, R. and Brown, T. (2005) 'Digital video as research practice: methodology for the millennium', *Journal of Research Practice* [online journal] 1(2). Available at http://jrp.icaap.org/content/v1.1/shrum.html.

Simons, H. and Usher, R. (2000) *Situated Ethics in Educational Research*, London: Routledge.

Starr, J.A. and MacMillan, I.C. (1990) 'Resource cooptation via social contracting: resource acquisition strategies for new ventures', *Strategic Management Journal* 11: 79–92.

Stinchcombe, A.L. (1965) 'Social structure and organizations', in J.G. March (ed.) *Handbook of Organizations*, Chicago, IL: Rand-McNally, 142–193.

Strecker, I. (1997) 'The turbulence of images: on imagery, media and ethnographic discourse', *Visual Anthropology* 9: 207–227.

Suchman, M.C. (1995) 'Managing legitimacy: strategies and institutional approaches', *Academy of Management Review* 20: 571–610.

Tornikoski, E.T. and Newbert, S.L. (2007) 'Exploring the determinants of organizational emergence: a legitimacy perspective', *Journal of Business Venturing* 22: 311–335.

van Leeuwen, T. and Jewitt, C. (2001) *Handbook of Visual Analysis*, London: Sage.

Vecchio, R.P. (2003) 'Entrepreneurship and leadership: common trends and common threads', *Human Resource Management Review* 13(2): 303–327.

Warren, S. (2002) '"Show me how it feels to work here": using photography to research organizational aesthetics', *Theory and Politics in Organizations* 2: 224–245.

——(2009) 'Visual methods in organizational research', in A. Bryman and D. Buchanan (eds) *Handbook of Organizational Research Methods*, London: Sage.

Watson, T.J. (2000) 'Making sense of managerial work and organizational research processes with Caroline and Terry', *Organization* 7(3): 489–510.

Zimmerman, M.A. and Zeitz, G.J. (2002) 'Beyond survival: achieving new venture growth by building legitimacy', *Academy of Management Review* 27: 414–431.

Zott, C. and Huy, Q.N. (2007) 'How entrepreneurs use symbolic management to acquire resources', *Administrative Science Quarterly* 52: 70–105.

13
Ethnographic videography and filmmaking for consumer research

Ekant Veer

Introduction

It is becoming apparent that videography and filmmaking is increasingly central to ethnographic consumer research, as a means of collecting, analysing and disseminating data in order to understand consumers' lives and consumer culture. In this chapter, I share some insights from consumer research to develop greater understanding of the uses and misuses of videography as an aid to ethnographic research; that is, how can researchers use video-recording tools to better understand a culture and the nuances associated with it, which cannot be captured without videography.

Visual data and ethnography have a strong and longstanding history (Pink 2008; White 1963; Ball 1998; Russell 1999), but it is evident that, without effective videographic skills, many nuances associated with ethnographic research are being missed by researchers (Heider 2006). Filmmaking is no longer confined to documentary makers who distinguish themselves from academic research; videoethnographic methods are becoming, if not already, mainstream. In addition, advances in technology make videography equipment more accessible to many researchers, while advances in visual analysis are making visual data a fundamental part of ethnography. As a growing number of researchers adopt a variety of contexts in which to conduct ethnographies, there is increased demand for effective and efficient use of videography for research purposes. Ethnographic research is no longer the domain of anthropologists entering a forgotten tribe, but rather a methodology that permeates all aspects of culture and interaction. By using videographic data as part of the data collection, analysis and dissemination of the research, the ethnographer is able to capture a richer set of data as well as, some may argue, a more unbiased account of the culture under investigation, compared to fieldnotes from a single researcher.

Rather than make this chapter a deep exploration of the ethnographic methodology, I will focus on the means by which videography can be specifically used to aid ethnography, from data collection to analysis and dissemination of findings. I begin by discussing the means by which videography can be used to elucidate the nuances of a culture, specifically for business and organizational research (cf. Sanders 2003), and aid in the ethnographic process. I continue by discussing how filmmaking can be harnessed as a means of disseminating ethnographic findings. First, I explain why I engage with videoethnographic research.

Why videoethnography?

Videoethnography is not suited for every research project. It is not the new way forward and it is not essential for the qualitative researcher of the future. However, there are situations and scenarios where videoethnography not only makes data collection easier, but is sometimes the only means by which data can be collected. For example, when I studied the role of weddings in Indian culture, I realized that words could never adequately describe the jewellery, costume, sounds, chants and dynamism of an Indian wedding in sufficient detail. Video data needed to be collected. To be fair, even a video is still not a full representation of an Indian wedding, as one requires the smell, taste, touch and ambiance of an Indian wedding to fully appreciate the impact it has.

Videoethnography helps us to capture that which is indescribable in words. It is not solely a means of storing visual and audio data in a permanent form, but also offers a way of collecting large amounts of data that can subsequently be analysed from a multitude of perspectives. For instance, a narrative analyst would be able to incorporate tonality and inflexion far more effectively into his/her analysis; a body language analyst might focus on the role of subtle body movements into their analysis; an ethnographer can develop a fuller appreciation for a culture as a whole, by taking a varied approach to the site and analysing data from multiple perspectives. My research only draws on video data when it is needed. There is no reason to collect video data when text data would adequately describe a situation or scenario. When an ethnographic site contains so much rich data that can be analysed in multiple ways, the use of video-recording equipment is almost expected.

At this point, it is necessary to distinguish between filmmaking and using film as a research tool. Collecting video data as a means of creating a film for public dissemination will be undertaken in a very different manner from collecting video data for research analysis alone. I try to incorporate both into my research; however, as videoethnographers will tell you, much video data will end up not being shown publicly. The role of video in ethnographic research is primarily to collect data for analysis, so as to further understand the culture being investigated. Once this is completed, and if the videoethnographer considers the use of film as a means of disseminating findings to be appropriate, then an edited film text can be made using the raw data. Hence, videoethnographers are not documentary makers, where the primary purpose is entertainment and education of a third party. Instead, videoethnographers are ethnographers who use video to collect and analyse data; they are documentary makers first and entertainers second.

Ethnography and visual data

Ethnographic research is focused on understanding the culture of a setting, phenomena or social group (Van Maanen 1988; Agar 1986; Fetterman 1989; Marcus 1998). Ethnographers' use of visual data is longstanding, as illustrated by the extensive use of still photography in early anthropological ethnography. However, there has been a recent upsurge in videography as an aid to ethnographic research, especially in consumer research. Videography and filmmaking allows a multi-sensory approach to understanding a culture (Collier Jr. 1988). By incorporating both the auditory and the visual in a dynamic format, the researcher is able to capture a vast array of data that he/she would otherwise not have been able to absorb or record. Even a notetaker focused solely on recording non-verbal cues and interactions would be hard pressed to record all the information gathered by videography. The use of videography as a means of collecting videographic data offers a longer-lasting representation, untainted by subjective memory recall of events (Bennett-Levy and Powell 1980) once the researcher has left the site of investigation. The quantity of data generated can, however, be daunting.

This richness is evident in my very first experiment with videoethnography as an undergraduate student. Videography was used primarily as a data collection tool when I interviewed participants about their relationship with family photographs. At the time of the interviews, my focus was on the informants, listening attentively and focusing on how to draw greater meaning from their words. This was my only chance to talk with many of them, so I needed to make the most of it. When reviewing the video footage, I noticed something that I had completely missed during the interviews themselves. Many of the participants would caress the photos of loved ones while talking to them. My Westernized upbringing had encouraged me to conform to the social norm of making eye contact with my discussant during the interview, but, by doing this, I had missed a critical aspect of their interaction with the object. Without the visual data, this interaction would have been missed and the data incomplete.

In a second piece of research, the need for videography was more explicit. While I was investigating the use of consumerism in Indian weddings (Veer 2009), the sheer volume of data I was faced with meant it would be impossible to accurately record and recall every aspect of the elaborate Indian festivities without the visual data. The colours, the noise, the dynamism of the participants and the organized chaos meant that videography was not simply a cool addition to the research, but also a much-needed tool to ensure data completeness. With so much data encapsulated into each frame of video, the richness of the data meant that analysis could take multiple paths. However, had my own consciousness and some rough fieldnotes been the only record, the concepts that were salient to me at the time of data collection would have been the dominant focus of analysis, thereby restricting the research.

In the documentary 'Pushing the scene', Hietanan *et al.* (2011) capture the multifaceted nature of the underground dubstep movement and express it through film. Rather than simply rely on transcripts, the use of videography ensures that the music, the movement, the rawness of the culture is captured and disseminated in a way that is impossible in a print format. There exist a number of contexts where videoethnography are particularly useful. The following are examples of a few contexts and situations where video and visual data are of specific importance.

Data amount

Any context where it is expected that the data present would not be effectively captured without some form of formal recording requires videoethnographic data. If one was to look specifically at the visual or auditory aspects of a site, videography is an obvious choice. There may be occasions where the site contains so much 'action' and so many actors that taking notes of every occurrence would do a disservice to the many aspects that are not being focused upon.

Millen (2000) argues that the sheer volume of data can make some ethnographic studies uninteresting, and that a more focused approach to a field with a more defined scope would be a better use of the ethnographer's time and energy. However, restricting the amount of data collected in the hope that this conserves resources, in my view, limits the site of investigation and the potential of the research. I am, therefore, willing to observe hours of data in order to find the 'nugget of gold', as it is the unknown and the unexpected that makes the ethnography worthwhile, which cannot be achieved through the restriction of scope to make research easier and faster.

Experienced organizational ethnographers also understand that action can be found in many mundane contexts. For example, a boardroom discussion can become extremely animated as a contentious issue is raised. Having visual data to analyse all the participants' behaviour and voices can aid in understanding the cultural context within which this interaction takes place. Capturing these behavioural nuances without the aid of video data can make the behaviour extremely difficult to retain and recall for analysis purposes. The ethnographer can, if desired, minutely analyse each aspect of a video to search for patterns and processes that are meaningful, rather than rely on what was meaningful at the time of capturing the data, as is the nature of fieldnote recording, which is bound by one's subjective rationale at that moment (Van Maanen 1988).

Data richness

The adage 'a picture paints a thousand words' is at the heart of the motivation for using video data in ethnography. The nuances and complexity associated with video data can make it difficult to analyse without a means of effective capture (Pink 2001). If the site under investigation not only has a large amount of data, but also contains data that is very precise and intricate, videography as a means of recording actions is recommended. Observational data may only be able to provide some of the information necessary, but video data has the ability to offer far deeper and richer data for analysis. For example, if one is investigating routines and rituals at work, recording not just when employees take breaks, but also the way in which employees relax during a busy day would be of interest. This richness is also a downfall of video, as it can make it difficult to extrapolate patterns and themes, simply because of the variety of possible meanings associated with the data (Mackay *et al.* 1988). However, as a researcher, being afforded an excess of data via a media-rich format, such as video, is of huge benefit compared to having insufficient data (Gluckman 1961; LeCompte and Goetz 1982).

Data comparison

If a researcher is conducting a comparative study of a number of sites or how a site changes over time, the use of videographic data can also be advantageous. By comparing changes or similarities across sites and time through visual analysis, one is able to gain a greater appreciation for how nuanced a culture is. For example, videography of an organization as it transitions through its life may show that, as a business grows, it may employ more people, resources and space, but the culture of the organization is very similar to how it started. Alternatively, studying how people drink coffee at different *Starbucks* cafes around the world would show that, although the brand is the same, the culture within the brand is very different. When multiple authors and interpreters are involved, having a common capture method can avoid biases associated with data collection. Starting with a common means of data capture can then be followed by analysis and interpretation.

By drawing on visual data, the visual comparison method becomes another addition to one's ethnography and the story being told. Visual comparison techniques are extensive and can be approached in a number of ways (Cooper 1976; Breitmeyer and Ogmen 2000). However, without the visual data to begin with, the comparison becomes driven by the interpretation of the data collector rather than the stories of the culture being investigated. This is not to say that the interpretation of the data by the ethnographer is not encouraged, but videography allows for subjectivity to be more part of the data analysis, rather than the data collection.

Data presentation

If it is expected that the findings from the research cannot be conveyed in a manner that is easily expressed in traditional print format, capturing visual and auditory data is something to consider from the outset. For example, if one wished to analyse the culture of an organization in a foreign country, the use of videography could be beneficial in order to convey the different environment and cultural norms more easily than through print alone. If asked to express what New Delhi's streets looked and sounded like, I could write thousands of words and not do the site justice. Indeed, even video of the scene does not offer the plurality of senses that encompass the site, but it does offer a richer depiction of the setting than words alone. Similarly, if a researcher wishes to carry out research on Indian organizations, understanding the culture in which those organizations exist is necessary. Kozinets' (2002) work on the Burning Man Festival gives a wonderful insight into the world of counter-consumerism. Burning Man organizers state on their website: 'Trying to explain what Burning Man is to someone who has never been to the event is a bit like trying to explain what a particular colour looks like to someone who is blind' (www.burningman.com). In a context such as this, the use of video as part of the ethnography to accompany a printed article enables expression of far more about the culture than words alone. However, some regular attendees could attest that even the video is still insufficient compared as a proxy to visiting the festival and engaging with the culture of Burning Man.

Consequently, videography and filmmaking have become increasingly powerful means for ethnographers to capture and display the sites in which they operate and present data in a way that expresses greater visual and auditory nuance than enabled by traditional data formats. The aim of the videoethnographer is not to create an Oscar-winning documentary, but rather to use videography to aid ethnographic research. A certain level of quality is necessary to ensure that visual and auditory data can be analysed, but the key is to maintain the naturalness of the context. The following sections outline the necessary skills, equipment and technique for ethnographic data capture, analysis and dissemination.

The eye

The equipment necessary for videoethnography is relatively straightforward to use, but infinitely complex to master. Again, it is crucial to remember that the aim is to collect data suitable for analysis, rather than to create a blockbuster movie. The two major elements involved in this process are the researcher's eye and the filmmaking technology.

One element that distinguishes an excellent videoethnographer is his/her 'eye'. That is, his/her ability to notice what is important in a context, to focus upon that phenomena and capture it. Without a good eye, no amount of technology will improve the videoethnography. The filmmaker's eye is often discussed as an intangible gift that filmmakers have (Mercado 2010). However, it could be argued that researchers, especially ethnographers, have a similar gift that is honed and developed over time. Walcott (1999) argues that any ethnographer needs the intrinsic ability to see the world around him/her. Videography offers both a means of capturing what the ethnographer is focusing on, but also captures that which the ethnographer may not have seen while filming (Pink 2001). An ethnographer needs to be able to take an entire cultural setting, understand the setting and focus in on the nuances that make the site both interesting and relevant to a wider audience (Clammer 1984; Hammersley and Atkinson 1989; Rohner 1969). This is the eye. Taking a vast world of investigation and capturing it in a meaningful way that is likely to be of interest, both theoretically and theatrically, to a wider audience.

Without the researcher's or filmmaker's eye, the videography would simply be automated capture of experience. As discussed in the next section, this can be of interest and use, but the majority of meaningful videoethnographic data requires guidance from the researcher. Harnessing one's eye is as intangible as the concept itself. However, as a guide, the key is to focus not on capturing as much as possible, but to maintain a balance between capturing the site and the nuances within the site. For example, if one was to study the culture of an organization going through a cost-saving merger, the videographer could set the scene by focusing on the entire office. By doing this, he/she is able to capture interactions between participants, but at a distance. This offers benefits in showing movement, dynamism and, over time, repeated patterned behaviour. However, the wide-angle shot does not offer any depth as to what is contained within the interactions. An ethnographer who stands afar from a site can make assumptions of a culture from his/her own interpretation of the viewed experience, but, without engaging within the site, the ethnographer cannot gain the participants' own understanding of the phenomena (Schouten and McAlexander 1995). As such, wider capture of a setting, followed by many more focused captures of *interesting* aspects of the site is necessary. What is interesting is a matter of interpretation, at the discretion of the researcher. A deep fascination for a site is thus fundamental to videoethnography, but there is also a need for skills to effectively capture what is deemed fascinating.

The equipment

The technology needed to conduct a videoethnography must suit the purpose of the research. If the final aim is to make a mass distributed documentary with aesthetics at the fore, then high-quality, professional equipment is necessary. However, for most researchers, the balance between capturing data in an effective manner and not being too much of an imposition on the culture being investigated means that everyday consumer technology can suffice. The greater the intrusion, the greater the likelihood of researcher and social response biases entering into the study (Rohner 1969; White 1963). The key is to capture the moment. With High Definition Hard Disk Drive (HD HDD) cameras reasonably accessible to the public, this is the standard video camera used to capture the bulk of the data during a videographic study. However, sometimes it may be more appropriate to capture a novel and interesting phenomenon on a cell phone. Whatever your choice, having a device that will convert captured video and images easily to editing software, such as Adobe Premiere Pro, is also necessary for viewing data and editing the data into a film, if desired. The following is a short list of different videoethnographic purposes and the equipment used to capture each phenomenon.

Scene setting

When dealing with a new research site, one can often enter with relatively little knowledge of the setting or the behaviours that occur within it. One simple means to gather a large amount of data is to take a wide-angle shot of as much of a site as possible. This is excellent for understanding how a site operates as a whole, rather than focusing on smaller parts or functions. By seeing a culture operate as a whole, one is able to analyse the nuances and patterned behaviour as well as guide the researcher to see which areas to focus on first for deeper enquiry. Returning to the example of an organization undergoing a cost-saving merger, having a video or still images capturing as much of the organization as possible helps to understand the environment in which the participants operate. The pace of the office; the body language of the participants; the patterns of movement around the office; the areas where participants meet and converse;

the timing of behaviour; and general tone of the office would all be captured with some scene-setting shots. Again, these aspects could be captured with fieldnotes and researcher commentary, but with easy access to technology that can capture the data and not be subject to recall biases, which are filtered through the researcher's own cultural interpretation of the site. For me, this analysis should be reserved for when data is ready to be analysed, not at the data-collection stage.

Close analysis

From a wide angle, the areas of specific interest in a site can be ascertained. The researcher's eye will naturally be attracted to the specific sites for closer examination, at which point a closer shot should be taken and greater emphasis on the processual nature of a behaviour established. For example, if the researcher is focusing on certain types of behaviour, greater focus should be placed on not only the action itself, but also the process of how the action is carried out. Close analysis and capture aids in understanding not just the reason for the behaviour, but also the way in which the behaviour is carried out, which can often be hard for a participant to explain. For when I make breakfast, I usually just say 'I make breakfast', but videography of my morning pattern would yield far greater data about my behaviour, which can then be used for further analysis and interpretation.

One example of how videography can be used for close analysis comes from Starr and Fernandez's (2007) Mindcam methodology. Here, the researchers attach a covert camera to a participant and allow them to go shopping, while the camera films everything they see and examine. After the shopping experience, the participant is then interviewed while viewing their own footage to elucidate their thoughts and experiences. What makes videography so powerful, especially with this type of example, is that the participant is often unable to express their actions or unaware of their conscious actions until they are able to review the footage themselves. This is not to say that the Mindcam method is a replacement for close analysis in ethnography, but it is simply another way in which videography can be used to aid our understanding of a phenomenon. By drawing on video footage of behaviour, the participants are able to engage in a type of photo elicitation interview, where the participant is asked to explain their beliefs about a phenomenon based on the video-recording (Heisley and Levy 1991).

In an example from my research, an Indian bride was being adorned with matrimonial Henna (temporary tattoos) for the wedding ceremony. This was a key event in the wedding ceremony and a lot of attention was paid to the process by the family. During the ceremony, I was able to interview the bride, the Henna artist and the family members present to explain the symbolism, the rationale, the stories and the behaviour associated with the ceremony to get a rich set of data that was driven by the process. However, after the video had been captured, a number of other family members, who were not in attendance, were also shown the footage and their interpretation recorded to gain as much data as possible about the event.

Videography for interviews

Possibly the most common use of videography is for recording interviews. Video cameras can be used as a replacement for the traditional dictaphone to simply record the interview. However, far greater richness can be gained from a video interview, even if much of the time the participant is static or not engaged in any active behaviour. One key reason for using video for interviews is for analysis of body and especially facial language. A close analysis of not just *what* is said, but *how* a phrase is said gives greater emphasis and meaning to the interview. This is not to say that videoethnographers must be expert in facial expressions and body language, but, if the data is collected, this level of analysis can be carried out retrospectively.

However, one major disadvantage of using videography during personal interviews is that many participants feel uncomfortable being filmed. Speaking into a video camera on a tripod with a radio mic attached to one's lapel, or in front of a large microphone, is a daunting experience for many interviewees. Relaxing a participant in a videography setting therefore becomes crucial. Two techniques that aid in this are the charisma of the researcher, as well as the ability to focus the participant away from the camera. This is expertly shown in Lastovicka et al.'s (2009) movie 'Can buy me love'. In this ethnography on consumers' attachment to loved possessions, the researchers spend time where participants feel most comfortable: among their possessions. When the researchers talk to car enthusiasts at a car show about their cars, many of the participants forget the camera exists and simply talk. Placing a video camera away from you, as the researcher, and filming on a slight angle, so that you are able to maintain eye contact with the participant is also helpful. By making the participant feel comfortable and keeping the focus away from the camera, it is more likely that a natural experience is recorded.

Another technique that can help keep the camera out of the participant's eye line is the *shoot from the hip* hold. If it is not possible to use a dedicated camera operator during an interview, placing the camera at one's side and filming on a wide angle or up, towards the participant's face, can aid in easing the nerves of the participant and maintain a strong connection between the researcher and participant. Naturally, this angle does not yield footage that would offer an aesthetically pleasing shot, but it is effective in capturing data and putting a participant at ease. It is especially useful when a number of quick interviews are being conducted at a site. For example, a Masters student of mine interviewed a number of people at a rock concert in Kazakhstan. It would have been impossible to interview people for much time, as their focus was on the music. At the same time, it would have been impractical to spend time easing a participant's nerves. As such, she carried the camera around with her and chatted to people as naturally as she could and recorded the data for future analysis. The quality of the footage, both visually and audibly, was poor, but sufficient for data analysis and the basis for depth interviews later in the study.

Covert videography

One ethically ambiguous form of videography is that of *covert* or undetectable capture. Covert filming is a topic of significant discussion in academia and the public media, with the increasing worries of a surveillance society (Lyon 2001). However, covert capture can offer a wealth of data that is free from researcher reactive effect or social desirability biases. That is, with covert capture, there is a lesser chance that participants will behave in a manner that they feel they should behave in, because they are being studied. By studying the patterns of shoppers in a retail environment, researchers are able to map transit routes, analyse how shoppers engage with different displays and determine how shoppers' interactions with employees may influence their retail experience. One exemplar of covert surveillance in academic research came from Jayasinghe's (2009) doctoral research on how families watched TV in their homes. By covertly filming their interactions, with the families' permission, Jayasinghe was able to capture a wealth of data for analysis. At first, a family may be aware that the camera exists in the room, but, as time passes, the camera is ignored and naturalistic behaviour ensues. Having a researcher in the room for weeks at a time, watching a family's behaviour, would be a significant imposition that a camera is able to avoid. Covert surveillance may not pass a University's Ethics Committee easily, as full disclosure and informed consent is often not present, but it does offer advantages over traditional means of recording behaviour. If such behaviour did not offer any advantages, surveillance videography would not be used so heavily by the government, intelligence agencies or law enforcement. From a consumer research perspective, one can gain a lot of data from covert videography. However, it does yield a lot of unusable video footage and a lot of data that needs to be analysed without any understanding of why the behaviour is being carried out.

Videography analysis

Analysing videographic data is much the same as other forms of visual analysis. Many of these techniques are covered in depth in other chapters of this book. However, some analysis techniques are specifically valuable for the videoethnographer. This section will outline some of the key elements to focus on as an analyst of videoethnographic data.

The body

If engaging with human participants, the analysis of body movement, facial expression and gestures are necessary. Many of these are culturally specific and, therefore, cultural experts are needed to decipher expressions. For example, Italian participants are often known to communicate as much with hand gestures as they are with language (McNeill 1992); similarly, body movements in India are culturally specific in execution and meaning and often so subtle that they can be missed by the uninitiated researcher. One example of this comes from video I have collected with sufferers of eating disorders. When analysing transcripts from sufferers, one is able to understand the vocalized rationale and beliefs. However, when incorporated with body movement and facial expression, it is far clearer that some of the vocalized expression is actually ego defence mechanisms, designed to 'say the right thing', although they internally believe a different reality. That is, a sufferer may overtly say they know they are sick and need to gain weight, but physically look uncomfortable with such a statement and withdrawn from what they are saying. That is, they can be seen to be separating themselves from their words, although they know social response bias encourages them to 'say the right thing'. Such data would not have been collected from transcripts alone or audio recording. Analysing the body, in conjunction with the words, and watching this behaviour over time allow the researcher to gain a greater connection to the participants and their specific means of expression. It is important to maintain data integrity in one's interpretation of the data, and multiple coders and analysts are always recommended, especially in culturally specific phenomena. I have often learned much about a participant by reviewing an interview with an anthropologist or sociologist present, and recording their examination of body and facial expression. Collaborating with others who specialize in areas of body and narrative analysis allows the videoethnographer to gain a deeper appreciation of the presented material from a perspective that they had not engaged with previously.

The environment

The participant's interaction with their environment is also of importance in videoethnography. How a participant operates and moves through an environment or how their posture changes as the environment changes can all yield interesting phenomena for examination. For example, interviewing participants in their homes versus their workplaces, versus a neutral territory, even if the topic is the same, can yield very different results. Our identity can be affected by our surroundings and, as such, our concentration and focus change to suit the salient identity

(Forehand *et al.* 2002; Reed 2004; Veer *et al.* 2010). By conducting research in different environments and capturing the participant's interactions with the environment, another level of analysis is generated. An excellent organizational example of this can be seen in the cult movie *Office Space* (Judge 2009). Comparing the differences between the character's workplaces, home spaces and the local cafe shows the places and spaces where they feel able to express themselves in different ways. Without an appreciation for the impact that the environment plays on a participant's behaviour, much of the rationale for the behaviour may be lost.

Time

Finally, an appreciation for how a culture develops, behaviours change and participants express themselves differently as time passes is an additional benefit that videoethnography offers. By understanding the impact of how time passes for the participant and how the participant operates differently within a culture over time, the ethnographer gains a greater appreciation for the processual nature of the site. Of course, this is limited by the amount of time the researcher spends within the site, but, by offering a longitudinal perspective on the site, the researcher is able to understand more about the visualized and captured changes and how the changes impact the culture. My interviews with participants suffering from eating disorders were recorded over a period of years. Seeing their development and changes in their lives as some progressively improved, while others continued to struggle with the disorder offers a greater understanding of the individual and the phenomenon they are experiencing. In this research, old videos were not shown to participants, so as to not influence their recovery, but this is also a means by which time can impact the data collection and analysis. Interviewing participants as they reflect upon videos of their previous behaviour and interviews allows another level of analysis that can help a researcher better understand the participant's rationale and reasoning for their past behaviours.

Filmmaking

Again, rather than offering advice on how to create a film, which in such a short piece would be a disservice, I will focus here on how filmmaking can be adapted for academic purposes. Data capture in videoethnographic research does require footage to be of suitable quality for public viewing. However, if the researcher wishes to disseminate the research to a wider audience, there needs to be a balance between the theoretical and the theatrical (Kozinets and Belk 2006). That is, a wonderfully creative piece that is theatrically stunning, but offers little theoretical advancement is of little use as an academic piece that advances theory. However, a strong theoretical contribution without theatrical quality that would both entertain an audience and express the findings in a creative manner would likely not be received well as a film. Without theory, the ethnography lacks advancement; without theatre, the film becomes little more than a narrated article that could well be presented equally well via print.

Being able to translate videoethnographic data into a film appears, at first, a fun and relatively easy task. However, it is not easy. Creatively editing what could potentially be hundreds of hours of footage into a meaningful short documentary can be taxing and time consuming. Ensuring an outlet exists for your film can often be the first step in deciding whether a film is a necessary venture to undertake. The Association for Consumer Research has successfully run a film festival as part of their conferences and has received a number of excellent films that are both theoretically and artistically impactful.[1] Also, some journals accept video submissions as part of the traditional manuscript submission, such as the *Journal of Consumer Research*; *Consumption*

Markets & Culture; *Qualitative Research*; *Advances in Consumer Research*; and the *Journal of Research for Consumers*.

Yet there is a temptation among academics to create a film that replicates a paper format. That is, offering a brief introduction, an examination of the literature, followed by a method, and so forth. There is nothing explicitly wrong with structuring a film as an article, but one may question the reasoning for such an endeavour. Instead, it may be more in keeping with the benefits of film production to create a supplement to the academic article. That is, the article offers one view of the research, while the film offers another. By creating a film, the focus should be on the aspects that a film can offer that a paper cannot. That is, the film could concentrate on the visual and auditory cues and the dynamic nature of the site. The film can also focus on showing visual changes over time and the contrast between different cultural sites, which would be made more obvious through film than in a manuscript. A film that focuses on a person being interviewed in an office with no real visual or auditory appeal is, arguably, less relevant as a film. Film offers the ability to share a rich array of sound and visual data that cannot be communicated effectively or efficiently via text and this, in my mind, should be the domain where film excels. Using film simply because the technology is available is less effective, but mindfully using videography as a means of capturing a rich environment provides far greater depth to the setting and offers more data to be analysed.

A film, as with research, needs to have a story. The role of the filmmaker is to tell this story. The filmmaker is the creator of the narrative and the one who decides what will be included in the story and what will not. The ethnographer collects and analyses the data associated with a culture; the videographer collects video data in order to support data analysis; while the filmmaker creates the story that is then shown to others as a means of expressing some contribution of knowledge and/or entertainment. All three roles are very distinct, but often are carried out by the same person. When creating a film, it may be that the ethnographer needs to step aside and allow the creativity of the filmmaker to step in. Similarly, it may be the case that the filmmaker requires video footage that the videographer has not been able to collect and subsequent site visits are needed, not for analysis purposes, but for video footage recording to be used in the film. Traversing these multiple bodies and selves can be an interesting and often challenging experience.

The filmmaker can be a very passive voice in the film and allow the story to tell itself, or the film can be narrated. Whatever the choice of the researcher, the film will develop a story through the editing process. Editing footage in order to express an academic story is a laborious process, but an exciting one. As with a manuscript, peer review aids in refinement of the story; collaboration improves the quality of the film, and experience improves the efficiency of creating films. Watching other successful films, such as those recommended in this chapter, can improve your chances tremendously. The key is to maintain integrity of your participants, data and site in your film as well as to use the film to its fullest potential. Focus on those aspects that cannot be communicated effectively through print.

Conclusion

Filmmaking equipment is becoming so easily accessible that one could argue that all ethnography should incorporate some analysis of audio and visual data. However, I have argued here that having the right equipment is only one aspect of successful videoethnography. Without the researcher's eye, inquisitiveness and ability to effectively analyse visual data and use it to tell a story, it is unlikely that videography will add significantly to ethnographic consumer research. Consequently, the videoethnographer shapes the research process by guiding the camera and controlling the collection and analysis of data. Even in covert video data collection, the ethnographer decides where the camera is placed and when they record. Videography is thus an interpretive process that relies on the ethnographer's training, experience and curiosity. Finally, there are times when videography is far more effective in capturing and disseminating data, and others when videographic data is unnecessary. Knowing the difference between the two is the first question the filmmaker should ask. If the site, context, theories and participants lend themselves to videography, there is no doubt that the ready accessibility of videographic equipment makes this a research opportunity not to be missed.

Note

1. A selection of videos shown at the film festival can be found at http://vimeo.com/groups/136972.

References

Agar, M.H. (1986) *Speaking of Ethnography*, Beverly Hills, CA: Sage Publications Inc.

Ball, M. (1998) 'Remarks on visual competence as an integral part of ethnographic fieldwork practice: the visual availability of culture', in J. Prosser (ed.) *Image-Based Research: A Sourcebook for Qualitative Researchers*, London: Falmer Press.

Bennett-Levy, J. and Powell, G.E. (1980) 'The Subjective Memory Questionnaire (SMQ). An investigation into the self-reporting of "real-life" memory skills', *British Journal of Social and Clinical Psychology* 19: 177–188.

Breitmeyer, B. and Ogmen, H. (2000) 'Recent models and findings in visual backward masking: a comparison, review, and update', *Attention, Perception, & Psychophysics* 62: 1572–1595.

Clammer, J. (1984) 'Approaches to ethnographic research: introduction', in R.F. Ellen (ed.) *Ethnographic Research*, London: Academic Press Inc.

Collier Jr., J. (1988) 'Visual anthropology and the future of filmmaking', in J.R. Rollwagen (ed.) *Anthropological Filmmaking*, Amsterdam: Harwood Academic Publishers.

Cooper, L. (1976) 'Individual differences in visual comparison processes', *Attention, Perception, & Psychophysics* 19: 433–444.

Fetterman, D.M. (1989) *Ethnography Step by Step*, Newbury Park, CA: Sage.

Forehand, M.R., Deshpandé, R. and Reed, A. (2002) 'Identity salience and the influence of differential activation of the social self-schema on advertising responses', *Journal of Applied Psychology* 87: 1086–1099.

Gluckman, M. (1961) 'Ethnographic data in British social anthropology', *The Sociological Review* 9: 5–17.

Hammersley, M. and Atkinson, P. (1989) *Ethnography Principles in Practice*, London: Routledge.

Heider, K. (2006) *Ethnographic Film*, Austin, TX: University of Texas Press.

Heisley, D.D. and Levy, S.J. (1991) 'Autodriving: a photoelicitation technique', *Journal of Consumer Research* 18: 257–272.

Hietanan, J., Rokka, J. and Roman, R. (2011) 'Pushing the scene: tensions and emergence in an accelerated marketplace culture', *Advances in Consumer Research*. Available at http://vimeo.com/32192229.

Jayasinghe, L.D. (2009) An Ethnography of the Audiences for Television Advertising: A Study of Viewing Behaviour in Eight Australian Households, PhD Doctoral Thesis, University of Melbourne.

Judge, M. (Director) (2009) *Office Space*, USA: Twentieth Century-Fox Film Corporation.

Kozinets, R.V. (2002) 'Can consumers escape the market? Emancipatory illuminations from Burning Man', *Journal of Consumer Research* 29: 20–38.

Kozinets, R.V. and Belk, R.W. (2006) 'Camcorder society: quality videography in consumer and marketing research', in R.W. Belk (ed.) *Handbook of Qualitative Research Methods in Marketing*, Cheltenham: Edward Elgar Press.

Lastovicka, J.L., Sirianni, N.J. and Kunz, D. (2009) 'Can buy me love', *Advances in Consumer Research* 36: 801.

LeCompte, M.D. and Goetz, J.P. (1982) 'Ethnographic data collection in evaluation research', *Educational Evaluation and Policy Analysis* 4: 387–400.

Lyon, D. (2001) *Surveillance Society: Monitoring Everyday Life*, Buckingham: Open University Press.

Mackay, W.E., Guindon, R., Mantel, M.M., Suchman, L. and Tatar, D.G. (1988) 'Video: data for studying human-computer interaction', in J.J. O'Hare (ed.) *SIGCHI Conference on Human Factors in Computing Systems*, New York, NY: ACM, 133–137.

Marcus, G.E. (1998) 'Imagining the whole: ethnography's contemporary efforts to situate itself', in *Ethnography Through Thick & Thin*, Princeton, New Jersey: Princeton University Press.

McNeill, D. (1992) *Hand and Mind: What Gestures Reveal About Thought*, Chicago, IL: University of Chicago Press.

Mercado, G. (2010) *The Filmmaker's Eye: Learning (and Breaking) the Rules of Cinematic Composition*, Oxford, UK: Focal Press.

Millen, D.R. (2000) 'Rapid ethnography: time deepening strategies for HCI field research', in D. Boyarski, and W.A. Kellogg (eds) *Designing Interactive Systems: Processes, Practices, Methods, and Techniques* (DIS '00), 2000, New York, NY: ACM.

Pink, S. (2001) 'More visualising, more methodologies: on video, reflexivity and qualitative research', *Sociological Review* 49(4): 586–599.

——(2008) *Doing Visual Analysis*, London: Sage.

Reed, A. (2004) 'Activating the self-importance of consumer selves: exploring identity salience effects on judgements', *Journal of Consumer Research* 31: 286–295.

Rohner, R.P. (1969) *The Ethnography of Franz Boas*, Chicago: University of Chicago Press.

Russell, C. (1999) 'Experimental ethnography: the work of film in the age of video', *Canadian Journal of Film Studies* 9: 117–123.

Sanders, E. (2003) *Special Section: Ethnography in NPD Research: How 'Applied Ethnography' Can Improve Your NPD Research Process* [Online]. PDMA Website. Available at http://www.crito.uci.edu/noah/design/Ethno7%20Sanders.pdf.

Schouten, J.W. and McAlexander, J.H. (1995) 'Subcultures of consumption: an ethnography of the new biker', *Journal of Consumer Research* 22: 43–62.

Starr, R.G. and Fernandez, K.V. (2007) 'The Mindcam methodology: perceiving through the native's eye', *Qualitative Market Research: An International Journal* 10: 168–182.

Van Maanen, J. (1988) *Tales of the Field: On Writing Ethnography*, Chicago: The University of Chicago Press.

Veer, E. (2009) 'This day is to be special: the role of exaggerated contrast in an Indian wedding', *Advances in Consumer Research* 36: 801–802.

Veer, E., Becirovic, I. and Martin, B.A.S. (2010) 'If Kate voted Conservative, would you? The role of celebrity endorsements in political party advertising', *European Journal of Marketing* 44: 436–450.

Walcott, H.F. (1999) *Ethnography: A Way of Seeing*, Oxford: AltaMira Press.

White, L.A. (1963) *The Ethnography and Ethnology of Franz Boas*, Austin, TX: The Museum of the University of Texas.

14
Drawing as a method of organizational analysis

David R. Stiles

Introduction: origins, uses and definitions of drawing

Drawing pictures is one of the oldest and most universal forms of human expression. It predates the use of written language by thousands of years and is practised across almost all human cultures. It is also one of the most powerful and versatile means of communication, with the capacity to arouse strong emotions and provide a readily accessible conduit for ideas. Drawing has never been just about reproducing nature. Indeed, it is believed the first bison and reindeer pictures were drawn on cave walls not as decoration, but as magical devices to help the real animals succumb to the prowess of hunters (Gombrich 1995). Over millennia, drawings have provided a huge range of social functions, including developing imagination through play (Lowenfeld 1987); projecting deep-set mental states (Semeonoff 1976); supporting and critiquing social, religious and political ideas and enhancing and distorting perceptions (Gombrich 1982). Drawings also help convey technical and imaginative knowledge difficult to communicate in other ways (Meyer 1991). Yet, despite being an innate human activity, drawing is still uncommon in social and organizational research. As with other forms of image, this is partly because of concerns about intellectual property and reproduction costs in publishing. However, digitalization and the Internet have brought costs down considerably over the last decade, so more salient explanations may involve academic reluctance to embrace images. Fyfe and Law (1988) suggest images tend to be perceived as 'subversive' and are disregarded in sociology's search for a distinct identity from fields such as art. Although verbal discursive analysis has become much more widespread (see Ezzamel and Willmott 2008) in social sciences, dominant realist ontologies and positivist epistemologies continue the assumption that words and numbers somehow represent more 'scientific' modes of analysis (Stiles 2004a).

Reluctance to use drawings is compounded by ambiguity in their definition. The concept of drawing as a process and product is highly contested within art, as is what constitutes a painting, sculpture or installation. Categories are blurred and socially derived; reflecting prevailing assumptions about art (Chaplin 1994). Contemporary views often see drawings as visual forms produced by hand using simple instruments such as pencils, pens and crayons. Chalk, charcoal and other media can also be applied to two- or three-dimensional surfaces consisting of many materials, although two-dimensional drawings on paper are the most common. Paint has conventionally been excluded from the act of drawing, with painting seen as a distinct art form attracting its own practitioners and connoisseurs, although again this distinction is controversial (e.g. Wölfflin 1950). Because a drawing is widely regarded as a still image, it is also conventionally distinguished from moving images such as film and video – although single animation frames may be considered separate drawings. Drawing processes have also become more complex. Computer technology has dissolved boundaries, with animation, art and CAD-CAM (computer-aided design and computer-aided manufacturing) software packages, and printers, screens, websites, cameras, phones and computer tablets assisting or even replacing the act of drawing by hand and of displaying and sharing its product.

We are concerned with a type of drawing known in organizational research as a 'freehand sketch' (Meyer 1991), 'pictorial representation' (Stiles 1998) or a 'participant-produced drawing' (Kearney and Hyle 2004). This is a self-composed, expressive, non-verbal, still, pictorial image or fabrication produced by hand using pen, pencil, crayon, digital or other non-painted means to enable people to articulate their feelings, perceptions and ideas about something. Here, the drawer takes the major responsibility for producing and explaining his/her own picture, with minimal instruction and interpretation by the researcher. Such an image is not intended to capture relationships between variables, as in an academic model; or provide a technical representation as does a diagram, chart or graphic. Rather, it helps people to express their emotions, beliefs and/or understanding about an organization, object or other phenomena. While an 'inner picture' is a mental record of a sense-experience, a drawing is a 'fabrication': a tangible, physical impression of that inner picture communicated by a person to an audience (Langer 1957). Technology can enable its production and dissemination, but at its simplest a drawing is a non-verbal pictorial image produced by hand using simple instruments.

Words, numbers and other discursive elements may be important in clarifying and communicating a drawing's meaning post-construction, and may be used in minor ways during drawing (Stiles 2004a); but these are generally discouraged by researchers in the initial act of drawing, since studies in art theory (Gombrich 1982), advertising (Smith 1996), semiology (the study of linguistic signs) and visual sociology (Chaplin 1994) confirm that pictures are powerful expressive forms in their own right. Brain physiology research also suggests pictures engage a different mode of expression from words based on spatial, synthesizing mental processes in the right cerebral hemisphere rather than analytical, verbal reasoning in the left (Koivisto and Revonsuo 2000); with drawing requiring a mental shift towards the right mode (Edwards 1981). Of course, it is difficult to conclusively show that drawing reveals alternative or deep-set mental constructs, although one study shows organizational perceptions not obtained by more traditional verbal questioning (Stiles 2004a) and others indicate it may help surface unconscious responses or feelings about organizational change (Kearney and Hyle 2004). Ultimately, it is reasonable to regard drawings, like other images, as essential components of a *relay* system of how humans develop meaning about their worlds. This means drawings are at least complementary and equal partners to words, numbers, symbols and other components of language, rather than a secondary or subservient medium, as an *anchorage* system of meaning implies (Barthes 1967). As a result, drawings can summarize and communicate complex ideas often more succinctly and with greater impact than verbal means alone (Stiles 1998).

Drawing in social and organizational research

Academic drawing methods have a much shorter history than those concerning other visual forms such as photographs. This is evident in semiology or semiotics (Barthes 1967, 1981; de Saussure 1966; Edeline *et al.* 1992; Peirce 1955; Penn 2000; Sonesson 1993); art theory

(Saint-Martin 1990); visual anthropology and sociology (Bateson and Mead 1942; Becker 1981; Chaplin 1994; Emmison and Smith 2000; Fyfe and Law 1988; Goffman 1979; Hall 1973; Latour 1990); and post-structural writing (Baudrillard 1975, 1983; Lyotard 1984). These texts have championed visualizations as a primary focus within a relay system of meaning (Barthes 1967). However, most analyse images already 'out there' in social discourse, such as still photographs and advertisements; and occasionally paintings (e.g. Hadjinicolaou 1978), film or video (e.g. Rose 2000). While this provides useful insights into society, it often means second-guessing the intent of the original image producers and transferring meaning to contexts other than their original site. Many images studied are produced indirectly as part of social discourse rather than for a particular research project. The result is a 'second-hand' view of pictures, rather than a more indirect engagement with images and their creators. Such visual forms may be seen as authentic, because they are produced by others in complex social and technological processes seemingly detached from the interventions of researchers, reinforcing their mystical appeal as 'legitimate technologies of summarisation' (Fyfe and Law 1988). However, it also leads to images being treated as cultural or historical artefacts subject to the interpretive biases of researchers; with the researcher cast as an expert analyst, rather than allowing people the freedom to construct and interpret their own pictures in response to particular research questions. In fact, Emmison and Smith regard a focus on photography as 'The major impediment to the development of a vibrant tradition in visual research' (2000: 2). In reducing analysis to a few technical parameters, some risk overlooking the subjective power of images completely. For example, Larsen *et al.* (2004) try to measure the iconic impact of advertising photographs and commercials in terms of angle of vision, abrupt cuts between cameras, and camera movement. These go some way towards providing rules on how and why images work, but only partly consider their individual emotive or aesthetic impact and the intent of their creators. Others (e.g. Chaplin 1994) construct their own pictures to represent the societies they study, rather than allowing those they study to do so.

Digitalization also brings particular problems about the authenticity of images. In this volume, Bell and McArthur (Chapter 23) follow Fleming's (2009) notion of visual *authenticity* in organizations to mean uncommodified goods and services and not fake, superficial or phoney practices. Bell and McArthur suggest short YouTube films about social and organizational change may be seen as more authentic if they involve home-made images using such processes as redaction (active involvement of the audience through editing existing content to add value) and an appropriate balance between playfulness and critical rational debate. Leonard (Chapter 20, this volume) also suggests in her chapter that authenticity is a key dimension of a successful corporate visual identity, along with consistency, visibility, distinctiveness and transparency. Discursive analysis of a filmmaker's intentions and client choices provides first-hand insights into this process in both chapters. However, as these authors also note, authenticity is a problematic concept, particularly where new social media are adding layers of complexity and blurring boundaries between actors and practices. For example, some corporate YouTube postings imitate video characteristics such as amateurishness in attempts to generate affinity with their organizations, obscuring both form and content of images. As Leonard notes, uncovering the regime of truth influencing user-generated content is a challenging task. In addition, redaction may change an image, but is each iteration an original, 'first-hand' image or, simply, the second-, third- or fourth-hand (etc.) modification, extension or reversal of another creator's intended meanings? Of course, soliciting first-hand drawings does not guarantee that ideas are authentic in the sense of being original – many would accept that few ideas are genuinely 'new' and redaction may itself result in highly original insights. However, social media and digital technologies may complicate the quest for authenticity in an era of increasing ocularcentrism.

Such creation and interpretation issues underline the importance of allowing people to produce and explain their own images directly for a researcher using as near to a 'blank sheet' as possible.

Drawings provide an accessible way of doing this. Like other visual forms, drawings have a recognized capacity to arouse emotions in both drawer and audience (Gombrich 1982). However, drawings have a particular advantage because of their simplicity and flexibility as a mode of expression and communication. These qualities enable drawings to connect profoundly with their creators and broad audiences. They require minimal, inexpensive, widely available and understood technology such as pens, pencils and paper. Drawings also utilize skills developed from an early age. Infants instinctively draw as part of play from around two years, going through a series of developmental stages from scribbling, through symbolic, narrative and naturalistic constructions (Lowenfeld 1987). Although drawing abilities vary and draughtsmanship may not improve further without training in adolescence, anybody with a normal degree of eyesight and eye–hand coordination, given some confidence and instruction, can produce a basic drawing (Edwards 1981). Some drawers are initially more reluctant (Kearney and Hyle 2004), but evidence suggests that, with 'warming-up' exercises and persuasion that technically proficient art is not required, almost all people will make an attempt (Stiles 2004a). Furthermore, drawings are a most versatile form of expression. While cave walls have long ceased to be a popular drawing surface and paper is the most-used medium, digital technology provides a means to capture, display and share drawings through cameras, scanners and computers.

Despite such advantages, if first-hand, relay-based drawings are rare in sociology generally, they are even more unusual in management and organizational theory. Photographs are created by the researcher to portray organizational life (Strati 2000) and video analyses exist of natural work interactions (Heath and Luff 1997), but an analysis of pictures 'already out there' generally supplements verbal text. For instance, a study of political newspaper cartoons helps reinforce a verbal discursive analysis of institutional struggles over immigration (Hardy and Phillips 1999); and famous paintings are used metaphorically to show how academics' ways of seeing shape their methodologies (Hatch and Yanow 2008). Where greater emphasis is placed on images, these are usually existing corporate artefacts analysed by an academic expert. Corporate newsletters and posters demonstrate corporate behaviour towards gender and race (Mills 1995); photographs on company websites (Lamertz et al. 2005) and in recruitment brochures (Hancock 2005) are shown to influence external public perceptions of an industry and organization; Disney's cartoon characters and souvenirs help convey the company's liability of foreignness (Brannen 2004); and advertisements and photographs depict persuasive marketing and branding processes (Floch 2001; Hussey and Duncombe 1999).

Bespoke first-hand drawings are limited to a handful of pioneering organizational studies (Kearney and Hyle 2004; Meyer 1991). Although used to surface individuals' feelings and constructs as projective methods in clinical and social psychology (Semeonoff 1976; Nolen-Hoeksema et al. 2009) and art therapy (Broussine 2008), they are seldom used to depict organizations. When they are, methods and results vary. Some researchers influence drawers and prestructure responses by specifying what is required in detail – such as formal diagrams of a hospital's environment (Meyer 1978). Zuboff (1988) asked workers to draw freehand sketches about their job-related feelings as a result of the introduction of new information technology. This was part of a wider ethnographic study of power relationships, in which images played a useful but relatively small part. Others allow drawers freer expression, stimulating greater creativity and imaginative insights, where traditional methods (including strategy techniques like SWOT) are over-used and lack creative potential (Stiles 2004a). Many of these studies sought, or their subjects provided, visual *metaphors*: asking respondents to express their feelings and perceptions about their organization as if it *were* something else, such as a matchstick person; since explaining a complex social phenomenon such as an organization beyond a few simple parameters such as size, location and products or services supplied often requires imaginative contortions beyond conventional descriptions (Morgan 2006). Vince and Broussine (1996) asked managers in healthcare and local government organizations to draw images reflecting feelings about change. Each drawer wrote down six to ten explanatory words/phrases, before exchanging interpretations in groups: an important research phase to examine whether individuals' perceptions are shared more widely in the organization. Change perceptions were illuminating, although fuller discursive explanations were not presented and images were not reproduced, making it unclear whether the relay principle was being applied – although later work did include some pictures from the study and a vignette from an MBA project (Broussine 2008). Kearney and Hyle (2004) followed Vince and Broussine's instructions to allow faculty and administrators freedom to draw any pictures revealing feelings about organizational change in a US technology school. This time pictures were presented alongside fuller verbal explanations, but the small number of participants (nine) meant a second, group stage was impractical. While the aim was not to prestructure responses, both sets of researchers explicitly told drawers that matchstick people were acceptable in a bid to calm nerves about drawing – and drawings show this may have influenced participants to draw such figures. Bryans and Mavin (2006: 118) instead asked three groups of students and female faculty to 'draw research or a researcher', resulting in twelve insightful pictures based on a rich set of metaphors – although verbal extracts were not provided alongside images, and group interpretations were sought rather than those of individual respondents.

Pictorial representation

A drawing method known as pictorial representation (Stiles 1995, 1998, 2004a, 2011) adopts five research principles seen as important in the discussion above. Pictorial representation (1) is based on the relay principle of equality between image and text; (2) relies on a simple and flexible mode of engagement between researcher and drawer; (3) emphasizes the centrality, freedom and agency of drawers in drawing and interpreting first-hand images; (4) promotes the use of metaphors in producing images; and (5) systematically connects individual and group level images within an organization. Pictorial representation has been used to uncover people's ideas about organizational identity. Although other applications are possible – Bryans and Mavin (2006), for example, draw heavily on the method in analysing perceptions of researchers – I outline this identity approach, with example images and verbal extracts shown from a longitudinal study of university business schools during 1992–2009.

Identity has social psychological origins as the relatively central, distinctive and enduring character of a human entity such as an individual, group or organization (Albert and Whetten 1985; Dutton and Dukerich 1991; Gioia *et al.* 2000) and identification as the social process by which individuals define themselves in relation to other entities (Tajfel and Turner 1985). Underlying the idea of organizational identity are fundamental questions about what an organization *is*. The researcher's aim is to understand how stakeholders in and around an organization conceptualize their organization's identity or identities, given that it is usual for organizations to have multiple identities in people's eyes (Stiles 2011). Unlike many of the second-hand methods above, pictorial representation decentres the analyst from a pivotal role in analysing images. The organizational member is regarded as an active rather than a passive actor in the image construction and interpretation process, composing images and providing a verbal explanation of why these represent the organization. The researcher provides a loose guiding framework based on a broad and universally understood metaphor – that of human personality – and searches for consistencies and inconsistencies in people's explanations of their drawings.

The approach is also consistent with the emerging social practice literature (Schatzki 2005), particularly strategy-as-practice (SAP or SP) research, which aims to discover how strategizing actually happens in organizations, rather than treating it as a 'black box' (Whittington 2006). Because of their simplicity, flexibility and expressive power, drawings help connect the rationalities of a range of strategy actors by providing an accessible way of revealing the local-specific (first order) use of language in an organization (Ezzamel and Willmott 2008). Individuals and groups are asked to draw pictures of the organization's *personality or personalities*: a metaphor that encourages people to reflect on identity by using everyday knowledge about people (Deaux 1991). Strategies can then be developed to address issues raised by stakeholders, grounded in rich perceptions of the organizational context.

Interviewees first complete 'warm-up' exercises to help them adopt a visual-spatial means of information processing by first drawing an imaginary human face, then its mirror image, before being asked to draw more creative figures (Edwards 1981). In the first-stage interviews with individuals, each person subsequently draws a *free-drawn personality image* of their organization, with care taken to ensure consistent instructions:

> Imagine that you're trying to communicate with someone who can't read or write. Some people say that each place you work in has its own personality. I want you to imagine that your organization has its own personality or personalities and do a rough sketch to try to explain to this person who can't read or write what that personality or personalities look like.

The conversation is otherwise unstructured to ensure ideas emerge without undue prompting. The characteristic of illiteracy discourages the use of words or numbers, and drawers interpret their own pictures immediately after drawing. These explanations are audio- or video-recorded: the latter useful in group settings to allow clearer attribution of text to individuals. Recordings are transcribed verbatim and analysed using Stiles' (2004a) approach, involving the search for patterns in visual and verbal data regarding variabilities and consistencies (shared accounts) in content or form, based on critical psychological approaches (Harré and Gillett 1994; Potter and Wetherell 1987). These variabilities and consistencies are grouped into themes, with data reproduced naturalistically. A grounded theory approach generates data until the point of theoretical saturation, i.e. where no new themes emerge (Glaser and Strauss 1967).

Internal and external stakeholder focus groups subsequently help to explore and validate initial interview data, construct collective organizational images and capture images of the organization over time. In this study, academics, managers, administrative staff, students and the business community were grouped separately to compare and contrast perceptions. The intensive nature of the method and the need to capture images to allow for substantive organizational change may mean making decisions as to appropriate intervals between follow-up interviews, so students were interviewed here at the beginning and end of their studies; and others at five-year intervals. This provided an invaluable perspective on change during the long study period. Five personality images and explanations from individual interviews were fed back into each focus group to provide a link between individual and group stages. Groups were asked to reach a consensus as to which, if any, of the five images represented the school. Groups were then free to explore their own ideas about the organization's identity and produce a *group free-drawn personality image*. Again following Stiles (2004a), consistencies and variabilities were identified across transcripts.

An extended report on the project reproduces all drawings and substantive verbal extracts from individual and group interviews to provide a full account (Potter and Wetherell 1987: 173).

This report offers participants the opportunity for feedback and reflection upon emerging themes. The final stage may be to communicate findings to a wider audience through academic or practitioner publications. These present particular style and format limitations, requiring greater summarizing and editing of data and findings than reports. However, the relay principle still demands substantive, naturalistic line-numbered (for easier reference) verbal extracts alongside images to 'let organizational voices speak for themselves'. Text from both researcher and respondents is included and material is only removed to shorten extracts for publication if this does not substantively change the context or meaning of the extract and to prevent individuals being identified. The analysis focuses on themes emerging from the data, with drawers' own explanations an important part of the overall narrative rather than just the researcher's reporting. I show examples from this study below to illustrate the method's application.

A case study: UK business school

As expected, drawings reflected multiple views of the organization's identity, varying between individuals, groups and over time. However, consistent identity themes also appeared. These themes were expressed in different ways, but common visual devices were evident. Overall, the business school was not depicted as a happy personality. The reasons for this are provided by interrelated identity themes that remained remarkably salient over the entire study period. People perceived the school personality as preoccupied with research, miserly owing to a lack of resources, disenfranchised and anonymous, fragmented, and overly male. At best, rather than showing stakeholders identifying strongly with the business school, many appeared to articulate schizo-identification (Elsbach 2001), where individuals in the organization actively and intensively identified and disidentified with different aspects of the school over the 17-year study.

Research preoccupation

The school personality was viewed as overly research focused. Although this was positive in the sense of achieving a scholarly mission for this premier UK research institution, it was also widely believed to be to the detriment of teaching and student interests, generating particular conflicts over identity. Albert and Whetten (1985) noted normative and utilitarian identity conflict may be an integral dimension of a professional school, but the school's strategy was seen to lead to manifest fragmentation: where protecting academic integrity conflicted with acquiring ever-tightening resources. A research preoccupation was amplified by intense pressures from successive externally driven research assessments encouraging the school to remain in the top research echelon, despite the importance of student income. Figure 14.1 exemplifies this theme.

Figure 14.1 Extract: Katie (lecturer)
1. K: Er, man in a white coat with a mortarboard. An academic more
2. concerned with research, er, it's supposed to signify...But he's
3. behind a door with 'DO NOT DISTURB'...notice on the handle,
4. which shows he doesn't really want to be bothered. He wants to be
5. getting on with his work.
6. R: Right. Right. Do not disturb. So, who is, is that a message
7. to anyone in particular then?
8. K: Er, everybody out there who isn't in academia.
9. R: Right. Right. What about to students as well?
10. K: Yeah.

David R. Stiles

Figure 14.1 Individual free-drawn personality image: Katie, lecturer

11. R: Or not?
12. K: Depends on what they wanted him for. If it was going to further
13.   his aims then he would be quite happy to see them.
14. R: Right. Right. So he's wearing a white coat?
15. K: Yeah, just to signify that he's interested in research – that's the, you
16.   know, the standard scientist.

Miserliness/meanness with money

An important linked characteristic was a strong sense of miserliness and financial hardship – as reducing government funding necessitated raising extra income through research grants contingent on a good research rating; and through student fees. Figures 14.1 and 14.2 depict currency signs in the figure's eyes and on a moneybag, with Figure 14.2 showing miserly attributes.

Figure 14.2 Extract 1: Darren (lecturer)
1. D: Uhm, secondly what you notice is that the person is holding on to
2.   its money, which is something that it does rather than spend it. It
3.   holds on to it…
4. R: Holding on to its money?

Figure 14.2 Individual free-drawn personality image: Darren, lecturer

Figure 14.3 Individual free-drawn personality image: Mark, full professor

5. D: If I can draw a grip better, I would have had it gripping and.
6. R: Not let it go?
7. D: Yeah, holding on to its money.

This meant meanness in terms of providing computer equipment and a feeling that academics were acting almost as sales representatives to attract student fees and grant income. Academics articulated this as a continuing pressure against engaging with students and conducting longer-term and practitioner-oriented research.

Disenfranchisement

Until he stepped down in the last 18 months of the study, the school had had a leader for an unusually long time. A theme emerging consistently across interviews and focus groups was the dominance of the leader in both strategic and operational decision-making, which was seen to exacerbate the school's fragmentation. At the start of the study, the leader was seen as a lone figure (Figure 14.3) trying to carry a burdensome administrative load, unwilling to delegate to others:

Figure 14.3 Extract: Mark (full professor)
1. M: It's a man. Probably [names leader]. He's carrying a great load,
2.   which is too big for him, so it's slipping. [pause] This is the
3.   different parts of the Business School. [pause] He should try to
4.   give bits away, but he won't.

In Figure 14.4, an MBA student group depicted social distance between leader and the body of the school through a long neck separating the head and body and folded arms to show a one-way flow of information, influence and communication:

Figure 14.4 Extract 1: MBA focus group
1. S1: The long neck was quite a good idea.
2. S2: Yeah.
3. S3: Yeah, I think so.
4. S4: Like the Student-Staff Panels. And you always hear that [pause]
5.   going into them, right, you hear [pause] but never have you seen any
6.   results from it. [pause] And it's almost like he's being closed-
7.   minded. They do this, they have the Student-Staff Panels, just for…
8. S3: Maybe his arms are folded. Unapproachable?
9. S4: Yeah. Yeah.
10. S1: Can you draw folded-up? [S3 draws folded arms on figure]
11.   [general laughter]
12. R: That's good. [pause] So this is the faculty folding their arms, is it?
13. S4: I say it's more that kind of the Business School Director.
14. R: Yeah.
15. S4: Kind of not getting the results.

Large size and scale/anonymity

Figure 14.2 portrayed the school as overweight because of large student numbers linked to the financial imperative through maximizing fee income. Figure 14.3 showed the school as a load

Drawing as a method of organizational analysis

Figure 14.4 Group free-drawn personality image: MBA students

too great for the leader to manage and many drawings referred to a sense of anonymity partly related to size, but with faculty, staff and students believing they had little voice because of the sense of disenfranchisement. An MBA group showed the school building as too small, with the roof pressing down on the character's head:

Figure 14.4 Extract 2: MBA focus group
1. S1:   I suppose we should have great big looking feet, 'cause there's too
2.   many sort of little legs in great big shoes: students to teachers.
3. S2:   I think this building is too small for a lot of people in it. I would have
4.   made it really cramped, like bending down. And all because I just
5.   think that [pause] the building can't accommodate this amount of
6.   people.
7. S3:   Yeah.
8. S4:   Make it a box just pressing down. [S5 draws low roof]
9. S6:   Oh, you are brilliant.
10. S1: Yeah. He'd crack his if he puts his head there.

Fragmentation

The idea of a split personality involved the school projecting contradictory characteristics internally and externally: most often expressed as a fundamental academic versus business mismatch. Conflicts between normative and utilitarian multiple identities were felt to result in a fragmented organizational identity, reminiscent of Elsbach's (2001) idea of schizo-identification. People actively articulated the idea of a split personality, with the character's portrayal suggesting a lack of belief in the business-oriented image the school portrayed through its publicity documents. Conflict between identities was intensified by the financial imperative, research prioritization and perceived disenfranchisement. Fabrications generally conveyed a sense of uncertainty as to the long-term strategies of the school, with the leader not providing a clear vision and fragmentation meaning individuals and groups pursued their own goals within extreme resource constraints and disenfranchised decision processes. Figure 14.2 articulates the notion of schizo-identification:

> **Figure 14.2 Extract 2: Darren (lecturer)**
> 1. D: I see the business school as essentially a schizophrenic organization but on
> 2. the one half you have got the sort of very academic academics who are sort
> 3. of favour the long hair, and the Levis 501s and trainers and the other hand
> 4. you have got the business academics who favour the suits and sort of pseudo
> 5. businessmen look and I think that is something that that is one of the things
> 6. that struck me when I first came.

Maleness

Pictures also reflected perceived gender imbalance at the school, based mainly on an overwhelming proportion of male faculty – although the influence of the male leader was also mentioned in Figure 14.4. The business side of the split personalities was also widely regarded as male, in contrast to the more balanced academic side. Male pronouns proliferated when describing the character, which usually had masculine clothing. The MBA focus group (Figure 14.4) reflected that:

> **Figure 14.4 Extract 3: MBA focus group**
> 1. S1: There's no females here.
> 2. S2: We don't have this many females, do we?
> 3. S3: Any teachers?
> 4. S1: No.
> 5. S3: Are they kidding?
> 6. S4: Really unbelievable.
> 7. S5: No, not really.
> 8. S1: There's [names female academic], but that's about the only female.
> 9. R: [pause] Yeah. Alright.
> 10. S5: And what type of business school, business joke. Your
> 11. mind really blows this mainly male world, you know? Mine does
> 12. anyway.

Overall, different images appeared to different stakeholders, but portrayed a generic identity of neutrality-unhappiness underpinned by these interwoven themes. Pictorial and textual discourse helped reveal competing images integral to the process of defining multiple organizational identities. Although confidentiality precludes giving specific details, specific research, teaching, marketing communication and human resource objectives and strategies were developed to address identity issues arising from this analysis. However, the researcher may be more concerned with helping stakeholders understand the organization's identities; gaining insights into how specific organizational activities, such as research, are conducted (Bryans and Mavin 2006); articulating feelings about organizational change (Kearney and Hyle 2004; Vince and Broussine 1996); or developing theory about wider social change (Stiles 2011).

Conclusion and future developments

This chapter has shown that, provided care is taken to address five research principles, drawing methods provide an accessible and flexible metaphor-based way of surfacing identities and other organizational aspects that alternative verbal and visual methods may find more difficult. Unlike conventional semiotic approaches, asking people to draw and explain their own images and presenting the resulting discourse through the relay principle decentres the researcher from the role of expert in judging what the drawer is conveying. It also helps avoid accusations of reification – that one is treating the personality drawing itself as real. In connecting individual and group level images within an organization, pictorial representation provides a bridge between different levels of analysis.

The simplicity and flexibility of pictorial representation is also to some extent its future-proofing. Film, video and other media also offer great possibilities for exploring organization and social processes (e.g. Heath and Luff 1997); but computer tablets, cloud computing, social networking and online journals also provide potential routes for the production and dissemination of drawings about organizations. These will become more important: tablet-based 'apps' already allow drawing via an intuitive touchscreen or stylus and camera-ready artwork for publications. Indeed, I experimented with 'pocket PC' devices in the early 2000s with prototypical drawing software, and currently use four drawing apps on my iPad. However, using more sophisticated image technology does not necessarily bring greater expression and may place unnecessary barriers between researcher and subject. Leonard (see Chapter 20, this volume) has already noted that the amateurish simplicity of video images involving such devices as stick people may help clarify messages in a way that more sophisticated technical products find difficult. Drawing using pen and paper allows one of the most direct, simple, first-hand modes of engagement with people. Even where technology such as compact cameras and cell phones enhances the first-hand construction and sharing of photographs and video, drawing will maintain an advantage as a viable 'low-tech' research approach. Taking a creative photograph or video of an organization requires greater knowledge and skills in image composition and manipulation than a simple line drawing.

Analysing the many website images being posted provides opportunities to research social discourse in new ways. Yet, positioning the researcher as an expert analyst risks ignoring or diminishing the voices that construct these images. Such images may also be disappointing in the depth of insight they provide. It is, of course, true that social media are employing image in ways that are both creative and unpredictable – as the Free Range Studios cases in this volume show (Bell and McArthur Chapter 23; Leonard Chapter 20). However, it is also the case that simplistic organizational stereotypes may inhibit deeper analysis – such as presenting CEOs as fat-bellied, money-fixated or giant, robotic characters. Issues of establishing authenticity make the analysis of social media images particularly problematic. In addition, most Internet images are currently used within routine activities such as sharing pictures of friends and families, email, seeking everyday information through search engines, and social networking (US Census 2011). No more than a third of young people – often seen as the most Internet-savvy demographic – have done anything more creative than set up a social networking page, pass comment on a website or construct a music playlist (Holmes 2011). Future social networking may involve people producing more critical first-hand web images about their social and organizational worlds; but a lack of more advanced imaging skills and motivation may mean most people are content to show personal snapshots. Recent concerns about employers' surveillance of employees' Internet activities (Halpern *et al.* 2008) provide another reason why more critical organizational images may only be revealed by the intervention of specific research projects.

Advancing the research agenda in drawing means applying methods in many more contexts, since only a handful of organizations have been explored. Longitudinal studies, such as the one outlined here, are also needed to show how identities and other social phenomena change over time. Although grounded theory means drawings are collected up to the point where no new themes emerge, researchers should ensure appropriate numbers of images are constructed to address the particular research question. Care must be taken to ensure the analysis process is robust, with researchers showing systematically how themes emerge directly from extracts and drawings, using respondents' own voices. Using other accessible and widely recognized metaphors besides personality may add important dimensions to work. While animals may, for example, have universal appeal (Stiles 2004b), people may find it more difficult to see their organization as a type of car or vegetable. Ultimately, drawings have great potential to add insights into our understanding of organizational and social processes; and researchers would be wise to consider this most ancient, universal and adaptable means of human expression.

References

Albert, S. and Whetten, D. (1985) 'Organizational identity', in L. Cummings and B. Straw (eds) *Research in Organizational Behavior*, Vol. 7, Greenwich, CT: JAI Press, 263–295.
Barthes, R. (1967) *Elements of Semiology*, trans. A. Lavers and C. Smith, New York: Hill and Wang.
——(1981) *Camera Lucida: Reflections on Photography*, New York: Hill and Wang.
Bateson, G. and Mead, M. (1942) *Balinese Character: A Photographic Analysis*, New York: New York Academy of Sciences.
Baudrillard, J. (1975) *The Mirror of Production*, trans. M. Poster, St Louis, MO: Telos Press.
——(1983) *Simulations*, trans. P. Foss, P. Patton and P. Beitchman, New York: Semiotext(e).
Becker, H. (1981) *Exploring Society Photographically*, Evanston, IL: Northwestern University Press.
Brannen, M. (2004) 'When Mickey loses face: recontextualization, semantic fit, and the semiotics of foreignness', *Academy of Management Review* 29(4): 593–616.
Broussine, M. (2008) 'Drawings and art', in M. Broussine (ed.) *Creative Methods in Organizational Research*, London, Thousand Oaks, CA and New Delhi: Sage, 70–91.
Bryans, P. and Mavin, S. (2006) 'Visual images: a technique to surface conceptions of research and researchers', *Qualitative Research in Organizations and Management* 1(2): 113–128.
Chaplin, E. (1994) *Sociology and Visual Representation*, London: Routledge.
Deaux, K. (1991) 'Social identities: thoughts on structure and change', in R. Curtis (ed.) *The Relational Self: Theoretical Convergences in Psychoanalysis and Social Psychology*, New York: Guilford Press, 77–93.
de Saussure, F. (1966) *Course in General Linguistics*, trans. W. Baskin, New York: McGraw Hill.
Dutton, J. and Dukerich, J. (1991) 'Keeping an eye on the mirror: image and identity in organizational adaptation', *Academy of Management Journal* 34(3): 517–554.
Edeline, F., Klinkenberg, J.-M. and Minguet, P. (1992) *Traité du Signe Visuel, pour une Rhétorique de l'Image*, Paris: Le Seuil.
Edwards, B. (1981) *Drawing on The Right Side of the Brain: How to Unlock your Hidden Artistic Talent*, London: Souvenir.
Elsbach, K. (2001) 'Coping with hybrid organizational identities: evidence from California legislative staff', *Advances in Qualitative Organization Research* 3: 59–90.
Emmison, M. and Smith, P. (2000) *Researching the Visual: Images, Objects, Contexts and Interactions in Social and Cultural Enquiry*, London, Thousand Oaks, CA and New Delhi: Sage.
Ezzamel, M. and Willmott, H. (2008) 'Strategy as discourse in a global retailer: a supplement to rationalist and interpretive accounts', *Organization Studies* 29(2): 191–217.
Fleming, P. (2009) *Authenticity and the Cultural Politics of Work: New Forms of Informal Control*, Oxford: Oxford University Press.
Floch, J.-M. (2001) *Semiotics, Marketing and Communication*, Basingstoke: Palgrave Macmillan.

Fyfe, G. and Law, J. (1988) *Picturing Power: Visual Depiction and Social Relations*, London: Routledge.
Gioia, D., Schultz, M. and Corley, K. (2000) 'Organizational identity, image, and adaptive instability', *Academy of Management Review* 25(1): 63–81.
Glaser, B. and Strauss, A. (1967) *The Discovery of Grounded Theory: Strategies for Qualitative Research*, New York: Alldine.
Goffman, E. (1979) *Gender Advertisements*, Basingstoke: Macmillan.
Gombrich, E. (1982) *The Image and the Eye: Further Studies in the Psychology of Pictorial Representation*, Oxford: Phaidon.
——(1995) *The Story of Art*, 16th ed., London: Phaidon.
Hadjinicolaou, N. (1978) *Art History and Class Struggle*, London: Pluto Press.
Hall, S. (1973) 'The determinations of news photographs', in S. Cohen and J. Young (eds) *The Manufacture of News: Deviance, Social Problems and the Mass Media*, London: Constable, 269–283.
Halpern, D., Reville, P. and Grunewald, D. (2008) 'Management and legal issues regarding electronic surveillance of employees in the workplace', *Journal of Business Ethics* 80(2): 175–180.
Hancock, P. (2005) 'Uncovering the semiotic in organizational aesthetics', *Organization* 12(1): 29–50.
Hardy, C. and Phillips, N. (1999) 'No joking matter: discursive struggle in the Canadian refugee system', *Organization Studies* 20(1): 1–24.
Harré, R. and Gillett, G. (1994) *The Discursive Mind*, Thousand Oaks, CA: Sage.
Hatch, M. and Yanow, D. (2008) 'Methodology by metaphor: ways of seeing in painting and research', *Organization Studies* 29(1): 23–44.
Heath, C. and Luff, P. (1997) 'Convergent activities: collaborative work and multimedia technology in London Underground line control rooms', in D. Middleton and Y. Engestrom (eds) *Cognition and Communication at Work: Distributed Cognition in the Workplace*, Cambridge: Cambridge University Press.
Holmes, J. (2011). 'Cyberkids or divided generations? Characterising young people's Internet use in the UK with generic, continuum or typological models', *New Media & Society* 13(7): 1104–1122.
Hussey, M. and Duncombe, N. (1999) 'Projecting the right image: using projective techniques to measure brand image', *Qualitative Market Research* 2(1): 22–30.
Kearney, K. and Hyle, A. (2004) 'Drawing out emotions: the use of participant-produced drawings in qualitative enquiry', *Qualitative Research* 4(3): 361–382.
Koivisto, M. and Revonsuo, A. (2000) 'Semantic priming by pictures and words in the cerebral hemispheres', *Cognitive Brain Research* 10(1–2): 91–98.
Lamertz, K., Pursey, P., Heugens, A. and Calmet, L. (2005) 'The configuration of organizational images among firms in the Canadian beer brewing industry', *Journal of Management Studies* 42(4): 817–843.
Langer, S. (1957) *Philosophy in a New Key*, Cambridge, MA: Harvard University Press.
Larsen, V., Luna, D. and Peracchio, D. (2004) 'Point of view and pieces of time: a taxonomy of image attributes', *Journal of Consumer Research* 31(6): 102–111.
Latour, B. (1990) 'Drawing things together', in M. Lynch and S. Woolgar (eds) *Representation in Scientific Practice*, Cambridge, MA: MIT Press, 19–68.
Lowenfeld, V. (1987) *Creative and Mental Growth*, 8th ed., London: Collier Macmillan.
Lyotard, J.-F. (1984) *Driftworks*, New York: Semiotext(e).
Meyer, A. (1978) 'Management and strategy', in R. Miles and C. Snow (eds) *Organizational Strategy, Structure, and Process*, New York: McGraw Hill.
——(1991) 'Visual data in organizational research', *Organization Science* 2(2): 218–236.
Mills, A. (1995) 'Man/aging subjectivity, silencing diversity: organizational imagery in the airline industry. The case of British Airways', *Organization* 2(2): 243–269.
Morgan, G. (2006) *Images of Organization*, 2nd ed., Newbury Park, CA: Sage.
Nolen-Hoeksema, B., Frederickson, B., Loftus, G. and Wagenaar, W. (2009) *Atkinson & Hilgard's Introduction to Psychology*, 15th ed., Andover: Wadsworth Cengage Learning.
Peirce, C. (1955) *Philosophical Writings of Peirce*, New York: Dover.
Penn, G. (2000) 'Semiotic analysis of still images', in M. Bauer and G. Gaskell (ed.) *Qualitative Researching with Text, Image and Sound*, London, Thousand Oaks, CA and New Delhi: Sage, 227–245.
Potter, J. and Wetherell, M. (1987) *Discourse Analysis and Social Psychology: Beyond Attitudes and Behaviour*, London: Sage.
Rose, D. (2000) 'Analysis of moving images', in M. Bauer and G. Gaskell (ed.) *Qualitative Researching with Text, Image and Sound*, London, Thousand Oaks, CA and New Delhi: Sage, 246–262.
Saint-Martin, F. (1990) *La Theorie de la Gestalt et l'Art Visuel*, Quebec: Presses de l'Université du Québec.
Schatzki, T. (2005) 'The sites of organizations', *Organization Studies* 26(3): 465–484.

Semeonoff, B. (1976) *Projective Techniques*, London: Wiley.
Smith, P. (1996) *Marketing Communications – an Integrated Approach*, London: Kogan Page.
Sonesson, G. (1993) 'Pictorial semiotics, Gestalt theory, and the ecology of perception', *Semiotica* 99: 319–399.
Stiles, D. (1995) The Art of Organisations: Picturing UK and North American Business School Strategies in Four Dimensions, PhD thesis, Cardiff: University of Cardiff.
——(1998) 'Pictorial representation', in G. Symon and C. Cassell (eds) *Qualitative Methods in Organizational Research: A Practical Guide*, London, Thousand Oaks, CA and New Delhi: Sage, 190–210.
——(2004a) 'Pictorial representation', in C. Cassell and G. Symon (eds) *Essential Guide to Qualitative Methods in Organizational Research*, London, Thousand Oaks, CA and New Delhi: Sage, 127–139.
——(2004b) 'Picturing the beast inside: animals, organizational identity and metaphorical grafting', paper presented at the Academy of Management Annual Meeting, New Orleans, August 2004.
——(2011) 'Disorganization, disidentification and ideological fragmentation: verbal and pictorial evidence from a British business school', *Culture and Organization* 17(1): 5–30.
Strati, A. (2000) 'Putting people in the picture: art and aesthetics in photography and in understanding organizational life', *Organization Studies* 21 (Supplement): 53–69.
Tajfel, H. and Turner, J. (1985) 'The social identity theory of intergroup behaviour', in S. Worchel and W. Austin (eds) *The Psychology of Intergroup Relations*, Chicago: Nelson-Hall, 7–24.
US Census (2011) '1160. Typical Daily Internet Activities of Adult Internet Users: 2011', retrieved from http://www.census.gov/compendia/statab/2012/tables/12s1160.pdf.
Vince, R. and Broussine, M. (1996) 'Paradox, defense and attachment: accessing and working with emotions and relations underlying organizational change', *Organization Studies* 17(1): 1–21.
Whittington, R. (2006) 'Completing the practice turn in strategy research', *Organization Studies* 27(5): 613–634.
Wölfflin, H. (1950) *Principles of Art History*, New York: Dover.
Zuboff, S. (1988) *In the Age of the Smart Machine*, New York: Basic Books.

15

Visual sociology and work organization

An historical approach

Tim Strangleman

Introduction

The sociological approach to the visual understanding of work organizations is a rich, fascinating and, at times, contradictory one. Sociology has a long history of engaging with its subject matter visually but, as a discipline, it has often been reluctant to acknowledge this legacy and achievement. In this chapter, this history is explored in all its complexity and richness. Rather than suggesting that there is a coherent story, one of unfolding logic, it will show the different ways sociology and sociologists have engaged with the visual around the topic of work, workers and organizations. It is important to recognize that some of the material presented here goes beyond sociology, borrowing from disciplines as diverse as anthropology, art history and social policy; this is done to think more deeply about how work has been understood visually and how we might use this legacy in contemporary visual studies of organizations. This chapter aims to provide a number of insights. First, it is a selective account of visual representations of work. Second, it provides an overview of the visual sociology of work. Finally, it is a reflection on the methodological practices of the visual sociology of work and approaches to the types and nature of data in the field.

The chapter begins with a reflection on nineteenth-century visual studies of work, going on to look at the maturing corporate use of photography. It reflects on the high point of corporate photography in the post-war period before examining the ways organizations have been portrayed in the context of deindustrialization. Finally, the chapter examines ways in which we can use images in sociology of work, asking what the visual adds to our understanding of work.

A short history of the visual sociology of work

With the rise of visual sociology and visual methods in the late twentieth century, it is easy to forget that sociology has a long and distinguished history in the field. Historically, sociology and photography grew up and matured in parallel (see Stasz 1979; Chaplin 1994). Here we are concerned in particular with sociology and work organization, but, in doing so, we have to see this as part of a wider interest in modern society and its problems. It is also important not to fall into the trap of viewing the visual as simply photography. Some of the earliest visual engagement by social scientists can be seen in other media such as engraving and mapping. Take, for example, Henry Mayhew's (1985 [1865]) *London Life and the London Poor*, which is an important but arguably neglected early piece of social research that made extensive use of illustrations in the form of engraving alongside his prose (Yeo 1971, 2011). These engravings showed types of the various London workers that were discussed in the written text. Similarly, Gustave Doré, a French engraver, produced iconic images of work, workers and, by extension, their social conditions in *London: A Pilgrimage* in collaboration with essayist Blanchard Jerrold (Jerrold and Doré 2006 [1869]). In copious plates, Doré animates trades and aspects of working life in London in the mid-nineteenth century. Another non-photographic visual approach to exploring aspects of work in the nineteenth century was the mapping carried out by Charles Booth (1840–1916). His poverty maps of London were explicitly about social class and relative income, but are also a powerful way of visualizing occupational groups (see Bales 2011).

Photography was arguably the most important visual media during the nineteenth century, and work and labour were often captured by either design or by accident by early photographers. In the United States, two photographers' portfolios became synonymous with the representation of work. Jacob Riis (1849–1914) was a pioneering photographer of the conditions of the poor in New York during the later nineteenth century. Riis, a Danish immigrant, began taking photographs in New York after being hired by the *Tribune* and Associated Press as a reporter in 1877. He was quickly promoted to police reporter, gaining access to the ghettoes on the city's lower east side. Ten years later, Riis developed a lecture series that highlighted the wretched conditions of his subjects, which he began to illustrate with lantern slides. These pictures alongside a series of essays were published in 1890 in his *How the Other Half Lives* (Riis 1998; see also Yochelson 2001).

A second major figure in the tradition of photography of labour is Lewis Hine (1874–1940). Hine obtained a Master's degree in sociology at Columbia University. Socially committed, Hine spent his time taking photographs for a series of socially aware magazines and later for the National Child Labor Committee (NCLC). The NCLC used his photography in a very direct way as evidence of child exploitation (Gutman 1967; Goldberg 1999). Importantly for the purposes of this chapter, Hine's sociology and general academic training was influenced in part by American pragmatist thought, which stressed ideas of engagement and reflection on experience (see Trachtenberg 1989). One of Hine's lesser-known assignments was his involvement in the Pittsburgh Survey, a pioneering project combining photography with statistical data and interview material (Cohen 2011).

Rise of corporate photography

Lewis Hine's career as a photographer acts as a useful bridge in our story. His early work influenced by sociological purpose shifts after the Great War ended in 1918 towards his later work for corporate clients. There is continuity here with that earlier sociological imperative and a clue is offered in a reflection on his career: 'There were two things I wanted to do. I wanted to show the things that had to be corrected. I wanted to show the things that had to be appreciated' (Hine, quoted in Langer 1998: 20).

This second aspect of his craft celebrated labour and the worker in industrial society, subverting the notion that, in an industrial age, humans became mere appendages to their machines. Rather, Hine lionized heroic workers and labour, most famously in his series of photographs recording the construction of the Empire State Building in New York (Langer 1998; see also Doherty 1981; Gutman 1974; Hine 1977; Orvell 1995; Trachtenberg 1989).

Visual sociology and work organization

The shift in Hine's focus came at a time when corporations were increasingly aware of the power of photography and of the need to develop their own images with their customers, with politicians and with their own workers. The corporate use of imagery has generated a wealth of material on the workplace and labour, companies often employing the best photographers of the day. Images were created for publicity; for training purposes; as scientific management tools; as well as the act of record. This range and nature of corporate photography is a subject that is strangely neglected by sociologists, its exploration carried out mainly by historians and visual scholars remote from sociology (see Brown 2005 and the discussion below). This is all the more surprising given the fact that photography, sociology and the modern corporation emerged near simultaneously in the nineteenth century (Stasz 1979).

Industrialist Henry Ford, as in so many other respects, was a pioneer in the use of photography for corporate purposes. Having purchased a camera for personal use in 1896, he later set up the Ford Motor Company motion picture department in 1914. His moving and still pictures record many aspects of the organization and its workforce, including the handling of raw materials, detailed photography of the assembly lines as well as specialist engineering functions and the large bureaucracy that managed and organized Ford's plant. These images were used for internal training purposes as well as to promote the company to its customers and a wider public. The scale of this endeavour can be seen in the fact that, as early as 1963, the company presented the US National Archives with approximately 1.5 million feet of silent film and the collection of more than 75,000 stills from the company's Rouge plant taken from its opening in 1917 to 1941 (Bryan 2003: 246).

There is a growing literature on corporate photography and the use of images. David Nye's (1985) book *Image Worlds*, for example, examines the use of photography in the ideological construction of the General Electric Company in the USA. In turn, Nye looks at the way the company recorded its workforce, managers, products, factories, engineers, publicity and consumers. Nye's *Image Worlds* was and still is influential because it mapped the different purposes to which a corporate body put its images. General Electric early on recognized the different audiences it had, both internal and external, and the ways in which visual material could reach them. Nye is also important in the way he considers how one thinks about a vast corporate collection or archive. How do you make sense of a collection that may run into hundreds of thousands of plates? This is an issue we will return to later in the chapter (see also Sekula 1983).

Another influential author is Roland Marchand (1998), who, in his *Creating the Corporate Soul*, discussed the way corporations in the USA developed the practice of public relations, achieving this through both written and visual texts. This was made possible by the improvements in photographic technology and reproduction. Marchand argues that corporate America became aware of its ability to, and the necessity of, visual public relations in the Progressive era.

Elspeth Brown's *The Corporate Eye* (2005) also explores commercial use of photography for public relations purposes – including internal and external promotion to staff and customers. But Brown also maps a range of other purposes to which the camera was applied. She examines more generally the way various businesses, managers and the emerging discipline of management science in the USA made use of photography from the 1880s onwards. These included using photography to identify and screen potential workers based on their physiognomic features in order to exclude those with the wrong 'character'. As Brown notes, this particular branch of science and its use of the image petered out in the twentieth century, replaced by psychological and behavioural approaches. Another aspect of corporate photography which *The Corporate Eye* lights upon is its early adoption in another aspect of scientific management, namely the rationalization and standardization of work movement exemplified in the research of Frank and Lillian Gilbreth. The Gilbreths were influenced by F.W. Taylor and sought to show the way photography could be used as part of time and motion studies. These studies fragmented the labour process frame by frame, and represent work and labour in an abstract and decontextualized format in order that it might be better understood and rationally planned. Brown suggests that the Gilbreths developed their thinking from seeing photography as a form of:

> functional realism, according to which the image serves as an empirical substitute for the object, a type of evidence, to an instrumental realism, in this case, using the realist promise of the photograph as truth to restructure the ways in which work is performed.
>
> *(2005: 71)*

In a fascinating paper on the photographic study of movement, Corbett shows the way early techniques pioneered by Eadweard Muybridge were applied to work by the Gilbreths. As he notes:

> The Gilbreths' work was conducted at a time when the cult of efficiency had as fully infiltrated American work culture as it had in late 19th century France. ... The Gilbreths were concerned primarily with the elimination of 'wasted motion' and sought to create their 'own visual vocabulary of efficiency – one in which labour is finally made fully alienated and therefore manageable through and through'.
>
> *(Corwin 2003: 146, cited in Corbett 2008: 117)*

Another way of exploring corporate image making is by revisiting the sources themselves which have been reproduced for a variety of reasons. An interesting but limited discussion of the use of corporate photography can be found in Douglas Harper's (2001) *Changing Works*, which, in part, uses the archive of Standard Oil, which commissioned Roy Stryker to produce 'a photographic documentation of the uses of petroleum in America' (ibid.: 8). This project explicitly aimed at portraying the social aspect of the company's product from 1943 to 1950. The autonomy granted to the photographers involved in the project resulted in images of great beauty as well as lasting historical sociological value.

One element of the representation of work is the reproduction of classic corporate photography in nostalgic reflections on the past. These publications are not intended necessarily for academic use but act as a wonderful fund of material for those interested in the portrayal of labour. Bryan's (2003) book *Rouge* is a good example of this, as are Olsen and Cabadas' (2002) *The American Auto Factory* and Cabadas' (2004) *River Rouge: Ford's Industrial Colossus*. All of these volumes are ostensibly produced for automotive enthusiasts and are packed with images of labour taken by talented corporate photographers whose role was to capture both the mundane everyday shots of production as well as significant milestones of factory life. This audience for industrial heritage is echoed in various other sectors, including railways, steel and mining (see Swanson 2004; Wollman and Inman 1999).

Researchers have access to a growing body of corporate film material which has been commercially released to a general public or is held in archives. In Britain, the pioneering work of the Documentary Film Movement (DFM), whose members were employed directly for the Empire Marketing Board (EMB), the General Post Office (GPO) or later nationalized industries has been available for some time. While not exclusively about work, they are dominated by industrial labour and subjects include fishing, shipbuilding, steelmaking, coalmining and railway work among other trades and professions (see Swann 1989; Aitken 1998; Russell and Taylor 2010).[1]

It is important that we do not overlook the role of the state as a corporate sponsor of art and photography, and of course the GPO and EMB were both quasi-autonomous arms of the British state. During the interwar period in the United States, there were important developments in the use of documentary photography. This was stimulated by the creation of a series of photo magazines, newspapers and the state sponsorship of photographers during the Depression years of the 1930s through the Works Progress Administration (WPA) and later the Farm Security Administration (FSA). The FSA photography provided pictures that would support the work of the Resettlement Administration. Under the directorship of Roy Stryker, dozens of photographers recorded conditions of farmers, the unemployed and the working poor across America (Hurley 1972). The resultant images, which have become icons of American life during this time, were made available to magazines and newspapers. Importantly, the wide range of subjects covered by photographers included 'race', gender, domestic work as well as paid employment. The FSA collection was later housed in the US Library of Congress and amounts to 165,000 prints, a further 265,000 negatives, as well as 1,600 colour slides (Daniel *et al.* 1987; Orvell 2003). Aside from these pictures of working life and social conditions, the photographers were important as many went on to produce further images of work and labour in a variety of genres including corporate and propaganda settings. The US government was also a huge sponsor of non-photographic depictions of labour. For instance, the New Deal Programme established in 1934 a section that commissioned art for federal buildings. As Melissa Dabakis notes:

> Within New Deal visual culture, the image of the industrial worker took center stage. Borrowing from the tradition of worker imagery ... public images were deployed to new ends – most notably, but not always, as propaganda for federal programs. In so doing, the image of the heroic worker bolstered the notions of American individualism and self-sufficiency at the same time that it promoted the expanding role of the state in social welfare.
>
> *(1999: 223)*

Erika Doss (2002) has written an important overview of some of this material and, in particular, the way it portrays work and labour. As is so often the case, Doss is an art historian rather than a sociologist, emphasizing the absence of more sociologically focused attempts to theorize and understand visual material. Of critical importance when examining corporate photography is the need to keep a series of questions in mind about the intent of the commissioning body, the choice of subjects, the limits placed on artistic freedom and the subsequent selection, editing and cropping of material. All of these aspects of the production process of corporate photography are not neutral, but rather deliberate choices made by different people. We also need to be aware of the reuse and recycling of images. Good examples of reuse can be seen in the reissue of nostalgic collections mentioned above. In a recent paper, American Studies scholar David Gray (2006) highlights the way images produced as part of FSA projects were cropped and captioned for reuse as US propaganda posters during World War II. The point to stress as sociologists here is not simply to develop a critical awareness of image manipulation; it is also that, in discovering more about the process of fabrication, we come to a deeper understanding of the way labour is presented, represented and how these images are received (see Hurley 1980 for an overview).

Post-war images

Some of the most stunning corporate photography dates from the period after World War II. The reasons for this are complex and linked to economic, political and social factors.

In part, corporations felt the need to develop strong visual identities, often to improve their images in a post-war period dominated by welfare states and a sense that industrial relations were now to be less conflictual after the collective sacrifices of the war years (see Fones-Wolf 1994). At times, corporations such as Standard Oil (see Harper 2001) had to repair their reputations with the political class as well as the public. Harper describes the way Standard Oil commissioned a range of photographers during and after World War II to take pictures of rural life where their oil products were being used. This was to soften the company's image dented by their secret pre-war agreement with the German firm I.G. Farben. As Harper notes:

> Plattner quotes a Standard Oil official responsible for the project as asserting that the photographs were 'to concentrate on "the human part" of the company's work, particularly the everyday lives of its workers and their families … [to] foster the impression in the public mind that Standard Oil was composed of "human beings like everybody else" … Standard Oil sought to project a public image as a company that 'is a good citizen … that always works in the public interest.'
>
> *(quoted in Harper 2001: 8)*

Harper's *Changing Works* makes extensive use of these images in various ways for illustration and as part of the interviews he carries out for his own later project. On both sides of the Atlantic, companies spent considerable sums on photography to promote their products, goods and services and in the process employed some of the most talented photographers of the day. These include photographers such as the German Walter Nurnberg (1954), who worked for the steel, textiles and brewing industries among others; Maurice Broomfield (2009), whose work included photography for the steel, engineering, paper and textile industries and was responsible for the so-called 'New Look' in industrial photography; and the American Arthur D'Arazien (2002), who is best known for his stunning images of the North American steel industry. These photographers and others produced images of organizations and the work processes for a variety of purposes. Like Standard Oil, these companies were attempting to go beyond simply recording what went on in their factories, mills and shops. They were attempting to communicate a range of stories about what they did and the value it had for the wider community. These images also help to contribute to a narrative of the value placed on work and industry in the post-war period; they speak to a desire to project and build a positive image of organizations and work but also of an audience ready and willing to consume such images.

It is important that we look beyond still photography in this discussion. One of the defining things about the decades after World War II was the flowering of industrial filmmaking. This is a huge field in its own right. As we saw above, the roots of post-war industrial film in the UK can be seen in the pre-war DFM, headed by John Grierson (see Aitken 1990; Swann 1989). The DFM produced many films on a range of social and economic themes but often dwelt on organizational and corporate issues; this was not surprising since their funding came from public and private corporations. Many of those involved in the pre-war DFM themselves later graduated into corporate filmmaking after 1945. These films were commissioned both by the public and private sectors in the UK. For example, nationalized industries commissioned or funded many films in the 1940s through to the 1960s and 1970s. These were sometimes training films but often were meant as short features to be played in cinemas and church halls. Their aim was to explain industrial processes and organizational change, stressing, in the case of the state-owned industries, the value of nationalization and the efficiency it would bring (see Russell and Taylor 2010). This trend was by no means exclusive to the UK with corporate filmmaking common in Europe and North America during the period (see, for example, Hediger and Vonderau 2009).

Both still and moving images were part of sophisticated and highly creative public relations strategies adopted in the period. But it would be wrong to see these images as crude propaganda, certainly in the case of the UK (see Fones-Wolf 1994 for a discussion of the context in the USA). Often the artists who made these images were informed by left politics with social consciousness and, likewise, they were often afforded huge amounts of discretion as to the style and content of their art. For these reasons, many of the images from the 1950s and 1960s retain their power because of the production values that created them.

Visualizing work and organizations in decline

One of the fascinating features of the last three decades for those interested in issues of work and organization has been the process of deindustrialization. Arguably, the visual has played an important part in charting this process and shaping the reaction to it. Deindustrialization paradoxically tells us a lot about work and organizations. The empty buildings and vacant lots serve both as reminders and prompts for thinking about the nature and value of employment. Visual images of deindustrialized sites, especially certain Rust Belt cities such as Detroit, for example, proliferate in today's media. Clearly, there are marked differences between such accounts. An early example of this genre was *Journey to Nowhere: The Saga of the New Underclass* by Dale Maharidge, who worked alongside photographer Michael Williamson to record the effect of job loss and industrial change in the USA. Originally published in 1985, *Journey to Nowhere* illustrates both the journeys laid-off workers made to find new jobs as well as the settlements destroyed as a result of economic change. In a later edition of the book, Bruce Springsteen writes a powerful introduction, telling of how he was inspired late one night to produce his own representation of labour in his songs 'Youngstown' and 'The New Timer' on his album *The Ghost of Tom Joad* (see also Maharidge and Williamson 2011).

The pictures of abandonment are certainly beautiful and aesthetically rich. What often marks out later books on deindustrialization is the absence of people in the images chosen. James Jeffery Higgins' (1999) *Images of the Rust Belt* is a good example of this trend, with the nearly 50 colour plates completely devoid of people, even in the context where part or the entire site being photographed is still active. It is also important to note that this desire to capture abandoned industrial space is not unique to the USA. In Britain, for example, we could point to Julian Germain's *Steelworks* (1990), which takes for its subject the town of Consett in the northeast of England; *Ming Jue* (2008) by Stuart Whipps, which shows the abandoned former Rover car plant in Birmingham (as well as its rebirth in China); and finally *Billancourt* by Bon and Stéphani (2003), showing inside and external images of a disused Renault plant near Paris just prior to its demolition.

In the USA, there are a growing number of urban explorer-inspired[2] coffee-table books in part or exclusively about former industrial space, and nowhere is more explored than Detroit, which may no longer produce the world's cars, but does provide the raw material for countless books on ruins. These include *The Ruins of Detroit* by Marchand and Meffre (2011); *Lost Detroit: The Stories Behind the Motor City's Majestic Ruins* by Dan Austin and Sean Doerr (2010); and *Detroit Disassembled* by photographer Andrew Moore (2010). Other examples of the genre would include *Forbidden Places: Exploring our Abandoned Heritage* by Margaine and Margaine (2009); Dan Dubowitz (2010) *Wastelands*; and *Beauty in Decay* by RomanyWG (2011). Trying to summarize these publications is difficult because they are so varied and are designed for different audiences. Some are clearly academic, others are meant as local and regional or even industrial history. Others fall into the category of fine art that happens to draw on industrial subjects. Related to this type of account are those by and for the urban explorer movement.

The commentary in each is similarly varied with some giving a great deal of attention to the former industries and people that the ruins once housed, and this can be even true of those books aimed at a fine art audience. Julian Germain's book, for example, combines his images of Consett post-closure with a wide variety of professional and amateur photography, which tells a complex narrative of this former steel town. Often, these books will include forewords or more substantive pieces either reflecting simply on the photographs or providing a wider analysis of the context of closure. The value of these books and publications in the context of this chapter is that they add a new dimension to the way we can read organizations visually. One of the best theorizations of the power and role of ruins can be seen in the writing of Tim Edensor (2005). In *Industrial Ruins*, he reflects of the meaning and role of abandoned industrial sites and importantly theorizes both the physicality of space as well as the absent labour that formerly populated the buildings he encounters. As he notes:

> photographs are never merely visual but in fact conjure up synaesthetic and kinaesthetic effects, for the visual provokes other sensory responses. The textures and tactilities, smells, atmospheres and sounds of ruined spaces, together with the signs and objects they accommodate, can be empathetically conjured up by visual material in the absence of any realistic way of conveying these sensations, other than through words and images.
>
> *(Edensor 2005: 16)*

We need to think expansively about the range and quality of visual material on offer to us on the subject of work and organizations. Such material is not always obvious, and is often produced by artists and others for very different reasons than ours here (see, for example, Chatterley *et al.* 2000). The point, though, is that photography and other visual media make an intervention that is different to the written text; it allows access to different meanings and understandings. Mention of Edensor brings us nicely to the point where we can discuss the more formally sociological account of work in and through visual media.

Visual sociology and work

In this part of the chapter, I want to develop this discussion further by looking at the way sociologists look at work and organizations, and how they actually produce accounts of work visually through their own practice. An early example of a sociologist using visual material to look at work is Francis Klingender and his pioneering *Art and the Industrial Revolution* (1972 [1947]), which examined the impact of new technology and industry on the English landscape (see also Pooke 2008). It is possible to argue that a visual sociology of work really begins to emerge during the 1980s, as part of a more general interest on the part of sociologists in the visual (see, for example, Rose 2012; Chaplin 1994; see Strangleman 2004, 2008 for a review). Work sociologists had used visual approaches before this time, Berger and Mohr's (1975) *A Seventh Man* dealing with migrant labour is a good example. Images of labour had also been used as illustration in studies of work: Jeremy Tunstall's (1962) *The Fishermen* is extensively illustrated with pictures of labour being carried out at sea and on land. Another example would be Ray Pahl's (1984) *Divisions of Labour*. The point is that the visual is not a method of research or analysis as such, but does represent more than simple illustration.

In the UK, an early sociological pioneer who did adopt visual approaches in a more developed sense was Huw Beynon. Known most famously for his ethnography of a car plant *Working for Ford* (1973), he is less well remembered for his book with photographer Nick Hedges *Born to Work* (Hedges and Beynon 1982). After the passage of three decades, *Born to Work* is both dated and remarkably fresh. The book acts as a time capsule revealing in its pages a lost world of work, exploring in its images the life-world of labour in light manufacturing in the English West Midlands. This was the same terrain on which Paul Willis' (1977) 'lads' began their working life in *Learning to Labour*, and the same industrial space that was decimated during the 1980s (Dolby *et al.* 2004). Crucially, the book is a combination of words and pictures: the one exemplifying the other. The images used here are not simple eye-wipes, introduced to break up text. Nor is the text there to act as an extended caption for the photographs themselves. Perhaps one of the most notable things about *Born to Work* is that it seems to have had so little influence on industrial or work sociology; this is even more inexplicable given Beynon's central place in that sub-discipline. This lack of influence is possibly due to the conservatism of work sociology and the discipline more widely (see Strangleman 2005; Halford and Strangleman 2009).

An example of where academics explore what the visual adds to research is the collaboration of photographer Bill Bamberger and English scholar Cathy Davidson on their 1998 book *Closing: The Life and Death of an American Factory*, which tells the story of the end of production at the White Furniture Company factory in North Carolina. Mixing images with interview material from the workers and interweaving this with a history of the plant, *Closing* is a model of how narrative and imagery can be combined to increase our understanding and empathy with the subjects of study. The authors used the photography at the end of the book to stimulate final reflection from the workers sometime after closure occurred and this is perhaps the most poignant part of the volume. Here workers' life narratives embedded in and by work and then disembedded by layoff speak to a sense of loss not simply at the level of community but also at the level of the nation. There is a sense here of mourning for a lost industrial era. In an epilogue entitled 'Does anybody *make* anything anymore', Davidson writes:

> White's wasn't perfect, and none of the workers says it was. Yet metaphors of death run through the comments so many of the workers make about the closing precisely because people felt that something of themselves died when White Furniture closed.
> *(Bamberger and Davidson 1998: 168)*

Any discussion of the visual sociology of work has to consider the writing of American visual sociologist Douglas Harper. Through a series of books and articles, Harper has used work as a focus around which he explores what the visual can add to a sociological understanding of social forms and practice. His engagement with work as a subject began tangentially with his *Good Company* (1982), a study of tramping and the world of the tramp (see also the revised and expanded edition, Harper 2006). His later book *Working Knowledge* (1987) was an in-depth study of a mechanic in a small machine shop. Harper, using photo elicitation techniques, sought to understand notions of skill and working knowledge embedded in an experienced worker. More recently still, Harper's (2001) *Changing Works*, mentioned previously, was a comparative study in mechanization and rural agricultural life and labour. This again used a range of visual techniques including photo elicitation but included the use of images from a corporate archive. This sense in which Harper shifts the focus of his research between different types of work and also in the mix of the visual techniques he employs has produced a rich body of material. This variety helps capture both different forms of work but also different moments of economic life, freezing and making intelligible elements of culture and interaction, the detailed minutiae of labour and in the process gains important insights into work identity and meaning.

There are a variety of work and organizational sociologists now using visual approaches as part of their teaching and research. Examples include Carol Wolkowitz (2006) in her pioneering

Bodies at Work, which employs visual material and approaches in looking at a range of body work; and organizational sociologist Susan Halford, who draws on visual material in a number of her studies (Halford and Knowles 2005). Other organizational sociologists working in the field include videoethnographers such as Heath and Luff (2000; see also Hindmarsh 2009 for a review). In my own work, I make extensive use of visual material and methods. In my research on the Guinness brewery at Park Royal in West London, I combine various photographic and other material, which has been self-generated, taken by photographers I have collaborated with or derived from company archives (see Stangleman 2010, 2012).

How do we make sense of the visual and work?

So far, we have seen a variety of examples of the visual interrogation of work by a great range of people, both academics and non-academics. We have seen that work has been a recurring subject that has attracted people researching in visual media. In this section, I want to examine how we make sense of this material, asking questions about how we analyse it and what uses we can put it to for a sociological understanding of work and organizations. It will look at the visual as illustration, in reflection theory, content analysis, photo elicitation, semiology and iconology, and visual ethnography.

As illustration

We could look at the visual record of work in terms of illustration, as representing an historical record of bygone ways of working or organizational structure. What all visual media have in common is that they freeze in time an image of work or a workplace. We can return to them to learn a variety of things. There has been an understandable tendency to downplay this aspect of the visual as, quite rightly, we have learned to be suspicious of images as telling a 'truth'. We expect to ask questions about the choice of subject, the selection of the field, the cropping and framing, all of which leads us to a sophisticated rejection of images as 'simply' doing anything. While we must be alert to all of these points, we should not dismiss the important potential of the image archive to provide us with a rich array of historical material ranging from images of vast spaces of production through to detailed studies of craft skill and knowledge. Although ironically this is probably the most common form in which the visual makes an appearance in work sociology, at least historically, it is also the least reflected on (see Burke 2001; Samuel 1994; Miller 1992). As we saw above, many sociological publications concerned with work do employ visual material. In the 1960s and through to the 1980s, this was not really reflected on as deeply as it might have been. In many ways, work sociology, and the wider discipline for that matter, lacked the critical language to interrogate and make use of visual material in any sustained way. There was arguably a deep-rooted suspicion of images and what one could say with them, linked to an overwhelming desire to privilege text-based evidence (see Stasz 1979; for an account of British sociological historiography, see also Savage 2010).

Reflection theory

This leads us on to reflection theory itself. Victoria Alexander provides us with a useful definition of the approach: 'Researchers who study visual documents, especially media texts, often rely implicitly on "reflection theory". They believe that visual documents mirror, or tell us something about, society' (2008: 464).

It is important to note that reflection theory alerts us to the relationship between an image and the society that produces and consumes it, but does not establish an objective account of the truth. Rather, reflection theory allows us to study how a society's values, fact, fiction and fantasy may be read into a particular image or collection. The sociology of work and organizations can look at a set of images and start to ask questions about what this tells about work in the past. What are the aesthetic tropes drawn on, why was an image produced, by whom was it commissioned, and what was the intended audience? Reflection theory – although that term is very rarely used by sociologists of work – alongside illustration are historically the most commonly adopted approaches to images. Theoretically, sociologists have tended to look to other disciplines for a visual vocabulary. Interestingly, it is the increasing presence of other sub-disciplines in the area of work that has introduced a greater confidence to reflect on visual material; the best illustration of this is in the case of the sociology of the body (see Wolkowitz 2006).

Content analysis

An approach related to reflection theory is that of content analysis. Here the researcher takes a sample of material from an archive and tries to discern patterns within the content. A good illustration of this would be if one were interested in looking at front covers of company or trade union publications. The researcher could look at a selection, or indeed all of a run, of magazines. You could look for patterns, similarities and differences across time. You could ask questions about the types of things that feature on the covers: do these include people, if so, what sort of people – men, women, what is the presence of ethnic minorities? Of course, if you had the time and resources, you could extend your analysis to the inside of the magazines themselves (see Wall 2008). Both Sekula (1983) and Nye (1985) are good examples of where researchers tackle the question of how to make sense of large archives of material on work. In Nye's *Image Worlds*, for example, he explores the problem of how to think analytically and critically about a huge corporate archive:

> I therefore took the entire archives as my subject. It made no sense, however, to view the photographs in isolation, as matters of pure form. I began to examine the company's publications to see where different images had appeared and to see what sorts of stories accompanied them. These in turn led me into the literature of technological history. At the same time I moved in quite a different direction to understand photography as a technology and as a means of communication. Thus the research bifurcated, and I began to see the archives in two quite different ways. Corporate and institutional history offered one analytical framework; the literatures on photography, communication, and semiotic theory suggested another.
>
> *(1985: x–xi)*

There are a number of points to be made here. Material can be ordered and understood in many different ways. In part, this ordering is a function of the disciplinary background and the literature the researcher uses. The quote also shows how the study of corporate photography is inherently interdisciplinary in terms of methods, approach and the substantive subject of the archive – in Nye's case, electrical engineering and machinery. In this sense, we cannot be just an historian, sociologist or semiologist. The richness of an interpretation emerges from a willingness to combine and transcend disciplinary silos.

Photo elicitation

Again, a related method is that of photo elicitation whereby images (usually photographs) are explicitly deployed as part of the interview process itself. The images elicit ideas, reflections and comments from the interviewee, and are a useful probe to garner more information than would usually be the case. There are a number of examples where this has been applied to studies of work and organization; the various projects in which Douglas Harper has been involved are perhaps the best examples. Importantly, photo elicitation techniques have the added advantage that they create a more democratic relationship between interviewer and interviewee; as Harper says:

> The researcher gains a phenomenological sense as the informant explains what the objects in the photograph mean, where they have come, or developed from, and what elements may be missing, or what photographs in a sequence may be missing. This method provides a way in which the interview can move from the concrete (a cataloguing of the objects in the photograph) to the socially abstract (what the objects in the photograph mean to the individual being interviewed).
>
> *(Harper 1986: 25)*

Bolton *et al.* (2001) provide another example of photo elicitation techniques where researchers gave child worker respondents cameras and then interviewed them using the images they had taken as a basis for the discussion about their lived reality and meanings. In their essay 'The visual and the verbal', David Byrne and Aidan Doyle use visual images of industrial landscape as an integral aspect of their method. They were especially interested in the salience of images of coalmining landscapes and the effect on the local communities they studied. Using images of destruction and ruin, they ran focus groups of local residents of deindustrialized spaces, attempting to get at 'structures of feeling' and the 'actual lived experience of change' (Byrne and Doyle 2004: 167). As they argue: 'Images of change – images of how things had been and how they are now – could be used to elicit people's response to those changes' (ibid.).

In all these examples, what is valuable here is precisely the subjective understandings that photographic and other types of images offer up. The images bring to life latent ideas about aspects of experience. This type of methodological approach is one, in all its variety, that is becoming increasingly popular with sociologists of work.

Semiology, semiotics and iconology

Perhaps the least used form of visual analysis in terms of work sociology are the various forms of analytic deconstruction associated with semiology, semiotics and iconology. Such an approach allows the researcher to think in detail about how an image is constructed and how it works, as in how meanings are attached to symbols. This allows us to understand and appreciate the taken-for-granted assumptions about images and their meanings. Work and organizations are subjects that have produced powerful images across the years as we have seen, and this type of approach is a significant one for understanding the relationship between society and the economic sphere (see Rose 2012). David Nye's *Image Worlds* is a good example of where a researcher has used semiotic approaches in combination with other methods. The issue with these detailed deconstructive techniques is that they may not allow the researcher to do justice to the sheer volume of a particular archive. Nye tells how he produced a catalogue of 7,000 images from the General Electric archives, stressing that this was a selection from one million photographs.

Visual ethnography

Finally, sociologists of work have used what is known as visual ethnography to explore the topic of work. This takes a number of forms such as videoethnography, where researchers record workplaces to understand the relationship between formal and informal work cultures, detailed interaction and the relationship between the said and the unsaid in workplace interaction (see Heath and Luff 2000; Hindmarsh 2009). Some studies use still photography to explore the workplace; often the images are used to expand the ethnographic imagination and add to the richness of the evidence and analysis. Finally, a popular version of visual ethnography is to ask one's respondents to take images of their own workplace. These images are then used in photo elicitation interviews to gain greater insight into the complexity of organizational life.

Conclusions

This chapter has done a number of things. It set out to examine how the visual study of work had emerged in the nineteenth century as a by-product of the desire on the part of Victorians to better understand their society. There was a concern with the social condition of people brought on by the rapid expansion of industry and creation of large cities. A variety of visual media helped in this recording and examination from engraving and mapping through photography and film. Later still, we saw the way in which the visual was drawn upon by corporations to promote their own self-image to consumers and others, and they also used images to rationalize, control and organize work and their employees. The chapter then looked at the ways social scientists have used the visual in order to better understand work in a variety of ways – as historical record, as mode of investigation, as stimulus to reflection or as a tool of analysis.

The visual offers the sociologist of work a very powerful way of understanding work historically. By drawing on photography and other visual media, we can understand far more about how work is organized, carried out and managed as well as opening up knowledge about the meanings and identities that have attached to labour. By exploring formal archives as well as private collections, we gain insight into how work is valued, perceived, made up and received by different actors. We learn about the politics of production as well as those of consumption. We come to a fuller appreciation of the changing meaning of work for society across time and space.

Contemporary society is saturated with images of work and organizations. We live in an incredibly rich visual moment and are privileged in our unprecedented ability to access archival material bequeathed to us from previous generations of image makers. The Internet has opened up a treasure trove of corporate photography and films are readily available to study and enjoy. All of these developments mean that sociologists of work have immense possibilities to understand work in so many new and exciting ways. The visual is a powerful way to unlock cultural and social meanings in and around employment. It allows new ways to explore how organizations develop and promote themselves, how this changes over time and also how they used visual methods to rationalize their own systems of organization. What is also exciting is that, while the social science of the visual is over a century and a half old, it still seems a very new area.

Notes

1 The British Film Institute has recently issued a comprehensive collection of 40 British Documentary Films on DVD, *Land of Promise: The British Documentary Movement 1930–1950*. See also two further

collections from the BFI, *Portrait of a Miner*, a collection of films from the *National Coal Board Collection* (2009), and *Tales from the Shipyard* (2011).
2 Urban explorers are individuals or groups who visit industrial and other ruins and in the process often take still or moving images. For more details, see Ninjalicious (2005).

References

Aitken, I. (1990) *Film and Reform: John Grierson and the Documentary Film Movement*, London: Routledge.
Aitken, I. (ed.) (1998) *The Documentary Film Movement: An Anthology*, Edinburgh: Edinburgh University Press.
Alexander, V. (2008) 'Analysing visual materials', in N. Gilbert (ed.) *Researching Social Life*, London: Sage.
Austin, D. and Doerr, S. (2010) *Lost Detroit: The Stories Behind the Motor City's Majestic Ruins*, Charleston: History Press.
Bales, K. (2011) 'Charles Booth's survey of life and labour of the people in London 1889–1903', in M. Bulmer, K. Bales, and K.K. Sklar (eds) *The Social Survey in Historical Perspective 1880–1940*, Cambridge: Cambridge University Press.
Bamberger, B. and Davidson, C. (1998) *Closing: The Life and Death of an American Factory*, New York: Norton.
Berger, J. and Mohr, J. (1975) *A Seventh Man: The Story of a Migrant Worker in Europe*, London: Penguin.
Beynon, H. (1973) *Working for Ford*, London: Penguin.
Bolton, A., Pole, C. and Mizen, P. (2001) 'Picture this: researching child workers', *Sociology* 35(2): 501–518.
Bon, F. and Stéphani, A. (2003) *Billancourt*, Paris: Editions Cercle d'Art.
Broomfield, M. (2009) *Photographs*, London: Foto8.
Brown, E. (2005) *The Corporate Eye: Photography and the Rationalization of American Commercial Culture, 1884–1929*, Baltimore: The Johns Hopkins University Press.
Bryan, F. (2003) *Rouge: Pictured in its Prime*, Dearborn: Ford Books.
Burke, P. (2001) *Eyewitnessing: The Use of Images as Historical Evidence*, London: Reaktion.
Byrne, D. and Doyle, A. (2004) 'The visual and the verbal', in C. Knowles and P. Sweetman (eds) *Picturing the Social Landscape: Visual Methods and the Sociological Imagination*, London: Routledge.
Cabadas, J. (2004) *River Rouge: Ford's Industrial Colossus*, St Paul: MBI Publishing.
Chaplin, E. (1994) *Sociology and Visual Representation*, London: Routledge.
Chatterley, C., Rouverol, A. and Cole, S. (2000) *'I Was Content and Not Content': The Story of Linda Lord and the Closing of Penobscot Poultry*, Carbondale: Southern Illinois University Press.
Cohen, S. (2011) 'The Pittsburgh survey and the social survey movement: a sociological road not taken', in M. Bulmer, K. Bales and K.K. Sklar (eds) *The Social Survey in Historical Perspective 1880–1940*, Cambridge: Cambridge University Press.
Corbett, M. (2008) 'Towards neuroscientific management? Geometric chronophotography and the thin-slicing of the labouring body', *Management and Organizational History* 3(2): 107–125.
Corwin, S. (2003) 'Picturing efficiency: precisionism, scientific management, and the effacement of labour', *Representations* 84: 139–165.
Dabakis, M. (1999) *Visualizing Labor: American Sculpture*, Cambridge: Cambridge University Press.
Daniel, P., Foresta, M., Stange, M. and Stein, S. (1987) *Official Images: New Deal Photography*, Washington: Smithsonian Institution Press.
D'Arazien, A. (2002) *Big Picture: The Artistry of D'Arazien*, Kent, OH: Kent State University Press.
Doherty, J. (ed.) (1981) *Women at Work: 153 Photos by Lewis Hine*, New York: Dover.
Dolby, N., Dimitriadis, G. and Willis, P. (eds) (2004) *Learning to Labor in New Times*, London: Routledge Falmer.
Doss, E. (2002) 'Design, culture, identity: the Wolfsonian Collection', *The Journal of Decorative and Propaganda Arts* 24: 230–257.
Dubowitz, D. (2010) *Wastelands*, Stockport: Dewi Lewis Publishing.
Edensor, T. (2005) *Industrial Ruins: Space, Aesthetics and Materiality*, Oxford: Berg.
Fones-Wolf, E. (1994) *Selling Free Enterprise: The Business Assault on Labor and Liberalism 1945–60*, Chicago: University of Illinois.
Germain, J. (1990) *Steelworks: Consett, from Steel to Tortilla Chips*, London: Why Not Publishing.
Goldberg, V. (1999) *Lewis Hine: Children at Work*, New York: Prestel.
Gray, D. (2006) 'New uses for old photos: renovating FSA photographs in World War II posters', *American Studies* 47(3/4): 5–34.

Gutman, J. (1967) *Lewis Hine and the American Social Conscience*, New York: Walker.
——(1974) *Lewis Hine 1874–1940: Two Perspectives*, New York: Grossman.
Halford, S. and Knowles, C. (2005) 'More than words: some reflections on working visually', *Sociological Research Online* 10(1).
Halford, S. and Strangleman, T. (2009) 'In search of the sociology of work: past present and future', *Sociology* 43(5): 811–828.
Harper, D. (1982) *Good Company*, Chicago: Chicago University Press.
——(1986) 'Meaning and work: a study in photo elicitation', *Current Sociology* 34(3): 24–46.
——(1987) *Working Knowledge: Skill and Community in a Small Shop*, Berkeley: University of California Press.
——(2001) *Changing Works: Visions of a Lost Agriculture*, Chicago: Chicago University Press.
——(2006) *Good Company: A Tramp Life*, Boulder: Paradigm.
Heath, C. and Luff, P. (2000) *Technology in Action*, Cambridge: Cambridge University Press.
Hedges, N. and Beynon, H. (1982) *Born to Work: Images of Factory Life*, London: Pluto.
Hediger, V. and Vonderau, P. (eds) (2009) *Films that Work: Industrial Film and the Productivity of Media*, Amsterdam: Amsterdam University Press.
Higgins, J. (1999) *Images of the Rust Belt*, Kent: Kent State University Press.
Hindmarsh, J. (2009) 'Work and the moving image: past, present and future', *Sociology* 43(5): 990–996.
Hine, L. (1977) *Men at Work*, New York: Dover.
Hurley, F.J. (1972) *Portrait of a Decade: Roy Stryker and the Development of Documentary Photography in the Thirties*, Baton Rouge: Louisiana State University Press.
——(ed.) (1980) *Industry and the Photographic Image: 153 Great Prints from 1850 to the Present*, New York: Dover.
Jerrold, B. and Doré, G. (2006 [1869]) *London: A Pilgrimage*, London: Anthem.
Klingender, F. (1972 [1947]) *Art and the Industrial Revolution*, St Albans: Paladin.
Langer, F. (1998) *Lewis W. Hine: The Empire State Building*, London: Prestel.
Maharidge, D. (1985) *Journey to Nowhere: The Saga of the New Underclass*, New York: Hyperion.
Maharidge, D. and Williamson, M. (2011) *Someplace Like America: Tales from the New Great Depression*, Berkeley: University of California.
Marchand, R. (1998) *Creating the Corporate Soul: The Rise of Public Relations and Corporate Imagery in American Big Business*, Berkeley: University of California Press.
Marchand, Y. and Meffre, R. (2011) *The Ruins of Detroit*, Göttingen: Steidl.
Margaine, S. and Margaine, D. (2009) *Forbidden Places: Exploring our Abandoned Heritage*, Tours: Jonglez.
Mayhew, H. (1985 [1865]) *London Life and the London Poor*, London: Penguin.
Miller, J.H. (1992) *Illustration*, London: Reaktion.
Moore, A. (2010) *Detroit Disassembled*, Akron: Akron Art Museum.
Ninjalicious (2005) *Access All Areas: A User's Guide to the Art of Urban Exploration*, Infiltration.
Nurnberg, W. (1954) *Men and Machines*, London: Keliher Hudson and Kearns.
Nye, D. (1985) *Image Worlds: Corporate Identity at General Electric*, Cambridge: MIT Press.
Olsen, B. and Cabadas, J. (2002) *The American Auto Factory*, St Paul: MBI Publishing.
Orvell, M. (1995) *After the Machine: Visual Arts and the Erasing of Cultural Boundaries*, Jackson: University Press of Mississippi.
——(2003) *American Photography*, Oxford: Oxford University Press.
Pahl, R. (1984) *Divisions of Labour*, Oxford: Blackwell.
Pooke, G. (2008) *Francis Klingender 1907–1955: A Marxist Art Historian Out of Time*, London: Gill Vista Marx Press.
Riis, J. (1998) *How the Other Half Lives*, London: Penguin.
RomanyWG (2011) *Beauty in Decay*, Darlington: Carpet Bombing Culture.
Rose, G. (2012) *Visual Methodologies: An Introduction to the Interpretation of Visual Materials*, 3rd ed., London: Sage.
Russell, P. and Taylor, J. (eds) (2010) *Shadows of Progress: Documentary Film in Post-war Britain*, Basingstoke: Palgrave.
Samuel, R. (1994) *Theatres of Memory: Past and Present in Contemporary Culture*, London: Verso.
Savage, M. (2010) *Identities and Social Change in Britain since 1940: The Politics of Method*, Oxford: Oxford University Press.
Sekula, A. (1983) 'Photography between labour and capital', in *Mining Photographs and Other Pictures: A Selection from the Negative Archives of Shedden Studio, Glace Bay, Cape Breton 1948–1968*, Glace Bay: NSCAD/UCCB Press.

Stasz, C. (1979) 'The early history of visual sociology', in J. Wagner (ed.) *Images of Information: Still Photography in the Social Sciences*, London: Sage.

Strangleman, T. (2004) 'Ways of (not) seeing work: The visual as a blind spot in WES?', *Work, Employment and Society* 18(1): 179–192.

——(2005) 'Sociological futures and the sociology of work', *Sociological Research Online* 10(4). Available at http://www.socresonline.org.uk/10/4/strangleman.html.

——(2008) 'Representations of labour: visual sociology and work', *Sociological Compass* 2(4): 1491–1505.

——(2010) 'Food, drink and the cultures of work: consumption in the life and death of an English factory', *Food, Culture and Society* 13(2): 257–278.

——(2012) 'Picturing work in an industrial landscape: visualising labour, place and space', *Sociological Research Online* 17(2). Available at http://www.socresonline.org.uk/17/2/20.html.

Swann, P. (1989) *The British Documentary Film Movement, 1926–1946*, Cambridge: Cambridge University Press.

Swanson, C. (2004) *Faces of Railroading: Portraits of America's Greatest Industry*, Waukesha: Kalmbach Publishing.

Trachtenberg, A. (1989) *Reading American Photographs: Images as History Mathew Brady to Walker Evans*, New York: Hill and Wang.

Tunstall, J. (1962) *The Fishermen: The Sociology of an Extreme Occupation*, London: MacGibbon and Kee.

Wall, C. (2008) 'Picturing an occupational identity: images of teachers in careers and trade union publications 1940–2000', *History of Education* 37(2): 317–340.

Whipps, S. (2008) *Ming Jue: Photographs of Longbridge and Nanjing*, Walsall: The New Art Gallery Walsall.

Willis, P. (1977) *Learning to Labour: How Working Class Kids Get Working Class Jobs*, Farnborough: Gower.

Wolkowitz, C. (2006) *Bodies at Work*, London: Sage.

Wollman, D. and Inman, D. (1999) *Portraits in Steel: An Illustrated History of Jones and Laughlin Steel Corporation*, Kent, OH: Kent State University Press.

Yeo, E. (1971) 'Mayhew as a social investigator', in E.P. Thompson and E. Yeo (eds) *The Unknown Mayhew: Selections from the Morning Chronicle 1849–50*, London: Penguin.

——(2011) 'The social survey in social perspective 1830–1930', in M. Bulmer, K. Bales and K.K. Sklar (eds) *The Social Survey in Historical Perspective 1880–1940*, Cambridge: Cambridge University Press.

Yochelson, B. (2001) *Jacob Riis*, London: Phaidon.

Part IV
Visual identities and practices

16
Arts-based interventions and organizational development
It's what you don't see

Ariane Berthoin Antal, Steven S. Taylor and Donna Ladkin

Recent years have witnessed a flurry of experimentation with processes that bring people, products and practices from the world of the arts into organizations of all kinds around the world (Darsø 2004; Berthoin Antal 2009; Laaksonen 2011; Schiuma 2011). The primary drivers behind these experiments with artistic interventions are a sense that there is an urgent need for new and innovative ways of developing organizations and that, through their ability to engage emotional and aesthetic ways of knowing, the arts can stimulate individual and collective learning and change (Schumpeter 2011; Taylor and Ladkin 2009; Strati 2010). The objective of this chapter is to explore the connections between the values and practices of organizational development[1] (OD), and those characterizing the emerging field of artistic interventions in organizations (sometimes also called arts-based initiatives (Schiuma 2011) or workarts (Barry and Meisiek 2010)). In doing so, the chapter demonstrates that both approaches enable assumptions and values to be revealed and thus worked with in explicit ways. However, the chapter also shows that artistic interventions can run the risk of allowing vital values and assumptions to remain invisible, and thus they may not fully realize their potential power as catalysts for change in organizations.

Our argument begins with a brief explication of the history of OD and the forces that have shaped its practices to set the scene for examining how artistic interventions have come to play a role within organization change initiatives. We then present two specific instances of such interventions in order to illustrate the ways visible and invisible aspects of their design and execution contribute to their eventual impact. Our analysis of the examples positions the visible artefacts as vehicles with which the participants – and we researchers – can gain access to the invisible features that play themselves out at the workplace: the values, diversity of interests and power dynamics. The chapter ends by discussing the implications of these examples for the stakeholders engaged in artistic interventions to more explicitly consider issues of transparency, visibility and invisibility in their design and enactment.

The values of OD

Given the strong similarities in the values that drove the birth of the OD movement and the humanistic values associated with the arts, today's artistic interventions in organizations might be considered a direct descendant, even a love-child, of OD pioneers. Art Kleiner (1996) characterized the beginnings of the OD movement in the late 1940s and 1950s as 'The Age of Heretics', because the founding generation dared to challenge the dominant views of organization and relations at work. David Jamieson and Christopher Worley summarize the context and the resultant aspirations succinctly:

> The practice of OD is more than 50 years old. Before World War II, organizations typically operated on principles of mechanistic and bureaucratic system, including authority and obedience, division of labor, hierarchical supervision, formalized procedures and rules, and impersonality (and many still do). After the war, increasing interest in social change, attitudes about democracy, and self-actualization brought distinctly different values that were a counterforce to the extant organizational values in use. OD grew in popularity by offering a more holistic view of people and organizations, with an emphasis on humanistic and democratic values and the belief that this different perspective was better not only for people but also for organization performance.
>
> *(2008: 100)*

The theory and practice of OD have not stood still since the inception of the field, spawning new approaches and intense debates about which features to keep or shed in light of changes in the socio-economic context and under the influence of ideas from scholars of human and organizational behaviour (Cummings 2008; Kegan 1971; Quinn and Sonenshein 2008). In 'second generation' OD (French and Bell 1999: 46), there has been a focus on organizational transformation, with interest in such areas as total quality management (TQM) and quality of working life (QWL), organizational culture, organizational learning, systems thinking, visioning and appreciative enquiry (French and Bell 1999: 46–50). One of the characteristics that the newer practices share is that 'instead of attempting to solely leverage techno-structural or human processes for change, they implicitly focus on meaning making, language and "discursive phenomena" as the central medium and target for changing mindsets and consciousness' (Marshak and Grant 2008: S11). In other words, a key informing principle of the OD field overall has been the commitment to render invisible forces within organizations, i.e. 'meaning-making', 'assumptions' and 'values', visible through processes that enable people within organizations to give voice to them. Newton Margulies and Anthony Raia enumerate those values particularly clearly:

1. Providing opportunities for people to function as human beings rather than as resources in the productive process.
2. Providing opportunities for each organization member, as well as for the organization itself, to develop to his full potential.
3. Seeking to increase the effectiveness of the organization in terms of all of its goals.
4. Attempting to create an environment in which it is possible to find exciting and challenging work.
5. Providing opportunities for people in organizations to influence the way in which they relate to work, the organization, and the environment.
6. Treating each human being as a person with a complex set of needs, all of which are important in his work and in his life.

(1972: 3)

In summary, the field of OD has matured and continues to spawn new ways of enabling learning and change in organizations. The humanistic values from the founding generation still inform the aspirations of many practitioners, impacting on how they undertake interventions. However, there are a number of pressures on the field and its ability to adhere to its founding principles. For instance, there is increasing demand for a stronger bottom-line orientation than at its outset. And, of course, there is often a demand for newness – the latest and greatest – which currently may be artistic interventions.

Artistic interventions in organizations

Large and small companies, as well as public sector and non-governmental organizations, are drawing on all forms of art – visual, performing, literary – as central features of interventions lasting a few hours, a couple of days, several months, or sometimes even years (for overviews, see Berthoin Antal 2009; Biehl-Missal 2011; Darsø 2004; Schnugg 2010). They entail bringing 'people, practices and products from the world of the arts into the world of organisations' with a more or less explicit orientation to stimulating collaborative learning processes (Berthoin Antal 2009: 4). In addition to these artistic interventions in organizations, there is also extensive use of the arts for individual training and development (Taylor and Ladkin 2009) as well as corporate art collections (Barry and Meisiek 2010). However, we limit our focus here to artistic interventions that seek to engage the larger organization much in the way OD efforts have.

It is important to point out a key distinction between the drivers of the OD movement and those involved with bringing artistic interventions into organizational settings. The founders of OD were largely academics with a strong interest in practice,[2] whereas a range of people, including artists, managers, intermediaries and policymakers, have been instrumental in bringing arts-based processes into organizations. Each of these different contributors has a particular reasoning and starting point for engaging in this work (Berthoin Antal 2009, 2011, forthcoming). What is interesting for our purposes here is to notice how those different, invisible agendas impact on the visible interventions they bring into organizational contexts.

The most visible interests on the agenda are those of the managers who invite artists into organizations. They have various motives for doing so, particularly developing creativity, communication and leadership skills of employees at various levels of the organization. Some managers may have no particular objective, but rather an open learning approach like 'let's see what happens' (Berthoin Antal 2012).

The artists who engage in artistic interventions do so for many reasons: some see in organizations the material and space with which to create art; others want to offer their skills to develop employees' creativity and communication skills and by doing so enhance an organization's capacity for innovation; some artists have socio-political motives and work in organizations in order to influence society more generally (Berthoin Antal 2009).

Of course, employees are intimately involved with the realization of artistic interventions but their interests remain largely invisible, having received little attention from research or from management. They are not positioned as drivers of the field, nor (to our knowledge) asked in advance whether they would like to participate in the process.[3] Their participation in interventions is sometimes mandatory (for example, when an intervention is designed for a specific unit, a whole organization, or a particular level of employees in an organization), and in other cases participation is (at least officially) voluntary. Depending on the art form and the method chosen by the artist and/or the provider, employees are sometimes involved in co-designing and running an intervention that management has chosen, and they are typically, but not always, asked after the fact how they felt about the experience.

Another set of actors with visible interests are the intermediaries, whose business it is to link the world of the arts with the world of organizations (such as TILLT in Sweden, Conexiones improbables in Spain and Interact in the UK (see Berthoin Antal 2011, 2012)), as well as the consulting companies that are enriching their services by involving artists in their change projects (such as KGD Kronberg in Germany and Ashridge Consulting in the UK).

An increasingly active stakeholder in the field are policymakers, who are discovering artistic interventions in organizations as potential sources of stimulation for innovation and competitiveness at the local, national and European level. They are pressing intermediaries to provide evidence of the effectiveness of artistic interventions, with the aim of persuading more managers to use them and to legitimize the use of public funds to support them.

We now turn to two specific artistic interventions in organizations to show some of the differences in values that this diversity of stakeholders and interests produces. In particular, we attend to the way invisible values become more visible through the way in which interventions unfold in practice. The first is the case of a theatre company hired for half a day by a CEO to work with employees on how the organization could better live its values. The second is a year-long 'artist-in-residence'[4] project in a manufacturing company, accompanied by an intermediary organization. Neither of the two cases was explicitly positioned as an OD project, although both could have made that claim.

A theatrical intervention

The CEO of a medium-sized French company in a knowledge-based industry wanted to address how the members of the organization could better live their values around diversity. He contacted a theatre company that specializes in artistic interventions, and, after briefing the director, provided him with the names and phone numbers of ten employees to call about their experiences in the organization. The way in which their responses would be used was not disclosed to those interviewed, in fact they were (mis)led to believe the interviews would be used for marketing purposes. He also arranged with the works council to use two-thirds of a day during an off-site event. Members of the theatre company developed scripts that encapsulated the preferred ways of enacting a more tolerant handling of diversity issues within the company, for which they drew on their knowledge of the subject in general, the outcomes of their interviews with employees, and additional input from the CEO. All the employees were required to attend the off-site event, but none knew what was planned for the day. The idea was to surprise the employees with an engaging way of addressing the serious matter of diversity in the workplace.

The off-site day opened with a brief introduction by the CEO, who then handed over the floor to the 'experts in diversity'. The employees soon realized that the speakers were actors and they started recognizing details about their own organization in the scene, which they found surprising and amusing. The introductory session was followed by a series of exercises that the actors led in small mixed groups, which the CEO had designated. The employees talked about their experiences at work with various aspects of diversity (gender, age, profession, class, country, etc.), from which they created sketches under the guidance of the actors. After lunch, the groups performed their sketches for the plenary. Not everybody had to play a role, but those who did act had to take a role that was unlike their normal position in the organization (e.g. the CEO played a secretary). At the end of the afternoon, the artists left and the CEO and the director of the supervisory board spoke to the employees. The CEO presented the organization's values in a new format and gave every employee a personally engraved wooden box with the values in a little booklet. He illustrated what he meant by living the values with examples of situations in which he had recently acted inappropriately and situations in which employees had behaved in keeping with the values.

It is interesting to note the number of 'invisible' aspects of the organization that were rendered 'visible' through this intervention. First, the desired way of dealing with diversity issues was given a physical, visible form that people could observe. Its power was perhaps accentuated by its genesis from their own (until that moment) organizationally hidden viewpoints. The CEO's disclosures provided a material touchstone by which employees could compare their own behaviours with his. Finally, the small wooden box engraved with the company's values provided a material artefact upon which employees could reflect on an ongoing basis.

Interviews with the CEO, the director of the theatre company, and with numerous employees from different departments over the course of the following months revealed diverse thoughts and feelings about the experience as a learning event.[5] Most employees in the first round of interviews (several weeks after the event) were very enthusiastic: they had learned a lot about different ways their colleagues experienced things in the organization, the acting was daunting for some, but fun for others, and many mentioned how impressed they were with the untapped acting skills they had discovered among their colleagues. Many specifically mentioned how positively surprised they had been by the CEO participating alongside them and playing the role of secretary, which showed a human side they had not yet seen in him. Most people said that the speeches at the end of the day had been clear and they remembered the values. Only a few critical voices emerged in the first round of interviews, mostly around the perceived risk of acting in front of everyone in the organization, particularly in front of management, because acting engages the entire body, revealing the whole person.

Over the following months, repeated rounds of interviews with employees, sometimes including people from earlier rounds, revealed a gradual shift towards more critical perspectives on the experience. Nevertheless, positive responses dominated. A year later, employees remembered the fun and innovative aspects of the event. The little wooden boxes were visible in many people's offices. Employees still referred to the surprisingly human participation of the CEO in the role play. The CEO reflected that the shared experience of that off-site event had probably been a significant factor in the ability of the organization to collectively deal emotionally with a very serious accident that occurred during the year. Employees commented that his response to that event had been very caring.

Let us contrast this example of a short theatre-based artistic intervention with a longer intervention, in which interactions between the 'visible' and the 'invisible' are apparent and play important roles in the way in which the event was experienced.

Artist-in-residence[6]

The head of human resources for Scandinavia in a company that produces insulation materials was quite sceptical when he first heard about TILLT's year-long programme bringing an artist to work on an organization's challenges with employees.[7] But the presentation by the director of TILLT (a former dancer) was infectiously enthusiastic, and the very fact that it was an unusual method triggered him to take the idea seriously. Together with the other members of the board, and with the agreement of the unions, he formulated the objectives for the residency:

- increase knowledge and pride in being in an environmental company;
- increase pride in own work;

- increase cooperation across the board in the company;
- facilitate organizational and leadership development;
- increase innovation.

The employees were initially as sceptical about the idea of working with an artist as the human resource manager had been when he first heard about it. One of the employees who became a leader of the project remembered having been so irritated and bored by the idea that he had fallen asleep during the management's presentation of the project. However, he was struck that, when the artist entered the meeting, her energy changed the space and alerted people to the sense that something new and different could happen.

The artist started off in April by visiting all departments and all shifts. The project team put up special noticeboards for the project and idea boxes all around the factory. The project group then decided which to deal with. Among the proposed projects that they got off the ground before the summer were a documentation of work at the factory with photographs of employees, recording sounds in the factory, a competition for photography, short stories and poems.

After the summer vacation, there were kickoff events in a special tent. The idea was to bring people together from different parts of the plant not only to learn about the objectives and the action plan but also to engage with each other in new ways, initiated by the artist. One of the key problems facing this site was how to encourage employees from two different companies to work together after they had been merged as part of an acquisition. Employees who had competed against each other for generations were now expected to work together. Resentment dominated as employees from the two former companies refused to interact together at work, let alone cooperate.

The kickoff exercises involved a lot of physical contact – the artist felt it was important to break the ice and to get people to have fun at work. Everyone in the company participated in these kickoff events in groups of 40. Employees reported that the impact was powerful. 'Imagine, some had not even shaken hands in over 30 years, but you can't walk past anyone any more in the company and pretend they are not there after you have been cheek to cheek with them!'

The human resource manager and the employees interviewed agreed that this project got conversations going between the two plants on the site that had not been possible beforehand – 'people can now address issues that had not been discussable before' – including sharing shift work.

What was the role of the artist? An employee remembered that the artist had presented herself as a 'cultural project catalyst'. Most of the ideas for activities in the project came from the employees, but they all stressed that 'she was the energy'. One of them explained: 'We've been here for many years, we know the routines. We know how the collective mind works. We needed someone to open the box, even throw the box away.' The artist in this case, as in most other TILLT projects, does not create art in the process, she 'brings in my artistic way of working and my artistic energy'. One way of thinking about what the artist contributed is that, through her very way of being, she demonstrated the possibility of acting differently – with enthusiasm and vitality. As an intermediary person from TILLT explained, 'I see the artists as "the sand and oil in the machine" – it is important that they do both, and sometimes I have to push them to be more of the sand.' By her way of being in the world, the artist showed people how to be more of the 'sand' and 'oil'.

Looking back at the process and its outcomes, the artist's ambition to get 55 employees involved had not been completely met. As with any change initiative, there were a variety of reactions in assessing its impact. Some members of the project team felt that top management had not exhibited a degree of visibility that would have indicated the project to be of high priority. Others, however, felt that the fact the project had started top-down had impeded buy-in from other employees, particularly because there were other top-down projects running at the same time.

In retrospect, the employees saw that it had been helpful for the organization, but at the time they had not felt that it made their work easier in the change process. Overall, they agreed with the human resource manager that a significant cultural shift had happened on the site over the course of the year. A forklift operator was particularly eloquent in expressing what the artistic intervention project had offered the organization: 'Culture is what we do as humans that enriches our lives. We come to work to get the salary that allows us to lead our lives. We do our work, we take pride in it – why not enrich our lives at work too? We wanted to mix the worlds of work, which is cold, structured, in which we spend our days and the world of culture in which we spend our free time, which is human.'

Employees had plans to continue developing some of the creative projects that had been launched during the artistic intervention, and the company was looking into initiating projects in more sites in future.

The human resource manager was reluctant to attribute organizational effects directly to the artistic intervention, pointing out that many other activities had been undertaken during the same year. But he had been struck by the fact that the auditors had reported a significant shift in the way employees responded to their visit on site, showing much more interest and willingness to talk about their work than they had before the artistic intervention. Also, an increase of 24 per cent in efficiency in production had been recorded in this period. Lastly, he mentioned that the project had generated quite a bit of media interest in the company, which had not been an objective but that feedback had served to encourage people that they were doing something interesting.

In summary, this artistic intervention was intended to support a complex organizational change process on a production site, into which the artist brought energy that stimulated new ways of thinking and behaving. This intervention was effective at revealing and releasing pent-up, 'invisible' resentments, which had had a detrimental effect on people's working relationships, thus allowing them to work more collaboratively. The arts-based approach offers an additional dimension that reaches beyond traditional OD interventions: the artist's energy itself made visible an alternative approach to engaging with difficult issues within the company, providing material evidence that a different way was indeed possible. This energetic enactment seemed to create a lasting impression on employees at the company, as they remembered the way in which she seemed to catalyse them into a different way of engaging with their work and one another.

Discussion of the cases

These two examples are very different and thereby are characteristic of the field of artistic interventions in the sense that there are no 'typical' interventions. In the first case, the short intervention was managed by the CEO without the help of an intermediary. The artists left the scene after delivering their services and the transition from the artistic intervention to the presentation by management was seamless. In the second, the artist engaged with the organization over a year-long learning process and was supported by an experienced intermediary (TILLT). The extent to which the humanistic values specified above (Margulies and Raia 1972: 3) were lived up to in the cases differs significantly. In both organizations, the senior management made great efforts to make the artistic intervention happen and they evidently cared about their employees and their welfare in the organization. However, in one organization, the lack of transparency and of organized reflection on the experience contradicts the key values of OD, whereas the process in the other organization gave employees ample space to shape the intervention according to their needs and interests.

In neither case did management arrange for formal evaluations to assess the impact of the artistic intervention, but, in both cases, significant positive effects were mentioned in subsequent interviews with management and employees. These included unexpected side effects such as the enhanced ability of the CEO and other organizational members to deal with an accident, and the auditors' report of finding employees much more forthcoming in talking about their work in the company. In the first case, the manager seemed unaware of employees' concerns about the process and its effects. In the second case, there was open discussion in which employees expressed both agreement and disagreement with the perspective of management and management appeared to take those views on board. This observation may arise from the different contexts in which each case is set: one a production facility in a relatively egalitarian society; the other a knowledge-based company in a relatively hierarchical culture. In neither case did management, the employees or the artists seek to challenge the organizational power structure. However, in both cases, the employees felt that they had been able to say and do things that were not normally addressed or expected in the organizational culture. Furthermore, in the second case, the artistic intervention stimulated not only employees but also the plant managers from the previously competing companies to meet and talk in ways they had not previously done, thereby dismantling a power blockage that had affected the entire organization.

Opportunities and challenges ahead

The cases described here illustrate how artistic interventions in organizations can be used for organizational development even without the input of OD specialists in their design or realization. The effectiveness of both cases may lie in the activation of two of the potential advantages of working with the arts that Elliot Eisner has identified: 'through art we come to feel, very often, what we cannot see directly' (2008: 8) and 'images rendered in artistically expressive form often generate a kind of empathy that makes action possible' (ibid.: 11). In both cases, the employees discovered features of their colleagues (creativity, humanity) that they had not seen before, and the experience spurred them on to undertake interactions in the organization that they had not envisaged earlier.

Nevertheless, the cases are not unqualified OD successes and they help to specify some of the challenges in the field of artistic interventions relating specifically to the issues of what is and is not made visible. The theatre example, in particular, is problematic, namely the CEO's secretive approach that the artists colluded with and the lack of reflection in and on the process. There is in the field a naive temptation to assume that, because the arts are 'a way of enriching our awareness and expanding our humanity' (Eisner 2008: 11), artistic interventions will automatically operate in organizations according to the humanistic principles that underpin the field of OD (Margulies and Raia 1972: 3). However, we would argue that, because OD has had its genesis in a relatively coherent body of humanistically based philosophy, the way in which these interventions become embodied, that is, the way in which they take visible form, are more likely to reflect these humanistic principles. The field of OD has matured over decades, with training programmes and publications that have developed a body of thought and expertise in systemic intervention processes and roles. By contrast, there is no coherence among the myriad of stakeholders engaging in artistic interventions, so a similar set of values cannot be drawn up to guide them. Formulating an explicit shared set of values would, in fact, undermine the potential inherent in the arts because the advantage of bringing in artists lies in their difference from the world of organizations. They have the potential to provide 'a fresh perspective so that our old habits of mind do not dominate our reactions with stock response ... and new ways with which to perceive and interpret the world, ways that make vivid realities that would otherwise go unknown' (Eisner 2008: 11).

The challenge for the stakeholders of artistic interventions lies in surfacing and grappling with the tensions between values and interests in organizations in new ways, rather than naively overlooking them or instrumentally suppressing them. This is not easy because one of the desired features of engaging with the arts is a temporary suspension of critical thinking and judgement, in order to enable employees to break free of routine ways of seeing and doing things in the organization and 'take a ride on the wings that art forms provide: the arts are ways to get a natural high' (Eisner 2008: 3–4). Suspending judgement and enacting or reflecting conflicting values is in general not a problem for art that is done within the art world. In fact, part of the power of art comes from its ability to make visible and hold seemingly contradictory elements. But the theatrical intervention case illustrates that, when artists move out of their world and into organizations, power and conflicting values may be masked rather than revealed (see also Clark and Mangham 2004). In the absence of an organized process of reflection, the contradiction between working on values of diversity and ending the day with a top-down presentation on a fixed set of organizational values remained unaddressed. Support from an intermediary who could have bridged between the world of the arts and the world of organizations might have made this problem visible and addressable.

The demand for novel approaches to developing organizations appears to be growing. Although artistic interventions are not positioned as OD, there are significant overlaps between the two and those initiating artistic interventions could benefit from the knowledge of the OD field. In particular, an awareness of critical discussion about the humanist values around transparency and engagement inherent to OD might appropriately inform arts-based work. Such an awareness, for instance, might have prompted the theatre company working with the first organization illustrated here to rethink its willingness to obfuscate the purpose of the initial interviews it carried out (or perhaps problematize that aspect of the process in their performance if that was part of their agenda as artists). It is impossible to know if a more transparent approach to how that intervention was established would have made a significant difference to the way in which it was experienced, but OD theory would suggest coherence in such matters is vital.

Transparency and enacting values in the process become even more important when the pressure on organizations to provide evidence of the cost-effectiveness of their activities is high. Obviously – or paradoxically – such pressure may be particularly high in areas that appear 'soft and fuzzy' and difficult to assess, such as artistic interventions. OD practitioners have been observing this trend towards a stronger orientation to the bottom line, some welcoming it (e.g. Burke 2008: 19) and others criticizing it (French and Bell 1999). The lack of exposure to the discourse about this issue among the stakeholders of artistic interventions leaves them ill prepared to deal with it. They may unwittingly fall into the trap identified by Mats Alvesson (1982) for OD, namely presenting the objectives of efficiency and humanization as completely compatible rather than making visible where they diverge and where choices need to be made.

Artists running interventions may find it easy to 'embrace collaborative and generative assumptions about change in human systems' (Marshak and Grant 2008: S17), thereby masking problems and issues of power. The danger is real because (unsurprisingly) so much of the practitioner literature describes the artistic interventions in glowing terms that are intended to motivate organizations to engage in them (e.g. VanGundy and Naiman 2003; Zander and Zander 2000). The difficulties encountered in the process remain invisible (although informal conversations are spiced with anecdotes about them), and the potential negative effects for individuals, organizations or artists are not addressed. The absence of rigorous critical studies by academics (with the exception of a few articles such as Clark and Mangham 2004; Meisiek and Barry 2007; Rae 2011) contributes to keeping problems in the shadows and maintaining an unbalanced view of arts-based processes and their inherent risks.

It is striking that, in the field of artistic interventions, the pressure to generate 'hard evidence' for business outcomes arises from policymakers wanting to use the data to convince other key stakeholders, while the managers who have experience with artistic interventions seldom conduct formal quantitative assessments of the impact of these processes. Instead, they rely on their – often bodily – observations of the situation in the organization and they point to the multiple factors affecting the situation that make attribution of causality questionable. They can 'see' the results, but have trouble communicating what they see to others in organizationally legitimate ways. Bodily ways of knowing are not officially recognized formats for reporting effects in organizations, leaving most people ill equipped to answer the crucial question: 'how do we know it was worth it?' Artists are well placed to help managers and employees develop and use multiple ways of knowing by drawing on their aesthetic sensibilities and extended repertoire of expression. Scholars of aesthetics are also experienced in dealing with this challenge. 'Aesthetics embraces its subjectivity and thus leaves little room for theories of organization that claim generalizable knowledge that can lead to prediction and control of organizational phenomena' (Taylor and Carboni 2008: 221).

It's what you don't see

Despite the issues mentioned above, we see great possibilities in artistic interventions as a form of organizational development. The two cases presented point towards different ways that artistic interventions can support learning and change in organizations. The first intervention used theatre as an unusual tool within a day-long traditional change effort. It was an effective approach in that people remembered it a year later – it was 'sticky'. It also allowed people within the organization to see each other in ways that they hadn't before. However, it was used within a top-down process designed to implement management's agenda for the organization. In contrast, the artist-in-residence intervention had artistic processes as the heart of the change process. They were open-ended, and responsive to agendas other than management's. Although neither was explicitly an OD effort, the artist-in-residence programme captured more of the values of OD than the theatrical intervention did. In both cases, our focus has not been on the work of art, the visible artefact of the process, but rather on what one does not see – the process, the values, the diversity of interests, the power dynamics.

Artistic interventions may create visible (and audible) artefacts such as the performance in the theatrical intervention or the photographs, short stories, and poems with the artist-in-residence. But these visible artefacts are simply that – artefacts, leftovers that remind the stakeholders what is really important – that which they do not see. Whether it is the memories of the CEO playing the role of a secretary, or the energy of the artist-in-residence, or the embodied knowing of the managers, artistic interventions work with the powerful intangible forces in people and organizations.

Notes

1 The term organizational development first appeared around 1956 and is usually attributed to Robert Blake and his colleagues when they recognized that they were shifting their primary focus from individual development to improving the organization (Kleiner 1996: 53; also French and Bell 1999: 41).
2 Key figures included: Kurt Lewin, Edgar Schein, Douglas McGregor, Herbert Shepard, Robert Blake, Jane Mouton, Richard Beckhard, Chris Argyris, Warren Bennis and Eva Schindler-Rainman.
3 Depending on the governance of the organization, union or work council representatives may be involved in the decision, particularly if it affects blue-collar workers.
4 The term 'artist-in-residence' was initially used by the intermediary TILLT, when it introduced this approach to artistic interventions. The term is presented in quotation marks here, because, unlike traditional artist-in-residence programmes, the objective here does not include the production of a work of art by the artist.
5 The interviews about this project were initiated spontaneously by employees when they heard that Ariane Berthoin Antal was conducting research on artistic interventions in organizations. The CEO was willing to be interviewed as well, and he provided access to the director of the theatre company. However, he did not want a formal follow-up study in the company, which he feared might interfere with the process. Subsequent rounds of interviews with employees were therefore conducted informally with people who wanted to talk about the experience.
6 This case is based on interviews Ariane Berthoin Antal conducted at the company in Sweden in 2009 with the human resource manager, six blue-collar employees, an artist and members of the intermediary organization, as well as on presentations by the human resource manager and an employee from the project team at a conference in Brussels in December 2009.
7 For more information about TILLT's method, see www.tillt.se; Berthoin Antal 2011: 21–42; Styhre and Eriksson 2008.

References

Alvesson, M. (1982) 'The limits and shortcomings of humanistic organization theory', *Acta Sociologica* 25(2): 117–131.
Barry, D. and Meisiek, S. (2010) 'Sensemaking, mindfulness and the workarts: seeing more and seeing differently', *Organization Studies* 31(11): 1505–1530.
Berthoin Antal, A. (2009) *A Research Framework for Evaluating the Effects of Artistic Interventions in Organizations*, Gothenburg: TILLT Europe.
——(with Gómez de la Iglesia, R. and Vives Almandoz, M.) (2011) *Managing Artistic Interventions in Organisations: A Comparative Study of Programmes in Europe*, 2nd revised and expanded ed., Gothenburg: TILLT Europe.
——(2012) 'Artistic intervention residencies and their intermediaries: a comparative analysis', *Organization Aesthetics* 1(1): 44–67.
——(forthcoming) 'When arts enter organizational spaces: implications for organizational learning', in P. Meusburger, A. Berthoin Antal and L. Suarsana (eds) *Learning Organizations: Extending the Field*, Dordrecht: Springer Verlag.
Biehl-Missal, B. (2011) *Wirtschaftsästhetik. Wie Unternehmen die Kunst als Inspiration und Werkzeug nutzen* [Business aesthetics: how organizations use art as inspiration and tool], Wiesbaden: Gabler Verlag.
Burke, W.W. (2008) 'A contemporary view of organization development', in T.G. Cummings (ed.) *Handbook of Organization Development*, Thousand Oaks: Sage, 13–38.
Clark, T. and Mangham, I. (2004) 'Stripping to the undercoat: a review and reflections on a piece of organization theatre', *Organization Studies* 25(5): 841–851.
Cummings, T.G. (ed.) (2008) *Handbook of Organization Development*, Thousand Oaks: Sage.
Darsø, L. (2004) *Artful Creation: Learning-tales of Arts-in-business*, Frederiksberg, DK: Samfundslitteratur.
Eisner, E. (2008) 'Art and knowledge', in J.G. Knowles and A.L. Cole (eds) *Handbook of the Arts in Qualitative Research*, Los Angeles: Sage, 3–12.
French, W. and Bell, C. (1999) *Organization Development: Behavioral Science Interventions for Organization Improvement*, 6th ed., Upper Saddle River: Prentice-Hall.
Jamieson, D.W. and Worley, C.G. (2008) 'The practice of organization development', in T.G. Cummings (ed.) *Handbook of Organization Development*, Thousand Oaks: Sage, 99–121.

Kegan, Daniel L. (1971) 'Organizational development: description, issues, and some research results', *Academy of Management Journal* 14(4): 453–464.

Kleiner, A. (1996) *The Age of Heretics: Heroes, Outlaws, and the Forerunners of Corporate Change*, New York: Currency Doubleday.

Laaksonen, A. (2011) 'Creative intersections: partnerships between the arts, culture and other sectors', *D'Art Topics in Arts Policy*, No. 41, International Federation of Arts Councils and Culture Agencies, Sydney. Retrieved 1 November 2011 from www.ifacca.org/topic/creative-intersections/.

Marshak, R.J. and Grant, D. (2008) 'Organizational discourse and new organization development practices', *British Journal of Management* 19: S7–S19.

Margulies, N. and Raia, A.P. (1972) *Organizational Development: Values, Process, and Technology*, New York, NY: McGraw-Hill.

Meisiek, S. and Barry, D. (2007) 'Looking through the looking glass of organisational theatre: analogically mediated inquiry in organisations', *Organization Studies* 28(12): 1805–1827.

Quinn, R.E. and Sonenshein, S. (2008) 'Four general strategies for changing human systems', in T.G. Cummings (ed.) *Handbook of Organization Development*, Thousand Oaks, CA: Sage, 69–78.

Rae, J.E. (2011) A Study of the Use of Organisational Theatre: The Case of Forum Theatre, Doctoral thesis, Durham University. Retrieved 12 February 2012 from http://etheses.dur.ac.uk/3268/.

Schiuma, G. (2011) *The Value of Arts for Business*, Cambridge, UK: Cambridge University Press.

Schnugg, C. (2010) *Kunst in Organisationen. Analyse und Kritik des Wissenschaftsdiskurses zu Wirkung künstlerischer Interventionen im organisationalen Kontext* [Art in organisations. Analysis and critique of the scientific discourse about the effects of artistic interventions in organisational contexts], PhD Thesis, Johannes Keppler Universität Linz, Austria.

Schumpeter (2011) 'The art of management: business has much to learn from the arts', *Economist*, 17 February 2011. Retrieved 20 February 2011 from http://www.economist.com/node/18175675.

Strati, A. (2010) 'Aesthetic understanding of work and organizational life: approaches and research developments', *Sociology Compass* 4(10): 880–893.

Styhre, A. and Eriksson, M. (2008) 'Bring in the arts and get the creativity for free: a study of the Artists in Residence project', *Creativity and Innovation Management* 17(1): 47–57.

Taylor, S.S. and Carboni, I. (2008) 'Technique and practices from the arts: expressive verbs, feelings, and action', in D. Barry and H. Hansen (eds) *The Sage Handbook of New Approaches in Management and Organization*, Los Angeles: Sage, 220–228.

Taylor, S.S. and Ladkin, D. (2009) 'Understanding arts based methods in managerial development', *Academy of Management Learning* 8(11): 55–69.

VanGundy, A.B. and Naiman, L. (2003) *Orchestrating Collaboration at Work. Using Music, Improv, Storytelling, and Other Arts to Improve Teamwork*, San Francisco: Wiley, Jossey-Bass, Pfeiffer.

Zander, R. and Zander, B. (2000) *The Art of Possibility: Transforming Professional and Personal Life*, Boston: Harvard Business School Press.

17
Towards an understanding of corporate web identity

Carole Elliott and Sarah Robinson

Introduction

The study of the role of organizational websites in the communication of corporate identity is still in its infancy. Yet, for many of its potential stakeholders, the first encounter with an organization is through its webpages (Coupland and Brown 2004; Pablo and Hardy 2009). Websites provide stakeholders with information, are a means of transmitting (Segars and Kohut 2001), and sometimes responding to, high-level management messages (Coupland and Brown 2004), and project the wider 'look and feel' of an organization (Pablo and Hardy 2009). Given the strategic importance of websites as global communication tools, calls have been made to gain a deeper understanding of their role as a component part of corporate identity, especially in terms of communicating messages and shaping perceptions of organizations worldwide (Melewar and Karaosmanoglu 2006; Warren 2009).

This chapter starts by examining how corporate identity has been defined and applied. We argue that its sub-concept, corporate visual identity (CVI), is not sufficiently broad to encompass, appreciate and evaluate holistically the complex medium of websites and the importance of corporate web presence. Working therefore towards developing the specific concept of corporate web identity (CWI), we examine existing work on the nature, role and purpose of organizational websites and identify five major features of contemporary corporate websites, which, it could be argued, constitute an emergent CWI. Different methodological approaches to website research and their suitability and efficiency for the study of this specific and complex medium are considered. A short study of a corporate webpage is then presented and the issues we encountered in researching its web identity are discussed. Finally, we identify emergent future research avenues and discuss possible methodological strategies for future organizational website research.

Websites and corporate identity

Various definitions of corporate identity have been developed within the extant literature. Gray and Balmer (1998: 697) view corporate identity as the 'immediate mental picture' that audiences have of an organization. Melewar and Karaosmanoglu, through an extensive study of managers' views, suggested that corporate identity is 'the presentation of an organisation to every stakeholder' and 'it is what makes an organisation unique' (2006: 864). Bartholme and Melewar summarized the concept of corporate identity as 'the set of meanings by which a company allows itself to be known and through which it allows people to describe, remember and relate to it' (2011: 53).

There have also been attempts to break down this 'mental picture' into component parts. Melewar (1993), for example, identifies seven main dimensions of corporate identity: corporate communication, corporate design, corporate culture, behaviour, corporate structure, industry identity and corporate strategy. Image and visual presentations of the organization certainly play a significant role in this framework. Indeed, Melewar and Karaosmanoglu claim that the literature makes a 'profound link' between corporate image and corporate identity, stating that image is the 'collective perception that the stakeholders have of corporate identity' (2006: 848).

Corporate image is deeply connected to a specific element of corporate identity, namely CVI, which has been described as 'the most tangible facet of corporate identity' (Simões *et al.* 2005: 158) in that it provides a 'visibility and recognizability' (Balmer and Gray 2000) of a given organization. It has been defined as consisting of five main elements: company name, symbol and/or logotype, typography, colour and slogan that 'reflect the company culture and values and that create physical recognition for the organisation' (Simões *et al.* 2005: 158; see also Melewar and Akel 2005: 44; Bartholme and Melewar 2011: 54). These elements have long been present in organizational artefacts, for example, annual reports and letterheads, and are now also important elements in the design of corporate websites (see also Leonard, Chapter 20, this volume). Schmitt *et al.* (1995) provide a framework for developing and managing CVI, involving paying attention to the 'four Ps of aesthetics management', namely, properties, products, presentations and publications, as key components of corporate image management (in Bartholme and Melewar 2011: 56).

Certainly, comprising many of the elements of CVI discussed above, websites have been described as 'carriers' of visual identity (van den Bosch *et al.* 2006: 139). However, if we start to apply Schmitt *et al.*'s (1995) framework to corporate websites, we see potential problems as: (1) websites are not solely a visual medium; and (2) as part of wider social media, they cannot be so easily controlled by the organization. Websites are, in fact, multi-modal and, as such, their role in engaging with an organization's diverse stakeholders and shaping their perceptions of the organization (Melewar and Karaosmanoglu 2006: 853) goes beyond reflecting, transmitting and protecting visual identity.

Given these issues, it is perhaps time to explore whether an organization's web presence needs a new framework to guide its creation and to evaluate its performance. At the very least, contemporary research needs to develop an awareness of: (1) how the design of an organization's website conveys corporate identity; (2) how it is open to the multiple interpretations of a diverse and global audience; and (3) how stakeholders experience and make sense of their 'visit' to a given website.

A key issue for consideration, as Melewar and Karaosmanoglu (2006: 850) remind us, is that corporate communication can be both 'controlled and uncontrolled in nature', the former being 'communication intentionally instigated by management with the aim of improving stakeholder relationships', and the latter communication that 'takes place when organisations influence stakeholders' perceptions unintentionally' (see also Price *et al.* 2008). Developing the notion of CWI allows us to explore the roles and purposes of websites and the emerging facets of their distinct identities starting with issues highlighted in contemporary research.

Towards an understanding of emergent CWI

Websites serve many different stakeholders and play a wide variety of roles. As such, they contain different combinations of visual, textual and interactive media. Early in their evolution, websites tended to consist of elements that existed in the same order elsewhere, in paper formats, for example, such as brochures and prospectuses (Coupland and Brown 2004). Criticism of traditional website design has been that 'in mimicking paper forms of communication, the user under-utilizes the power of the new electronic medium' (Dillon and Gushrowski 2000, in Coupland and Brown 2004), while Chaudhri and Wang (2007: 242) in their study of the role of websites in CSR reporting in India noted a 'lack of creativity' in exploiting multimedia and interactivity in supporting corporate messages. However, although the traditional website genre, containing mainly a mixture of text and photos and other images, is still quite prevalent, corporate websites are becoming increasingly sophisticated, containing videos, podcasts, blogs and fora, and so are becoming more interactive and, as such, boundaries between corporate and public more blurred (see Coupland and Brown 2004; Pablo and Hardy 2009; Leonard, Chapter 20, this volume). In this section, we identify from the existing literature five emergent elements which, we argue, could constitute an initial framework for conceptualizing CWI. These are: mobility, accessibility, interactivity, visuality and customization.

Mobility

A striking feature of contemporary corporate webpages is that of *mobility*, that is the movement both of the site itself and of the way in which visitors can navigate freely around it. An innovation away from the 'brochure' model of web design is the use of revolving text and picture boxes and 'headlines', which allows for much more information to be transmitted in a short space of time. However, this also means that what a new user will see on first accessing the site can never be accurately predicted (Elliott and Robinson 2012). Further increasingly sophisticated features of websites are the navigability features and opportunities provided through portals, portlets[1] and hyperlinks (Kalyanaraman and Sundar 2008; Pablo and Hardy 2009). These imply that, in contrast to a printed text where the reader's journey is relatively linear, visitors can choose to navigate webpages in different ways according to their own needs and preferences and thus each user's journey is likely to be unique.

This feeling of movement and personal agency is reinforced by the language associated with websites, which is active and evokes personal exploration. A person 'visits' a 'home' page, is welcomed and invited to 'enter', 'explore', 'navigate' and 'browse'. Such activities suggest a very different type of experience from the reading of a brochure or a prospectus, and require more 'physical' engagement on the part of the visitor (Kivinen 2006). In addition, there are the evocations of hosting and welcoming, so to what extent is it possible for visitors to feel at home on the site and find and take in the information and/or the experience they are searching for, a feature we broadly term *accessibility*, discussed below?

Accessibility

This feature of web identity relates to how visitors are able to find what they are looking for, how they are able to navigate through a mass of information and how they receive, react to, and make sense of, the information and messages available.

Corporate websites are increasingly 'multi-purpose' and multi-activity, transmitting corporate information, on the one hand, and facilitating corporate activity by the public, on the other, for example, through online shopping. Many organizations, in fact, have two websites, one of which we term the 'informational' and which, in the case of the UK supermarket Waitrose, outlines its history and relationship to the wider John Lewis Partnership, providing information about its head office, management team, constitution, principles, strategy and suppliers.[2]

The other website, which we refer to as a 'functional' site, provides access to online shopping.[3] In the Waitrose example, the informational site has embedded links to the functional site, whereas links to the informational site from the functional site are quite difficult to find, as they are positioned right at the end of the site in grey. In this case, these are effectively two different portals – the John Lewis informational portal and the Waitrose shopping portal.

The role of portals in facilitating both visitor mobility and accessibility is significant. Portals are defined as 'sites that serve as a point of access to information from diverse sources' (Pablo and Hardy 2009: 822). Portals are also used by 'umbrella' organizations, for example the World Bank, to bring together organizations under a common theme such as international development (Pablo and Hardy 2009). One of the main roles of portals, it is claimed, is to 'help to make sense of information avalanches by establishing gatekeeping guidelines and streamlining information flow' (Kalyanaraman and Sundar 2008: 239).

Although these can be highly structured and controlled, some portal functionality, for example customization, also implies a degree of agency and control on the part of the visitor. Kalyanaraman and Sundar argue that they 'empower users to construct personal information systems that are receptive to individual needs by their ability to respond in an interactive manner' (2008: 246).

Several different roles and functions of portals have been conceptualized as 'five different but inter-related metaphorical conceptions – gateways, billboards, networks, niches, and brands – which, in turn, suggest five dominant features of portal sites: customization, content, control, community, and commerce' (ibid.: 239). Pablo and Hardy (2009) also research use of and engagement with metaphor through a study of 29 web portals, established through a World Bank-sponsored project – the Development Gateway. They identified three metaphors – 'expert', 'market' and 'community' – which were recurrent either on their own or in combination across this wide data set. They discovered that the use of such metaphors may sometimes be inadvertent but are also sometimes consciously constructed and adopted by organizations. However, on other occasions, the audience may play an active part in the implementation of a new metaphor. Pablo and Hardy (2009) identify patterns in the way these metaphors are used and coexist, allowing organizations to address multiple stakeholders and audiences at the same time.

Other types of accessibility include issues of cultural appropriateness and relevance. For example, Singh *et al.* argue that 'the web is not a culturally neutral medium, but it is full of cultural markers that give country-specific websites a look and feel unique to that local culture' (2003: 63). In their content analysis of American companies' domestic websites and Chinese websites, they found cultural adaptation that spoke to assumed cultural difference, e.g. collectivism, was still at the early stages of development. However, the domestic and Chinese websites were significantly different in terms of structure and appearance, namely in the use of bold colour and animation (ibid.: 75) (for discussion on cultural customization of websites, see 'Customization and communication of "special"/strategic messages' below).

Interactivity

Another active role played by the website visitor is that of dialogue facilitated through multiple channels of communication such as blogs and discussion fora. The inclusion of such interactive spaces within webpages means that individual stakeholders can connect publicly with an organization and other organizational stakeholders and be directly and publicly replied to. Esrock and Leichty (1998) also noted the usefulness of such interaction in that it allows companies to engage in multi-stakeholder dialogue, which is often seen, for example, as a practical challenge of CSR communication. However, such communication can be difficult to control and risky for the projection of a corporate image. For example, Coupland and Brown studied two email exchanges posted on Royal Dutch Shell's website in order to investigate how organizational identities are constructed through processes of 'description, questioning, contestation and defence' (2004: 1325). Employing a discourse analytic methodology they study how what they term 'identity-as-argument' is enacted. They suggest that organizational identities are to a certain extent shaped by such interactions: 'Our suggestion is that organizations are best characterized as having multiple identities, and that these identities are authored in conversations between notional "insiders", and between notional "insiders" and "outsiders"' (ibid.).

As demonstrated by Coupland and Brown (2004), such interactions can highlight some of the tensions and contradictions in corporate identity. However, such co-creation can also be very positive as pointed out by Afuah (2003), as in the example of Cisco, which 'allowed its customers to form virtual communities in which they could exchange ideas and experiences on how to better use Cisco's products in their own systems' (*Economist* 1999, in Afuah 2003: 40).

Another use of this two-way conversation is the appearance of customer reviews, ratings and blogs on corporate websites, which, although generally quite positive, and very useful for the potential consumer, also sometimes contain scathing comments about wider aspects of the organization. For example, a comment on a recipe (posted 27 October 2011) on the website of Waitrose supermarket details frustration with the shopping experience in terms of not being able to find the given ingredients in store and disappointment at the behaviour of staff when asking for help. It is interesting how such a damning indictment is allowed to stay on a corporate website, albeit buried in a rather niche area, for 12 months at the time of writing.

Another connected form of dialogue is that which takes place through an intermediary website, e.g. Trip Advisor.[4] Here customers rate and describe their experiences, e.g. of restaurants and hotels, which organizational representatives can respond to directly or, as is often suspected, indirectly (for example, posing as a happy customer with a counter experience). Such examples pose questions as to what extent organizations feel it necessary to police, edit and respond to such input and how a balance is maintained, although such issues are beyond the scope of the present chapter.

Visuality

Webpages contain images, logos, text, videos and so on, and the aesthetics of, and interface between, these elements are all worthy of study. However, the visual function is significant in its own right, so we use the term *visuality*, namely what is able to be seen by the eye, to refer to this element of CWI. In this limited space, we briefly explore two interrelated issues concerning website visuality, namely: (1) the use of the visual to replace or reinforce feelings and emotions engendered by other organizational artefacts, e.g. buildings; and (2) the interaction between visuality and the transmission of organizational values and strategy and the creation of a unique organizational visual identity.

First, there is the issue of how an organization can be represented virtually. For example, how can a website take the place of a physical building (e.g. company headquarters) as the public face and focal point of the first encounter between the organization and the public? What feelings do they evoke in the visitor? This question relates in part to what has been termed a 'visual monumentality' (Harris 1996: 460), in that corporate buildings have been designed to convey many different things including trust, wealth, power (see Dale and Burrell 2008) and dependability. So can such reactions (and others) be evoked through webpage design and functionality? In this vein, Schroeder studied the design of the webpages of banks, noting how the World Wide Web is already 'infused with architectural metaphors' (2002: 93), such as portals, firewalls and soon. He examined how ten US banks expressed their 'trustworthiness' on their webpages. He found that over half of the banks studied drew on architectural images, including buildings, and bank headquarters. The choice of these images, Schroeder argues, 'represent strategic choices' (ibid.: 111), as most other organizations do not show images of their headquarters on their webpages.

However, such images are predominantly external. Internal work environments have also been designed to engender certain feelings and encourage specific roles within staff, customers and other users. Hancock and Spicer (2011), for example, study the interplay between 'forms of identity' and internal design in relation to a new university library. In addition, in some cases, corporate designs have been developed to have a 'houselike' environment (Pelkonen 2011: 39) to promote both employee morale as well as identification with corporate ends. This home image is, in fact, often conveyed on websites, first through language, as discussed above, but also through use of colour and relaxing images; internal pictures of organizations are often of lounges, waiting areas and so on. On websites, the inside and outside is conflated as to a certain extent is the concept of internal and external stakeholders in that both groups use, and are affected by, the corporate website.

Second, we consider the interaction between visuality and the transmission of organization values and strategy. Two traditional ways in which organizations have done this is: (1) through company's annual reports; and (2) through CSR reporting. There are now many studies of image use within text-based corporate reporting (see, for example, Preston *et al.* 1996; Preston and Young 2000; Benschop and Meihuizen 2002; Davison 2007) and Campbell *et al.* (2009) point to the ever-increasing use of images and, more specifically, the use of 'faces' in annual reports.

However, there is still surprisingly little work that focuses specifically on websites' role in transmitting such messages (some exceptions include: Chaudhri and Wang 2007; Coope 2004; Chapple and Moon 2005). In addition, Pollach's study of CSR reporting on corporate websites identified different 'persuasive appeals' relating to Aristotle's three argumentative appeals: appeal to source credibility (ethos), appeal to reason (logos), and appeal to the audience's emotions (pathos) (2003: 283). Pollach argues that companies concerned with CSR seek 'to project the image of a good corporate citizen' (ibid.: 278), although she does not focus specifically on the use of visuality to achieve this.

Other text-based studies demonstrate how strategic uses of images certainly complement such discursive strategies. Logos and images appeal to contemporary audiences in different ways and are changed and adapted over time in terms of their 'projected images' (Price *et al.* 2008). Changes in representation can be traced, for example, in the changing face of Oxfam (see Davison 2007; Chouliaraki 2012b) and other humanitarian organizations (see Chouliaraki 2011, 2012a). For example, in October 2012, the homepage of Oxfam's website[5] had the caption: 'We can make it: a future without poverty for everyone'. This was accompanied by a picture of smiling children with hands raised in a positive gesture. The page was framed by a combination of bright primary colours. The former famous tagline 'be humankind' (see Chouliaraki 2011) was no longer in evidence. This was in contrast with the more sombre image of children used in its 2003/2004 annual report, where they were 'dignified, neither happy nor sad, in harmony with objectives of support through self-help' (Davison 2007: 145). Such changes also point to the changing role of the 'spectator'/audience (Chouliaraki 2011, 2012a, 2012b), especially in terms of what it is that the multiple audiences are meant to do and feel.

More widely, image also plays a key role in directing/enticing people through portals, which makes an interesting element in web accessibility (see Pablo and Hardy 2009). The collage or visual patchwork structure of portals is an emerging feature of website design. The choice, appropriateness and juxtaposition of images is often intriguing and, in some cases, puzzling (see RBS case study below). This visuality in portal use has been described as a 'veritable gallery that serves as a billboard advertising a diversity of content, both informational and commercial' (Kalyanaraman and Sundar 2008: 243). This gallery can include photos, pictures, graphics, sometimes eclectic and non-conformist in terms of colour and design, and so could actually be seen as a challenge to the control of CVI.

This diversity of image can lead to what Price *et al.* (2008) term the problem of 'scattered images', which occurs because 'there are many potentially disparate or competing images, interpretations, and understandings of one focal organization' (ibid.: 174). The challenge then is how organizational websites can be designed, shaped and customized to speak to a specific target audience.

Customization and communication of 'special'/strategic messages

With so much variety of design, visual genre, informational input and flexibility (of interaction) available, it is a challenge for organizations to ensure that the communication of key messages is achieved. The major themes, activities and distinctiveness of an organization can be subsumed by the sheer mass of messages and information available on the webpages (see Elliott and Robinson 2012). This is complicated by the question of audience and the perceived need to communicate with diverse groups with different informational needs: in the case of university business schools, for example, these would include potential students, current students, alumni, staff, the wider academic community, business communities and so on.

Portals in particular have the potential to target certain specialized consumers. Kalyanaraman and Sundar explain how

> horizontal portals cover a wide array of topics and features, and also act as repositories for an extensive range of information. In contrast, vertical portals, or vortals, are considered to represent category leaders in a given topical group or cater to a specific segment of users.
>
> *(2008: 244)*

Certainly web messaging affords some freedoms, for, as Chaudhri and Wang point out, 'the Web also offers organizations the opportunity to design messages that do not have to follow the dictates of gatekeepers as with print and electronic media' (2007: 235). Rolland and O'Keefe Bazzoni argue that 'online messages can be carefully targeted in meaningful ways to specific stakeholders, be they internal or external, primary or secondary within national or global settings' (2009: 259).

Esrock and Leichty claim that 'The World Wide Web provides organizations an opportunity to communicate with a multiplicity of audiences at a single point in time through one medium, but in a manner that is somewhat customized to each public' (1999: 465). An example of this is IKEA (2012)[6] where every country's homepage is different and customization occurs not only at the level of language but also in terms of the look, feel and presentation of main messages, although most of the supporting images are actually taken from the generic catalogue. However, with the different audiences in mind, it would be interesting to explore further the differences in colour use and choice of content in developing the way the organization is portrayed for its specific (national) audience. Continuing the IKEA example, other small differences arise in the look and organization of the website per country. For example, the interactive questioning feature in some countries becomes 'Ask Anna', 'the automated online assistant'. The image of Anna changes per country. For example, in the UK, Ireland and Germany, she is blonde, while, in Spain, Iceland and China, she is brown-haired. In other countries, for example, Bulgaria, Greece and Finland, the same feature exists (without the 'ask Anna' tag) and is accompanied by a blank head and shoulders image. In another group of countries – France, Italy, Poland, UAE – this feature is not available at all. This suggests an *'audience sensitivity'* (Hyland 2007, in Price *et al.* 2008: 174), although, as in this example, it is not always clear to the external observer how messages are being tailored so that they 'resonate with recipients' (Price *et al.* 2008: 174). However, given that web accessibility is more and more open, it is not only 'the intended' audience who can access the different iterations. As Price *et al.* point out, it could be the case that 'Organizational communicators often seem to underplay the degree to which unintended audiences receive the messages they are sending' (ibid.). It would seem, therefore, that this is an area worthy of more research activity.

Towards an understanding of CWI: implications for research and practice

The discussion of the concept of CWI has highlighted five distinct areas of corporate website activity which could be taken as constituting emergent web identities. In evaluating and researching the strength of web identity and its relation to corporate identity, the following questions could be posed of the websites (and perhaps, by reflection, of the organization more generally): *How mobile or navigable* is the website? *How accessible* is it to its multiple stakeholders? *How interactive* and facilitative of two-way conversations? How *visible* does the organization make itself – what messages might the visual images be portraying? How *flexible* and strategic is its messaging in terms of customization to the needs of multiple audiences? Certainly, as Coupland and Brown argue, organizational researchers need to be alert to the 'persuasive techniques' that organizations can deploy 'in their efforts to render hegemonic their versions of an organization's identity' (2004: 1325), and posing such questions is an interesting way of interrogating the role and purpose of corporate identity. In fact, as our discussion and examples above illustrate, it is actually quite difficult for organizations to maintain hegemonic positions through websites (see also Price *et al.* 2008). How then can an organization's web identity be researched? If we see CWI as a 'sub-construct' of an organization's corporate identity (Coupland and Brown 2004: 1325), how are the organization's wider aims and intentions reflected through their web presence and its design? The constant flux between the part and the whole is certainly a research challenge and arguably one which has not been adequately addressed. This is because most research focuses on discrete aspects of an organization's web presence. Another issue to add to the research focus is the choice of method and disciplinary orientation.

It has been argued that the study of corporate identity more generally needs a 'multidisciplinary approach' (Melewar and Karaosmanoglu 2006: 848), and, although corporate website research is young, there are already innovative transdisciplinary approaches emerging, focusing on different features and roles of webpages. The nascent discipline of Internet studies is very much interdisciplinary in orientation (McLemee 2001; Wellman, 2004). For example, the *Journal of New Media and Society* claims to publish work from the subject areas of 'communication, media and cultural studies, sociology, geography, anthropology, political and information sciences and humanities'.[7] Work emerging from this new discipline ranges from the design and security of websites, through studies of online communities and culture, to the sociology of the Internet and computer-mediated communication.[8]

However, much of the work drawn on in this chapter uses methods traditionally associated with textual research, for example discourse and content analysis, focusing on discrete issues, such as the use of metaphor and quantitative work on cultural suitability (see Table 17.1 for an overview).

We suggest that, although such research has identified some significant issues and raised important questions, website methodologies remain rather limited and there remains a 'brochure' approach (i.e. treating it as a written text) to website research, even though the medium itself has developed and diversified considerably. It is time then to consider the development of more global research designs, which could address website's multi-modal nature and capture some of the complexities of web identity.

Construction of a research approach: adaption of 'visual semiotic' method

In previous research, we took a holistic and 'layered' approach to website complexity (Elliott and Robinson 2012). Focusing on the internationalization of management education, we studied four business school websites, which we contrasted with student interviews from the same institutions. We employed a four-stage hermeneutic cycle of analysis: (1) first impressions; (2) stakeholder views; (3) a visual semiotic approach; and (4) our reflexive account of our interpretations. Although distinctive approaches to internationalization at each institution are identified through student interviews, these are somewhat lost through the mass of information on the webpages. Our analysis also revealed that webpages portray mixed messages that do not necessarily support each school's distinct approach in terms of students' learning, pedagogy or curriculum.

In the next section, using a worked example, we demonstrate how using a multi-layered analytical method can uncover intended and unintended meanings and shed light on the workings of the different elements of CWI.

In examining organizations' communication of their corporate identity through their webpages, we are working from the assumption that webpages constitute a form of 'text' in the widest hermeneutic sense (see Prasad 2002), and draw on Kress and van Leeuwen's (2006) visual semiotic method. This approach claims that any one image (e.g. an advertisement, a painting) not only represents the world, but is also involved in interaction with a viewer. Visual semiotics has been described as 'the study of the ways in which visual images produce social meaning' (Scollon and Scollon 2003: 217). Kress and van Leeuwen's visual grammar (2006) focuses on four main semiotic systems: *representational meaning*; *modality*; *composition*; and *interactive participants* as a means of interpreting this meaning.

Representational meaning is conveyed by the participants in a visual image and can include people, objects or places. Panofsky (1970) refers to representational meaning as the recognition of what is represented based on the viewer's practical experience, 'taking into account the stylistic conventions and the technical transformations involved in the representation' (van Leeuwen, 2000: 100). For example, we understand that photography is unable to represent the world's three-dimensionality. Images, therefore, 'involve two kinds of participants, represented participants', and 'interactive participants' (Kress and van Leeuwen 2006: 114). In taking a visual semiotic approach to the analysis of webpages, we draw attention to the different relationships between these two kinds of participants, 'the people who communicate with each other *through* images, the producers and viewers of images' (ibid., original emphasis), as a means to explore the emergent CWI.

Table 17.1 Summary of different foci, approaches and methodology

Authors	Research site	Research focus	Methods used	Findings/type of web identity
Segars and Kohut (2001)	CEO letters	Effectiveness of letters	Q sort analysis	Evidence of credibility, efficacy, commitment, responsibility
Singh, Zhao and Hu (2003)	Chinese/American websites	American companies' domestic websites and Chinese websites	Content analysis	Slight differences in terms of perceived cultural differences but considerable difference in terms of brightness of colour and animation on Chinese websites
Schroeder (2003)	Ten US banks' websites	Representations of trustworthiness on the WWW	Content analysis	Half of websites studied included images of buildings to represent banks' trustworthiness
Coupland and Brown (2004)	Royal Dutch/Shell	Identity creation through dialogue	Discourse analysis	Organizational identities are constructed through interactive processes of 'description, questioning, contestation and defence'
Kivinen (2006)	Two energy companies' home webpages	The concept of home and the different ways in which boundaries of identity and difference are drawn	Lefebvre's concept of space: social, physical and mental	A 'home' is constructed through the collection of ideas, objects and people within the space. But exclusion also takes place even though images of the environment are present on the website
Chaudhri and Wang (2007)	100 IT companies in India	Analytical focus on the dimensions of prominence of communication, extent of information and style of presentation	Content analysis	Very little CSR information put on site and interactive opportunities not generally leveraged
Kalyanaraman and Sundar (2008)	Portals (different types)	Metaphorical conceptions connected to web portals	Content analysis	Five dominant features of portal sites – customization, content, control, community and commerce
Pablo and Hardy (2009)	A comparative study of 29 web portals	The functionality of web portals and the use of metaphors in relation to them	Systematic analysis of the linguistic, visual and interactive features of web portals	The metaphor of expert, market and community
Elliott and Robinson (2012)	Four UK business schools' MBA webpages	Portrayal of internationalization	Visual semiotics Critical hermeneutics	Mixed and confused messages. Organizational distinctiveness obscured by mass of information and not congruent with stated student experiences.

Modality refers to the degree to which a photograph appears 'credible' or real in a naturalistic sense. Naturalistic modality means that the greater the congruence between what the viewer sees in a visual image, and what the viewer sees in reality, the higher the modality of that image. Visual images can represent people, places and objects as if they are real, or as if they are not – 'as though they are imaginings, fantasies, caricatures, etc.' (Kress and van Leeuwen 2006: 156). In that sense, how we judge the modality of an image is inherently social as it depends on 'what is considered real (or true, or sacred) in the social group for which the representation is primarily intended' (ibid.).

Composition: van Leeuwen (2005) refers to composition as the arranging of elements, whether these are people, objects, diagrams, either in or on a semiotic space, which can range from a page or a canvas to a city.

Interactive meaning indicates relationships with the viewer, in that images can create particular relations between viewers and the world inside the image. For example, in photographs of individuals in advertising texts, those individuals look directly at the viewer in an attempt to 'make contact' with them, to 'establish an (imaginary) relation with them' (Jewitt and Oyama 2001: 145). Images can also keep the viewer at a distance, just as in everyday interactions social norms play a role in determining how close we stand in relation to one another. In photography, 'this translates into the "size frame" of shots' (ibid.: 146), so a close-up shot of an individual, for example, suggests intimacy (Elliott and Robinson 2012; see also Campbell *et al.* 2009).

Corporate websites in action: Royal Bank of Scotland (RBS)

In this section, we employ a visual semiotic analysis to the current homepage of RBS (2012). We chose this organization's webpage because it represents a sector that, following the financial crisis from 2008 onwards, is facing difficult times as well as public criticism and scrutiny. Therefore, there is a need to study its corporate identity and to evaluate how has this been achieved.

In contrast to Schroeder's (2003) analysis of architectural language on bank websites, which identifies the presence of bank headquarters' images on six of the ten banks studied, the RBS Group global portal's homepage does not feature any images of its headquarters. Nevertheless, the top quarter of the webpage, dominated by a table of information, includes a photograph of the Forth Bridge, a well-known Scottish landmark.

If we consider the *representational meaning* of the RBS webpage's imagery, the table of information can be seen as an organizing device offering windows through which the viewer can enter in order to access different areas of RBS activity. Each 'window' of information contains an image underlined by explanatory text. The photographic images used are realist in nature, whereas the 'running of the bulls' image appears to be a pencil drawing, and the invitation to read RBS's annual review is more abstract. Considered as a whole image, the table of information is a form of covert taxonomy (Kress and van Leeuwen 2006: 79). It shows the variety of areas that RBS is choosing to associate with. As a taxonomy, it is ranking different categories of activity, and, with the facilities available to us through Internet-based technology, the viewer can access what lies underneath the homepage headline. Curiously, though, when the lower four windows are clicked on to access further information, the linked pages are image-free, consisting of standard text that reads like press releases.

Given the turbulence of the banking and financial sectors since 2008, banks are less trusted than when Schroeder (2003) conducted his examination of banks' use of architectural imagery

Carole Elliott and Sarah Robinson

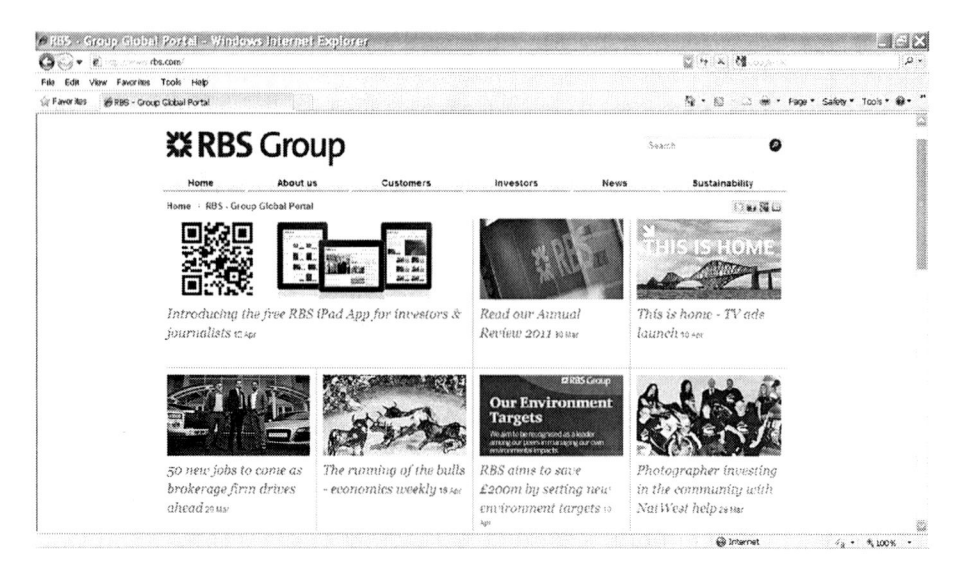

Figure 17.1 Royal Bank of Scotland, website homepage, 10 November 2012

on webpages to represent trust and stability. The presence of images and text relating to different aspects of RBS's activity in the taxonomy discussed above, and the corresponding absence of overt representations of RBS buildings on the homepage, moves us to consider the reliability of the images presented, the degree to which we can trust what we see, that is the *modality* of the home webpage. The images used in the table-based taxonomy are mobilized in different ways, but, in terms of their modality, are all, apart from the image of three iPads, used in symbolic ways. This includes the photograph accompanying the '50 new jobs to come as brokerage firm drives ahead' text, which shows three men in suits standing between, and at the front of, two expensive cars. Whether the cars are intended to symbolize the 'drive ahead', or the brokerage firm's wealth, is unclear; but they are nevertheless overt symbols of wealth. The photograph above the 'photographer investing in the community with NatWest help' text is ambiguous. The text does not provide any clues as to why a motorbike should feature in a piece about a photographer's relationship with the community. The drawing representing the running of bulls is a curious choice for a bank heavily criticized for its role in precipitating the current economic recession. A bull market is associated with increased investor confidence in anticipation of future price increases, and 'the running of the bulls' is a controversial practice that occurs annually in some Spanish towns and villages. The Forth Bridge is used clearly here, as it is in other contexts, to symbolize Scottish identity and RBS as a Scottish bank.

The *composition* of the RBS homepage is structured along a vertical axis. The space above the vertical axis is dominated by the table-taxonomy, and the space below consists of more factual information relating to RBS. The webpage's overall composition affects the relationship with the viewer, meaning that its *interactive meaning* is complex. The RBS webpage includes a number of images in its composition that are elements in the overall layout. As we argue above, this makes the visual analysis of websites, particularly the interactive meaning they invoke, more complicated than the analysis of a single painting, photograph or magazine advertisement that are literally static. In the RBS case, the table dominating the upper part of the page gives the effect of an organized collage, or different windows through which to discover more about RBS activities.

Visual semiotics and CWI

In applying a visual semiotic analysis to explore 'the grammar' (Kress and van Leeuwen 2006) of organizations' website design, we are working to the assumption that webpages constitute a significant element in the evolution of organizations' aesthetic environments. That is, we suggest that a visual semiotic analysis of organizations' webpages moves us to a deeper understanding of the role of CVI, and an appreciation of emerging corporate web identities, whereas text-based analyses of websites focus on specific aspects of website content only.

The analysis of the RBS case, and the examples we have drawn upon earlier in this chapter, reveal that organizations' CWI, as evoked through the grammar of the webpages' design, emerges in relation to their real or imagined stakeholders and audience. The use of the table-taxonomy of information in the RBS case hints at the organization's awareness of stakeholder/viewer diversity. The amount of information included on homepages, including hyperlinks, suggests the organization is also aware of viewer agency; any viewer can move swiftly from one bank's website to another at the click of a mouse, so key corporate messages need to feature prominently and be visually striking. Unlike corporate brochures or other marketing materials, websites present organizations with the dilemma of choice. Through Web 2.0 technology, they are able to include not only static images and text, but also access to social media and film (see also Leonard, Chapter 20, and Bell and McArthur, Chapter 23, this volume). This can compromise the coherence and uniformity of corporate identity as each viewer practises their own 'mash up' of engagement with the website, as they choose the amount of time spent, and routes into, through, between and out of the webpages.

By applying a visual semiotic method to analyse webpages, we have attempted to provide insights into webpages as a form of visual communication. Visual social semiotics regards visual resources as developed 'to do specific kinds of semiotic work' (Jewitt and Oyama 2001: 140); so the image of the Forth Bridge represents Scottish identity, and the image of a blonde woman (in the IKEA example) is intended to evoke Swedish identity. As a method, however, visual semiotics was developed prior to Internet-based technologies of communication, which leads to difficulties when trying to analyse the multiplicity of static and moving images common to many webpages. Do we focus on the page as a whole and examine its composition, or do we focus on specific images and sections of any one webpage? In our analysis of RBS above, we have looked at webpages through four semiotic systems. As the method lends itself to very detailed considerations of static images, we are aware that doing so has led us to undertake a somewhat fleeting analysis, but one that we hope sheds some insights on how webpages communicate an organization's corporate identity.

Conclusions: emergent research issues and suggested ways forward

Investigating the relationship between websites and corporate identity has revealed methodological, conceptual and practical questions. We began the chapter by examining how corporate identity has been defined and applied, and argued that the sub-concept corporate visual identity (CVI) is not sufficiently broad to appreciate and evaluate the complex medium of websites; their multi-modal nature requires the introduction of a new concept that we term corporate web identity (CWI).

In terms of methodology, there seems no one best method to undertake a qualitative exploration of how organizations communicate a corporate identity through their websites. Our analysis, for example, could have focused exclusively upon the *composition* of the two websites or their *interactive meaning*; but this would not have revealed the complexity of analysing a multi-modal communication technology.[9] Visual semiotics offers one approach, but, while organizations might seek to control the messages they send out through websites, they are not necessarily in control of the semiotics. There is further work to be done, therefore, on developing methodologies that take account of the viewer's experience of, and relationship to, organizations' CWI, as well as the viewer's role in shaping CWI.

To conclude, earlier in this chapter, we suggested the need for research that develops an awareness of: (1) how organization website design conveys corporate identities; (2) how websites are open to the multiple interpretations of a diverse and global audience; and (3) how stakeholders experience and make sense of their 'visit' to a specific website. In our attempt to attend to these areas we have proposed: (1) an analytic framework, which, drawing on visual semiotics, uses a four-stage process to focus upon the different ways in which images, and webpages' visual design, convey meaning. In addressing (2), we have drawn attention to ways in which organizations' (e.g. IKEA's) corporate web identities are customized according to the nationality/culture of the audience to whom they are communicating. To work towards an understanding of how stakeholders experience and make sense of their website visits, we have identified five questions that can be used as an analytic guide to investigate the features of CWI:

- How *mobile* and *navigable* is the website?
- How *accessible* it is to multiple stakeholders?
- How *interactive* is it and does it facilitate dialogue?
- How *visible* does the organization make itself through the images it uses?
- How do organizations *customize* and *communicate* their strategic messages?

Posing these questions of websites, we suggest, draws attention to the significance of images in shaping corporate web identities, and websites' role in communicating to organization stakeholders.

Notes

1 These are small editable information applications, or boxes, which typically are accessed from the right or left side bars of a page for example, calendar, events, recent items and so on.
2 For example, see http://www.johnlewispartnership.co.uk/about/waitrose.html.
3 See http://www.waitrose.com/.
4 http://www.tripadvisor.co.uk.
5 http://www.oxfam.org.uk/ (accessed on 28 October 2012).
6 http://www.ikea.com/.
7 http://nms.sagepub.com/.
8 See also *International Journal of Internet Science*: http://www.ijis.net/.
9 The Singapore-based Multimodal Analysis Lab (www.multimodal-analysis-lab.org) is unusual in bringing together social scientists and computer scientists and has, as a key objective, the development of interactive media technology for the analysis of images, video texts and interactive digital sites.

References

Afuah, A. (2003) 'Redefining firm boundaries in the face of the Internet: are firms really shrinking?' *Academy of Management Review* 28(1): 34–53.
Balmer, J.M.T. and Gray, E.R. (2000) 'Corporate identity and corporate communications: creating a competitive advantage', *Industrial and Commercial Training* 32(7): 256–262.
Bartholme, R.H. and Melewar, T.C. (2011) 'Remodelling the corporate visual identity construct: a reference to the sensory and auditory dimension', *Corporate Communications: An International Journal* 16(1): 53–64.

Benschop, Y. and Meihuizen, H.E. (2002) 'Keeping up gendered appearances: representations of gender in financial annual reports', *Accounting, Organizations and Society* 27(7): 611–636.

Campbell, D., McPhail, K. and Slack, R. (2009) 'Face work in annual reports: a study of the management of encounter through annual reports, informed by Levinas and Bauman', *Accounting, Auditing & Accountability Journal* 22(6): 907–932.

Chapple, W. and Moon, J. (2005) 'Corporate social responsibility (CSR) in Asia: a seven-country study of CSR web site reporting', *Business and Society* 44: 415.

Chaudhri, V. and Wang, J. (2007) 'Communicating corporate social responsibility on the Internet: a case study of the top 100 information technology companies in India', *Management Communication Quarterly* 21(2): 232–247.

Chouliaraki, L. (2011) '"Improper distance": towards a critical account of solidarity as irony', *International Journal of Cultural Studies* 14(4): 363–381.

——(2012a) 'The theatricality of humanitarianism: a critique of celebrity advocacy', *Communication and Critical/Cultural Studies* 9(1): 1–21.

——(2012b) *The Ironic Spectator: Solidarity in the Age of Post-Humanitarianism*, London: Polity.

Coope, R. (2004) 'Seeing the "net potential" of online CSR communications', *Corporate Responsibility Management* 1: 20–25.

Coupland, C. and Brown, A. (2004) 'Constructing organizational identities on the web: a case study of Royal Dutch/Shell', *Journal of Management Studies* 41(8): 1325–1347.

Dale, K. and Burrell, G. (2008) *The Spaces of Organization and the Organization of Space: Power Identity and Materiality at Work*, Basingstoke: Palgrave Macmillan.

Davison, J. (2007) 'Photographs and accountability: cracking the codes of an NGO', *Accounting, Auditing & Accountability Journal* 20(1): 133–158.

Dillon, A. and Gushrowski, B.A. (2000) 'Genres and the web: is the personal home page the first uniquely digital genre?' *Journal of the American Society for Information Science* 51(2): 202–205.

Elliott, C. and Robinson, S. (2012) 'MBA imaginaries: projections of internationalization', *Management Learning* 43(2): 157–181.

Esrock, S.L. and Leichty, G.B. (1998) 'Social responsibility and corporate web pages: self presentation or agenda-setting?' *Public Relations Review* 24: 305–319.

Esrock, S.L. and Leichty, G.B. (1999) 'Corporate World Wide Web pages: serving the news media and other publics', *Journalism and Mass Communication Quarterly* 76: 456–467.

Gray, E.R. and Balmer, J.M.T. (1998) 'Managing corporate image and corporate reputation', *Long Range Planning* (30)5: 695–702.

Hancock, P. and Spicer, A. (2011) 'Academic architecture and the construction of the new model worker', *Culture and Organization* 17(2): 91–105.

Harris, N. (1996) 'Architecture and the business corporation', in C. Kaysen (ed.) *The American Corporation Today*, Oxford: Oxford University Press, 436–486.

Hyland, K. (2007) 'Applying a gloss: exemplifying and reformulating in academic discourse', *Applied Linguistics* 28: 266–285.

Jewitt, C. and R. Oyama (2001) 'Visual meaning: a social semiotic approach', in T. van Leeuwen and C. Jewitt (eds) *Handbook of Visual Analysis*, London: Sage.

Kalyanaraman, S. and Sundar, S.S. (2008) 'Portrait of the portal as a metaphor: explicating web portals for communication research', *Journalism & Mass Communication Quarterly* 85: 239–256.

Kivinen, N. (2006) *Entering Organizations: Essays on Image, Space and Difference*, Finland: Abo Akademi Turku.

Kress, G. and van Leeuwen, T. (2006) *Reading Images: The Grammar of Visual Design*, 2nd ed., London: Routledge.

McLemee, S. (2001) 'Internet studies 1.0: a discipline is born', *The Chronicle of Higher Education* 47(29): 24.

Melewar, T.C. (1993) 'Determinants of the corporate identity concept: a review of literature', *Journal of Marketing Communications* 9(4): 195–220.

Melewar, T.C. and Akel, S. (2005) 'The role of corporate identity in the higher education sector: a case study', *Corporate Communications: An International Journal* 10(1): 41–57.

Melewar, T.C. and Karaosmanoglu, E. (2006) 'Seven dimensions of corporate identity: a categorisation from the practitioners' perspective', *European Journal of Marketing* 40(7/8): 846–869.

Pablo, Z. and Hardy, C. (2009) 'Merging, masquerading and morphing: metaphors and the World Wide Web', *Organization Studies* 30(8): 821–843.

Panofsky, E. (1970) *Meaning in the Visual Arts*, Harmondsworth: Penguin.

Pelkonen, E.-L. (2011) *Kevin Roche: Architecture as Environment*, New Haven and London: Yale University Press.

Pollach, I. (2003) 'Communicating corporate ethics on the World Wide Web: a discourse analysis of selected company web sites', *Business & Society* 42: 277–287.

Prasad, A. (2002) 'The contest over meaning: hermeneutics as an interpretive methodology for understanding texts', *Organizational Research Methods* 5(1): 12–33.

Preston, A. and Young, J. (2000) 'Constructing the global corporation and corporate constructions of the global: a picture essay', *Accounting, Organizations and Society* 25(4/5): 427–449.

Preston, A., Wright, C. and Young, J. (1996) 'Imag[in]ing annual reports', *Accounting, Organizations and Society* 21(1): 113–137.

Price, K.N., Gioia, D.A. and Corley, K.G. (2008) 'Reconciling scattered images: managing disparate organizational expressions and impressions', *Journal of Management Inquiry* 17(3): 173–185.

Rolland, D. and O'Keefe Bazzoni, J. (2009) 'Greening corporate identity: CSR online corporate identity reporting', *Corporate Communications: An International Journal* 14(3): 249–263.

Schmitt, B.H., Simonson, A. and Marcus, J. (1995) 'Managing corporate image and identity', *Long Range Planning* 28(5): 82–92.

Schroeder, J. (2002) *Visual Consumption*, Abingdon: Routledge.

——(2003) 'Building brands: architectural expression in the electronic age', in L. Scott and R. Batra (eds) *Persuasive Imagery: A Consumer Response Perspective*, New Jersey: Lawrence Erlbaum.

Scollon, R. and Scollon, S. (2003) *Discourses in Place: Language in the Material World*, London: Routledge.

Segars, A.H. and Kohut, G.F. (2001) 'Strategic communication through the World Wide Web: an empirical model of effectiveness in the CEO's letters to stakeholders', *Journal of Management Studies* 38(4): 535–557.

Simões C., Dibb, S. and Fisk, R.P. (2005) 'Managing corporate identity – an internal perspective', *Journal of the Academy of Marketing Science* 33(2): 153–168.

Singh, N., Zhao, H. and Hu, X. (2003) 'Cultural adaptation on the web: a study of American companies' domestic and Chinese websites', *Journal of Global Information Management* 11(3): 63–80.

van den Bosch, A.L.M., De Jong, M.D.T. and Elving, W.J.L. (2006) 'Managing corporate visual identity – exploring the difference between manufacturing and service, and profit-making and nonprofit organizations', *Journal of Business Communication* 43(2): 138–157.

van Leeuwen, T. (2000) 'Semiotics and iconography', in T. van Leeuwen and C. Jewitt (eds) *Handbook of Visual Analysis*, London: Sage, 92–118.

van Leeuwen, T. (2005) *Introducing Social Semiotics*, London: Routledge.

Warren, S. (2009) 'Visual methods in organizational research', in D.A. Buchanan and A. Bryman (eds) *The Sage Handbook of Organizational Research Methods*, London: Sage, 566–582.

Wellman, B. (2004) 'The three ages of Internet studies: ten, five and zero years ago', *New Media and Society* 6(1): 123–129.

18

Visual workplace identities

Objects, emotion and resistance

Harriet Shortt, Jan Betts and Samantha Warren

Introduction

In this chapter, we present data that show how personal and organizational objects serve important purposes for individuals at work, depending on the degree to which these objects and their meanings are visible to others. We develop empirical themes relating to how workspaces look, drawing on three case studies, demonstrating that the visual dimensions of objects at work – on a continuum from transparent to opaque – are of particular importance in the lived experiences of people at work, organizing relationships between self, other and the organization at large. As such, it is that capacity of objects to symbolize personal and organizational meanings that constitutes the 'visual organization' for those who work there. Paying attention to what we do or do not see in organizations allows analysis of the micro-processes that make up organizational life.

We begin with a review of approaches to studying the visual dimensions of objects at work, before presenting our case studies. The first relates to personal objects as they are deliberately displayed. Samantha's study of workstations discusses the largely transparent meaning of personal objects as they are displayed for others to see. These objects act as points of connection between people, demonstrating that discretion over the personalization of workspace facilitates a sense of individual belonging, and group cohesiveness at work. Second, we consider more obscure objects. Harriet's research with hairdressers addresses more mundane and/or functional tools of work whose significance for their users is not obvious from their appearance. Here, objects provided by the organization gave rise to individuals' feelings of embarrassment and pride, on account of a congruence between the organization's projected identity and their own personal sense of self. Lastly, we move away from the display of objects – whether personal possessions or work tools – to consider the significance of objects that are kept *hidden* at work. Jan's study of public and private sector workers in a range of different occupations highlights how objects hidden from view – or objects with hidden meanings – help resist colonization of the self by corporate cultures.

We then flesh out the themes outlined above, discussing how the visual organization of workplaces by employees enriches our understanding of the lived experience of work. The chapter concludes by considering where the visual study of objects might develop in the future in a world where the visual appearance of things in advanced consumer culture represents 'symbolic work' in the service of identity construction (Willis 2000), increasingly enacted through (visual) digital media technologies and in contexts where mobile-working is blurring boundaries between work, home and leisure.

Researching organizational objects visually

Attention to objects has been gaining prominence in studies of organization for some time now, arguably beginning with Latour and Woolgar's (1979) work on scientific laboratories as characterized by non-human as well as human components. Material and technological objects (non-human) and people (human) are all considered part of a network – one that is therefore both social and material – that affects who we are and what we do in organizations. These ideas later developed into actor-network theory or ANT (Latour and Callon 1981; Law 1997; Law and Hassard 1999). Organizational research informed by ANT spans a variety of subject specialisms and is used in different ways; the exploration of management accounting and accounting technologies (Ezzamel and Robson 1995); the examination of leadership in organizations (Nohria 1998); and research into the architecture, artefacts and embodiment in hairdressing salons (Chugh and Hancock 2009). Indeed, Chugh and Hancock discuss the significance of the inter-relationships between salon tools, aesthetics, the hairdressers and clients themselves, and how these broader considerations of the environment provide meaningful investigations into labour processes. This use of ANT as a framework in the study of the materiality of organizations is one that foregrounds objects not as passive parts of the working world, but as visible and *active* (Dale and Burrell 2008).

However, ANT does not emphasize how individuals interact with objects at work at a micro-level, and their precise role in labour processes. O'Toole and Were (2008) take up this theme in relation to the role of objects in maintaining power structures in a manufacturing firm, and Molotch and McClain (2008) report on the (mis)use of employer-provided tools by American subway workers – explaining how the function of these objects is determined in use (as opposed to design) and essential to the enactment of their work, often contrary to explicit organizational rules. Both these studies used ethnography, but were augmented by photographs of the objects discussed, some of which are displayed in the published articles. Indeed, objects can be visual artefacts in and of themselves. Practices such as architecture and the medical profession rely heavily on visual objects to share meaning and professional knowledge, such as models, diagrams, scanner outputs and the like (Ewenstein and Whyte 2009; Styhre 2010, 2011). Similarly, the workplace studies of Luff *et al.* (2000) apply principles of conversation analysis to video footage of workers carrying out their everyday tasks with the aim of seeing how work is produced through material interactions (Heath *et al.* 2010; Hindmarsh and Heath 2000). They utilize video (as opposed to traditional observation) in order to rewind, pause, speed up and slow down what the camera observes, isolating salient patterns of interactions with specific objects.

Moving to research that explores special objects in the workplace, such as possessions and owned artefacts, shifts attention away from the labour process function of things and considers how they are imbued with emotional attachments, personal stories, histories and identities (Tian and Belk 2005). Recent research has shown these to be important elements in the display of identity at work and that, in the case of employees who work in non-territorial workplaces, where no permanent area of work is owned and the display of objects cannot be realized, a *loss* of identity can be felt (Elsbach 2003, 2004). These are both themes that we pick up in our case studies later in this chapter. Studies of workplace possessions have roots in consumer research (Schultz Kleine *et al.* 1995; Belk 1988) and, more broadly, in material culture studies

(Dant 1999; Ingold 2010; Miller 2005, 2009a; Turkle 2007), but there are also useful insights to be gained from investigations into souvenir practices (Morgan and Pritchard 2005), migrants' choices of objects carried with them when leaving their homelands (Parkin 1999; Mehta and Belk 1991), and from the relationships between people and objects in museum studies (Dudley et al. 2011).

The study of special objects moves us away from the functional role of objects in the workplace and towards the realm of the affective-aesthetic, whereby the symbolic and/or representational features of objects are of prime importance. This connects with a further field of research concerned with (re)materializing organization, that of organizational aesthetics. This approach has given rise to a body of literature on how sensory aspects of organizations, and, more specifically here, *visual* aspects – artefacts, objects and things – are full of social meaning and symbolism on both an individual level as well as the wider cultural meanings associated with the organization itself (Gagliardi 1990; Hatch 1990; Strati 1999; Linstead and Höpfl 2000; Warren 2002). For example, Strati (1999) examines how particular items are signs and symbols or, indeed, say something about the nature of the organization's identity as a whole (Hatch 1990; Campbell, Chapter 8, this volume). Furniture, artefacts and paintings are used by organizations to visually communicate corporate identities and enhance feelings of adherence, or indeed resistance (Martin and Siehl 1983; Betts 2006).

Importantly for our purposes here, we contend that a strong 'visual' thread runs through all these variants of object-related organizational research. Ewenstein and Whyte (2009) and Styhre's (2010, 2011) research explicitly surfaces the visibility of objects and the act of vision, Luff and colleagues' (2000) workplace studies stress the importance of documenting the nuances of interaction through video, and, although broadly ethnographic, many studies of workplace objects and personal possessions use photographs to 'capture' something of the materiality of their subject matter in order to better communicate it to the reader. Likewise, studies of organizational aesthetics have drawn on visual methodologies (Warren 2008; Strati 2000). By contrast, the ethnographic accounts of Daniel Miller (e.g. 2009b) and Sherry Turkle (2007) use a poetic, richly descriptive narrative prose to help the reader visualize the scenes they portray *without* the aid of images, but we suggest this further supports our contention that 'the visual' (whether image or imagination) is of considerable importance when it comes to the material dimension of organization studies.

So, while we do not wish to downplay the solid, multi-sensory and experiential dimension of objects, in this chapter we are particularly interested in objects as markers of identity at work, as apprehended visually, either as physically displayed in workplaces, or indeed *hidden* from view This is what unites the three cases presented below. Within them, we explore the tacit personal and organizational meanings that objects hold, whether they are displayed on a desk, shared work tools or hidden away. In each of the studies, a photographic methodology was used to gather data. Participants were issued with cameras (either digital or traditional film) and asked to take photographs in response to a question posed by the researcher. The subsequent images were then used as stimuli for qualitative interviews from which the data we present here emerged. Further methodological detail is given under each case, but here it is appropriate to consider why photo-interviewing is particularly apposite for studying objects in organizational settings.

First, photography serves as a kind of 'removed observation' and is especially useful for taking an inventory of scenes that would be impractical to observe or discuss for sufficient time and/or in appropriate depth, in 'real time'. Asking participants to make photographs for later discussion also forces them to make choices between objects that are more or less important to them (and therefore worthy of photographing), emphasizing their subjectivity in the process

(Vince and Warren 2012). This, in turn, raises the 'voice' of the participant in the research since they are literally showing the researcher how the world is through their eyes (Wang and Burris 1997; Warren 2005). Finally, photography also allows for context to be drawn into the research, since photographs capture background scenes as well as the foreground 'subject', which may lead to 'unintentional' but important data being made available for later analysis (Shortt and Warren 2012).

We now turn to our three case studies, beginning with Samantha's investigation of personal possessions displayed in an office environment.

Displayed objects: personalization and community

The paraphernalia with which we surround ourselves at work was the subject of a qualitative photographic study of why individuals in Dept. X – a 'new media' department of a large IT firm – felt the need to colonize shared desk-space in a hot-desking environment (Warren 2006). The study was carried out in 2001, when hot-desking was a fairly novel working arrangement, enabled by technological advances and organizational drives to make the most of increasingly expensive office space. Thirty-one members of the department took part and were asked to take a photograph of the 'workspace' for later discussion with the researcher (see Figure 18.1).

Part of a wider investigation into workplace aesthetics (Warren 2005), the study was motivated by Samantha's observation that, despite an espoused clear desk policy and the operation of hot-desking at Dept. X, many of the workstations were covered in personal effects, giving the impression that these spaces were very much owned, and 'lived in' by their occupants on more than a daily, transient basis. Some displayed only a few personal items, whereas others exhibited what Scheiberg calls the '*rampant personalization of space*' (1990: 332).

During the interviews, participants were asked to 'talk the researcher round' the desk-spaces depicted in the photographs, explaining the significance of the objects that were visible. As is common with the use of photo-interviewing of this kind, Samantha questioned the participants about objects in the photographs that she found interesting, as well as listening to the participants' narratives about what they considered important. This led to rich and wide-ranging data

Figure 18.1 Rampant personalization of space

that demonstrated how these workers were using objects to anchor a sense of self at work, in opposition to the hot-desking policy, which was widely disliked.

'Familiarity', 'comfort', 'putting down roots' and not being 'dislocated' were widely cited as reasons why certain objects were on display on individuals' desks. These concepts were invoked to explain how the hot-desking policy was disliked because it prevented individuals from feeling settled at work, and the metaphor of the home was often used to convey this need to belong in one's workspace, as the following extract from the study shows:

> *Yep, [you've] gotta have some greenery. I dunno, my desk is – everyone says 'Oh your desk always looks identical to wherever you go' but I dunno I, well it's your desk at work and I like having some pictures I like it to be sort of homely, I mean some people's desk is ... just a mess and there's no pictures up and there's no nothing and I don't ... when you're spending every day at your desk, I like it to feel vaguely homely.*

Thus, objects were chosen to show a sense of belonging to the desk enabling its occupant to feel settled (see Figure 18.2). Yet, as we note above, items are deliberately chosen for *display*, and as such they acted as conversation-starters with visitors to the desk, giving them a decidedly social function too. This is illustrated by a quotation from a study participant talking about a photograph of Ponte Vecchio, Florence, where he used to live and work:

> *You know people are image conscious on the whole – they do put something up because they want other people to see it, or um, even as a talking point or something – somebody'll come past and say 'Oh!' you know – just like you did – 'Ooh look, Florence' and then of course I can go off on one talking about Florence.*

Figure 18.2 Homely desks

Figure 18.3 Objects as talking points

In the study, Samantha found that this 'small talk' was a source of relational identity construction within the department. Personalization was an expression of, and way to maintain, a sense of self at work – even the decision not to personalize space was recognized by participants as saying something about 'who they were'. But, beyond this, there also seemed to be a 'group identity' function of the act of personalization itself – certain norms were apparent among different sections of the department.

This personalization fostered and maintained a sense of community within Dept. X, which was seen by participants as vital to their happiness at work and ultimately their productivity. This socializing power of objects (Csikszentmihalyi and Rochberg-Halton 1981) – that is to say, the importance of displaying personal objects in forming group norms – and the extent to which personalization in Dept. X was a culturally related practice is illustrated by the following comments from an individual currently sitting in a different area of the office from usual. He spoke of the 'pressure' he felt to personalize his desk, yet he also spoke at length about how positive he felt about the fact that this part of the department had a community identity through their prolific displays of personal objects:

> *I've never been one for, um, photos and cuddly toys at work, I'm there to do a job ... now and again I might put a couple of things up but I'm very aware that I'm doing it and it doesn't feel quite – it feels a bit 'officey', feels a bit 'why am I doing this? Am I doing this because everyone else is? And also what statement am I making about myself? I'm a crazy guy cos ... y'know?'*

Taken together, these data show that it is not just the object that matters at work, but also its *visibility* – facilitating the interactions that socialize organizational members into community cultures that help them feel they belong, have permanence and stability. All of which were of considerable importance to the individuals in Samantha's study.

We have seen from the above how hot-desking individuals resisted this requirement of their jobs, but nonetheless because of the nature of their work – sitting at one desk, every day – they were able to do so through their visual-material practices. But what happens when organizational members do not have their own space to colonize? In the next section, we outline Harriet's study of hairdressers who do not have access to any traditionally conceived personal space – potential or otherwise – in their workplace.

Obscure objects: workplace tools and identity

Harriet's research study examined meaningful objects in the lives of hairdressers working in hair salons in the UK. Specifically she investigated how mundane and/or functional tools of their work are salient to the hairdresser's identity, for example, chairs and towel baskets that are not special, owned possessions, but rather objects that are ostensibly ordinary, commonplace and often *shared* by all in the salon. Here, we explore how the hairdressers have acute associations and disassociations with the appearance of such objects in the salon, linking this to their feelings of professionalism, and how this, in turn, connects to clashes (feelings of embarrassment) and matches (prideful feelings) between their individual identity and the organization's projected identity.

In total, 42 male and female hairdressers, aged from 17 to 50, took part in the research across 5 UK salons of varying size and 'prestige'. The sample included junior hairdressers (those still in training) and experienced stylists and colourists (those specializing in cutting/styling or colouring hair). Once again, as in Samantha's study, participants were given a camera and asked to take up to 12 photographs of objects and 'things' that were most meaningful to them and that said something about who they are. After the photographs were developed, one-to-one, face-to-face, photo-interviews were conducted with each participant, where their images were discussed and stories about their objects emerged.

These images evoked embarrassment in the hairdresser who captured it: he felt that this 'clutter' reflected him as 'unprofessional' and was fearful others (his clients) would 'judge' him:

> So, we'll group all these ones together … and what I don't like here is the clutter, the stuff … and it takes something away from the salon and the space. I can't bear it. Look at this table, these bits, this hosepipe hanging down outside. It's so unprofessional and people look at that think, well … our clients don't come here 'cos they want a haircut, they come here because they have decided to treat themselves. You want the clients to be impressed … gobsmacked! You don't go to a Gordon Ramsay restaurant because you're hungry, do you? And this, well, it's embarrassing and it sends the wrong message about who we are and who I am.

Importantly, these objects are 'on display' and essentially form a public spectacle, seen by others (or at least are at risk of being seen). Since the hairdressers have constructed particular social expectations of themselves and how they would *like* to be seen by others, when such objects fail in conveying this impression, the emotion of embarrassment is experienced, something which is objectionable for them. More specifically, feelings of embarrassment appear to trigger reservations and doubts about the hairdressers' own sense of professionalism, with a corresponding serious concern about how 'others' (visitors and clients in the salon) might judge them.

In contrast, however, other everyday workplace tools engendered feelings of pride. For example, some hairdressers captured images of staircases in their salons. Each described how they deliberately showed these staircases to clients and family members in order to visually illustrate

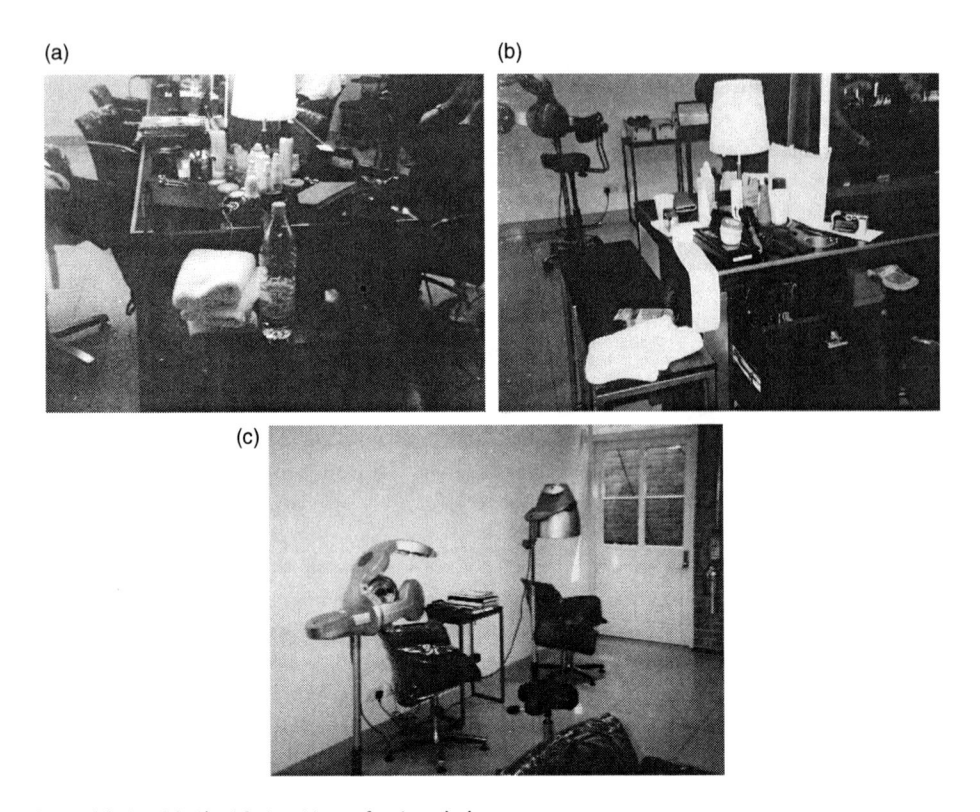

Figure 18.4a, 18.4b, 18.4c Unprofessional clutter

the grandeur and quality of their salon. In addition, 'ordinary' objects, such as plant tubs, towels and trolleys, were also discussed with a sense of delight or 'showing off'. The hairdressers enjoy being associated with 'high-quality' objects, regarding them as signs and symbols of a 'professional' and proficient self.

Thus, just as we saw in the discussion of embarrassment, the social emotion of pride is once again connected to the hairdressers' sense of how they are judged by others (here, by their clients and family members). Essentially, it is the visible image of the salon – on show to the public – of which the hairdressers seem most proud.

Hidden objects: self and resistance

So far, we have considered ways in which objects either on display or found overtly in the workplace have importance for researching organizations. Here, in a case study from Jan's research (Betts 2012), we consider the opposite of visualizing – hiding – either as objects that are literally obscured from view, or as objects displayed, but with hidden meanings.

In this project, a variety of full-time, part-time, professional and blue-collar workers were asked to photograph all the objects in their immediate working spaces that had meaning for them. As in our previous case studies, participants were then asked why each object was chosen as meaningful during interviews, using the photographs as stimuli. However, using Kelly's (1955) Repertory Grid technique, the participants were subsequently presented with the photographs

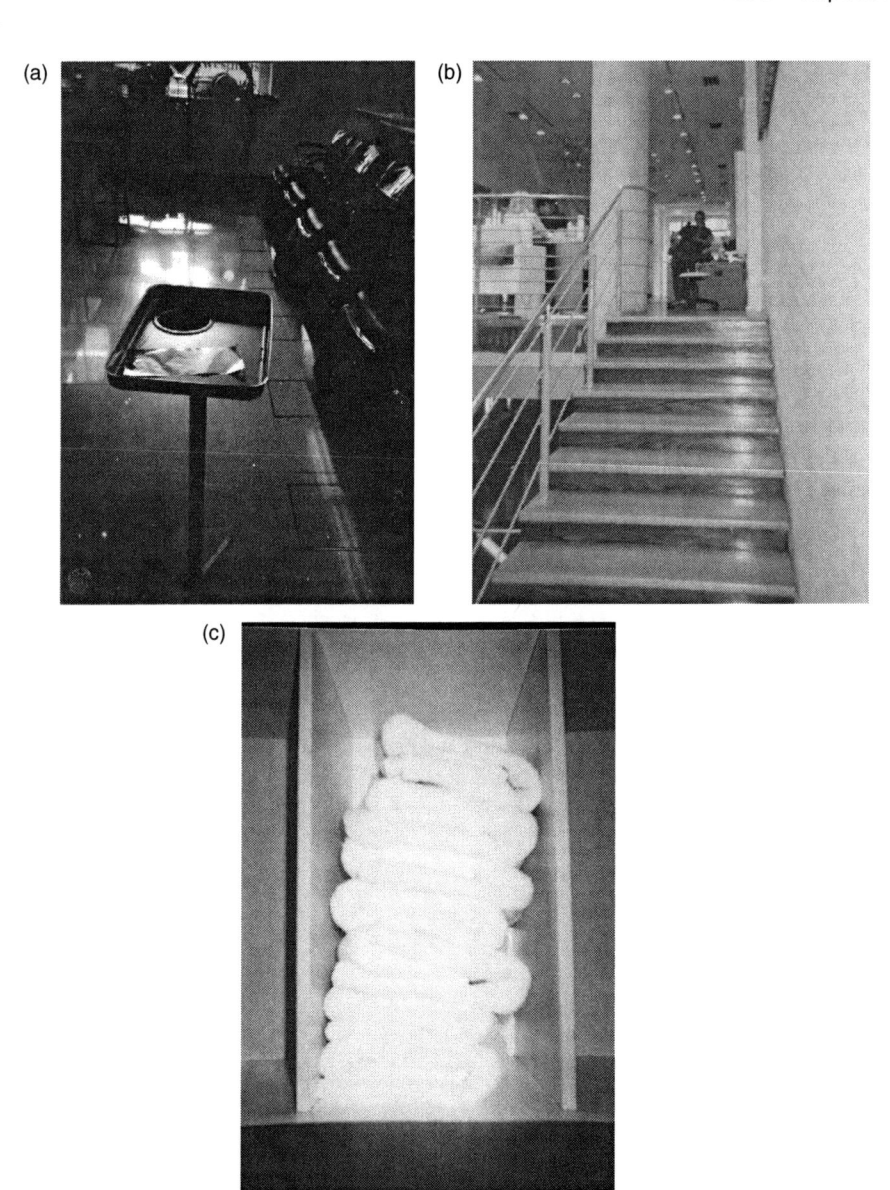

Figure 18.5a, 18.5b, 18.5c Professional and proficient

in random sets of three and asked to express ways in which any two were alike but different from the third. The purpose of this was to encourage participants to mine deeper meanings across the set of photos, explaining what distinguished one photo from another and why this was important to them. From these two sets of data, various themes emerged, one of which was 'hiddenness'. This is far from a single concept, both in its expression and its function: the data show a number of ways in which hiddenness manifests itself.

First, hiddenness is expressed through objects that are literally kept sheltered from public gaze – being covered up or in a drawer, for example. Sarah, a senior manager, has a briefcase that is quite bright, but she hides it among a pile of old papers. In it are things she has collected from her working life in various jobs, such as thank-you cards, pieces of work of which she was particularly proud and mementoes of social events. She told Jan that she absolutely would not want people to see it if anything happened to her, and after the interview she resolved to put a note on the front to say it should be collected by her husband in the event of unforeseen eventualities:

> *This one, I guess because it's just bits of stuff that there's nowhere to put. Well I don't really want to throw them away, but I don't quite know what to do with them, so they could just go back in the bottom of the cupboard I guess, out of the way. Interestingly, though, this is a box that I brought from the old offices ... I've kept it in the garage at home, virtually everywhere I've worked I've taken it.*

Ann, an academic, had a small pencil case, similarly 'hidden-in-plain-sight', which was a memento of her childhood abroad and a constant in her life. It had gone with her to every job, nestled behind or under a file, and will in time be passed on to her grandson. The contact with both past and future was significant, offering her reassurance about a life outside work where other values ruled her. In the same vein, Jane, a senior manager in a local authority, had a beer-mat in her drawer from a particular holiday, which, for many reasons, reminded her to 'check in with her heart' sometimes, to reflect on the values that threatened to engulf her at work and to measure them against her personal values.

Lastly, Jim, a cleaner, had a list of football fixtures inside his locker door, which he looked at deliberately during the day as a way of distracting himself from work, of thinking about something important to him, but which he didn't discuss with the other mostly female cleaners. In a previous job, he had pictures of his son on the inner lid of his toolbox, which, again, he never showed to others, but looked at himself when he wanted to be reminded of life outside work.

In a slightly different vein were meaningful objects that were in plain sight but which reflected something private and which the owner did not want to express openly. For example, Susan, a young personnel manager, asked for a nice pen as a present from her mother, because she felt

Figure 18.6 Hidden briefcase

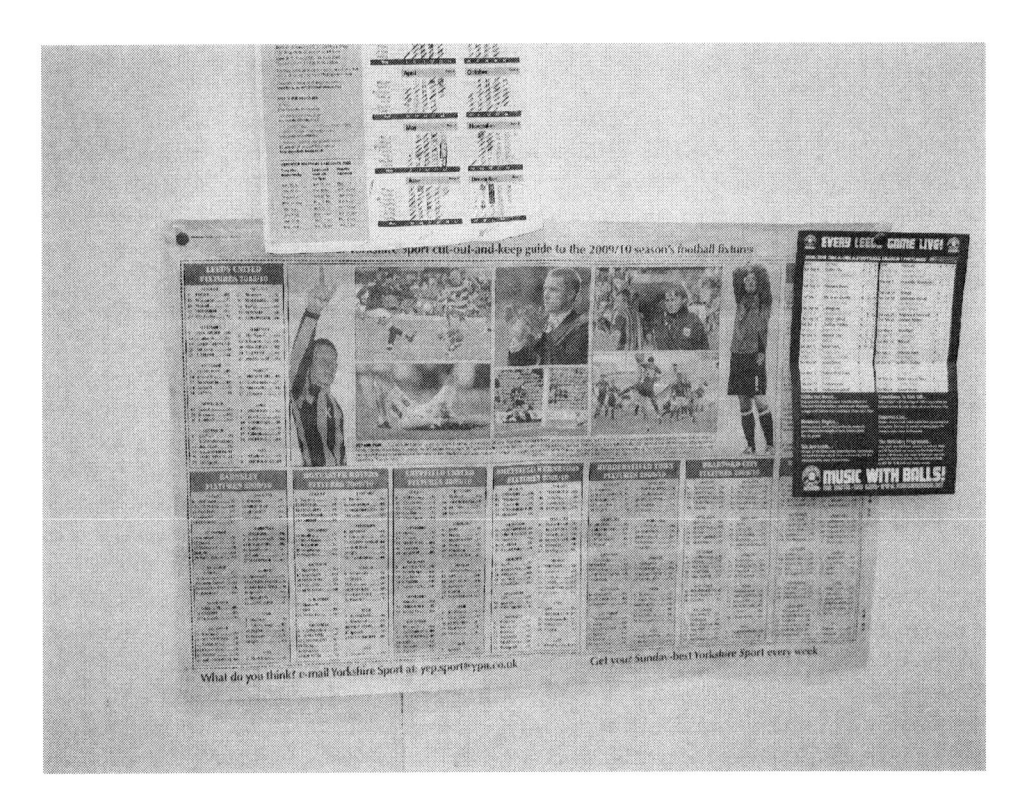

Figure 18.7 Football fixtures

Figure 18.8 Brian's monkey

it signalled that she is someone to be taken seriously in meetings with those more experienced than she is and it had the reassurance of being given to her by her mother, whom she values greatly. If she had told anyone about this, the weight of this meaning would have surprised those she worked with; as she herself said, 'it's a lot to put on one small pen'. But having it with her at all meetings is very important as a way of signalling to herself that her contribution to the organization is significant, despite how others make her feel.

A similar but much more 'confident' object sits in the office of Brian, a senior partner in a law firm.

Quietly scathing about the management of the organization, Brian took a picture of a toy monkey on his desk, which was his name for the (often young) managers who 'told him what to do'. During conversations he felt were overly managerial, he explained to Jan that he invented a 'conspiracy' between him and the monkey enacted by a sideways glance. Brian's desk had a number of toys on it, reflective both of work and home, so the monkey did not stand out, but yet it had a quiet and very strong message for him of resistance against certain organizational diktats.

All these examples represent an interface between the individual and the organization, which is of significance. Clearest of all the messages coming from the interactions is a need to feel that, at some level, personal values override organizational values and a need to feel some sense of recognition as competent people at work. In the face of increasingly impersonal working environments, these are crucial psychological requirements, which may not be recognized by the organization because of the hidden ways in which they are expressed. The very hiddenness is the core of the sense of self, which is being preserved against organizational intrusion and ownership, or, as Ng and Höpfl (2011) put it, to ameliorate the experience of work as 'exile'.

Discussion: visual workplace identities

The above vignettes highlight ways in which the extent to which certain objects are visible to others in the workplace has particular organizing effects for the individuals who work there. In this section, we turn our attention to how these analyses tell us something useful about contemporary organizational life. In common with Stolte *et al.*'s (2001) call for a sociological miniaturism, and Scheff's (1990) insistence on a 'micro-sociology', we suggest that examining the dense visual textures of workplace life might shed light on wider organizational processes. In the same way that Fine and Hallett (2003: 2) connect the commonplace substance, dust, to 'gender, political economy, work and nationalism', we suggest that the detail of everyday objects gives us clues as to how the 'big' topics of organizational analysis – labour process, identity, motivation, culture, and so on – are grounded in the tiny details of *material micro-interactions*.

Samantha's study shows how the consciously constructed visual appearance of personal space is an important element of both psychological satisfaction and social affiliation at work – a finding supported by Nathan and Doyle, who found that 'flexible workspaces may be making some employees unhappy by denying them their territory' (2002: 24). The workers in Dept. X invested time and effort in selecting and maintaining their object-displays, which, in turn, said much about them as individuals, and their desire to affiliate with a workplace community (Suchman 2005). Wolfram Cox and Minahan (2005: 530) note that, far from being surface trivialities, adornment and decoration connote dignity and value, as was the original Latin meaning of the terms. Moreover, Willis (2000) argues that the accumulation and careful arrangement of objects in displays is a form of 'symbolic work' – which we can study as a labour process in itself, noting who 'produces' and who 'consumes', and how and where value is produced in the process, which could represent a rich vein for future research (Warren 2012). Indeed, this raises additional questions about possessions and tools 'at work' when we consider *where* work is conducted in today's fragmented, fluid and often digital working world; what objects are important when we work from home? Are they different to those at the office or those when we are working 'on the move'? With increasingly blurry boundaries between work, home and leisure, what objects say something about who we are and what meanings do they hold?

Harriet's study turns attention away from personal objects chosen for display by the individuals, and towards interactions with organizationally provided objects. Harriet's data evoke Cooley's (1964 [1902]) 'looking-glass self' to suggest that the image of the salon reflects the image of the participants themselves. When positive – as in the instances of pride described above – this affiliation with the organization can offer a sense of order, stability and clarity to the hairdressers' identity (Alvesson 2006). It has been proposed that pride itself 'is the sign of an intact bond' (Scheff 1990: 15), whereby feelings of pride are experienced when individuals sense an engagement with social norms and expectations. Likewise, it seems that the embarrassing aspects of the salon objects reflect what Alvesson *et al.* define as 'anti-identities ... visions of the "other" or dis-identification, all of which constitute the self around what it is not' (2008: 19).

The everyday tools the hairdressers use are visible gestures (Yanow 2006) between the hairdressers and their clients – intimately linked to the hairdressers' sense of professional identity. The clients make judgements about the competence and skill of the hairdressers and quality of the salon by looking at these tools just as much as by regarding the hairdressers' personal grooming and appearance as 'branded selves', a topic that has received much more attention in literature investigating aesthetic labour (e.g. Pettinger 2004). Importantly for our purposes here, it is the hairdressers themselves who place expectations and values on these mundane objects, investing them with the power to embarrass. While others may simply see a hairdryer, or towel basket, the hairdressers see an affront to their professionalism. The level of visual organization in this case is more obscure.

Moving further still away from the idea of display, Jan's study shows how objects can still be imbued with a sense of identity for the worker, yet remain hidden, as also pointed out by Miller (2009a). Pratt and Rafaeli (2006) argue that we relate to objects on account of their instrumentality, their aesthetic pleasure and their symbolic meaning, which may be largely or totally opaque to others. However, although Schein (2004) refers to hidden assumptions in his work on culture, which includes the impact of objects, hiddenness has, on the whole, received scant attention in organization studies with the hidden nature of the impact of objects more implied than explicit (see, for example, Fenwick 2010; Tyler and Cohen 2010; Berlin and Carlstrom 2010). Ng and Höpfl's study seems, thus far, to be alone in addressing hidden intimate spaces and objects in what they describe as 'exile': 'the introduction of artefacts which have no place within that order, both challenge and subvert the prevailing notion of order and its arbitrariness' (2011: 762).

This echoes Jan's data, in particular, that discretion over how workspaces appear to others and control over what they *don't* see holds potential for employees to keep something of themselves *for* themselves as they are required to give more of their whole person in the service of a potentially alienating labour process. As Tian and Belk (2005) propose, objects work as boundaries, to create complementary selves in different arenas. For example, work and home interlink through objects that remind people of home when at work (and perhaps vice versa) regardless of whether they are on display or not. They help to keep a sense of a self with a past and a future that lies outside work and the controlled environment in which work happens. We could even frame this as resistance, albeit in a subtle and perhaps unexplicit way. Hiding things away at work may not bring about a revolution, but it nonetheless makes working life more bearable for these employees, at least.

Conclusion

We have presented three sets of empirical data that support our argument that practices around the appearance of workplaces – from the transparent to the opaque – constitute a form of visual organization at the micro-level of employees' everyday lives. In sum, we have shown that:

- questioning how employees arrange their own workspaces for display helps understanding of their ties with others and the purposes this serves for them, e.g. a sense of identity, belonging, solidarity and so on;
- paying attention to employees' perceptions of aspects of workplace appearance outside their sphere of influence illuminates the relationship between the individual and their identification with the organization; and
- enquiring after hidden objects shows how employees regain a measure of consolation and control in increasingly colonizing corporate cultures.

These substantive themes are of contemporary organizational importance, as leafing through the pages of any management journal will attest. However, it is not our intention for the above themes to rest on a functionalist foundation. The objects do fulfil a function in the lives of each of the individuals: that is why they have chosen to photograph them. However, the function cannot simply be read off from similar objects – for example, work tools produce pride or shame, soft toys attract admiring or derisory attention – but is a combination of both the work context and the subjective understanding of the photographer. The gaze and the understanding of the photographer create the function, or indeed functions, not the gaze and understanding of the viewer.

We also propose that they are likely to warrant further investigation in the light of technological developments. Internet technologies have given rise to new forms of working, where, in some cases, employees no longer need to be co-located in order to accomplish their tasks. Given our emphasis on the appearance of workspace in this chapter, it will be fascinating to chart how the need to display, signal and hide certain aspects of selves-at-work through the visual-material world might change. Do mobile workers enact the same visual practices in their homes as they do in their offices? Does the sign value of objects increase or recede in importance when working in non-traditional workspaces, such as the home, a train carriage, shared flexible office or a coffee-shop, or is it transformed into a more complex synthesis of self-work-leisure? In particular, how do new entrants to professions become socialized under such conditions? Mobile workers connect to each other through interactive software such as email, Skype, Google Docs, and social media platforms, to name just a few emerging technologies, and so perhaps we might witness a shift from *material* visual organization to a set of *virtual* visual practices involving preferences for certain fonts, icons, badges and identification images that these programs enable. Other chapters in this volume are beginning to explore these fascinating issues from an organizational perspective (see Leonard, Chapter 20; Bell and McArthur, Chapter 23; Elliott and Robinson, Chapter 17) and, concomitantly, we wonder, how does one construct a working *self* in a virtual organizational world?

Although it was not our main aim in this chapter, we also hope to have demonstrated that photographic methods can fruitfully examine people's relationships with their material environments (see Shortt and Warren 2012; Warren 2008). This is also due, in large part, to digital image technologies that make it easier, cheaper and more intuitive to collect visual data on workplace life. However, even when elements of this may not actually be in view, visual methodologies hold promise. As we have shown in this chapter, visual organization encompasses both visible and invisible practices, indicating the need to qualitatively interrogate how and why people hide or reveal certain objects at work, so going beyond the surface of what we can actually see. Visual organization studies should be just as concerned with *non*-representational visual practices, then, as with analysing the manifest content of images (Scarles 2009). 'Seeing is believing' reflects a common ideology in contemporary Western society (see Kavanagh, Chapter 4, this volume) but we caution against the seductive power of the image to mask other equally important data that may not be so visible. However, in the same way that shadow cannot be seen without light, we argue that paying attention to the visible world helps us access what is *in*visible, and why.

References

Alvesson, M. (2006) 'Shakers, strugglers, story-tellers, surfers and others: varieties of perspectives on identities', Conference Paper: 22nd EGOS Conference, Bergen, Sweden.
Alvesson, M., Ashcraft, K.L. and Thomas, R. (2008) 'Identity matters: reflections on the construction of identity scholarship in organization studies', *Organization* 15(5): 5–28.
Belk, R. (1988) 'Possessions and the extended self', *Journal of Consumer Research* 15(2): 139–168.
Berlin, J. and Carlstrom, E. (2010) 'From artefact to effect: the organising effects of artefacts on teams', *Journal of Health Organization and Management* 24(4): 412–427.
Betts, J. (2006) 'Framing power: the case of the boardroom', *Consumption Markets & Culture* 9(2): 157–167.
——(2012) 'Moving objects', paper presented to the 30th Standing Conference on Organizational Symbolism, Barcelona, Spain, 14–17 July 2012.
Chugh, S. and Hancock, P. (2009) 'Networks of aestheticization: the architecture, artefacts and embodiment of hairdressing salons', *Work Employment Society* 23(3): 460–476.
Cooley, C.H. (1964 [1902]) *Human Nature and the Social Order*, New York: Schocken.
Csikszentmihalyi, M. and Rochberg-Halton, E. (1981) *The Meaning of Things: Domestic Symbols and the Self*, Cambridge University Press: Cambridge.
Dale, K. and Burrell, G. (2008) *The Spaces of Organisations and the Organisation of Space: Power, Identity and Materiality at Work*, Hampshire: Palgrave Macmillan.
Dant, T. (1999) *Material Culture in the Social World: Values, Activities, Lifestyles*, Milton Keynes: Open University Press.
Dudley, S., Barnes, A., Binnie, J., Petrov, J. and Walklate, J. (2011) *The Thing about Museums: Objects and Experience, Representation and Contestation*, London: Routledge.
Elsbach, K.D. (2003) 'Managing threats to workplace identity: a study of a non territorial office environment', Working Paper, Davis: University of California.
——(2004) 'Interpreting workplace identities: the role of office décor', *Journal of Organizational Behaviour* 25(1): 99–128.
Ewenstein, B. and Whyte, J. (2009) 'Knowledge practices in design: the role of visual representations as "epistemic objects"', *Organization Studies* 30(1): 7–30.
Ezzamel, M. and Robson, K. (1995) 'Accounting in time: organizational time-reckoning and accounting practices', *Critical Perspectives on Accounting* 6(2): 149–170.
Fenwick, T. (2010) 'Re-thinking the "thing": sociomaterial approaches to understanding and researching learning at work', *Journal of Workplace Learning* 22(1/2): 104–116.
Fine, G. and Hallett, T. (2003) 'Dust: a study in sociological miniaturism', *The Sociological Quarterly* 44(1): 1–15.
Gagliardi, P. (1990) 'Artifacts as pathways and remains of organizational life', in P. Gagliardi (ed.) *Symbols and Artifacts: Views of the Corporate Landscape*, New York: Aldine de Gruyter.
Hatch, M.J. (1990) 'The symbolics of office design: an empirical exploration', in P. Gagliardi (ed.) *Symbols and Artifacts: Views of the Corporate Landscape*, New York: Aldine de Gruyter.
Heath, C., Luff, P. and Hindmarsh, J. (2010) *Video in Qualitative Research*, London: Sage.
Hindmarsh, J. and Heath, C. (2000) 'Sharing the tools of the trade: the interactional constitution of workplace objects', *Journal of Contemporary Ethnography* 29(5): 523–562.

Ingold, T. (2010) 'Bringing things to life: creative entanglements in a world of materials', *Realities Working Paper Series No. 15*. Available at http://www.socialsciences.manchester.ac.uk/realities/publications/workingpapers/15-2010-07-realities-bringing-things-to-life.pdf (accessed 31 July 2012).

Kelly, G.A. (1955) *The Psychology of Personal Constructs*, New York: Norton.

Latour, B and Callon, M. (1981) 'Unscrewing the Big Leviathan: how actors macrostructure reality and how sociologists help them to do so', in *Advances in Social Theory and Methodology: Toward an Integration of Micro- and Macro-Sociologies*, London: Routledge & Kegan Paul, 277–303.

Latour, B. and Woolgar, S. (1979) *Laboratory Life: The Social Construction of Scientific Facts*, London: Sage.

Law, J. (1997) 'Traduction/Trahison: Notes on ANT', Department of Sociology, Lancaster University. Available at http://www.lancs.ac.uk/fass/sociology//research/publications/papers/law-traduction-trahison.pdf (accessed 12 May 2012).

Law, J. and Hassard, J. (eds) (1999) *Actor Network Theory and After*, Oxford and Keele: Blackwell and the Sociological Review.

Linstead, S. and Höpfl, H. (eds) (2000) *The Aesthetics of Organization*, London: Sage.

Luff, P., Hindmarsh, J. and Heath, C. (2000) *Workplace Studies: Recovering Work Practice and Informing System Design*, Cambridge: Cambridge University Press.

Martin, J. and Siehl, C. (1983) 'Organizational culture and counterculture: an uneasy symbiosis', *Organizational Dynamics* 12(2): 52–64.

Mehta, R. and Belk, R.W. (1991) 'Artifacts, identity, and transition: favourite possessions of Indians and Indian Immigrants to the United States', *Journal of Consumer Research* 17(4): 398–411.

Miller, D. (2005) *Materiality*, Durham: Duke University Press.

——(2009a) *Stuff*, London: Polity Press.

——(2009b) *The Comfort of Things*, London: Polity Press.

Molotch, H. and McClain, N. (2008) 'Things at work: informal social-material mechanisms for getting the job done', *Journal of Consumer Culture* 8(1): 35–67

Morgan, N. and Pritchard, A. (2005) 'On souvenirs and metonymy: narratives of memory, metaphor and materiality', *Tourist Studies* 5(1): 29–53.

Nathan, M. and Doyle, J. (2002) *The State of the Office: The Politics and Geography of Working Space*, London: Futures Publication in The Industrial Society.

Ng, R. and Höpfl, H. (2011) 'Objects in exile: the intimate structures of resistance and consolation', *Journal of Organizational Change Management* 24(6): 751–766.

Nohria, N. (1998) 'Is a network perspective a useful way of studying organizations?', in G. Hickman (ed.) *Leading Organizations: Perspectives for a New Era*, London: Sage.

O'Toole, P. and Were, P. (2008) 'Observing places: using space and material culture in qualitative research', *Qualitative Research* 8(4): 616–634.

Parkin, D. (1999) 'Mementoes as transitional objects in human displacement', *Journal of Material Culture* 4(3): 303–320.

Pettinger, L. (2004) 'Brand culture and branded workers: service work and aesthetic labour in fashion retail', *Consumption Markets & Culture* 7(2): 165–184.

Pratt, M. and Rafaeli, A. (2006) 'Understanding our "object-ive" reality', in A. Rafaeli and M. Pratt (2006) *Artefacts and Organizations: Beyond Mere Symbolism*, New Jersey: Lawrence Erlbaum.

Scarles C. (2009) 'Becoming tourist: renegotiating the visual in the tourist experience', *Environment and Planning D – Society & Space* 27(3): 465–488.

Scheff, T.J. (1990) *Microsociology: Discourse, Emotion and Social Structure*, Chicago: University of Chicago Press.

Scheiberg, S. (1990) 'Emotions on display: the personal decoration of workspace', *American Behavioral Scientist* 33(3): 330–338.

Schein, E.H. (2004) *Organizational culture and leadership*, 3rd ed., San Francisco: Jossey Bass.

Schultz Kleine, S., Kleine, R.E. and Allen, C.T. (1995) 'How is a possession "me" or "not me"? Characterizing types and an antecedent of material possession attachment', *Journal of Consumer Research* 22(3): 327–343.

Shortt, H. and Warren, S. (2012) 'Fringe benefits: valuing the visual in narratives of hairdressers' identities at work', *Visual Studies* 27(1): 18–34.

Stolte, J., Fine, G. and Cook, K. (2001) 'Sociological miniaturism: seeing the big through the small in social psychology', *Annual Review of Sociology* 27 (Aug): 387–413.

Strati, A. (1999) *Organization and Aesthetics*, London: Sage.

—— (2000) 'Putting people in the picture: art and aesthetics in understanding organizational life', *Organization Studies* 21: 53–69.
Styhre, A. (2010) 'Knowledge work and practices of seeing: epistemologies of the eye, gaze, and professional vision', *Culture and Organization* 16(4): 361–376.
—— (2011) 'The architect's gaze: the maintenance of collective professional vision in the work of the architect', *Culture and Organization* 17(4): 253–269.
Suchman, L. (2005) 'Affiliative objects', *Organization* 12(3): 379–399.
Tian, K. and Belk, R.W. (2005) 'Extended self and possessions in the workplace', *Journal of Consumer Research* 32: 297–310.
Turkle, S. (ed.) (2007) *Evocative Objects: Things We Think With*, Boston: MIT Press.
Tyler, M. and Cohen, L. (2010) 'Gender in/visibility and organizational space', in P. Lewis and R. Simpson (eds) *Revealing and Concealing Gender*, London: Palgrave, 23–38.
Vince, R. and Warren, S. (2012) 'Qualitative, participatory visual methods', in C. Cassell and G. Symons (eds) *The Practice of Qualitative Organizational Research: Core Methods and Current Challenges*, London: Sage, 275–295.
Wang, C. and Burris, M.A. (1997) 'Photovoice: concept, methodology and use for participatory needs assessment', *Health and Behaviour* 24(3): 369–387.
Warren, S. (2002) 'Show me how it feels to work here: using photography to research organizational aesthetics', *ephemera: theory & politics in organization* 2(3): 224–245.
—— (2005) 'Photography and voice in critical qualitative management research', *Accounting, Auditing & Accountability Journal* 18(6): 861–882.
—— (2006) 'Hot nesting? A visual exploration of personalised workspaces in a 'hot-desk' office environment', in P. Case, S. Lilley and T. Owens (eds) *The Speed of Organization*, Oslo/Copenhagen: Liber/Copenhagen Business School Press, 119–146.
—— (2008) 'Empirical challenges in organizational aesthetics research: towards a sensual methodology', *Organization Studies* 19(4): 559–580.
—— (2012) 'Having an eye for it: aesthetics, ethnography and the senses', *Journal of Organizational Ethnography* 1(1): 107–118.
Willis, P. (2000) *The Aesthetic Imagination*, London: Sage.
Wolfram Cox, J. and Minahan, S. (2005) 'Organization, decoration', *Organization* 12(4): 529–548.
Yanow, D. (2006) 'How built spaces mean: a semiotics of space', in D. Yanow and P. Schwartz-Shea (eds) *Interpretation and Methods: Empirical Research Methods and the Interpretive Turn*, New York: M.E. Sharpe.

19
Managing operations and teams visually

Nicola Bateman and Sarah Lethbridge

This chapter explores current practice in organizations at an operational level, and particularly teams who use visual tools in their decision-making. We focus on the field of operations management, and the management of everyday processes. The dominating paradigm within operations management has been lean operations and this has a large visual component known as 'visual management'. This chapter will draw mainly from these fields and provide examples of visual tools. We outline how design principles in the field of visual management were developed and give an example of how this has been applied in a company – Assa Abloy. We present four further examples of visual management and then conclude by setting out an agenda for how this approach to decision-making can be applied and the challenges that lie ahead.

Visual management in lean enterprises

Lean operations are primarily concerned with reduction of waste and delivery of customer value. The lean approach was initially developed in the automotive sector in Japan from the 1940s but started to become well known in a wide range of industries in the 1980s and then spread into the service sector in the 1990s (Womack and Jones 1996). As such, lean and its associated ideas have become mainstream and incorporated in the way that many organizations are run (Radnor 2010). One of the core ideas of lean is continuous improvement, whereby everyone in the organization is tasked with suggesting and implementing ideas for removing waste and adding value to processes. This is not done in an extemporized way but through the use of a range of formal tools and techniques.

Visual management is one of the ways, in a lean organization, in which the working environment is designed to allow the identification of waste and to support people in their quest for continuous improvement. Traditionally, knowledge of elements of processes is held by individuals alone, solely relating to aspects that affect them and their work. Organizations then rely on these individuals being considerate enough to share their knowledge with others who have an interest. Visual management socializes the work and data relating to the work, and this 'knowledge' becomes a collective responsibility. This is achieved by making the work visible, so organizations do not have to rely on individuals to remember all the detailed aspects of work tasks. In addition, very few work processes are dealt with in their entirety by one person and, if work is made visible within a shared space, individuals have a more consistent view of what is collectively required. This approach also better manages between shifts or when an employee is absent. For example, a human resources officer has phoned in sick and is likely to be away from work for a whole week. If that officer had indicated what work they had planned for the forthcoming week (attending interviews, staff meetings, etc.) via the means of a shared visual board in the office, colleagues could then easily make arrangements to cover their tasks. In a factory, if one shift have experienced a quality defect because of a broken tool on a machine, they would note the problem and what solution was put in place on a whiteboard, alerting the next shift to take extra care with this machine to make sure the quality problem did not reoccur.

If work is managed visually, everybody in the organization is responsible for ensuring that work progresses well, as everyone has been given responsibility for it. Work made more visible allows a deeper understanding of existing processes and their shortcomings, and so employees can appreciate the types of problems that occur and thus reduce the cause of such problems. So, in essence, the idea behind visual management is that the workplace should be organized to allow the team who work there to be able to identify when they are doing well, how the work is flowing, and when problems are about to arise. It can take the form of organizing the physical equipment in a visual way and also using visual tools such as graphs and tables to provide a snapshot of the current status of the work area and allow the operational team to plan work. This approach to organizing the workplace is not unique to a lean approach (Greif 1991); indeed, lean practitioners are very happy to incorporate ideas from many sources, provided it supports the core idea of identifying waste. To summarize, the purpose of visual management is to:

- make work visible;
- understand the current situation so as to improve;
- encourage and enable a better flow of work through:
   ○ the ability to detect normal versus abnormal
   ○ the identification of waste
   ○ highlighting of problems;
- facilitate team problem-solving;
- increase communication between teams;
- enable organizational learning.

Visual management principles

The principles were developed by the authors to allow non-experts at graphic design – such as production cell leaders – to develop their own graphical materials effectively. A number of sources were used to develop these principles, which had to be easily applicable by cell leaders who would not have access to sophisticated software, experience in design or a great deal of time to develop materials. Thus, they had to be pragmatically based.

The work of Edward Tufte (2001) and the contributions to the related website of Graphics Press[1] provided some key ideas into the development of the principles. The website provides a lively and informed debating forum where many of the challenges of developing usable graphical materials in a business environment are discussed. One of Tufte's key ideas is data to ink ratio, which is concerned with ensuring any graphical marks convey data. He translates this into the concept of data density, which is measured in data points (data matrix) per m^2: the higher the data density, the better the graphic communication 'Data graphics should often be based on large rather than small data matrices and have a high rather than low data density' (2001: 168). This sits well with the lean approach because of its focus on waste reduction. Another key idea from Tufte is to use colour sparingly – many software packages encourage us to use highly coloured, vibrant hues and this can obscure the key message we want to convey – Tufte suggests using colour to just highlight key pieces of information.

Cognitive psychology is a useful area for the development of guidelines. Shah and Hoeffner (2002) explore the best ways to display data, which was of particular interest to the authors because it was accessible to us as non-psychologists and addressed the type of graphical material likely to be developed by cell leaders, such as bar graphs and line graphs. However, some of the material, while useful background for us and providing a wealth of references of original sources, was still too detailed for use by cell leaders; examples include consideration of aspect ratio and animation. With their more general guidelines, such as 'line graphs are good for depicting x-y trends, bar graphs for discrete comparisons and pie chart for relative proportions' (2002: 53), Shah and Hoeffner provided a useful starting point for the development of the visual management principles.

Many of these principles from Shah and Hoeffner are shown by Few (2006) in his book on dashboard design. Dashboard design is an area allied to communications board design, except it uses a medium of electronic presentation. Few's book particularly focuses on visual perception in chapter 4 and provides many pictorial examples.

The work of Miller (1956) regarding cognitive workspace is informative in terms of the breadth of ideas that people can manage. His observations can help to inform the layout and data structure of visual tools, such as ensuring not too many elements are presented at once. The ideas of Miller and Tufte on first inspection do appear to contradict: Miller suggests simplicity, ensuring that no more than six elements are presented at once, whereas Tufte suggests that high levels of data density provide a depth of interest, authenticity and relevance to the user. The authors reconcile this conflict by ensuring not too many elements are presented at once but that the data density of the elements can be quite high.

This literature of how to present visual material was summarized by the researchers and, as part of a 'Lean University' project at Cardiff University, developed as a poster shown in Figure 19.1.

The use of visual management to inform and manage the workplace has been utilized in a range of organizations and outlined below is a case study of Assa Abloy, a lock company, who have implemented visual management ideas on their shop floor. The specific principles developed for their organization are outlined below.

Visual management at Assa Abloy

Assa Abloy is a multinational company with sites in Europe, USA and China. It makes a wide range of locks from padlocks to complex electronic locking systems and allied door products such as emergency-exit bars. This section is based on work that took place on the Portobello site in Willenhall in the West Midlands, near Birmingham, UK. Assa Abloy took over ownership of the site in 2001. The area of Willenhall has been associated with lock manufacture for three centuries, which has been long established at the Portobello site. Lock manufacture at Portobello is conventional, consisting of production of component parts and then assembly into a wide range of products, such as padlocks or door locks.

The Portobello site has been updating its approach to manufacturing through the incorporation of lean ideas since 2006. As such, the shop floor is organized into cells where each cell focuses on making a family of products, such as small padlocks or night latches. The cell has a

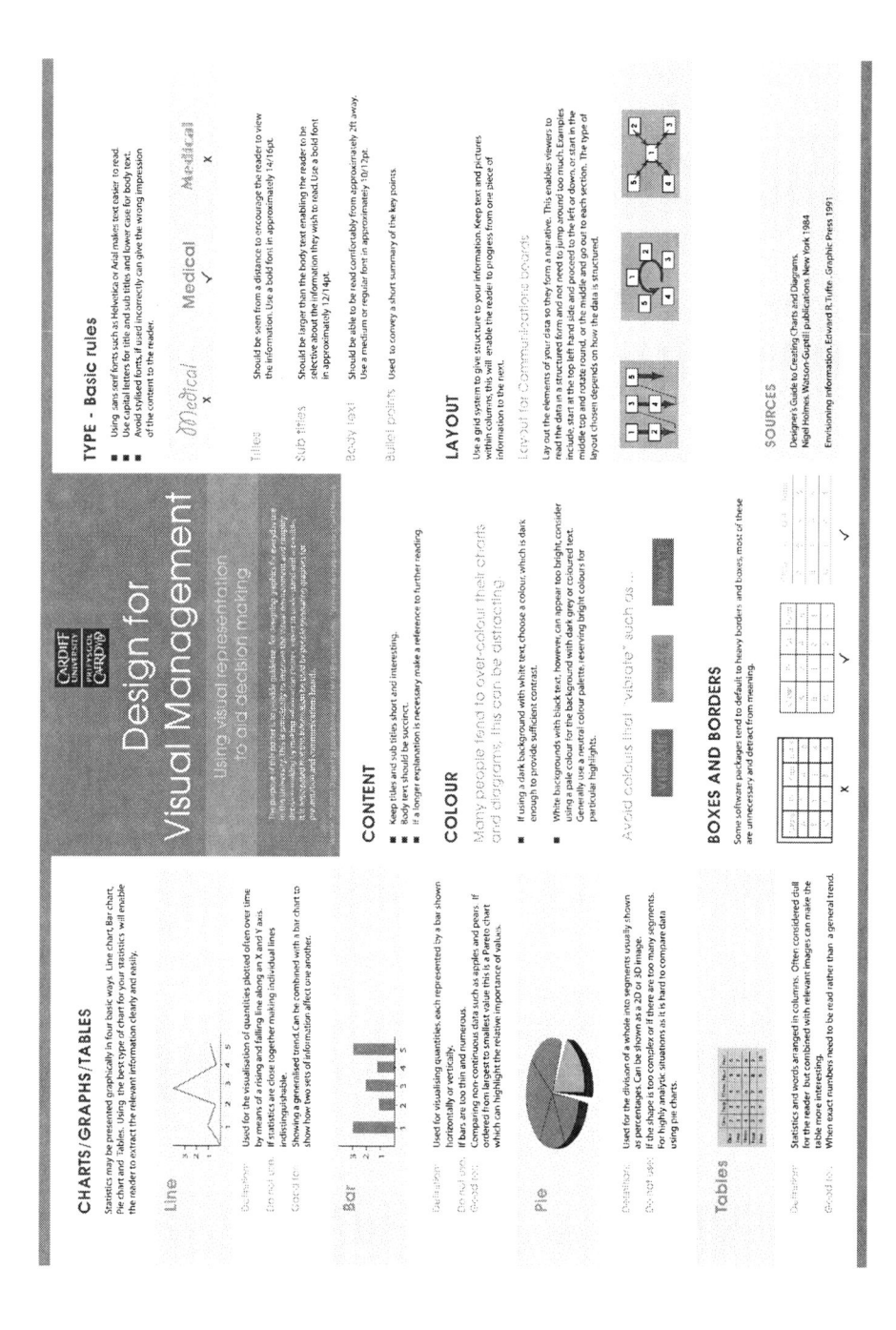

Figure 19.1 Visual Management Principles, developed by Cardiff University, of 'Lean University' project

number of operators, typically 8–12, and a cell leader who manages the cell. The operations director wanted to improve visual management within the cells particularly the communications boards used by the cell leaders. He wanted to develop boards that would enable cell leaders to have better control of their cells, in terms of meeting customer orders more reliably, and also enabling cell leaders and their teams to identify areas for improvement. Communications boards are commonly used by many different organizations, in cells and other areas where teams operate, to provide a focus where information about the cell can be displayed and discussed daily by the team. It would usually consist of: graphs of performance measures, details of the team – such as skills, workload planning tools and improvement activities. Further examples can be found from Rich et al. (2006).

Research methodology

This section documents action research that took place over a period of four years and, as such, it addresses activities that took place at two levels: the action taken by Assa Abloy and the research conducted to investigate this process. The action taken by Assa Abloy encompassed the design of the boards, their implementation and ongoing use. This process is represented in Figure 19.2, which shows that initial objectives were selected. This was followed by a design phase that set the proposed format and contents of the communications board. This design then moved to an implementation phase that was rolled out across all the cells in the shop floor.

Figure 19.2 Implementation in Assa Abloy

Once in place for nine months, the design of the board was reviewed by analysing its use. The following year, the ongoing use of the boards was again reviewed.

The second level – associated with action research – is the research process that overlays the action taken by the subject organization (Assa Abloy) shown in Figure 19.3. The initial visual management principles developed by the authors were introduced at the meeting where the objectives of the implementation were specified. The design stage was observed and documented by one of the authors, by notetaking and photographs. Review 1 looked at how the boards were

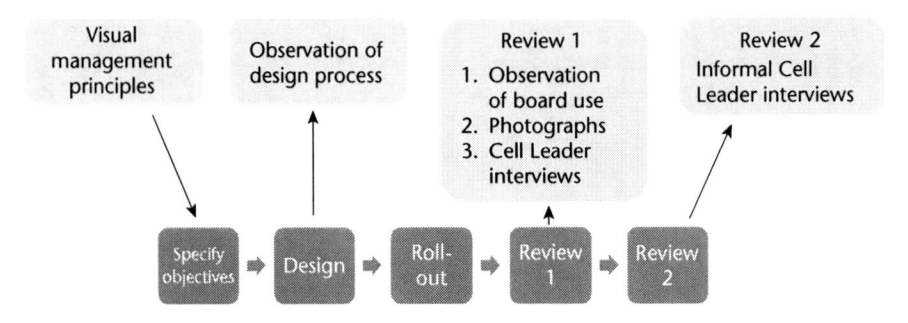

Figure 19.3 Research overlaying implementation

being used as part of everyday shop-floor life. This review consisted of: observations of the day-to-day meeting where the cell leaders used their board to interact with their team; photographs of each of the boards; and interviews with six cell leaders to provide their opinion on aspects of the use of the board. Of particular interest in this context are the methods used in review 1, where photographic materials were created.

These photographic materials were images of the communications boards that had been in use for at least nine months across the shop floor, images were taken from fourteen cells. The photographs were taken by the researcher at the end of each observation of the board use. These photographs were used in two ways; first, an overall analysis of the content and, second, an analysis of the content over time. The analysis of the content was conducted by looking at the elements in the photographs and comparing them to the original design. The researcher looked at how the elements on the board related to each other in terms of data flow from high-level strategic material down to low-level causes of occurrences of problems and the associated problem-solving. It was possible to examine data added to the boards over time from a single photograph rather than from a series of chronological photographs (as one might expect) because of the way that data was recorded on the various graphs. Most graphs required the cell leaders to add data each week, plotting the performance of an aspect of operations over time. This means that a single photograph shows plots of time-phased data, enabling the researcher to assess use of data over a year. In addition, the researcher could use these photographs to assess levels of data density. This was done by selecting the potentially most data-dense graphics, measuring their size and counting the number of data points required to produce the graphic.

Review 2 was less extensive than review 1 and consisted of an informal meeting with the cell leaders who updated the researcher as to ongoing changes of use of the board. Further details of the action research approach taken can be found in Bateman *et al.* (2009a). The next section reports the findings from the research process.

Board design process

The process of designing the new board and its deployment in the cells is documented below. The Assa Abloy boards had two sides, a production analysis board (PAB) side, and a key performance indicator (KPI) side. The PAB side deals with the daily plan to allow cell leaders to organize their day, while the KPI side gives a longer-term view to allow trend analysis and, hence, problem-solving. We shall track the development of the KPI side.

To design the KPI side, a team of cell leaders were drawn together, and a facilitator was appointed to help the design process. Not utilizing a graphics designer to develop the board may seem an unusual approach, but it has a number of advantages over employing a design expert. First, cell leaders need to have ownership of the design and are more likely to encourage other cell leaders to adopt the design and for operators to use and update the information held within it. Second, cell leaders are much more likely than an external designer to create a board that meets their needs, and, finally, in line with continuous improvement ideas, it was expected that the design would evolve and this was more likely to happen if control of the design was in the cell leaders' hands. Once the decision not to use a designer has been made, it is necessary to support the cell leaders with help to produce a design in line with visual management principles and also to provide them with technical support to use any software required to develop proformas. This is where a facilitator is able to play an important role. The facilitator was external to Assa Abloy and had an ongoing relationship with the company, working with them to embed lean ideas at the Portobello site. He worked for SMMT Industry Forum as an engineer, and, as such, was not a design specialist but was experienced in facilitating teams and providing visual tools to support them.

In addition to the Industry Forum engineer's skills, some visual management principles were developed for this project to aid the design process; these principles evolved from those identified in Figure 19.1:

1. Using the right graphical tool to convey data – when and where bar charts are appropriate, when and where line charts, etc. The difference between discrete and continuous data, etc.
2. Using colour sparingly – just to highlight key features.
3. Avoid using excess borders and boxes – looking at minimum ink to data ratio.
4. Using a board layout that reflects the flow and structure of the information to be presented. The layout should act as a visual agenda for meetings providing appropriate structure.

The design process involved four cell leaders and a quality engineer and took three and half days over a period of a couple of months. The cell leaders took the process seriously and much earnest debate ensued about what should be included and what existing material could be modified to suit the needs of the cell leaders. They also took note of the visual management principles and tried to incorporate them into their development of the designs. A more detailed account of the design process is documented in Bateman *et al.* (2009b). It should be noted that the support by the facilitator took two forms: first, guiding the team leaders through the design process and, second, to produce the graphic proformas to populate the boards and then organize the physical boards. This second input was considerable and required an additional eleven and a half days by the facilitator.

Explanation of KPI board design

The board (Figure 19.4) follows a specific flow, adhering to principle 4, with cell overview information in the left-hand column (a), including the cell team, product range, the process flow, attendance monitor and team skills. The second column (b) addresses the detailed performance of the cell and has five KPIs recorded graphically week by week. These KPIs are 'On Time In Full' (OTIF) deliveries, 'quality concerns', 'downtime', health and safety monitor, and '5S' score, which is a measure of workplace organization. The third column (c) provides some insight into the causes of the scores for the KPI level and looks at reasons for variation. The fourth column (d) provides additional performance data in terms of arrears, scrap, efficiency, cell status in terms of overall competency and a log of 'yellow tags'. Yellow tags highlight equipment that needs intervention in terms of maintenance or modification.

The fifth and final column (e) provides an overview of performance with site performance both in terms of OTIF and an accompanying narrative of performance and site activities, cell improvement actions and a visual history of improvements.

Thus, the KPI board flows (left to right) from background through specific performance and its causes to overall performance and its history, safety and workplace organization.

Within this, there are horizontal themes, the first row (f) documents OTIF and its converse arrears, the remaining rows cover customer concerns, efficiency, health and safety. It should be noted that this design of the board (documented in April 2010) uses computer-generated proformas (largely for columns two and three) but the actual data is filled in by hand. This is common practice for these types of board and is based on the assumption that having the cell leader write by hand means that the data is more 'involving' than computer-generated material; it also means that a single sheet can be used to collect six months of data, providing the teams

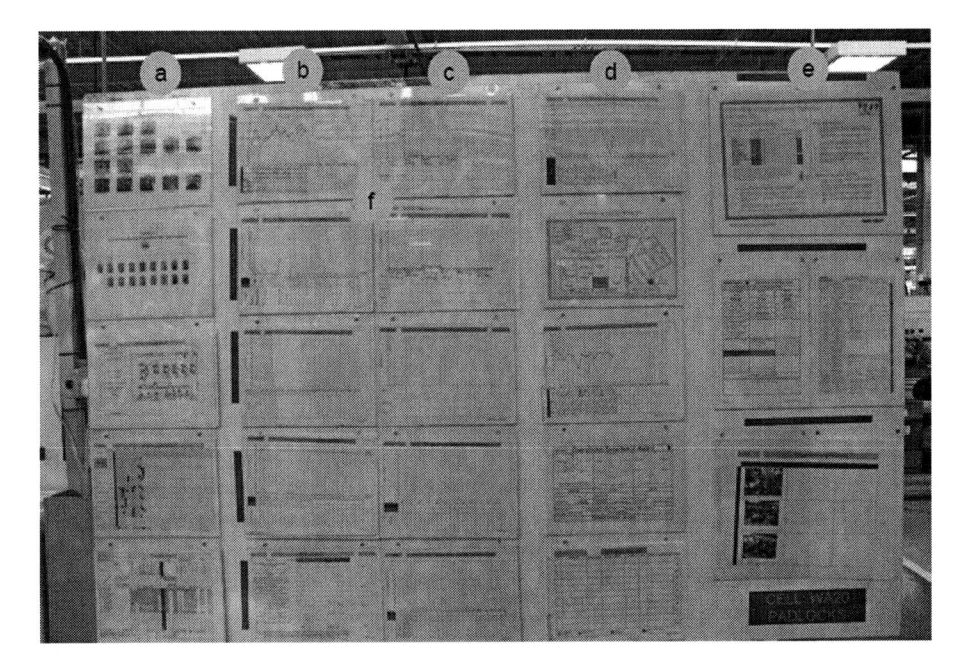

Figure 19.4 Assa Abloy communications board, KPI side

with the ability to analyse trends. If the graphs were generated by computer, a new printout would need to be made each time data was added. It is more accessible for operators to update the information by hand on a regular basis. This encourages interaction with the board, in a way, 'socializing' it.

Use of board on the shop floor

After the design of the board had been decided, it was rolled out across 23 cells on the shop floor; the process was again supported by the Industry Forum engineer and required considerable support. Further research was conducted that examined how the boards were being used and achieving their aim of participation in improvement by cell leaders.

Observation of board use indicated that ten out of the fourteen cell leaders used the data on their boards as part of their daily brief by interacting with the graphs. Ten cell leaders (with an overlap of nine with the previous group) used the briefing process to problem-solve. In addition, it became evident that two methods of using the board had emerged. The intention of having the board is to conduct a daily brief with the cell team and appropriate support staff such as maintenance engineers and component supply. However, one group of cell leaders, who had an area manager – their line manager – in common, were briefing as a single group in the staff canteen (away from their boards), rather than separately with their cell teams.

The analysis of photographs taken as part of review 1 (see Figure 19.3) showed that the KPIs were being extensively completed by the cell leaders, with four of the primary KPIs being completed by all the cells and the remaining four primary KPIs being completed by more than half the cells. Data density calculations revealed that the densest chart was the time planner with 251,819 data points per m^2, equivalent to sophisticated graphics used in academic journals. This demonstrates that this group of cell leaders are comfortable using quite high levels of data density, supporting Tufte's theory that data dense graphics are suitable in this context.

Development of visual management at Assa Abloy

Since the observations of the board use (April 2010), the methods that the cell leaders use, both in terms of the design of the board, and how it is updated and utilized by the team, have continued to evolve as identified in review 2. The canteen group and non-canteen group approaches have been merged, and the cell leaders meet together daily in groups by area. The boards for each cell are still completed in the locale of each cell. The area meeting of the cell leaders provides opportunities to support each other in terms of sharing workers, and also means support functions, such as supplies, quality and engineering, can attend fewer area meetings rather than every cell meeting. How new data is added to the board has also changed, instead of being completed by hand it is printed out by computer.

Further examples of visual management

This section shows four examples of visual tools used to aid decision-making and to manage teams. The examples chosen are from a range of sectors to demonstrate the applicability of this approach and include a web team at the University of St Andrews, Her Majesty's Courts Service in Sefton (Merseyside), and two examples from the UK's National Health Service, one for planning patient stays at Calderdale and Huddersfield NHS Trust and one for managing prescriptions piloted at St Mary's Hospital London. The authors of the chapter took no active part in the development of these visual tools. They were independently developed by the different organizations who interpreted existing visual approaches. All but St Mary's Hospital did this within a lean remit.

We included these examples to show the range of approaches available both in development and execution of visual tools, and also to show how they solve common problems within the contemporary workplace. Thus, the examples show the range of possibilities for implementation and highlight contrasting approaches.

University of St Andrews – Web Team's visual management board

In 2006/2007, the University of St Andrews established a 'Lean University' programme, its aim being to 'eliminate non value adding activity so that the University can focus its energies on Teaching and Research'.[2] It seeks to achieve this by creating a 'culture of continuous improvement' where 'respect for people' is paramount. A central team was established to act as a 'change management consultancy' for the institution, leading improvement projects, developing improvement skills in staff and offering advice and support to those practising improvement work within their everyday work roles. After several years, the University has achieved some substantial results as a consequence of their improvement efforts. In a December 2009 audit, staff working on lean teams had enabled the release of an estimated 3,500 days of time on an annual basis.

The introduction of visual management has proved to be an integral part of their improvement approach. The University's Web Team use visual management to help them to see the tasks that they have to complete and when they need to be completed. This is an example where visual management is providing a team of people with a shared vision of a complex and changing situation to provide a clear sense of the priority in which those tasks need to be completed. Without it, individuals might not appreciate the critical tasks that need to be completed from an organizational perspective, but might merely focus on the tasks that they are aware of. By converting the task that needs to be done into a visual medium, a collective understanding of the work ahead of the team can be discussed in a proactive way.

Managing operations and teams visually

Different tasks are represented by different-coloured sticky notes (g) and then allocated to different team members to complete these tasks (h). Sticky notes are used so that the tasks can easily be moved around. A section of the board asks team members to examine how many tasks received from the CMS (their helpdesk) and emails they have completed and how long it took them to solve that task (i). The board forms the basis of their team meetings, a kind of agenda. To aid the team meeting, an aide memoire has been added to provide structure (j): 1. What did you do yesterday? 2. What do you need to do today? 3. Any problems? 4. Any new requests? 5. Any outstanding CMS (helpdesk) calls? A set of questions exists to facilitate a weekly review, which asks the team to consider who should be responsible for different tasks, who should do what task and to update the project board accordingly.

The board is highly valued by the team. They regularly seek to improve the design of the board in order to make it more useful. Their latest addition is a section which is designed to help them to plan long term, so the board now helps them to manage their work on a daily, weekly and monthly basis.

Having been enabled to have greater visibility of the tasks ahead of them, the Web Team can better prioritize and plan. First, the abstract process of managing tasks and processes is made more tangible by having a physical manifestation on the board, and this makes it easier to see the scope of the week ahead. In addition, when the team is experiencing difficulties in solving tasks, visual management acts as a vehicle to help them to collectively problem-solve, particularly starting to uncover the underlying causes of recurring problems. For example, '*we are always waiting for a response from Department X*'; the team can then ask the question: '*why does this reoccur with this department?*' The team could then approach Department X with real data and information collected from the board about the number of times a project is delayed because

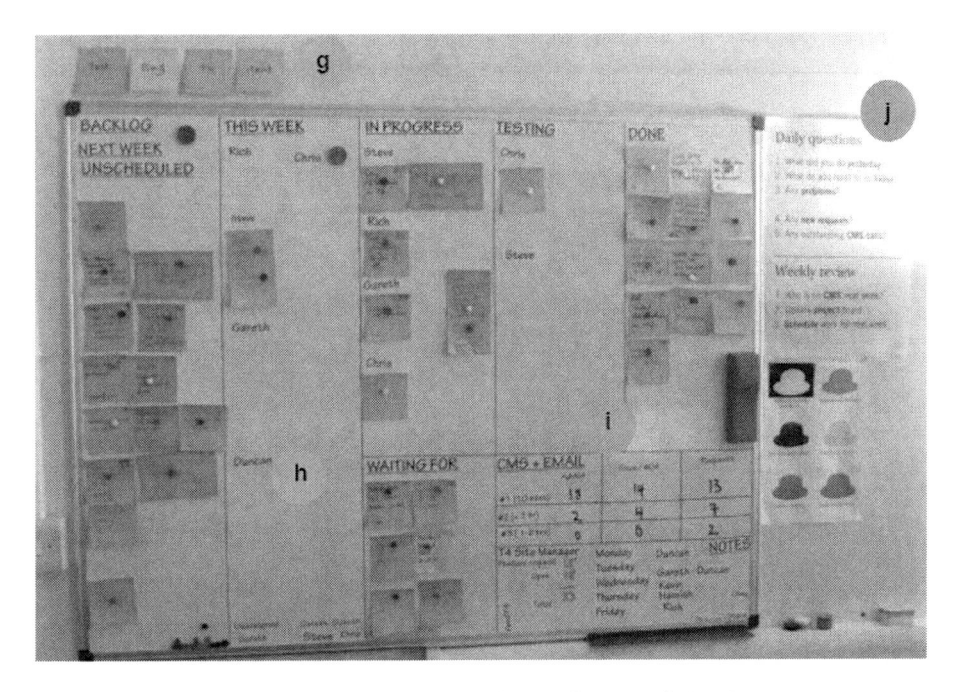

Figure 19.5 Management board for University of St Andrews Web Services
Source: © University of St Andrews. Created by University of St Andrews Web Services and Lean Team

they have not provided them with the necessary input, and they could also communicate the consequence of these delays. This conversation could then lead to a discussion about the reasons why the delay occurs. Perhaps, Department X do not really understand what they were asked to provide or why this information was important. Collectively, the two teams, when armed with accurate data, can decide a way forward, to facilitate a better flow of work.

Such discussions build collaboration and encourage deep organizational learning. All of these activities help the team to complete tasks within a quicker timeframe, one of the key objectives of a lean approach. If tasks are done to a high level of quality, within a shorter timeframe, capacity is released, enabling the organization to do more and to deliver increased value to its customers and stakeholders. Visual management facilitates the pursuit of better quality to shorter delivery timeframes by providing teams with the data, often in graphical form, that they need to improve.

Her Majesty's Courts Service visual management

The example in Figure 19.6 is from Sefton Magistrates' Court. The team at Sefton greatly valued the introduction of the board and would not wish to return to a time where visual management was not used. They stated that they 'couldn't imagine' how they managed to get the work done before the introduction of the board, as it allows them to effectively allocate work, depending on the volume and type of work received. They also greatly appreciated being able to understand, in a more robust way, the types of problems that they were encountering. The board would enable them to collect quality information, which provided them with the data needed to conduct problem-solving techniques.

The board records, on a daily basis, the volume and variety of work that comes into the court. These pieces of work are categorized into different types of task and some calculations are made to establish how much time will be needed to complete these tasks (k). The team are then able to allocate employees to work on these tasks accordingly. Other sections of the board

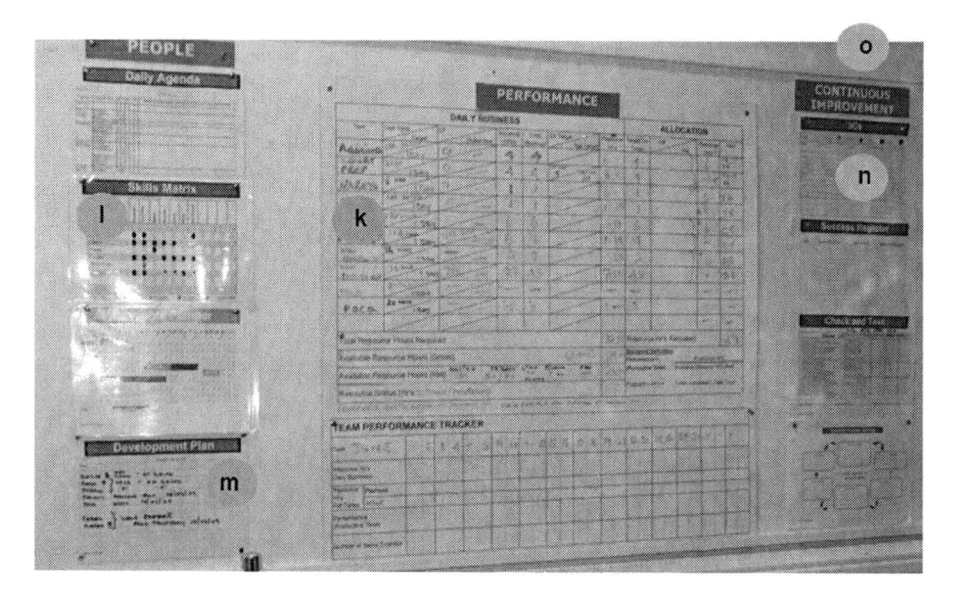

Figure 19.6 Sefton Magistrates' Court's team information board
Source: © HMCS. Created by Sefton Magistrates' Court Lean Team

Managing operations and teams visually

identify the different skills of team members (relating to their capability to respond to the different tasks) (l) and a development plan exists to address any gaps (m). The board also encourages team members to analyse where they have experienced problems within the completion of tasks (n). In fact, the entire right section of the board is dedicated to continuous improvement (o). So, to summarize, the board offers the team at the court the opportunity to reflect on their performance of previous work, to actively plan current work, and also to improve for the future.

Calderdale and Huddersfield NHS visual management

Calderdale and Huddersfield NHS have embraced visual management to help bring about operational improvement, to the extent that, with the assistance of external consultants, they plan to create a 'Visual Hospital'. The improvement team realized that, in order for their hospital to effectively deal with as many patients as possible, they would need to focus on making sure that patients spend no more time in hospital than they needed to. As such, improvement plans were put together to make sure that they effectively used all of the beds that were available to them. Figure 19.7 illustrates the visual bed management aspect of the project.

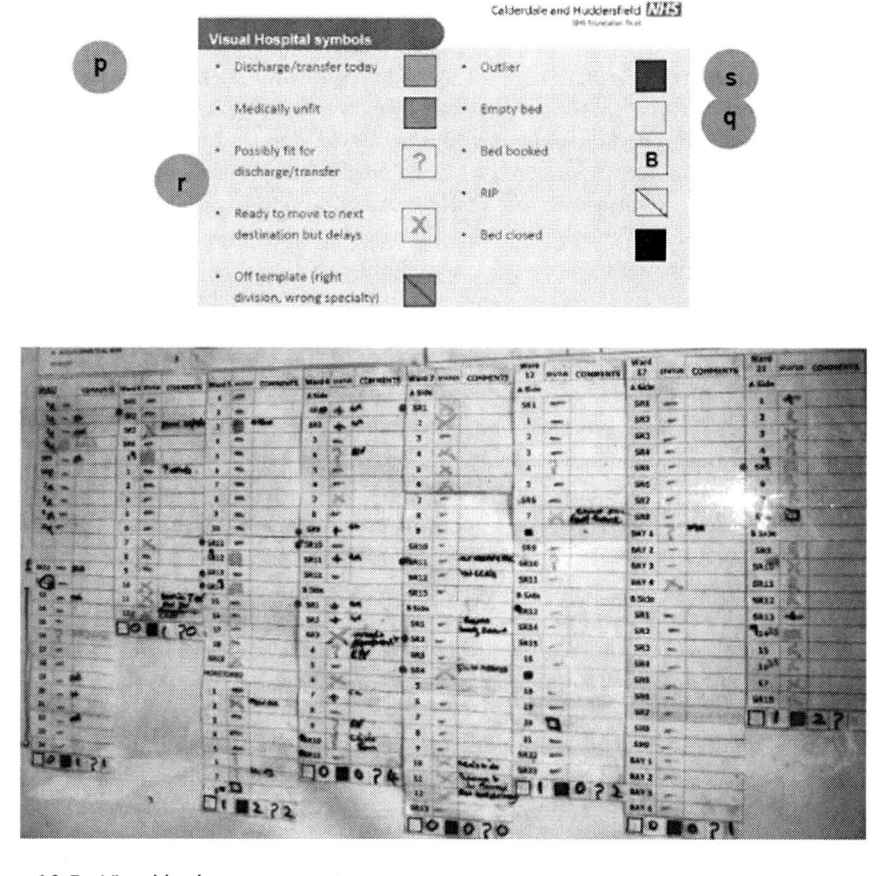

Figure 19.7 Visual bed management
Source: © Calderdale and Huddersfield NHS Trust. Created by Calderdale and Huddersfield NHS Trust Lean Team and Marc Baker and Ian Taylor from Lean Enterprise Academy

This board shows all of the beds that are available in the hospital on different wards. Using the key provided, the status of all beds can be quickly ascertained. The chart helps the bed management team to:

- fill empty beds (p);
- work with ward staff to ensure that all those due to leave the hospital that day do so (q);
- actively assist wards to solve any patient problems so that they can leave (r);
- identify patient outliers (s) so that they can be monitored more closely (patient outliers are a category of patient that require special attention).

As a result of their efforts (including the bed management project), the average length of stay in their medicine and elderly care division moved from 6.1 days to 4.4 days – a considerable reduction, which benefits not only the productivity of the hospital, but also the patients who are keen to return home. Typical delays that previously occurred were due to transportation home not being booked and secured, or because 'take-home medication' had not been processed.

Prescription chart at Imperial College Healthcare – IDEAS

This example is different from the previous examples in that it did not evolve from within a lean environment. It developed out of the thinking from 'nudge' psychology (Dolan et al. 2010) and is concerned with applying these ideas to the problems that exist to patient prescribing within hospitals. Nevertheless, it is included here because it encompasses similar problems to the other visual tools presented. It uses a different approach to the development and design of the tools, reflecting the different academic perspectives from which IDEAS originated, principally the MINDSPACE approach (Dolan et al. 2010). The detailed solutions and guidelines developed in IDEAS follow similar lines to the previous visual management approach, such as structuring elements in an appropriate order, and only highlighting key elements, indicating considerable crossover in subject matter in potential of cross-fertilization of approaches.

The IDEAS prescription chart was developed to address the issues of errors associated with the writing of prescriptions in hospital. Most hospitals use handwritten paper-based prescription charts as a method of recording medications that have been prescribed and given. This process is subject to the usual errors associated with handwriting, such as illegibility and incomplete data. These problems are compounded by the hospital environment where considerable time pressures on staff exist and different teams work round the clock. In addition, different hospital trusts use different charts (only Wales has a standard prescription chart), making it difficult for bank staff, agency staff and new recruits to adjust to local procedures.

The IDEAS approach was to apply thinking from the 'nudge' approach to human decision-making – this would support clinicians to better prescribe. Using the MINDSPACE framework developed by the Cabinet Office for 'robust non-coercive effects on behaviour' (Dolan et al. 2010), a new design for a prescription chart was developed, initially using a review of the current NHS charts, including analysis of focus groups. These findings were then used in a design stage using the MINDSPACE approach, and so the design developed is currently being piloted.

Figure 19.8 shows an example from the regular prescriptions section of the IDEAS chart. It uses colour in a visual management way, having blue as a neutral tone and only using red for highlights (see Figure 19.9). Figure 19.8 (t) prompts the user to use appropriate units and provides a contact bleep for queries (u).

The approach used embraces visual management techniques, such as ensuring an appropriate flow, and increasing the data to ink ratio, but it also encompasses the specific issues associated

Managing operations and teams visually

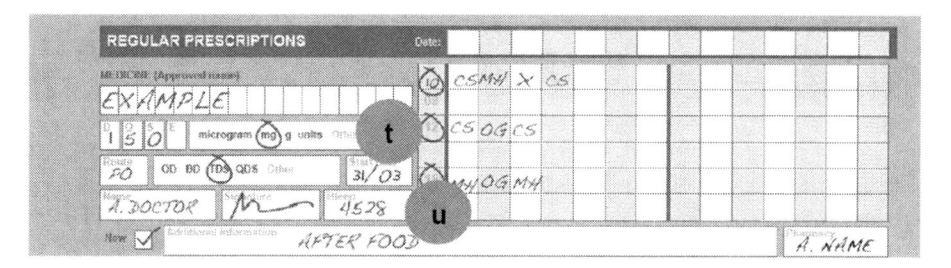

Figure 19.8 Example of page 7 from IDEAS prescription chart

Figure 19.9 Use of red to highlight key features

with prescribing, such as duration of dose and review dates and also the complexity of hospital patient prescribing; hence, it runs to 16 pages instead of the single sheets utilized by the other examples shown in this chapter.

Discussion and conclusions

This chapter documents how visual management has been used in a range of industries and sectors. The development of visual management principles draws on wider thinking from graphic design and cognitive psychology and refines the approach to developing visual tools. The Assa Abloy example illustrates the application of these ideas.

The examples from the University of St Andrews, Her Majesty's Courts Service and Calderdale and Huddersfield NHS Trust provide service sector examples of how teams use visual tools to manage their processes and demonstrate how visual tools can assist decision-making and reduce the burden of managing teams in a complex environment.

The final example of the IDEAS prescription chart is in contrast to the previous examples and principally draws from a 'nudge' psychology standpoint as opposed to a lean approach. However, it tackles similar problems of shared knowledge and decision-making and also finds common solutions such as use of colour, the benefit of consistency and leads the users through a well-structured process. Thus, it demonstrates the board applicability of visual tools both in and out of a lean environment.

The above examples highlight the visual management approach and also the different ways it can be implemented. The Assa Abloy example also has highlighted some of the challenges and areas to explore further with this approach. For example, is it best to handwrite data, which is regarded as more involving, or is it better to use computer printouts from a single data source? A comment from the University of St Andrews team expresses this dilemma well:

> While I am attracted to the idea of a centralized, available-anywhere online tool to manage our workload – there is actually something very satisfying and valuable about physically moving a ticket from

319

one column to the next; in a way it makes that task feel more real. It's also a much quicker, more flexible system that doesn't require a PC to be booted up, or software to be installed or reconfigured before you do anything. And using a methodology that encourages change ... that's got to be a good thing!

In addition, the best way of designing the visual tools is in question; for example, do the visual management guidelines developed for Assa Abloy help to develop better visual tools that justify the additional design effort? And, contrasting the Assa Abloy process of design development with the IDEAS prescription chart, what effect does relinquishing the design processes to an external designer have on the design outcome, effort required and the subsequent evolution and management of the design? Does having an external designer actually reduce ownership by the organization's decision-makers and to what extent does it inhibit continuous improvement? The questions are yet to be answered in this field of enquiry; however, the further application of visual tools in organizations seems likely to continue to spread.

Each of the organizations in the examples outlined above has devoted considerable effort to the development of their visual tools. New organizations considering this approach should not underestimate the time required both to design and implement visual tools. Nevertheless, the examples clearly demonstrate the power of visual management in helping teams to conduct their work efficiently and effectively and to help improvement to occur.

Acknowledgements

Thanks to: Lee Philp at Assa Abloy and all the cell leaders; Harry Warrender, formerly at SMMT Industry Forum, now Assa Abloy; Steve Yorkstone at University of St Andrews; Deborah McLaughlin at Her Majesty's Courts Service; Tania King at Calderdale and Huddersfield NHS Trust; Marc Baker and Ian Taylor from Lean Enterprise Academy; and Dr Dominic King at Imperial College London.

Notes

1 http://www.edwardtufte.com/tufte/.
2 www.st-andrews.ac.uk/lean.

References

Bateman, N., Philp, L. and Warrender, H. (2009a) 'Visual management and KPI board design in a lean environment', paper presented at the British Academy of Management Conference Brighton, September.

Bateman, N., Philp, L. and Warrender, H. (2009b) 'Visual management and shopfloor teams – utilising shopfloor knowledge', paper presented at the European Operations Management Association (EUROMA), Gothenburg, July.

Dolan, P., Hallsworth, M., Halpern, D., King, D. and Vlaev, I. (2010) 'MINDSPACE: influencing behaviour through public policy', London: Cabinet Office.

Few, S. (2006) *Information Dashboard Design: The Effective Visual Communication of Data*, Sebastopol, CA: O'Reilly Media, Inc.

Greif, M. (1991) *The Visual Factory*, Portland, OR: Productivity Press.

Miller, G.A. (1956) 'The magic number seven, plus or minus two: some limits on our capacity for processing information', *Psychological Review* 101(2): 343–352.

Radnor, Z. (2010) *Review of Business Improvement Methodologies in Public Services*, London: Advanced Institute of Management (AIM) Research.

Rich, N., Bateman, N., Esain, A., Massey, L. and Samuel, D. (2006) *Lean Evolution*, Cambridge: Cambridge University Press.

Shah, P. and Hoeffner, J. (2002) 'Review of graph comprehension research: implications for instruction', *Educational Psychology Review* 14: 47–69.
Tufte, E.R. (2001) *The Visual Display of Quantitative Information*, 2nd ed., Cheshire, CT, USA: Graphics Press.
Womack, J. and Jones, D. (1996) *Lean Thinking: Banish Waste and Create Wealth in Your Corporation*, New York: Simon & Schuster.

20
Social media and organizations

Pauline Leonard

Introduction

This chapter explores the use of social media and the Web in the making of organizational visual identities and practices. I draw on ongoing empirical research[1] to focus on the ways in which social media are stretching understandings of the visual in organizations and extending paradigms of identity construction and meaning-making. In particular, I focus on a case study of the use of YouTube to argue that social media are influencing an organizational rethink on visual practices, as well as relationships with clients. Increasingly, as contemporary organizations are reshaping into '*org/borgs*' (Haraway 1991; Consalvo 2003), their use of social media is contributing to a blurring of, and even a challenge to, previously established boundaries in organizational practices, positions and identities. Yet, while on the one hand, the democratic nature of these digital tools can be read as opening up directions of communicative flow and power and, as such, flattening relations; on the other hand, I argue that social media may, in fact, be additional forms of social and cultural capital by which organizations compete for relative advantage within organizational fields (Bourdieu 1984; Bennett *et al.* 2009).

Background

The rapid development of digital information and communication technologies and the affordances of the World Wide Web are enabling some significant transformations in, and challenges to, organizational practices and relations, not least in terms of their ownership and control of their visual identities (V. Miller 2011). A defining feature of contemporary Internet activity, particularly in its Web 2.0 and social media forms, is its 'for the people' democratic and participatory culture, whereby ordinary people are linked together in social and collective conversational and interactive webs (Fournier and Avery 2011: 193). This foundation underlines the fact that Web 2.0 was not in any way initially created as an instrument for organizations, or to boost corporate power. Rather, through interactive websites such as YouTube, Facebook and Twitter, new relationships between producers and consumers, organizations and clients are emerging, which are unsettling understandings of influence and form (Jensen 1998). Indeed, the bottom-up nature of digital culture means that corporate presence is not always welcome, but, rather, that organizations are often suspiciously regarded as 'uninvited crashers of the Web 2.0 party' (Fournier and Avery 2011: 193). On the other hand, as Elliott and Robinson also note in Chapter 17, the participatory nature of Web 2.0 means that any user (albeit with skills in this direction) can interact with the technology to reinterpret and re-present images and content in ways that may actually be counter to organizational purposes or ambitions (Burgess and Green 2009), and powerful multinational corporations are often seen by social media users as particularly enjoyable targets for extra-textual parody. At the same time, however, the economic potential of the Web for organizations is enormous: brand building, marketing and consumer engagement can all be enhanced, unrestricted by time and space, through the creation of (global) social networks and an organizational 'community'. It is thus becoming increasingly evident to organizations across the private, public and voluntary sectors that they must, somehow, find a way to join Web 2.0 activity as legitimate, or even honoured, guests and embrace social media as an integral part of their organizational digital strategy (Kaplan and Haenlein 2010).

Conceptualizing social media as organizational visual practice

In 1991, the feminist academic Donna Haraway proposed the metaphorical model of the 'cyborg' in order to disrupt the artificial dualisms in human thinking (Haraway 1991; Consalvo 2003). The cyborg is neither all machine nor all human, and as such challenges the purity of both categories as well as the binary and oppositional nature of knowledge based on dualisms. Haraway argued that technology, and its role in our futures, should be embraced, 'as to do otherwise is to cede control of that potentially destructive force to dominant, conservative forces already in charge' (Consalvo 2003: 70). Stone (1996) also argued that our increasing reliance on digital communication in our lives has turned us all into cyborgs and, certainly, now over 15 years on from his original book, we can agree that digital culture has significantly and irrevocably influenced methods of visual as well as oral and textual communication at the full range of scales: personally, organizationally, nationally and globally. Our increasing reliance on these systems thus turns us all into cyborgs, and the more that these are used and integrated into daily practice, the more they become essential to what we do. Organizations are certainly no exception here: as new technologies increasingly influence working lives and organizational practices, organizations too can be conceptualized as cyborgs or '*org/borgs*'. Further, the increasingly pervasive use of social media by organizational members from the bottom to the top of organizational hierarchies is contributing to the boundary-blurring that is marking contemporary working life more generally; and as the dichotomies of organization/client, professionalism/amateurism, work identity/personal identity and work-time/leisure-time are gradually becoming less distinct, organizational identities – who can do what, when and how – are being reconfigured.

Central to the above, therefore, is the acknowledgement that use of digital technologies and the Internet are being thoroughly embedded in organizational and personal daily practice. As such, *practice theory* is also useful to understanding social media as a visual form (Bourdieu 1977; Ardevol et al. 2010). A key aspect of social media is that content produced by amateurs is displayed and distributed alongside that produced by media professionals. In other words, ordinary people's media practices, such as the regular uploading and sharing of content, mix with institutionalized practices to define cultural production (Ardevol et al. 2010). On the face of it, this is a move towards democratization – but to what extent, and how, are these new and multiple forms of media practice leading to any real changes in the distribution of power and inequalities within and between organizations and other users? Bourdieu's concept of '*capital*' is useful here, as it encourages us to move away from 'the idea of fixed advantages associated with pre-defined groups and focuses instead on "the set of actually usable resources and powers" (Bourdieu 1984:122) that can be mobilized to achieve advantage and classify social distinctions' (Halford and Savage 2010: 944). This may allow us to explore how '*digital capital*', the technical skills in social media, can be converted by people/organizations into gaining advantage in competitive contexts.

The ways in which technology and organizations shape each other to *co-construct* outcomes is developed further through Actor Network Theory (ANT) (Law and Hassard 1999; Latour 2005). This focuses on the interdependency between human and non-human actors, and the ways in which these come together and combine into networks to produce outcomes. Challenging any Bourdieusian notion of fixity, however, ANT sees the nature of networks as fluid, diverse and heterogeneous, and, as such, outcomes can never be certain or ever simply be read off from actors' intentions. Using social media cannot therefore *predetermine* advantage for organizations or other users, nor achieve any predictable stability in positioning. However, in so much as their use may produce certain networks that may be enacted with some consistency, 'temporary stabilizing effects' may result from these associations (Law 2008). ANT recommends using case studies to trace such effects and outcomes of particular networks, and this is the approach of this chapter.

I have discussed above how social media can be seen both as a form of practice and as a producer of networks. In these conceptualizations, useful connections can also be made with Foucault's concept of discourse. Discourses are 'forms of knowledge or powerful sets of assumptions, expectations and explanations, governing mainstream social and cultural practices. They are systematic ways of making sense of the world by inscribing and shaping power relations within texts' (Baxter 2003: 7). Discourses are, in turn, closely associated with the social practices they produce, as well as the power relations constructed through these. Crucially, Foucault conceptualizes power not as a repressive force, held by one particular subject, but as a 'net-like organisation', which 'weaves itself through social organisations, meanings, relations … and identities' (Baxter 2003: 8). Thus while, as I will show, social media have come to be governed by a powerful set of discourses that frame the ways in which they are used, they also form a highly productive and dynamic set of networks in which individuals are simultaneously undergoing and exercising power (Foucault 1980).

These four theoretical strands interweave to offer a useful conceptual framework by which to explore the complex texture of social media. I now turn to the ways in which this may be used in organizational visual practice and identity making.

Organizational visual practice and social media

Existing 'visual identity' theories and models stress that corporate visual identity (CVI) is achieved through a very strategic approach, albeit one that is 'hardly noticeable to outsiders' (van den Bosch and de Jong 2005: 108). CVI itself is here seen to reflect 'the essence' of an organization: 'what it stands for, what its aims are, in what respect it differs from others' (ibid.: 109). It is only once these aspects are known that the 'design process' can start, the desired result being a 'visual identity system that fits the organisation' (ibid.). Although, within this conceptualization, a visual identity architecture is relatively easy to implement, 'CVI management is needed to ensure consistency'. Indeed, consistency is seen to be an integral dimension of a successful CVI, along with visibility, distinctiveness, transparency and authenticity (Fombrun and Van Riel 2004). These are achieved through the management of such visual techniques, such as company logos, signage of buildings and vehicles, billboards, business cards and letterheads, etc., the design of which is usually tightly managed by the marketing department and perhaps outsourced to an (often expensive) 'professional' public relations agency. Further, on the face of it, these are understood to be non-interactive artefacts by which to deliver a consistent and powerful message and identity.

In many ways, social media invert this approach. In contrast to this predominantly unidirectional model of CVI, social media content can be used and created by *any* Internet user, hosted as they are by a range of inexpensive and easy-to-use digital tools such as Facebook, Twitter, YouTube, Wikipedia and blogs. The opportunity for management and control is lost, as social media sites are inherently social and participative in nature, attracting and developing 'communities' of users who engage around the content, creating and sharing comments, stories, plans, videos, photos and other visual images. The potential for activity that may be counter to the vision of identity an organization may have for itself is nicely illustrated by Elliott and Robinson in Chapter 17 in this volume, when they discuss some negative comments posted on Waitrose's website. It is through activities such as these that people connect to one another, formulating online communities or 'hubs' that influence social networks. While these networks may not be as large as is sometimes assumed (Huberman *et al.* 2008), they can make things 'go viral': that is, when vast numbers of people watch a video or read a blog (Kaplan and Haenlein 2011). In terms of their potential for organizations and their CVI, therefore, social media offer exciting new opportunities in terms of reach, but there are also challenges. Thus, on the one hand, they can open up avenues for communication: tools such as YouTube and Twitter can act as *conversation starters*; wikis and Google Groups can act as *collaboration tools*; and social networking sites such as Facebook, LinkedIn and Twitter can act as *network builders* (Kanter and Fine 2010; D. Miller 2011; Kietzmann *et al.* 2011). On the other hand, however, as any user can create content, anybody could join in the production of an organization's CVI. The aim of managing consistency, therefore, may be lost.

To date, the real experts in social media have not been organizations but 'free agents' – 'individuals working outside of organizations to organize, mobilize, raise funds and communicate with constituents' (Kanter and Fine 2010: 15). Some of these work on behalf of, in particular, voluntary and charity organizations, helping to build and develop networks, raise money and promote their causes. Increasingly, however, organizational employees are themselves developing the toolkit of free agents and simulating their methods to promote organizational aims (Java *et al.* 2007). What is interesting here is that 'hub status does not happen because of a person's position on an organization chart' (Kanter and Fine 2010: 28). Anyone within an organization, regardless of position, can become a Twitter user or blogger, and be very good at it, creating a large following and developing a lively network. In this way, boundaries between the relatively powerful and the relatively powerless in an organization can become blurred; and someone at the bottom of the organizational hierarchy may be far better networked than someone at the top. As Kanter and Fine (2010) argue, *social capital* works differently online, and, as such, an individual may be more trusted than an organization. Although their content may be more *amateurish* in quality, they are likely to be regarded as more *authentic*, and, as such, have the ability to create powerful communities of *affinity*. In turn, the hierarchical distribution of organizations' social capital may also be challenged by social media presence. In the UK, for instance, recent research has demonstrated that, when the top 25 fundraising charities are compared with the top 25 FTSE companies by market capitalization, charities are far ahead in terms of use of social media, with three times as many YouTube subscribers, eight times as many Twitter followers and ten times as many Facebook 'likes' on average (nfpSynergy 2011). As this research argues, social media are a great leveller when it comes to communications, as they offer a cheap and simple way to reach out and engage supporters. Not only is this true in the developed world, but also increasingly in the less developed world (D. Miller 2011). As such, the boundaries between organization and power, rich and poor can become blurred, as small charities mobilize the resources of amateurism, authenticity and affinity to compete successfully with major corporations for online presence.

As I will now go on to suggest, it is these three discourses – amateurism, authenticity and affinity – that frame the design aesthetics of social media and work to define the parameters within which the visual is constructed. In other words, the *cultural capital* of contemporary social media may also be challenging organizations and the ways in which their CVI was previously constructed, particularly in the ways in which they traditionally used the visual to achieve distinction and status (Bourdieu 1984). The design of much social media takes a different form to the high-budget/professional approaches that have dominated organizational image-making practices. The ways in which, for example, Facebook/Twitter profile pictures are increasingly personalized means that a specific, arguably even narcissistic, genre is emerging, which users must either subscribe to or resist (Marshall 2006; Hills 2009; V. Miller 2011). However, this is *not* to argue that there is one completely distinctive 'design aesthetic' that differentiates social media or digital culture from other forms of media (Lister *et al.* 2009). In contrast, in the ways in which the digital interplays intertextually with established media forms, social media draw on visual culture and extend the interactivity of their relationship with audiences. My discussion of this will focus in particular on YouTube, arguably the least text-based form of social media. Drawing on a broadly ANT approach, I will explore new case study empirical material to trace some of the visual practices and resources that may be employed by organizations, as well as some of the outcomes, both planned and unplanned, which may be produced.

YouTube

YouTube, owned by Google since 2006, is the most prominent video-sharing website in the Western, English-speaking world and is consistently in the top ten of most visited websites globally (Burgess and Green 2009). Users upload video content to the website and audiences engage around that content, through comments and often reacting with new content of their own. In relation to this, a key discourse by which the site is positioned is that of '*amateurism*'; i.e. YouTube is primarily about the sharing of the mundane and the everyday through videos of often indifferent quality, rather than the promotion of the highly professional or corporate interests. As a result, the site has a somewhat vernacular culture with much of the content having a 'home made' character, albeit often playing intertextually with other cultural forms through inference and parody (Burgess and Green 2009). However, the fact that YouTube is very successfully able to reach a wide and diverse audience in a very short time period means that many organizations, including professional media producers, are increasingly becoming interested in exploiting its potential. As such:

> the contributors are a diverse group of participants – from large media producers and rights owners such as television stations, sports companies and major advertisers, to small-to-medium enterprises looking for cheap distribution or alternatives to mainstream broadcast systems, cultural institutions, artists, media literate fans, non-professional and amateur media producers. Each of these participants approaches YouTube with their own purposes and aims and collectively shape YouTube as a dynamic cultural system: YouTube is a site of participatory culture.
>
> *(Burgess and Green 2009: vii)*

Organizational presence, with its structural position in status hierarchies as well as its ability to produce high-quality video content, sits somewhat uneasily within this participatory culture therefore. If institutions are to be successful in exploiting the visual potential of YouTube as a means of promoting organizational aims, they may need to perform a nuanced balancing act. On the one hand, if they present too polished a video to push commercial interests, they risk transgressing the 'amateur' identity of the site and alienating many of its users. On the other hand, if they produce content which is too 'down with the kids', they risk not only tarnishing their professional image but also being positioned negatively by another of the key discourses that frame the site: that of *authenticity*. Connected with the amateurism discourse is the claim that YouTube is a vehicle for authentic and individualistic self-expression, and as such suspected violators are outed swiftly. However, as Jenkins (2009) notes, in a hybrid space such as YouTube, it is often difficult to ascertain what regimes of truth govern different genres of user-generated content in practice. For example, the emergence of what is dubbed 'Astroturf': 'fake grassroots media content produced by commercial media companies and special interest groups but passed off as coming from individual amateurs' means that the 'goals of communicators can no longer be simply read off the channels of communication' (2009: 122). Although, as Jenkins concludes, 'historically, these powerful interests could exert overt control over broadcast media but now, they often have to mask their power in order to operate within network culture' (ibid.: 122–123), it is clear that YouTube presents new challenges to organizations in the construction and negotiation of the visual. If they are to succeed, they may need to explore different techniques of self-representation that play with the vernacular and the low brow.

However, there is a third aspect of YouTube, which offers more opportunity for organizations: its potential for *affiliation* (Lange 2009). Lange defines affiliation as both 'feelings of membership in a social network, and feelings of attraction to people, things or ideas' (2009: 71). Videos of affinity try to establish communicative connections between people, and, as such, can facilitate large business-oriented networks alongside small personal ones (Lange 2009). This is a powerful way in which organizations can use the visual in order to build and maintain a community to which it can continuously promote its image and message. However, as Lange goes on to argue, this takes work, as, in order to maintain connections and relationships, attention has to be both captured and kept. Ideally, 'viewers to whom the video is addressed may respond and help maintain a field of connection between creator and viewer' (ibid.: 73). In this way, if organizations are successful in moving in this direction, the relationship between organization and user can become flattened, and even participatory. Users also enter the creative space, commenting positively or negatively on content, suggesting ideas, posting clips or even engaging in 'redaction': editing existing content to produce new content (Hartley 2008: 112; Burgess and Green 2009). This is the achievement of the organizations in the research case study to which I now turn.

Case study: Free Range Studios and The Story of Stuff

An organization that has very successfully drawn upon all three discourses of amateurism, authenticity and affinity is Free Range Studios, a 'value-centred organization' based in the US, which produces films and videos, principally via YouTube, for a range of environmental and ethical not-for-profit organizations. Over the last couple of years, Emma Bell and I have conducted a range of interviews with key personnel at both Free Range Studios and one of its key clients The Story of Stuff, predominantly via Skype. In these, we have explored the highly networked relationships between the two organizations and the ways YouTube and other forms of social media have been exploited to promote the identity and ethos of each organization as well as an environmental agenda. Our methodology of 'virtual ethnography' (Hine 2000) has also included regularly monitoring the website, the organizations' Facebook pages, blogs and Twitter feeds, as well as analysing the YouTube videos and comments themselves. While Emma and McArthur, a partner at Free Range Studios, explore the concept of 'authenticity' more broadly in Chapter 23 in this volume, here I will discuss the ways in which the three concepts interplay in their films and videos.

Free Range Studios has had phenomenal success with its YouTube postings, many of which have 'gone viral' overnight. Co-founder and CEO Jonah Sachs explains that this is because they have been extremely careful with both the messages that they have agreed to promote, as well as the choices they have made in terms of the visual style and text to convey these. By making intertextual connections with mainstream cult movies, such as *The Matrix* and *Star Wars*, yet retaining a simple and almost amateurish range of cinematic techniques, the videos produced by Free Range Studios have appealed to a wide and diverse film-buff audience as well as to an already networked (green) community, which is passionate about its cause. The participatory nature of the YouTube audience and existing social/environmental networks have thus been successfully garnered to help propagate the product, and, in the process, the status and identity of Free Range Studios. This now has its own loyal networked community with which the organization maintains contact through social media such as Twitter and blogs as part of its regular practice (Bourdieu 1977). Jonah Sachs explains how creating videos of affinity, which worked on their behalf by commenting on videos and retweeting, have been central to their success:

> If people were going to be choosing what they broadcast to their communities instead of just being broadcast to, then potentially messages of passion as opposed to messages of just straight marketing would have kind of a natural advantage that they never had before. Usually cause-based messages had been shut out of the marketplace because of money basically and also because gatekeepers were sensitive to controversial messages. Now we thought people could try building social capital and more passionately sharing things that they cared about rather than just kind of professional messages that were blasted to them and demanded that they passed them along. So we just started experimenting and playing with different ways that we could realize that dream for social change clients and non-profits and socially responsible businesses and that led us pretty quickly to … what our passion had been to begin with, which was creating movies and considering what the audience's passions were and how that fit in with what our clients were trying to achieve and then creating a whole range of different storytelling devices to break the traditional expectations of what you can do with limited budget.

Key to the success of the organization has also been a desire to differentiate itself from large, profit-driven corporates and, from the start, the visual possibilities of the Internet were used to achieve this aim.

> When we put up our first website, the first thing it said was 'We only serve non-profits.' That was the first thing on the website and just the response from the community at the time and their response to our commitment was really huge. So I think that was sort of an accidental differentiator which we really needed as a start-up.

Sachs recognizes that using the Internet means other factors come into play that are equally important in determining success as the technical quality of the visual product.

This understanding stems from the fact that they have been engaging with the visual possibilities of the Internet for well over a decade, i.e. before Web 2.0. In these early days, the amateurish simplicity of their visual images, then by necessity, was made forgivable by their novelty, leading Sachs to realize that the cultural capital and power of the Internet may be more a result of clarity of message and good timing as in a highly sophisticated technical product:

> We had some viral successes very early on, but it was very much pre-YouTube. Some of the early things I think worked not even because they were great pieces, but because they were some of the few things that actually moved and made noise on the Internet, so it kind of was a novelty at the time. And so there's always something novel that's going on, but back then, you know, Internet cartoons and videos were novel. We were even doing this before video was a viable option. We were doing it when you needed a cartoon that was less than 200 kilobytes to hope anyone would see it. So it's changed a tremendous amount and the ability to just use viral as your main strategy is now much less well placed than maybe it used to be, where if you were willing to put your video into the mix you could be one of 50 videos that were circulating at that time. And now you really can't set out to say 'Well, we're going to make something that 5 million people are going to see,' because it's expensive and throwing a dart with your eyes closed at the dartboard and just hoping it lands. So that has definitely changed, although the power of great stories and the power of bringing complex information into simplified versions is still very strong. You just can't expect that you're going to just immediately rise above the din just because you've created a story.

The dominant cultural capital of social media and the Internet may, to some extent, therefore, challenge the existing 'visual identity' theories and models, which, as I discussed above, dominate mainstream organizational studies and marketing practices; requiring organizations to rethink their visual strategies for corporate identity-making. Digital culture and social media are not in the main about a highly specified technical or aesthetically sophisticated product, but about amusing images and powerful but simple messages. For this reason, those organizations who may be the most successful users of social media are often those with less explicitly profit-oriented aims and small budgets that need to be exploited to the maximum. Indeed, voluntary and campaign organizations with clear ideologies have emerged as particularly successful users of social media, drawing on their connective properties to create and mobilize communities and increase impact (Kanter and Fine 2010). In this vein, Free Range's success is, in part, due to the fact that they have carefully built on their early positioning to maintain a location away from any identification with the profit-driven corporate sector. This is achieved visually in their videos by the clear use of signs to connote an antipathy to the excesses of capitalism (Barthes 1982 [1964]). As discussed by Davison in Chapter 2 in this volume, Barthes (1982 [1964]) shows how signs and stereotypes are used to transmit powerful ideas and messages, often in repetitive ways. This is a technique perfected by Free Range: through the use of recurring cartoon characters such as a top-hatted, fat-bellied CEO with dollar signs on his chest, and a giant iron man/robot, big business is represented as villainous and all-consuming.

One of the most successful arms of Free Range Studios' work has been for the environmental campaign organization The Story of Stuff. Together, they have produced several videos, all of which have gone viral, which are unified by the powerful visual theme of amateurish simplicity. The videos draw on a range of images that act as signs to connote the impact of big business on the environment. Childlike pictures of stick figures, line drawings of objects such as buildings and material products, and simple cartoons punch out uncompromising messages about the damage that many large corporations are inflicting on the planet. The Executive Producer at The Story of Stuff explains how this iconic style came about:

> A big part of the style actually arose out of necessity. I mean we wanted something that was going to be really simple and easy for people to take in because the information is so robust; and also from a production standpoint, an animation production and kind of budget, etc. – from that standpoint we had to come up with a style that we could make 20 minutes of it without it costing like a gazillion dollars and that was how we sort of reinvented the stick figure in that project.

The first video, itself called *The Story of Stuff*, thus deployed a style of artwork that tapped into the amateurish culture that prevails on YouTube, which was then animated and, in a juxtaposition of the sort that Sørenson discusses in Chapter 3 in this volume, supported by a 'real' presenter. This is Annie Leonard, the co-director at The Story of Stuff, who addresses the camera with the manner of a primary-school teacher giving a geography lesson. The clarity and conjunction of image and talk thus played intertextually with childish media forms to convey the message that the story here is simple: our consumption of everyday 'stuff' – bottled water, mobile phones and jeans – is damaging the planet and ruining our lives. In fact, however, it was not Free Range Studios that came up with this design, but Annie Leonard herself. The Director of Projects at The Story of Stuff explains:

> Annie had been working on these issues for a long time, but she had always kind of communicated it in a bit kind of nerdier way. You know, talking about parts per billion and toxics in the materials flow and she did a year-long workshop with a bunch of other activists and leaders and they just gave her a lot of really authentic feedback about how she could make her kind of rap, so to speak, more accessible and she really took it to heart ... she was super frustrated by her inability to communicate the information in a way that resonated with people, so, almost as a joke, when she was giving her presentation she started putting up these stick figures and these little kind of line drawings to tell her story and it immediately became apparent that that was such a better way to tell the story and she started getting invited places to go and give her talk using the stick figure drawings and everyone kept saying to her like 'You should make a film of this. You should make a film of this.'

This blurring of highly professional knowledge with amateurish style resonated with viewers to such an extent that a large online community of affinity was quickly developed. As discussed above, a key aspect of social media is its participatory culture and the interactivity of its networks, such that the whole experience of 'audiencehood' has been dramatically redefined (Burgess and Green 2009). In particular, participants of YouTube routinely engage in new forms of publishing as a way of identifying and communicating their own experiences in relation to the community's. Hartley (2009) argues that, through this process of 'redaction', 'the origin of meaning has migrated along the "value-chain" of the cultural industries, from the "author," the "producer," and the text, to the "citizen-consumer," so that "consumption" is a source of value creation, and not only its destination' (Burgess and Green 2009: 48). In the ways in which social media engage audiences as well as connect them into a network based on an affinity to a particular set of ideas, the relationship between organizations and clients is thus blurred. The latter are now more actively and directly engaged in the production of visual practices and, consequently, the identity of an organization. However, the heterogeneity of networks means that outcomes are often quite unpredictable, as is illustrated well by the Director of Projects at The Story of Stuff:

> We have a very engaged audience. We call them a community instead of an audience because they really do ... You know, it was really interesting with this last *Story of Citizens United* film that we did. We had folks complete some survey questions for us and we had them watch a series of videos both for and against the decision and then give us some feedback around what messages were coming through ... to try and get a sense from them in terms of what information would be useful as we tried to tell the story. It's [also] a very diverse audience ... it's very popular with Catholic nuns in the mid-west and here in Oakland there's like a youth group of colour that has adopted *Story of Stuff* into like a hip-hop poetry dance.

The unpredictable and uncontrollable nature of networks and audience participation are thus aspects of social media that organizations have to take on board. However, redactions produced within and by the community of affinity, such as those mentioned in the above quote, may add to the authenticity of the content produced in ways which augment its visual appeal to users, as well as, by association, the appeal of the organization. The creative designer at Free Range Studios explains how these developments in the interactive possibilities of social media mean that organizations are now in a creative arena where they are only one among multiple producers of their online content:

> One of the great things about the teenagers who are talking is that actually you can YouTube their response. I think it's hysterical, smart ... they got on and they said 'Hi, we're here to talk about *The Story of Stuff*. My name's Annie,' and then they had people kind of pop out from the side that said 'But Annie, what's a toxin?' and 'What about this?' and 'What about this?' It was really the fact that their minds were so interested and so engaged, but yet they had some really solid thoughtful critiquing, sometimes tough questions and that kind of ability that they could respond and ask those is a totally different dialogue than just Free Range broadcasting something out. I mean *The Meatrix* [an early film] was put out in some ways similar to a television model, where you have a source of the content and it broadcasts out to a wide stream. Obviously it can go viral in a way that TV can't, but it's still the model of one to many, versus when we started doing *The Story of Stuff* all of a sudden you're having one to many and many can come back to one, and many can go to each other and so it's a whole new game, which I think it's just really exciting from a creative standpoint.

Redactions may not always be produced by the community of affinity, however, but by other actors in the broader network. As mentioned above, the various videos produced by the Free Range Studios/Story of Stuff partnership have tackled a range of unsustainable corporate practices in ways that, in some cases, have clearly rattled some viewers. For example, in a critique of *The Story of Stuff*, the video is overlaid with symbols of communist regimes with a Russian army uniform superimposed on the image of Annie herself.[2] Other 'free agents' have also produced competing videos in which *The Story of Stuff* is parodied and charged with being communist and treacherous:

> There's been quite a backlash – people thinking that we're indoctrinating children, that we're socialists, which, you know, might as well be a four letter word ... [some] people just

think Annie's a liar and then make just the most outrageous claims like Annie's making millions off of this and she's attacking big business.

However, generating publicity-starting conversations and then developing and maintaining them in whatever direction and through diverse means are fundamental functions of social media, and the Free Range Studios/Story of Stuff case studies reveal the complex and contradictory ways in which this is performed. Further, the interactivity does not stop with YouTube: it is picked up, repackaged and re-circulated through other social media tools and networks such as Facebook, Twitter and blogs. While these, in turn, have their own visual regimes, the three key discourses of authenticity, amateurism and affinity are still influential. Thus, the Free Range Studios' Facebook page conforms to the dominant design aesthetic of Facebook by consisting of low-quality, un-photoshopped photographs of its employees going about their everyday lives accompanied by a chatty, intimate and youthful style of text, as well as links to other organizations and film clips that can be seen as occupying the same ideological terrain: Amnesty International, Alliance for Climate Change Education, etc. The Twitter feed also provides a constant stream of links to various YouTube videos. The key visual feature of these forms of social media is not high-brow aesthetics but constant engagement, and to this end the boundaries between work-based issues and identities and personal/leisure-based ones are increasingly being blurred by practitioners. Facebook postings and Tweets frequently intersect comments on personal lives and habits with work-based events and links in an effort to increase the quantity of communication and, hopefully, 'followers' and 'likes'. It is perhaps most through this need for a constant drip feed of communication that social media are not only challenging organizations' visual practices but also their organizational identities across the board.

Concluding discussion

In this chapter, I have shown that social media offer organizations both opportunities and challenges to their visual practices and identities. In that social media and the Web are now thoroughly embedded into many people's daily practices, those organizations that fail to perform as *org/borgs* and establish social capital by engaging with these new media forms are losing the possibilities of creating a significant and contemporary identity for themselves as well as securing their place in the market (Bourdieu 1984; Haraway 1991). However, as ANT theorists argue, those organizations that do interact with the Web must do so on the understanding that the outcomes are far from certain or predictable. While the Web undoubtedly reproduces established forms of power and inequality, its discursive regimes and technological affordances also have the potential to produce new forms of social and political relations (Foucault 1980). Changing notions of cultural and social capital are challenging understandings of who can do what, when and how. Through these new and diverse interplays of people, organizations, digital culture and visual aesthetics, dichotomies of powerful/powerless, organization/client, professionalism/amateurism, work identity/personal identity and work-time/leisure-time are thus being reshaped. However, while some of these reconfigurations are leading to the flattening of older hierarchies, the extent to which social media are upturning more entrenched patterns of inequality is still being worked out (Halford and Savage 2010). What is clear is that organizations using social media as part of their visual practice need to embrace risk in order to exploit the Web's ability to build networks, generate debate and promote interactivity. As such, social media offer organizations a new lens from which to understand and use both the visual and themselves. It will be interesting to see which organizations decide to join the party.

Notes

1 The research on YouTube has been conducted with Emma Bell and we are grateful to the University of Exeter for financial assistance with this project.
2 These images can be seen in the accompanying online resources.

References

Ardevol, E., Roig, A., San Cornelio, G., Pages, R. and Alsina, P. (2010) 'Playful practices: theorising "new media" cultural production', in B. Bräuchler and J. Postill (eds) *Theorising Media and Practice*, New York: Berghahn Books.
Barthes, R. (1982 [1964]) 'Rhetorique de l'image', in *L'obvie et l'obtus*, Paris: Le Seuil, 43–61. (Barthes, R. (1977) 'Rhetoric of the Image', in *Image, Music, Text*, trans. S. Heath, London: Fontana Press, 52–68.)
Baxter, J. (2003) *Positioning Gender in Discourse*, Basingstoke: Palgrave.
Bennett, T., Savage, M., Silva, E., Warde, A., Gayo-Cal, M. and Wright, D. (2009) *Culture, Class, Distinction*, London: Routledge.
Bourdieu, P. (1977) *Outline of a Theory of Practice*, Cambridge: Cambridge University Press.
——(1984) *Distinction*, London: Routledge.
Burgess, J. and Green, J. (2009) *YouTube: Online Video and Participatory Culture*, Cambridge: Polity Press.
Consalvo, M. (2003) 'Cyber-slaying media fans: code, digital poaching and corporate control of the internet', *Journal of Communication Inquiry* 27: 67–86.
Fombrun, C. and Van Riel, C. (2004) *Fame and Fortune: How Successful Companies Build Winning Reputations*, Upper Saddle River, NJ: Financial Times/Prentice Hall.
Foucault, M. (1980) *Power/Knowledge*, Brighton: Harvester Press.
Fournier, S. and Avery, J. (2011) 'The uninvited brand', *Business Horizons* 54(3): 193–207.
Halford, S. and Savage, M. (2010) 'Reconceptualizing digital social inequality information', *Communication and Society* 13(7): 937–955.
Haraway, D. (1991) *Simians, Cyborgs and Women*, New York: Routledge.
Hartley, J. (2008) *Television Truths: Forms of Knowledge in Popular Culture*, London: Blackwell.
——(2009) 'Uses of YouTube – digital literacy and the growth of knowledge', in J. Burgess and J. Green, *YouTube: Online Video and Participatory Culture*, Cambridge: Polity Press.
Hills, M. (2009) 'Participatory culture: mobility, interactivity and identity', in G. Creeber and R. Martin (eds) *Digital Cultures: Understanding New Media*, New York: McGraw Hill Open University Press, 30–38.
Hine, C. (2000) *Virtual Ethnography*, London: Sage.
Huberman, B., Romero, D. and Wu, F. (2008) 'Social networks that matter: Twitter under the microscope'. Available at http://arxiv.org/pdf/0812.1045.pdf (downloaded 23 April 2012).
Java, A., Finin, T., Song, Z. and Tseng, B. (2007) 'Why we Twitter: understanding micro-blogging usage and communities'. Available at http://aisl.umbc.edu/resources/369.pdf (downloaded 23 April 2012).
Jenkins, H. (2009) 'What happened before YouTube', in J. Burgess and J. Green, *YouTube: Online Video and Participatory Culture*, Cambridge: Polity Press.
Jensen, J. (1998) 'Interactivity: tracing a new concept in media and communication studies', *Nordicam Review* 19(1): 185–204.
Kanter, B. and Fine, A.H. (2010) *The Networked Nonprofit: Connecting with Social Media to Drive Change*, San Francisco: Jossey Bass/John Wiley and Sons.
Kaplan, A. and Haenlein, M. (2010) 'Users of the world unite! The challenges and opportunities of social media', *Business Horizons* 53(3): 59–68.
Kaplan, A. and Haenlein, M. (2011) 'Two hearts in three-quarter time: how to waltz the social media/viral marketing dance', *Business Horizons* 54(3): 253–263.
Kietzmann, J., Hermkens, K., McCarthy, I. and Silvestre, B. (2011) 'Social media? Get serious! Understanding the functional building blocks of social media', *Business Horizons* 54(3): 241–251.
Lange, P. (2009) 'Videos of affinity on YouTube', in P. Sinckars and P. Vonderau (eds) *The YouTube Reader*, Stockholm: National Library of Sweden.
Latour, B. (2005) *Reassembling the Social: An Introduction to Actor Network Theory*, New York: Oxford University Press.
Law, J. (2008) 'On sociology and STS', *Sociological Review* 56(4): 623–649.
Law, J. and Hassard, J. (1999) *Actor Network Theory and After*, Oxford: Blackwell.

Lister, M., Dovey, J., Giddings, S., Grant, I. and Kelly, K. (2009) *New Media: A Critical Introduction*, London: Routledge.
Marshall, P.D. (2006) 'New media, new self: the changing power of the celebrity', in P.D. Marshall (ed.) *The Celebrity Culture Reader*, London: Routledge, 634–644.
Miller, D. (2011) *Tales from Facebook*, Cambridge: Polity Press.
Miller, V. (2011) *Understanding Digital Culture*, London: Sage.
nfpSynergy (2011) *Social Media League Table*. Available at http://nfpsynergy.net/social-media-league-table.
Stone, A.R. (1996) *The War of Desire and Technology at the Close of the Mechanical Age*, Cambridge, MA: MIT Press.
van den Bosch, A. and de Jong, M. (2005) 'How corporate visual identity supports reputation', *Corporate Communications: An International Journal* 10(2): 108–116.

21
Simulated realities
(Or, why boxers and Artificial Intelligence scientists do mostly the same thing)

Steve G. Hoffman

Simulations are a strikingly regular feature of group life, organizational practice, and popular culture, yet most analyses of them completely miss how widespread they have become. Simulations are more than just sophisticated computer techniques for testing scientific theories. The social analysis of simulation is anemic if we only conceive of them as metaphor for symbolic economy and referential ambiguity. At both a more mundane and profound level, simulations are a central way that groups, organizations, and workplaces confront difficult tasks when direct experience is hard to come by. This chapter explores how two quite different groups develop and use simulation techniques and technologies to manage (although just as often exacerbate or create *de novo*) core organizational problems. That is, when Artificial Intelligence scientists and boxing coaches develop simulations, whether to study human-level intelligence or to prepare for an upcoming competitive match, they engage in a process of reality control that transforms particular organizational ambiguities into legible and tractable bits. This chapter shows the distinctive mechanisms of this process and argues that these simplified solutions develop complex social lives all their own. It concludes with a discussion of how the empirical study of simulated realities can help draw out a deep synthesis between the physical and the virtual, visual representation and organizational process, and lay and scientific expertise.

Introduction

On a humid but otherwise uneventful August afternoon in Chicago, IL, a friendly sparring session became a real fight. The stage for this transformation was Harlien's Gym, a municipally funded amateur boxing program on the city's North Side. Two teenaged boys, 13-year-old Keshawn and 14-year-old Lamar, had the starring roles. The two boys are regular training partners and friends outside the gym. Head coach Al Levinsky, a handful of young boxers, and me, Al's assistant trainer, monitor the exercise.

Physical props, from the visual management tools highlighted by Bateman and Lethbridge (Chapter 19, this volume) to the ring ropes at Harlien's Gym, focus group attention toward 'where the action is,' to borrow Goffman's famous phrase. We have all positioned ourselves around the ring ropes to maximize our sightlines and thus make the interaction available to collective manipulation. At the midpoint of the second round, we can all see and hear that Keshawn is breathing heavily. To compensate, the young boxer starts throwing noticeably harder, but fewer, punches. In boxing terms, he is 'loading up.' Al tells him to 'take it easy.' Instead, Keshawn connects with a hard punch that snaps Lamar's head back. A bit shook, Lamar fixes his twisted headgear and tries to respond in kind. Al instructs the boys to 'keep your cool,' but the intensity escalates. Both are falling out of their better form, creating openings for the counterpunches of their opponent and the critiques of their coaches and fellow boxers.

Outside the ring, boxer Reginald, a frequent rabble-rouser, looks to me and says with a grin, 'It's a fight, now! They're really fighting, Steve! You better stop it.' The round is nearly over. I glance at Al, who raises his palm to signal that he can handle this. Soon, the gym timer blares its round-ending bell. The boys part ways but Lamar gives Keshawn a little shove on the shoulder. This subtle escalation, far more benign than the punches that have just preceded it, draws the ire of Al, who yells, 'STOP!' In a cadence reminiscent of the drill sergeant in the movie *Full Metal Jacket*, Al commands, 'That's it. Take off your gloves. Now! Shake hands. Both of you.' Lamar refuses. Keshawn shrugs and walks to his locker. Al allows the situation to pass. Later that evening, however, the coach informs them that they will not be sparring for two weeks. Lamar's scheduled match in one week will be cancelled. The coach summarizes, 'Your sparring partner is your friend. You can't do that stuff.'

There is something odd about the scenario I have just described. You have an activity, competitive boxing, where the main goal is to instruct adolescents how to punch their opponent harder and more often than they punch back. So, when Reginald says 'it's a fight now!', that might strike you as a rather bizarre restatement of the obvious. If an alien visitor observed this scene, armed with a language translation app, it would find the definition of 'fight' to be perfectly well captured in the phrase 'a hostile encounter.' Our space alien might then be confident in classifying all sparring matches as clear examples of hostile encounters and would be rightly confused when Reginald violated that classification by implying that the one between Keshawn and Lamar had only recently become such a thing. Something is happening here. An act of interpretive flexibility is occurring *in situ*. There must be 'invisible factors' contributing to this interaction that the explicit performance does not immediately reveal (Berthoin Antol *et al.*, Chapter 16, this volume). What is the logic of this exchange? What background knowledge and implicit rules govern this negotiated order? For now, I bracket this scene at Harlien's so as to return to it with some better analytic tools.

These tools will involve the empirical life of simulation techniques and technologies in group and organizational settings. This is not the typical way that social analysts discuss simulation. The most common research literature on them is largely practical in orientation. It treats simulations as sophisticated computer systems for testing theories or providing rich visual and aural mediums for the exploration of data (Bainbridge *et al.* 1994; Gilbert and Troitzsch 2005; Sawyer 2005; Winsberg 2010).[1] While this is clearly an important epistemological and methodological development, this way of conceptualizing simulation provides a very limited analysis of its broader social, political, economic, and organizational repercussions. That is, if we focus primarily on the implications of simulation for the philosophy of science, we miss their quotidian character.

Another common way that scholars have discussed simulation is as a metaphor for a broad social transformation of Western societies. Here, simulation provides the basis for a postmodernist metaphysics attentive to the ascendency of symbolic economy in late capitalist, global, and information-based societies (Baudrillard 1994 [1981]; Bogard 1996; Hayles 1996). This poststructuralist approach has proven theoretically anemic, however, because it tends to simplify empirical variation, erase historical contingency, and ignore contextual specificity, despite its adherents' philosophical proposition to do just the opposite. While Baudrillard insists that we understand how postmodernism creates the world-as-simulation, the approach I offer suggests we focus instead on how simulations create worlds by asking a fundamental if jarringly straightforward question: Why do social actors create simulations and what do they do with them?

The main answer is that simulations are a key mechanism that groups and members of organizations use to manage the problem of 'stingy' or 'thin' experience (March *et al.* 1991). That is, simulations are used when some indexed reality (e.g. a 'real' boxing match, the impact of a hurricane on a metropolitan area, the role of analogy in human cognition, 'best practices' in lean enterprise, etc.) is unavailable to routine experience. Simulation transforms the extraordinary into the mundane by rendering an indexed reality tractable and legible through a series of simplified 'best guesses' on key sources of complexity. These guesses are then used to construct an interactive, repeatable, and highly portable situation, activity, or model. However, partial interventions can create new dilemmas and unintended consequences. Simulations can and often do exacerbate the very problems they were created to solve, especially when they serve as depositories for solutions that are uncoupled from the initial dilemma (see Cohen *et al.* 1972). Simulations forge new realities with risks, uncertainties, and ambiguities all their own.

One finds simulations in an enormous variety of empirical settings and they have become increasingly common in both scientific and organizational settings. In this chapter, I present ethnographic data on two groups that are quite different in purpose and personnel – boxing gyms and academic Artificial Intelligence (AI) labs. I argue that, despite their substantive distance, both groups are centrally in the business of designing simulation techniques and technologies. These techniques necessarily rely heavily upon visualization, whether of the physical (e.g. ring ropes) or virtual (graphical design) sort. As many of the authors in this volume point out, visualization props render group practices and identities explicit by foregrounding certain characteristics while framing out others. In boxing, coaches and boxers mostly engage with *physical* simulations, like sparring, hitting punching bags, or shadowboxing, although trainers and athletes also incorporate virtual inputs as well (e.g. watching YouTube clips of potential opponents). In AI, scientists primarily engage in research and development of *virtual* simulations like storytellers, battle-planning assistants, and other decision-making 'helpers' that exhibit intelligent behavior or decision-making capacity. They, in turn, profoundly rely on physical inputs (e.g. conceptual drawings on whiteboards, notes scrawled on paper, the electrical current required to run their computers) to refine their technical artifacts. What unites these two groups is that they both engage in a sense-making process, worked out through the medium of simulation, of reality control. Lab and gym life are both organized around policing the interpretive borders of the simulation and their indexed realities, subtly transforming both and, in the process, creating all new social worlds.

Data and methods

My observations of simulations as an empirical process began at Harlien's Gym, a city-funded park district boxing program in Chicago for youth ages 9 to 17. It is located in an inner-city neighborhood well known for its ethnic, religious, and economic diversity, although most members of the gym are African-American, white, or Latino boys who come from working-class or working-poor homes. My long background in the sport helped forge a niche within the gym, where I became an assistant coach for the youth program. After the conclusion of my ethnographic observations, I started an adult boxing program, which I ran for six years. In the two years I worked as an assistant coach, I openly took notes during and after regular workouts, two to three times per week, travelled with the team to hundreds of amateur competitions around the Chicago region, and took several long-distance trips to regional and national boxing tournaments. I relied on a digital recorder to record training sessions while I worked 'hand in glove' with my boxers.

Approximately two years after finishing my observations at Harlien's, I began a three-year ethnography of two academic labs working on Artificial Intelligence technology to observe the production of simulations within a science and engineering setting. Unlike my background in boxing, I had no expertise in AI or computer science beyond a baseline familiarity with computer technology. Nonetheless, both labs were welcoming due primarily, I believe, to my academic credentials, and I quickly settled into a role as a sounding board for ideas and de facto editor of rough drafts of lab papers.

Both labs are part of the same Department of Computer Science at a well-endowed private research university in the American Midwest. I was allowed to share an office at the IntelliLab with an advanced graduate student. I observed both labs approximately two to three times per week for this period, although for several month-long periods I came nearly every day. I participated in weekly project meetings and other brainstorming sessions and remain in semi-frequent contact with several members of the labs. I conducted over 50 one- to three-hour interviews with all the members of the labs along with shorter follow-up interviews. I also include in my data set several thousand pages of email, pictures, lab papers, and website materials, along with hours of online video content produced by the labs.

The two AI labs map onto two key subfields within contemporary AI. The IntelliLab is an information-processing lab that focuses on information classification and retrieval, drawing on an array of AI techniques but based primarily in the subfield of case-based reasoning. The lab and its leaders were professionalized within a well-known tradition in AI science known as 'script theory.' The vast majority of its research projects are externally funded by the IT industry, the arts and entertainment industry, and venture capitalists. The co-directors of the IntelliLab maintain extensive social and professional networks within these fields.

QualGroup is a lab working on computer systems that can reason using analogy, and is based in the AI subfields of 'knowledge representation' and 'qualitative reasoning.' The QualGroup was, by far, the most well-endowed and largest CS lab on campus. It received the vast majority of its funding from the US Department of Defense, the US Naval Academy, the National Science Foundation, and the US Department of Homeland Security, and the head of the lab maintained both thick and thin ties to research scientists working at these agencies, other researchers in the field of cognitive psychology and cognitive AI, and with military commanders (some of whom were university alumni).

Simulation as an empirical process

Before moving into a discussion of how simulation shapes out in these settings, I first set out a formalized definition. Simulations are *sets of activities or techniques that members of a self-delimited group or organization mutually recognize as a simplification of some more real entity, experience, or goal state.* These simplifications operate in one of the following two distinct ways: *(1) segmented pre-enactments of the bracketed reality designed as a means-to-an-end; or (2) self-contained, self-referential experiences for knowledge exploration or entertainment that is designed as an end-in-itself.*

Simulation, as defined above, is incredibly commonplace. Cooks commonly rehearse a new recipe before preparing it for dinner guests, with the reactions of intimates serving as an impromptu simulation for more consequential tastings in the future. Adjustments in flavoring, ingredients, timing, and visual presentation are all affordances that can be manipulated within the simulation to fine-tune the model (which in this example is the recipe). Simulation technologies have become an increasingly important component of disaster and risk analysis, mobilized to prepare for hurricanes, earthquakes, deep-sea oil spills, or evacuation planning.[2] The United States military designed full-scale simulations of Iraqi villages complete with insurgents in the Mohave Desert (Filkins and Burns 2006), and the testing and maintenance of nuclear weapon stockpiles relies almost exclusively on simulation technologies (Gusterson 2001; Masco 2006). Advertising firms offer simulation techniques for product testing. Scientists use simulations to derive data on phenomena that is either cost forbidding or simply beyond the reach of traditional scientific techniques. The entire field of experimental particle physics is organized around large-scale physical and virtual simulation techniques (Traweek 1988).

A suggestive literature for understanding the social life of simulation can be found in organizational decision-making theory. For example, both the Carnegie School tradition and Mertonian-style institutional analysis demonstrated some of the mechanisms that groups and organizations use to learn from paltry precedent (March et al. 1991). Members of organizations either develop a deep and rich analysis of the small number of cases they have at their disposal or figure out how to imagine the wider array of possible alternative histories that could have transpired but did not yet happen. Simulation is of the latter mechanisms. Another generic reason why simulations arise is when goals are ambiguous. That is, when groups and organizations set out to accomplish something that is so complex, risky, or multivalent that information flows are slow, inefficient or costly. There are varied literatures that speak to this issue, including work on stochastic decision-making in anarchic organizations (Cohen 2007; Cohen and March 1974; Cohen et al. 1972), work on the normalization of risk (Heimer 1985; Perrow 1999; Vaughan 1996), or contingency theories that treat decision-making as a function of what information is available at any particular time (Stinchcombe 1990). Herbert Simon (1957) provided a nice summary of this problem when he said that goals are ambiguous when accumulating sufficient information to maximize on them would require 'powers of prescience and capacities for computation resembling those we usually attribute to God'. To be sure, simulation is not the only way that organizations manage ambiguity. Familiar ways include administrative record keeping, organizational hierarchy, the segmenting of tasks into discrete parts, quantification, and even the 'heedful interrelating' described in Weick's case studies of occupational sense-making (Weick et al. 2005).

Simulation adds two novel aspects to these previously identified mechanisms for managing ambiguity. First, it provides a clear focus on what we might refer to as the performative infrastructure of reality. It draws attention to the ways that actors consciously and unconsciously frame some situations as less real than others, and then derive behavioral cues from those distinctions (Bateson 2000 [1972]; Goffman 1974). This interpretive bracketing creates the situational possibilities for action that are otherwise unavailable, very much akin to the 'liminal spaces' famously identified by cultural anthropologists (Gennep 1960 [1909]; Turner 1977 [1969]). Second, simulation is an intermediary mechanism between innovation and routine, as well as between protocol and practice.

In the next section, I argue that simulations vary across three interrelated dimensions. Then I discuss how these axes can help us get analytic leverage on the central dilemmas animating boxing gyms and AI labs as well as a wide spectrum of groups and organizations in the business of reality control.

Three dimensions of simulation

Simulations imitate many different things – a complex task or game; a physical, chemical, or mental phenomenon; an exciting or evocative experience; an ecosystem, a social system, a world, a universe. For example, both climate modelers and baseball coaches regularly use simulation to make guesses about how best to predict the future. Thus, an empirical analysis of simulation requires tools that can cover both scientific forecasting and competitive sports, at the very least. To develop such tools, I argue that simulations vary on three main dimensions.[3]

Experiential modality

Perhaps the most obvious source of variation involves the visual and material interface of a simulation – whether it is physical or virtual. This is what I call the *experiential modality*, or the visual and material modality through which a user interacts with a simulated technique, technology, process, experience, or world.

At Harlien's, physical simulations include shadowboxing in front of mirrors, or hitting a range of different leather punching bags, or running through many different sorts of punch combinations and defensive tactics with a coach on punch mitts. These various simulations form a hierarchy of space and substance within the gym, so that only the most accomplished boxers have free access to all of them. Initiates are typically relegated to the peripheral zones of the gym and, for quite a long time, to sparring first their own mirror image and then the inanimate bodies of punching bags.

The most 'serious' or complex simulation, and the one that comes closest to an actual match, is a sparring session. But here too there are many variations on the theme. Some sparring matches are highly choreographed, in which one boxer is only supposed to throw a certain combination and nothing else, or mimics a coach's demonstration, or partners are told to only hit each other to the body. This forms a continuum all the way to sessions that are nearly indistinguishable from a competitive match except for the fact that the session is not scored and does not have an external audience to witness it.

In contrast to physical simulation, virtual simulation abstracts and formalizes an indexed reality in algorithmic and programming language and is represented through computer visualization. The modality is free of the constraints that govern Newtonian physics unless those constraints are programmed in. Visual representations replace physical surroundings, as in the case of virtual and 3-D environments. An example of a primarily virtual simulation discussed below is a tactical battle plan simulator that assists military commanders in battle scenarios, with an interface that mimics the plastic overlay and grease pencil-based Course of Action, or COA, diagrams used by commanders. Physical and virtual are not mutually exclusive properties as most simulations include both. We tend to forget the vast physical networks, from the chair that users sit in to the electrical circuits that undergird all virtual modalities. Thus, it is best to think of modality as an ordinal tendency, not a binary.

Referential frame

The second dimension of simulation is its *referential frame*, or the purpose of the simulation relative to the reality it indexes. The primary distinction here is between pre-enactment and self-referential simulation. Pre-enactment is a simplified mock-up that helps prepare people for some future scenario or task, such as a sparring session, or a difficult military battle scenario, or the impact of a nuclear explosion. It is a means-to-an-end.

There also exist simulations that are not so much a means-to-an-end but an experiential end-in-itself. For a mostly physical simulation, consider Civil War re-enactments. It is clear that their purpose is not to prepare people for nineteenth-century musket battle. Rather, they are done for a variety of more internal reasons – to provide a more embodied experience of war than film or games provide, to relive and reaffirm one's imagined community, or as a personal hobby.

Self-referential physical simulation, such as war re-enactments, tend to be rare. Self-referential virtual simulation, in contrast, is quite common. First-person shooter video games are a common example. Another is the IntelliLab's Murmur system, which simulates a storyteller. The AI system is not oriented to improving future storytelling. Rather, it is an attempt to create an engaging storytelling experience. This system was installed at a popular comedy club in Chicago and provided the technical infrastructure and 'life-world' for lab members to write and publish papers on the semantic properties of story generation. Many of the simulations used for scholarly inquiry are self-referential in orientation, in the sense that they are aimed at gathering knowledge about an indexed reality (often a hypothesis, model, or theory), not preparing for future events.

Perceived realism

The third dimension of simulation is their *perceived realism*, or the extent to which the audience and users of a simulation consider it an accurate representation of the reality it imitates. In Irwin's (2005) study of military training, for example, the most realistic simulations involved live ammunition, and were necessarily used sparingly. In competitive boxing, full-exchange sparring is considered the most realistic simulation of a match, with lots of degrees of freedom for how realistic it gets. In virtual simulations, the realism of the digitized environment is a key limitation, especially in terms of the disproportionate amount of visual versus tactile stimuli (a key reason why surgical simulators must rely on both virtual and physical elements, given that surgical skill is such a profoundly tactile craft).

Mapping simulations

A three-dimensional Cartesian grid can bring these three dimensions into a single heuristic space, something like Figure 21.1.

The x axis is the modality. The z axis is the referential frame – pre-enactment on one end and self-referential on the other. The y axis is the degree of perceived realism. With this grid, one can plot any given simulation along each axis across the three continuous dimensions. Take a sparring session. It is mostly physical, so would go on the far right of the x axis. It is usually oriented to pre-enactment, so, for argument's sake, we place it high on the z axis. How realistic it is involves the interpretation of those who are engaging or witnessing the event, so one would need to evaluate different perspectives before plotting it along the y axis.

The three intersecting axes yield eight different condition states of simulation. If we move left to right and top to bottom, Octant I resides at the top left position (mostly virtual, pre-enacted, and realistic), Octant II at the top right (mostly physical, pre-enacted, and realistic), Octant III in the lower left, Octant IV in the lower right. If you flip the figure around, the four octants begin with octant V (mostly physical, pre-enacted, and low realism), and so forth. Each of the eight conditions states are suggestive of rough tendencies that characterize variation across different empirical examples of simulation. One could then plot a large number of cases to create a mapping of the social organization of simulation across multiple empirical sites.

There would be, however, a significant epistemological tension embedded in that task. How do we know if and when one object is more realistic than another? Two answers are typically offered. An outcome-based analysis would make analytic choices that are reasonable,

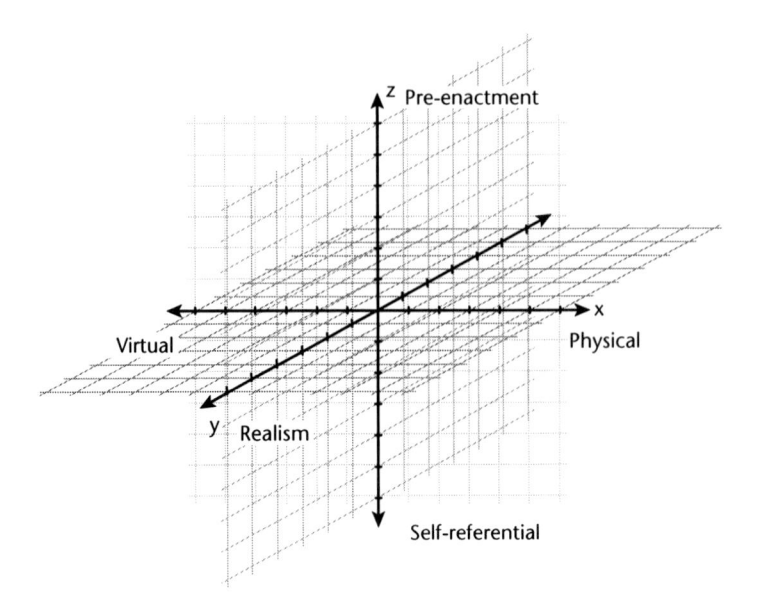

Figure 21.1 Three dimensions of simulation

logical, and behaviorally justified. The other answer, and the one I pursue for the remainder of this chapter, is to utilize epistemological uncertainties as empirical opportunities for understanding group and organizational level dilemmas wrought by simulation.

That is, it turns out that the descriptive uncertainties over empirical cases are typically mirrored in the normative uncertainties that members of groups have around what kind of simulation the case *should* be. The background knowledge and implicit rules governing the kind of interpretive conflict that occurred in the opening scenario at Harlien's Gym, I will suggest, makes sense if we understand it as an uncertainty over what octant any given simulation belongs. A tremendous amount of group and organizational effort goes into figuring out the right amount of physicality vs. virtuality to build into an AI system's interface or a boxing technique, as well as its purpose and perceived reality.

Dilemma 1: debating the modality of a newscast simulator

The single most common and recurrent dilemma I observed at the IntelliLab involved negotiations and conflicts over how much and what kinds of virtual and physical elements should be added to a developing technology's interface. Regular debates occurred around visual presentation issues, typically as follows: if a user provides too much direct input to the technology (via keyboard strokes, voice recognition interface, hand gestures), then that system might be dismissed by skeptics as getting fed the answers. If so, the computer agent will be seen as doing nothing authentically or autonomously intelligent. On the other hand, if the system is entirely self-reliant, it will probably not be interactive enough to intrigue an audience. As Latour (1995) has pointed out, when non-human technologies (e.g. hydraulic door closers) do their work reliably and well, their social agency is forgotten. Conversations about the inputs and modalities of an interface are examples of how members of the IntelliLab continually tweak computer-based utility functions in a way that balances exciting virtual capabilities with some degree of human–machine interactivity. There is no straightforward recipe for how to do this, no perfect preference set to maximize the constraints of the embedded algorithm.

An IntelliLab system called 'YourNews' provides a nice example of how this dilemma played out in practice.

YourNews automatically generates a newscast based on the top news stories of the day, using categorization and search techniques to match textual content with pictures and video, all compiled in real time. It is a virtual simulation of a newscast. Once the initial functionality and visual aspects of the system were in place, the question that continually arose at meetings involved how to get an audience to actually watch the show. The group concluded that an engaging visual representation of a newscaster was essential, but not sufficient. A human audience requires more than just captivating images to maintain its interest. An audience requires the performance to convey meaning, which, the scientist-designers of YourNews suggested, is found in the dynamic interaction between the viewer, the subject matter, and the presentational medium. It was important to get a large audience for the newscast because audience interaction would be mined and used for research publications. An input database could create a feedback loop to steadily improve the newscast as well as refine the linguistic classification schemes that provided the backbone of scientific knowledge claims coming out of the project.

One of the more creative ways the design group sought to hook in an audience was by leveraging the virtual modality of the system to playfully subvert the conventional structure of traditional newscasts. The host of YourNews is Alyx Vance, a popular avatar from the video game *Half Life*. In some of the newscasts, Vance is distracted from telling the news by invading space zombies, a bit of light-hearted whimsy. Interestingly, in one newscast I watched in real time, this stock scenario followed immediately after the system displayed a grisly image of a genocide victim in Darfur. This was not a deliberate juxtaposition on the part of the designers (the system itself 'decides' the progression and images displayed in real time). However, it does demonstrate a kind of callous if unintended randomness inherent in the sorting and classification algorithms embedded in these kinds of technologies.

YourNews can narrowcast by providing a content that is specifically tailored to individual viewers through physical input via keyboard strokes and the tracking of 'clicks.' The design team spent a lot of time debating the best interface modality for eliciting user preferences. Embedded in these interface debates were important group and organizational dilemmas: how can systems like this attract a large enough audience to create a scientifically credible database, get the positive attention of funders (in this case, the focus was on the telecommunications industry), yet also be understood as doing something credibly intelligent? It was assumed that the modality of YourNews would be mostly virtual, but the designer's work still involved figuring out how to add physical input elements to leverage the narrowcasting functionality. YourNews was, like all virtual simulations, a hybrid of virtual and physical elements. To return to Figure 21.1, one way to understand the group's dilemma is that the development team struggled to figure out where YourNews should be placed along the x axis.

Figuring this out involved a tremendous amount of negotiated and emergent sense-making. Regular group meetings and brainstorming sessions were held where prototypes were demoed and discussed. Ultimately, projects like YourNews led to the creation of a new subgenre of research within the IntelliLab roster for projects that emphasized visualization, art, and media delivery over formal knowledge representation and classification. This organizational subdivision created a lasting symbolic and material boundary, and, according to some members, a source of intra-organizational stratification that persists to this day.

Dilemma 2: representing the referential frame of a 'nerd sidekick'

I turn now to a more emotionally charged scenario involving how members of the QualGroup lab disputed the referential frame of a simulation system.

The day after a site visit from representatives of DARPA – the primary research agency of the Department of Defense and primary funder of the QualGroup's most ambitious development, the Colleague Project – lab head Keith Fender called for a post-site visit meeting to evaluate how their presentation went. Overall, Keith was not too happy. There were too many glitches in the demonstrations. While he stated that DARPA will most likely 'keep the spigot open,' meaning they would continue to fund his research team, they would need to develop better 'learning metrics.' Don, a senior graduate student, suggested that designing evaluation tools is what DARPA should do, not them. Keith replied with considerable annoyance, even disbelief, in his voice, 'Oh, no, no, nooo!' He stressed that there are 'serious dangers to turning over your evaluation scheme to the funding organization.' The QualGroup does not want to get into a relationship with DARPA where they are getting subcontracted to build a narrow or 'deployable' technology. Keith stated definitively, 'You either plan or are planned for!' He advised his lab, 'If we design our own metrics, and do it right, you can do real science and have work that is publishable, and they [DARPA representatives] are happy too.'

Keith's warning about not allowing DARPA to impose their evaluation scheme involved a concern for professional autonomy and centrally concerned an uncertainty over the purpose of their technologies. Where should the Colleague Project fall on the z axis of Figure 21.1? Is this simulation a pre-enactment or is it self-referential?

The head of the QualGroup half-jokingly refers to the Colleague Project as a 'nerd sidekick.' It is designed to have deep expertise in a couple of well-defined areas, particularly in physical geometry and tactical battle planning. The key aspect of the system that Keith does not want to give up, and that is central to his goal as a research scientist, is to build a system that continuously learns about that domain based on its interactions with human users, compiling data based on analogical reasoning techniques in real time. He does not want to build a sophisticated expert system, in other words, but rather a system that learns from the bottom up, through observation of unpredictable but patterned user behavior. What he feared about DARPA's evaluation scheme is that they would be too narrowly scoped on a single military task. He doesn't want to create a simulation that pre-enacts a single scenario. His goals are much broader, and far more ambiguous – to derive scientific understanding on the role of analogy in human-level cognition.

Keith's warning was a normative statement about the sort of simulations his lab should be building. He does not want his group to make simulations that are too far into Octant I of Figure 21.1. He wants them to be oriented to pre-enactment enough to keep his funders satisfied, but still solidly anchored in Octant III. If the Colleague Project were to simply simulate a future, well-specified task, they might lose sight of the goal of creating thinking agents that are able to respond to a complex and ever-changing world.

Dilemma 3: policing the boundaries of a 'real fight'

Some of the most salient tensions, uncertainties, and dilemmas in both boxing gyms and AI labs have to do with contested perceptions of realism. Central to the determination of realism is intersubjective perceptions of how realistic something looks. Here, especially in terms of virtual simulations, visualization is a central focus.

Realism also goes to the very heart of the most salient professional legitimacy dilemma in AI science. AI scientists have been frequently dismissed by philosophers and neuroscientists

(Dreyfus 1972; Searle 1980), social scientists (Collins and Kusch 1998), and even members of their own discipline (Weizenbaum 1976), as creators of machines that do computational tricks that do not tell us much about how human-level cognition operates. AI research continues to have a bit of the lurid quest of Dr. Frankenstein about it, perhaps reflecting the naive dream of building life from the lifeless. To be sure, this is a seductive notion that AI scientists themselves play with when they make bold predictions that non-human agents will eventually conquer human-level intelligence (Kurzweil 1999; Moravec 1988) – the kinds of predictions, many of my research subjects admitted, that are used mostly to stimulate interest and funding, not because they think they can actually accomplish them in their lifetime. Still others think that their colleagues make such predictions to the peril of the field, continually dooming the enterprise to the failure of unmet expectations.

Realism is a central problem for boxers and their coaches too. A punching bag, for example, is a horribly imperfect piece of training equipment since a bag looks nothing like a human being and cannot hit back. Boxers often forget about their defense and punch placement while hitting a bag. Heavy-bag manufacturers have attempted a variety of innovations on this front. One bag includes the outline of a human form. Another includes padded bars that protrude like zombie arms. Still another, made of thick foam, is molded into a human torso. Some trainers stand behind the bag while whipping a towel in the face and body of the athlete. Affordances are crafted and re-crafted to compensate for the native limitations of the simulation. This is simulation in empirical action – forging new social networks that meld human and non-human agency.

Now we can return to the conflict at Harlien's Gym with which I began this chapter. Recall that Reginald declared that a 'fight' had broken out between Keshawn and Lamar. After the round ends, the boys refuse to shake hands, and later Al punishes them by barring sparring for two weeks and scrubbing Lamar's upcoming match. This sparring session created an uncertainty on two of the three dimensions of Figure 21.1. First, it was unclear to members of Harlien's where to place the sparring session on the y axis. Was this just a highly realistic simulation of a boxing match, and therefore belonged within Octant II (a simulation that is mostly physical, highly pre-enacted, and very realistic)? Or did Keshawn's hard punches and Lamar's wild response actually make the sparring session too unrealistic, so that it belonged to Octant V instead (mostly physical, highly pre-enacted, but not very realistic).

It was also unclear what the purpose of the sparring session had become. Was it still oriented to cooperative training for future competition or had it transformed into an end-in-itself? Perhaps the boys were engaged in a 'fight' now, in Reginald's terms, precisely because they were no longer trying to pre-enact what might happen in the future but were rather working something out in the here and now.

This suggests an altogether different possibility. Maybe what had happened took the situation out of a simulation frame altogether. Perhaps it was no longer 'less real' than some bracketed reality outside the situation. In this sense, the conflict was not about which octant the simulation should be in, but about whether it belonged in Figure 21.1 at all. The sparring match was now, as Reginald implied, a 'hostile encounter,' in the dictionary sense of the term, which raised the stakes of the exchange by making the desired outcome more open-ended and consequential.

This may be the most accurate explanation. However, the normative violation occurred in the context of an organization in which simulations are *the* central feature of the negotiated order. On a near-daily basis, boxers are reminded of slogans like, 'your sparring partner is your friend' or that 'nobody wins or loses in here.' What happened, then, was that it was no longer clear to the observers of the sparring session whether it remained a simulation in the minds of Keshawn and Lamar. In the minds of the rest of us, and, most importantly, in the mind of authority figure Al, there was no doubt that it *should* be a simulation.

345

Al's attempt to get them to shake hands was an attempt to reconstitute a negotiated order that necessarily involves frequent rituals of mutual respect and masculine civility. The forced complicity with this ritual was an attempt to remind both boys, and perhaps even more importantly the audience, that the punches exchanged in the gym are not really real, even if they are just as physically or psychically damaging as the punches exchanged in a 'real fight.' Thus, Lamar's slight push was a far more egregious violation than were the much more vicious blows exchanged just seconds before. As a famous saying in amateur boxing goes, 'It is better to bleed in the gym than in the streets.' The athlete's subsequent punishment was further reminder of this principle. Cross the line of realism too far and valued group resources will be withheld.

In this sense, then, what happened between Keshawn and Lamar is that their exchange of punches became so realistic that it violated the Price is Right Rule of physical, pre-enactment simulation. That is, in physical simulations oriented toward preparation for highly risky, highly unpredictable, and highly interdependent tasks, the logic of the simulated frame involves getting as close as possible to the indexed reality without going over, just as Bob Barker instructed contestants on *The Price is Right* game show to guess a price that was as close as possible to the actual price of a consumer item, without going over.[4] The problem with Keshawn and Lamar's sparring session, then, was that it violated this iterative norm.

Interestingly, the Price is Right Rule does not govern virtual simulations, which often try to get either as close as possible to the indexed reality, or, better yet, to surpass it. YourNews is a good example of this, in which it is both an approximation of a traditional newscast, but also surpasses it in several ways. Alyx Vance can shoot down space zombies in between telling the news, the modality can lend itself to the emergence of new and problematic blurring of physical and virtual imagery, and the broadcast itself can be narrowcast to a user's specific interests – all features that enable the simulation to actually surpass the indexed reality albeit in calculated ways.

Conclusion

I have argued that simulations can be broken down into three dimensions – by modality, frame orientation, and perceived realism. Next I suggested that figuring out where to place a simulation along these dimensions is not simply an analytic problem for social inquiry but is also an opportunity to explain how and why certain kinds of group and organizational dilemmas routinely arise. I have described the simulated realities that groups engage in when they design simulations to manage ambiguous or uncertain goals. We see this playing out in the tensions between physicality and virtuality in the development of YourNews. We see it in the tension between the QualGroup's scientific goals and a fear that those goals might be compromised if DARPA is allowed to set the terms of evaluation. We also see it in the tension between training boys how to fight while making sure that they don't get in a real one. These are all ways that group members bracket out metaphysical questions around 'what exactly is our goal' and 'what is reality' and get on with everyday guesses that segment forbiddingly complex realities in more digestible bits. Simulation techniques and technologies, across its main dimensions, provide a powerful, and remarkably common, way to render the uncertain and ambiguous legible and tractable.

It is likely that simulation, especially virtual ones, will become increasingly prominent features of organizational and scientific practice throughout the twenty-first century. As noted earlier, entire professions are based on simulation techniques, from climate science to atomic energy. Simulations are also popular techniques in employee instruction. Pilot training is almost entirely a simulated enterprise and surgical training is following suit. Liberal arts classes are likely not far behind and already incorporate some elements of simulation and modeling in them (one might argue that distance learning courses are already there). Simulation techniques that can constrain uncertainty in order to prepare for risk, provide novel experiences, or engender new forms of knowledge production will be increasingly monetized, pre-packaged, and marketed as the ubiquitous technologies of 'forward looking' organizations. *Star Trek*'s fabled 'holodeck' already seems less like a fantastical dream and more a quaint forecast of the even more luminous organizational experiences of our not-so-distant future lives. All that said, we are meaning-making creatures. The bracketing of the real from the imitation that lies beneath the interpretive policing that I have documented in this chapter will not simply disappear. The distinctions will be reconfigured again and again, in a fractal nature, as computer technology continues to subvert modernity's tidy demarcations between 'nature' and 'culture' and 'representation' and the 'real.' We will continue to mark certain realities as more authentic and rich than others, forging new categories of thought as we go.

This leads me to a concluding point about interpretative inquiry, visualization, and simulation. In 'A Theory of Play and Fantasy,' Gregory Bateson (2000 [1972]) shows that the cognitive ability to recognize one set of activities as 'play' in opposition to something that is not play – 'the serious' or 'the real' – is something in which children and even chimpanzees regularly engage. He then shows us what a wondrous and far-reaching ability this is. By marking off a set of activities or an environment as related to a more real one, an unserious activity enables actors to engage with a playful representation, changing the nature and scope of the initial reality. At its most fundamental, Bateson sees this as a basis for second-order learning and meta-cognition – the ability to learn about learning. Put into contemporary methodological terms, there is an endogenous relationship between learning and meta-cognition. This points to the rather serious side of child's play.

Simulations are quite similar to moments of liminality, but, in Victor Turner's terminology, they are not instances of anti-structure. They are experimental and potentially subversive, but not anti-normative. They do not involve a total reversal of the agreed-upon rules. On the other hand, simulations are far more serious than pure game. They also involve enough experiential dimensionality that move beyond the assumed artifice of visual representation. In short, they provide a fundamental modality through which rules of interactive engagement are tentatively worked out. Calling attention to their empirical realities is, in this sense, a way of suggesting that a tremendous amount of social life has this kind of highly fragile, tentative, and provisional nature. Simulations are 'loose structures' in which the possibilities for individual and collective agency, and, by extension, innovation, are a bit more open-ended than they might otherwise be. They provide moments in which we can see social structure for what it is – never quite a Weberian iron cage, but more like the permeable, though remarkably elastic membrane of an amoeba, growing in odd directions but always re-synthesizing its forms and functions in response to its changing environment.

Humans are not much like rock-em, sock-em robots who maximize on a codified set of behavioral plans. I doubt we will ever devise a sufficient means–ends analysis, or visual schematics, that can satisfactorily capture the emergent quality of social interaction, despite the best efforts of some of my friends in AI and organizational studies alike. Yet it is also true that we do not get to reinvent the rules every time we re-enter the game. What we do instead is occasionally engage in a bit of child's play with those rules, and then incorporate traces of that play, for good or evil, into the formal set. To paraphrase Goffman (1974), a focus on processes of representation and recognition enables us to get an inkling of just how startling a thing social experience really is.

Steve G. Hoffman

Acknowledgements

This research benefited from the support of the MacArthur Foundation, the Mellon Foundation, the Kaplan Center for the Humanities and the Sociology Department at Northwestern University. The Sociology Department at the University at Buffalo, SUNY, has provided a generous and supportive home for the writing process. Many colleagues have provided critical feedback that has helped refine my thinking about the sociology of simulation. I have generously decided not to blame any of them for my persistent shortcomings.

Notes

1 What distinguishes a model from a simulation? In this chapter, I consider a model a hypothesis or a lay hunch about how an indexed reality operates or how to achieve it. This could take the form of a formalized theory, such as structure mapping theory of analogical reasoning, or a discussion of how to perform within a behavioral idiom or style (for example, it is common in boxing circles to discuss differences between 'stylish boxers' and 'brawlers'). Simulations are sets of activities that put a model in motion in a real-time process. Models, then, refer to static representations of an indexed reality and will tend to vary by their degree of formal codification and by representational idiom (written, visual, figurative, ideational, etc.). Simulations are an attempt to execute the process through which the model's indexed reality unfolds. Simulation proves particularly adept at identifying emergent processes that are unanticipated in the model or by the modeler.
2 Too often within high-risk fields simulations are put to rhetorical, not substantive, use (Clarke 1999), as was the case with the underfunded and incomplete Hurricane Pam simulation shortly before the Katrina disaster of 2005.
3 For a more elaborated discussion, see Hoffman (2006, 2007).
4 I thank Lars Jarkko for this fun and illuminating analogy.

References

Bainbridge, W.S., Brent, E.E., Carley, K.M., Heise, D.R., Macy, M.W., Markovsky, B. and Skvoretz, J. (1994) 'Artificial social intelligence', *Annual Review of Sociology* 20: 407–436.
Bateson, G. (2000 [1972]) 'A Theory of Play and Fantasy' in G. Bateson (ed.) *Steps to an Ecology of Mind*, Chicago, IL: University of Chicago Press, 177–193.
Baudrillard, J. (1994 [1981]) *Simulacra and Simulation*, Ann Arbor: University of Michigan Press.
Bogard, W. (1996) *The Simulation of Surveillance: Hypercontrol in Telematic Societies*, New York: Cambridge University Press.
Clarke, L. (1999) *Mission Improbable: Using Fantasy Documents to Tame Disaster*, Chicago: University of Chicago Press.
Cohen, M.D. (2007) 'Reading Dewey: reflections on the study of routine', *Organization Studies* 28: 773–786.
Cohen, M.D. and March, J.G. (1974) *Leadership and Ambiguity: The American College President*, New York, NY: McGraw-Hill.
Cohen, M.D., March, J.G. and Olsen, J.P. (1972) 'A garbage can model of organizational choice', *Administrative Science Quarterly* 17: 1–25.
Collins, H.M. and Kusch, M. (1998) *The Shape of Actions: What Humans and Machines Can Do*, Cambridge, MA: MIT Press.
Dreyfus, H. (1972) *What Computers Can't Do: The Limits of Artificial Intelligence*, Berkeley: University of California Press.
Filkins, D. and Burns, J.F. (2006) 'Mock Iraqi villages in Mojave prepare troops for battle', *New York Times*, 1 May. Available at http://www.nytimes.com/2006/05/01/world/americas/01insurgency.html?pagewanted=all.
Gennep, A.V. (1960 [1909]) *The Rites of Passage*, Chicago: University of Chicago Press.
Gilbert, N. and Troitzsch, K.G. (2005) *Simulation for the Social Scientist*, Philadelphia, PA: Open University Press.
Goffman, E. (1974) *Frame Analysis: An Essay on the Organization of Experience*, Cambridge, MA: Harvard University Press.

Gusterson, H. (2001) 'The virtual nuclear weapons laboratory in the new world order', *American Ethnologist* 28: 417–437.
Hayles, K. (1996) 'Simulated nature and natural simulations: rethinking the relation between the beholder and the world,' in W. Cronon (ed.) *Uncommon Ground: Rethinking the Human Place in Nature*, New York: W.W. Norton, 409–425.
Heimer, C.A. (1985) 'Substitutes for experience-based information: the case of offshore oil insurance in the North Sea', in A.L. Stinchcombe and C.A. Heimer (eds) *Organizational Theory and Project Management: Administering Uncertainty in Norwegian Offshore Oil*, Oxford: Norwegian University Press, 172–224.
Hoffman, S.G. (2006) 'How to punch someone and stay friends: an inductive theory of simulation', *Sociological Theory*, 24: 170–193.
——(2007) 'Simulation as a social process in organizations', *Sociology Compass* 1: 613–636.
Irwin, A. (2005) 'The problem of realism and reality in military training exercises', in E. Ouellet (eds) *New Directions in Military Sociology*, Willowdale, Ontario: de Sitter, 93–133.
Kurzweil, R. (1999) *The Age of Spiritual Machines: When Computers Exceed Human Intelligence*, New York: Penguin.
Latour, B. (1995) 'Mixing humans and nonhumans together: the sociology of a door closer', in S.L. Star (ed.) *Ecologies of Knowledge: Work and Politics in Science and Technology*, New York: SUNY Press, 257–280.
March, J.G., Sproull, L.S. and Tamuz, M. (1991) 'Learning from samples of one or fewer', *Organization Science* 2: 1–13.
Masco, J. (2006) *The Nuclear Borderlands: The Manhattan Project in Post-Cold War New Mexico*, Princeton, NJ: Princeton University Press.
Moravec, H. (1988) *Mind Children: The Future of Robot and Human Intelligence*, Cambridge: MA: Harvard University Press.
Perrow, C. (1999) *Normal Accidents: Living with High-Risk Technologies*, Princeton, NJ: Princeton University Press.
Sawyer, R.K. (2005) *Social Emergence: Societies as Complex Systems*, New York: Cambridge University Press.
Searle, J.R. (1980) 'Minds, brains, and programs', *Behavioral and Brain Sciences* 3: 417–457.
Simon, H. (1957) *Models of Man*, New York: Wiley.
Stinchcombe, A.L. (1990) *Information and Organizations*, Berkeley: University of California Press.
Traweek, S. (1988) *Beamtimes and Lifetimes: The World of High Energy Physicists*, Cambridge, MA: Harvard University Press.
Turner, V. (1977 [1969]) *The Ritual Process: Structure and Anti-Structure*, Ithaca, NY: Cornell University Press.
Vaughan, D. (1996) *The Challenger Launch Decision: Risky Technology, Culture, and Deviance and NASA*, Chicago: University of Chicago Press.
Weick, K., Sutcliffe, K. and Obstfeld, D. (2005) 'Organizing and the process of sensemaking', *Organizational Science*, 16: 409–421.
Weizenbaum, J. (1976) *Computer Power and Human Reason: From Judgment to Calculation*, San Francisco, CA: W.H. Freeman.
Winsberg, E. (2010) *Science in the Age of Computer Simulation*, Chicago: University of Chicago Press.

Part V
Visual representations of organization

22
The organization of vision within professions

Alexander Styhre

Introduction: Visual cultures and the epistemology of the eye

In the Western tradition of thinking, the tradition of Plato and Descartes, the separation between the human intellectual faculties and the sensuous faculties has influenced everyday thinking about perception. Human cognition, the capacity of reason and critical thinking, has always been privileged over the sense impressions. In Platonist ontology, the world of appearances is separated from the world of ideas and, consequently, what is observed and perceived is at peril of being deceptive. Therefore, one must not put too much emphasis on what is seen; only critical reflection based on systematic doubt is to be trusted. In addition, until at least the mid-nineteenth century, Crary (1990) argues, human visual perception was rendered unproblematic as it was conceived of as a mere registration of external events. The *camera obscura*, a device known since at least the medieval period, served as a model for human visual perception. In the mid-eighteenth century, however, both philosophers, such as Arthur Schopenhauer, and scientists, such as the German scientist Herman von Helmholtz, started to theorize on human visual perception. They began to conceive of human vision as a form of trained capacity and a matter of attention rather than a passive registering of the external world. Instead of being a universally shared human capacity, vision was portrayed as a subjective and highly personal skill bound up with other cognitive and perceptual systems. For instance, the ability to concentrate the gaze for longer periods of time was found to be a matter of training and personal interest and not an inherent capacity.

This shift in focus from the cognitive to the visual occurred in a period of time characterized by swift urbanization and the development of new visual media. As Friedrich Kittler (1990) has emphasized, during the nineteenth century, the telegraph, the photograph, the cinema, and the gramophone were invented and developed. These new media shifted the focus from the printed book – the principal medium by the year 1800 – to other media and consequently to other senses. In the urbanized nineteenth century, there was an almost insatiable demand for visual media and entertainment such as theatre, cabarets, cinema, and other forms of spectacle. During that century, the visual culture that predominates today in the age of the Internet and social media was founded. In a nutshell, with urbanization and modernity of the nineteenth century, first observable in metropolitan areas of London, Paris and New York, came a shift in focus from the linear text and human cognition to visual media and human perception.

In organization studies, there has been a recent interest in concepts such as the 'aesthetic economy' (Böhme 2003), 'the attention economy' (Davenport and Beck 2001), or the 'creative industries' (Caves 2000). These conceptual elaborations all emphasize the central role and importance of aesthetic, visual, perceptual (e.g. tactile, olfactory and gustatory skills) and sensual capacities. In the contemporary economy, economic value is no longer strictly a matter of transforming natural resources into commodities or services but also derives from the capacity to attract attention from consumers and the public. The film theorist Jonathan Beller, using a Marxist vocabulary, speaks about the 'cinematic mode of production' and the 'the production value of attention' (Beller 2006: 108, original emphasis omitted) that underlines the perceptual constitution of economic value in the contemporary period. In the present era, when consumers dwell in a world saturated with information, messages and impressions, the capacity to attract attention is of central importance. Attention, not information or knowledge, is what is in short supply, as several scholars have remarked (Lanham 2006; Eriksen 2001).

The term 'visual culture' is used in this chapter to refer to the totality of practices, traditions, beliefs and assumptions pertaining to vision and visuality in organizations (Styhre 2010). Vision and visuality include a variety of elements including what Daston and Galison (2007: 368) term, on the one hand, the 'practice of seeing' – the actual work to use visual perception in everyday life – and, on the other, 'theories of vision' – the underlying ontological and epistemological framework constituting an integrated image of vision. 'Visual culture' is, therefore, a somewhat loose term that seeks to accommodate a series of discourses and debates regarding the role of visual perception in organizations. More specifically, professional expertise, in many cases, is constituted by the capacity of shared practices of seeing, being able to make credible and authoritative statements on the basis of visual materials. Such professional expertise, ultimately rooted in what Lave and Wenger (1991) term 'communities of practice', is accomplished and rendered credible by combining visual inspection and descriptions and explanations of what is visually displayed. To serve as a member of a professional or organizational community is thus to enact certain ways of perceiving the world.

This chapter also presents case study material to demonstrate how visual cultures are constitutive of economic value and worth in the contemporary period. Rather than taking visual cultures for granted, I suggest they need to be understood as forms of collective professional vision or enskilled vision that rests on underlying beliefs and assumptions regarding how and what to observe in day-to-day work. The observing subject, say, an architect, a scientist or a physician, all execute a specific disciplined, professional vision in order to accomplish their work. That is, vision is both collective and situated: what one specialist physician (e.g. a radiologist) sees may be different from what another specialist (e.g. a surgeon) observes because they arrive at different conclusions on the basis of varying underlying bases of knowledge and expertise; their observations are theory-laden (Hanson 1958). At the same time, the radiologist or the surgeon needs to share visual practices with other members of their community; no radiologist observes Magnetic Resonance Imaging (MRI) plates representing the patient's body in isolation but always articulates his/her diagnosis on the basis of visual practices that are collective and disciplined in every sense of the term. When it comes to professional fields where there is less scientific evidence guiding visual practices, say, in the area of fashion journalism or art criticism, visual practices become even more precarious, being bound up with institutional arrangements and a specific economic regime of 'credibility' (Karpik 2010; Velthuis 2003). However, in all cases, any claim to expertise resides in the capacity of seeing and saying

(Foucault 1973), of combining visual perception and discursive resources rendering the observations meaningful.

The chapter is structured as follows: in the first section, the concept of aesthetics and its role in shaping vision and ways of seeing is examined. The second section, where the core argument of the chapter is put forth, addresses how vision is mediated through the use of various tools and technologies (e.g. the microscope and other medical visualization technologies), and stresses that vision is always simultaneously an individual competence – a learned professional skill – and a collective capacity. Drawing primarily on studies of scientific and medical practices, the chapter makes a distinction between *visual cultures*, based on the use of certain media and visualization technologies, and *professional vision*, as defined on the basis of an underlying theoretical framework used when examining a material substratum; visual cultures may thus accommodate many forms of professional vision.

Aesthetics and visual cultures

During the last decade, interest in the influence of art and aesthetics on organizing has been repeatedly articulated (Barry and Meisiek 2010; Carr and Hancock 2003). This literature suggests that the arts by no means serve only a decorative function in society, but that they, and aesthetics more broadly, serve as a production factor in the contemporary economy. While the arts have always been supplementary to commerce and finance, in today's attention economy, creativity and aesthetics are brought to the fore. Taylor (2002) and Taylor and Hansen (2005) use the term 'aesthetic knowledge', while Strati (2007) introduces the term 'sensible knowledge'. Such a source of knowledge that '[e]nables us to see in a new way' (Taylor and Hansen 2005: 1213) may be used to inform research on both professional work commonly associated with aesthetics, such as architects (Ewenstein and Whyte 2007), but also in potentially unexpected domains such as the finance industry (Guve 2007) or software engineering (Piñeiro 2007). While the professional vision, for example, of scientific communities seeks consistency across time and space, industries dominated by aesthetic and sensible knowledge are less concerned about similarity and consistency, and more with novelty. If a hundred architecture competition submissions offer a hundred alternative solutions to prescribed problems, it is not a failure for the community of architects but is instead indicative of the heterogeneity and creativity of the field. On the other hand, if a hundred psychiatrists articulate, say, fourteen different diagnoses of one single patient, it would not benefit the credibility of the profession. Moreover, a common concern for both architects and the evaluators of their work is that there is *too little* variation in their proposals. Architects themselves tend to deplore the 'conformism' and 'lack of creativity' of the profession, in many cases blaming contractors for not recognizing the value of qualitative architecture.

Speaking in terms of visual cultures, in the case of architects, there may be too strong an emphasis on adhering to past accomplishments and enacting analytical frameworks, a tendency informed by modernism and functionalism in large parts of the Western world. Drawing on recent research in neurology, Stafford emphasizes that, rather than being an act of simply perceiving the world, consciousness '[p]roduces its own content, i.e., the world' (2009: 281). That is, what we have previously seen, the experiences we have acquired over the course of a lifetime, shape our sense impressions. In Bergsonian terms, perception does not begin with sense impression leading to the engagement of the memory function stored in the human brain, but, on the contrary, it is memory that precedes and triggers perception (Bergson 1988 [1910]). The attention needed to perceive an object or an event in the external world is derived from memory and cognition, not from the visual apparatus. Consequently, the human brain and more specifically the limbic system, Stafford says, 'reinforces certain perceptual and cognitive constants of reality' (2009: 282). This means that the human brain and its accompanying visual apparatus *make us see what is previously seen*. For creative and innovative professional groups, this imposes certain problems that need to be overcome. In fact, Stafford suggests 'creativity may well lie in escaping, not giving in to, our autopoetic machinery and focusing carefully on the world' (ibid.: 289).

Adults are often charmed by small children's questions regarding why 'the sky is blue and not pink', and so forth, and both Gregory Bateson (1972) and Gilles Deleuze and Félix Guattari (1983) have written about the peculiar life-world of schizophrenia patients, perceiving the world so differently from other human beings. Children soon enough learn how the world is constituted and refrain from asking such questions as their attention is directed elsewhere and, while taking a romantic view of psychological disorders must be resisted, the ability to 'see things differently' is commonly praised as a skill. When Picasso was told by a woman that she, in fact, did not look as she was portrayed, he snapped that she may eventually do so, seeking to defend the artist's right to see beyond what is immediately present. Stafford (2009) warns that aesthetic knowledge is the capacity to transcend everyday life experiences and perceive the world in entirely new terms. Our perceptual competencies, acquired over years of training and practical experience, may, in fact, be our prison, a delimited field containing a set of possibilities that should be explored. In professions dominated by aesthetic knowledge and in the domain of innovation and in entrepreneurship, this capacity for seeing the world in new terms is highly acclaimed, even a source of veneration. However, the difference between *ex ante* and *ex post* needs to be recognized; innovative thinking and creative work may be praised in hindsight when they are rediscovered (the works of Mendel and van Gogh here being standard references), while their originators may have been ignored or even scorned during their lifetimes. Seeing differently, outside of conventions and well-charted routes is thus both a curse and a blessing. In avant-garde communities, there is a sense of shared obligation to recognize such alternative perspectives, and experts on innovation emphasize the need to provide space for mavericks in mainstream settings (e.g. R&D divisions in large corporations). However, being an innovator is of necessity to operate in hostile territories, potentially undermining the status and positions of certain groups (e.g. Dougherty and Hardy 1996). Consequently, the innovator may expect little understanding of his/her endeavours until the innovation has proven its market value and starts to generate an income. Under all conditions, innovators in industries and fields determined by aesthetic knowledge should pay attention to Stafford's (2009) warning that our ways of seeing restrict new thinking as our limbic system prevents us from seeing the world differently. Just as professional vision is an accomplishment in its own right, so is the capacity to transcend its boundaries.

A key point here is to avoid thinking of the concepts of aesthetic knowledge and sensible knowledge as reserved for artistic and cultural activities and forms of production. Rather, we should look to the etymology of aesthetics as first formulated by Alexander Baumgarten, as 'the whole region of human perception and sensation' (Eagleton 1990: 13). All forms of practices of seeing are based on the capacity to discern and identify differences and variation in visual objects. The work of a radiologist inspecting photographic plates is, in this respect, not very different from the art dealer's examination of a painting, inasmuch as both of them draw on specific professional ways of seeing that, in turn, include attentiveness to aesthetic features of the image observed. Practices of seeing in both cases are trained yet collective capacities that, by and large, constitute professional expertise. Aesthetic and sensible knowledge is part of all forms of human perception, in the 'ways of seeing' enacted by different professional communities.

Ways of seeing

Biologically speaking, visual perception is based on a number of interrelated perceptual and cognitive systems (see Gregory 2004a, 2004b for an overview). While vision *qua* sense impression is 'given' as a biological process, the ability to discriminate between elements in the visual field demands intricate cognitive systems. Experimental psychologists such as Lev Vygotsky have shown that small children may identify elements in a picture but basically see them in isolation. As the child grows older, developing their cognitive capacities and integrating perceptual apparatus and vocabulary, they are able to tell stories of what is about to happen in an image or what may have happened previously. Studies of primates show no such development and the visual field remains strictly limited to what is observed. Vygotsky and other developmental psychologists thus conceive of human intelligence not as a single capacity but as the interrelation and mutual constitution of a variety of perceptual and cognitive systems. Enskilled and qualified visual practices are therefore a matter of training and expertise, often in collaboration with other members of the professional community.

Visualization technology in medicine

Foucault's (1973) study of medicine emphasizes the integration of visual practices and articulation. A physician, touching and looking at the patient's body, draws on formal training and conceptual vocabularies as well as previous experience when articulating his/her diagnosis. In some cases, in common and recurring illnesses, the diagnosis is unproblematic as the physician travels well-charted territories, while, in other cases, the symptoms and stories told about the illness by the patient are less easily interpreted and related to the entrenched medical framework. Under all conditions, Foucault writes, the physician must transform him/herself into a 'speaking eye', maintaining a close connection between 'seeing and saying'. In fact, the professional expertise and authority of the practising physician reside in the ability to visually observe, to draw conclusions on the basis of observations, and to point to adequate therapies. In this view, seeing never occurs in isolation from the operative vocabularies employed; the one is constitutive of the other. Foucault's case is deceptively simple, yet illustrative. First, it portrays the physician as operating in isolation in his/her practice, individually making inferences from the inspection of the patient. Second, the diagnosis is unmediated, in that it occurs separated from instruments and technologies, the various 'vision machines' that increasingly shape and form human perception (Virilio 1989). In many cases, especially in healthcare practices, vision is collective and mediated.

At the end of the nineteenth century, new medical instruments for visualizing the human body were developed. The X-ray, developed by Wilhelm Röntgen, enabled the medical gaze to enter the interiority of the human body. In the community of physicians, this new technology was not praised from the very beginning as cases of malpractice would be more easily detected and X-ray plates could be used as evidence in court (Golan 2004). Little wonder then that lawyers embraced the X-ray as 'a silent witness', 'speaking for itself' as it lay bare the human body in the form of a photograph. In addition, new professional groups within the community of physicians such as orthopaedic surgeons could advance their position as their work was supported by the use of X-ray images. The introduction of X-ray as a visual medium indicates that new technologies destabilize dominant institutional arrangements and open up new ways of working. The naive but appealing idea that X-ray plates 'speak for themselves' is an assumption that accompanies virtually all visual media, well into the contemporary period. Dumit (2004) examines the use of Positron Emission Tomography (PET), providing colourful images of the activities of the human brain. In the trial of John Hinckley, the man who attempted to assassinate President Ronald Reagan in 1981 to impress his idol, the actress Jodie Foster, Hinckley's defence invoked PET images of his brain as evidence of a psychological disorder. In Dumit's view, this is a precarious juridical practice as such images never speak for themselves. The PET images are what Dumit calls 'expert images'; that is, they demand highly skilled expertise in interpreting, and, as soon as they are 'interpreted' by the expert, they no longer serve their role in the court as being self-evident proofs:

> Expert images are objects produced with mechanical assistance that require help in interpreting even though they may appear to be legible to laypersons. The paradox of expert images in a trial is that if they are legible, then they should not need interpretation, but if they need interpretation, then they probably should not be shown to juries.
>
> *(Dumit 2004: 112)*

Hinckley's defence, on the one hand, assumed that the images could speak for themselves, demonstrating their client's inability to be held responsible for his actions, while at the same time the lawyers conceived of the PET images as being an authoritative account of the underlying material substratum, i.e. Hinckley's brain, and, arguably, his psychological condition.

Hinckley's defence is here guilty of assuming that visual media are developed and used in isolation from wider social interests and concerns. As Gaston Bachelard (1984 [1934]) has emphasized, scientific technologies always already embody a series of assumptions of the community developing and using the technology; scientific technologies do not fall from the sky or emerge from some 'extra-social' domain but are always of necessity products of this world, and consequently they cannot be conceived of as being in a position to provide absolutely objectively true images of material substrata. Seen in this view, PET images may be helpful in diagnosing and prescribing relevant therapies (e.g. surgery or medication), but it would be problematic to use such images, complicated as they are to interpret, to provide evidence for psychological disorders. More recently, Daemmrich (1998) has pointed out that traces of DNA at crime scenes are never *per se* evidence of anything; instead, they need to be accompanied by explanations and commentaries from experts in court. Again, similar to the case of the PET images, as soon as 'expert witnesses' are needed to explain the uses of scientific instruments and their images, the juridical value as evidence is lowered as there is always of necessity an element of interpretation. Expressed differently, the scientific discourse relying on systematic doubt and the juridical discourse favouring unambiguous evidence are largely incompatible discourses; they constitute what Stark (2009: 19) would call an *heterarchy*, a field characterized by 'dissonance' and 'diverse principles of evaluation'.

Studies of visual practices in professional communities more or less support the view of perception held by the first generation of experimental psychologists, that visual skills are trained and acquired and embedded in concentration and attention rather than being natural-born competencies. Studies of the uses of MRI have demonstrated the skills needed to account for what is observable in the images (Beaulieu 2002; Burri 2008). Alac (2008) argues that radiologists working with MRI brain scans encounter a two-dimensional image on the computer screen, but that they are trained to think of the brain as a three-dimensional organ and therefore project their theoretical understanding of it onto the screen when making their assessment of the photographic plates. The entire visual practice is, therefore, Alac suggests, an *embodied* experience wherein radiologists use their hands and bodies to explain to themselves and one another how images are to be interpreted. In Alac's account, the radiologists are engaging in an iterative process, wherein the two-dimensional image of the screen, the three-dimensional conceptual image they have acquired through their formal training, and their bodies are folded into one another. Similar to the practice of surgeons as studied by Hirschauer (1991), the actual body of the patient and the virtual and abstract model of the 'typical' human body are interrelated; deviances from the prescribed typical model need to be corrected. Alac's (2008) study of the uses of MRI supports the view of Dumit (2004) that expert images are by no means devoid of inconsistencies and ambiguities. In fact, one needs substantial formal training and years of experience to be able to execute the professional vision of the visual culture one is taking part in. 'Expert seers' such as radiologists strongly dislike when other professional groups ignore the skills needed to interpret and decode the images, suggesting that such images are to be 'read like an open book'. As one radiologist says:

> Orthopedists might comprehend something about orthopedics but they do not have a generalized gaze. Other clinicians do not understand the meaning of the images, since there is a lot of hidden information which they overlook. Internists should leave it to radiologists to get that information out of the message.
>
> *(quoted in Burri 2008: 48)*

Individual and collective vision

This skill in seeing as a professional, to execute *professional vision* (Goodwin 1994, 1995) or *enskilled vision* (Grasseni 2004), has been of special interest to students of technoscience. In science and technology studies, Rheinberger (2010) has declared a shift in focus from a Kuhnian view of *science as theory* (i.e. the gradual advancement of new theories being tested and verified empirically) to a Fleckian (after the Polish philosopher of science Ludwik Fleck) view of *science as experimentation*, the actual work to stabilize what Rheinberger calls 'experimental systems' and accompanying epistemic objects. Within this new perspective, the *process* rather than the *output* is emphasized and, consequently, there is more focus on how actual research work is organized. The historian of science Lorraine Daston cites Fleck and what Fleck referred to (writing in German) as *Denkkolletiv*, a 'thought collective', and *Denkenstile* (a thought style), as the communal resources being drawn on in joint research work. For Daston, one of the principal challenges for the neophyte is to acquire the capacity of seeing as a member of the professional community.

Again, rather than being a natural-born capacity, a form of 'gift' or 'talent', the learner arrives at such competencies through months or even years of training: 'The novice sees only blurs and blobs under the microscope; experience and training are required in order to make sense of this visual chaos, in order to be able "to see things"', as Daston (2008: 99) says. Kruse's (2006) ethnographic study of the work in a bioscience laboratory in Sweden nicely illustrates how a newcomer to a field is expected to learn to execute a specific form of professional vision – Kruse (2006) speaks of the 'ability to look', which sounds like a deceptively simple practice – while getting little help from a senior researcher on how to acquire such skills:

> Just how much this ability to look was a product of practice and experience did not become clear to me until I watched a doctoral student try to make sense of the raw data from an analysis she had just completed for the first time ... Senior colleagues she asked for help gave her advice like 'You have to look at them' ... The doctoral student became quite frustrated about her failure to understand how others reasoned when interpreting results and about their inability to explain. 'I don't have the experience,' she said,

adding that she would have to learn and that interpreting this kind of data probably would be easy once she had grasped it, but right now it was really difficult. An experienced person, on the other hand, could tell with a glance whether a result was good or worthless, including additional factors into her judgment: something may have gone wrong with the sample being analysed, or the machine might be out of calibration or might simply behave 'strangely,' which the experienced person could tell by the same glance.

(2006: 111–112)

One of the great paradoxes in both scientific and aesthetic work like the arts is that the skilled practitioner, on the one hand, must be able to see things like a member of a particular community, while, on the other hand, must also be able to transcend this disciplined gaze in order to advance what is new and creative. However, prior to any digressions, the neophyte must submit to the disciplined gaze of the professional community:

[S]cientific perception – especially when elevated to the level of systematic observation, often in carefully designed setups – is disciplined in every sense of the word: instilled by education and practice, checked and cross-checked both by other observers and with other instruments, communicated in forms – text, image, table – designed by and for a scientific collective over decades and sometimes centuries.

(Daston 2008: 102)

In Daston's Fleckian view of scientific observations, Kantian terms such as 'subjective' and 'objective' (and terms like 'objectivity', derived from these terms) are of less relevance when understanding scientific work. The difference between skilled and commonsensical vision is not a matter of the former being more (or less) 'objective', but is framed in terms of being experienced and related to legitimate and corroborated, widely shared analytical frameworks.

Professional vision is thus not so much a matter of looking and speaking 'objectively' – if that were the case, it would not be a problem to use statements from scientists in courts – but as looking and speaking in the same manner as other scientists would do under the same conditions. That is, scientific thought communities are characterized by *consistency* rather than the capacity to tell what is objectively true (Timmermans 2008: 170). This goes also for other visual cultures such as the British naturalists studying moss (an expertise formally labelled *bryology*) examined by Ellis: '[V]ision itself emerges through associated rituals of participation and a sharing of socially aesthetic sensibilities' (2011: 772). She continues:

[W]ays of seeing cannot be extricated from the socio-cultural and political forces through which they are shaped. In such accounts, the forces of discipline and control – a hegemony of standards – appear to activate or trigger the relationships required to generate a shared visual account of the world in the face of potential perceptual differences.

(ibid.: 785)

At the same time, some visual cultures are more vulnerable to weakly developed professional standards of visuality than others. In some cases, such as where diagnoses in medicine differ across time and space, the entire discipline may be discredited. Psychiatry is a good example, having historically been subject to much criticism as the diagnoses of certain psychological illnesses have differed between for example the US and the UK (Lakoff 2006: 29). Where American psychologists diagnosed schizophrenia, the British diagnosed manic depression, leading critics to suggest that there is a low degree of 'disease-specificity' in psychiatry, making the diagnosis a highly situated and contingent practice by and large uncorrelated with the diagnoses of other psychiatrists. In another famous experiment, the so-called Rosenhan experiment, David Rosenhan sent eight sane colleagues with no previous experience from psychiatric institutions to twelve mental hospitals to investigate how they would be handled by the psychiatrists. The outcome was surprising:

> Of the 12 separate diagnoses, 11 found schizophrenia. Once admitted to the hospital, the 'pseudo-patients' acted normally, evincing no other symptoms of the diagnosis. However, the average time spent interned by the experimenters extended to 19 days, with the longest lasting a full 52 days. During their time, their normal behaviour was often recorded as symptoms of their disease ... As Rosenhan and others learned, the only way to convince the staff of their normality was to agree with the diagnosis, submit to treatment, and then act as if they were making progress toward overcoming the disorder.
>
> *(Strand 2011: 294)*

In Daston's (2008) terms, the field of psychiatry could not, at least at this point in time, draw on a shared professional vision including both guidelines for how to look and how to articulate diagnoses that are consistent over time and space. What we learn from this case is that, in some disciplines, there are loose couplings between, on the one hand, the observational practices and, on the other, the analytical framework.

When shifting focus from the sciences and healthcare to the performing arts and the domain of aesthetics, there is an even more ambiguous relationship between professional vision and 'objective accounts'. For instance, there is a seemingly longstanding rift between the architecture favoured by professional architects and the architecture favoured by the proverbial man on the street. In the liberal arts and in art critique, works acclaimed by critics are not necessarily appreciated by the public and bestsellers are not necessarily held in esteem by critics. 'Elite preferences' and 'public taste' do not always converge. As Pierre Bourdieu (1993) has argued, for the untrained eye, modern and especially non-figurative art is complicated to decode and understand. Instead, Bourdieu suggests, people with little experience of modern art favour figurative art portraying landscapes and buildings, images that can be understood on the basis of the life-world of the spectator. The spectator's gaze is thus of necessity always already constituted by previous experiences and personal biographies, and consequently common-sense thinking resists objects of art that cannot easily be decoded within the present horizon of understanding. Again, similar to the scientists studied by Daston (2008) and Kruse (2006), the gaze of the spectator needs to be disciplined to be able to decode the messages of both photographic plates generated by visual media and art objects.

Concluding remarks

In summary, being a member of a visual culture means to almost effortlessly participate in specific visual practices. A visual culture as it is used here still needs to be distinguished from professional vision. It is a broader term that stresses the uses of certain visualization technologies (e.g. MRI, PET or genomics technologies), but one visual culture may include many forms of professional vision. For instance, a computational chemist seeking to create patterns or structures on the basis of large genomics or proteomics data sets, i.e. a form of structural and formalist analysis (Styhre 2011), perceives the genomics data differently from a protein crystallographer who seeks to construct morphological models of individual proteins (Myers 2008). Both professional categories draw on the same visualization technologies (genomics and proteomics) but they pursue different ends. Visual technologies provide empirical data in the form of images, photographic plates and other representations, but professional vision is always already theory-laden and derived from specific knowledge interests.

Once acquired, the capacity of seeing as a scientist, radiologist, art dealer, cattle breeder or bryologist may be taken for granted as it is part of the actor's professional expertise, but, when encountering newcomers and trainees, there is once again a need for the actor to reflect on his/her 'ways of seeing'. However, there is commonly an element of what Jordan and Lynch (1992: 91) term 'autoreification' in professional vision, meaning that, 'once "you suddenly seem to be able to do your work", you already take it for granted, without being able to fully articulate its "inner logic"'. That is, executing professional vision is one thing; teaching others how to do it (as demonstrated by Kruse 2006) is quite another. Imperatives such as 'just look!' are, as Wittgenstein (1953) has suggested, not very useful when teaching visual practices because they already assume too much regarding the experience of the newcomer. Ultimately, 'there is no such thing as just looking', as Elkins (1996: 31) contends.

Vision and visual cultures remain relatively little studied in mainstream organization theory. Instead, sociology, science and technology studies, history and anthropology are disciplines where vision has been examined. In addition to visual perception, four more senses (or seven, in Elkins' (1996) view) are used to guide human beings in their day-to-day life. In addition, these senses have their own epistemologies and practices, adhering to certain norms, standards and institutional arrangements, being translated into domains of expertise that are part of the contemporary economy and society. This volume is dedicated to visual practices and visual cultures, but, in many cases, experiences rely on the combination of one or more senses. For instance, sight and sound are part of the cinematic and digital media that dominate the Internet, and the restaurant business and food industry pays much attention not only to how the food tastes and smells but also to how it looks. When using concepts such as aesthetic knowledge, it may be problematic to examine various forms of perception in isolation, as human beings enter the world ceaselessly perceiving it through the totality of their senses (Grosz 2008: 82). In fact, sight, sound and the other senses in many ways are interrelated, as one sense impression may reinforce the other, courtesy of the limbic system and its ability to structure and organize our experiences in our life-worlds. Regardless of such methodological concerns, a number of studies, some reported in this chapter, point to the importance of a more systematic analysis of the role that professional vision and visual cultures play in contemporary organizations and the production of economic value.

References

Alac, M. (2008) 'Working with brain scans: digital images and gestural interaction in FMRI laboratory', *Social Studies of Science* 38(4): 483–508.
Bachelard, G. (1984 [1934]) *The New Scientific Spirit*, Boston: Beacon Press.
Barry, Daved and Meisiek, Stefan (2010) 'Seeing more and seeing differently: sensemaking, mindfulness, and the workarts', *Organization Studies* 31(11): 1505–1530
Bateson, G. (1972) *Steps to an Ecology of Mind*, Chicago: University of Chicago Press.
Beaulieu, A. (2002) 'Images are not the (only) truth: brain mapping, visual knowledge and iconoclasm', *Science, Technology and Human Values* 27: 53–86.
Beller, J. (2006) *The Cinematic Mode of Production: Attention Economy and the Society of the Spectacle*, Duke Hanover: Dartmouth College Press.
Bergson, H. (1988 [1910]) *Matter and Memory*, New York: Zone Books.
Böhme, G. (2003) 'Contribution to the critique of the aesthetic economy', *Thesis Eleven* 73: 72–82.
Bourdieu, P. (1993) *The Field of Cultural Production: Essays on Art and Literature*, edited by Randall Johnson, Cambridge: Polity Press.

Burri, R.V. (2008) 'Doing distinctions: boundary work and symbolic capital in radiology', *Social Studies of Science* 38: 35–62.
Carr, A. and Hancock, P. (eds) (2003) *Art and Aesthetics at Work*, Basingstoke and New York: Palgrave.
Caves, R.E. (2000) *Creative Industries*, Cambridge and London: Harvard University Press.
Crary, J. (1990) *Techniques of the Observer: On Vision and Modernity in the Nineteenth Century*, Cambridge and London: MIT Press.
Daemmrich, A. (1998) 'The evidence does not speak for itself: expert witnesses and the organization of DNA-typing companies', *Social Studies of Science* 28: 741–772.
Daston, L. (2008) 'On scientific observation', *Isis* 99: 97–110.
Daston, L. and Galison, P. (2007) *Objectivity*, New York: Zone Books.
Davenport, T. and Beck, J. (2001) *The Attention Economy*, Cambridge: Harvard Business School Press.
Deleuze, G. and Guattari, F. (1983) *Anti-Oedipus: Capitalism and Schizophrenia*, Minneapolis: University of Minnesota Press.
Dougherty, D. and Hardy, C. (1996) 'Sustained product innovation in large mature organizations: overcoming innovation-to-organization problems', *Academy of Management Journal* 39(5): 1120–1153.
Dumit, J. (2004) *Picturing Personhood: Brain Scans and Biomedical Identity*, Princeton: Princeton University Press.
Eagleton, T. (1990) *The Ideology of the Aesthetics*, Oxford and Cambridge: Blackwell.
Elkins, J. (1996) *The Object Stares Back: On the Nature of Seeing*, New York: Simon & Schuster.
Ellis, R. (2011) 'Jizz and the joy of pattern recognition: virtuosity, discipline and agency of insights in UK naturalists' arts of seeing', *Social Studies of Science* 41(6): 769–790.
Eriksen, T.H. (2001) *Tyranny of the Moment*, London and Sterling: Pluto Press.
Ewenstein, B. and Whyte, J. (2007) 'Beyond words: aesthetic knowledge and knowing in organizations', *Organization Studies* 28(5): 689–708.
Foucault, M. (1973) *The Birth of the Clinic*, London and New York: Routledge.
Golan, T. (2004) 'The emergence of the silent witness: the legal and medical reception of X-ray in the USA', *Social Studies of Science* 34: 469–499.
Goodwin, C. (1994) 'Professional vision', *American Anthropologist* 96(3): 606–633.
——(1995) 'Seeing in depth', *Social Studies of Science* 25: 237–274.
Grasseni, C. (2004) 'Skilled vision: an apprenticeship in breeding aesthetics', *Social Anthropology* 121: 41–55.
Gregory, R.L. (ed.) (2004a) 'Visual system: organization', in *The Oxford Companion to the Mind*, 2nd ed., Oxford and New York: Oxford University Press, 931–937.
——(ed.) (2004b) 'Perception', in *The Oxford Companion to the Mind*, 2nd ed., Oxford and New York: Oxford University Press, 707–710.
Grosz, E. (2008) *Chaos, Territory, Art: Deleuze and the Framing of the Earth*, New York: Columbia University Press.
Guve, B.G. (2007) 'Aesthetics of financial judgments: on risk capitalists' confidence', in P. Guillet de Monthoux, C. Gustafsson and S.-E. Sjöstrand (eds) *Aesthetic Leadership: Managing Fields of Flow in Art and Business*, Basingstoke: Palgrave Macmillan, 128–140.
Hanson, N.R. (1958) *Patterns of Discovery: An Inquiry into the Conceptual Foundations of Science*, Cambridge: Cambridge at the University Press.
Hirschauer, S. (1991) 'The manufacture of human bodies in surgery', *Social Studies of Science* 21(2): 279–319.
Jordan, K. and Lynch, M. (1992) 'The sociology of a genetic engineering technique: ritual and rationality in the performance of the "plasmic prep"', in A.E. Clarke and J.H. Fujimura (eds) *The Right Tools for the Job: At Work in Twentieth-Century Life Sciences*, Princeton: Princeton University Press, 77–114.
Karpik, L. (2010) *Valuing the Unique: The Economics of Singularities*, Princeton: Princeton University Press.
Kittler, F. (1990) *Discourse Networks 1800/1900*, trans. M. Metteer and C. Cullens, Stanford: Stanford University Press.
Kruse, C. (2006) The Making of Valid Data: People and Machines in Genetic Research Practice, PhD Thesis, Linköping University.
Lakoff, A. (2006) *Pharmaceutical Reason: Knowledge and Value in Global Psychiatry*, Cambridge: Cambridge University Press.
Lanham, R. (2006) *The Economics of Attention: Style and Substance in the Age of Information*, Chicago and London: University of Chicago Press.
Lave, J. and Wenger, E. (1991) *Situated Learning: Legitimate Peripheral Participation*, Cambridge: Cambridge University Press.

Myers, N. (2008) 'Molecular embodiments and the body-work of modeling in protein crystallography', *Social Studies of Science* 38: 163–199.
Piñeiro, E. (2007) 'Aesthetics at the heart of logic: on the role of beauty in computing innovation', P. Guillet de Monthoux, C. Gustafsson and S.-E. Sjöstrand (eds) *Aesthetic Leadership: Managing Fields of Flow in Art and Business*, Basingstoke: Palgrave Macmillan, 105–127.
Rheinberger, H.-J. (2010) *The Epistemology of the Concrete: Twentieth-century Histories of Life*, Durham and London: Duke University Press.
Stafford, B.M. (2009) 'Thoughts not our own: whatever happened to selective attention?', *Theory, Culture & Society* 26(2–3): 275–293.
Stark, D. (2009) *The Sense of Dissonance: Accounts of Worth in Economic Life*, Princeton: Princeton University Press.
Strand, M. (2011) 'Where do classifications come from? The DSM-III, the transformation of American psychiatry, and the problem of origin in the sociology of knowledge', *Theory and Society* 40: 273–313.
Strati, A. (2007) 'Sensible knowledge and practice-based learning', *Management Learning* 38(1): 61–77.
Styhre, A. (2010) *Visual Culture in Organizations: Theory and Cases*, London and New York: Routledge.
——(2011) 'Institutionalizing technoscience: post-genomic technologies and the case of systems biology', *Scandinavian Journal of Management* 27(4): 375–388.
Taylor, S. (2002) 'Overcoming aesthetic muteness: researching organizational members' aesthetic experience', *Human Relations* 55(7): 821–840.
Taylor, S. and Hansen, H. (2005) 'Finding form: looking at the field of organizational aesthetics', *Journal of Management Studies* 42(6): 1211–1231.
Timmermans, S. (2008) 'Professions and their work: do market shelters protect professional interests?' *Work and Occupations* 35(2): 164–188.
Velthuis, O. (2003) 'Symbolic meanings of prices: constructing the value of contemporary art in Amsterdam and New York', *Theory and Society* 32: 181–215.
Virilio, P. (1989) *War and Cinema: The Logistics of Perception*, trans. Patrick Camiller, London and New York: Verso.
Wittgenstein, L. (1953) *Philosophical Investigations*, Oxford: Blackwell.

23
Visual authenticity and organizational sustainability

Emma Bell and McArthur

Introduction

The rising prevalence of screen-based media has contributed to a growing ocularcentrism or image saturation in contemporary culture. In this, the era of the manufactured image, visual authenticity has become a contested terrain which is open to ongoing manipulation and interpretation. For example, one need only look to the fashion industry and the way that images of female models are routinely digitally manipulated, or 'photoshopped' to reflect an ideal of beauty favoured by the industry.[1] At the same time, as a consequence of the shift away from traditional forms of mass-media communication, such as TV advertising, and towards social media technologies that invite a greater degree of audience response and participation, audiences are provided with a potential means of playing a more active role as recipients of image-based meaning.

Videocy, defined as the ability to think critically and use images effectively (Goldfarb 2002), has thereby become increasingly important for individuals and organizations, as a means of mediating and challenging the contemporary image world. In this context, the ability of consumers and publics to assess the authenticity of images by critically appraising the claims made by image producers, such as marketers and brand creators, is of increasing importance. Marketers and brand creators have in turn responded to opportunities afforded by new social technologies by using images in a manner that is intended to demonstrate their authenticity, as 'beyond the artificially constructed world of typical corporate communication' (Schroeder 2012: 129). Such practices of 'calculated sincerity' (Thrift 2008) are intended to convey an impression of unstaged spontaneity, thereby encouraging the viewer to suspend judgement of any manipulative intent.

The concept of organizational authenticity has also come to be associated with issues relating to sustainability and corporate social responsibility. Much of the debate around corporate greening revolves around the extent to which organizational practices are authentic, or whether corporations are perceived instead to be cynically and deliberately manipulating information in order to conceal less environmentally and ethically responsible aspects of their practice; in other words, engaging with sustainability in a manner which is inauthentic. If an organization is not perceived to be genuine in its actions, through social actors having 'a felt sense of responsibility, triggered by guilt or shame, for the consequences of their actions' (Fineman 1996: 480), a truly authentic culture of sustainability cannot exist.

Writers such as Peterson (2005) suggest the management of impressions of authenticity is of particular importance in the creative industries. For Peterson and others, authenticity is understood to be socially constructed and 'used as a renewable resource for securing audiences, performance or exhibition outlets and relationships with key brokers by participants in the milieu' (Jones et al. 2005: 893). Guthey and Jackson (2005) suggest organizations explicitly seek to demonstrate authenticity through visibility, for example, in the form of CEO portrait photographs. They also identify what they call the 'authenticity paradox', which arises from the constructed nature of such visual representations and has the potential to expose a corporation's chronic lack of authenticity. The power of representations of authenticity using visual means arises partly from the perceived objective realism of the image, which is sometimes naively understood as providing an unmediated window on the truth (Pink 2001). The reality of organizational authenticity is thus presumed to be visible, observable and recordable using contemporary technologies, in a manner that is not enabled by written and spoken words alone.

In this chapter, we explore these issues by analysing the representational and discursive practices used by one creative design company to define and communicate messages about organizational authenticity. The organization on which we focus is Free Range Studios, a US-based creative design company, which, for over a decade, has produced and distributed short films about social and organizational change that are watched by millions of people around the world, via the online film delivery platform YouTube. We concentrate intensively on this single case study because it provides the opportunity to develop knowledge about new forms of organizational communication that rely on new social media technologies. Using a combination of intrinsic and instrumental case analysis (Stake 2005), we identify the particular strategies of visual film production adopted by this organization and locate them relative to the technological affordances of Web 2.0. Through this, we show how organizational authenticity has been repeatedly linked to notions of environmental sustainability and corporate social responsibility. Using an example of a film that focused on the production and consumption of bottled water, we will suggest that the notion of organizational authenticity is potentially valuable, as a means of assessing the competing claims of organizational image producers as they seek to assert their dominance in this field. We further consider the challenges and tensions that members of this organization face in establishing and maintaining the meaning of authenticity in this context. Finally, we suggest that the social construction of visual authenticity in organizations relies on contrast with less authentic organizations, through which the matter as well as the manner of authenticity is highlighted.

The chapter is written as a dialogical reflection through which we seek to overcome the divisions between our respective researcher and practitioner perspectives. McArthur has been a partner at Free Range Studios since 2000. She managed the growth of the organization from a small, 2-person design studio to a highly prestigious 25-person strategic communications firm with offices in Berkeley, California and Washington DC. Emma is a UK-based management researcher and educator employed by a university. In 2009, she contacted McArthur to try to establish a research relationship with Free Range to understand how and why they made these films and the audience receptions they generate. Emma subsequently invited a creative director from Free Range to speak at a management research conference in 2010.[2] This was followed by a series of research interviews carried out on Skype with organization members and one of Free Range's key clients.[3] This collaborative research project was thus based on cooperation between a researcher, who studies social problems and issues, and a practitioner, who acts on these problems and issues, based on their shared concern and interest in organizations and how they might do things better (Denis and Lehoux 2009; Heron and Reason 2001). This participatory approach was used to bring together experiential and scientific knowledge and avoid the construction of an authoritative critical researcher subject position which is detrimental to the development of more equal power relations between researchers and research participants (Wray-Bliss 2003). This involved building a reciprocal research relationship where understanding and knowledge was based on exchange and mutuality of interests (Bell and Bryman 2007) and the goal was 'to contribute to the emergence and maintenance of a more cooperative world' (Denis and Lehoux 2009: 365).

The ethics of authenticity

The modern value of authenticity is widely recognized to be a pervasive feature of contemporary cultural life. Its rise on the cultural stage can be traced historically to the virtue of sincerity, which in Medieval Europe constituted a response to modernity, and the feelings of alienation and meaninglessness associated with social and geographical mobility (Lindholm 2008). Lindholm also suggests that interest in personal authenticity arose from the alienation of workers under capitalism; 'the workplace came to be pictured as a battleground, where combatants must put on carapaces and conceal their true feeling selves behind standardized roles' (2008: 6). In the twentieth century, this lack gave rise to the commodification of authenticity, as a means whereby organizations and marketers could invite consumers to realize their authentic inner identity through the possession of particular goods and services; 'reacting to the dehumanizing effects of mass (re)production and the rationalization of labor, the American general public increasingly strove to achieve some kind of secure identity space through the consumption and display of objects radiating authenticity' (ibid.: 55), the promotion of Coke as 'genuine' or the 'real thing' providing just one illustration of this. This, in turn, gave rise to an emotivistic, narcissistic philosophy of authenticity, wherein the only measure of authentic action was whether or not it felt right to the individual (MacIntyre 1981).

Yet, for Canadian philosopher Charles Taylor, authenticity is more than simply an inward-looking, self-directed search for meaning and purpose, although in its lesser forms he acknowledges it can become a wholly narcissistic project. In talking about the ideal of authenticity, Taylor begins by highlighting the malaises of modernity that trouble us. First is individualism, or the ability to choose one's path in life, which comes at the expense of interconnectedness and a sense of moral purpose. Second is the primacy of instrumental reason, epitomized by Weber's metaphor of the disenchanted 'iron cage', wherein decisions in modern culture are based on economic calculations and technologies, and presented as solutions to human problems. As a consequence, Taylor argues, individuals have become increasingly atomized, locked into a 'culture of authenticity', which is self-absorbed and self-absorbing – a form of authenticity that can be identified readily in popular self-help literature (Guignon 2004). However, the answer, Taylor suggests, is not to condemn authenticity but instead to retrieve it, by searching for the moral ideal that lies behind it, which includes a commitment to holistic appreciation of our dependence on the natural world: 'If authenticity is being true to ourselves, is recovering our own "sentiment de l'existence," then perhaps we can only achieve it integrally if we recognize that this sentiment connects us to a wider whole' (1991: 91).

In order to achieve this, we need to distinguish between the *matter* and the *manner* of authenticity. For Taylor, the problem is that authenticity has become a goal in itself, an ethic related to personal desires and aspirations that is good in and of itself. In other words, authenticity has become a manner of being that focuses on the purely personal project of self-fulfilment. This overlooks the matter of authenticity, or the purposes it serves. Instead, he argues, 'we ought to attempt to raise its practice by making more palpable to its participants what the ethic they subscribe to really involves' (ibid.: 72). Hence, the struggle should not be '*over* authenticity but *about* it' (ibid.: 73, original emphasis). This, he suggests, would enable a break with the cultural pessimism that leads to the condemnation of authenticity and open up the possibility of responsibilization, whereby the ideal of authenticity could encourage a more self-responsible form of life.

Taylor uses the example of Romantic art to illustrate how the subjectivation of manner need not necessarily preclude consideration of an order beyond the self, including issues related to human predicament and our place in the universe. The retrieval of authenticity could thus be immensely valuable in helping us to address pressing ecological issues of our time, by getting beyond environmental policies founded on anthropocentric ethics that assume nature is simply a set of resources for human beings to use (Curry 2011). Hence,

> We don't need to see ourselves as set in a universe that we can consider simply as a source of raw materials for our projects. We may still need to see ourselves as part of a larger order that can make claims on us. Indeed this latter may be thought of as urgent. It would greatly help to stave off ecological disaster if we could recover a sense of the demand that our natural surroundings and wilderness make on us.
>
> *(Taylor 1991: 89–90)*

Such a perspective potentially enables a move away from managerialist forms of environmentalism and corporate social responsibility. Some suggest sustainability has become a popular cultural fashion, part of the logic of late capitalism, a resource used by the corporate world to generate economic value through ecobranding (Parr 2009). Underlying this managerialist approach to environmentalism is a faith in technologies as the solution to ecological problems, and failure to acknowledge that impossibility of an indefinitely and continually growing economic system within a finite ecological system (Jackson 2009). As Curry (2011) argues, such a shift is reliant on an emotional as well as a rational commitment in determining the value of species and environments based on a more ecocentric set of ethical beliefs. For Taylor, the potential benefits associated with the ideal of authenticity arise from overcoming the polarized debate between the 'boosters' and 'knockers' of authenticity and moving away from the disengaged model of the human subject in order to reconnect with 'our bodily constitution, our dialogical situation, our emotions, and our traditional life forms' (1991: 102). The ideal of authenticity, he concludes, reduces the risk of fragmentation in modern democratic society and enhances citizens' capacity to form, and act upon, a common purpose.

Yet, in the context of debates about the modern workplace, authenticity is presumed to be a highly elusive, if not an impossible ideal. For critical writers such as Fleming (2009), authenticity is understood as a managerialist guise for dealing with the self-alienation caused by modern work, a means of dealing palliatively with the disenchantment caused by rational instrumentalist forms of organization. This has given rise to a managerial self-help literature that claims individuals are obliged 'to participate in a world of jobs where many of us spend a good deal of time not being truly happy' and suggest that we need 'a new model for business' that 'delivers our needs for self actualization' (Crofts 2003: 20–30). For Fleming, this 'celebration of authenticity' in organizations is simply 'an articulation of domination' (2009: 9).

What are we to make of this cynical viewpoint? It may be, as Fleming's study of call centres suggests, that the type of authenticity that has been adopted in some organizations is of the superficial, individualistic, 'just be yourself' kind. However, like Taylor (1991), we do not agree that this is the only type of authenticity that can be pursued within organizations. Nor do we think that the only reason that authenticity is 'pushed onto the corporate stage' (Fleming 2009: 4) is because of the inherent inauthenticity of the employment experience in profit-seeking firms. Rather, we suggest that the contested terrain surrounding discourses of authenticity about and in organizations exposes the duplicity associated with some organizational practices, particularly those relating to ethics and sustainability, and through this it opens up discussion about alternative forms of organization (Parker *et al.* 2007).

In this chapter, we want to get beyond debates between the self-help 'boosters' and the 'knockers' (Taylor 1991) of organizational authenticity in order to explore how the ideal of authenticity might be pursued in a way that is more ethically productive. However, just as at an individual level the notion of authenticity can be used to imply an essentialist notion of selfhood and identity that is deeply problematic, our analysis of organizational authenticity seeks to avoid the suggestion that there can be any truly authentic organization in an absolute sense. Instead, we see organizational authenticity as a socially accomplished phenomenon.

Organizational authenticity and sustainability

Authenticity is of particular concern in relation to issues of corporate social responsibility and sustainability where organizations have been accused of 'greenwashing', branding themselves as environmentally and socially responsible in order to draw attention away from their more ethically dubious business practices (Laufer 2003; Ramus and Montiel 2005; Urbany 2005). Fleming (2009) argues that concerns about corporate social responsibility are a key element of contemporary organizational authenticity. He further claims that they constitute an organizational response to consumer-led pressures for authentic (i.e. uncommodified) goods and services and authentic (i.e. not fake, superficial or phoney) marketing practices. Corporate greenwashing, a term coined by environmental activists, refers to strategic practices of organizational reputation management intended to promote a favourable public image of business ethics through deception (Beder 1997), by restricting and deliberately manipulating information that would reveal backstage activities that could undermine this reputation. This has the potential to 'give an organization the appearance of ethicality and leadership, when no such commitment exists' (Laufer 2003: 257). Such practices may be understood as an attempt to fabricate organizational authenticity in order to bolster the reputation of the brand among employees and consumers (Fleming 2009). The contemporary obsession with authenticity is also related to the recent popularity of notions of organizational 'soul', which exposes ethical tensions arising from the disjuncture between stated moral values and corporate practices (Bell *et al.* 2012).

Much of the literature emphasizes the potential disjuncture between the stated rhetoric of an organization's published social and environmental accounting processes, policy or value statements and the practical reality as evidenced by their material greening practices (Ramus and Montiel 2005; Urbany 2005). This gap is suggested to be detrimental to an organization's credibility. The analytical focus of visual researchers has so far mainly been on top-down, or one-way organizational modes of communication, such as corporate annual reports, which are used to manage corporate reputation for internal and external audiences. Examples include Cho *et al.*'s (2009) study of how corporate websites enable use of 'richer' (i.e. more complex and ambiguous) multimedia in social and environmental responsibility disclosures and Davison's (2007) analysis of the use of photographs in corporate annual reports. Such research demonstrates how visual communication can be used by companies and non-profit organizations to enhance their reputation on corporate social responsibility and sustainability issues.

However, organizations are finding it increasingly difficult to control the reputational messages they seek to convey as a consequence of the rise of more informal and interactive channels of communication enabled by the Internet and new social media such as Facebook and YouTube. These Internet technologies enable consumers to talk to one another, as well as back to the corporate image producer. Business reputation management, including practices of greenwashing, must therefore be understood in the context of the emergence of participatory culture (Burgess and Green 2009; Jenkins 2006), which involves the use of digital technologies in the creation and circulation of content and challenges established commercial relationships between media industries and consumers. These new technologies open up possibilities for more two-way organizational communications between corporations and environmental organizations and consumer groups, through which the reputational claims of both may be challenged.

Defining authenticity at Free Range Studios

The identity work involved in constructing organizational authenticity is evident at Free Range Studios, which describes its mission as working to sell revolutionary ideas and products that build a more just and sustainable world, in contrast to traditional creative agencies that just work to sell stuff (Sachs and Finkelpearl 2010). In explaining the company's creative approach, Sachs argues that facts and information alone are insufficient as a basis for stimulating social change because humans tend not to be rational actors (Sachs and Finkelpearl 2010). These views are congruent with research which suggests that pro-environmental organizational changes rely on the emotional meanings that key actors attach to greening (Fineman 1996). The company thus advocates a method of identity-based storytelling that can be used to change behaviour, rather than to sell a product. In 2008, Fast Company named the co-founder of Free Range Studios as one of fifty people who might save the planet. And, in 2010, the company was nominated for a National Design Award from the Smithsonian.

The ideal of authenticity is expressed in relation to the creative outputs that Free Range Studios produces, the clients it chooses to work for, and the way the company is organized internally. When asked what authenticity meant at Free Range, McArthur explained:

> As more and more companies want to reach into this authentic sustainability world space, then we have to decide whether we're willing to work for them. There's a wide range of opinions at Free Range about who we work for and how authentic they have to be.

McArthur also spoke of the challenges in assessing client authenticity particularly as a growing number of Free Range's current enquiries are from businesses, rather than non-profit-making organizations. When asked how Free Range assesses the authenticity of prospective clients, she said:

> It's really hard and frankly tricky. If you're in the non-profit sector we tend to be more casual. We'll read your mission statement and say 'Right, okay, that's great.' But if you're a business, then we are not only looking at your mission statement, but also how you treat employees or what your supply chain is, and we don't do that for a non-profit. We don't go into a non-profit and say 'Can you tell me whether you give your employees good healthcare?' As a society we don't hold non-profits to the same standards. We've been much more demanding of businesses than we have been of non-profits, even though they are on the same slippery slope of authenticity.

For McArthur, a crucial aspect of organizational authenticity involves the cultivation of scepticism through which authenticity is explored and debated as part of an ongoing process reflection.

> I don't think these issues are ever resolved. I think it's an on-going question and discussion. Even yesterday I was talking with our Studio Director and she was saying 'Do we want to work for Coke? You know, the fact is their very nature is a product that's not good for people, right? So how do we feel about pushing a product that's not good for people?' That said, people are always going to drink Coke. We're not going to change the world and say 'People, this is bad for you.' And so if Coke, a brand which is ubiquitous, is willing to change how they do business and change the plastics that are in their bottles, isn't that at least better than the business status quo? These are conversations that come up frequently at Free Range and we have a wide spectrum of people who have different ideas all the way from 'Absolutely not, any commercial product – I don't want to do' all the way to people saying 'I'm willing to be team mates with anyone who's being authentic, even if it is motivated by the bottom line, even if it means they're producing a product that I don't particularly think is good for people, I'm willing to play with them if they can effect real world change'. That's a large stretch to reconcile – and we have to make frequent decisions about who to take on as a client.

As this illustrates, authenticity is constructed dialogically within Free Range Studios, through exchanges between organization members. When asked what constitutes organizational authenticity, McArthur said:

> Authenticity around sustainability to me means it's not just greenwashing. So you're not just slapping a sticker on something to make it appear as if it were more environmentally or people friendly than it is. And, when I say sustainable, I don't just mean in an environmental way. I mean sustainable for people as well. And so if you're just glossing over the yucky stuff and pulling out a few highlights that are good, with the intent to mislead the consumer, then that's not authentic in my mind. Authentic is sincerely trying to have a product or a cause that is good for people, planet and profits. For me, it doesn't have to be perfect – it just has to be intentional. And for most large-scale businesses, there is no way to be perfect in your supply chain. OK, I get that. But you can have the intention to improve, the intention to care about more than just making money. Don't get me wrong – I am completely fine with profits as the motivator as long as those other two things – people and planet – are part of the measure of success. For example, I like Green Mountain Coffee Roasters' approach in their annual report, where they explain what they've tried, how they've succeeded and failed, and why they made certain decisions. I appreciate that kind of authenticity.

Visual authenticity on YouTube

A key aspect of Free Range's work involves the production of short films, popularly referred to as 'viral videos' (Wolfe 2009), which contain animated content and are almost exclusively disseminated online via websites and social media including YouTube and Facebook. Free Range films have received significant media attention from TV networks including Fox News and CNN and newspapers (*The New York Times*, *Washington Post* and *LA Times*). One of the highest-profile and earliest of the company's successes was a three-minute-long cartoon-style animated film entitled *The Meatrix* (2003). *The Meatrix* offers a critique of corporate industrial agriculture that addresses issues of 'animal cruelty, pollution, food safety and the destruction of American family farming' (Wolfe 2009: 318). Donated by Free Range to the Global Resource Centre for the Environment, the film was produced pro-bono and released onto the Internet in November 2003. The manner of the film's production, whereby Free Range was prepared to produce the film without receiving a fee, was seen by members and audiences as crucial in demonstrating the organization's commitment to authenticity. In its first week, the film attracted 350,000 individual viewers; by January 2005, this had risen to 5 million and, by 2008, the count was over 20 million; it has now been translated into over 40 languages. The film was followed in 2006 by two sequels, *Meatrix 2* and *Meatrix 2.5*. This provided the foundations for many other Free Range films that critique the relationship between business and the environment including *The Story of Stuff* (2007), commissioned by environmental activist, author and campaigner Annie Leonard, and its sequels including *The Story of Bottled Water* (2010), *The Story of Electronics* (2010) and *Citizens United v. FEC* (2011). The core message of *The Story of Stuff* is that globalized corporations are fuelling an unsustainable commodity culture based on an unethical materials economy that is profoundly exploitative of people and the natural world.

Part of the appeal of these texts derives from the childish, playful nature of the stories, as illustrated by the stick figures in *The Story of Stuff*. The films also rely on a high degree of intertextuality, deliberately drawing on other films that audiences are likely to be familiar with. Intertextuality is inherently historical, drawing on film texts from the past and remaking them in ways that reflect contemporary concerns and interests (Frow 2006). For example, Hollywood science fiction films, such as *Star Wars* and *The Matrix*, were used to enable the juxtaposition of good (Moopheus in *The Meatrix*) against evil forces (Darth Tater, *Grocery Store Wars*, 2005). These popular, iconic images help to denote the righteousness of the cause championed by the film. They can thus be seen as exemplars of environmental social movements' use of 'kitsch' to generate collective sentiment and commitment; 'though we know they are kitsch, we also sense that maybe they are effective, and therefore justifiable' (Newton and Harte 1997: 82).

They also rely on narrative construction of an eco-hero(ine), in this case Annie Leonard, who provided the original inspiration for, and is a central character in, the *The Story of Stuff* film. Leonard has since written a book based on these ideas (Leonard 2010). She has also been the focus of many audience responses to *The Story of Stuff*, some of which involve challenging her personal authenticity, others potentially reinforcing it. An example of the latter involved a situation where a group of American high-school students watched the film and then created their own YouTube film response to it, as a means of asking Leonard questions. Leonard subsequently visited their school and answered their questions on her blog. As this example illustrates, these new technologies provide the possibility for more robust conversations about organizational authenticity.

Authenticity is a concept that has particular currency within new social media such as YouTube. This is, in part, because of the ease with which identities can be manipulated within the medium. One such example concerns the case of 'Lonelygirl15', who purported to be the teenage daughter of religious parents, who 'vlogged' (made an autobiographical video diary delivered straight-to-camera) about her fraught relationship with a teenage boy and fellow vlogger. The posts, which attracted a large YouTube following, were subsequently discovered to be the result of a filmmaking experiment that had been carefully scripted and professionally acted, prompting considerable backlash from viewers. There are also examples of perceived corporate inauthenticity on YouTube. One of the most prominent concerns the film *Al Gore's Penguin Army*,[4] a spoof of the film *An Inconvenient Truth* (2006) featuring former Democratic Vice President of the United States Al Gore, talking about the effects of climate change.

Al Gore's Penguin Army displays many grammatical features typical of YouTube and draws on semiotic resources of vernacular culture including home-madeness, intertextuality and provenance (Burgess and Green 2009). The film also draws on the popular feature film *March of the Penguins* (2005) and uses parody to disrupt and ridicule (Wolfe 2009). The film was posted on YouTube in June 2006 and to date has generated 616,563 views. However, it was subsequently exposed as having been produced by a public relations and lobbying firm named the DCI Group whose clients include ExxonMobil and General Motors.[5]

These examples highlight the contested terrain of visual authenticity within YouTube, including the importance of perceived realness and the willingness of audiences to challenge performances that are perceived to be inauthentic (Burgess and Green 2009). Recently, there have also been concerns that encroaching corporate interests threaten the authenticity of YouTube through the shift from 'bottom-up' to 'top-down' determination of content and the difficulties in finding user-generated content as opposed to that provided by commercial partners. Such concerns reflect subcultural norms that have emerged in relation to the YouTube community and the values that members hold.[6] This has led websites such as 'YouTube Stars' to compile lists of non-corporate films, while complaining that 'lately, it seems that most of the videos on the Most Viewed page on YouTube are made by slick Corporations'.[7] Trying to establish how much of YouTube content is genuinely authentic and uncovering inauthentic authenticity has thus become part of the participatory cultural repertoire within YouTube (Burgess and Green 2009).

Uncovering organizational inauthenticity: *The Story of Bottled Water*

One strategy used by YouTube audiences to challenge perceived inauthenticity involves redaction, the practice of active audience engagement through content editing (Hartley 2008, in Burgess and Green 2009). This involves editing existing content to add value, often by subverting the message originally intended by the producer. It builds on an already established strategy of visual organizational resistance in the form of culture jamming, involving the artistic appropriation of advertising and branding images to disrupt meaning (Klein 2000). Viral films can be understood as potentially more writerly (Barthes 1975) than other texts such as feature film because they blur the boundaries between the roles of media producer and consumer through involving them more closely in the production of meaning (Bell 2008). This is of particular relevance to companies and marketers who seek to exploit the promotional potential of YouTube. An example involves the car company Chevy, which invited audiences to take clips of their new vehicle, the Tahoe, and make their own animated commercial.[8] The results were far from what the organization intended, in that they deliberately parodied the design features of the SUV in a way that drew attention to its negative environmental impact.

The Free Range film *The Story of Bottled Water* (2010) traces the production and consumption costs, including environmental and social impact associated with drinking bottled, as opposed to tap, water. It builds on the success of *The Story of Stuff*, which, since its release in 2007, has generated 12 million recorded YouTube views and is distributed across 220 countries and territories. Released onto YouTube three years later, *The Story of Bottled Water* also attracted large YouTube audiences, recording 1.3 million YouTube views. However, within weeks of the release of the film, the International Bottled Water Association produced a response, in the form of a viral film entitled *Conflicted Consumer* (2010),[9] which provided a counter-argument to the claims made in *The Story of Bottled Water* by highlighting the consumer health and safety benefits associated with drinking bottled water and promoting the industry's commitment to sustainability (e.g. through bottle recycling). The film is a day in the life of a bottled water consumer as she struggles with her devilish doubts about drinking bottled water and eventually sides with the angel on her shoulder in realizing its benefits. However, the film 'boomeranged' (Lazarsfeld et al. 1968); its meaning was turned around by audiences who read it in a way that reversed the message the producer intended, as comments such as this one on YouTube illustrate:

> Wow ... what an excellent video ... It tells you exactly WHY you SHOULD NOT be drinking bottled water. How ironic that the angels is selfish – after having seen this, I too am going to continue polluting because my convenience is WAY more important than common good!!!

These views were confirmed by members of Free Range and The Story of Stuff, who spoke of the resistance to the films as an indication of audience impact.

> You know a project is a success in the viral model, you know, if it starts being talked about and if it starts to create a bit of a [buzz] ... if something initiates a debate or really sparks a conversation, you know, lots of good, heated conversation, we like that.
> *(Free Range executive producer)*

> That was such a funny video that they made, my goodness. So with *The Story of Bottled Water*, kind of much as you would expect, we got some push-back from the industry and they actually attempted to make their own video to kind of counter ours and talk about the 'real' story of bottled water and how bottled water's so good for you and blah, blah, blah, but it was so tragically badly done that it really just made us look a lot better ... On some level, you know, we can wear it as a badge of honour that our work is meaningful enough and powerful enough that ... people are paying attention to it.
> *(Story of Stuff director)*

> It was awful and it was hilariously bad ... The production value was terrible. The message was so transparently bad. It was ... it was grasping at straws and anyone with half a brain could see right through it ... If we receive backlash on what we've done, then we've done our job.
> *(Free Range creative director)*

Indeed, these counterclaims were perceived to be so inauthentic that, for a while, Free Range included a link to *Conflicted Consumer* on its own website under 'Current News'. Under the auspices of the industry coalition 'Bottled Water Matters',[10] a number of related films were made and posted on YouTube including *It's Mr Watercooler!*[11] Despite these efforts, the success of these films never approached that of *The Story of Bottled Water*,[12] which, in March 2010, was at number seven in the viral video chart.[13] While the films produced by Bottled Water Matters display the grammatical features associated with authenticity on YouTube, i.e. they appear homemade, involve cultural redaction,[14] and a degree of playfulness rather than critical-rational debate (Burgess and Green 2009), it is clear that they miss the mark in terms of effectively representing organizational authenticity in a visual form. At the same time, *The Story of Bottled Water* gave other organizations an opportunity to live up to their authenticity claims. For example, in interviews members of Free Range Studios told a story about the owners of an independent organic health food store in the Berkeley, California area who, after watching the film, cleared the shelves of all bottled water products. Instead, on the commercially valuable shelf space they placed a TV and ran the film continuously for a week to explain to shoppers why they no longer stocked bottled water. As this example illustrates, the ripple effect of organizational authenticity claims can be significant. However, many companies flounder in the face of trying to express authentic messages about sustainability and corporate social responsibility. In some ways, this illustrates how little organizations have changed over the past decade and a half in their response to greening pressures, and many continue to react with emotional hostility towards environmental pressure groups (Fineman 1996).

As responses to *The Story of Bottled Water* also show, organizations increasingly seek to engage emotionally and symbolically, rather than just intellectually, with greening issues, by telling morality stories that try to capture hearts and minds rather than making rational counterclaims in the battle for organizational authenticity. However, it may be that these attempts fail for a different reason. As Fineman (1996: 495) argues, managers may be pressured towards organizational greening as a means of avoiding the emotional discomfort that arises from pressure groups that 'worry away at executive intransigence and sensibilities'. That *The Story of Bottled Water* precipitated this response from the bottled water industry could be interpreted as a sign that it touched an emotional nerve, which might ultimately result in shaming or embarrassing them into action.

However, new technologies of visual communication like YouTube are commercial enterprises as well as platforms for cultural participation. There are growing signs that commercial interests are seeking to curb the unruly nature of participatory culture's unintended consequences, and in the longer term this may represent a threat to 'bottom-up' user-generated content (Burgess and Green 2009). However, the cultural and economic value of new social media relies partially on participants for the creation of content. Consequently, 'any platform's capacity to produce value relies on the active involvement of communities of co-creative users' (ibid.: 98). This places certain limits on the ability of corporations to manage the collective agency of users in generating and manipulating these visual texts.

Concluding thoughts

The pursuit of authenticity in the image world has been a longstanding organizational ambition. In recent years, corporations have sought to respond to contemporary anxieties about environmental degradation, climate change, post-peak-oil survival and global population expansion by promoting their practices as authentically sustainable and responsible, using visual forms of communication to convey this message. However, visual authenticity is an increasingly contested terrain, and organizations are not able to control these messages as effectively as they once did. This is, in part, a consequence of new technologies of film production and consumption, which have resulted in more distributed patterns of message production than those associated with traditional channels of mass-media marketing. It may also be a consequence of increased visual literacy, wherein consumers and activists are able to subject organizational authenticity claims to greater critical scrutiny by employing techniques of image production and distribution.

In the Hollywood movie *Wall Street* (1987), there is a scene where Gordon Gekko shows off his multi-million-dollar modern art collection to his guests. The scene is meant to imply that the artistic image has been completely commodified, an observation related to the film's overall narrative about the explosion of hyperreal consumption in a postmodern world (Denzin 1991). The image world in *Wall Street* is thus entirely symbolic, an illusion or a simulacrum that gives the impression of reality but is simultaneously fictional. Within this, Gekko is the archetypal postmodern person, a restless voyeur who stares restlessly at images on computer screens and pictures on the wall, simultaneously mesmerized and bored by the illusions that his capitalist lifestyle produces. Such representations suggest that image work in the globalized capitalist landscape is profoundly inauthentic because it involves the disconnection of the signifier from any meaning or concept that it is understood to represent. Wall Street, as Denzin (1991) notes, is thus not a real place, but an imagined, computerized one, where meaning and value is constructed through the flow of imaginary numbers that represent imaginary things.

Yet the collapse of traditional conceptions of authenticity does not necessarily mean that visual authenticity is in crisis. Assessments of authenticity continue to be made on the basis of whether an object, person or organization is what it purports to be, in other words, on the basis of identity or 'content' more than 'origin' (Lindholm 2008). Parody and appropriation in the image world does not, therefore, automatically represent a threat to authenticity; instead, it can constitute a potential means of challenging, verifying and thereby enhancing its robustness. Nowhere is this more apparent than in the context of organizations that have been subject to numerous satirical critiques of visual authenticity (see Klein 2000); examples include American artist Ron English, who appropriates corporate mascots like McDonald's Ronald McDonald and Disney's Mickey Mouse[15] in order to challenge the ethics of their marketing practices, and UK street artist Banksy, whose powerful images critiquing the ethics of multinational corporate interests have been highly commmodified, yet he claims not to be a brand and asserts that he does not make merchandise such as greeting cards, T-shirts or mugs.[16]

Debates about organizational authenticity, therefore, need to explore the matter, or the purposes that authenticity serves, in addition to the manner of its communication. Organizational authenticity must also be understood as an ideal, rather than an actuality, which may be founded on responsibilization and communitarianism rather than narcissistic individuality. In this chapter, we have shown how such a project might be developed and how notions of visual authenticity might be usefully and productively understood.

Notes

1 See http://www.youtube.com/watch?v=EBiA5d77HTg (accessed 27 February 2012).
2 'What's Wrong with this Picture? Critical Documentary Film as a Catalyst for Change', Professional Development Workshop at the Academy of Management Meeting, Montreal, August 2010.
3 A total of six interviews were carried out by Emma and her research collaborator on the project, Pauline Leonard. These were transcribed verbatim and analysed in conjunction with the film texts and websites.
4 Available at http://www.youtube.com/watch?v=IZSqXUSwHRI (accessed 9 August 2011).
5 Regalado, A. and Searcey, D. (2006) 'Where did that video spoofing Gore's film come from?', *Wall Street Journal*, 3 August 3. Available at http://online.wsj.com/public/article/SB115457177198425388-0TpYE6bU6EGvfSqtP8_hHjJJ77I_20060810.html?mod=blogs (accessed 5 April 2011).
6 See Mike Wesch's Library of Congress lecture *An Anthropological Introduction to YouTube* for an excellent introduction to the values, norms and practices of YouTubers. Available at http://www.youtube.com/watch?v=TPAO-lZ4_hU (accessed 9 August 2011).
7 See http://www.bkserv.net/YTS/YTMostViewed.aspx/FlagCorp.aspx?c=olo567 (accessed 9 August 2011).
8 http://www.youtube.com/watch?v=4oNedC3j0e4 (accessed 09 August 2011).
9 http://www.youtube.com/watch?v=eklg6j2G2pk (accessed 09 August 2011).
10 See http://www.bottledwatermatters.org/ (accessed 09 August 2011).
11 http://www.youtube.com/watch?v=uL2VzMl0M0g (accessed 09 August 2011).
12 As of April 2010, *Conflicted Consumer* showed on YouTube as having 3,190 views, while *The Story of Bottled Water* has 1,543,829.
13 See http://viralvideochart.unrulymedia.com/ (accessed 09 August 2011).
14 For example, *I am Bottled Water* refers to the 'I am Windows' marketing campaign http://www.youtube.com/watch?v=lSkkZj5xFRw (accessed 09 August 2011).
15 http://www.popaganda.com/blog1.php (accessed 27 February 2012).

16 http://www.banksy.co.uk/ (accessed 27 February 2012).

References

Barthes, R. (1975) *The Pleasure of the Text*, New York: Hill & Wang.
Beder, S. (1997) *Global Spin: The Corporate Assault on Environmentalism*, Chelsea Green, White River Junction: VT.
Bell, E. (2008) *Reading Management and Organization in Film*, Basingstoke: Palgrave.
Bell, E. and Bryman, A. (2007) 'The ethics of management research: an exploratory content analysis', *British Journal of Management* 18(1): 63–77.
Bell, E., Taylor, S. and Driscoll, C. (2012) 'Varieties of organizational soul: the ethics of belief in organizations', *Organization*, doi:10.1177/1350508411411759.
Burgess, J. and Green, J. (2009) *YouTube: Online Video and Participatory Culture*, Cambridge: Polity.
Cho, C.H., Phillips, J.R., Hageman, A.M. and Patten, D.M. (2009) 'Media richness, user trust and perceptions of corporate social responsibility', *Accounting, Auditing & Accountability Journal* 22(6): 933–952.
Crofts, N. (2003) *Authentic: How to Make a Living by Being Yourself*, Chichester: Capstone.
Curry, P. (2011) *Ecological Ethics*, Cambridge: Polity.
Davison, J. (2007) 'Photographs and accountability: cracking the codes of an NGO', *Accounting, Auditing & Accountability Journal* 20(1): 133–158.
Denis, J.L. and Lehoux, P. (2009) 'Collaborative research: renewing action and governing science', in D. Buchanan and A. Bryman (eds) *The Sage Handbook of Organizational Research*, London: Sage, 363–380.
Denzin, N. (1991) *Images of Postmodern Society: Social Theory and Contemporary Cinema*, London: Sage.
Fineman, S. (1996) 'Emotional subtexts in corporate greening', *Organization Studies* 17(3): 479–500.
Fleming, P. (2009) *Authenticity and the Cultural Politics of Work: New Forms of Informal Control*, Oxford: Oxford University Press.
Frow, J. (2006) *Genre*, London: Routledge.
Goldfarb, B. (2002) *Visual Pedagogy: Media Cultures in and Beyond the Classroom*, Durham: Duke University Press.
Guignon, C. (2004) *On Being Authentic*, London: Routledge.
Guthey, E. and Jackson, B. (2005) 'CEO portraits and the authenticity paradox', *Journal of Management Studies* 42(5): 1057–1082.
Heron, J. and Reason, P. (2001) 'The practice of co-operative inquiry: research with rather than on people', in P. Reason and H. Bradbury (eds) *Handbook of Action Research: Participative Inquiry and Practice*, London: Sage, 179–188.
Jackson, T. (2009) *Prosperity without Growth: Economics for a Finite Planet*, London: Earthscan.
Jenkins, H. (2006) *Convergence Culture: Where Old and New Media Collide*, New York: New York University Press.
Jones, C., Anand, N. and Alvarez, J.L. (2005) 'Manufactured authenticity and creative voice in the cultural industries', *Journal of Management Studies* 42(5): 893–899.
Klein, N. (2000) *No Logo*, London: Flamingo.
Laufer, W.S. (2003) 'Social accountability and corporate greenwashing', *Journal of Business Ethics* 43(3): 253–262.
Lazarsfeld, P., Berelson, B. and Gaudet, H. (1968) *The People's Choice: How the Voter Makes up his Mind in a Presidential Campaign*, New York: Columbia University Press.
Leonard, A. (2010) *The Story of Stuff*, London: Constable.
Lindholm, C. (2008) *Culture and Authenticity*, Oxford: Blackwell.
MacIntyre, A. (1981) *After Virtue: A Study in Moral Theory*, London: Duckworth.
Newton, T. and Harte, G. (1997) 'Green business: technicist kitsch?' *Journal of Management Studies* 34(1): 75–98.
Parker, M., Fournier, V. and Reedy, P. (2007) *The Dictionary of Alternatives: Utopianism and Organization*, London: Zed Books.
Parr, A. (2009) *Hijacking Sustainability*, Cambridge, MA: MIT Press.
Peterson, R.A. (2005) 'In search of authenticity', *Journal of Management Studies* 42(5): 1083–1098.
Pink, S. (2001) *Doing Visual Ethnography*, London: Sage.
Ramus, C.A. and Montiel, I. (2005) 'When are corporate environmental policies a form of greenwashing?' *Business and Society* 44(4): 377–405.

Sachs, J. and Finkelpearl, S. (2010) 'From selling soap to selling sustainability: social marketing', in Worldwatch Institute, *State of the World, Transforming Cultures: From Consumerism to Sustainability*, New York: W.W. Norton.

Schroeder, J.E. (2012) 'Style and strategy: snapshot aesthetics in brand culture', in C. McLean, P. Quattrone, F.-R. Puyou and N. Thrift (eds) *Imagining Organisations: Performative Imagery in Business and Beyond*, London: Routledge, 129–151.

Stake, R.E. (2005) 'Qualitative case studies', in N.K. Denzin and Y.S. Lincoln (eds) *The Sage Handbook of Qualitative Research*, 3rd ed., Thousand Oaks: Sage.

Taylor, C. (1991) *The Ethics of Authenticity*, Cambridge, MA: Harvard University Press.

Thrift, N. (2008) 'The material practices of glamour', *Journal of Cultural Economy* 1(1): 9–23.

Urbany, J.E. (2005) 'Inspiration and cynicism in values statements', *Journal of Business Ethics* 62(2): 169–181.

Wolfe, D. (2009) 'The video rhizome: taking technology seriously in *The Meatrix*', *Environmental Communication* 3(3): 317–334.

Wray-Bliss, E. (2003) 'Research subjects/research subjections: the politics and ethics of critical research', *Organization* 10(2): 307–325.

24

(Seeing) organizing in popular culture

Discipline and method

Martin Parker

Culture, in its widest anthropological sense, cannot be reduced to the visual.[1] This much seems obvious, since culture also comprises of smell, hearing, taste and touch. Even if we restrict the definition of culture to the consumption and production of goods within the service sector, I can't think of many examples of culture which are one-dimensional in sensory terms. When we visit a white cube art gallery or a music festival, go to the cinema, play a video game or eat a Double Whopper with cheese, we are immersed in a bath of the senses. It might be possible to say that one of those senses is a dominant one – sound in the case of the music festival, for example – but we would find it hard to understand the music festival without also acknowledging what it looked like, smelled like and so on. The mud and the toilets are just as much constitutive of experience as what happens on stage.

To make the point, take the example of a comic book, a predominantly visual medium. The one I am holding now is titled *The Adventures of Unemployed Man* (Origen and Golen 2010). It's a soft-cover graphic novel, satirically echoing the golden age of superhero comic books in its rather grandiloquent tone, art, panel arrangement and lettering. There are even mock full-page adverts for magic rings, crystals and other superhero comics. It could be reproduced visually in this book, or on a screen. However, as any comic book fan will tell you, that is not all that matters here. Comics often have a particular feel to them because of the heavily inked and oversized paper. They *feel* different from magazines, which are usually glossier, newspapers, which are thinner and larger, and books, which are smaller and denser. Comics also often smell like comics, again probably because of the thickness and variety of inks on poor-quality paper. As you turn the page, you can hear the rustle of the paper, higher pitched than you get from a book, and feel the rather unwieldy way that it sits in your hand. With less robust covers than a book, it flops and curls, and means that you sometimes have to spread your fingers to support it, or fold it at the spine so that you can read one page at a time. It can also, if you are careless with your comics, be rolled and slid into a pocket. And this is just the object, because most fans would also tell you about their favourite comic book shops, or the yearly conventions they visit, or their friends who they argue with about the relative merits of *2000AD* stories, the best artist, and the merits or problems with the latest Marvel film adaptation of a classic superhero story.

Just as cultural forms and processes spill into one another, so do the ways in which they are experienced, so it isn't really possible to write a chapter about cultural representations of organization which only considers the visual. Of course, the reverse is also true too, so I will assume that all the arguments about the neglect of the visual within studies of organizations and more widely are simply accepted. However, and this is important to my argument below, one of the reasons that studies of organizing have tended to have an impoverished sense of the visual is precisely because they were working with highly particularized and containerized senses of what organizations are. No wonder that we see so few examples of visual research in this area when the organization chart was often enough taken to be reflective of power relations and decision-making, or what a manager said to an interviewer was assumed to reflect practice within a workplace. Such one-dimensional assumptions led to one-dimensional methods and, in turn, to one-dimensional representations.

This chapter considers the relationship between disciplinary assumptions and their objects of enquiry in order to try to explain the relevance of *The Adventures of Unemployed Man* for academics interested in organizations. I begin with a history of ideas of culture, which moves us from colonial anthropology to the business school, noting as we go how different meanings of 'culture' are inflected by their disciplinary origins. This is followed by an exploration of the popular culture of organization, of which I think this comic is an example, followed by some thoughts on methods, disciplines and institutions. If we want to understand why the visual has often been a problem for social science research, particularly where organizations are concerned, it is necessary to show how institutions provide what the art theorist John Berger (1972) famously called 'ways of seeing'. The places we look from are not innocent, but shape what we can see, what we can't see, and how we see things at all.

Culture: mass, popular, organizational

Culture, like many words, can mean many things (Williams 1976: 87). In its most general sense, it refers to an anthropological understanding of the way of life of a people, and implicitly suggests some sort of distinctiveness between what different sorts of people do in different places and at different times. In that wide sense, it includes forms of song, dance, myth and so on, but also topics which many commentators might put in other boxes – such as kinship relations, technology, economy and so on. That is to say that the anthropological sense of culture would, in principle, leave nothing out. It represents an attempt to capture a whole way of life without making any particular distinctions between different parts of that life. This is simply because, as with the example of the senses above, the different forms of anthropological culture intermingle. A visual representation of different gods might also tell us something about different lineages, and hence who can marry and inherit. Or a comic book might contain a critique of free market assumptions and the liberal individualism that they imply, but also be sold for $14.99 by a capitalist publishing firm. Wherever we begin, every other aspect of that life is implicated, because the social world does not come with dotted lines that allow us to separate economics, from politics, from culture and so on.

However, it seems to have been easier to maintain this holistic sense of culture when the object of enquiry was 'others'. Anthropology grew out of the colonial encounter which identified 'them' as different from 'us', and perhaps it was easier to see *their* lives as undivided when 'we' viewed them from a distance. Once the social sciences began to emerge in the imperial nations in the second half of the nineteenth century, processes of division and distinction begin to produce diverse fields of enquiry which made a series of increasingly definitive claims about the separation of different elements of human life. The disciplines of economics, psychology, politics, sociology and so on were each predicated on the idea that they were investigating distinctive sites or institutions. At the same time, the humanities were increasingly demarcating those aspects of cultural life with which they are concerned – history, literature, music, visual art and so on. While such distinctions were certainly helpful for academic claims to expertise and producing a way of seeing, they also decisively fragmented the possibilities for knowing, producing a wide range of images of humankind.

In the case of the humanities, they also sedimented the idea of an implicit class distinction, which became a way of understanding who has culture and who does not. We can see this in the second common meaning of culture as a label for *particular* and *preferred* cultural forms and practices – opera and not popular song, literature and not dime novels or penny dreadfuls. In general terms, this implies an epistemological distinction between 'art' and the everyday, and, hence, a distinctive set of research sites where such work could be done – museums, galleries, certain theatres and universities themselves. To speak of someone as 'cultured' means that they are knowledgeable about what Matthew Arnold called 'the best that has been thought and said' (Storey 1994: 6). More generally, it also becomes a way of gesturing towards the manners of the upper and middle classes,[2] referring to particular forms of supposedly timeless comportment and attitude. The raucous and ephemeral vulgarities of the people after the Industrial Revolution were hence not culture at all in this second sense, and certainly not worthy of serious study. To put it bluntly, since trivia had nothing timeless to say about the human condition, it could easily be consigned to the dustbin of history as 'mass' culture.

Combining disciplinary division with a cultural politics based on exclusion meant that academic ideas about culture have tended to be fragmented and multiple. Within studies of organizations, for example, the use of the term culture begins to be applied in quite specific ways from the 1980s onwards. Though earlier writers from organizational sociology, occupational psychology and industrial anthropology had referred to organizational 'climate', 'atmosphere' and 'personality', the development of the idea of 'organizational' culture within the growing business school was driven by the claim that culture could be a source of excellence (Parker 2000). In practice, what was being studied was an epistemologically demarcated version of culture, because the interest was largely in the fit between strategy and attitudes, and the accounts were usually those of management and professionals. Yet even the work that continued an older tradition of shop-floor ethnography tended to be shaped by its origins in different ways. The organization tended to be imagined as a container, a time and place where a particular sort of culture happened. Despite Linda Smircich's (1983) often-repeated insistence that organizations don't *have* cultures, they *are* cultures, the tendency was to assume that culture began at nine and ended at five, and could be found within the boundaries of the workplace. The multiple intersections between the symbolic universe of a particular organization and that of a wider culture were hence rarely explored, perhaps because they were assumed not to be relevant for a business school audience. If it was work and organizations that were being studied, the research needed to take place *in* work organizations, and not across, between or outside them.

Such a disciplinary focus should not surprise us, but the late 1960s saw a series of movements in sociology, history and literature that were beginning to undo both the epistemological and institutional divisions that had produced such a complex terrain for a reasonably simple concept.[3] The result was what is now usually called cultural studies, and (to simplify considerably) this was a new interdisciplinary space where an anthropological definition of culture was being applied to the way of life of the people of modern societies. Social historians began to investigate the common people, rather than kings and generals, cultural sociologists began to relax the distinction between culture and structure, which had produced their discipline, and literary critics began to pay attention to chap-books, popular ballads and comics (Storey 1993;

Lewis 2008). The result was an opening for a different way of seeing culture, one which refused epistemological and disciplinary difference in favour of an engagement with everyday materials, with the celebration of the popular rather than the denigration of the mass. One might have imagined that this would include work, but, in practice, organizations were rarely considered to be of interest in themselves in early cultural studies, more the backdrop to research on shopping, schooling and policing, or the unexamined sites which somehow produced clothes, TV programmes, pop music and so on. In a sense, the focus was what happened outside work, in the 'leisure' time of the weekend and the spaces of the shopping mall, in the places of consumption rather than the places of production (Parker 2006).

And so now we can return to where we began, with the question of how to deal with *The Adventures of Unemployed Man*. The problem has been that this sort of cultural form tends to fall between the gaps. It is a comic, so not of immediate interest to those working in the visual arts or literature because it can't be clearly located within certain epistemological or institutional assumptions. It is clearly 'about' work and organizations, but not produced within or for the business school, or for those working in any particular organization. Indeed, its tone is very hostile to the ideological claims made by the proponents of free markets, a knowledge economy, self-management and so on. In some sense, it could be argued that it is a leisure product, yet its content does not celebrate a particular form of consumption or an escapist life outside work, so it seems not to harmonize with the temper of cultural studies. It seems that this piece of popular culture doesn't fit well into the sorts of boxes that the university provides, which makes it interesting in all sorts of ways.

The popular culture of organization

I will assume that the lack of fit is a problem with the university rather than with this comic. In other words, that the problem is with the way that we classify the world, and not with the world itself. In order to understand this object, to be able to 'see' it as something other than trivia or a category mistake, we need to have a way of placing it, and of applying some sort of method (perhaps visual) to it. In an anthropological sense, it is clearly culture. It also seems fairly obvious that it is a form of popular culture, because it is not epistemologically privileged or associated with particularly elevated institutions. So I'm going to suggest that this represents part of the 'popular culture of organizing' – a genre of cultural representation that comments on work, management and business, but in ways that are often satirical and broadly hostile to authority.

The suggestion here is that the counter-culture can be set against a 'culture *for* organizing', which contains many images of work and management that are broadly positive. Think of the sorts of ideas you find in orthodox textbooks, in the marketing claims made by business schools, business magazines and newspapers, and the shelves full of glossy one-minute manager books. Rather like the utopian dreams of escape offered by musicals, fashion, holidays or betting shops in popular culture, this is mirrored in an elitist set of representations that combine first-class lounges, expensive watches and exclusive credit cards with the idea of being a special person. Certain people are part of the star system within this arena – management consultants with international tours delivered to packed conference rooms in expensive hotels, 'outlaw' entrepreneurs who can afford private jets, business school professors who can charge extraordinary fees for their wisdom. Embedding these images are other more mundane ones – well-dressed people looking at laptops, workplaces with water coolers and dress-down Fridays, and apartments offering lifestyle living in the heart of the city. This is all part of a cultural genre in which organizations, management and work are regarded as central to the reproduction of what is good, and the smile of an executive gazing out of an aeroplane window as a (female) member of the aircrew passes by smiling tells us what our dreams should be.

However, as is obvious, this culture for organizing is hugely contested. *The Adventures of Unemployed Man* is just one example here. It tells the story of a smug middle-aged white superhero – 'Ultimatum' – who passes through the city at night with messages of self-help for the poor and deviant. However, after being fired from a company he thought he owned and realizing that he can't get another job, he gradually comes to realize that the problem is the inequalities of capitalism, and not the indolence of the poor. Fighting the forces of the 'Invisible Hand' and 'The Free Marketeers', he becomes 'Unemployed Man' and defeats evil through collective organization. Just about everything in this comic contests the corporation, neoliberalism, consumer credit and the individualism which underpins pro-managerialism utopianism. Yet I do not believe that this is an unusual or anomalous example. Indeed, I would argue that the counter-culture of organizing is actually just as important and widespread as that which it opposes, and perhaps even more so. The interesting question is just why these cultural artefacts and practices tend not to be visible, but more on that in a moment.

Just to take some examples – in films as diverse as *Brazil* (1985), *What Women Want* (2000), *Monsters Inc.* (2001) and *Fun with Dick and Jane* (2005), we have plots that are organized around the idea that the work organization is the problem.[4] In popular film, most organizations are managed by bureaucrats, careerists or criminals, and freedom can only be found by telling the boss what you really think and then walking out, or pushing him/her out of the window of the skyscraper. In much storytelling, this is now no more than the deployment of a very common stereotype. If you want a bad guy, then make him a company executive (Bell 2008: 65 *passim*). So, when *The Muppets* film was being made in 2012, the plot revolved around an evil oil baron called Tex Richman. Even in science fiction movies, which we might imagine to be most divorced from such grubby questions of power and wealth, many now classic films have shadowy evil corporations as the ultimate source of the problem that needs to be overcome – The Tyrell Corporation in *Bladerunner*, Omnicorp in *Robocop*, Skynet in *Terminator* and The Weyland-Yutani Corporation in the *Alien* films. Our heroes are pirates and outlaws who fight against organizations (Parker 2012), and films about work are explorations of the meaninglessness of routine, boredom and humiliation – *Clerks* (1994), *Office Space* (1999), *Waydowntown* (2000), *I Really Hate My Job* (2007), *Horrible Bosses* (2011) and many others.

I think we can add to this list of films a whole series of less publicized ways in which the same generalized scepticism is routinely deployed in endless acts of production and consumption. For example, there is something fascinating about a 'Fuck Work' badge. I have one, and think of it as an impossible object (or, at least, a hypocritical one) since it, in some sense, attempts to deny the very labour that went into its production. Someone imagined it, and then other people designed it and chose a colour and typeface that someone else had designed, marketed it, optimized the production schedule, pressed the button that made the machines run, packed it, designed a website, distributed it, sold it and collected the profit, or even the interest from their investment. While the 'Fuck Work' example is rather extreme, a lot of money is clearly made through selling other examples of the counter-culture of organization. C. Northcote Parkinson's *Parkinson's Law* (1958) was an early example of a book-length view of organizations as inane bureaucracies populated by pompous and stupid men in suits. More recent examples are *Bureaucrats: How to Annoy Them* (Fishall 1981); *The Official Rules of Work* (Dickson 1996); the *Bluffer's Guide to Management* (Courtis 2000); *The Little Book of Management Bollocks* (Beaton 2001); *The Little Book of Office Bollocks* (Gelfer 2002); and *Bullshit Bingo* (Edmonds 2005). Found in a similar place in the book or gift shop might be *Mr Mean's Guide to Management* (Hargreaves 2000); *The Tiny Book of Boss Jokes* (Philips 2002); or *250*

Dumb Dares for the Workplace, which is 'guaranteed to keep the office entertained'. *The Office Kama Sutra* (Balmain 2001) contains instructions for the 'dance of a thousand sticky notes' and suggests many ways in which offices can become sites of libidinous excess. Rather deliciously, it also has a reversible book jacket that will allow you to pretend that you are actually reading a book called *Getting What you Want at Work: Ten Steps from Fantasy to Reality*. Or you might choose 'Voodoo Lou's Office Voodoo Kit' containing a corporate doll (with male and female sides), pins and 'Executive Spellbook'. The book explains what is wrong with bosses (playing golf, eating big lunches, driving a Lexus), their assistants, the computer nerd and so on. It then proposes various voodoo remedies that will deal with them, and provide the owner with 'your ticket to the corporate high life'. The same is probably not true of the 'Office Profanity Kit', containing a mini talking punchbag which swears at you when you hit it, and three stamps with the mottos – 'This is F**CKING URGENT'; 'Complete and Utter BULLSHIT'; and 'I haven't got time to read this CRAP'.

Television is another place to find examples of similar sentiments, such as the 2004–2005 US reality TV show *I Hate My Job*. A similar show was aired the year before in the UK – *Office Monkey*. Each episode was a TV version of giving the boss the finger.

> Offices are dull dreary places where nothing ever happens. That's why we bribed two members of offices around the country to disrupt their work places in the funniest ways possible. The winner gets a holiday, and the right to call themselves: Office Monkey.
> *(http://www.princess.uk.com/programmes/individual/recent/office.htm#)*[5]

The squirming embarrassment that accompanied victory was painful to watch, but tapped into some deeply rooted assumptions about what work is, and what work does to people. Office humour is generally spiteful, a form of vengeance that punishes hypocrisy and pomposity. This has been exploited by many British situation comedies in their portrayal of figures of authority.[6] *On The Buses* (1969–1973), *Are You Being Served?* (1972–1983), and the Reginald Perrin shows (1976–1979) all contained various supervisory or management characters whose vacuous vanity is regularly exposed (Hancock 2008). Often, these dramas were also post-war satires of social class in an era of accelerated social mobility, particularly of the 'jobsworth' who is acting up in terms of status and authority. So, Captain Mainwaring, the bank manager in *Dad's Army* (1968–1977) or the leisure centre manager Gordon Brittas in *The Brittas Empire* (1991–1997) are both claiming airs and graces that they clearly do not possess. Nowhere was this better satirized recently than in the mock-reality TV show *The Office*, which ran for two series on the BBC between 2001 and 2003, and then was remade for US TV in 2005 with eight series made at the time of writing. The US show, featuring the Dunder Mifflin company, has led to a video game, board game, nodding models of the characters, T-shirts, fake Dunder Mifflin websites and parodies of motivational posters.

The other iconic anti-work satire of the last few decades has been the Dilbert cartoons by Scott Adams. Co-opted by an entire generation of management academics and trainers, Adams' syndicated strip explores the stupidities of office life through the eyes of a naive junior (Ackroyd and Thompson 1999: 116–118). Many episodes of *The Simpsons* picked up on similar themes concerning Homer's work at Mr Burns' power plant and the characteristics of the various professionals who work in Springfield (Rhodes 2001; Ellis 2008). These ideas were prefigured in Matt Groening's 1980s cartoons such as the *Work is Hell* collection (2004). Senior managers read articles titled 'How to Make the Veins in your Forehead Throb Alarmingly' in a magazine called 'Lonely Tyrant'. An even more surreal portrayal of work is David Rees' *My New Filing Technique is Unstoppable* (2004), which contains assorted employees abusing each other about their filing systems, computers that insult you in the most profane fashion, and a character called Dr Niles Fanderbiles from the Quality Perfection Department who delivers self-righteous homilies in a Chinese accent. These satirical portrayals of work can also be found in plenty of underground comics and zines, such as the sad quietness of Stephen Knowles' *Five Days Out of Seven* (2004). Celebrations of sabotage and slacking, and descriptions of alienation and boss hatred are a powerful theme, as Stephen Duncombe catalogues (1997: 79 *passim*). Less ribald, but just as powerfully, Matanle *et al.* (2008) have also shown how Japanese salaryman manga comics can represent popular challenges to management authority.

Given its easy access at most workplaces and relative anonymity, it is hardly surprising that the Internet has become a site for the popular culture of organizing, as well as many ways to practically avoid working. The circulation of various anti-management spam mails is now a routine part of office life. Surfing during work time is a problem for organizations in itself, and various snooping technologies have been developed to prevent it, just as other counter-technologies have been developed to allow rapid movement between illicit web trivia and 'real' work on the computer. After all, if you were playing 'Whack Your Boss', you would almost certainly not want your superiors to know. This is a downloadable game that lets you kill your boss by using common office equipment.

> So one can enjoy the numerous ways of whacking your boss. You can smash his head to the wall repeatedly, you can squish his egg head in the drawers of your office table. There are actually twenty different types of whacking your boss.
>
> *(http://whackyourboss.info/)*[7]

Bored with watching the blood splatter, you might go and have a look at websites and blogs like i-resign.com, worktotallysucks.com, and mybossisanidiot.com. The last allows you to send a letter from the site to your boss, anonymously of course, and helpfully provides templates and examples of other people's letters. There are some particularly nice examples on the site workrant.com, which encourages obscene venting of various kinds. This, for example, from 'Killy Killkill', in IT and based in the UK.

> Dear Manager
> A quick question – HOW THE FUCK CAN YOU BE SO FUCKING INCOMPETENT WITHOUT ACTUALLY DYING OF IT??? And one comments, which needs to be branded across your stupid fucking face – backwards, so even a fucking mong like you can read it in the mirror – NO YOU DON'T UNDERSTAND MY FRUSTRATION BECAUSE EVERY SINGLE FUCKING FRUSTRATION I HAVE IS ENTIRELY DUE TO YOU. …
> I feel better for that, thank you.

All these examples work so well precisely because the popular culture of organization is embedded into so many assumptions about what work is and what it is not. We don't need to employ a huge amount of interpretive labour to make sense of them, or to explore their assumptions. For example, an advert for cheap flights suggested that you could 'Tell the boss to stick it … where the sun don't shine' because holidays are articulated as a way of escaping from work. A promotion for Christmas parties is called 'P45' (the UK tax form you get when leaving, or being sacked from, work), 'because you never liked your boss anyway'. Or even the advertising for Kit Kat chocolate bars ('Have a break. Have a Kit Kat'), because even having a break from work is part of the routine of work itself. Almost any leisure-related product can make a useful reference to the repressive structure of the working week, such as the restaurant chain 'TGI Friday' (Thank God It's ...), the TV show *TFI Friday*, or the hundred and one pop songs that have Friday on their mind, and are waiting for the weekend when we can dance, party, escape or be together with the one we love (Rhodes 2007).

This could never be anything like an exhaustive list, but it has indicated something about the variety and scale of the popular culture of organizing. This in itself underscores the ways in which certain disciplinary, institutional and epistemological distinctions are quite capable of making certain matters almost invisible, even when they are as common and noisy as the things I have collected here. Or, if they are seen at all, they can be dismissed as 'not belonging here' – not art, not business, not politics, not leisure. This metaphor of seeing is useful in another way too, because it presses us to think about questions of method.

Methods, and the visual

As is becoming clear, as well as falling between various different disciplinary divisions, the popular culture of organizing is methodologically problematic too. This is another way of understanding why it doesn't fit well within classifications, because very often what we understand to be appropriate as a method is determined by the definition of the object in the first place. So those who study texts, in the narrow sense of written words, have developed a body of literary theory which explores the ways in which those texts can be approached and explicated (Eagleton 2008, for example). Those who study visual art, or dance, or sculpture, or architecture have similarly developed ways of understanding what it means to work with the visual elements of their objects of enquiry. The social sciences, on the other hand, have tended to work with ideas of what 'accounts' – interviews, questionnaires, ethnographies and so on – can reveal about the relationship between beliefs and behaviours. As this volume illustrates, though these accounts may involve the production of visual data – graphs, kinship diagrams, photographs, NVivo diagrams of relationships, nodes and attributes – these are not usually taken to be visual *per se*, but rather the indicators of something else. That is to say, the visual tends to be thought of as useful insofar as it can tell us about some 'deeper' layer of explanation, or be used to triangulate a particular account.

In general, then, different disciplines come with deeply embedded assumptions about what 'data' looks like, what its epistemological status is, and what sorts of methods are legitimate to apply to it. Of course, these might themselves be the subject of much contest within the discipline – such as the dull and longstanding comparison between quantitative and qualitative work – but even then there is usually still some agreement about the 'object', even if there is disagreement about its nature. The popular culture of organization is clearly not amenable to such partitioning. Assuming that it is accepted that I was presenting a more or less coherent body of examples in the previous section – and it might not be – then it is obvious that this phenomenon presents itself in a wide variety of ways. Certainly, it is visual, in the examples of comic books, Internet pages and TV cartoons, but sometimes it is not visual at all, in the examples of popular song and radio programmes. Sometimes it is material and tactile, in a book, a badge or office toy, and sometimes it is virtual, as spam, a TV show or a video game. Most often, it is a form of culture that simply refuses being reduced to one category – just as films are concerned with sight and sound, so do they produce merchandising that is pirated as materials in cheap markets in cities across the world, and parodies which rapidly go virtual and viral.

Just as importantly, the popular culture of organizing is found in different sites – on the noticeboards of offices and sellotaped to walls in factories, or in bookshops, car boot sales, cinemas and homes. There isn't a definitive place you could go to in order to find this cultural form, and neither can you say much reliably about who produces it. It might be on the back of a truck, a handmade sign that says 'Mr Friday Night'. It might be a cultural product manufactured by the culture industries – Fox Broadcasting Company (a subsidiary of Rupert Murdoch's News International Corporation) makes *The Simpsons* and the US version of *The Office* is made by Universal TV, part of the NBC TV network. Ironically, these television shows which endlessly parody the big company are financed and produced by big companies. On the other hand, the spam emails and endlessly photocopied satirical notices have no clear source, but we can probably safely say they don't come from the boss. Some products, such as the 'Friday on my Mind'-type pop song, might originate with alienated office boys in garage bands, but then are reproduced and distributed by multinational corporations. As I noted before, an anthropological understanding of culture messes up the boundaries between economics, sociology, politics and so on. It also confuses the methodological distinctions that are embedded in different disciplines.

Insofar as these matters have been treated as worthy of note within cultural studies itself, I think the tendency has been to take on a broadly literary theory method and say that they can all be treated as 'texts'. This visual but rather typographic metaphor can certainly be useful because it stresses the work of 'reading', which inevitably goes into any account of cultural practices and products (Hall and Jefferson 1976; Hall 1980). Parts of cultural studies (particularly those influenced by literary and social theory) develop this into broadly semiotic approaches to meaning, in which words, images, sounds and so on can be treated as elements of a sign system. Since all forms of culture putatively have meaning, the task is to produce convincing 'readings' that combine evidence with sophistication and verve (Barthes 1972). Other parts of cultural studies (often the more sociologically inclined work) tend to look at behaviours in a broadly ethnographic fashion, documenting and interpreting what happens in local contexts (Willis 1977), or concentrating on 'reader response' audience studies of particular cultural texts (Morley 1980; Ang 1985).

It seems to me that any attempt to study the popular culture of organization must involve the same sort of pluralism in both method and analysis. If we take the English cultural studies classic *Resistance Through Rituals* (Hall and Jefferson 1976) as an example, we can see a set of approaches to the study of youth cultures that are very eclectic indeed. After some theoretically dense positioning essays, there is a section (titled 'ethnography') that presents historically informed readings of the dress and attitudes of Teds, Mods and Rastas, a literary and ethnographic account of the Skins, and ethnographies of what it means to hang around on the street doing nothing, and of Hippy drug-taking. There is also a typology of communes, and theoretically informed reading of black music, and of the 'mugging' panic. These essays are followed by others on style, class and generation, girls, marginality, politics and methods. Many of these essays are illustrated by full-page black and white photos of various youth cultures in full dress, as well as various diagrams with arrows and rectangles, and even boxes with mock writing from fieldnotes.

It is a messy book. It uses a wide variety of techniques for documenting and warranting its claims, evidence which ranges from song lyrics to participant observation, as well as very different writing styles by the 25 authors involved. Interestingly, much about the text is concerned with the visual (the 'look' of clothes and so on) and is presented in a visual way. The text is largely set in a courier typeface which echoes the manually typed working paper series from the Centre for Contemporary Cultural Studies and which forms most of the content of the book. It looks urgent, rather rough and unpolished, with connotations of authentic unmediated experience. The photographs themselves are largely illustrative, and not analysed in any detail, but the very fact that there are grainy black and white images of kids

Martin Parker

hanging around looking cool provides the book with a dimension that the usual academic text lacks. In an anthropological sense, this book is culture too of course – material culture, visual culture – a culture which reflexively comments on its own epistemological preferences.

So there are certainly openings in cultural studies for a consideration of popular culture as visual but not much interest in work organizations as sites or topics for popular culture. There are also plenty of examples of the popular culture of organization, but little interest in them as a legitimate topic for people who work in business schools. The question that remains concerns a way of seeing, and consequently the sort of methods and analysis that might be appropriate to explore matters that have fallen into the shadows of institutions and disciplines.

Against method

The most obvious objection to what I have suggested here is to say that the collection of materials and practices that I have chosen to call the 'popular culture of organizing' is not a coherent one. In other words, like Borges' famous list from Foucault's *Order of Things* (1989: xvi), it is not a set of things that makes any sense to collect together. It might be said that it would be better to segment the field I have produced and send the different classes of things back to the boxes where they belong. Texts go to literature, songs to music, pictures to visual art and so on. In this way, the problems go away and the disciplines are restored as *tabula*, which allow 'thought to operate on the entities of our world, to put them in order, to divide them into classes, to group them according to names that designate their similarities and differences' (ibid.: xix). Foucault's consistent concern in his book is how things come to be ordered, and what principles are used to produce different sorts of knowledge to speak about human beings and other materials. This is both a question of deciding when things belong together and when they belong apart, and also what sorts of methods can and should be used on the different categories thereby produced.

For a structural anthropologist like Mary Douglas, these are matters that also reflect the existence and structure of various sorts of institutions. Universities, galleries, newspapers, publishers and so on are all examples of *How Institutions Think* (1987). The hierarchies, departments and processes that are embedded in organizing and organizations encourage us to think in ways that follow those established channels, and also to observe which sort of things belong in different sorts of places. Douglas, of course, has also written about mess as 'matter out of place' (1966), her point being that there is no 'mess' unless we have already decided on a preferred order. The world as it presents itself to us is not disordered, it just *is*, but we begin to perceive it as disordered as soon as we insist on fitting it into the boxes that we provide. John Law plays on similar themes in *After Method* (2004), which begins with an attempt to describe a complex visual illustration. If the world is multiple, fluid, elusive and hybrid, he says, then we need messy imaginative methods to cope with the messy pictures we face. In the social sciences, method and analysis must, to some extent, be mimetic of the conditions that it seeks to reveal, and not always assuming that order lies beneath the surface. It simply isn't possible to say what these methods or forms of analysis should look like, because that would already be to close down the possibility of producing something interesting by looking somewhere unusual. In that sense, any method should be treated with suspicion.

It seems to me that the question of the 'popular culture of organization', within a book that seeks to explore the idea that 'the visual' is a neglected and useful method for studying organization, presents this classification problem in a complex and nested way. The very idea of popular culture is a troubling one to begin with, since it originates as a residual category from that which is not 'high' culture. If 'mass' culture was denigrated, then popular culture is celebrated precisely because it questions the epistemology and politics that make opera worth more than *The X Factor*, and sometimes questions the very institutions that produce elite culture. However, it would be easy enough to say that 'popular' here means numerical popularity, and that is going to be a problem. *Five Days Out of Seven* was self-published, and probably printed in a very limited run. Compared to, for example, the attendance at a major city art gallery, Knowles' comic is very selective in its appeal. Deciding what is popular culture is itself then a problem, particularly with regard to a contrast with the 'culture for organizing', which, it could be argued, is a form of popular culture too in numerical terms, since it is not always elite in its appeal (ten Bos 2000). Neither can we make a clear distinction in terms of some sort of ideological commitment, simply because there are plenty of examples of 'high' culture that articulate a critique of industrial societies and modern organizations – Blake, Ruskin, Dickens, Morris, Kafka and so on (Parker 2005).

Yet, even if a stable object called 'popular culture' could be produced, it is by no means obvious why any particular method would be more appropriate than others for studying it. Popular culture is certainly partly a visual medium, and studying it will be impoverished if it neglects this aspect, but it is by no means exclusively visual and indeed is in some ways less visual than certain other cultural categories – such as white cube art, sculpture or ballet. The key point is that an anthropological definition of culture doesn't exclude anything in principle, which is both generous in its ambition and impossible to achieve in practice. The result is unlikely to be tidy and, hence, as Law suggests and *Resistance Through Rituals* demonstrates, a range of messy methods are most likely to be able to cope with a messy world. This degree of imprecision might be unsatisfying to those who prefer order and organization, but is less likely to ignore elements that don't fit into categories that have already been established by particular epistemologies, institutions and methods. In *The Adventures of Unemployed Man*, there is a mock advert for 'Blind-o-Vision' goggles, which 'will allow you to block out negative sights and get on with what's most important'. Disciplines make those decisions for us too, because different ways of seeing produce different objects. They fit them into the shape of the institutions we work in, and encourage the use of certain methods over others.

The organizational shaping of thought, and hence of what is made visible and invisible, is inevitable. We cannot easily do away with institutions, and, even if we don't like the ones we have, it is likely that we will replace them with others that shape how we think and see. So there is no solution to the relationship between location and vision, but simply the reminder that we are always in a location, looking from somewhere and hence never able to see everything. But, that being admitted, it doesn't stop us from asking just how 'Fuck Work' badges might be interesting for people who work in business schools, or why visual methods will always be needed, and at the same time never enough, to understand *The Adventures of Unemployed Man*.

Notes

1. Thanks to Emma Bell for her helpful comments on this chapter.
2. Not just class, though this does seem to have been the most important organizing concept, but also gender, race and ethnicity.
3. I'm not sure that culture is a particularly complex concept. Rather, its wide application results in its being a word with many different antonyms, prefixes and suffixes, which results in its being a family of inflected terms rather than a single word.
4. This section is adapted from Chapter 8 in Parker 2012.
5. This site was accessed some time in 2004, but seems to have disappeared, which is an interesting comment on artefacts and method itself.

6   Apologies for the ethnocentricity of the following examples. Popular culture of the TV variety is rarely genuinely global.
7   These websites were accessed in November 2011.

References

Ackroyd, S. and Thompson, P. (1999) *Organisational Misbehaviour*, London: Sage.
Ang, I. (1985) *Watching Dallas*, London: Methuen.
Barthes, R. (1972) *Mythologies*, London: Paladin.
Bell, E. (2008) *Reading Management and Organization in Film*, Basingstoke: Palgrave.
Berger, J. (1972) *Ways of Seeing*, Harmondsworth: Penguin/BBC.
Douglas, M. (1966) *Purity and Danger: An Analysis of Concepts of Pollution and Taboo*, London: Routledge and Kegan Paul.
——(1987) *How Institutions Think*, London: Routledge and Kegan Paul.
Duncombe, S. (1997) *Notes from Underground*, Bloomington, IN: Microcosm Publishing.
Eagleton, T. (2008) *Literary Theory*, Oxford: Wiley Blackwell.
Ellis, N. (2008) 'What the hell is *that?*' *Organization* 15(5): 705–723.
Foucault, M. (1989) *The Order of Things*, Abingdon: Routledge.
Hall, S. (1980) 'Encoding/decoding', in S. Hall, D. Hobson, A. Lowe and P. Willis (eds) *Culture, Media, Language*, London: Hutchinson, 128–138.
Hall, S. and Jefferson, T. (1976) (eds) *Resistance Through Rituals*, London: Hutchinson.
Hancock, P. (2008) 'Fear and (self) loathing in Coleridge Close', *Organization* 15(5): 685–703.
Knowles, S. (2004) *Five Days Out of Seven*, Falmouth: R. Booth Ltd.
Law, J. (2004) *After Method: Mess in Social Science Research*, Abingdon: Routledge.
Lewis, J. (2008) *Cultural Studies*, London: Sage.
Matanle, P., McCann, L. and Ashmore, D. (2008) 'Men under pressure', *Organization* 15(5): 639–664.
Morley, D. (1980) *The Nationwide Audience*, London: British Film Institute.
Origen, E. and Golen, G. (2010) *The Adventures of Unemployed Man*, New York: Little, Brown and Company.
Parker, M. (2000) *Organizational Culture and Identity*, London: Sage.
——(2005) 'Organizational Gothic', *Culture and Organization* 11(3): 153–166.
——(2006) 'The counter culture of organization: towards a cultural studies of representations of work', *Consumption Markets & Culture* 9(1): 1–15.
——(2012) *Alternative Business: Outlaws, Crime and Culture*, London: Routledge.
Rhodes, C. (2001) 'D'oh: *The Simpsons*, popular culture and the organizational carnival', *Journal of Management Inquiry* 10(4): 374–383.
——(2007) 'Outside the gates of Eden: utopia and work in rock music', *Group and Organization Management* 32(1): 22–49.
Smircich, L. (1983) 'Concepts of culture and organizational analysis', *Administrative Science Quarterly* 28: 339–359.
Storey, J. (1993) *An Introductory Guide to Cultural Theory and Popular Culture*, Hemel Hempstead: Harvester Wheatsheaf.
——(ed.) (1994) *Cultural Theory and Popular Culture: A Reader*, Hemel Hempstead: Harvester Wheatsheaf.
ten Bos, R. (2000) *Fashion and Utopia in Management Thinking*, Amsterdam: Benjamins.
Williams, R. (1976) *Keywords*, London: Fontana.
Willis, P. (1977) *Learning to Labour*, Farnborough: Saxon House.

Index

Note: Page numbers in **bold** type refer to **figures**
Page numbers in *italic* type refer to *tables*
Page numbers followed by 'n' refer to notes

Aalbaek, P. 54–7
Abrams, M.H. 67
accountancy 33–4; role 36
accountants: image 10
accounting practices 22–3
Acevedo, B. 7, 116–29
action research 310
actor network theory (ANT) 70, 290, 324, 326, 332
acts 178
Adenhauer, K. 148
Adventures of Unemployed Man, The (Origan and Golen) 379, 380, 382, 383, 389
advertisements 195, 229; freezer 133
advertising 7; agencies 133; and American culture 131; ancestral models 134; campaigns 104; and capitalism 138; as communication 133–5; definition 130–1; future 140–1; hierarchy of effects 134; and ideology 138–40; images 34; medical 131; neurological 134; photographs 229; productive consumption 103–5; recruitment 139–40; scientific 131; signs' history 132–3; signs and semiotics 130–45; spending 131; visual aspects 82–3
aesthetic(s) 7, 49, 61, 100–1, 102, 146, 147, 361; classical strategies 146, 147–52; consumption 96, 100–2; economy 354; knowledge 355, 356; marketing 153–4; organizational 291; products 127; relational 159; spatial 107; state 151, 155; turn 146; and visual cultures 355–6
affiliation 327
Africa Remix (Hayward Gallery 2005) 40
agency 199n
agriculture 251
Ahuvia, A. 198
Ai Weiwei 158, 159
Al Gore's Penguin Army (2006) 372–3
Alac, M. 358–9

Alexander the Great 117–18
Alexander, V. 252
Alliance for Climate Change Education 332
Althusser, L. 139
Alvesson, M. 49; *et al* 301
amateurism 326, 327
American culture: and advertising 131
Amnesty International (AI) 332
analysis 6, 46–7, 61
anchorage 34
anchoring 42
Anderson, K. 93
Andersson, R. 160
Angelus Novus (Klee) 48, 58, **59**
anti-identities 301
anti-work satires 383–5
Apple 105, 139–40, **140**
architects 355
architecture: digital 104–5
Arendt, H. 70
Aristotle 278
Arnould, E.: *et al* 91
art 61, 104, 108, 141, 146–63, 263, 268, 361, 381; federal buildings 247; function 119; history 156; juxtaposition 50; mass-media 147; organizations as 147–8; Platonic idea 155; power 127, 269; product design as 153–86; projects 7–8; Renaissance 104; role 150; romantic 368; spaces 158; and state 152; visual 157; of visual inquiry 28
Art & Copy 131
artefacts 173, 180; and meaning 171, 172–3, **173**; production 193; spatial 174; text 170
Artificial Intelligence 335, 341, 342, 347; labs 337, 338, 339, 344–5
artist marketers 155–6
artist-in-residency project 264, 265–7, 270, 271n
artist-organizer 148–50

391

Index

artistic interventions 48, 268, 269, 270; in organizations 263–4; and policymakers 264, 270
artists 160; avant-garde 50; installation 159; as reality coaches 158; role 266
arts 101, 355; performing 361
arts-based interventions 261–72
Asch, T. 166
Assa Abloy 306, 308, 310–14, **310**, 319, 320; communications boards 311–12, 313, **313**; key performance indicator side 311, 312, 313, **313**; production analysis board 311; visual management 314
Association for Consumer Research 223
Astroturf 327
attention economy 354
audience: participation 331; role 12; sensitivity 280
audiencehood 330
audit society 73
authenticity 12, 229, 327, 328, 365–78; client 370; ethics 367–9; and organizational sustainability 365–78; paradox 366; YouTube 371–3
authority 53; figures and television representations 384
Avery, J.: and Fournier, S. 322, 323
Avolio, B.J.: and Gardner, W.L. 204
Azoulay, A. 195

Bacon, F. 123
Bak, S. 59
Balmer, J.M.T.: and Gray, E.R. 273–4
Bamberger, B.: and Davidson, C. 251
banks: webpages 278
Banksy 376
Barnhurst, K.G.: et al 188
Barthes, R. 5, 33–45, 51, 132, 136, 141, 329; *Camera Lucida* 33, 34, 37–9, 43, *43*; *Rhetoric of the Image* 33, 34–5, 43, *43*
Bateman, N.: and Lethbridge, S. 11, 306–21
Bateson, G. 166, 347
Baudrillard, J. 103, 104; and Fleming, J. 73
Baxandall, M. 121, 122, 123, 124, 125, 194
Baxter, J. 324
Beaton, C. 124
bed management 317–18, **317**
Beethoven, L. 150, 151
Beijing Olympic Stadium 159
Belk, R.W. 73, 92
Bell, E.: and McArthur 12, 365–78; Warren, S. and Schroeder, J.E. 1–16
Beller, J. 354
Belova, O. 5
Benjamin, W. 58, 63, 104, 119, 147
Berger, J. 6, 66, 104, 122, 165, 180, 195
Bergson, H. 69–70
Berthoin Antal, A. 263; et al 10, 261–72
Betts, J.: Warren, S. and Shortt, H. 11, 289–305

Betty Crocker cake mix 133
Beuys, J. 156
Beynon, H. 250; and Hedges, N. 250–1
Bhabha, H.K. 57
Bhopal tragedy 28, 50
Billancourt (Bon and Stéphani) 249
Birchall, C. 22
Blanchette, A. 84
blogs 325, 328, 332
Blösche, J. 58
Boden, D. 6
Bolla, P. de 20
Bon, F.: and Stéphani, A. 249
books: comic 379, 380, 383, 386
Booth, C. 244
Borgerson, J.L.: and Schroeder, J.E. 107, 138
Born to Work (Hedges and Beynon) 250–1
Bote & Bock 148
Bourdieu, P. 323–4, 361
Bourriaud, N. 159
boxing: coaches 335, 345; gyms 337, 344–5; and realism 345
brand 1, 98, 106, 140; culture 106; identity 12; images 99
branding 10; sensory 74
British Empire 57
Britton, T.: and La Salle, D. 1
Bronson, P. 57
Broomfield, M. 248
Broussine, M.: and Vince, R. 231
Brown, A.: and Coupland, C. 277
Brown, E. 245, 246
Brown, S.: and Maclaran, P. 73
Bryans, P.: and Mavin, S. 231
Bryman, A. 121
Building Blocks (Siemens) 137–8, **137**
buildings 169
Burgess, J.: and Green, J. 326
Burgin, V. 1
Burke, E. 71
Burke, K. 172
Burning Man Festival 218
Burrell, G. 50
Burri, R.V. 4, 359
business: leaders 126; reputation management 370; schools' websites 281
Byrne, D.: and Doyle, A. 254

Calderdale and Huddersfield NHS: visual management 317–18, **317**, 319
call centres 368–9
Camera Lucida (Barthes) 33, 34, 37–9, 43, *43*
camera obscura 353
Campbell, D.: et al 10
Campbell, J. 169
Campbell, N. 7, 130–45
Can Buy Me Love (Lastovicka et al) 221

capital 323–4; cultural 99, 105, 326, 329, 332; digital 324; social 325, 332
capitalism 329, 367; and advertising 138; and images 105; industrial 132; late 368; post-industrial 104
Caravaggio, M.M. da 48, 53–4; *Conversion of Saint Paul* 48, 50, **52**, 51–3
cartoons 169–70, 172, 173, 181; political 230; television 386
Cartwright, L.: and Sturken, M. 6
Cataldi, S. 25
Catholic Church 51–3, 118, 125, 126
Ceccarelli, L. 193
Centre for Contemporary Cultural Studies 387
CEO portraits 124–5, 126, 203, 366
change 267, 270; perceptions 231; social 71–2
Changing Works (Harper) 251
charisma 7, 53, 116–17, 118, 119, 120; routinization 116, 117, 119–21
charismatic leadership 116–29
charities 325
Chaudhri, V.: and Wang, J. 279
Chia, R. 70
chiasmic flesh 25–7
children 39, 42
Cisco 277
Citroën DS 136, 143n
Civil War 191; re-enactments 340–1
Clarke, J. 9, 202–13
class 381, 384; creative 53
classical aesthetic strategies 146, 147–52
client authenticity 370
Closing (Bamberger and Davidson) 251
co-creation 7
coaches: boxing 335, 345; reality 158
cognitive workspace 308
collaboration tools 325
collective instruction 60
collective memory 51
Collier, J.: and Collier, M. 85, 206
comic books 379, 380, 383, 386
communication 2, 8, 9, 12, 188–201; advertising as 133–5; corporate 274; informational theory 134; philosophy 33; text-based 202; theories 134; tools 205; visual 2, 8, 9, 12, 188–201, 202
communications boards 310; Assa Abloy 311–12, 313, **313**; design 311–12
communism 331
company websites 10
comparison techniques 217
competence: social 204–5
complexity 142
composition 283, 284, 285
computer: gaming industry 74
computer technology 347; and drawing 228
conflict: identity 237–8

Conflicted Consumer (2010) 373–4
connotations 34, 35, 36, 42–3, 136
Consalvo, M. 323
conservatism 71
constructivism 70
Consumer Culture Theory 81; Conference (2011) 93
consumer research 7, 9, 83, 93; ethnographic 88; ethnographic videography 214–26; filmmaking 214–26
consumerism: Indian weddings 216
consumers 7, 79–95, 98–9, 100, 101, 102, 103, 138; culture 84, 99, 101, 102, 108, 214; empowerment 108; motivations 154; productive consumption 106–7; researchers 91; visual 7, 79–95
consuming representation: definition 103
consumption 7, 19, 80–1, 86, 89, 91–3, 135, 195, 330; aesthetic 96, 100–2; images 96–115; marketplace image 96, 102–7; visual 7, 19, 97, 102, 105–6
consumption, *see also* productive consumption
contemporary aesthetic strategies 146–7, 156–9
content analysis 8, 197–8, 253
conversation starters 325
Cooper, R. 61; and Law, J. 70
Corbett, M. 246
corporate annual reports 5, 369
corporate communication 274
corporate ethnographers 87–90, 92
corporate identity 280, 281, 285; management 11; and websites 273–4
corporate image 246, 274
corporate photography 9, 243, 244–7, 255
corporate social responsibility (CSR) 40, 277, 278, 365–6, 368, 369, 375; websites 275
corporate sustainability reports 22
corporate visual ethnographers 93
corporate visual identity (CVI) 11, 273, 285, 324, 325
corporate web identity 10, 273–88, *282*; accessibility 275–6; customization 279–80; interactivity 276–7; mobility 275; visuality 277–9
corporate websites 369
corporations: modern 53
Costea, B.: *et al* 53
Coupland, C.: and Brown, A. 277
creative class 53
creative industries 354
creators 171, 172
Culler, J.D. 33
cultural capital 99, 105, 326, 329, 332
cultural intermediaries 97, 98, 99, 101
cultural knowledge 5
cultural production 96–115, 195
cultural products 98, 100, 103

Index

cultural studies 195, 381–2, 387, 388; definition 194
culture 12, 19, 194–5, 197, 267–8, 353–5, 361–2, 380–2; and aesthetics 355–6; American 131; brand 106; consumer 84, 99, 101, 102, 108, 214; digital 322–3, 329, 332; high 388, 389; popular 379–90; visual 355–6; youth 387
cyborg 323
cynical distance 56
Czarniawska, B. 1

Dabakis, M. 247
Daimler-Chrysler 134
Dali, S. 156
D'Arazien, A. 248
DARPA 344, 346
Daston, L. 359, 360, 361
data 8, 81, 84, 86, 166, 167, 217, 386; density 307–8, 313; display 308; and ethnography 215–18; genres logic 178; representation 183n; video 208–9, 210, 215
Davidson, C.: and Bamberger, B. 251
Davison, J. 5, 33–45; and Warren, S. 26
decision-making theory 339
defamiliarization 49, 60
deindustrialization 243, 249–50
deindustrialized spaces 254
Deleuze, G. 47; and Guattari, F. 48
democratization 323
denotation 34, 42
depression: manic 360
Derrida, J. 66–7, 72
Descartes, R. 65–6, 353
design: logic 178; product 105, 106, 153–86; social media 326
deskwork 168, 179, 180
Detroit 249
development 21, 261–70, 271n; values 261–3
Development Gateway 276
Dewey, G. 101
diabetes 87–9, **88**, **89**
Dickinson, G. 191–2; and Ott, B.L. 191
digital architecture 104–5
digital capital 324
digital culture 322–3, 329, 332
digitalization 13, 229, 230
Dikovitskaya, M. 194
discourse 324; political 71–2; voice 69
Disney 107, 230
distancing 66
diversity 264–5
Divisions of Labour (Pahl) 250
DNA: crime scenes 358
dOCUMENTA 157–8
Documentary Film Movement (DFM) 246, 248
documentary photography 247
Doré, G. 244

Doss, E. 247
Douglas, M. 388
Doyle, A.: and Byrne, D. 254
Doyle, J.: and Nathan, M. 300
drawing 9, 227–42; and computer technology 228; social and organizational research 228–31; UK business school case study 233–9
Drucker, J. 170
Dumit, J. 358, 359

e-vision 65, **66**, 72
eating disorders 222
economic science 53
Economic and Social Research Council (ESRC) 3
economy 79; aesthetic 354; attention 354; visual 79
Edensor, T. 250
Eisenstein, S. 147–8
Eisner, E. 268, 269
Eliasson, O. 158, 159
Elkins, J. 194, 196, 362
Elliott, C.: and Robinson, S. 10–11, 273–88
Ellis, R. 360
embodied perception 25
embodiment 24, 25
Emmison, M.: and Smith, P. 229
emotion: and organizations 74
Empire Marketing Board (EMB) 246, 247
Empire State Building: construction 244
empiricism: materialistic 24
empowerment: consumers 108
enframed vision 23–4
English, R. 376
engraving 244
Enlightenment 65, 66, 67, 68, 69, 73
enskilled vision 359
entrepreneurial interactions: visual symbols 203–5
entrepreneurship 9, 57, 356; communication tools 205; and videoethnography 202–13
environment 329–30
environmental social movements 372
epistemology: modern 68
Ernst & Young 5, 33; Annual Review front covers 35–7, 42–3
Esrock, S.L.: and Leichty, G.B. 279
Esso 133
ethics: authenticity 367–9; marketing 376; situated 208; video research 207–8; visuality 48
ethnographers 81; corporate 87–90, 92, 93
ethnographic consumer research 88
ethnographic film 91
ethnographic videoethnography 9
ethnographic videography: consumer research 214–26
ethnography 81, 206, 207, 255; academic constructions 84–7; corporate constructions 87–90; data amount 216–17; data comparison 217;

394

data presentation 218; data richness 217; observation 88; and visual data 215–18
European Institute for Advanced Studies in Management (EIASM) 3
expert images 358
expert seers 359
eyes: ascendancy 65–7; epistemologies 20

Facebook 2, 93, 322, 325, 326, 332, 370, 371
Farm Security Administration (FSA) 247
Fascism 119
fashion industry 365
Fast, O. 157
federal buildings: art 247
Fender, K. 344
Fernandez, K.V.: and Starr, R.G. 220
Few, S. 308
fieldnotes 86
fieldwork 168, 178; analytic triad **172**
film 166, 173, 181, 383, 386; ethnographic 91
filmmaking 223–4; consumer research 214–26; industrial 248
Fine, G.: and Hallett, T. 300
Finkelpearl, S.: and Sachs, J. 370
Finnegan, C.A. 196, 197
Fischer, M.M.J.: and Marcus, G.E. 46, 49, 50, 51
Fisher, D.: and Fowler, S. 126
Fishermen, The (Tunstall) 250
Fleming, J.: and Baudrillard, J. 73
Fleming, P. 368–9; and Spicer, A. 56
flesh: chiasmic 25–7
Flewitt, R. 208
Florida, R. 53
Flusser, V. 6
Ford, H. 245
Ford Motor Company 245
Forester, J. 179–80
form 151
Foss, S. 192, 193
Foucault, M. 68, 72, 120, 324, 357, 388
Four Nigerians 55–7, **56**
Fournier, S.: and Avery, J. 322, 323
Fowler, S.: and Fisher, D. 126
frame 122, 124
Free Range Studios 327–32, 366, 370–4
free-drawn personality image 232, **234**, **235**, **237**
freezer advertisements 133
functionalism 355
Fyfe, G.: and Law, J. 227, 229

Gabriel, Y. 74
Gallagher, V.J.: *et al* 196
Galliano, J. 155
Gardner, W.L.: and Avolio, B.J. 204
gaze 122
genealogy 122, 125
General Electric Company (GEC) 245

General Post Office (GPO) 246, 247
geographic logic 175
Germain, J. 249, 250
Germany: national anthem 148
Giddens, A. 71
Gilbreth, F.: and Gilbreth, L. 245–6
Glasnapp, J.: and Isaacs, E. 90
glass cage metaphor 74
globalization 73; and advertising 142–3
goals: ambiguous 339
Goethe, J.W. 149, 150, 151–2
Goffman, E. 204
Goldman, R.: *et al* 142
Golen, G.: and Origan, E. 379, 380, 382, 383, 389
Goodwin, C. 21
Google 131, 326; Groups 325
Gore, A. 372–3
governmentality 68
Grant, D.: and Marshak, R.J. 262, 269
Graphics Press 307
Gray, E.R.: and Balmer, J.M.T. 273–4
Gray, R.: *et al* 42
Great Exhibition (1851) 105
Green, J.: and Burgess, J. 326
greenwashing 369, 370
Grint, K. 126
group identity 294
Groys, B. 159
Gruber, R.E. 170
Guantánamo Bay 168
Guattari, F.: and Deleuze, G. 48
Guba, E.G.: and Lincoln, Y.S. 199
Guillet de Monthoux, P. 7–8, 146–63
Guinness brewery 252
Gulick, R. van 165
Guthey, E.: and Jackson, B. 116, 119, 121, 122, 123, 124–5, 203, 366
gyms: boxing 337, 344–5; Harlien's 335, 337–8, 340, 342, 345–6

Habermas, J. 69, 72
Habsburg dynasty 118
hair salons 295–6, **296**, 301
Halbwachs, M. 51
Half Life 343
Halford, S. 252
Hall, S. 194
Hallett, T.: and Fine, G. 300
Haraway, D. 71, 137, 323
Harlien's Gym 335, 337–8, 340, 342, 345–6
Harper, D. 246, 248, 251, 254
Hawaii: marketing 107
Haydn, J. 148–9, 150, 151, 153
Hedges, N.: and Beynon, H. 250–1
Hegel, G.W.F. 152
Heidegger, M. 23–4, 70

395

Index

Her Majesty's Court Service: visual management 316–17, **316**, 319
hermeneutics 170–1, 181
Herzele, A. van: and van Woerkum, C.M.J. 175
Heuss, T. 148
hidden objects 296–300, **298**, **299**, 301, 302
Hidden Persuaders, The (Packard) 133
Hietanan, J.: *et al* 216
Higgins, J. 249
Hinckley, J. 358
Hine, L. 244, 245
Hitler, A. 147, 152
Hoeffner, J.: and Shah, P. 308
Hoffman, S.G. 11, 335–49
Holocaust 60, 148
Höpfl, H.: and Matilal, S. 50; and Ng, R. 300, 301
human: actions 170; body 138; cognition 353; visual perception 353
Hume, D. 154
Hummer 106
Hyde, A.: and Kearney, K. 231

iconology 254
IDEAS 318–19, **319**, 320
identification: schizo- 233, 238
identity 10, 10–11, 99, 231–3, 238, 277, 324; brand 12; conflict 237–8; corporate 11, 273–4, 280, 281, 285; corporate visual (CVI) 11, 273, 285, 324, 325; group 294; organizations 165–6, 231, 232, 238, 277; social 26–7; theories 329; web 280; and workplace tools 295–6, **296**, *see also* corporate web identity
identity construction 138; and social media 322
ideology: and advertising 138–40
Iedema, R. 209
IKEA 279–80, 285, 286
illustration 252
Image Worlds (Nye) 245, 253, 254
image-based research 10
imagery 7, 91, 209; corporate use 245
image(s) 4–6, 8, 102, 108, 122, 141, 175, 227, 278; accountants 10; advertising 34; and capitalism 105; consumption 96–115; corporate 246, 274; double contextualization 92; expert 358; free-drawn personality image 232, **234**, **235**, **237**; management 1–2; marketplace 96, 102–7; meanings 97; organizations 12; post-war 247–9; production and consumption 107–8; reuse 247; scattered 279; self- 120; as species 141–2; surplus value 141; video 239; visual 122
Images of the Rust Belt (Higgins) 249
Imperial College Healthcare 318–19, **319**
impressionism 119
inauthenticity 373–5
Indian weddings: consumerism 216
indiscipline 188
industrial capitalism 132

industrial filmmaking 248
industrial mechanization 155
Industrial Ruins (Edensor) 250
industrial sites: abandoned 250
industry 250
information technology 41
Innocent X, Pope 116, 117, 118, 119, 122, 123–5, 126
innovation 356
inquiry: logics *176*, *177*
Inspire 5
installation artists 159
institutions 388
instruction: collective 60
intangible values 26
IntelliLab 338, 341, 342, 343
inter-visuality 29
interactive meaning 283, 284, 285
intermittence 36
Internet 323, 328, 353; activity 322; power 329; studies 280–1; technologies 302
interpellation 139, 140
interpretive research 170
intertextuality 12, 372, 373
interviews: semi-structured 9; videography 220–1
intuition 28
invisibility 4, 25–7
inVisio 3
iron cage metaphor 367
Isaacs, E.: and Glasnapp, J. 90
Israel Corporation of Community Centers 173

Jackson, B.: and Guthey, E. 116, 119, 121, 122, 123, 124–5, 203, 366
Jamieson, D.W.: and Worley, C.G. 262
Jay, M. 68, 69
Jayasinghe, L.D. 221
Jenkins, H. 327
Jenkins, M. 118
Jewish Ghetto (Warsaw 1943) 58–60, **58**, **59**
Jewitt, C.: and van Leeuwen, T. 135
Jhally, S. 82
John Lewis Partnership 276
Jonas, H. 66
Journal of New Media and Society 280
Journey to Nowhere (Maharidge) 249
Joy, A.: *et al* 91
Jung, C. 169
juxtaposition 28, 46–63; art 50; cross-cultural 49; method 48–53

Kalyanaraman, S.: and Sundar, S.S. 276, 279
Kant, I. 152, 153, 154, 157, 159
Karaosmanoglu, E.: and Melewar, T.C. 274
Kavanagh, D. 5, 64–76
Kearney, K.: and Hyde, A. 231

Index

Kelly's Repertory Grid technique 296
King, I. 49, 50
Kirshenblatt-Gimblett, B. 165
Kittler, F. 353
Klee, P. 48, 58, 60
Kleiner, A. 262
Klingender, F. 250
knowledge: aesthetic 355, 356; cultural 5; sensible 355, 356; spectator theory 68
Knowles, C.: and Sweetman, P. 8
Knowles, J.G.: *et al* 28
Kozinets, R.V. 218
Kress, G.: and van Leeuwen, T. 281, 283
Kruse, C. 359–60
Kubrick, S. 148
Küpers, W. 4, 19–32

La Salle, D.: and Britton, T. 1
labour: division 61; migrant 250
Laclau, E.: and Mouffe, C. 71–2
Ladkin, D. 120
Landscapes of Capital project (1998–2003) 142
language 69, 174, 178; non-verbal 174
Larsen, V.: *et al* 229
Lastovicka, J.L.: *et al* 221
Law, J. 388, 389; and Cooper, R. 70; and Fyfe, G. 227, 229
leadership 120, 121, 125, 127; charismatic 116–29; research 121
lean enterprises: visual management 306–7
Lean University project 308, **309**, 314
learning 316; and meta-cognition 347; multicultural 80
Learning to Labour (Willis) 251
Lears, T.J.J. 133
Leeuwen, T. van: and Jewitt, C. 135; and Kress, G. 281, 283
legitimacy 204
Leichty, G.B.: and Esrock, S.L. 279
lenses 27
Leonard, A. 330, 372
Leonard, P. 11, 322–34
Lethbridge, S.: and Bateman, N. 11, 306–21
Levine, P. 57
liminal spaces 339
Lincoln, Y.S.: and Guba, E.G. 199
Lindholm, C. 367, 376
Lindstrom, M. 74
linguistic turn 2–3, 46, 69
linguistics 34, 42
LinkedIn 325
literacy 4, 13, 83, 90, 198, 375; projects 40
lock manufacture 308, 310–14
logos 278, 324
London Life and the London Poor (Mayhew) 244
longitudinal studies 240
looking: systematic ways 175–80

m-vision 65, **66**, 72
McArthur: and Bell, E. 12, 365–78
McCracken, G. 97, 98, 135
Maclaran, P.: and Brown, S. 73
McLuhan, M. 67, 142
Mad Men 131
magnetic resonance imaging (MRI) 358–9
Magritte, R. 156, 168, 169, 183n
Maharidge, D. 249
management 10, 55–6, 306–21; boards 11; corporate identity 11; lean enterprises 306–7; operations 306–21; principles 307–8, **309**, 312; scientific 8, 49; total quality (TQM) 262; visual 317–18, **317**, 319
managers: postmodern 54–7
manic depression: diagnosis 360
mapping 244
Marchand, R. 132, 245
Marcus, G.E.: and Fischer, M.M.J. 46, 49, 50, 51
Margulies, N.: and Raia, A.P. 262
marketers: artist 155–6
marketing 7, 72–3, 98, 105, 154; aesthetic 147, 153–4; ethics 376; Hawaii 107; sensory 74; strategy 80, 89, 96
marketplace image: consumption 96, 102–7
Marshak, R.J.: and Grant, D. 262, 269
Marx, K. 53, 56, 71, 154–5
mass-media art 147
materialistic empiricism 24
materials 169, 174, 175, 178, 181, 182, 182n; analysis 179; genres *167*
Matilal, S.: and Höpfl, H. 50
matter 151
Mavin, S.: and Bryans, P. 231
Maximilian, Emperor 118
Mayhew, H. 244
Mead, M. 49, 166
Meamber, L.A. 7, 96–115
meaning: construction 124; locating 170–4
Meatrix, The (2003) 372
mechanization 251; industrial 155
media 92, 255; new 142; visual 92, 255, 353, *see also* social media
medical advertising 131
medical professionals 12, 354, 355, 357–9
medicine: visualization technology 357–9
Melewar, T.C. 274; and Karaosmanoglu, E. 274
member-generated materials 178–9
memory 61; collective 51
Mendelssohn-Bartholdy, F. 151–2, 153
Merleau-Ponty, M. 4, 20, 23–5, 26, 28
meta-cognition: and learning 347
metaphors 64, 66, 230–1; glass cage 74; iron cage 367; ocular 5, 64, 65, 66, 67, 68, 74; visual 230–1
metaphysics 70
metatexte 35
method 6, 9, 28, 166, 168

397

methodology 9, 168
metonymy 36
Michelis, A. 29
Mick, D.G.: *et al* 135–6, 138
Microsoft 139–40, **139**
migrant labour 250
military training 341
Miller, G.A. 308
Mills, C.W. 92
Mindcam method 220
MINDSPACE 318
Ming Jue (Whipps) 249
Mintzberg, H. 48, 50, 51–3; basic model of organization **52**
Mirzoeff, N. 196
Mitchell, W.J.T. 141–2, 197
mobile workers 302
modality 283, 284
models 348n
modernism 355
modernity 54, 72, 124, 132, 353; late 41, 46, 74
Moisander, J.: and Valtonen, A. 84
Morgan, D. 175
Mouffe, C.: and Laclau, E. 71–2
Mozart, W.A. 149–50, 151
Müller, M. 197
multicultural learning 80

nanotechnology 193
Nathan, M.: and Doyle, J. 300
nation state 147–8
National Child Labor Committee (NCLC) 244
National Western Stock Show and Rodeo 82, **83**
nationalism 67, 71
natives: colonial view 57
Nazism 119; ideology 147
networks 331; builders 325; social 240, 323
neurological advertising 134
New Deal Programme 247
new obscurity 72
New World 118
newscast simulator: modality 342–3
Ng, R.: and Höpfl, H. 300, 301
Nietzsche, F.W. 47, 68, 152
Nigerians: Four 54–7, **56**
Norris Martin, K. 9, 188–201
nudge psychology 318, 319
Nurnberg, W. 248
Nye, D.: *Image Worlds* 245, 253, 254

Obama, B. 125
objects 178, 301; organizational 290–2; workplace 292–5
observations 182
ocular metaphors 5, 64, 65, 66, 67, 68, 74
ocularcentrism 229, 365; displaced 64, 68–72; extended 64, 67–8; inverted 65, 72–3, **72**;

metatheoretical trajectories 64–5, **64**; and organization 64–76
Office Space (2009) 223
O'Keefe Bazzoni, J.: and Rolland, D. 279
Olivetti, D. 166
Olson, L.C.: *et al* 192
One Day with Peter (Tréhin-Marçot) 54, **54**, **56**
operations management 306–21
operator 37, 39, 43
optics 66
org/borgs 322, 323, 332
Organizational Memory Studies 51
organization(s) 1–16, 26, 303; as art 147–8; buildings 169; future 13–14; identity 165–6, 231, 232, 238, 277; image 12; strategies 5–8; studies 47, 49, 51
Origan, E.: and Golen, G. 379, 380, 382, 383, 389
Orwell, G. 130
Oswick, C. 21
Other Americas (Salgado) 80
Ott, B.L.: and Dickinson, G. 191
overidentification: parodic 57
ownership 180
Oxfam 34; Annual Review front cover 39–43; website 278

Packard, V. 132–3
Pahl, R. 250
paintings 180, 181, 229
Pandemonium (Burrell) 50
PARC 90
Parker, M. 12–13, 379–90
parking areas 90
parodic overidentification 57
participatory sense-making 29
Parviainen, J.: and Ropo, A. 121
Paul, Saint 46–8, 52–3
Peñaloza, L. 82; and Thompson, A. 7, 79–95
perception 24, 29, 355–6, 357, 362; embodied 25; scientific 360
performance 204; appraisals 23
period eye 122–3, 125
personalization: of space 292–5, **292**, **293**, **294**
perspectivism 66
Peter Pauper Press 105–6
phantasmagoria 21–2
phenomenology 19, 20, 23, 26, 27, 29, 181
philosophers: process 69–71
photo elicitation 254
photographs 35, 51, 79, 86, 92, 173, 181–2, 195, 229, 311; advertising 229; eidetic science 37; logic 58; sentiment 38
photography 6, 13, 85, 104–5, 166, 255, 302–3; corporate 9, 243, 244–7, 255; documentary 247; and dramatic arts 41; practice 37; removed observation 291–2
physical simulations 337, 340–1, 346

pictorial representation 231–3, 239
pictures 228, 229
pilot training 346–7
Pink, S. 86, 208, 210
Pistoletto, Michelangelo 156
Plato 65, 68, 155, 353
Platonic idea 155
play 151, 347
pleasure 195; principle 154
policymakers: and artistic interventions 264, 270
political cartoons 230
political discourse 71–2
politics: visibility 22–3
Pollach, I. 278
Pollock, J. 181
Poole, D. 79–80, 81, 91, 92
popular culture 379–90
Porat, D. 60
portals 276, 279
portraits 7, 116–29; analysis 121–3, *123*; leaders 10
Positron Emission Tomography (PET) 357–8
post-structuralism 33
post-war images 247–9
postmodern managers 54–7
postmodern radicals 71
postmodernism 73, 336–7
postmodernity 72
poverty 80
power 68, 120, 180–1, 195, 324; art 127, 269; Internet 329; portraits 117–19; relationships 196
practice theory 323
practices 11; collective 354
prescription chart 318–19, **319**, 320
presentation: self- 120
Price is Right, The 346
Price, K.N.: *et al* 279
print technology 67
process philosophers 69–71
product design 105, 106; as art 153–86
product placement 140
productive consumption 96, 97–100, 105–6, 108–9; advertising 103–5; consumer experiences 106–7; products and brands 105–6
professional vision 21, 355, 359, 360, 362
progress 58–9
propaganda 148; US WWII posters 247
psychiatry 360–1
psychoanalysis 3–4, 47
psychology: nudge 318, 319
public relations 245, 249
Punctum 38, 39, 41–3
Pushing the Scene (Hietanan *et al*) 216

QualGroup 338, 344, 346
quality of working life (QWL) 262

race 79, 80
radical democratic theory 72
radicals: postmodern 71
radiologists 359
Raia, A.P.: and Margulies, N. 262
Ramirez, R. 146
rationalism 67, 71
REACT (Rapid Ethnographic Assessment and Communication Technique) 90
readers 171, 172
realism 346; and boxing 345; perceived 341, 344–5; scientific 86
reality coaches: artists as 158
reception studies 193
recognition 23
recordings 166
recruitment: advertising 139–40
recycling 40
reflection theory 252–3
reflexive turn 68
reflexivity 91, 92, 93
relational aesthetics 159
relay 34, 42
Renaissance 118–19, 124; art 104
representation 11–13, 194, 209–10; data 183n; meaning 28; pictorial 231–3, 239
research 7, 188–201, **189**, **190**, 202–3, 207, 229, 380; action 310; ethnographic consumer 88; interpretive 170; leadership 121; phase logic 178; projects 174, 175; strategy-as-practice (SAP) 232; video 9, 207–8, 209; vision 27, *see also* consumer research
researchers: consumers 91
Reynolds, J. 119
Rheinberger, H-J. 359
rhetoric 9, 191–4, 197, 198
Rhetoric of the Image (Barthes) 33, 34–5, 43, *44*
Riefenstahl, L. 147
Riis, J. 244
Robinson, S.: and Elliott, C. 10–11, 273–88
Rolland, A.A. 152
Rolland, D.: and O'Keefe Bazzoni, J. 279
romantic art 368
Romanticism 67, 68, 71, 73
Ropo, A.: and Parviainen, J. 121
Rorty, R. 69, 72
Rose, G. 124, 141
Rosenhan, D. 361
Royal Bank of Scotland (RBS): website 283–5, **284**
Royal Dutch Shell 277
Ruby, J. 91, 93

Sachs, J. 327, 328, 329; and Finkelpearl, S. 370
St Andrews University 314–16, **315**, 319
Salgado, S. 80
Samoa 49

Index

satires: anti-work 383–5
Saussure, F. de 69
scattered images 279
Scheiberg, S. 292
Schiller, G.F. 151, 152, 154
schizo-identification 233, 238
schizophrenia: diagnosis 360; patients 356
Schoeneborn, D. 26
Schroeder, J.E. 101–6, 141, 278, 365; Bell, E. and Warren, S. 1–16; and Borgerson, J.L. 107, 138
science: as experimentation 359; images 137; social 9, 386; as theory 359
scientific advertising 131
scientific management 8, 49
scientific observations 360
scientific perception 360
scientific realism 86
scopic regimes 4
Scott, L.M.: and Vargas, P. 82–3
Scottish Parliament building 169
script theory 338
seeing: practices 20, 21–2, 29, 354; ways 357–61, 362
seeing and knowing: methodological ways 165–87
Sefton Magistrate's Court 316–17, **316**
self-image 120
self-presentation 120
semi-structured interviewing 9
semiology 254
semiotics 132, 135, 136, 254; and corporate web identity (CWI) 285, 286; method 281–3
sense-making: participatory 29
sensible knowledge 355, 356
sensoriality 29
sensory branding 74
sensory marketing 74
Sex and the City 140
Shah, P.: and Hoeffner, J. 308
Shannon, C. 134
shopping experience 107
Shortt, H.: Betts, J. and Warren, S. 11, 289–305
Siemens: *Building Blocks* advertisement 137–8, **137**
sight 5, 65, 66, 82, 181
Simon, H. 198, 339
simulations 10, 11, 335–49, 348n; dimensions 339–41, **342**; empirical process 338–9; experiential modality 340; mapping 341–2, **342**; perceived realism 341, 344–5; physical 337, 340–1, 346; referential frame 340–1; virtual 337, 340–1, 346
Singh, N.: et al 276
situated ethics 208
Skype 327
Smith, A. 153–4, 159
Smith, K.: et al 188
Smith, P.: and Emmison, M. 229
SMMT Industry Forum 311
smoothness 136

social capital 325, 332
social change 71–2
social competence 204–5
social identities 26–7
social media 10, 92, 108, 229, 302, 353, 365, 370, 372, 375; design 326; Facebook 2, 93, 322, 325, 326, 332, 370, 371; and identity construction 322; as organizational visual practice 323–4; and organizations 322–34; Twitter 2, 131, 322, 325, 326, 328, 332, *see also* YouTube
social networks 240, 323
social sciences 9, 386
socialism 67, 71
sociology: and work organization 243–58
Solomon, M.R. 97
Sontag, S. 1, 51, 58, 60, 87
Sorensen, B.M. 5, 46–63
spaces: art 158; deindustrialized 254; liminal 339; personalization 292–5, **292**, **293**, **294**
spatial aesthetics 107
spatial artefacts 174
spectator 37, 38, 39, 40, 41, 42
spectrum 37, 39, 43
Spicer, A.: and Fleming, P. 56
Spoelstra, S. 21–2
Springsteen, B. 249
Stafford, B.M. 355, 356
Standard Oil 246, 248
Star Wars 372
Starbucks 191–2
Starr, R.G.: and Fernandez, K.V. 220
state: aesthetics 150–2; and art 152
statistical data 170
status 180–1
Steelworks (Germain) 249, 250
Stéphani, A.: and Bon, F. 249
Stewart, A. 117, 118, 120
Stiles, D.R. 9, 227–42
Story of Bottled Water, The (2010) 372, 373–5
Story of Stuff, The (2007) 327, 329, 330, 331, 372, 373, 374
Strand, M. 361
Strangleman, T. 9, 243–58
strategy-as-practice (SAP) research 232
Strati, A. 74
structuralism 33, 69
studies 9, 166, 193, 194–7, 198
Studium 38, 39, 40, 41, 42, 43
Sturken, M.: and Cartwright, L. 6
Styhre, A. 12, 353–64
Suchman, M.C. 204
Sundar, S.S.: and Kalyanaraman, S. 276, 279
supervision 68
surveillance 13, 73, 203; covert 221–2
sustainability 368, 375; and visual authenticity 365–78
Sweetman, P.: and Knowles, C. 8

400

symbolic work 300–1
symbols 82, 208, 209; in entrepreneurial interactions 203–5

Taylor, C. 47, 367–8, 369
technology 137–8, 239, 250, 362; computer 228, 347; information 41; Internet 302; print 67
television: authority figure representation 384; cartoons 386; programming 195; viewing 221; work parodies 387
text: artifacts 170; meaning 171
text-analogue 171
textwork 168, 179, 180
theatrical intervention 264–5, 270
theoria 70
Thompson, A. 89; and Peñaloza, L. 7, 79–95
TILLT 264, 265, 266, 267, 271n
time and motion studies 166, 246
tools 314, 319, 320
total quality management (TQM) 262
Toulouse-Lautrec, H. de 156
tourism 107
Toyota Motor Corporation 98
training: military 341; pilot 346–7
transferability 199
transparency 22, 269
trauma: culture 100
Tréhin-Marçot, P.: *One Day with Peter* 54, **54**, **56**
Trier, L. von 54
Trimble, D. 67, 71
Trip Advisor 277
Tufte, E.R. 307–8, 313
Tunstall, J. 250
turn 2, 9, 46, 202
Twitter 2, 131, 322, 325, 326, 328, 332

United Kingdom (UK): business school case study 233–9
United Nations (UN): Convention (1948) 39
United States of America (USA): Detroit 249; military simulations 339
University of St Andrews: web team's visual management board 314–16, **315**, 319
urbanization 353

Valtonen, A. van: and Moisander, J. 84
values: intangible 26
Vargas, P.: and Scott, L.M. 82–3
Vecchio, R.P. 204–5
Veer, E. 9, 209, 214–26
Velázquez, D. 116, 117, 123–5, 126
video 182, 203, 205–6, 210; of affinity 328; images 239; viral 371
video data 210, 215; analysis 208–9
video research 9, 209; ethical issues 207–8
videocy 4; definition 365
videoethnographers 218–19

videoethnography 215; close analysis 220; and entrepreneurship 202–13; equipment 219–22; ethnographic 9; scene setting 219–20
videography 28, 87, 214, 216, 224–5; analysis 222–3; body movements 222; covert 221–2; environment 222–3; interviews 220–1; time 223
Vince, R.: and Broussine, M. 231
viral videos 371
virtual ethnography 328
virtual simulations 337, 340–1, 346
visibility 19; politics 22–3
visio-corporeality 20
vision 23, 26, 29, 68, 357, 362; collective 359–61; enframed 23–4; enskilled 359; ethical issue 47; individual 359–61; professional 21, 353–64, 359, 360, 362; research 27; role 19–20, 21–2
Visual Communication 202
Visual Hospital 317
Visual Studies 195, 202
visuality: critical phenomenology 28; ethical issue 48
visualization: limits 64–76; technology in medicine 357–9
voice discourse 69

Wagner, R. 152
Waitrose 276, 277, 325
Wall Street (1987) 375–6
Wang, J.: and Chaudhri, V. 279
Warhol, A. 155, 156
Warren, S. 37; and Davison, J. 26; Schroeder, J.E. and Bell, E. 1–16; Shortt, H. and Betts, J. 11, 289–305
water: bottled 373–4
Web 2.0 technologies 322, 323
web: accessibility 279; identity 280
Weber, M. 53, 116, 117, 119–20, 367
webpages: banks 278
websites 273; business schools 281; company 10; corporate 275, 369; and corporate identity 273–4; Oxfam 278; Royal Bank of Scotland (RBS) 283–5, **284**
Weick, K. 339
wellbeing 196
Whipps, S. 249
White Furniture Company 251
Whitehead, A.N. 70
Wikipedia 325
Williams, R. 139
Willis, P. 251, 300
Woerkum, C.M.J. van: and Van Herzele, A. 175
Wolkowitz, C. 251–2
women: full-figured 84
word theory 66
work: as exile 300; film representations 383; organization and visual sociology 243–58; representations 246, 247; symbolic 300–1; television representations 384

Index

workers: mobile 302
Working for Ford (Beynon) 250
workplace 381; authenticity 368; identities 11, 289–305; objects 292–5
workplace tools 302; and identity 295–6, **296**
workspace: cognitive 308
World Bank 276
World War, Second (1939–45): US propaganda posters 247
Worley, C.G.: and Jamieson, D.W. 262

x-ray 357

Yanow, D. 8, 9, 165–87
YourNews 343, 346
youth cultures 387
YouTube 131, 229, 322, 325–8, 330, 332, 337, 366, 370, 375; visual authenticity 371–3
Yukl, G. 120

Zentropa 48, 54, 57
Zizek, S. 56–7, 59